From Normandy to the Ruhr

With the
116th Panzer Division
in World War II

Heinz Günther Guderian

THE ABERJONA PRESS
Bedford, Pennsylvania

Editor: Keith E. Bonn
Translators: Ulrich Abele, Esther Abele, and Keith E. Bonn
Production: Patricia K. Bonn
Photos: Kurt Wendt
Printer: Mercersburg Printing

The Aberjona Press is an imprint of Aegis Consulting Group, Inc.,
    Bedford, Pennsylvania 15522

ISBN: 0-9666389-7-2

Contents

List of Maps   *vii*
Editor's Preface   *xix*
Translators' and Editor's Notes   *xi*
Acknowledgments   *xiii*
Rank Equivalences   *xiv*

1. Phoenix from the Ashes: The Creation of the 116th Panzer Division   1

2. Awaiting the Invasion   16

3. The Landing: The Battles in Normandy from 6 June to 18 July 1944   26

4. Awaiting Action   35

5. The Battle for Normandy   54

6. Withdrawal   92

7. Aachen   129

8. Autumn Battles   189
    Part 1: Arnhem   189
    Part 2: Aachen Once Again   208
    Part 3: The Hürtgen Forest   233
    Part 4: Scattered   271

9. The Ardennes Offensive   283
    Part 1: Planning and Preparation   283
    Part 2: The Attack   302
    Part 3: Defense and Retreat   343

10. Defensive Combat Between Rhine and Maas   369

11. The Ruhr Cauldron   412

12. The End in the Harz Mountains   472

Appendices   479

  1. Organization Diagram, Panzer Division 44 479

  2. Roster of Officers and Duty Positions of the 116th Panzer
    Division (to the extent they can be determined today) and the
    Division's Knight's Cross Recipients 480

    a. Commanders and Staffs, 116th Panzer Division
      (as of June/July 1944) 480

    b. Commanders and Staffs, 116th Panzer Division
      (as of about 16 December 1944) 485

    c. Commanders and Staffs, 116th Panzer Division
      (as of about 15 March 1945) 489

    d. Soldiers Who Received the Knight's Cross While Assigned to
      the 116th Panzer Division 494

    e. Recipients of the Knight's Cross Who Served in the
      116th Panzer Division After the Medal was Awarded 495

  3. Appeal by the Führer to the Soldiers in the West 496

  4. Order, 116th Panzer Division, 12 June 1944 497

  5. Order for Deployment of 116th Panzer Division by
    Headquarters, LXVII Corps, 13 June 1944 498

  6. Order, 116th Panzer Division to Panzer-Grenadier Regiment 60,
    23 July 1944 500

  7. Letter by Commander, 116th Panzer Division to His Subordinate
    Commanders, 9 August 1944 501

  8. Appeal by Gauleiter Grohé of Cologne–Aachen to the Border
    Population, approximately 11 or 12 August 1944 502

  9. Appeal by the Committee for the Temporary Administration of
    the City of Aachen, 14 September 1944 504

 10. Organization Diagram, 116th Panzer Division,
    15 September 1944 505

 11. Organization Diagram, 116th Panzer Division,
    24 September 1944 506

 12. Order for the Installation of a Battle Commandant for the City of
    Aachen, 116th Panzer Division, 25 September 1944 507

13. Order for the Release of the 116th Panzer Division, Headquarters, LXXXI Corps, 26 September 1944 508

14. Order for the Relief of Panzer-Grenadier Regiment 156, 116th Panzer Division, 26 September 1944 510

15. Order of the Day to the Soldiers of the Army Group B from Generalfeldmarschall Model, Early October 1944 511

16. Directives for Conduct of Battle for the 5th Panzer Army in the Ardennes Offensive (Excerpt) 513

17. Order for Operation "Adelheid," LVIII Panzer Corps, 12 October 1944 (Excerpt) 519

18. Situation Report, 2d Battalion, Armored Artillery Regiment 146, 15 December 1944 522

19. Order, 116th Panzer Division, 16 December 1944 523

20. Personnel and Equipment Status Reports, 116th Panzer Division, 29 December 1944 524

21. Order for Reorganization of Units in Accordance with the Panzer Division 45 Structure, General Inspector of Panzer Troops, 25 March 1945 526

22. Organization of 2d Battalion, Panzer-Grenadier Regiment 156 Under the New Structure, 17 March 1945 529

23. Battle Order #1, Battle Commandant "Harz," 11 April 1945 532

Notes 534

Index 580

Maps

About the Author

List of Maps

1. Overview of the Situation in the Supreme Command - West Area of Operations as of 6 June 1944 and Rommel's proposal of 3 May for Deployment of I SS-Panzer and III Anti-Aircraft Corps

2. Disposition of the 116th Panzer Division Northwest of Paris, late April–12 June, and after the Retreat Across the Seine, late August 1944

3. The Landing of 6 June 1944

4. 116th Panzer Division Area of Operations Behind the Coast South of Abbeville, 13 June–19 July 1944

5. 116th Panzer Division Area of Operations Behind the Front of I SS-Panzer Corps Near Caen, 22–28 July 1944

6. Combat Northeast of Percy, 30–31 July 1944

7. Combat in the Le Gast–St. Pois–Sée sector, 1–4 August 1944.

8. Combat in the Champ-du-Boult–Perriers-en-Beauficel–Chérancé-le-Roussel Sector and Counterattack Toward Avranches, 5–11 August 1944

9. Combat in the Sée–Argentan–Trun–Le Bourg–St. Léonard Sector, 12–20 August, and Breakout of 116th Panzer Division from the Pocket Southeast of Falaise on the Night, 20–21 August 1944

10. Combat in the Seine Bridgehead of the Rouen, 23–27 August 1944

11. Retreat Through Northern France and Western Belgium, 30 August–3 September 1944

12. Retreat Through Belgium up to the Meuse, 4–8 September 1944

13. Retreat to the Border of the Reich, 9–12 September 1944

14. Situation Near Aachen on 24 September 1944, and American Attacks, 13–21 September 1944

15. Counterattack from the Bridgehead South of Arnhem, 1–5 October 1944

16. Aachen, Battle for Würselen, 11–22 October 1944

17. Combat in the Hürtgen Forest, 2–15 November 1944

18. Combat Groups of the 116th Panzer Division Defend Against the American Offensive Against the Roer, 16–23 December 1944

19. Planning for the Ardennes Offensive

20. The Attack in the Ardennes, 16–26 December 1944

21. Defense and Withdrawal in the Ardennes, 3–16 January 1944

22. Combat between Reichswald and Xantener Hochwald,
     12 February–3 March 1945

23. The Wesel Bridgehead, 5–9 March 1945

24. The Ruhr Cauldron, combat with the front toward the west, 25 March–
     1 April 1945

25. The Ruhr Cauldron, combat with the front toward the east,
     1–16 April 1945

26. The End in the Harz Mountains, 10–21 April 1945

Editor's Preface

Generalmajor Heinz Gunther Guderian has given the world a rare gift. In an era characterized by the availability of a huge variety of privately- and commercially-published WWII memoirs, he has crafted something entirely apart. *From Normandy to the Ruhr* is both a deeply-researched scholarly history of one of the key German Army units of WWII and a multi-tiered memoir (and collection of others' memoirs, contemporary diaries, and personal notes) of combat in some of the most significant battles of the 20th century.

General Guderian, who served as the 1st General Staff Officer of the 116th Panzer Division from its organization through the end of the war, wrote this book for a variety of reasons. Fully recognizing the effects of the "fog of war," he wanted his comrades from the "Greyhound Division" to possess a definitive history of wartime events which affected them throughout their combat service with the Division. A retired *Bundeswehr* general officer himself, General Guderian wanted to help modern *Bundeswehr* soldiers, and modern Germans in general, better understand the tactical and other challenges their forebears faced in the last year of the war in the West.

With the translation of his book into the English language, General Guderian has now reached a far larger audience, with different interests and perspectives. The 116th Panzer Division was the only German unit to fight in all of the most famous battles on the Western Front in 1944–45. Normandy, Falaise, Aachen, Arnhem, the Hürtgen Forest, the Ardennes Offensive, the *Reichswald,* and the Ruhr Pocket are battles known to every English-speaking student of the war and to every American, British, and Canadian veteran who fought in them. Veterans of these battles will be engrossed by the author's honest evaluations of both their units' combat proficiency and by his detailed description of what was happening on "the other side of the hill." Amidst all of the ongoing debates about these battles and the issues surrounding them, there is now, finally, a professional soldier's comprehensive and candid report about German operations in these key events.

Much more than a chronology of tactical events as they unfolded for the 116th and associated units, General Guderian has incorporated his insights into the reasons for and issues behind the tactical and operational decisions which dictated the course of his Division's combat. Many readers will be surprised by his analysis of each of the Division's battles, and perhaps even stunned by the successes and failures General Guderian so candidly recounts. From the truly historic revelations about the political reasons behind the deployment of the Panzer divisions in the West before the Allied landings in Normandy, to the amazing details of the Division Commander's plans to disband the Division upon reaching German soil, to the repeated, nearly-complete annihilation of the Division's combat units, this is much more than a simple military history. In an era when historians and, at least in the United States, ranking soldiers, sometimes hotly debate the relative merits and proficiency of the opposing sides in the West in 1944–45, this book will raise eyebrows and inevitably fuel further disputation on the subject. Since much affecting the future of several armies may rest on this debate, General Guderian's work has relevance and import far beyond that of most unit histories.

Beyond the author's precious insights into leadership, organization, tactics, and decisionmaking provided in this thoughtful, provocative book, for modern students of war and military professionalism perhaps the most critical subject illuminated by the author is the role of political correctness. The intellectual and moral dishonesty of the National Socialist regime and its adherents is clearly documented, and the corollary disastrous impact on a variety of fundamental military factors—from unit reporting, to relationships between leaders and led, to tactical decisionmaking—are all abundantly apparent. Although not an explicit theme of the book, there is a clear undercurrent of the author's disdain for the backstabbing, sycophancy, and dishonesty which sometimes resulted from the influence of the Nazi regime and philosophy at surprisingly low levels within the Army. For the leaders and soldiers of the armies of democratic nations, this book is a glimpse into the abyss of professional and moral corruption which results from the politicization of military organizations.

Finally, General Guderian's treatment of the human side of war provides both inspiration and a warning. The pervasive valor, steadfast professionalism, and overwhelming commitment of most of the soldiers of the 116th Panzer Division, in the face of continuous defeats and disappointments, can only inspire soldiers everywhere. As General Guderian wrote, the combat dead of the 116th Panzer Division should be remembered with reverence. How and why such individual and even collective military virtue was ultimately incompletely rewarded should serve as an admonition for soldiers and civilians everywhere, today and in the future.

Keith E. Bonn, Editor

Translators' and Editor's Notes

Translation is both an art and a science. We have most earnestly endeavored to retain the author's voice and, as with all Aberjona Press books, have tried to retain absolute authenticity of terms, tone, and structure. These efforts have been balanced by our consideration of the English-language audience for this book.

Thus, we have retained some German terms, such as "*Panzer* Division," because we believe that practically all of the readers of this book will easily understand their exact meaning. In other cases, we have retained some slightly more obscure German terms, such as "*Panzerjäger*" *Battalion 228,* because there is no precise translation in the English language, that is, since its combat elements consisted of both tank destroyers and anti-tank guns, such an organization was neither a "tank destroyer" nor an "anti-tank gun" battalion in the American sense of the term. (Such terms are described parenthetically in the text.)

In the case of terms which are, in our judgment, likely to be obscure to most readers (or at least would be distracting to many, even if their meaning was discerned), such as "*Landesschützen-Ausbildung*" battalions, we have used the closest American military terms possible; in this case, "militia training battalion." Similarly, with more common military—especially tactical—terms, we have used the American military terms which most closely correspond with their German equivalents. Inevitably, especially in view of the many English-language readers who are extremely familiar with and enjoy using German military terminology, there will be those who are disappointed that we did not use more actual German language terms. At the same time, there will be other readers who will be frustrated that we have used as many German words as we have. Suffice it to say that we have attempted to gauge the needs and desires of as many readers as possible, and tried to find the most suitable middle ground. Overall, wherever there seemed to be a conflict between the benefits of enlightening readers with more exotic German military terms and effectively conveying the substance of the author's work to the greatest part of the book's audience, we have leaned toward the latter.

A life-long professional soldier, General Guderian wrote the original German-language text for this book in the style of the accomplished military professional he is, and was very concerned that his style be preserved in this translation. Along with its magnificent utility for stirring drama, pungent disputation, engrossing narrative, and evocative poetry, German is also a great language for military reports and orders. Its word structure allows the creation of precise, self-explanatory terms which, in other languages, require hyphenations, phrases, or even whole sentences to convey. Its nominative, accusative, dative, and genitive cases facilitate the creation of sentences which are both extremely comprehensive and precise in their meaning.

Unfortunately, exact or direct translation of such German terms and sentences into the English language can create prose that is stilted at best, and labyrinthine to the point of meaninglessness at worst. The differences between the English and German languages are such that a literal or nearly-literal translation neither preserves the author's true style, nor adequately conveys the author's meaning. At the same time, converting General Guderian's German to purely common-usage English would detract too much from the flavor of his style and deprive readers of the important opportunities to gain insight into the author's personality, cultural background, and mind. General Guderian is an educated and experienced German soldier and student of war, and our translation portrays him as one. Certainly, he should not sound like an American or Englishman. Our intent has thus been to strike a balance that preserves his style and accurately reveals his thoughts while making the text readable for the English-language audience.

A few technical notes and details are in order. Since so many units and commanders' titles are used throughout the text, for simplicity's sake we have used the somewhat unusual convention of capitalizing the first letter of the word referring to either the *116th Panzer Division* (the "Division") or its commanding general (the "Commander" or "Commanding General"). Also, we have used the full and correct names of each unit, German or allied, throughout the book. German units have been italicized, and allied units appear in regular font; since the overwhelming majority of the allied units encountered by the *116th Panzer Division* were from the US Army, these are not specifically labeled as such. However, we have specified when a unit is British, French, or Polish, unless it is obvious from the name of the unit, such as the "43d (Wessex) Division" or "4th Canadian Armoured Division."

To ensure that the English-language notes correspond to the original notes in the German version, we have used another unusual technique. Rather than cause confusion by placing some note numbers in the middle of sentences—as they sometimes are in the German version of this book—we have placed them at the end of each sentence, per the American convention. Therefore, on rare occasion, there will be two, or even three note numbers at the end of some sentences. While the 14th Edition of the *Chicago Manual of Style* indicates that this is to be "rigorously avoided," we have decided that this measure will facilitate cross-checking with the original German version for researchers or those who wish to check the sources (most of which come from the Federal German Archives).

Although General Guderian has reviewed this translation and has graciously identified linguistic issues and made corrections, there were ultimately a very few minor disagreements about some usages or phrases. Any or all genuine mistakes of translation are the sole responsibility of the editor.

Keith E. Bonn

Acknowledgments

The Author wishes to express his heartfelt thanks to everyone who assisted him in the completion of this book, especially the leaders and staff of the Federal German Military Historical Bureau, who provided materials which were key to the research for this work.

The Editor wishes to acknowledge the contributions of the following to the completion of the translation:

Ulrich and Esther Abele, for their magnificent translation of the text and facilitation of practically every aspect of the completion of this project.

Generalmajor Heinz Gunther Guderian, Federal German Armed Forces (Retired), for his careful and detailed review of the translated text, and his patient and enthusiastic cooperation throughout the course of this project.

The Count and Countess von der Schulenburg, for their gracious and kind assistance with logistical and communications requirements during the latter portions of this project.

Herr Kurt Wendt, former tactical draftsman for the 116th Panzer Division and assistant to the author during World War II, for his unequivocal and enthusiastic provision of every one of the photos included in this book.

Major Mike Giangregorio, US Army (Retired), Staff Sergeant Tom Houlihan, USMC (Retired) Lieutenant Colonel Hugh Foster, US Army (Retired), James Anderson, and Susie Cucura for their excellent re-renderings of the maps crucial for reader understanding of this book.

Lieutenant Colonel Jim McDonald, US Army (Retired), a WWII veteran of the 8th Armored Division, for his expert evaluation and suggestions regarding the photo captions of this book.

Dr. Jochen Seeliger, a World War II veteran of the 6th SS-Mountain Division, provided technical advice regarding translation of numerous terms in the appendices.

Rank Equivalences

Officer

US Army	German Army	Waffen SS
General of the Army	Generalfeldmarschall	
General	Generaloberst	Oberstgruppenführer
Lieutenant General	General der Infanterie, General der Panzertruppen, etc.	Obergruppenführer
Major General	Generalleutnant	Gruppenführer
Brigadier General	Generalmajor	Brigadeführer
No equivalent	No equivalent	Oberführer
Colonel	Oberst	Standartenführer
Lieutenant Coloonel	Oberstleutnant	Obersturmbannführer
Major	Major	Sturmbannführer
Captain	Hauptmann	Hauptsturmführer
First Lieutenant	Oberleutnant	Oberstrumführer
Second Lieutenant	Leutnant	Unterstrumführer

Enlisted

US Army	German Army	Waffen SS
Master Sergeant First Sergeant	Stabsfeldwebel	Sturmscharführer
Technical Sergeant Staff Sergeant/ Technician 3d Grade	Oberfeldwebel	Hauptscharführer
	Feldwebel	Oberscharführer
Sergeant/ Technician 4th Grade	Unterfeldwebel	Scharführer
Corporal/ Technician 5th Grade	Unteroffizier	Unterscharführer
Private First Class	Gefreiter/Obergefreiter	Rottenführer
Private	Soldat (Grenadier in the Infantry, Kanonier in the field artillery, etc.)	SS Mann

From Normandy
to the Ruhr

CHAPTER 1

Phoenix from the Ashes:
The Creation of the 116th Panzer Division

The *116th Panzer Division* was formed in the spring of 1944 from the *16th Panzer-Grenadier Division.* After suffering losses in battles in the East, the remnants of this division were transferred to France. There, with the incorporation of the *179th Reserve Panzer Division,* the unit was newly established as a *Panzer* division.

In August 1940, the *16th Infantry Division (Motorized)* was composed of detachments of varied origin, including parts from several different divisions and formerly separate units. After 23 June 1943, this formation was redesignated the *16th Panzer-Grenadier Division.* The *60th Infantry Regiment* and the *1st Battalion, Artillery Regiment 146* came from the old *16th Infantry Division.* The *60th* was formed from *Wehrkreis VI* in Münster, and thus initially received its replacements mainly from its conscription area in the Rhineland-Westphalia region of Germany.[1] Thus, whenever *Wehrmacht* bulletins were issued or awards of the Knight's Cross of the Iron Cross were announced, the Division was referred to as a "Rhenish-Westphalian division." This remained so, even after its reorganization as a *Panzer* division.

The *16th Infantry Division (Motorized)* had to evolve from very distinct units. It received its baptism of fire in the spring of 1941 during the campaign against Yugoslavia, and took part in the war against the Soviet Union almost without interruption from the first day. It quickly fused into a strong, cohesive outfit, which achieved a good reputation, with friends as well as enemies, through its accomplishments. The Division achieved its great successes on the Kalmuk Steppe in 1942, and most of all in 1943 during the battles on the Mius River and at the Zaporozhe bridgehead. The Division's achievements were specifically recognized in the *Wehrmacht* bulletins of 17 January, 25 August, and 27 October 1943.

The initiative to move the *16th Panzer-Grenadier Division* to the West, and its subsequent reorganization as a *Panzer* division may have been due to a letter written by *Generalleutnant* Count von Schwerin to Hitler on 29 June 1943. He announced it the same day in a Division order:

> After returning from home leave, I have resumed command of the Division and I am glad to be back with you. Soldiers from the Rhineland and Westphalia! You know what the enemy has done to your homeland. It is indescribable and unimaginable. Therefore, I have on this day, addressed the following letter to the *Führer:*

1

"As commander of a Rhineland-Westphalian Division, I beg you, my *Führer*, in view of the indescribable conditions wrought upon our western German homeland by the British-American air raid terror, to order that the Division be afforded the opportunity to confront Anglo-American forces as soon as the situation of the war allows it. I am obligated to present this request in consideration of the morale of my soldiers. We have to settle the score with the English and the Americans in a special way."

Soldiers, I hope I acted in your interest with this petition. The fulfillment of our wish depends on the war situation and the decision of the *Führer*. Furthermore, the Division will at once find out in which way we can help the families of our comrades who suffered from the terror of the enemy's air raids.[2]

On 13 July 1943, Schwerin wrote to Hitler's adjutant, *Oberstleutnant* Engel, "We hope the *Führer* will grant us our . . . wish to let us fight the English and Americans, the destroyers of our Rhineland-Westphalian homeland, quite soon. We will take great pleasure in soundly beating the hell out of those fellows in every way we can, according to the rules of warfare."[3]

For many months, there was no perceptible reaction to Schwerin's petition. The heavy fighting in the East continued; this was where the Division was needed and committed. In early 1944, in accordance with orders from the Division Commander, *Major* Tebbe (Commanding Officer of the Division's *Panzer Battalion 116*) held exploratory discussions at *OKH* with the Inspector General of *Panzer* Troops and with other departments in the homeland aimed at reorganization as a *Panzer* division, but initially, these produced no tangible result. However, with the consent of the Inspector General, Tebbe traveled to the headquarters of *Reserve Panzer Battalion 1* in France, in hope of procuring it as the *2d Battalion* of the *Panzer* regiment around which the newly-organized Division could be formed. Those plans, however, were laid aside due to catastrophic developments of the situation in the southern part of the Eastern Front.

During the first days of February 1944, the Division was sucked into the vortex of the Russian breakthrough at the bend of the Dnepr River north of Nikopol. In spite of the Division staff's warning that its soldiers were exhausted and without their usual tenacity, and regardless of the fact that the Soviet buildup was under observation by the Division and being reported as such, leaders at higher headquarters did not want to believe that such a proven Division had finally come to the end of its rope. The Division's capabilities were so overrated that an adjacent infantry division was subordinated to its command, with the expectation that the *16th*'s armored elements would be able to support them as well. But when the circumstances went too far, and melting snow and rain turned the Ukrainian soil into sticky mud that made any movements with vehicles impossible, the unavoidable happened. The Division's front line broke up. Almost all motorized vehicles were lost. A weak line of defense could be established only with the greatest of pains. Later, on 9 February 1944, the Division Commander and I (the First General Staff Officer, or *Ia*) were relieved. [The *Ia*, or "First General Staff

Officer," was the division operations officer, and at the division level, also functioned as the chief of staff—*Editor.*]

Count Schwerin fought for the reconstitution of the Division. Although the award of the Swords to his Knight's Cross had been approved on 4 November, he announced that he would refuse to accept them during the ceremony planned for 15 February. He informed the Chief of Administration–Group P1 of the Army Personnel Office, *Generalmajor* Linnarz, of his decision, as well as the Chief of the Operations Section of *OKH, Generalleutnant* Heusinger. On 18 February, he also informed the Inspector General of *Panzer* Troops, *Generaloberst* Guderian.

By 29 February, the general opinion in the *Führer's* headquarters was that the calamity which had befallen the *16th Panzer-Grenadier Division* was not entirely the responsibility of the Division's leadership. On that day, Linnarz wrote to Schwerin, "Your case is in the best of hands. *Generalleutenant* Schmundt (Chief Adjutant of the *Wehrmacht* with the *Führer* and Chief of the Army Personnel Office) wants you to know you should recuperate with calm. No one is going to dispute the honor of your Division."[4]

Referring to an order by the Organization Office dated 20 February, on 24 February the Operations Office issued an order to move *Panzer Battalion 116* "after its extrication" from the front "to Grafenwöhr for rearmament."[5]

Tebbe's efforts seemed to have paid off. This action may have been the first sign of a favorable turn for the entire Division. In early 1944, developments elsewhere had forced the forces in the West to be diminished. The heavy battles on the Eastern Front (mainly in Southern Russia), the deteriorating situation in Italy, and the German occupation of Hungary had all taken their toll. The forces that had been withdrawn had to be replaced. The Western Powers' initiation of a "Second Front" in Europe was to be expected in the spring of 1944. (The Italian theater was not considered as such by the enemy.) These circumstances forced *OKW* to create new units quickly. The potential for using the three reserve *Panzer* divisions located in the West to this end was first mentioned in the *OKW Kriegstagebuch* (organizational daily journal, hereafter referred to as "the journal.") on 6 March 1944. On 11 March, the decision was made to use these to constitute three new *Panzer* divisions: the *OKW* journal reads, "For this, the cadres of divisions used for the rescue of *Army Group South* should be used, that is, the *9th Panzer* and *10th* and *16th Panzer-Grenadier Divisions.*"[6]

The order for "Reconstitution" came down on 11 March 1944, from "*Der Führer*–Chief *OKW*/Army Staff." The detailed instructions issued by the Organization Section of the Army General Staff on 15 March 1944 referred to this order. It directed the rehabilitation of the *9th Panzer* and the *10th* and *16th Panzer-Grenadier Divisions* using the *155th, 179th,* and *273d Reserve Panzer Divisions.* It further specified that the *16th* should be combat ready no later than 15 May 1944.[7]

Meanwhile, the Division Commander accepted the Swords from Hitler and was familiarized with the plans for his Division. In his "Instructions for

Commanders" on 19 March 1944, he declared, "The Division's reconstitution as a *Panzer* division takes effect under my command."[8]

In a Division order on the same day, Count Schwerin announced the rehabilitation of the Division through Hitler:

> After the unfortunate battles in the vicinity of Pavlopya-Kamenka-Michailovka, I had to leave the Division due to a strong rebuke from our superiors. The Division was blamed for the breakdown of the front in the eastern bend of the Dnepr River. I disputed this unbearable, insulting reproach to the honor of the Division. At the same time, I announced that as long as such blame was brought against me, I was not in a position to accept the award of the Swords to the Knights Cross from the hand of the *Führer*. After examining the incident, the *Führer* decided that the accusations were made without justification; that the Division command and troops are free from any blame; and that I may remain your commander. I am profoundly happy to announce the *Führer*'s decision to all of you.[9]

At about that time, *Generaloberst* Guderian wrote to Schwerin that he was convinced that the name Schwerin would "guarantee the reappearance of numerous members of the old Division."[10]

The issuance of orders now began with full force by *OKH*, principally those from the Organization Section of the Army General Staff and from the General Army Office with the Chief of Army Equipment and Commander of the Replacement Army.

On 28 March 1944, the deadline for combat readiness for all three new *Panzer* divisions was moved up two weeks, to 1 May 1944.[11] At the same time, the *16th Panzer-Grenadier Division* was officially redesignated the *116th Panzer Division*.

For each newly constituted field unit of the *116th Panzer Division,* a corresponding unit in the *179th Reserve Panzer Division* was designated to handle organizational responsibilities. The relationships were as follows:

179th Reserve Panzer Division	**116th Panzer Division**
Reserve Panzer-Grenadier Regiment 81	*Panzer-Grenadier Regiment 60*
Reserve Grenadier Regiment 29	*Panzer-Grenadier Regiment 156*
Reserve Armored Reconnaissance Battalion 1	*Armored Reconnaissance Battalion 116*
Reserve Panzerjäger Battalion 9	*Panzerjäger Battalion 228**
Reserve Artillery Battalion 29	*Armored Artillery Regiment 146*[12]

---

*Although elsewhere in the text we translate the term *Panzerjäger* as "tank destroyer" (which is the US Army equivalent vehicle, being an armored vehicle mounting an antitank gun, designed specifically to fight tanks), this is only when the word is used in reference to individual vehicles or to organizations which contained only these vehicles. Unlike US tank destroyer battalions, a German WWII Divisional *Panzerjäger* battalion possessed

Reserve Panzer Battalion 1 was transferred in its entirety. It was equipped with *Panzer IVs,* and was temporarily renamed *"2d Battalion, Panzer Regiment 116."* The gun sections of the self-propelled artillery battalion of the armored artillery regiment trained separately at the firing range area at Gross Born in Pomerania. In mid-May, they joined the Division in France.[13]

Until the end of March 1944, some subunits of the three divisions being reconstituted were still assigned to *Army Group A* on the Eastern Front. However, on 30 March the order was finally given for all of them to be transferred immediately to the West.[14] Furthermore, it was decided to reorganize the three divisions under the *"Panzer Division 1944* (free organization)" structure, and a "temporary organization" was subsequently established. Final organization and wartime establishment were still being worked on and were to be forwarded when finalized.

New features of this "free organization" included the consolidation, at battalion level, of the logistics elements formerly assigned to the companies. On 15 August 1944, the Inspector General of *Panzer* Troops issued a table of organization for *Panzer Division 1944.*[15] (see Appendix 1) In several respects, it was different from the "temporary classification" of 30 March 1944. First, it was not specified that each *Panzer* regiment would possess a battalion equipped with Panthers. The creation of the army-anti aircraft battalion was also initially omitted. The *1st Battalion* (Self-Propelled) of the armored artillery regiment was to consist of two heavy batteries (equipped with *Hummel,* or "Bumblebee" self-propelled 150mm howitzers) and one light battery (equipped with *Wespe,* or "Wasp" self-propelled 105mm howitzers). The *2d Battalion* was structured with three batteries of four guns each, instead of two batteries of six guns each.[16] The *Panzer* regiment received the numerical designation *"116,"* and the other remaining units retained their old numbers.

On 2 May 1944, we were ordered to incorporate the staff of *Panzer Regiment 69* into *Panzer Regiment 116.*[17] On 20 May, the regiment was redesignated as *"Panzer Regiment 16."*[18] *Panzer Battalion 116* remained in Grafenwöhr, and became *1st Battalion, Panzer Regiment 16.* On 29 June, this unit was ordered to be reequipped with Panthers and be made combat-ready to join the Division no later than 15 October 1944.[19] In its place, from early May until the beginning of July, the *1st Battalion, Panzer Regiment "Grossdeutschland"* was attached to the Division.[20] From 14 June until the return of *Panzer Regiment 16's 1st Battalion* in November 1944, the *1st Battalion, Panzer Regiment 24* was attached to the Division.[21] The men of this battalion were loyal comrades, enduring all the heavy battles of the summer and autumn with us.

---

both tank destroyers and towed antitank guns. Similarly, since US regimental antitank companies or battalion antitank platoons possessed only towed antitank guns, the translation "Antitank Battalion" would also be misleading and imprecise. Thus, when *Panzerjäger* is used in reference to the divisional unit especially designed to fight tanks, we refer to it by its German nomenclature.

The decision for the reorganization of the *16th Panzer-Grenadier Division* as a *Panzer* division was soon known to the members of the Division still in the East. *Major* Vogelsang, the Division *IIa* (Adjutant) expressed this quite vividly in his diary. On the morning of 14 March, while in Olgopol, Vogelsang wrote:

> Last evening, we got a pleasant surprise when *Major* Tebbe (Commander of the *Panzer* battalion) called us from Vosnesensk, to tell us that by "decision of the *Führer,*" Count Schwerin will remain our Division Commander and will be vindicated. At the same time, *Major* Wolf (the "Second General Staff Officer," or *Ib* [Supply Officer]), who also arrived here, learned that in spite of the intentions of the *6th Army* staff, the Division will not be disbanded under any circumstances. Now the soldiers will pass the word from position to position; this should really boost the morale of those members of the Division who gradually despair about leadership and justice. . . . (20 March 1944)
>
> The remaining elements of the Division were concretely identified. They were split up among units of various sizes, with the *15th Infantry, 258th Infantry,* and *24th Panzer Divisions, Group Pean,* and at the bridgehead at Vosnesensk. (The latter had, by the personal order of the *Führer,* been declared a "Fortress," and thus the units there were tightly bound to their mission.) Part of the Division trains, some of the maintenance units, a few specialists, and the sick are being organized in the collection area west of the Bug river. . . ." (Vosnesensk, 17 March 1944, 1900 hrs.)
>
> The march to the collection area has commenced according to plan. Having been informed by telephone or messengers, all march units are on their way. Right now, we are still short 45 officers and 1,000 enlisted men who were incorporated into other units in action. At this point, the battalion made available to the battle commandant and a medical company remain at the bridgehead. The stream of individual stragglers has almost ceased. (20 March 1944, 1030 hrs)[22]

On 22 March 1944, by *OKH* directive, the Commander of *6th Army* ordered the formation of a reinforced regimental combat group from the elements of the *16th Panzer-Grenadier Division* that were still available for attachment to the *24th Panzer Division.*[23] The execution of this order would have meant that except for some logistical support units, hardly any members of the Division would have been transferred to the new formation. At the same time the order from *6th Army* arrived, the aforementioned orders from Count Schwerin in Germany also came in. Vogelsang reported in the diary:

> Here we were unpleasantly surprised by the arrival of a spy from *6th Army* headquarters, who had been detailed to supervise the formation of the combat group. He brought written orders from *6th Army* to this effect. According to them, we were now to assign all infantrymen and combat engineers to this *ad hoc* outfit. Only the remaining staff members and some mechanics could stay. What was to happen with the establishment of the new *Panzer* Division? For now, there was nothing to do but pass on the orders about the combat group. We sent the officer away and forbade any control over us.

At the same time, we received an order from Count Schwerin with additional instructions for the commanders. . . . Our first step was again to hold a commanders' conference for the announcement of his order, the disposition of the *6th Army* and the . . . order for the formation of the combat group. . . . It looks quite grim, especially in the case of the infantry, combat engineers, and armored reconnaissance personnel. We try as hard as we knew how to convince our superior commanders to settle for a reduction, as small as possible, of the cadre for the combat group we were to form. (Chernovo, northeast of Issayevo on the Tiligul, 22 March 1944)

Yesterday, we worked on the strength and organization of the combat group all day. . . . *Major* Grollmann arrived today and learned that since he was the only one among the available commanders who was healthy, he had to take command of the combat group. Naturally, he was shaken, as anyone probably would be in this case, and vehemently opposed the idea. Psychologically, it was a bad start for the members of this formation who had to stay behind to watch their comrades marching off to the West; for them, a three-year-old dream would not come to pass.

Yesterday, just at the right moment, a group of 450 convalescent replacements arrived from the homeland. They were immediately integrated into the combat group to relieve some of the men who had suffered most during the recent fighting. At this moment, the *Ia* conveys a warning order. We are to march cross country to Ismail on the Danube in Rumania to embark on trains. A 200- to 300-kilometer march—that will be a hard nut to crack for our already mostly sick men! (25 March 1944, 1800 hrs.)

The combat group is now ready, with an assigned strength of 700 German soldiers, plus a number of Russian volunteers (*Hiwis*). Now, all that's needed is the replenishment of the supply of weapons and equipment. . . . The rest of the Division is in five march units . . . [they] marched off and should reach the vicinity of Causani in Bessarbia—about 130–140 kilometers. (27 March 1944.)

From Bessarabia, the foot march continued to entrain at the railroad station in Rumania.

Under the provisions of the aforementioned 30 March order by *OKH,* the withdrawal and departure of the combat group to France was now also ordered. The foot march to the vicinity of Galatz on the Danube River took about two weeks. In the second week of April, the troops were loaded on trains in Braila, and two weeks later they reached their destination in France. *Major* Vogelsang closes this part of his diary with the following sentences:

During the coming days, little by little, undisturbed but totally exhausted, the "Division" arrived in Galatz without vehicles, heavy weapons, or tanks, and was loaded on trains. Throughout almost all of April, the individual transports rumbled westward. To our greatest joy, we found *Major* Grollmann and his combat group on the last transport.

All of this must be understood if one was to understand how *"Phoenix 116"* could be so quickly resurrected from the ashes of the *16th Panzer-Grenadier Division.* To actually appreciate this, one must also comprehend the indescribable difficulties, the efforts required, and the ability for improvisation of all involved, from all levels. (Nuremberg, 6 April 1944)

It was here where the strong cohesion of the Greyhounds and the camaraderie of the unit was proven, after three years of hard fighting with the enemy. Its men held together and joyfully returned to their old units when they learned that they were to be reconstituted in the West.

The transports reached the designated railroad stations west of Paris during the last ten days of April.[24] After disembarking, the men were taken to the corresponding units of the *179th Reserve Panzer Division,* which had been situated northwest of Paris since the end of March. Most of its units were north of the Seine, and its headquarters was in Meulan.[25] As shown in the division status report of 8 April 1944, it had already conducted good preparations under the supervision of the Commander of *Panzer Group West, General der Panzertruppe* Leo, *Reichsfreiherr* (Imperial Baron) Geyr von Schweppenburg.[26]

On 24 April, the *Panzer Group* announced that the *116th Panzer Division* already had a personnel strength of 13,500 men, reckoned as follows:

Arrived from the East	7,500 men
Recovered from wounds or returned from leave	2,000
German Ethnic Category III[27]	1,000
Members of the 179th Reserve *Panzer* Division	3,000[28]

Thus, actually only a little over one-third of the original 8,500 men from the *179th Reserve Panzer Division* had to be absorbed into the *116th.*

The equipment also started to come in. According to the 24 April report of *Panzer Group West,* equipment arriving between 8 and 22 April included *inter alia* 59 *Panzer IVs* with long 75mm main guns and 32 armored personnel carriers.

Vogelsang rushed ahead by airplane to take care of personnel questions with the personnel staff and with the reserve units. He arrived on 21 April in Meulan:

Today, I have been traveling all day long—visiting the *179th Reserve Panzer Division, Oberst* Voigtsberger, as well as all the staff sections of the Division that are already here. Toward evening, we occupied the Villa Hardancouria, a quaint little castle with an overgrown, park-like garden, making it the adjutants' quarters. There is more than enough work. . . . Right now, there is an alarm. The others [A polite euphemism for "the enemy"—*Editor*] systematically bomb all the railroad stations and airfields. At noon, it was Mantes' turn. We could hear substantial noise from the explosions. (22 April 1944, evening)

It is very unpleasant for us to find out that, according to orders, the *179th Reserve Panzer Division* is to be constituted instead of ours. . . . One could hardly have expected our Division to bring back more than about 3,000 soldiers from the Soviet Union, but this is now the reason being given for the preference for the *179th.* Now, thanks to all our efforts in every imaginable way, more members of the *16th Panzer-Grenadier Division* are arriving from the East and from the homeland, from training units, field hospitals, convalescent leave, and even from assignments to different units; all had arrived or sent word of their status. Thus, there was no good reason to integrate us into a different formation or to be reorganized by it. (23 April 1944, evening)

The transport carrying the Division command and communications staff arrived on 24 April. Now Vogelsang could really get to work. On 27 April, he traveled to Les Mureaux, on the south bank of the Seine, and achieved the independence of our division personnel from the *179th*:

> A clear situation after all! After the arrival of *Panzer-Grenadier Regiment 60*, we can be manned, with a few exceptions, by 1 May.
>
> A lengthy commanders' conference was held today, concerning all essential questions. Everything has gotten off to a pleasant start. Hopefully, the equipment will come too. The invasion is not going to be delayed much longer.
>
> This morning, we had a total of six air-raid warnings. The supply depot in Mantes was bombed twice in two days. One railroad station after another and many airports were attacked. The nights are getting to be more uneasy; low-flying aircraft are firing at single vehicles. Yesterday, one of our *Oberleutnants* was wounded. (28 April 1944)
>
> Meanwhile, all leaves were cancelled. It seems as if the situation is leading more and more toward the expected invasion. (29 April 1944)

Luckily, almost all members of the Division had received their leave during the previous twelve months.[29] On 30 April, Vogelsang wrote:

> All that could be foreseen in this situation, and whatever else is in the wind, points toward an invasion. We count on surprises every day. Hopefully, we still have time to achieve full combat readiness. Right now, we do have the men, but not much else, especially no motorized vehicles. We have been reinforced (temporarily) by the full-strength tank battalion from the *"Grossdeutschland" Division*. As a result, we appear to be in good shape as far as tanks go. There is also supposed to be a great deal of equipment on its way to us, but since the others bomb one railroad station after the other, the trains cannot reach us. All the transports that were to arrive from Russia are here by now!

The goal of being combat ready by 1 May could not be achieved. The principal problem was a shortage of equipment, and training had also only just begun. According to a memorandum in the files of the Inspector General of *Panzer* Troops, the target date had been postponed to 10 July.[30] In reference to all of the *Panzer* units then undergoing reconstitution, on 10 May the Inspector General announced to Hitler that it would be at least six weeks until they achieved a measurable degree of mobility and battleworthiness.[31] By this standard, this milestone would reached on or about 20 June.

On 29 April, the Division was placed under the tactical command of *Army Group B*, commanded by *Generalfeldmarschall* Rommel.[32] For issues related to training and organization, it remained answerable to *General* Geyr von Schweppenburg's *Panzer Group West*. On 26 May, *XLVII Panzer Corps* became our intermediate tactical headquarters, but this did not affect the Division until the beginning of the invasion.[33] For logistical support, commencing 18 April the Division was subordinated to *I SS-Panzer Corps*; from 2 May, it was supported by *15th Army*; and from 26 May, from the Military Commander of France.[34, 35, 36] On 3 May the staff of the *116th Panzer Division* officially assumed command of the units of the *16th Panzer-Grenadier* and *179th Reserve Panzer Divisions*.[37]

In the beginning of May, the Division delivered its first status report since moving to the West.[38] The Division's personnel strength was at nearly 100 percent. However, there were substantial shortcomings in equipment. Only the *2d Battalion, Panzer Regiment 16* possessed its full complement of *Panzer IVs*. Only 30–40 percent of the Division's authorized quantities of tank destroyers, artillery, antitank guns, and machine guns were on hand. Only 40 percent of the required quantity of armored personnel carriers were present. The biggest weakness, however, was in the quantity of wheeled vehicles, especially tactical trucks and prime movers. Only about six percent of trucks and prime movers had been delivered. The stocks of personnel vehicles and motorcycles reached 45 percent, but only four percent of the assigned off-road vehicles were present. The supply of prime movers reached only 0.4 percent of authorized.

In the "Commander's Summary" of this initial status report, Schwerin reached the following conclusion:

> Due to the protracted, heavy combat it experienced in the East, the training level of the Division is inadequate. The units lack cohesion. Because of the still ongoing retraining and special instruction of personnel, and because the units are still only partially equipped, unit combat readiness is limited. To restore full combat readiness, the Division requires thorough individual and collective training.

The morale and attitude of the troops was rated as "good and positive," but the degree of mobility of the Division was only 7.5 percent. The Division's battleworthiness at this moment was not great, "Because of the paucity of motorized vehicles and equipment, the Division is only capable of limited attack assignments and only with weak units (combat groups)."

On 3 May, Schwerin was welcomed to the Division "with music and flowers." "One is impressed again and again by his personality," Vogelsang noted on 4 May. The next day, the Division Commander reported to Army Group headquarters in La Roche-Guyon on the Seine. On that day, Rommel dictated his personal "daily report" to his aide.[39] "Today I had a conference with . . . *Generalleutnant* Count von Schwerin, the Division Commander of the *116th Panzer Division*, which is now also subordinated to the Army Group."

On 7 May, Vogelsang wrote that "the commander of our new *Panzer* regiment staff," *Oberstleutnant* von Trotha, reported for duty. Vogelsang continued, "He came from a bombed-out camp, where 228 were killed and several hundred wounded. The staff also suffered nine dead, and lost all its motorized vehicles and much equipment."

Trotha came from Mailly-le-Camp (70 kilometers south-southeast of Reims), where the Panther battalions being formed in the West were located. The attack on this installation could have had more serious consequences if *General* Geyr von Schweppenburg had not had the foresight to move most units out of the cantonment area and into the surrounding villages and woods.[40]

Bombs also fell on the Division's individual cantonments, such as the attack on the encampment of *Panzer Pioneer Battalion 675* at Mantes on 7 May. The losses were minor: throughout May, the Division lost only eight dead and eight wounded.[41]

As we have seen, the mobility of the Division was still quite poor. Since we could not depend upon substantial deliveries of motorized vehicles from the homeland, the *Supreme Commander–West* received the order to pull out trucks from his units' stocks to equip the *9th, 11th,* and *116th Panzer Divisions.* This decision required the wisdom of Solomon. The prospects for its success had to be very carefully evaluated, as the situation regarding motorized vehicles in the West was already tense.[42]

Between 13 and 15 May, the Division was transferred northwest into the area southeast of Rouen.[43] This area extended almost as far as Mantes and Meulan in the southeast.

The Division command post was in Bernouville and Bézu-St. Eloi (six kilometers northwest of Gisors). The Division Commander was housed a little outside the area in a small castle which had once been Clemenceau's country home. On 16 May, the commander again visited Army Group headquarters; he reported the completion of the Division's displacement and informed the Army Group Chief of Staff, *Generalleutnant* Dr. Speidel, about the progress of the Division's reconstitution. By now, 55 percent of the authorized quantity of wheeled vehicles were present, but there were still numerous vital commodities missing, such as the equipment for maintenance shops and recovery operations, as well as prime movers. Only 30 percent of the field kitchens had arrived. There was also a lack of communications equipment. The fuel situation presented a particular problem. The transfer had used up so much of the Division's already small supply that training with vehicles came to a dead stop. *Army Group B* and *Panzer Group West* did make efforts to remedy the fuel situation; on 19 May, the *Supreme Commander–West* allocated 100 cubic meters of fuel to the Division.[44]

Stragglers from the East continued to arrive at the Division, including several Division staff officers. The *Ic* (Intelligence Officer), *Hauptmann der Reserve* Dr. Holtermann and the *IIb* (Adjutant for Enlisted Men), *Hauptmann der Reserve* Stukenberg, were followed finally on 25 May by me. Vogelsang describes the reunion:

Yesterday, in Paris, *Major i.G.* Wolf* and I picked up the little Guderian, our old, esteemed *Ia*, known and loved throughout the Division. Thus, the last of the old group that had been relieved and run about were with us once again. After the unbelievable events at Krivoi Rog, and all the ensuing suffering, the last stone had been turned in the reconstitution of the Division. We are all together again! There is great joy. Among the commanders, the welcome at the Division headquarters was equally joyful. (26 May 1944)

The day before, Vogelsang commented upon the Division's situation:

The formation of the Division made good progress. A large part of the weapons are now with the unit. Wheeled vehicles have also arrived, but are in very poor condition. In addition, the self-propelled artillery battalion has been established. With certain limitations, the majority of the Division is combat ready. If the Tommies and Americans wait a little while longer, we and the other two *Panzer* divisions will be completely prepared! (25 May 1944)

Now we have 80 percent of the machine guns and 70 percent of the wheeled vehicles. In three more weeks we will be quite well put together, contrary to other predictions. (26 May 1944)

On 24 May, Vogelsang produced the order for the formation of *Field Replacement Battalion 146.*[45] It was to be formed into a headquarters, two half-battalions, and one staff company (doubling as the Division combat training school). The two half-battalions were formed from the remnants of the *3d Battalions* of both *Panzer-Grenadier* regiments, and were to signify "the continuation of stability and tradition." In this manner, the Division Commander wanted to maintain the continuity of these battalions, which otherwise would have been eliminated under the new table of organization. Vogelsang wrote, "This required a new internal appraisal of personnel strength within the Division, and a new organization of the wartime structure, with cross-assignments and changes to duty positions in many areas of the Division."

The Division combat training school commenced operations on 14 June, after the Normandy landings. Under the command of *Hauptmann* Winter, the first course was conducted from 27 June to 25 July 1944. The mission of the school was to train squad and platoon leaders:

From experience, the attrition of junior leaders could not be covered adequately by replacements assigned from the homeland, either in quantity or in quality. It is further necessary to select and train the next generation of junior leaders from our own ranks. . . . The objective is to produce leaders who set an excellent example of combat spirit and proficiency for their men.[46]

---

*"*i.G.*" stood for "im Generalstab," signifying that the officer is a member of the German General Staff Corps, a carefully trained and managed group of specially selected officers assigned to the most demanding command and staff positions.

After they moved into their quarters, units began systematic training. Special attention was paid to firming up the lax discipline acquired during the Eastern campaign, as well to training specialists.[47] The training with heavy equipment, individually and collectively, suffered due to missing or slowly arriving equipment; it was also limited by insufficient fuel.

After the Division's transfer into the area southeast of Rouen in mid-May, all units received the order to defend their cantonments against enemy airborne assault. For that reason, alarm systems were planned; reaction units were established; positions reinforced; and in open areas, suitable for drop zones, anti-parachutist obstacles were rammed into the ground. These stakes were usually called "Rommel stakes" or "Rommel asparagus," because their installation was initiated by the *Generalfeldmarschall* himself. Naturally, training was further impeded by these measures.[48]

Still, commanders sought every opportunity for training. For example, there is evidence in Vogelsang's diary that on 11 May, *Panzer-Grenadier Regiment 156* conducted a very educational tactical exercise, in which all of the Division's commanders and adjutants participated. The topic was division operations in the event of the invasion. At the end, we listened to a lecture about parachute units and airborne landings by a general staff officer. On 26 May, Vogelsang wrote, "I'm often alone or on the road with the general to visit tactical exercises and troop units. On 2 June, *Armored Engineer Battalion 675* conducted a tactical exercise in Heuqueville. Ultimately, the Division prepared a planning exercise concerning the advance and deployment of the Division in the event of a landing between the mouth of the Somme and Le Havre. However, it was cancelled when the invasion occurred."

In late May, *Armored Artillery Regiment 146* conducted several live fire exercises. The results in the *5th Battery,* for example, revealed that "the battery may well be combat ready, but needs a lot more practice to get back into the old swing of things, due to new men and replacements who have not received very good training."[49]

Training, building defensive positions, and emergency reaction tasks were a difficult combination for the unit, but the diaries also speak of recreation, of movies and variety shows, of soccer games, visits to Paris, and social gatherings.

On 1 June, the Division was almost at full strength. Only the Army anti-aircraft battalion, the *Panzer* signal battalion, and the supply troops were still short of men. The equipment situation showed considerable improvements, but also significant shortcomings. Thus, the Division's equipment fill was approximately as follows:

Armored personnel carriers, armored reconnaissance vehicles, and armored artillery observation vehicles,	65%
Tank destroyers	55%
Heavy artillery	30%
Motorcycles	20%

All terrain wheeled vehicles (which were inadequately replaced from commercial sources)	15%
Total truck capacity	70%
Prime Movers	20%
Anti-aircraft cannon	0%

The "Commander's Summary" of the last situation report before the beginning of the invasion stated the following:

1. The training status of the Division has improved at the time of this report, but is not yet sufficient. While good progress has been made in the individual and platoon training, there are still deficiencies, mainly in collective and combined arms operations.
2. Morale of the troops is good and their attitude positive, in spite of the impressions made by enemy air superiority.
3. Special difficulties:
   —Lack of collective training opportunities.
   —The deficiency of radio sites and shortages of personnel vehicles and motorcycles degrade the mobility of the Division's leaders.
   —The non-combat ready status of *Army Anti-Aircraft Battalion 281,* especially in view of the situation in the air in the West.
   —The shortage of scout vehicles limits reconnaissance capabilities.
   —Obsolescence of a large proportion of the wheeled vehicles, the lack of spare parts, and a combat readiness rate among the repair crews of only about 50 percent, all combine to augur a heavy loss of vehicles in the next deployment.
   —The shortage of tires prevents full use of cargo volume.
4. Degree of mobility: 70 percent.
5. Due to incomplete collective training, the Division is only suitable for limited offensive operations.[50]

Appendix 2a is a roster of officers and their assignments, down to and including company commanders, as of mid June 1944. Some positions could not be filled. Further, officer assignments from 16 December 1944 to 15 March 1945, and a roster of Knight's Cross recipients are listed, in Appendices 2b through 2e.

On 4 June, the Commander, *Ia,* and *Ib,* of the *116th Panzer Division* drove to a conference with the *Army Group B* Chief of Staff in La Roche-Guyon.[51] First, Speidel oriented us on Rommel's intention "to advance the Division to approximately the line of Neufchatel–Rosay–Cleris–Malaunay–Rouen, with a general thrust toward Dieppe." He based this intention on the belief that *General* Cramer, who had recently returned from British captivity, also assumed the bulk of the allied invasion would be on "both sides of the River Somme." With this, two topics were addressed which required further discussion, namely the location of the enemy landing, and Rommel's authority to place the formations under his tactical command where he wanted to, both during preparation for deployment and during the deployment itself. From Speidel's interpretation, one could deduce that Rommel also expected the enemy to land on both sides of the Somme. Furthermore, one could conclude that Rommel was rightfully entitled to advance the Division closer to the coast, or at least that he did not expect objections from his superiors. Such a disposition would have brought the Division about 20 kilometers closer to the coast. Its advanced units would thus have been about 25 kilometers behind Dieppe.

After this information by Speidel, I delivered the Division status report. I declared that *Panzer Regiment 16,* including the *Panther Battalion "Grossdeutschland"* were combat ready, but both *Panzer-Grenadier* regiments still lacked heavy self-propelled infantry guns and some of the armored personnel carriers; the ones that had been delivered had no machine guns. I also stated that the *Panzer* reconnaissance battalion had not yet received its armored cars, nor the half-tracks with cannon that it was authorized; it was also short of specialists in its heavy company. The *Panzerjäger* battalion had 12 antitank guns without prime movers; it also had six assault guns and six tank destroyers belonging to the *179th Reserve Panzer Division,* but these were supposed to be returned to their rightful owners. I suggested that they remain with the *116th Panzer Division,* and to provide the 12 antitank guns to the *Panzer-Grenadier* regiments, which had the capability to tow them behind their own vehicles. The artillery was not mentioned in the report. The report further stated that with a few exceptions, the anti-aircraft battalion was combat ready from a personnel perspective and that the guns were all present. However, the battalion lacked "all other vehicles and, most importantly, the optical sights" for the weapons. In this regard, the report was in error. Unfortunately, the anti-aircraft battalion actually had no guns. They were only delivered after the withdrawal from France.[52] I concluded by again noting the paucity of communications equipment for the Division signal battalion, as well as radios in the rest of the Division's signal units.

Accordingly, the *116th Panzer Division* was not able to complete its reconstitution by early June 1944. The Inspector General of *Panzer* Troops' estimate that limited combat readiness would only be possible by about 20 June turned out to be realistic. In spite of this, the Division already had achieved respectable battleworthiness; the tank regiment alone, with its two tank battalions, represented significant combat power. Both battalions were ahead of the rest of the Division in their preparations; unlike the other divisional units, they had not returned, shattered, from the Eastern Front only five weeks earlier. However, even the other divisional units were again looking better. All of this had been achieved within about six weeks.

At this point, the work that was done in the homeland should also be remembered. In spite of the hail of bombs, people produced innumerable products that were then shipped by the railroad workers to the front, which consumed everything they sent. The sacrifice made by all those women and men who contributed to the effort with little public recognition should hereby be acknowledged. They behaved like the soldiers at the front, for the good of their country, and many gave their lives.

CHAPTER 2

Awaiting the Invasion

What thoughts were going through the minds of the soldiers during these weeks of spring 1944? What was the leadership doing to defend against an invasion? What were the opponents planning?

First of all, the soldiers of the *Windhund Division* who came to France from the East all took a deep breath and thanked their Creator for having survived the tortuous battles of defense and retreat from the bend of the Dnjepr River to Bessarabia. They really enjoyed the break in action as well as the spring sunshine in beautiful France. Almost everywhere, relations between the French and the German soldiers were friendly.

A young *Panzer* officer, *Leutnant* Janske Drost, wrote of the atmosphere in France:

> In the evenings, we often sit together under the big chestnut tree. For dessert, *Madame* Dupont would serve salad or strawberries and in exchange for it, *Monsieur* would get a cigarette. Then we have a glass of red wine and our conversation deals with the war, its context, and side effects. The people insist that they did not want this war and did not feel any animosity towards Germany. This is not just politeness or caution towards the enemy billeted among them. In fact, I heard the same all over the country. Certainly, personal contact between the French civilians and our military in general—indeed the conduct and the appearance of the German soldier in particular—influenced French public opinion, and mostly to our benefit. But I do believe that, in fact, the old hatred against the "sworn enemy" was no longer prevalent among the majority of the French populace by 1939. One cannot change a deeply-rooted opinion that quickly; that is, by 1944. We soon recognized those who were convinced of the insurmountable differences between our peoples and persisted in the old animosity. With impressive pride, they show us ice-cold rejection. They are mostly teachers, clergy, physicians, and lawyers. This is all the more significant considering that, despite their great influence, another opinion keeps growing.[1]

In a company newsletter from 15 May 1944, company commander *Oberleutnant* Weiss appealed to his soldiers with an article, titled "Conduct":

> Today, we are all over Europe and every one of us is a personal representative of the German people. You can be sure that all Europe looks upon us with critical and watchful eyes. If any of you believe that mistakes, blunders, injustices, and impudence would be benevolently overlooked and hushed up, you are definitely on the wrong track.[2]

In his diary, Vogelsang also occupied himself with the relationship between the German soldiers and the French people. On 29 April, he visited an old acquaintance from 1941, in Paris:

> After the long time in Russia, I was received and entertained by him and his kin with surprise, joy, and affection, like a member of his family. He himself and his father's family were bombed out. They curse the English and the Americans. (29 April 1944)
>
> How France will conduct itself in case of an invasion is very debatable. The two sides are in serious opposition. Disturbances can be expected with certainty. Pétain's proclamation regarding the critical internal political situation was very clear. The majority of the population may be relatively indifferent, or above board with us. Some have very friendly attitudes, while others are totally hostile. This is mainly true for the Communists. (30 April 1944)

On 6 May, along with a married couple, Vogelsang and Count Schwerin were invited to dinner by the Division Commander's hosts. During the "very cozy" and "stimulating conversation," the problems of the French became clear: "Our hosts are afraid of a possible German departure. They are afraid of the underground, mostly of the Communists and their vengeance and envy toward property owners. Paris would turn into a witch's cauldron." (7 May 1944)

Despite of all social distractions, which next to work would soon develop into a "constant burden," (14 May 1944) the reality of war was ever present: "According to private tips from the general's circle of friends, we had expected the invasion for yesterday morning. But it did not happen." (14 May 1944)

Streams of enemy aircraft roared over the troops daily and unloaded their bombs on airports, traffic installations, and mainly the French railroad system, as well as the bridges over the Seine. At the same time, the German homeland also suffered from heavy air raids, specifically aimed at the aircraft industry and fuel production.

Vogelsang penetratingly described the tremendous activity of the allied air forces:

> We have air raid alarms once or twice daily. About 200 American planes, in packs of fifty each, flew over us in Meaux. If they would have unloaded on us!—But better here than at home! (24 April 1944)
>
> During the night from 6 to 7 May we observed a heavy air raid on Mantes, with innumerable parachute flares, search lights, and detonating bombs. Unfortunately, the engineers suffered losses. The paymaster is dead, one company commander and the physician are wounded. The next attack has already taken place today at noon. (7 May 1944)
>
> In general, many air raid alarms and non-stop attacks during the day and night throughout the whole area. (20 May 1944)
>
> The flyers are ever so zealous as they cause substantial damage to the railroad system and bridges, as well as to industry. The supply of provisions for Paris has

become difficult. Most of the industry lays dormant due to lack of coal and electricity.

Unfortunately, the Division suffered more losses because of low-flying aircraft. They had a special preference for attacking single vehicles and convoys on the big and open national roads. Yesterday, one man from *Regiment 60* was shot, and one wounded. Almost daily, bomber formations pass over us, with from 30 to 150 planes. Today again, bombs fell in our proximity. (22 May 1944)

Finally, the sun came out again—sadly, this also brought more enemy aircraft. In tight swarms, they fly over us and bomb the railroad stations that are still intact or had been repaired. Single fighters and fighter bombers prowl over all important roads and railroad lines and render those areas unsafe. Unfortunately, the losses are mounting quite noticeably. (24 May 1944)

Again, the Americans attacked a passenger train with fighter bombers. Besides a number of French civilians, a soldier from the *Field Replacement Battalion* was also killed. After a series of others, the Gisors railroad station has now also been blown to pieces! Air activity is increasing. One must be very careful on every trip, even on side roads." (26 May 1944)

None of those who were present will forget how, on 28 May, we sat in the church of Les Andelys on the Seine, during a Pentecost service that was also a memorial service for our fallen comrades, while swarms of bombers buzzed above us without interruption.[3] The drone of their engines mixed into the organ music and the singing, and almost overpowered the voice of the minister. We knew that the bridges over the Seine were preferred targets. Was it now the turn for the bridge of Les Andelys? We asked ourselves if we should not at once cut the church service short, but on this day, not one bomb fell on Les Adelys. God probably listened to the prayers and rewarded the worshippers. At this point, we remembered our two clergymen with gratitude: The Protestant minister's name was Baedeker, and the Catholic priest's name was Strickstrock.

"The air war increased day by day," Vogelsang wrote in the evening of the same day. "One by one, all the bridges, airfields, and railroad stations are being destroyed. Supply is difficult, industry lies dormant, electricity is scarce, all roads are hunting grounds." (28 May 1944) On 30 May, he wrote his last entry before the invasion:

> The air war continued during the days of Pentecost with unrelenting force. The last two bridges between Paris and Rouen are now gone too. Good thing that we moved out of Mureaux in time because there, along with the bridge, parts of the village were taken out. During Pentecost, France is said to have suffered 5,000 deaths. Two flyers who bailed out were almost beaten to death by an embittered mob in Amiens.

Shortly after an air raid on Rouen, which had already suffered heavy destruction and losses to its population on 24 April, the author spoke with a French woman whose house was still intact. Pointing a finger to the sky, she said, "They'll bomb us until we turn German."

The increasing number of air raids on the countryside inland from the coast during the last days of May indicated that the invasion was not far away. There was no way of determining a specific concentration behind any particular sector of the coast. As we know today, to mislead the German command, air raids for the specific preparation of the invasion began about 60 days before the landing, and they were divided between Normandy and the area north of the Seine, in a ratio of one to two. The actual landing areas at the coast were bombed only shortly before the invasion itself.[4]

In view of the coming invasion, every thinking soldier started to reflect on the war situation. Considering the growing superiority of the Soviets since the autumn of 1943, the fear arose that the German forces in the East could not withstand that pressure for long. The situation in the Mediterranean was not delightful, either. North Africa, Sicily, and southern Italy were in the enemy's hands. After the fall of Mussolini, Italy switched sides. The successes of the *U*-boats had diminished. In the air war, a great, still-growing superiority of the Western opponents was evident. We witnessed it in France every day.

The days of shining victories were gone. Since the start of 1943, there were almost only failures. If the Anglo-Americans were successful with their invasion in the West, the war would be lost. Should the invasion be repelled, it would create a new situation that could perhaps allow a political solution, with hopes for a bearable termination of the war. Therefore, every effort had to be made to thwart the invasion—unless one had already conceded the certain loss of the war for the purpose of toppling the government. But only a very few came to that conclusion.

On 3 November 1943, in an accurate evaluation of the general situation at large, Hitler issued Edict 51, which began as follows:

> The tough and costly combat of the last two and a half years against Bolshevism has taken an extreme toll on the larger part of the military forces and its efforts. This is a result of the magnitude of the danger and the overall situation. In the meantime, the situation has evolved. The danger in the East has remained, but a larger one in the West is starting to emerge: the Anglo-Saxon landing. In an extreme case, a loss of a large area of land in the East could be tolerated, without causing mortal damage to German life.
>
> It is different in the West! If the enemy can penetrate our defenses on a broad front, the consequences will be immeasurable. All signs point to the fact that the enemy will attack the western front of Europe in the spring at the latest, and perhaps earlier.[5]

Corollary to this evaluation, the forces available to *Generalfeldmarschall* von Rundstedt, *Supreme Commander–West* had to be reinforced. In consonance with this, the reconstitution of the *116th* and of two other *Panzer* divisions in France was as evident as the enforced completion of the Atlantic Wall.[6] *Generalfeldmarschall* Rommel's inspection of the readiness of the defenses along the coast from Denmark to Brittany was also evidence of this.[7] In pursuit of this mission, on 1 January 1944, Rommel and his *Army Group B* assumed command of the sector from the Netherlands to the mouth of the Loire, and went to work energetically.[8]

Ultimately, there were 58 divisions in the West, ten of which were armored.[9] Three infantry divisions were deployed on the coast of the Netherlands. Between Oosterschelde and Dives, *15th Army* deployed 17 infantry divisions—11 directly on the coast, with 6 behind them in reserve. Bordering the Loire to its left (south), *7th Army* deployed nine and a half divisions along the coast, with five and a half divisions behind them in reserve. *Army Group G* covered the area of southern France with 13 infantry divisions.

OKW retained four of the ten armored divisions as a reserve, namely the *1st SS-Panzer Division,* north of Brussels; the *12th SS-Panzer Division,* south of the line Elbeuf–Bernay–Vimoutiers; the *Panzer Lehr Division,* between Chartres and Le Mans; and the *17th SS-Panzer-Grenadier Division* near Niort, south of the Loire.[10]

Three *Panzer* divisions, the *2d SS, 9th,* and *11th,* were under the command of *Army Group G,* while three others were under the command of *Army Group B.* The *2d Panzer Division* was at the Somme between Amiens and Abbeville; the *116th* was east of Rouen; the *21st* was at Caen, but had elements already deployed in the sectors of the coastal divisions, in accordance with the wishes of the Army Group commander.

On the German side, knowledge about the enemy was insufficient. Reconnaissance by the *Luftwaffe* and German Navy was an almost total failure. German intelligence calculated that there were more than twice as many enemy troops available as there were: instead of the actual 37 divisions available to the enemy, the *OKH* intelligence section responsible for analyzing the enemy order of battle in the West estimated there were 79.[11] This miscalculation helped validate the enemy's deception operations and, as will be seen, led to terrible consequences during the invasion.[12]

The questions on every leader's mind were the time and place of the opponent's landing. The one thing on which everyone agreed was that the landing would be in the spring. From the observation of enemy landing exercises, everyone concluded that the enemy would most likely land with a rising tide to allow transit past the beach obstacles, which would be submerged at high tide. Since the landing fleet would probably not approach in total darkness, based on the different times of tides, one could calculate when a landing at dawn would be favorable in each respective coastal sector.[13]

On the German side, there were varying predictions about the location in which the landing would take place. The prevalent opinion was that the enemy would land on the Channel coast between the strait of Dover and Le Havre, in the sector defended by the *15th Army.* At this point, the opponent had the shortest sea distance to cover and the fastest way into the *Reich.* This is also where the launching sites for the "V," or *Vergeltungswaffen* ["Vengeance weapons"] were being built.[14] To this end, this sector was more heavily fortified and units were more densely deployed than in the other sectors.

The bay of the Seine in Normandy was also considered to be in danger. This opinion was shared by the leadership of the German Navy. They came to the conclusion that a landing on the Channel coast would be most probable; they further opined that the Cotentin Peninsula was an unlikely venue for the main attack, although they admitted that location was suitable for a diversionary operation in support of the main invasion.[15]

Hitler was most intensively preoccupied with Normandy. Several times, he pointed out the danger and the significance of the Cotentin with the main port of Cherbourg at its tip. Hitler demanded and achieved reinforcements for that area, against partial resistance from the commanders in the West.[16]

In retrospect, it was asserted that *Generalfeldmarschall* Rommel also believed that Normandy was especially imperiled and proposed its reinforcement.[17] The contemporary war records do not convey this impression. On 2 May 1944, when Hitler once again demanded reinforcements for Normandy, Rommel used the opportunity to gain influence over the *OKW* reserves, namely *I SS-Panzer Corps* with the *Panzer Lehr* and *12th SS-Panzer Divisions*. He requested their subordination to *Army Group B* and demanded that they be transferred to the vicinity of Lisieux–east of Rennes–Alençon. Neither the *Supreme Commander–West* nor *OKW* wanted to give up their reserve prematurely.[18] Map 1 shows that the area requested by Rommel would not have meant fundamental changes. Furthermore, the *Panzer* divisions from *OKW* Reserve, except for the *12th SS-Panzer Division*, were stationed exactly where Rommel wanted them in his request of 10 April 1944.[19] The *Panzer Lehr Division* had just arrived in the west from Hungary! Rommel also failed in his 12 May attempt to get *General* Jodl, Chief of the *Wehrmacht* Operations Staff, to agree to the deployment of the *12th SS-Panzer Division* south of the Cotentin Peninsula.[20] This location would hardly have been a better place, probably even worse than near Bernay.

The Atlantic Wall, reinforced by efforts of the Army, presented quite an imposing fortification, but its construction included significant discrepancies. The most strongly fortified sector lay between Dunkirk and Le Touquet, and the remaining portions of the Channel coast were built up more than the bay of the Seine and the other coastal regions. Between the strongest positions, Rommel had the troops build field fortifications and erect obstacles on the beach. In the areas behind the coast that would lend themselves to airborne landings, the troops installed the aforementioned "Rommel Asparagus," and as far as possible, the areas were secured by reserves. Wherever possible, flooded regions and swamps were created.[21]

There was unity regarding conduct of the battle in the event of an invasion, to the extent that there was hope of repelling the enemy during his approach to the coast. For that reason, Rommel wanted to deploy the armored divisions close behind the most threatened coastline sectors. As mentioned before, the *OKW* subordinated only three *Panzer* divisions to him, but stationed the *OKW* reserve largely per Rommel's requests. Jodl wanted to keep these "modest reserves" for

"operational command," that is, to affect the outcome not just of individual battles near the beach, but of the entire campaign. He promised Rommel he would
release them without being asked, "as soon as the intentions and the main attack
of the enemy became clear."[22] Apparently, nobody approached the subject of
redeploying the three *Panzer* divisions stationed in southern France to the badly
endangered front of *Army Group B*. In his book *Invasion 1944, Generalleutnant*
Dr. Speidel, *Army Group B* Chief of Staff, concluded his considerations about the
use of the operational reserves with the following, "For *political* reasons, it
seemed appropriate to the *Feldmarschall* to have reliable *Panzer* units at hand for
possible upcoming events." [emphasis by the Editor][23]

The *2d* and *116th Panzer Divisions* were available for just this sort of contin-
gency. They were subordinated to *Army Group B* and were led by commanders
whom Speidel considered approachable.[24] The leadership of the *Panzer Lehr
Division* was perhaps the only one of the *OKW* reserve that was similar in this
regard; there was no question about the attitude of the leadership of the three *SS*
divisions.

On 8 May, *Generalfeldmarschall* von Rundstedt assembled his commanders in
the West to "orient them on the common mission." He stated one could be confident, "because there are all kinds of powerful results achieved by commanders
and troops alike; new ideas for the further improvement for the coastal defense
had been practically applied, thanks to the initiative of *Feldmarschall* Rommel,
so that one can look forward to the impending battles with complete calm."[25]

Similar utterances have been handed down about Rommel. On 6 May, he
wrote to his wife, "I am looking forward to the battle with great confidence,
maybe by 15 May, maybe by the end of the month."[26]

On the previous day, after receiving the report from Count Schwerin, he dictated in his personal daily report that, "The area behind the coast is now, after all,
quite strong in regard to troops and my confidence has grown even more. If the
English give us two more weeks, I will have no more worries."[27]

On 14 May, during a speech to representatives of all branches of the armed
forces and *Organization Todt* at Le Touquet in the Atlantic Wall, Rommel
expressed his confidence about the upcoming decisive battle.[28] On the evening of
this day, he dictated to his aide-de-camp, "In regard to the upcoming decisive battle in the West, I hope that my words will arouse confidence not only among the
soldiers, but also in the homeland."[29]

During these days, Count Schwerin visited the units of the *116th Panzer
Division*. On 6 May, the men of the *3d Battalion, Armored Artillery Regiment 146*
stood in formation for roll call on the castle grounds of Villette, not far from
Meulan. Schwerin spoke in "clear and earnest words."[30]

> The fight has been hard, but it will get harder still, and we must not have false
> hopes. Our enemies are pursuing the total destruction of the German people, and we
> are called upon to annihilate this . . . desire for our destruction. This requires the

cooperation of every single German person, as well as tremendous strength. Whatever may happen, there will be no capitulation as there was in 1918. We will persevere and fight until the victory is ours.[31]

In 1977, Schwerin opined that this report by *Leutnant* Poth did not correspond with the speeches he made at that time, and he presented a different view in the *Memoirs of the Former Commander of the 116th Panzer Division.* [Written in the third person, "He" refers to Schwerin—*Editor*]

> He could count on the men of his Division and they would follow him anywhere, because they trusted his decisions. After his return, he had visited all the units and told them openly and honestly that it is now strictly about the honor of the German soldier, which would have to be maintained for the sake of the future of Germany, regardless of whether it was an advance or a retreat. At a time when one was only supposed to drivel about the upcoming victory, that was quite risky. The soldiers understood very well what the *General* was trying to tell them. None of them committed treason. Now they knew what it was about and what was demanded of them. They were willing to carry out their duty and to keep the shield of honor of the German soldier, and especially of their Division, unblemished.[32]

How can the same event be interpreted so differently? The young lieutenant cannot be further questioned about his interpretation; he was killed in action. His comrades remember him as being enthusiastic. He may have written down his impression of the speech, maybe in some formulations following his own manner of expression, but without the intent to falsify anything. His text indicates the possibility that, at that time, the majority of the German soldiers hardly understood the hidden indications of a mind like Count Schwerin's that thought in other ways.

Other members of the Division were worried that the kind of speeches made by their commander would not properly prepare the troops for what was to come. Unlike *Leutnant* Poth, they sensed the ambiguity of Count Schwerin's speeches. After my return to the Division, I heard about these officers' concerns. I asked Count Schwerin if it was correct to talk to the men only about the fight for the honor of the German soldier; would it not be more important to call on them to defend against the coming invasion? (Today one would say "to motivate them.") I also expressed the opinion that there might be a chance to repel the invasion, which would then present a more favorable situation. At that time, the Division Commander answered this question only with, "Is that what you think?" I answered that I did, indeed, believe it. I found myself in agreement with what the soldiers had to be told in this situation, as well as with what the leadership in the West proclaimed, and, evidently to a large extent, believed. It is well known among soldiers that troops can sense when their leader has lost his faith in success. Their fighting spirit suffers, which again seems to validate the opinion of the leader involved.

In 1959, Vice Admiral Ruge recalled his opinion of those days. "Sober consideration mandated that only total rebuff of a major invasion attempt could lead to real respite and relief. In turn, this could even lead to a sort of bearable conclusion of the war, in spite of all requests by the statesmen of the opposing side for an unconditional surrender."[33]

Here, he is indicating that he had thoughts similar to mine, and wrote them down 15 years later.

For many months, the Americans and the English prepared their invasion to the last detail.[34] Immense numbers of ships, airplanes, and equipment stood ready to transport the invasion troops to the beach, to support them by fire, and to supply them. On the first day ("D-Day") alone, this would include three airborne divisions and five infantry divisions. To facilitate this, 163 new airfields had been built in England. Beginning in January 1944, the allied air forces prepared for the invasion by systematically eliminating the German *Luftwaffe* and by destroying the aircraft industry. Next, they attacked German fuel supplies and thus, long before the invasion began, the Allies established air superiority. With that accomplished, they began attacking the transportation system and the airfields in France.

Based on the experience gained from the failed attempt to land at Dieppe in 1942, the enemy knew they should conduct the landing on an open coast. Accordingly, the allies developed two artificial ports and planned an underwater pipeline. The "wind-protected" bay of the Seine in Normandy, between the River Orne and north of the mouth of the River Vire, was chosen as the landing site. From there, the allies calculated that the ports of Cherbourg and Brittany would be conquered quickly.

The time of the landing would be determined by the following criteria: moonlight on the night before the landings to better enable the airborne operation and crossing of the massive fleet; low tide at dawn for the first landings; and a rising tide for the following hours. The operation was named OVERLORD. General Eisenhower was responsible for overall command of the operation, while the invasion troops were led by the British Field Marshal Montgomery.

Every last detail was thought out, but the opponent's leadership did not consider the invasion to be a leisurely stroll, despite all their overwhelming preparations and forces. Churchill called it "the most difficult and the most complicated operation that ever took place." Later, in his report about the invasion, Eisenhower said, "With Operation 'Overlord', we built our foundation on unknown factors and in hindsight, our fate on games."[35] He also stated:

> When we moved into France, we had all the tactical information that a competent intelligence service could acquire, but we had to reckon with the activities of the enemy. We had to undertake the largest invasion in history against a coastline spiked with the most modern fortifications, and behind this coast stood the German army in the west that since the dark days of 1940 had not fought a battle.[36]

Eisenhower had already prepared an announcement to use in the event the invasion failed. It read:

> At our landing in the vicinity of Cherbourg-Le Havre, we were unable to establish an adequate foothold, and I have, therefore, brought our troops back. My decision to attack at this time in this area was based on the best available information. The Army, Air Force, and naval forces did everything that bravery and sense of duty can do. Any mistakes in this operation and any reprimand due are mine alone.[37]

CHAPTER 3

The Landing: The Battles in Normandy from 6 June to 18 July 1944

By the end of May 1944, the *Wehrmacht* believed itself to be relatively well disposed for its opponent's expected landings, however, the German Navy's coastal mine-laying effort was still "in a state of pronounced weakness."[1,2] Enemy combat power and the location and time of the landings remained unknown. Reconnaissance by the *Luftwaffe* and Navy was completely inadequate, and the reports from the intelligence service were of dubious character.[3,4] Even though it was presumed that the opponent would probably land at dawn during rising tides, it was calculated in the West that there would be no danger for the days of 5 to 6 June . . . which were exactly the days selected by the enemy.[5,6] The tide for a landing in the bay of the Seine was favorable, but not at the channel coast, from the strait of Dover to the mouth of the Somme. Because of this, and because on 4 June the weather was not good, *Generalfeldmarschall* Rommel believed he could drive home. He hoped he would then be called for a report to Hitler, in which he personally wanted to present his proposal from 3 May, about pulling the *Panzer* divisions of the *OKW* reserve closer to the coast.[7]

During the evening of 5 June, Rommel was not the only one absent from his command post. Several other high leaders and important general staff officers were also away.[8] The Navy had no patrol vessels at sea, even though the weather forecast for the night of 5/6 June indicated such operations were feasible.[9] It was a bright night, one day before the full moon. As on many previous days, the *Luftwaffe* did not conduct reconnaissance flights.

All this happened even though the *Wehrmacht* Operations Staff considered the days from 5 to 13 June to be favorable for a landing, and the intelligence services at the front predicted the landing precisely.[10,11] But *Supreme Command–West* and *Army Group B* gave no credence to these reports; they later proffered the excuse that there had been too many similar warnings in the past.[12] Even when the warnings for the French sabotage organization were broadcast by London radio in the evening, the two headquarters did not issue an alert.[13] Only *15th Army,* which directly received the warning from the intelligence service at the front, alerted its troops and informed *Army Group B.*[14] *Generalleutnant* Dr. Speidel had someone query *Supreme Command–West,* and was told that no alert should be issued.[15] Intercepted weather reports for the enemy air force were disregarded.[16] These decisions combined to stifle any warning for the threatened *7th Army*. All in all, this was an almost incomprehensible failure of the German leadership in the West, as well as of the *Luftwaffe* and the Navy.

This was the situation when the event for which the German Army in France had been preparing finally happened. Unfortunate circumstances were combined with inadequacy.

It was especially tragic that Rommel, who had lived and worked exclusively for the day of the invasion, was not at his post during the decisive hours. Perhaps his actions could have saved something. It was not until 0730 hours on 6 June that he was informed about airborne landings, and he was told even then that it was not clear if this was the beginning of the invasion. Only when Rommel called Speidel on his own initiative at 1000 hours that he learned that the commencement of the invasion was being acknowledged. Following this, Rommel returned to France and arrived at his command post in the evening.[17]

The allied landing started around midnight with heavy air attacks on coastal fortifications in the Bay of the Seine. At 0030 hours, in moonlight, large airborne landings took place on both sides of the mouth of the Orne and on the Cotentin Peninsula, north of the mouth of the River Vire. They continued throughout the whole night.[18] Two American airborne divisions landed on the Cotentin Peninsula, and one British airborne division landed on either side of the mouth of the River Orne.[19]

Very soon, strong naval convoys were identified north of Cherbourg and the sound of engines could be heard coming from offshore.[20] At 0215 hours, the *7th Army* Chief of Staff, *Generalmajor* Pemsel, expressed his opinion to Speidel that the "airborne landings are the opening act to larger enemy action," but was not able to convince him.[21] At 0350 hours, the Chief of Staff of *Supreme Command–West, General der Infanterie* Blumentritt, came to the conclusion that the airborne landings constituted a major operation.[22] At 0445 hours, he reported accordingly to *OKW* and requested release of the *Panzer* divisions of the *OKW* Reserve "just in case." He ordered these divisions, the *12th SS-Panzer,* the *Panzer Lehr,* and the *17th SS-Panzer-Grenadier,* to prepare to move out. At 0505 hours, *Supreme Command–West* subordinated the *12th SS-Panzer Division* to *Army Group B,* which was directed to move it to the sector of the coastal division in place east of the river Orne, in such a manner "that immediate action against the enemy landing there would be possible." *Army Group B* moved the division forward "into the area of Bernay-Lisieux-Vimoutiers."[23] That placed the forward units of the division about 20 kilometers closer to the coast.

The Commander of *15th Army* urged *Army Group B* to deploy the division in a strike against the enemy airborne forces that landed east of the Orne, but did not find any support.[24] Speidel subordinated the *21st Panzer Division* from *Army Group B* to the *7th Army* only after Pemsel reported at 0615 hours that the opponent opened fire from the sea.[25]

Meanwhile, after heavy preparatory bombardment, the seaborne units began landing at 0600, shortly after low tide in each location. Thus, the landing took place in intervals from west to east. At the outset, one American infantry division landed north of the mouth of the Vire in the sector "Utah," while another landed east of the Vire in the sector "Omaha." Two British and one Canadian division landed further east, between Arromanches and the Orne, in the sectors "Gold," "Juno," and "Sword." All landing troops were supported by amphibious tanks. The forces landing in sector "Omaha" achieved only little effect against the brave men of the *352nd Infantry Division*. In the remaining sectors, however, the landings and subsequent linkups with the airborne units were successful. By the evening, considerable beachheads were established in the sectors "Utah," "Gold," "Juno," and "Sword." "Gold" and "Juno" were connected and occupied an area of 20 kilometers wide and nine kilometers deep.[26]

None of the German counterattacks had any significant effect. The attack of the *21st Panzer Division* west of the Orne in the afternoon was not successful. Since the *21st*'s troops that had been placed within the coastal divisions' sectors were involved in the fighting, only the *Panzer* and one *Panzer-Grenadier* regiment were available for an attack. The *Panzer* regiment soon encountered strong resistance, including tanks, northeast of Caen; its attack ground to a halt. The other combat group, however, reached the coast near Luc-sur-Mer by 1900 hours, between the "Sword" and "Juno" beachheads. Yet its success was in vain, and it was withdrawn during the night.[27]

Neither the *12th SS-Panzer* nor the *Panzer Lehr Divisions* were deployed on 6 June. At about 0900 hours, *OKW* refused to release their mobile reserve.[28] The reports from *Army Group B* and *Supreme Command–West* were not sufficiently clear. Time and again, the doubt surfaced: *Supreme Command–West's* "First Estimate of the Situation," issued first at 0935 hours makes it clear that, in their opinion, there was not sufficient intelligence to determine whether this was a major diversionary operation or the main attack; a similar estimate was issued again at 1100 hours.[29] In spite of urgent pleas from Headquarters, *7th Army*, Speidel could not decide before 1305 hours to request the release of the *12th SS-Panzer Division* for deployment toward the mouth of Orne.[30] The situation was only finally declared urgent by *Generalfeldmarschall* von Rundstedt in a report at 1415 hours; at once, *OKW* released the *12th-SS* and *Panzer Lehr Divisions*, including the Headquarters, *I SS-Panzer Corps*.[31]

While the displacements towards the front on most of 6 June were only hampered to a small extent from the air, beginning in the late afternoon, and continuing through the night and throughout next day, the full weight of the enemy's interdictory airpower fell upon the *Panzer Lehr Division*.[32] Consequently, the division could not launch a coherent counterattack on 7 June. It was planned for 1600 hours, but had to be postponed until the following day. Nevertheless, the *12th SS-Panzer Division* entered the battle at the appropriate time to beat back a Canadian attack west of Caen.

No counterattack was successful on 8 June. During the night, Bayeux fell into the hands of the enemy. West of the city, the English and Americans linked up, establishing a bridgehead 60 kilometers wide and 10 to 15 kilometers deep. Despite all reinforcements, the *7th Army* was compelled to assume a defensive posture. The same was true for the battles on the Cotentin Peninsula.[33]

Thanks to the information gained from a captured copy of an order from the VII Corps (the Corps that led the invasion on the Peninsula), the intentions of the enemy were completely evident, but the fear that this might not be the "real" invasion lingered with every staff from *Army Group B* up.[34] Different evaluations of this issue could not gain any traction. On 8 June, *Generaloberst* Jodl told Rommel that there would be no second invasion. Rommel disagreed.[35] Rommel also hesitated to move available forces of the *15th Army* across the Seine, where he could deploy them to eliminate the enemy east of the Orne, and thereby ease the burden of the *7th Army*.[36] Thus, the *116th Panzer Division* also remained north of the Seine and drove towards the Channel coast in two short displacements, to be explained later in more detail.

Nevertheless, on 7 and 8 June, *Supreme Command–West* ordered reinforcements forward. With the concurrence of *OKW*, these included the *17th SS-Panzer-Grenadier Division* on 7 June and the *2nd Panzer, 1st SS-Panzer,* and *2nd SS-Panzer Divisions* on the following day. Additionally, *Supreme Command*–West ordered *Army Group B* to designate two infantry divisions that could be sent to Normandy at once.[37] The *7th Army* took all forces that could be spared from Brittany and from its part of the Atlantic front, and moved them up, but the *15th Army* remained untouched.[38]

On 11 June, after the bridgeheads on both sides of the Vire linked up, there were indications that the Americans would thrust westward to cut off the Cotentin Peninsula.[39] There was hardly any time to assemble sufficient forces to prevent such a development.

Hitler now ordered the transfer of *II SS-Panzer Corps* with its *9th* and *10th SS-Panzer Divisions* from the Eastern Front to Normandy. At the same time he ordered the piecemeal destruction of the beachhead, as if these divisions had already arrived.[40] Instead of deploying the *116th Panzer Division* to Normandy, Rommel transferred it during the night of 13/14 June toward the mouth of the Somme. He did not seek the concurrence of *Supreme Command–West,* nor that of *OKW* for this order. The newly arrived *6th Parachute Division* was also directed towards the mouth of the Somme.[41]

On 15 June, Rundstedt presented another estimate of the situation to *OKW*. It warned of the impending isolation of German forces on the Cotentin Peninsula and asked "for a general directive with a prognosis for the near future."[42] With this, Hitler decided to travel to the West. On 17 June, Hitler and Jodl, Rundstedt and Blumentritt, Rommel and Speidel, each with a few assistants, met in the improved command post near Margival (ten kilometers northeast of Soissons). The record written by an *Army Group B* general staff officer reflects the objective course of the discussion.[43] It mainly dealt with the conduct of the battle of Cherbourg. The breakthrough to the west coast of the Cotentin Peninsula was imminent. Hitler demanded that fortress Cherbourg be occupied with sufficiently strong forces and held as long as possible.

Hitler considered a second invasion unlikely. He thought that, at most, the 15 June commencement of V-1 bombardments could force the enemy into it. Hitler accepted the plans presented by Rundstedt to halt across from the bridgehead and to prepare the reserves in such a way that they could "break up the bridgehead east of St. Lô, and then, depending on the situation, expand east or west." A suggestion by Rommel to not directly attack the bridgehead, but after a limited detour to attack the enemy's flanks, was not discussed, but it was later incorporated to a certain degree in Hitler's written order.[44]

Hitler's directive about the course of battle on the Cotentin Peninsula contained reasonable guidelines. The corollary order from *Supreme Command–West* however, placed less importance on the defense of the Cherbourg fortress than on the ongoing battle on the Peninsula.[45] The Commander of *Army Group B* expanded on this concept in his orders to the *7th Army* and incorporated the troops that ultimately were to defend the fortress into a 42-kilometer-long line across the Cotentin Peninsula, south of Cherbourg.[46] Despite vehement objections by *General* Dollmann, Commander of the *7th Army,* and his chief of staff, it was issued as an order by the *Führer*.[47]

The Americans broke through to the west coast of the peninsula on 18 June. A line oriented toward the north was established south of the point of breakthrough. The main forces of the Americans turned north and arrived at Cherbourg on 21 June. Only minor German forces were able to reach the fortress for its defense; it fell on 27 June.[48] The defenders managed to destroy the port facilities to the extent that they could not be used by the allies until August.[49] Thus, the invasion army had to continue to depend on its temporary ports.

The fall of Cherbourg concluded the first phase of the invasion. The fight for Caen began next. The English started the attack west of this city on 25 June and threatened to break through. Following this, the newly-arrived *II SS-Panzer Corps* was deployed for a counterattack, even before it was fully assembled. Actually, it should have been disposed for a thrust into the flanks of an enemy attack. The corps moved into action hastily on 29 June and was stalled by the following day.[50]

This settled the issue of how to employ the last reserve. Nevertheless, from 20 June forward, a discussion continued between *OKW* and the leadership in the West about initiating a new counterattack. "To reach a decision," Rundstedt and Rommel were ordered to the *Führer*'s headquarters in Berchtesgaden.[51] Yet the opinions in the *OKW* were contradictory even before their arrival. On 24 June, the *Wehrmacht* Operations Staff proposed that the attack be conducted "on about 5 July with forces that are gained from further withdrawals from other fronts." It was established that the leadership in the West "was unwilling to assume the required risks."[52] On the other hand, on 26 June, *OKW* ordered *Supreme Command–West* to reinforce the reserves between the Somme and the Seine because the divisions in that area (*116th Panzer Division* and *84th Infantry Division*) "were not sufficient."[53] Once again, fear of a second cross-Channel invasion haunted them, even as Hitler again opined to Jodl that there was no danger, "unless the opponent . . .wants to get his hands on the V-1 launch sites." But then, Hitler was still afraid of another invasion in Britanny.[54]

The result of the discussion at Berchtesgaden on 29 June was to forgo an attack. The mission for the near future was established as follows: "Conduct a flank attack to destroy enemy forces advancing via Baron towards the Orne."[55]

Baron is ten kilometers southwest of Caen. The British attack there was already under way, but the forces for a thrust against its flanks were not available. The moment for weakening the *15th Army* had not yet been perceived. However, hasty crossings of the Seine should have been prepared. Hitler declared that under no circumstances should the situation be allowed to become fluid, because with the opponent's air superiority, high degree of motorization, and fuel reserves, the opponent was far more mobile. For this reason, success depended upon interrupting the opponent's logistical support, "because it is incomparably more effective to sink a whole shipload, than to later have to destroy the unloaded material and fight the personnel one by one."[56]

Interdicting the allies' sea lines of communication could only be accomplished by the Navy or *Luftwaffe,* but neither was up to the task. Thus, all remained theory.

On 30 June, when Rommel returned to his staff, he was presented with the estimates of the situation by the ranking commanders in Normandy. They requested permission to withdraw from the Caen bridgehead west of the Orne, to prevent the exhaustion of the *Panzer* divisions and gain an opportunity to rest and rebuild them for future operations. This concept was championed by the Commander of *Panzer Group West, General der Panzertruppe* Imperial Baron Geyr von Schweppenburg, and by General of the *Waffen-SS* Hausser, who had assumed command of *7th Army* after Dollmann's death. Rommel endorsed the idea, and passed the request on to Rundstedt.[57] Rundstedt, in turn, forwarded them on 1 July to *OKW*, but Hitler objected.[58] Then, *General* Geyr von Schweppenburg reported:

> If the line is not straightened as requested within the next few days, the *9th, 10th, 12th SS-Panzer Divisions,* and the *Panzer Lehr Division* will burn out beyond usefulness.
>
> This is not a case of "running away," but of a sensible and planned extraction of forces from [the effects of] naval gunfire, where the men are only targets.
>
> The same message has been sent to *Generaloberst* Guderian.[59]

This message was passed, *verbatim,* through Speidel and Blumentritt to *OKW*, and led to the immediate relief of *General* Geyr von Schweppenburg; *General der Panzertruppe* Eberbach succeeded him. At the same time, Rundstedt was also relieved and replaced by *Generalfeldmarschall* von Kluge. The two new commanders arrived to assume command on 3 July.[60] Kluge immediately addressed

Rommel in person, giving him advice. This led to a violent confrontation and caused Rommel to write down "observations." He sent the first of these reports to Hitler's adjutant, *Generalleutnant* Schmundt. Kluge received the second copy, a rather unusual procedure.[61] On 7 July, the *Ia* for *Supreme Command–West* took a position regarding the issue, which corrected some of Rommel's distorted points.[62]

Kluge's intentions for the course of the battle were:

1. Defense! Unconditional retention of the current front line.
2. Improve the line forward, through attack after most careful preparation, where it is truly advantageous.
3. Improvement of rear areas.[63]

The only promising opportunity, namely a flank attack, as Rommel and, at times, *OKW* had mentioned, was missing.

Beginning in July, the alternating attacks of the British near Caen and the Americans between Vire and the west coast of the Cotentin Peninsula had unpleasant effects at the front of the beachhead. On 7 July, the American attacks reached such force that the *2nd SS-Panzer* and *Panzer Lehr Divisions* had to be moved to the sector they were threatening.[64] On 8 July, *Supreme Command–West* received a new *Führer* directive for the course of battle.[65] It was similar to the order of 29 June. As before, a second invasion was still feared, which required strong reserves to remain behind the *15th Army*. In Normandy, they were to stand fast, because "no operational mobility of equal value" existed. There was a request for the relief of the *Panzer* divisions by infantry, to facilitate preparations for a limited objective attack which would drive a wedge into the enemy's beachhead, to divide it and destroy its forces.

The process which had proven to be unsuitable was maintained. No infantry divisions relieved the *Panzer* divisions. Eberbach's calls for them faded away.[66]

On 10 July, when Kluge suggested that *Army Group B* evacuate Caen—thus reinstating the proposals of 30 June and also gaining the agreement of Jodl—Rommel reversed his previous position and disagreed.[67] On this day, the northern part of Caen up to the Orne fell to the British. The fighting subsided temporarily, but preparations for a new offensive were evident. The American attacks on St. Lô continued without surcease; counterattacks had hardly any success. A crisis was to be expected. On 13 July, when *OKW* declined to move the *11th Panzer Division* up from southern France, Kluge warned Jodl of impending havoc.[68]

On 15 July, *Army Group B* headquarters issued "Observations of the Situation," which hinted at the upcoming crisis. The last two sentences were authored by Rommel personally:

> Everywhere, the soldiers are fighting heroically, but the uneven fight is drawing to a close. In my opinion it is necessary to bring up the consequences of this situation. As Army Group Commander, I feel it is my duty to make this clear.[69]

Actually, Rommel initially wrote, "the political consequences" but the word "political" was later crossed out.[70] These "Observations of the Situation," often known as Rommel's "ultimatum," were sent to Kluge, not directly to Hitler, on 16 July. Not until *21 July* did Kluge forward the document to Hitler, along with his own notes.[71][Editor's emphasis]

On 17 July, after describing the deteriorating situation, Kluge had a conversation with *General der Artillerie* Warlimont, the acting Chief of the *Wehrmacht* Operations Staff. He closed with the following words, "It is very questionable if the forces available to us will be sufficient, but we are facing the situation calmly."[72]

That same day, Rommel's car was strafed by low-flying aircraft and hit a tree. Rommel was severely wounded and became incapacitated. The previous day, at Headquarters, *Panzer Group West,* he had indicated to *General* Eberbach that he was thinking about opposing Hitler. *General* Eberbach remembers that Rommel said that the best course of action in the West was to conduct a fighting withdrawal, to pull out as many *Panzer* divisions as possible, and throw them against the Russians.[73] He added that on its way east, a reliable *Panzer* division should arrest Hitler. He should then be brought before a court of law, to avoid rumors of a stab in the back. When Eberbach asked, "But how would you avoid a civil war?" Rommel is said to have answered, "We will talk about that next time." But the "next time" never came.

On the evening of 17 July, Speidel reported Rommel's injury to Headquarters, *Supreme Command–West,* and also advised them about the danger at St. Lô, where the Americans had achieved deep penetrations.[74] He proposed moving the *12th SS-Panzer Division "Hitler Youth"*—which had been pulled out of its heroic battle at Caen and was in reserve behind *Panzer Group West*—toward the *7th Army.* He added that the only *Army Group B* asset left for such a mission was the *116th Panzer Division. Supreme Command–West* did not concur with the proposal.

The following day, the British attacked east of the Orne toward the south.

After the heaviest bombardment—over 2,200 aircraft delivering 8,000 tons of bombs, augmented by naval gunfire—five divisions were committed. They achieved a considerable penetration, but were finally brought to a standstill.[75] The *12th SS-Panzer Division* was released by *Supreme Command–West* for a new mission. Kluge, who by now had also taken command of the Army Group, issued a distinct order that under all circumstances, the enemy was to be thrown back toward his original positions.[76] The American attack near St. Lô continued; on 19 July, the city was in the hands of the enemy.[77]

On 18 July, at 2330 hours, Speidel again mentioned the *116th Panzer Division* to Kluge. Kluge ordered Blumentritt to request the release of the Division from *OKW,* and he added, "The *116th Panzer* has to be brought across the Seine immediately. . . . It is *Panzers* we need."[78] Kluge's telegram to Jodl contained the following text:

1. Situation southeast of Caen serious.
2. I request immediate release of the *116th Panzer Division* for deployment vicinity Caen. Quickest decision is essential, because *326th* and *363d Infantry Divisions* will not be available for several days and combat against Anglo-Americans requires above all use of tanks.
3. Extremely urgent you expedite sufficient replacement of armor. Send more *Panzer-Grenadier* unit replacements.[79]

At 0055 hours on 19 July, permission to commit the *116th Panzer Division* arrived at *Army Group B* headquarters. Now we will see what the *116th Panzer Division* had been doing in the six weeks leading up to that date.

CHAPTER 4

Awaiting Action

As reported in Chapter 1, on 5 June the *116th Panzer Division* was deployed southeast of Rouen, where it was refitting and securing the area against enemy airborne landings. The routes toward the coast had been explored in the *LXXXI Corps* sector near Le Tréport–Le Havre, and communications had been established. However, tactically, on 26 May the Division was placed under the command of *XLVII Panzer Corps,* which also had responsibility for refitting and training. By 5 June, this latter headquarters had made little use of its powers as a superior headquarters.

It was a cool and rainy day.[1] Nothing unusual happened, and there were no indications of the upcoming events. The alert order from *15th Army* did not reach the Division, even though it was in its sector. *Army Group B* did not pass the warning on to its other subordinate units, nor did anything come from *LXXXI Corps.* No one noticed anything that took place in the first hours of 6 June in Normandy, despite the fact that the distance from our sector to the mouth of the Orne was only a little over 100 kilometers.

The Division was not alerted until 0230 hours that morning. The highest degree of readiness, a "Level II" alert, was ordered and at once passed on to the units.[2] The first situation report we received indicated that the enemy had begun the invasion between Le Havre and Cherbourg.[3] *LXXXI Corps* requested that the *12th SS-Panzer Division* send reconnaissance patrols toward the coast in the sector of the *711th Infantry Division,* south of the Seine, as early as 0200 hours.[4] At 0212 hours, *LXXXI Corps* requested that *15th Army* also dispatch patrols from the *116th Panzer Division.* At 0320, *LXXXI Corps* was informed by Headquarters, *15th Army,* that the *116th Panzer Division* was still under the control of *Army Group B,* and that patrols could not be released; the *12th SS-Panzer Division* deployed reconnaissance elements. Still, as a precaution, *LXXXI Corps* asked the *116th Panzer Division* to prepare a reconnaissance plan, and *Armored Reconnaissance Battalion 116* was tasked accordingly. This was later cancelled.

The most important mission of the Division now was to form combat ready units from elements which had not yet been fully reconstituted or refitted. At 1030 hours, the Division Commander reported to *LXXXI Corps,* and probably also to *XLVII Panzer Corps,* that the following were combat ready:

Two *Panzer-Grenadier* Regiments
The *Panzer* Regiment
Most of the Armored Reconnaissance Battalion

The Armored Engineer Battalion
Strong artillery units[5]

The artillery units received orders to establish liaison with the regiments they were to support: The *1st Battalion,* equipped with self propelled artillery, would support *Panzer Regiment 16*; the *2d Battalion* was to support *Panzer-Grenadier Regiment 60*; and the *3d Battalion* was to support *Panzer-Grenadier Regiment 156*. During the day, the battalions were subordinated to "their" regiments. The *2d* and *3d Battalions* each exchanged one battery. This resulted in the *2d Battalion* having two batteries of light and one battery of heavy field howitzers, while *3d Battalion* consisted of its *7th Battery* (with 105mm field guns) and one battery of light field howitzers from *2d Battalion.* One of the *3d Battalion's* batteries had not yet been equipped with its heavy field howitzers.[6]

If they had not already done so, the units now moved out of the villages and into open terrain, where they prepared to defend. They continued training to the extent the continuous alert conditions permitted. In his diary, Vogelsang noted:

So now the war has started for us as well. . . . The opponent landed in the area of Caen by air and by sea. One unit south of Villers sur Mer is nearing decimation. Apparently, heavy fighting is occurring southwest of the mouth of the Orne, where the enemy landed along a broad front. It is still quiet where we are. We still assume this to only be a sideshow of the invasion, and that the main attack will come at the mouth of the Somme. The destruction of the Seine bridges is now making itself felt in an extremely uncomfortable way.

The flyers are active. For an hour now, English and American planes have been circling and firing at anything that moves. By now, the war should finally be decided. So be it! (6 June 1944, 1200 hours)

The *"Führer's* appeal to the soldiers in the West" had to be announced to the troops and destroyed afterwards (Appendix 3).[7]

Army Group B intended to deploy the Division closer to Rouen; at 1105 hours, *Generalleutnant* Dr. Speidel so apprised *15th Army.* These intentions must have been turned into an order quickly, because on the same day, parts of *"Combat Group Fischer"* marched to a new location. The whole Division was ordered into the following area: Bosquentin–Hodeng–Hodenger (included)–Neufchâtel-en-Bray (included)–Grigneuseville (included)–Roncherolles–Pont St. Pierre (included).[8,9,10]

This new area coincided to a large extent with the one that the Division already occupied. Therefore, not all units of the Division had to be moved. As far as could be established, only *"Battle Group Fischer"* (*Panzer-Grenadier Regiment 156; Panzerjäger Battalion 228; 3d Battalion, Panzer Artillery Regiment 146*) was the only combat unit that was to move out of the area near Gisors to the northeast of Rouen. Early on 7 June, the Division command post displaced to Perriers-sur-Andelle into the facility formerly occupied by the staff of *Panzer-Grenadier Regiment 60.* Vogelsang reports:

Around 0800 hours we drove here and found good accommodations. Again, the General is living outside the town, in a very pretty chateau. It is still quiet here, nothing happened in our sector of the coast.

Heavy fighting between Le Havre and Cherbourg. Immense employment of weapons, bombs, and naval gunfire. The enemy is now in possession of a larger beachhead from Caen to Bayeux, and three smaller ones up to the Cotentin Peninsula. Supplies are continuously arriving by sea and air. It is time to straighten out the situation. Today, for the first time, we noticed some stronger activity by the *Luftwaffe*. By tomorrow, the *Panzer Lehr Division* and the *SS-Division HJ* should arrive at the points where the enemy landed. I hope they are successful. (7 June 1944, evening).

The Division order of 7 June read,

> As long as the situation seems to allow enemy landing attempts north of the Seine, the Division has to count on being ready for action in the present area. On the other hand, the developments in Normandy or in other places may warrant withdrawing the Division for use elsewhere.[11]

The Division was now moved to the area which, on 4 June, Speidel already mentioned as the one planned for it by Rommel. It was therefore closer to Dieppe and Le Havre. *Army Group B* declined a 7 June request by *15th Army* to again move the *116th Panzer Division* further toward Dieppe, but approximately 15 kilometers southwest of the town.[12]

According to the Division's status report of that day, there were 78 Panthers, 66 *Panzer IVs* with long 75mm guns, and a combined total of 13 *Panzer IIIs* equipped with 50mm guns and *Panzer IVs* with short 75s available for commitment against the enemy.[13] Both *Panzer-Grenadier* regiments could each commit two battalions; in total, this amounted to eleven rifle companies (in *Panzer-Grenadier Regiment 60,* this included three borne in armored personnel carriers), two heavy companies, and two regimental engineer companies. The armored reconnaissance battalion had at its disposal two companies mounted in armored personnel carriers and one heavy company. The *Panzer-Grenadier* and reconnaissance battalions could field a combined total of 154 armored vehicles. The *Panzer-Grenadier* regiments were mostly short of heavy infantry howitzers, and the armored reconnaissance battalion needed its eight-wheeled-armored cars.

Since end of May, *7th Company, Panzer-Grenadier Regiment 156* (commanded by *Oberleutnant* Strackerjahn), had been guarding the headquarters of *Panzer Group West* in Paris; after the commencement of the invasion, it was deployed to the front in Normandy. On 10 June, its *3d Platoon* was almost completely destroyed in an air attack. Only after 19 June, when this company was replaced by one from *Field Replacement Battalion 146* (commanded by *Leutnant* Brockmeier) was it returned to the Division.[14]

The *Panzerjäger Battalion* was the least complete unit among the Division's combat elements. It lacked prime movers for its antitank guns, and the tank destroyer companies only had the vehicles that were left behind by the *179th Panzer Division,* as well as some assault guns, all of which should actually have been turned in. All together, ten guns were ready for employment.

The armored artillery regiment had 29 guns. It was short of one *Wespe,* five *Hummels,* one towed 105mm howitzer, four towed 150mm howitzers, and one 105mm field gun. Three companies of the armored engineer battalion were combat ready. *Army Anti-Aircraft Battalion 281* had, as reported earlier, neither guns, nor prime movers, nor command vehicles. The insufficient combat readiness (17 percent capable) of the radio company of *Armored Signal Battalion 228* was a special weakness. This was inadequate to control the Division in the field.

The day of 8 June 1944 passed without any significant events. Although the weather since 6 June had not been particularly good—the operations journal of *2d Battalion, Panzer Artillery Regiment 146* read "Cloudy and rainy"—all operations journals and diaries emphasized strong enemy air activity, including in the skies above the *116th Panzer Division.* Movement in daylight was only possible with losses. Even single vehicles were attacked.

On the evening of 8 June, the alarm was cancelled, and the Division was ordered to stand by to march on two hours' notice.[15] On the following day, the *Supreme Command–West* order mentioned in the previous chapter about moving forces to Normandy had an impact on the *116th Panzer Division.* In the late morning, I was called for a conference with the *LXXXI Corps* staff regarding restructuring within the corps; by evening, the Division was under this corps' control.[16] To facilitate the possible release of the *84th Infantry Division* from its front-line positions near Le Havre, *LXXXI Corps* and *15th Army* intended to displace the Division closer to the coast. The *116th Panzer Division* was to advance with its forward units to the line Neufchâtel-en-Bray–Tôtes, just a simple displacement. In the evening, the Division received the corresponding order. The following villages were designated as the boundaries of the new sector: Malaunay–Lyons-la-Fôret–Forges-les-Eaux.[17]

As on 6 and 7 June, this shift did not make much of a difference to a motorized unit. In fact, such moves cause more harm than they do good. Therefore, the Division tried to move only a few units. As far as could be established, during the night of 9/10 June, *Panzer Regiment 16* and *1st Battalion, Armored Artillery Regiment 146* moved north into the area southwest of Neufchâtel, while the armored engineer battalion displaced into the area southwest of La Feuillie.[18] Rommel did not agree with the larger shift west into the area of Yvetot, as planned by the *15th Army*; he wanted to retain the option of deploying the Division in the vicinity of Dieppe or at the mouth of the Somme.[19]

On 9 June, the Division received the order by *Supreme Command–West* to release the *1st Battalion* of *Panzer Regiment "Grossdeutschland."*[20] On the evening of this day, Vogelsang entrusted the following thoughts to his diary:

> Right now, very strong elements of the *Luftwaffe* are roaring westward over us at low altitude. The invasion is coming full circle, at least at its first landing site.

Through the air and by sea the enemy has already landed 20 to 30 divisions and has connected the original beachheads. Indeed it looks very threatening! The enemy's superiority in the air is so strong that it is almost impossible to move around in daylight. Our own forces are arriving slowly. . . . At times they have been ferried across the Seine with difficulty. It is now high time! And where is the much promised "vengeance?" We are moving a little closer to the coast, parts of the division are on their way already (9 June 1944, midnight). [*Major* Vogelsang's estimate of the Allied order of battle ashore was somewhat exaggerated. By D+3 (9 June), the Allies actually had 14 divisions and three separate maneuver brigades ashore— *Editor.*]

On June 10, at 1000 hours, the Division reported to *LXXXI Corps* that all displacements made during the night were complete. At 1100 hours the Division Commander conferred with the Corps Commander, *General der Panzertruppe* Kuntzen.[21] That day and the next, 11 June, passed uneventfully except for brisk activity of enemy aircraft over the Division area. The Division command post was attacked by low-flying aircraft, but did not suffer any damage.[22]

During the night of 10/11 June, *1st Battalion, Panzer Regiment "Grossdeutschland"* commenced its departure. It was to cross the Seine by ferries that apparently were to be built by our engineer battalion and its bridge section. On the morning of 11 June, I reported to *LXXXI Corps* that the crossing would take about three nights, and thus requested a second bridge section.[23] On that same day, the commander of the engineer battalion, *Hauptmann* Hossenfelder, was at the Seine, building ferries.[24] On 13 June, *Supreme Command–West* reversed itself and permitted the *1st Battalion, Panzer Regiment "Grossdeutschland,"* to remain attached to the *116th Panzer Division.*[25]

On the afternoon of 11 June, the Division received instructions for operations in the event of enemy landings in the *LXXXI Corps* area.[26] To learn more exact details about the situation in Normandy, not long after the invasion the Division Commander sent the *Ic* to confer with his opposite number at headquarters, *Army Group B.*[27] To the same end, he also dispatched a liaison officer to the command post of *I SS-Panzer Corps.*[28] The *Ia*-scribe, *Obergefreiter* Wendt, accompanied the liaison officer and reported:

> I accompanied the officer to assist him by graphically depicting the situation in a sketch. We were very well received by the staff of the *"Sepp Dietrich Corps,"* and were even received by him personally. . . . Iron discipline ruled the command post. Nobody was allowed to leave the concealment provided by the trees while moving around outdoors. I was warned that Sepp himself painstakingly enforced this. With the situation on a map overlay, we returned to our Division CP. Again and again, we had to duck off the roads on our way. Low-flying aircraft made our lives difficult.

Although *Naval Command–West* judged the situation differently, on 11 June, *Supreme Command–West*'s concern about a second landing in the area of the *15th Army* is evident in a passage in their operations journal:[29]

Situation Cotentin Peninsula intensified. . . . Heavy build-up towards Cherbourg is clearly recognizable because of continuous arrivals of strong forces and number of divisions deployed in the landing area. Landing in other area before achieving this goal unlikely.[30]

At 1200 hours on 12 June, the *Army Group B Ia* reported Rommel's thoughts to his opposite number at *15th Army.* Rommel perceived the greatest danger in the Boulogne–St. Valery-en-Caux sector (28 kilometers southwest of Dieppe), and therefore intended to transfer the *116th Panzer Division* to the vicinity of Feuquiéres–Eu–Envermeu–Senarpont.[31] At 1320 hours, Rommel personally spoke with *Generaloberst* von Salmuth, Commander, *15th Army,* and apprised him of his concern about the area on both sides of the Somme. Specifically, Rommel considered it unlikely that the English would attack further on the east bank of the Orne, that is, into the left wing of *15th Army.* Rommel rejected Salmuth's intention of moving the *84th Infantry Division* from Le Havre across the Seine, as he was not then concerned about an attack toward Le Havre. Salmuth's planned action was in accordance with the wishes of *OKW,* received through *Supreme Command–West,* whose first goal was to defeat the enemy east of the Orne. Rommel explained to Salmuth that it would be better to employ the arriving units of the *6th Parachute Division* on the Somme than to send them to Le Havre, and that the *116th Panzer Division* should be deployed to the northeast, behind the boundary between *LXVII* and *LXXXI Corps.*[32] At 1525, *LXXXI Corps* informed me of these plans.[33]

Shortly thereafter, *Generalfeldmarschall* Rommel appeared at the command post of the *116th Panzer Division* and oriented us on his concept of operations; he ordered the transfer of the Division to the prescribed area during the night of 13 June and issued the following specific missions:

1. Annihilate airborne landings in zone.
2. Destroy forces landing at the mouth of the Somme, by means of counterattacks near Le Tréport and Dieppe.[34]

Rommel's escort reported about the visit as follows:

1600 hours, conference of the Commander, *Army Group B,* at the command post of the *116th Panzer Division* in Perriers.

Division was informed in advance of the night movement toward the coast. The Army Group Commander ordered the Division to deploy during the night on both sides of the Bresle, behind the front line of the *348th* and *245th Divisions,* in the vicinity of Eu–Tully–Feuquieres–Gamaches–Melleville–Tourville–Touffreville; such a disposition enables it to attack towards Dieppe, as well as towards the Somme.

The Army Group Commander ordered displacement tonight so that positions could be occupied and prepared immediately, with movement to be finished by first light.

Units to be integrated as combat groups.[35]

Following this, the Division issued the operation order (Appendix 4).[36] The new area of operations indicated in Rommel's escort's report did not quite coincide with the one prescribed by *Army Group B, 15th Army,* and *LXVII* and *LXXXI Corps*; theirs was closer to the coast. This soon led to discrepancies. Vogelsang also portrayed this visit in his diary:

> Yesterday afternoon. . . . *Feldmarschall* Rommel visited us. I took part in the briefing. It was very interesting. . . . Since one could count on English air attacks and landings by sea in the area of the mouth of the Somme at any time, the Division had to be redeployed very quickly. . . . I remember that Rommel gave very short notice for the jump-off. Justifiably, the Division Commander expressed disagreement, which Rommel interrupted with words like "we know each other from Africa—the Division marches!" (13 June 1944)

The new command post was in Hélicourt near Gamaches on the Bresle. The V-1s were to be launched from their nearby ramps commencing the night of 12/13 June, but it did not work out well. Only a few of the flying bombs became airborne. Therefore, the date was postponed to the night of 15/16 June.[37]

At this point, the Division was being held as *15th Army* reserve, but was nevertheless subordinated to *LXVII Corps,* which controlled both sides of the mouth of the Somme. On the night of 12/13 June and throughout the day on 13 June, there was an alert for enemy airborne landings in the Belgian-French border region.[38] *LXVII Corps* issued the final order for the deployment of the Division on 13 June (Appendix 5).[39] Early that day, most of the Division arrived in the new area of operations. Units that did not get to their final destination before first light took cover wherever they were, and covered the rest of the distance during the night of 13/14 June.[40]

No entries in the journals of *Supreme Command–West* or those of *Army Group B* indicate that Rommel asked permission to or even reported his intention of moving the *116th Panzer Division*. The only indication of it appeared in the *Army Group B* daily report to *OKW* on 13 June, and that simply depicted the displacement as a *fait accompli*.[41] Neither *Supreme Command–West* nor *OKW* expressed objections, despite the clear threat of an American penetration toward the west coast of the Cotentin Peninsula—a threat which could lead to the loss of Cherbourg.[42] Even Rommel's decision to withold the *84th Infantry Division* was accepted without grumbling. All of this illustrates how much the fear of a second invasion dominated the minds of commanders at higher levels. *OKW* even substituted paratroopers for the *2d Panzer Division* at the mouth of the Somme. The *85th Infantry Division* was arrayed in depth north of the Seine.[43]

Besides the return of the *1st Battalion, Panzer Regiment "Grossdeutschland"* permitted by *Supreme Command–West*, 13 June brought three more positive developments for the Division. An ambulance platoon that had been turned over to the *711th Infantry Division* on 11 June was to be returned, and the creation of the armored anti-aircraft platoon for the command post of *Panzer Regiment 16* was announced.[44] The *9th Battery* of the artillery regiment received its 150mm howitzers, and in the night which followed, moved into the new firing positions, towed in part by locally requisitioned civilian vehicles. With this, all the batteries were in place.[45]

During the night of 13/14 June, the supporting assignments of the *2d* and *3d Battalions* of the artillery regiment switched, that is, the *2d* became subordinated to *Panzer-Grenadier Regiment 156*, while the *3d* was assigned to *Panzer-Grenadier Regiment 60*.[46]

The Division now had plenty to do. Its units had to get settled in the new area in a posture that could prevent an enemy airborne landing, and its commanders and staffs had to explore the various deployment options and issue the necessary preliminary orders. The Division had to establish contact with coastal defense forces, mainly the *348th Infantry Division*. Various courses of action for counterattack had to be agreed upon. The coastal divisions had already reconnoitered and selected alternate and supplementary positions. These positions were to be occupied by task-organized, combined arms units of the *116th Panzer Division*. The Division's artillery had to be emplaced in such a way that it could take part in the battle on the coast and also be able to go into action in any other direction. Its forward observers occupied various observation posts, some directly behind the coast, and adjusted fire at targets in various areas.[47]

On 14 June, the Division was notified that another Panther unit, namely *1st Battalion, Panzer Regiment 24,* was to be attached; its wheeled vehicles and repair shop were still missing. The Army Group achieved this rapid transfer from *Supreme Command–West*, despite some objections expressed by *OKH*.[48]

On 15 June, the commanding general, *LXVII Corps, General der Infanterie* Sponheimer, visited the Division and requested the following:

1. Units, staffs, supply installations, must in no way be surprised by air or sea landings. Units must be especially alert by night.
2. With all dispatch, emphasize construction of dug-in positions for tanks along all avenues of approach.
3. Every strongpoint, even in the hinterland, is to be defended to the last man and to the last round.
4. During level I or II alerts, all weapons that can easily be unloaded must be loaded; ammunition must be readily accessible for all remaining weapons.[49]

On 15 June, the Division command post displaced to Lignieres-en-Vimeu (three kilometers northeast of Senarpont), and at 2310 of the following night, V-1 launches began in full force.[50] *Stabsintendant* [an administrative officer with the rank of captain—*Editor*] Wolff-Boenisch of the engineer battalion wrote in his diary:

> Around 2400 hours a tremendous, thundering noise fills the air. We run into the street and in the dark we recognize several flying objects, trailed by long, fiery comet-like tails. Burning air planes? The French are shouting: "Les canards sauvages!" ("The wild ducks!") It is the "vengeance." All night long these "wild

ducks" fly over our heads. Suddenly the thunder over our village stops and one flying object falls silently to the ground. A dud? My God! Maybe all the houses here will blow up, but nothing happens.

Early in the morning, everybody runs to the place of impact near the edge of the village. Curious, but with some trepidation, we approach the monster, which broke into two parts. One could see nothing but levers, screws, dials, and hundreds of twisted, colorful wires. An absolute marvel! At noon, I drive to Division.

In the forest, we find a bomb crater, six meters across and equally deep, caused by a faulty V-1. We are somewhat disappointed, as we expected holes large enough for a three-story house.

On 16 June, we received the joyful news that *Panzerjäger Battalion 228* was to pick up all 21 tank destroyers due to it from the army ordnance department in Breslau.[51] The next day, *1st Battalion, Panzer Regiment "Grossdeutschland"* returned and was stationed in the right-hand sector of the division with *Panzer-Grenadier Regiment 60,* near Aigneville.[52] From that point, it could go into action anywhere in the open terrain north of the Bresle. On this day, *15th Army* allowed the *1st Battalion, Panzer Regiment 24* to be situated in the vicinity of Piquigny (12 kilometers northwest of Amiens), to defend this area against airborne landings.[53]

On 18 June, the *15th Army* Chief of Staff reported to Speidel that, "*15th Army* is counting on an early attack in this area because of the V-1," and added that there were no armored units left between the Seine and Scheldt. This was a surprising statement, since the addition of the *116th Panzer Division* to the *15th Army* and the arrival of *1st Battalion, Panzer Regiment 24* gave them more than 220 tanks in this very area. One can see from this report that not only were the leaders in higher commands afraid of a second landing, but that the commanders who would be involved in it actually fed the fear themselves.[54]

The tides were a certain cause for concern. On 16/17 June, the tides in the Dunkirk–Dieppe sector were identical to those which had existed in Normandy on the night of the invasion; two nights later, similar conditions would obtain in the Dieppe–Le Havre sector as well. However, there would be no full moon, but rather a waning moon close to a new moon in these areas at these times.[55]

Despite a dramatically worsening situation around Cherbourg on the Cotentin Peninsula, on 19 June Rommel visited the *116th Panzer Division* and the *6th Parachute Division* at the mouth of the Somme. The weather was cloudy and windy, and the sea was stormy. The temporary port facilities on the Normandy beaches sustained severe damage. Acute danger for a second landing, therefore, did not exist. The Commanders of *15th Army, LXVII Corps,* and the *348th Infantry Division,* which was positioned at the coast, were called to a conference.[56] Rommel declared:

> Experience in Normandy shows that, due to air superiority, moving up reserves is impossible. Therefore, reserves can only be advanced in a very specifically defined sector.

Since the English land their paratroopers and glider forces three to five kilometers behind the coast, these reserves have to be positioned sufficiently far forward to allow them to go into action against this enemy.

These are the words in the record created by the *Ia* of *LXVII Corps.* They continue:

Since the *Generalfeldmarschall* expects a landing of the opponent between the Somme and the Seine, and considers the area on both sides of Ault in the corps' sector to be especially endangered, the *116th Panzer Division* is to be moved forward even further than previously ordered.

He requested the same of the *Parachute Training Regiment* of the *6th Parachute Division* and persisted in his request, even when he was advised of objections by the *Luftwaffe.* [German parachute divisions were staffed and trained by the *Luftwaffe,* even though they generally operated under Army command in the field—*Editor.*] After a private conversation with Rommel, Salmuth complemented Rommel's directive by adding:

The immediate action of every leader is decisive when it comes to the employment of airborne troops by the enemy. . . . Use all means to destroy them at once. . . .

If heavy naval gunfire hits defensive strongpoints in the field, commanders may occupy alternate positions to the flanks, but only if the original avenue of approach can be controlled from the new position.

Furthermore, Salmuth ordered the *116th Panzer Division* and the *Parachute Training Regiment* to move up immediately. This was later postponed to the night of June 20/21. The 20 June order from *LXVII Corps* read as follows:

1. By verbal command of the Commander, *15th Army,* the most advanced units of the *116th Panzer Division* must move ahead immediately to the line Friville–Bouvaincourt. . . .
2. Missions remain the same.
3. Parts of the land front will be occupied by the *116th Panzer Division.* Elements of the *348th Infantry Division* will not be withdrawn from the front.
4. The advance will be completed by 0500 hours on 21 June.[57]

With this, Rommel advanced the Division in its right-hand sector as far forward as he had already verbally ordered on 12 June. It was emplaced there, mingled with units of the *348th Infantry Division.* The Division command post was moved forward again to Hélicourt. Nearby, the staff found finished bunkers built into a steep slope which could be used in case of emergency.[58]

On his way back from the conference, Rommel visited the command post of *LXXXI Corps,* the unit to the left of *LXVII Corps.* In this venue, he again stated that he believed the sector between Somme and Seine to be severely threatened and strongly anticipated a landing in that area. In this regard, his estimate did not differ with *Supreme Command–West* or *OKW,* although with regard to the fighting between the Dives and the Orne, he emphasized opinions that were at odds with those of Hitler and *OKW.*[59]

Given that the Division was now located in open terrain, training activities were resumed across the Division to the greatest extent possible.[60] This was especially important for the *1st Battalion, Panzer Regiment 24,* which was only beginning training at the platoon level. For this reason, the Division objected to moving this battalion all the way to the front; it also expressed misgivings about plans by the *15th Army* to move *1st Battalion, Panzer Regiment "Grossdeutschland"* to the north bank of the Somme.[61] This unit owned the only complete tank repair shop in the Division, and the engines of their tanks were already overused. However, no relief was granted.[62]

On 23 June, when Rommel was again near the mouth of the Somme, he decided that the *1st Battalion, Panzer Regiment 24* had to move up, and that no units of *Panzer Regiment 16* were to be transferred across the Somme to the north. Accordingly, during the night of 24/25 June, *1st Battalion, Panzer Regiment 24* moved forward into the sector of Vismes-au-Val.[63]

The whole *Panzer Regiment,* together with the *1st Battalion* (Self-Propelled) of the artillery regiment, was now disposed in suitable tank country, behind *Panzer-Grenadier Regiment 60. Panzer-Grenadier Regiment 156,* reinforced by *Panzerjäger Battalion 228,* lay south of the Bresle, while *Armored Reconnaissance Battalion 116* was disposed south of the Yéres, in the sector of *LXXXI Corps.*[64] "The Division," Vogelsang noted on 24 June, "is now engaged in forward coastal defense, practically 'in position' to duly oppose a possible airborne landing attack. The unit is digging in and camouflaging itself." Vogelsang's impressions of the Atlantic Wall are interesting:

> Early today I took a ride to the Atlantic Wall, to look at the positions of Ault and Le Tréport. . . . The fortifications are spread out, but by themselves, look quite stable. I was impressed by the immense bomb craters around the bunkers of a bombed out battery. A battalion of Armenian volunteers is positioned at Ault.
>
> The war in the air continues without surcease. Bombs are falling everywhere. They seem to be desperately searching for the positions of the V-1s, which are apparently very bothersome to them. (24 June 1944)

This was clear during an attack in bright daylight on 25 June, at 1640 hours, when 25 to 30 bombers hit Hélicourt.[65] As we found out later, a construction staff for the V-1 had occupied the little chateau prior to us, and this had obviously been the raiders' target.

Vogelsang reported this event vividly:

> As so often happened—almost unnoticed—a tremendous roaring started. I looked outside, but saw nothing. Suddenly, there was a rustling, a thunder—I just made it

out the door to the hallway on the third floor of the castle. All the walls were shaking as if they were ready to crumble. Windows shattered, cracks appeared in the walls, and all was dirt, smoke, dust. We ran down the stairs, but only got as far as the hallway before the second round hit. We took cover under the staircase. Again, shattering and thundering noise, 100-pound [Literally, "Zentnergewicht," meaning "100 pounds." A German "pound" is one-half kilo, or 1.1 pounds in English measurement - *Translator*] lumps of dirt, rocks, tree branches, falling everywhere. I ran into Guderian and together we hid behind the garden wall, where the next wave of detonations covered us with plaster and dirt. Our piece of the wall remained intact! By leaps, we made it to the safety of the bunker. . . .

Then it was quiet. When the smoke cleared, we saw the whole mess. There were tremendous craters all around the castle; the maintenance building was destroyed; everywhere were toppled trees, and a huge tree root crushed a car. The cemetery looked as if it had been overturned. A large tombstone broke through the roof and landed in the kitchen. After all, there must have been 50 heavy and medium bombs. We were unbelievably lucky! Only a few were not seriously wounded.

During the night there was an enormous racket! Finally, some of our own night fighters arrived, searchlights sent up their beams, and our own anti-aircraft guns fired extensively. In our area alone, 40 aircraft were shot down. It seems that all the castles in the area are being bombed day and night. We almost get the impression that we were accompanied by secret enemy radio operators who report every change of our position to the other side. For this reason, we only stay inside the castle during daylight, using good camouflage. We spend the nights in the roomy bunkers. (25 June 1944)

On 27 June, Vogelsang wrote:

Staying in the bunkers is absolutely safe, but nevertheless a damp and musty business. They are certainly more suitable for growing mushrooms. These bunkers are a system of tunnels, branching out 20 to 30 meters into the steep slope of the hillside. The main tunnel opened into another one crossing it, to which were connected nine rooms, hewn from the rock. The engineers are working diligently to finish the interior walls.

The following day, Vogelsang became ill and was taken to the field hospital. He did not return until September.

During the night of June 27/28, 500 to 600 four-engine bombers attacked the V-1 launching sites, and 500 of the same kind returned on 30 June.[66]

General von Salmuth was satisfied with what he found when he visited the Division on 29 June.[67] On 1 July, the journal of *2d Battalion, Armored Artillery Regiment 146* includes:

Moonlight and tides are favorable for large-scale enemy landings for a period of 10 days, starting on 1 July. Therefore, the Division has ordered heightened observation and combat readiness. The staffs have been made responsible for heightened readiness and must occupy bomb-proof shelters.

Due to this order, battalion staff has moved into a bunker with the vehicle crews. The readiness of the unit is continuously tested through alert and communications exercises. Completion of the positions goes on, in part using civilians. Each battery builds and maintains a dummy command post and a dummy observation post. Alternate positions are being built for immediate occupation and our main command post is being turned into a strongpoint, surrounded by infantry positions.[68]

This entry once again raises the issue of fears regarding a second landing. The *Foreign Armies–West* intelligence section continued to confuse the *Ic* with its erroneous perceptions (encouraged by the enemy's deception operations), which continued even after the invasion. On 26 June, in its "Situation West" summary, the section identified 21 allied divisions already on the continent and 60 more in Great Britain and Northern Ireland, not counting separate brigades and battalions.[69] On 8 July, *OKH* assumed that about 30 large formations were present in the Normandy beachhead.[70] *Foreign Armies–West* added that this "should not put to rest the assumption that the enemy command has resources ready for a new invasion," an opinion it maintained until the end of July. On 27 July, it stated halfheartedly that:

Army Group Patton [The strong enemy forces mistakenly assumed by German intelligence to be in Britain—*Author*] is thereby gradually losing effectiveness for large-scale operations, making it improbable that it will be deployed on short notice against a strongly fortified and occupied coastal sector. While giving up more forces to the elements deployed in Normandy, it will be kept in readiness to be able to attack a German sector of the Channel coast if or when a gap is evident for a prolonged period.

Thus, in the opinion of the department, Army Group Patton does not present an imminent danger, but one has to presume that the Americans will eventually replenish and reinforce it, and have it ready for larger combat operations.[71]

The commanders and staffs in the West were spellbound by this concept. The staff of *Army Group B* reached a similar conclusion, as indicated by Rommel's statements about the *15th Army* sector. He resisted withdrawing any forces from this Army and, on 25 June, sent a concrete message to *Supreme Command–West* in which he most strongly declined even very modest withdrawals from the area of the Channel coast.[72] No unit journals include indications of opposing opinions by Rommel or his staff.

Despite the steadily worsening situation in Normandy, the *116th Panzer Division* remained in its sector south of the mouth of the Somme. It made a special effort to gather experiences from the armored units that were fighting in Normandy.[73] On 5 July, *Leutnant* Borgert, the Adjutant of *Panzerjäger Battalion*

228, visited the *2d Panzer* and *Panzer Lehr Divisions*. Again and again, the most important concern was the enemy's domination of the air above the battle area. This was also highlighted by all directives issued by the higher command staffs. In retrospect, we have to admit that we should have been better prepared for the special challenges that were waiting for us. For example, we did not fully appreciate the impact that the bocage would have on the employment of armored forces, as was later obvious by the first attack in Normandy.

At the beginning of July, *1st Battalion, Panzer Regiment "Grossdeutschland"* was detached and sent to the Eastern Front. On the orders of *Army Group B, 1st Battalion, Panzer Regiment 24*—which until then had been deployed behind it— advanced into the vacated area.[74] To alleviate the shortage of convoys behind the invasion front, columns of trucks had to be delivered to Normandy. The Division was left with a hauling capacity of only about 100 tons. This, of course, had repercussions for the tactical employment of the Division.[75]

In general, relationships with the French populace remained amicable throughout this period. The French suffered with us from the air attacks of the Anglo-Americans. The Resistance made an occasional appearance. On 27 June, the journal of the *2d Battalion, Panzer Artillery Regiment 146,* stated:

> At the observation post of the *8th Battery* . . . in the night of 26/27 June, two terrorists were apprehended and handed over to the regiment for interrogation. Per Division order, *Oberleutnant* Prem established a patrol from the battalion's support troops to catch paratroopers and partisans. All battalion gun positions are to be closed off by guards day and night, to allow no vehicle or pedestrian to approach without identification. All roads were closed off by barricades.[76]

Given the situation in Normandy in the meantime, at the recommendation of *Generalleutnant* Dr. Speidel, *Generalfeldmarschall* von Kluge requested *OKW*'s permission to move up the *116th Panzer Division*. Permission was granted within minutes. This took place on 19 July, at 0055 hours. In a phone conversation with the Chief of Staff, *Supreme Command–West,* Kluge ordered, "Under all circumstances, the *116th* must be brought across the Seine tonight."[77]

Anyone who can imagine the situation at that time would be shocked by the lack of understanding connoted by such an order. On the night of 18/19 July, there were no elements of the Division on the move. Over the next several days, *Army Group B* and *Panzer Group West* continuously pressed for speed, without considering that all of the combat units of the Division had to cross the Seine using only the few ferries available, and at that, only during hours of darkness. The Division crossed the river during the nights of 19–24 July, spread out on both sides of Rouen, from the mouth of the Seine upstream to Vernon. On 24 July, the bulk of the Division had crossed and arrived in its sector behind *Panzer Group West*. This was a job well done.

The Division was assigned to the following sector, behind the *I SS-Panzer Corps,* southeast of Caen: Airan–forest southeast of St. Aignan-de-Cramesnil–

Maizieres–Escures-sur-Favieres.[78] The only subunits missing on 24 July were the *1st Battalion, Panzer Regiment 24* and the engineer battalion; by 26 July, the whole Division was assembled, and there were no serious losses.[79] The Field Replacement Battalion, along with the Division combat training school, were later transferred to the vicinity of Evreux–Conche.[80]

The mission for the Division was approximately as follows: Subordinated to *I SS-Panzer Corps,* the *116th Panzer Division* prepares in sector to repel an eventual enemy penetration through the line Airan–forest southeast of St. Aignan, and further prepares to attack to the north and west-northwest, on both sides of the forest west of Chicheboville.[81] The Division moved into an assembly area about eight kilometers behind the line occupied by the *1st* and *12th SS-Panzer Divisions,* ahead of the Muance brook, and established an armored group ready for immediate counterattack.[82] (See Appendix 6)

First, the Division Commander built a command post on Hill 62, south of Airan. When the staff arrived, the Division command post was erected in Escures. The command post of the artillery regiment was there as well. The command post of *Panzer-Grenadier Regiment 156* was located in Quatrepuits, while that of *Panzer-Grenadier Regiment 60* was in Le Bu-sur-Rouvres.[83]

The journal of *2d Battalion, Panzer Artillery Regiment 146* describes the situation:

> The battalion's mission is to support the defense of the emplaced division, in accordance with the fire missions of the Arko [Arko = Artillery commander, *I SS-Panzer Corps—Author*] and if necessary, contribute to the blocking fires of the *1st* and *12th SS-Panzer Divisions.*
>
> In the event of an enemy penetration of the main line of resistance of both *SS* divisions, the batteries support the counterattack by *Panzer-Grenadier Regiment 60* (reinforced with a *Panzer* battalion) with a smoke screen on the flanks. Alternate positions are to be reconnoitered and constructed. (23 July 1944).
>
> The night generally passed quietly.
>
> Again, our own strong bomber squadrons (Junkers 88s) are bombing installations in the enemy's rear.
>
> Towards 0300 hours, the enemy began pounding the main line of resistance and main battle area with a strong artillery preparatory fires.
>
> From 0500 hours, the barrage intensified and continued with undiminished force until 0700. Harassing fires into our own rear areas are fired by the heaviest caliber naval gunfire.
>
> Strong enemy bomber formations appear above the main line of resistance around 0730 hours, dropping bombs of all sizes on the positions of the *SS-Hitler Youth Division.*
>
> It is impossible to view the sector from the battalion's rearward observation posts, since the whole area is covered by fumes and smoke from the drumfire barrage. Reports from the front indicate that the enemy has not started the major attack that was expected.

The heavy barrage has subsided and the enemy is firing only scattered heavy rounds at targets in the main battle area of the *SS-Hitler Youth Division.* Fighter-bombers and fighters are continuously in the air, looking over our positions. (25 July 1944)

Despite its weakness, the *Luftwaffe* obviously did its utmost in the nights until the end of July; on 20 July, even the journal of *Army Group B* mentioned its success in night operations.[84]

In a letter dated 26 July, Count Schwerin related his view of the situation to *Major* Tebbe, the commander of *1st Battalion, Panzer Regiment 16* in Grafenwöhr:

The Division overcame the very difficult move from its old sector into its new one south of Caen. We were tremendously fortunate to have caught a period of bad weather, which allowed us to march in daylight. The Division is now combat ready, in reserve behind *I (SS) Panzer Corps,* expecting a large-scale British attack. I have the impression that this will not happen here at all. Perhaps the British will do something totally different. In any case, they did not miss the fact that we reinforced our presence in this area.[85]

He was correct in his judgment of the situation. The new attack by the Americans, west of the Vire on 25 July, was an indication that could not be overlooked.

On 20 July, while the Division was on the move, the attempt to assassinate Hitler took place. It had no effect within the Division. The facts became known only little by little. Soldiers who were about to go into battle showed little understanding. They had no knowledge of the crimes that were committed behind their backs: these only became clear after the war. Individual events may have been known to a few individuals, but they were pushed aside by men at the front who were fighting for very existence of their people.

The Division was ordered to move on the day before the assassination attempt. The Division Commander drove ahead with a small staff. While in the vicinity of La Roche-Guyon, he dictated a letter for *Generalleutnant* Speidel to his sergeant major, *Oberfeldwebel* Lademann. *Unteroffizier* Trauden, a motorcycle messenger for the general, delivered the letter in a sealed envelope to Speidel personally, who mentions the letter on page 126 in his book, *Invasion 1944.*[86] In 1977, Count Schwerin wrote about the contents of his letter:

With this, the general offered an assessment of the situation, which culminated in his statement that this was the last chance for *Army Group B* to intervene in favor of an immediate termination of the fighting. In light of the catastrophic development of the overall situation in all theaters of war, this had to be demanded. The Division still was, without limitations, at the disposal of the field marshal. It would no longer be available, once it disappeared in the witches' cauldron of the invasion.[87]

Oberfeldwebel Lademann remembers:

The general notified Army Group that the Division was again combat ready as far as the circumstances allowed. He took this opportunity to request that the Division only be deployed in case of an emergency, since this Division was one of the few that had complete trust in its leaders and could be relied upon in case of a change in the highest command. The general bade General Speidel to rest assured that he could strongly count on him and the Division in any situation.

The participants also reported these events to David Irving, who used the information in his book, *Rommel.*[88] Irving reproaches Speidel about holding back the *116th Panzer Division* from invasion front for the purpose of having it available for participation in a *coup d'etat*. He also refers to Speidel's book, where it says, "Also out of political concerns, the Field Marshal deemed it wise to have reliable *Panzer* units at hand for possible future events."[89]

In 1978, *General* Count Schwerin sent a sworn statement to me.[90] It reads:

1. I have absolutely no doubt that I, as the commander of *116th Panzer Division*, was informed by the appropriate authority that the detention of my Division in the sector of the mouth of the Somme before and during the battle of the invasion in Normandy was done for two reasons:

   a. The possibility of a second invasion on both sides of the mouth of the Somme, for which certain signs were believed to be visible by higher levels. These signs were considered to be valid by the *Führer*'s headquarters, by *OKW*, and by other higher command staffs, even long after the landing in Normandy.

   b. The secret plans of Rommel's staff, naturally limited to a few confidants, for the conclusion of an immediate truce with the Western powers, if necessary against Hitler's will. This was to be combined with Hitler's arrest, his delivery to a German court of law, and the elimination of the Nazi regime. . . . In case of "internal disturbances," Rommel's staff wanted to have a reliable unit at hand.

Count Schwerin could not remember exactly who confided the "secret plans from Rommel's headquarters" to him, but said that it could only have been Speidel or *General* Geyr von Schweppenburg. Geyr can be excluded with almost complete certainty. His relationship with Rommel was extremely tense, and after the war he declared that he only heard of those plans from Speidel during his imprisonment.

Schwerin's statement further specifies that his letter to Speidel could hardly be explained "without knowledge of the secret plans," these, as well as the plans by Beck for the elimination of Hitler "received my full consent in view of the strategically and politically hopeless situation."

In a letter to me, Speidel expressed his opinion on the matter:

One has to differentiate between the time before and the time during the Invasion.

It is correct that before the start of the battle of the Invasion, thoughts were weighed to have "reliable *Panzer* units available for possible, coming events" (*Invasion 1944*, page 71), and that the *2d Panzer Division* under Baron von

Lüttwitz, and the *116th Panzer Division* under Count Schwerin were considered. These considerations took place in connection with the then-disputed formation of *Panzer* units. I wrote about that in *Invasion 1944,* but to avoid repetition, I did not go into this in detail in my memoirs.

After the initiation of the invasion, one cannot talk about "detaining" the *116th Panzer Division* for such reasons. That the *116th Panzer Division* was not released for deployment by *OKW* until 19 July 1944 was probably due to the incomplete reconstitution you mentioned, but also due to the expectation of a second landing in the sector Seine/Somme, referred to by Count Schwerin in 1a [of his sworn statement].[91]

The *2nd Panzer Division* was ordered by *Supreme Command–West* to the invasion front on 8 June.[92] This eliminated it from political plans, unless one suspects a political motive behind the initiation of the division's withdrawal from the front, near Caumont, and its subsequent assembly south of Caen, on 16 July.[93] In any case, one cannot assert that this division was kept away from the battle in Normandy. Does this also apply to the *116th Panzer Division?*

I asked *General* Speidel and *General* Count von Schwerin that they, as the only witnesses, jointly clarify the situation. Unfortunately, they both declined. Therefore, history may never have a complete clarification of the "secret plans."

As evidence of his position, *General* Dr. Speidel presented the fact that *Army Group B* could not exercise free reign over the *116th Panzer Division*. This certainly does not hold true of the beginning of the invasion; at that time, *Army Group B* repositioned the Division several times, without asking permission from the higher command. After the conference at Berchtesgaden, the climate with *OKW* became so tense that the freedom of the higher commands in the West diminished continually and therefore, permission should have been requested. But before the evening of 17 July, when Rommel was wounded, such a request was never made.

I have reported extensively about the fear of a second invasion, and presented the roles of the individual commanders and staffs regarding this question. One could posit the incomplete reconstitution of the Division as a reason for witholding it from combat, but this deficiency was resolved by 1 July. After all this, only the fear of a landing between Somme and Seine could be used as an argument, unless the "secret plans" indeed had a part in the decision to detain the Division at the mouth of the Somme. Amazingly, only directly following Rommel's injuries was Speidel affected by this situation. If the plans could no longer be realized, would not employing the *116th Panzer Division* near the mouth of the Somme become senseless?

This question cannot be answered clearly. On the evening of 19 July, in reference to *15th Army's* release of the *116th Panzer Division,* Warlimont said to Blumentritt, "The risk has to be taken." On 24 July, Kluge declared to Hausser, "All in all, I wish to evaluate the situation by expressing my belief that the opponent never considered undertaking a more extensive landing anywhere else, and probably will only try to extend his bridgehead."[94]

Two days later, Blumentritt and Speidel contemplated the withdrawal and subsequent advancement of more forces from *15th Army,* "since a separate landing is becoming more and more unlikely." Additionally, they talked about the release of one *Panzer* division and one infantry division from *Army Group G.*[95]

On 27 July, conclusions were drawn from this realization and a request was sent to the *OKW* to extract forces from the *15th Army.*[96] Three infantry divisions were relieved, and the *9th Panzer Division* along with another infantry division, were ordered in from southern France. Like most actions in the battle of Normandy, these actions also were implemented too late.

The sworn statement of *General* Count von Schwerin concludes:

Whenever needed, the *116th Panzer Division* would at once have been subordinated, without limitation, to the direct command of *Generalfeldmarschall* Rommel, and would also have accepted the orders of his Chief of Staff, Speidel. I am convinced that the Division would have obeyed all related orders without hesitation. A decision in this case would have been easy for me. In most units engaged in combat, including the *Waffen-SS,* an anti-Nazi mood was present, and most troop commanders were against Hitler and his conduct of war, since it would evidently lead to ruin.[97]

It is difficult to say today, if the Division would have, without hesitation, obeyed all these related orders. It could possibly have led to civil war. It is questionable if all the Division's subordinate commanders would have cooperated. They were, after all, not prepared, and at that time their faith was not as shaken as was later believed by their Division Commander. It would have depended on each one's individual situation. One also has to question the behavior of the young officers and the troops as a whole. At this point, one should be reminded of young *Leutnant* Poth's reaction to the Division Commander's speech at the reconstitution of the Division. (Chapter 2)

The 21 July entry in the diary of a veteran member of the Division states:

We received news of the assassination attempt on the *Führer.* It's hard to believe. This is how far it gotten in the German Army; high officers committing a murderous attack against their highest commander. Undoubtedly, officers and soldiers are fed up with the long war. Yet, one is outraged by this act, which will only lead us deeper into misery. Now more than ever, we must continue to fight! Are there really such fools, who think one could appease the Bolsheviks and calm down the Anglo-Americans? I am very sad.[98]

Surely, the writer was not the only one having such thoughts. The leader of one of the Division's *Panzer-Grenadier* companies, at the time 20 years old, conveyed his memories to the author:

The news of the attack on Hitler reached us during the march, somewhere between Seine and the first assembly area, east of Caen. It was devastating. If morale was not exactly high or the attitude eager for action after the honest words of the Division Commander, *General* Count Schwerin, during his visits before the expected invasion, it now slipped to zero. . . . "Should we not succeed in destroying the enemy during the invasion in front of the main line of resistance at the beach, then this war cannot be won. Then the only thing left for us to do is to conduct ourselves in such a manner as not to damage the reputation and honor of the German soldier!"

These were roughly the words of the commander.[99]

CHAPTER 5

The Battle for Normandy

While the *116th Panzer Division* was assembled behind the front line near Caen, and the *2d Panzer Division* was brought back there from the western flank of *Panzer Group West,* the American First Army had finished its preparation for an attack on the Cotentin Peninsula.[1,2] On 25 July, the VII Corps attack west of St. Lô began with a tremendous aerial bombardment. Three infantry divisions attacked, supported by concentrated artillery fire, while their air forces shifted their attacks into the depth of the German main battle area. The terrain gained was modest, but on 26 July, after renewed aerial and artillery preparations against the divisions in the front line, three fresh American units, including elements of two armored divisions, started their attack. They created a breach more than five kilometers deep that could not be closed.[3]

The American success was based on their overwhelming artillery preparatory bombardments; precise concentration of forces, that is, six divisions in a narrow sector; excellent cooperation between fighter bombers and ground forces; and finally, a technical improvisation called the "Rhinoceros." It consisted of four pointed steel teeth that were made from parts of German beach obstacles and attached to the front of many Sherman tanks. This enabled these tanks to rip openings in the hedgerows. Thereby, the attack was not limited to roads but was able to proceed on a wide front.[4]

On 26 July, the Americans started to advance toward the Peninsula's west coast against the northern front of *LXXXIV Corps.* They prosecuted this attack with VIII Corps, which led with three infantry divisions, followed by two armored divisions. The *LXXXIV Corps* situation became critical and no more reserves were available.[5] On 27 July, the Americans achieved a deep penetration toward the south and southwest. *Generalfeldmarschall* von Kluge ordered the *2d Panzer Division* and the headquarters of *XLVII Panzer Corps* to the *7th Army.* Early on 28 July, the *2d Panzer Division* was to close the gap between the left flank of *II Parachute Corps* (south of St. Lô) and the *Panzer Lehr Division* (near Dangy) by attacking from east to west.[6] The *2d Panzer* succeeded in crossing the Vire near Tessy and, with its most advanced units, it seized the intersection two kilometers west of Moyon (La Denisière). This intersection was the object of heavy fighting.[7]

Kluge spoke with Warlimont at 0925 on 28 July. He deemed it necessary to withdraw the *7th Army* to the line Caumont l'Eventé–Tessy–Percy–Gavray–Granville. Besides that, he declared his intention to transfer the *116th Panzer Division* to the west. Warlimont agreed.[8]

At 1010 hours, *Panzer Group West* received the corresponding order, according to which the Division was to be deployed to the area Vire–St. Sever-Calvados.[9] Shortly thereafter, Kluge complemented this order for *Generalleutnant* Gause, *Panzer Group West* Chief of Staff:

> The Army Group commander reported that the situation of the *7th Army* has become considerably worse. The *116th Panzer Division* must therefore at once commence marching to join the *7th Army* near Vire, with all energy and every possible assistance. The move should be conducted during daylight by individual march units if the air situation permits.[10]

In the afternoon, *7th Army* reported that its commanding general [*SS-Obergruppenführer* Paul Hausser–*Editor*] preferred to deploy the *116th Panzer Division* to the left of the *2d Panzer Division*.[11]

For its part, the staff of the *116th Panzer Division* recommended a careful withdrawal from its positions and assembly for redeployment. *Armored Reconnaissance Battalion 116* had already commenced its march at 1245 hours and most of the Division was to begin moving at 1730 hours. Three march units were formed: one moved north on the Falaise–Vire main road; the second one marched through Flers–Tinchebray, and one took the southern route through Putanges–Briouce–Mortain–St. Sever-Calvados. During daylight hours, they marched in smaller individual groups, keeping long distances between them.

On the morning of 29 July, with the benefit of fog, the Division reached its destination. This was a major accomplishment, since, for example, the route for the southern group had required marching over about 150 kilometers of secondary roads. Casualties and losses due to air activity were tolerable. Contrary to the estimates and orders of higher headquarters, the Division was not able to immediately conduct an attack alongside the *2d Panzer Division*. First, it had to reconsolidate. After this, it would have to prepare for the attack, in an area completely dominated by the enemy air force.[12]

On 28 July, the opponent reached the Tessy–Villebaudon–Bréhal road, west of Villebaudon, and sent some units northwest near Lengronne. The rest of *LXXXIV Corps* was threatened with encirclement and its units tried to break through in the direction of Percy–Villedieu-les-Poêles. There was an opening at the coast in the direction of Avranches.[13]

On this day, the Commanding General of the *116th Panzer Division* drove ahead to the command post of *II Parachute Corps*. *Armored Reconnaissance Battalion 116* followed him.[14] East of Percy, *Generalleutnant* Count von Schwerin found the corps staff at about 1700 hours. They knew little of the situation.

The command post of *XLVII Panzer Corps* was nearby. There, the Division Commander was informed of the situation by the corps commander, *General der Panzertruppe* Baron von Funck. Count Schwerin learned that the Division was subordinated to this corps, that enemy armored units were attacking Percy from the north, and that the *2d SS-Panzer Division* in the area east of Coutances was cut off and was supposed to fight its way back to *XLVII Panzer Corps*. Funck informed him that the *2d Panzer Division,* which was also subordinated to his command, was defending in front of Tessy. The *116th Panzer Division* was to prepare to counterattack to the northwest, to enable the *2d SS-Panzer Division* to break out.

Later, as darkness fell, the Division Commander traveled to Courson, to the command post of *Hauptmann* Zehner, the commander of *Armored Reconnaissance Battalion 116,* who had just arrived himself. The Division Commander ordered him to secure the main road from Villedieu to Pont-Farcy during the night and to be prepared to reconnoiter to the northwest at daybreak. Schwerin established his command post near Sept-Frères, and went to see the commander of the *Panzer Lehr Division,* who had just arrived in the area. Schwerin wanted to procure information about the situation and the terrain.

He found *Generalleutnant* Bayerlein visibly affected by the destructive blows his division had sustained. Remnants of the division stood along the road, northeast of Percy, facing a threat from enemy tanks; the few combat capable units were to assemble southeast of Percy. Bayerlein explained that the only open terrain favorable for armor laid to the north and northwest of Percy, while the area east of the road, from Percy to Villebaudon, presented difficult, hilly terrain with few roads. Thereafter, Count Schwerin ordered *Armored Reconnaissance Battalion 116* to occupy Mount Robin (Hill 276), northeast of Percy, at first light on 29 July. From there, the battalion was to make contact with the elements of the *Panzer Lehr Division* that were still in front of the hill, and to reconnoiter the enemy position north of Percy.

Meanwhile, I arrived and was sent to the corps command post with the proposal to lead the attack with the main effort in the vicinity of and west of Percy, basically toward the northwest. Here, the terrain permitted an advance across a broader front with multiple armored spearheads, while an attack from east to west from the area west of Tessy could only be launched through a narrow, restrictive corridor. Besides that, the rest of the *Panzer Lehr Division* was located near Percy and could have secured the line of departure for the *116th Panzer Division*'s attack. I was told to have the Division ready and to send strong units to the area near Villedieu, as it was reported that the enemy was advancing via Gavray toward Villedieu.

Fate did not smile on the *116th Panzer Division* during its first combat. A patrol of the armored reconnaissance battalion had already encountered the enemy at Mont Robin. The units of the *Panzer Lehr Division* which had been in the area on the previous evening had already been moved back to Percy.[15] *Hauptmann* Zehner, rushing ahead of his battalion to personally observe the action, missed the patrol, ran into the enemy, and was killed. After losing its leader, the battalion was unable to seize the hill. There they were confronted by elements of the 2d Armored Division, which, in the course of the day, were reinforced by a regiment of the 29th Infantry Division.[16] *Rittmeister* [Captain of Cavalry—*Editor*] Schliep assumed command of *Armored Reconnaissance Battalion 116.*

Higher command echelons did not possess a clear understanding of the operations of the *116th Panzer Division.* Based on the instructions from the evening before, the Division staff planned to attack with the Division's main effort toward the left. This is what I reported to corps. Furthermore, word was floating around that units of the Division should be diverted toward Villedieu. When Kluge heard of this plan by *7th Army,* he ordered, in part directly to Funck, to disregard it.[17] At 1055 hours on 29 July, *7th Army* received the order that *XLVII Panzer Corps* was not to secure the area around Hambye, but to attack on the same day to close the gaps there with the *116th* and *2d Panzer Divisions.* Subsequently, Kluge gave the order—again directly to Funck [that is, directly from army group commander to corps commander, bypassing the *7th Army* intermediate echelon—*Editor*]—to conduct the *116th Panzer Division*'s attack with a strong right wing toward Hambye, even if strong enemy forces were reported to be there.

At 1540 hours, Funck directly told Kluge about strong attacks on both sides of the Vire, that is, from north towards the corps, and also towards Percy. He stated that the *116th Panzer Division* was being hindered by aircraft but despite that, he was counting on its attack "still today." Based on monitored radio traffic which indicated that tanks of the *2d SS-Panzer Division* were still in the vicinity of Le Guislain, northwest of Villebaudon, Kluge changed the direction of the attack of *116th Panzer Division* again, at 1730 hours. The Division was to march, "still today," and reach Le Guislain with its right wing. But at 1900 hours, *7th Army* reported that the Division could not attack "today," but rather that it should roll in concert with the *2d Panzer Division* on the following morning (30 July). Meanwhile, the enemy attacked the *2d Panzer Division* not only from north, but also its southern flank near La Denisière, in an attempted encirclement. There, too, the 29th Infantry Division was the opponent.[18]

The leadership of the *116th Panzer Division* had no idea of the differences of opinion among their superiors, and only learned that the attack towards Villedieu was cancelled. They, therefore, adhered to their plan of attack, with the main effort on the left via Percy to the northwest, and reconnoitered accordingly. They also ordered *Panzer-Grenadiers* and artillery to move forward to the assembly area in individual groups and to secure the line of departure for the attack. The operations journal of the *2d Battalion* of the artillery regiment reads:

> Liaison instructions from the artillery regiment require immediate action of the battalion in the vicinity of Gouvets. . . . The Division goes into action directly from the move and opposes the enemy along the line Percy–Chevry. Both infantry regiments have already arrived in that area and taken up position in the main battleline.[19]

This was certainly expressed with some extenuation because the *Panzer-Grenadiers* did not fare much better than the artillery, whose operations journal continues, "All day long, the battalion remains in the forest near St. Sever due to fighter bombers. This area is continuously checked by low-flying aircraft. Any vehicle breaking cover is fired upon."

The battalion lost several vehicles. Its commander, *Hauptmann* Müller, was wounded.

At noon, the corps commander appeared at the Division's command post. He criticized the slow arrival of the Division and demanded that the attack still take place on 29 July, from the area northeast of Percy to the west. This attack was to take place in concert with that of the *2d Panzer Division,* to exploit their success at La Denisière.

This contradicted the Division's plans. The previous discussions with the corps staff, to begin the attack from the area of Percy to the northeast, were now declared by Funck as a "misunderstanding." All objections—terrain conditions, changes to the already-begun reconnaissance and unit movements—were ignored. Even though the staff declared that it was impossible to conduct the attack on the same day, Funck ordered the Division to advance immediately and to subsequently attack on the same evening.

The new plan of attack for the Division called for *Panzer-Grenadier Regiment 60* and *Panzer Regiment 16* to attack on the right, along the Tessy-sur-Vire–Villebaudon road, as the main effort in conjunction with the *2d Panzer Division,* as ordered. To the left, *Panzer-Grenadier Regiment 156* was to attack toward Mont Robin with *Panzerjäger Battalion 228,* along the road from St. Lô to Percy, north of La Tilandière. As already mentioned, the armored reconnaissance battalion was not successful in taking the hill in the course of the day. The enemy brought in reinforcements and it turned out that the hill was too steep for armored vehicles.

Even though the afternoon hours were used to prepare for the operation, time available limited opportunities for reconnaissance. In most cases, enemy air activity prevented movement into attack positions. Many of the units only settled into their designated positions during the night. The Division established a forward command post in La Benouvière les Monts (two kilometers southwest of Pont-Farcy). The Division Commander went there, while I stayed in Sept-Frères until the forward position was connected to the main command post by telephone line. In the evening of 29 July at 2120 hours, the corps commander telephoned me. The following are notes from that conversation:

Corps commander: The *2d Panzer Division* just reported that, according to *Major* Guderian, the *116th Panzer Division* would not be attacking any more today. Besides, one of its regimental commanders, *Oberst* Schneider, or similar (Fischer), explained to the *352d Infantry Division* that he would stay in the area of Gouvets and the hills southwest of it, and would not attack before early morning. This looks to me like pure obstruction and I am now quite sure that the *116th Panzer Division* does, indeed, not want to attack today. I demand, however, the strict execution of my orders and will not be afraid of changing the leadership of the Division so that my instructions will be carried out.

Ia: I did not tell the *2d Panzer Division* that the *116th* would not attack any more today. On the contrary, I said that this Division would do everything to help as quickly as possible, but that under the given circumstances, I doubted that the attack could still take place today. *Oberst* Fischer has the order to prepare an attack in the area of Gouvets and southwest of it, and immediately thereafter to drive to the Division Commander, who was at the forward command post near La Benouvière les Monts to control the attack from there.

Corps commander: What good is an attack position behind the firing positions of the artillery? Do you have your Division Commander on the line? Does he know my order of attack?

Ia: The attack order was sent to the Division Commander by radio, but besides that, I also sent the *O1* [the Assistant Division Operations Officer–*Editor*] to inform him precisely.

The statement of the *Ia* regarding heavy losses through continuous air attacks and his report that the first units of *Panzer-Grenadier Regiment 156* arrived in the designated attack positions by 1900 hours were no longer afforded recognition.[20]

Since *7th Army* had already reported to *Army Group B* at 1900 hours that the *116th Panzer Division* would not be attacking on 29 July, this conversation made sense only as intimidation. At 2219 hours, I reported the following to corps headquarters by telephone:

1st Battalion, Panzer Regiment 24 in attack position as of 2045 hours; likewise, at 2115 hours, the self-propelled battalion of *Panzer Artillery Regiment 146,* directly behind the armored personnel carrier-borne infantry battalion and *2d Battalion, Panzer Regiment 16.* So far, no report from *2d Battalion, Panzer-Grenadier Regiment 60.* Initial elements of *Panzer-Grenadier Regiment 156* in position, partially on foot.[21]

The last sentence shows that the Division made an effort to follow the order to still attack "today," even if it believed the order to be wrong, which the events proved by the time of the conversations. On 29 July, the enemy was, of course, still relatively weak, but in conjunction with its dominant air forces, it was strong enough that a piecemeal attack could not have broken through.

The formerly encircled units of the *2d SS-Panzer Division* arrived near Percy, which made the left flank of the Division more secure.

In the evening, *Army Group B* reported that it intended to close the gap between Villebaudon and Hambye with an attack by *XLVII Panzer Corps,* and to establish a "secure defensive front" from Hambye to the coast.[22] What incredible optimism, considering the strength of the enemy, the violent attacks against the *2d Panzer Division* and, most of all, the desperate condition of *LXXXIV Corps*!

In the morning of 30 July 1944, at 0500 hours, the *116th Panzer Division* commenced the attack.[23] After a successful beginning, the attack ground to a halt.

The *2d Battalion, Panzer-Grenadier Regiment 156,* under the command of *Hauptmann* Nitsch, achieved the greatest success, by attacking in the middle, away from the main roads. *Oberleutnant* Best advanced with *6th Company* to the Villebaudon–Percy road near La Guilleri. The company destroyed and captured a number of enemy weapons and vehicles.[24]

The regiment's *1st Battalion* no more succeeded in seizing Mont Robin than did the armored reconnaissance battalion on the day before. Even after some initial successes, the attack of the armored group within the right attack group of the Division had to be stopped. The attack was led by *1st Battalion, Panzer Regiment 24.* The activity report of this battalion characterizes the action as follows:

> Since this attack had to be carried out quickly, our orientation regarding enemy and friendly positions was poor, which led to difficulties even before the attack began. . . . The terrain for the attack was extremely unsuitable for armored vehicles. . . . The attack had to be conducted along a main road, lined on both sides with hedgerows and meadows with trees, where the maximum field of fire was 400 meters. Fighting with tanks was only possible if the commanders or platoon leaders proceeded dismounted through the obstructed terrain to reconnoiter enemy targets and friendly positions and then personally guided their tanks. The Panther was outstanding in traversing rough terrain. It playfully overcame high hedges and walls, on which older model tanks would have gotten stuck . . . .
>
> The attack by the *Grenadiers* and the *1st Company* [of *Panzer Regiment 24— Editor*] proceeded slowly because of the increasing resistance of the enemy, as well as the unfavorable terrain. Soon the first fighter bombers and artillery spotter planes arrived to take part in the ground action. . . . In the afternoon hours, the order came to cease the attack.[25]

The enemy now turned to counterattacks with infantry and tanks. He achieved small breaches on the extreme right flank, near Chevry, as well as on the road near La Tilandière.[26] A night attack by *Panzer-Grenadier Regiment 156* to take possession of Mont Robin and to interrupt the Percy–Villebaudon road achieved no results.[27]

The Division was denied success in its first action since its reorganization as a *Panzer* division. Nevertheless, it engaged opposing forces and thereby relieved the pressure on the badly distressed *LXXXIV Corps.*

The enemy forces opposing the Division consisted of most of Combat Command A of the 2d Armored Division, and the 115th and 175th Infantry Regiments of the 29th Infantry Division.[28]

An American officer reporting on XIX Corps operations, an attack by which covered the left flank of the US offensive between Vire and Percy, wrote, "On the evening of 30 July, the XIX Corps was still involved in heavy fighting in the area of Percy–Tessy. From the higher ground between the villages, the Germans had the American units effectively under fire and interdicted the roads in the area of Villebaudon as they chose."

After regrouping on the following morning, the *116th Panzer Division* intended to continue the attack. It pulled the armored group to the left flank to resume its original plan, to attack with the main effort via Percy towards the northwest.[29] Only one company of *1st Battalion, Panzer Regiment 24* remained with *Panzer-Grenadier Regiment 60* on the Villebaudon–Tessy road.[30] But this attack never materialized. The increasingly threatening situation in *LXXXIV Corps*, and the growing pressure upon the northern flank of the *2d Panzer Division* forced it to abandon the counterattack The opponent penetrated the thin line of defense between Gavray and the coast, moved towards Villedieu and stood in front of Avranches. In addition, the English attacked the left wing of *Panzer Group West* and achieved deep breaches south of Coumont.[31] On the morning of 31 July, Kluge spoke with Warlimont and demanded the delivery of reinforcements in taxis, *à la* Paris to the Marne in 1914.[32] Finally, there was an order to withdraw more forces from the *15th Army*.[33]

Too late!

Late in the afternoon of 30 July, the *116th Panzer Division* received an order to release at once an armored group and place it at the disposal of *LXXXIV Corps*. Under the leadership of the commander of *Panzer Regiment 16*, *Major* Lueder, this group was sent toward Villedieu. It consisted of a mixed armored battalion, the *2d Battalion, Panzer-Grenadier Regiment 60*; the *1st Battalion, Armored Artillery Regiment 146*, with one battery of *Wespe* and one battery of *Hummel* self-propelled howitzers; and units from *Armored Reconnaissance Battalion 116*. *Combat Group Lueder* was originally supposed to attack from Villedieu to the major intersection eleven kilometers west of the town. Obviously, this did not happen. On the morning of 31 July, we found them ten kilometers southwest of Villedieu.[34]

At this time, *7th Army* ordered that the entire *116th Panzer Division* be withdrawn under the cover of security forces, and sent into action toward Avranches. Since the opponent started to attack the Division in the morning hours, this plan had to be abandoned.[35] The remaining units of the Division were on the defensive the whole day. A breach near *Panzer-Grenadier Regiment 156* southwest of Montabot was sealed off.[36] *Panzer-Grenadier Regiment 60* repelled all attacks with the help of the *4th Company* of *Panzer Regiment 24*, under command of *Rittmeister* Weidemann, but in the evening, only three battleworthy Panthers were left.[37]

Although the Division was forced onto the defense after relinquishing half of its tanks, the commanding general of *XLVII Panzer Corps* [Baron von Funck— *Editor*] demanded a renewed attack to take Mont Robin. After two failures in the previous days, the Division deemed accomplishment of the plan impossible. Nevertheless, *2d Battalion, Panzer-Grenadier Regiment 156* was pulled out at noon on 31 July by shortening the front along the line Beaucoudray–west of Montabot, and was, along with assault units, prepared to attack the hill. The attack, however, did not materialize because the enemy again penetrated near *1st*

Battalion, and *2d Battalion* had to close off the hole toward the north. To reestablish the position, *Generalleutnant* Count Schwerin personally directed the counterattack from the command post of the armored reconnaissance battalion. At 1800 hours, *2d Battalion, Panzer-Grenadier Regiment 156,* supported by a platoon of tanks and a platoon of tank destroyers, executed the attack, and by 2100 hours the position was reestablished.[38] The commander of *1st Battalion, Panzer Regiment 24, Major* von Meyer, and his reinforced *1st Company,* were fighting east of Percy, where a gap towards the left neighbor opened up. They repelled all attacks.[39]

Group Lueder was deployed by *LXXXIV Corps* via Ste. Pience (eleven kilometers southwest of Villedieu) and Le Luot towards Sartilly on the Granville–Avranches road, twelve kilometers across enemy territory. But by noon, *Group Lueder* had already been pushed into the defense near Ste. Pience and found themselves isolated between Villedieu and Avranches. A regimental group from the *77th Infantry Division,* coming from the south, was supposed to plug up the hole. This failed, and the Sélune bridge near Pontaubault (six kilometers south of Avranches) fell undamaged into enemy hands.[40] This freed the way for the Third Army under Lieutenant General Patton, who assumed command of the western American corps on 1 August. Three American armored and four infantry divisions poured into the open between Villedieu and Avranches.

Combat Group Lueder was literally surrounded, because on 31 July the enemy turned toward the southeast with First Army's VII Corps (3d Armored,1st, 4th, and 9th Infantry Divisions).[41] South of Villedieu, the enemy advanced to Brécey in the evening. Lueder's command was deployed by *LXXXIV Corps* against the enemy near Brécey.[42] On the evening of 31 July, he received orders to break through toward the east. On 1 August, *Major* Sandkuhl wrote, "Breakthrough successful without enemy contact. In the course of the day, enemy moves eastward. Disengagement of the combat group toward St. Laurent."[43]

On the morning of 1 August, Lueder's command fought enemy tanks near St. Laurent-de-Cuves (northeast of Brécey). Some of his units, most likely from the armored reconnaissance battalion, secured an area near Montigny, ten kilometers southeast of Brécey, and later near Mortain.[44]

On the evening of 31 July, the Division received orders to displace to the area east of Villedieu after being relieved by the *2d Panzer Division*. The Division was to remain there, ready to commence a counterattack to the northwest or west.[45] To withdraw the *116th Panzer Division,* the front line of *XLVII Panzer Corps* was moved back to the line Tessy–Percy–Villedieu. During the night and in the morning hours of 1 August, most of the Division was relieved. During the day, the Division marched south in individual groups; units of *Panzer-Grenadiers,* mainly of *Regiment 156,* did not return from the front until evening, because heavy enemy attacks prevented their relief.[46]

The Division was now subordinated to *LXXXIV Corps*. The leadership took a breath of relief to have escaped the depressing influence of *General* von Funck.

Now the Division received the order to adopt a mobile, predominantly offensively-oriented tactical posture to prevent a further enemy advance to the east, between the left flank of the *353d Infantry Division* and the Avranches–Juvigny road. To this end, *Group Lueder* was returned to the Division. The sector was about 16 kilometers in width. It was not clear where the unit to the right was. One could hope that remnants of the *353d* would be east of Villedieu, on the road to Vire. Villedieu itself fell into enemy hands, and south of it, the opponent advanced to Le Gast and St. Pois.[47]

At 2210 hours on 1 August, *7th Army* reported to Kluge that the northern combat group of the *116th Panzer Division* had linked up with the *353d Infantry Division*, southeast of La Chapelle-Céceline, which it had seized. The group had received orders to push on to St. Martin, to the southwest. It could not be established if this report was correct, or to which group of the Division it pertained. According to the same report, Lueder was supposed to advance from St. Laurent to Brécey, to again close the road to the east. This was not achieved.[48]

The *116th Panzer Division* could not cover the whole area. Its staff therefore decided to do the next best thing and bring the northern enemy group to a standstill. To accomplish this mission, the Division deployed as follows:

Right: *Panzer-Grenadier Regiment 156* (*Oberst* Fischer) reinforced by *Panzerjäger Battalion 228* via Le Gast.

Left: *Panzer-Grenadier Regiment 60* (*Oberst* Voigtsberger) reinforced by *1st Battalion, Panzer Regiment 24* via St. Pois. In lieu of its *2d Battalion*, fighting with *Group Lueder*, *Armored Engineer Battalion 675* was attached.

On the afternoon of 1 August, the left group reached St. Pois before the enemy and moved patrols west to *Group Lueder*, near St. Laurent. Some of these were cut off by the enemy moving from the northwest to St. Pois, and had to fight their way back. The right group only arrived in its sector in the morning of 2 August and encountered the opponent, who was already in Le Gast. It seized the village and Hill 290, situated to the southwest. *Hauptmann* Nitsch wrote in his diary, "1300 hours attack on Hill 290 in spite of heavy enemy action, including from the air, a proud day for the battalion."[49]

The Division now intended to destroy the northern enemy group with a concentric attack on Coulouvray-Boisbenâtre by all three groups. The attacking elements were arrayed as follows:

Group Fischer from Le Gast to the west.

Group Voigtsberger from area north of St. Pois towards the northwest.

Group Lueder, about face from St. Laurent towards the north-northeast.

No further progress could be achieved near Le Gast. On the contrary, the opponent became stronger; but his assaults were stopped in their tracks by tank destroyers and artillery. *Major* Flecke, commanding the *1st Battalion, Panzer-Grenadier Regiment 156*, was wounded.[50]

The attack from St. Pois started to gain ground, but came to a halt at the intersection in Le Ny au Jan, before La Cour. Lueder came to within one kilometer of Coulouvray-Boisbenâtre, but he did not succeed in taking the village and cutting off the enemy ahead of the Division, because the enemy also turned around northwest of St. Pois and pushed into Lueder's right flank. He was forced to turn, and a violent tank battle ensued, with losses on both sides.[51] This is how full success was denied the Division on 2 August. Nevertheless, the enemy attack was defeated and did not resume with full force in this sector. The *1st Battalion, Panzer Regiment 24* alone destroyed 19 enemy tanks.[52]

The opponent was the 4th Infantry Division, reinforced by Combat Command B of the 3d Armored Division. His instructions were to seize St. Pois and Hill 211 southeast of the town, as well as to build a bridgehead at Chérencé-le-Roussel south of the Sée creek. He achieved nothing and therefore, on 3 August, sent Combat Command B via Cuves toward the south bank and from the south built a bridgehead on the north bank. This would later would cause a great deal of trouble for the *116th Panzer Division.*[53]

The southern sector of the Division was controlled by *Armored Reconnaissance Battalion 116.* Its men also reconnoitered further south. On 2 August, it reported the enemy in Cuves and near Juvigny-le-Tertre. Given this situation, the Division Commander suggested to *Generalleutnant* Elfeldt, the commanding general of *LXXXIV Corps,* to break off the action near Coulouvray-Boisbenâtre, and to take measures for the protection of the left flank. His evening report contained his opinion of the situation:

> After being observed moving up infantry and armored reinforcements in the vicinity of Brécey and to the southeast all day, between 1600 and 1700 hours the enemy moved to attack generally to the southeast after artillery bombardment and attacks by aircraft. I suppose that the enemy plans to take the high ground northeast of Reffuveille. He then has the option, as he tried to do yesterday, to advance further in bright moonlight, to which the major road to Juvigny lends itself very favorably.
>
> In view of this situation, I suggest forming a new and shorter line, thereby gaining the use of *Panzer* and motorized forces, which would be capable to effectively slow down an eventual advance by the enemy to Juvigny on the following day.[54]

He suggested a line from north of Coulouvray-Boisbenâtre to east of Cuves, and concluded, "With a thin but sufficient occupation of this line, protected by tanks, the Panther battalion and the half-track-borne *Panzer-Grenadier* battalion could be pulled out this evening and moved into the area west of Juvigny during the night. They would be combat-ready by tomorrow."

The suggestion to halt the attack was accepted and the line approved. The armored group was evidently not moved south over the Sée creek, as the enemy was already further than Schwerin had assumed. The Americans pushed forward at 1800 hours, from Juvigny to St. Barthélemy. About 75 enemy tanks attacked the defenses of the *275th Infantry Division* near Montigny.[55]

The higher command now became active. At 1645 hours, *7th Army* was permitted to move the northern front back during the night, to pull out the *2d Panzer Division*, and to deploy it as reinforcement of the *116th*. Something also happened on the southern flank of the Army. *Assault Gun Brigade 394* and *Armored Reconnaissance Battalion 116* were to be sent toward the enemy who moved east from Cuves and Juvigny. Units coming from southern France under *LXXXI Corps* were deployed on the far southern flank.[56] In the evening, *OKW* gave the order for the attack on Avranches:

> The breach by the enemy at the western flank of the beachhead can only be met with a decisive counterattack of our own strong armored forces. . . . Therefore, the *Führer* ordered that the front between the Orne and the Vire must be held mainly by infantry divisions. . . . The armored units that were deployed until now at the front must be withdrawn and, as a unit, join the left flank. With the attack of at least four armored units, the enemy armored forces that advanced east, southeast, and south are to be destroyed. Without consideration for the enemy which has broken into Brittany, the connection to the western coast of the Cotentin Peninsula near Avranches, or north of it, is to be reestablished.[57]

In theory, this order was correct, but it came too late. The time for replacement of the *Panzer* divisions by infantry had passed weeks ago. As late as 27/28 July, there may have been a small chance to withdraw *Panzer* divisions in time to fight a mobile battle and to keep the front of *Panzer Group West* strong, by straightening it out. Now a miracle would have been needed. The enemy would have had to make a mistake, by which he did not strike south to encircle to the east, but rather wasted his time and strength in Brittany. To a certain degree, this is what the enemy did, but on 3 August, the commander of the 12th Army Group, Lieutenant General Bradley, ordered Patton to be prepared for a thrust with strong armored forces to the east and southeast.[58]

The *116th Panzer Division* ceased attacking and went over to the defensive on the evening of 2 August. Le Gast was given up, to maintain contact toward the right.[59] The front line was established from east of Le Gast via St. Pois to Chérencé-le-Roussel; it continued from there with security positions in the Sée sector to south of Sourdeval.

The night remained quiet, but on 3 August, the enemy was reinforced in front of the Division and attacked near Le Gast, at St. Pois, and from Cuves. The Division repelled the attacks and a small breach near Le Gast was cleaned up. On 3 August, the daily reports of Army Group and *Supreme Command–West* read, "Southwest and south of Forêt de St. Sever, the *LXXXIV Corps,* by making use of the successful battles of the *116th Panzer Division* and with the help of the moved up units of the *363d Infantry Division* and parts of the *84th Infantry Division,* could establish a new defensive front and repel enemy attacks."[60]

In the evening, the enemy penetrated the lines of the unit to our right in St. Sever. Efforts to clarify the situation were unsuccessful. On the open southern flank, the *84th Infantry Division* arrived from the east in the area southeast of Sourdeval. Further southeast, the remnants of the *275th Infantry* and the *Panzer Lehr Divisions* secured the line. The *2d Panzer Division* was ready behind the front and was to deploy in the vicinity southwest of Sourdeval. The overall situation seemed to be somewhat firmed up.

On the morning of 4 August, the uneasy feelings about the action in the sector to our right were confirmed. The opponent pushed from north to south, through the forest, into the flank of *Panzer-Grenadier Regiment 156*. The unit on our flank yielded toward the southeast. Our own patrols were bypassed or taken by surprise. Soon, the opponent confronted the command post of the regiment at the southern rim of the forest. The right flank of the regiment near Le Gast was open. There was no chance to remedy this situation through an attack. The Division was glad to be able, under enemy pressure, to extricate *Regiment 156* from encirclement. This unit was still fairly intact, and in the evening, the Division established and maintained a new front along the line Champ-du-Boult–north of St. Pois. "Hundreds of fighter bombers" were in the air above this area and impeded movement; at times no movement was possible at all.

Our artillery fire and the assault guns of *Panzerjäger Battalion 228* prevented a fragmentation of the Division's right flank.[61] With support from *Panzer Regiment 16, Panzer-Grenadier Regiment 60* finally cleaned up a penetration north of St. Pois. A counterattack against the stronger opponent, who advanced to Hill 221 (two kilometers southeast of St. Pois) was initiated but made no headway because of the attacks of enemy fighter bombers.[62]

The northern front of *LXXXXIV Corps* was now moved back to the line Vire–Champ-du Boult–St. Pois, and in so doing, the staff of *XLVII Panzer Corps* was withdrawn. In the south, the *2d Panzer Division* south of the Sée creek connected with the left wing of the *116th* east of Chérencé-le-Roussel. The first units of the *84th Infantry Division* arrived during the night of 5 August and relieved the *2d Battalion, Panzer-Grenadier Regiment 156*. During the entire following day, the opponent conducted heavy attacks against the *116th Panzer Division* front. In the morning, they were mostly directed against *Panzer-Grenadier Regiment 60*, near and southeast of St. Pois. An attack with 25 tanks from Chérencé toward the northeast was driven back by the Division reserve, the *1st Battalion, Panzer Regiment 24* with one attached company from *Armored Engineer Battalion 675*, and the village of Le Fougeray was recaptured. The enemy renewed his attacks in the evening, southeast of St. Pois, and achieved breaches that could only be closed inadequately. Units of *1st Battalion, Panzer Regiment 24* cleared a breach near *1st Battalion, Panzer-Grenadier Regiment 156* at Champ-du Boult. On 5 and 6 August, the Division command post was situated in La Haule (northwest of Vengeons).[63]

In the meantime, plans for our own counterattack toward Avranches took concrete shape. The *7th Army* commander wanted to attack as soon as possible and counted on the following forces:

2d and *116th Panzer*—as well as the *2d SS-Panzer Division.*

One *SS-Panzer* division from *Panzer Group West* (namely, the *1st SS-Panzer*).

9th Panzer Division, which came from the south and was to be brought up via Mayenne to the southern wing.

Command and control of the attack was to be exercised by *XLVII Panzer Corps* and the arriving *84th Infantry Division* was to relieve the *116th.*

The German counterattack during the night of 6/7 August looked like an act of desperation. *OKW* lacked knowledge of the actual situation at the invasion front. It was living with illusions and *Supreme Command–West* did not do enough to clarify the matter. Differences arose between the leadership at *7th Army,* Kluge, and *OKW* regarding timing and the direction of attack. *OKW* wanted a later date to allow commitment of stronger forces. The *7th Army* staff and Kluge insisted on quick action, since they rightfully feared that the enemy might recognize the intention of an attack and would take countermeasures. *OKW,* and probably also Kluge, considered another assault aiming southwest, because they correctly expected weaker enemy resistance there.

The leadership of *7th Army* did not want to swing around that far, especially considering the weakness of the forces already committed directly toward Avranches. On 6 August at 1045 hours, during a conversation with *Oberst i.G.* von Gersdorff, whom Kluge had appointed to succeed Pemsel as *7th Army* Chief of Staff, Kluge criticized this development and directed the forces to be combined. He also found the commitment of the *116th Panzer Division* to the west to be a mistake, since the enemy would undoubtedly be very strong there. He wished to closely follow and support the *2d Panzer Division,* first attacking toward the south and then turning to the west.

Then Gersdorff explained the *7th Army* plan. The inadequacy of the roads in the area precluded deploying the divisions more closely together. The *116th Panzer Division* was to remain north of the Sée creek, to be able to support the *84th Infantry Division.* Its *Panzers* would be attached to the *2d Panzer Division.* From this conversation, it was already evident that *9th Panzer Division* would not take part in the attack, and that the *1st SS-Panzer Division* would only arrive with some units.[64]

During the night of 5/6 August, the *116th Panzer Division* was relieved by the *84th Infantry Division.* The *116th*'s artillery, however, remained in position so that it could support the infantry division. A breach west of Champ-du-Boult in early morning was temporarily cleared up, but then the village was lost. In the course of the relief, the curved line southeast of St. Pois was vacated. The Division was subordinated to *XLVII Panzer Corps,* which ordered the bulk of the *Panzers* from the *116th* to be transferred to *2d Panzer Division* for the attack. The *116th* received orders to support the attack planned for the night of 6/7 August north of the Sée creek, and to seize Chérencé-le-Roussel as its first objective. The *7th Army* left the *116th* north of the creek sector, since without it, the infantry north of the creek would be too weak.[65]

Thus, the task of the Division was anything but pleasant. Deprived of most of its tanks, it had to take Chérencé, which for days had been in enemy hands and from whence the enemy had already launched an attack toward Perriers-en-Beauficel on 5 August. According to orders and in its own interest, the Division continuously kept an eye on the development of the situation of the *84th Infantry Division,* which was in battle for the first time and was menaced by the enemy along the whole front from Champ-du-Boult to Perriers. The enemy achieved a deep breach there toward Gathemo, one which could only be stopped with the help of the *116th.* Therefore, the Division left *Panzer-Grenadier Regiment 156* (without the *2d Battalion,* which was attached to *Panzer-Grenadier Regiment 60*) with elements of *Panzerjäger Battalion 228* behind the front line of the *84th Infantry Division.* The artillery helped the *84th* the whole day. If the enemy had penetrated the line at Sourdeval, the *116th* and *84th* would have been cut off.

For the attack at Chérencé, only the reinforced *Panzer-Grenadier Regiment 60* was available. It was made ready east of Perriers-en-Beauficel. Toward evening, the enemy broke through to the eastern edge of Perriers and took nearby Hill 241. Since the *84th Infantry Division* was not up to the task by itself, ready units from *Panzer-Grenadier Regiment 60* had to be committed to clean up the penetration. Although this effort was successful, the attack ordered for 2100 hours could not commence as planned. The regiment did not gain much ground beyond the line created by the restoration of the breach.[66] Only *2d Battalion, Panzer-Grenadier Regiment 156,* attacking from the left wing, could advance. During the night, it reached the area south of Perriers in the Sée Valley.

At dawn, 7 August, through a narrow valley void of roads, the *7th Company* pushed toward Chérencé, along an intact railroad line. Its leader, *Oberleutnant* Strackerjahn, gave the following description from memory about the further course of the attack:

> The company advanced quickly along the old railroad tracks. . . . The men, still 35 of them, deployed right and left of the tracks and stormed ahead with "Hurrah!" The Americans were totally surprised. They left everything behind and fled in panic to the west. . . . A narrow path off the railroad tracks turned southwest toward Chérencé, on which we stormed forward. We reached the road to Perriers, crossed it, and suddenly stood in the middle of an American battery. Here too, they had dropped and left everything. . . . The left group, meanwhile, waded through a little creek towards the first houses of Chérencé and occupied them. Now, however, the opponent in Chérencé woke up and suddenly sprayed us with heavy fire from infantry weapons, tanks, and mortars, so that we had to dig in immediately. . . . Only now, our artillery started to bombard Chérencé with heavy rounds, which gave me some relief. . . . The opponent could not think of a counterattack from the village. Thanks to this fact alone, the position could be held for the day.[67]

Obviously, the report about the success of *2d Battalion, Panzer-Grenadier Regiment 156* did not reach the Division, or only much later, because in the operations journal of *7th Army,* it is noted that the *116th Panzer Division* did not gain any ground. Nor was it brought to the attention of the Division that the railroad tracks were passable, which would have allowed armor support for *2d Battalion, Panzer-Grenadier Regiment 156.* The commanding general of *XLVII Panzer Corps* [Baron von Funck—*Editor*] had no appreciation of the little success of the Division and criticized the *116th Panzer Division* for only deploying half of *Panzer-Grenadier Regiment 156.*

All of this again led to unpleasant disputes with Baron von Funck. On 6 August, at 2200 hours, he had already requested that Hausser relieve the Division Commander. Allegedly, the tanks from the *116th* had not yet arrived at the *2d Panzer Division,* and Funck complained that the Division always failed.[68] Nevertheless, the tanks of the *116th* fought at the tip of the attacking wedge of *2d Panzer Division.* Therefore, they must have arrived in time. The *116th Panzer Division* that was left at the north bank of the Sée creek was supposed to support the *84th Infantry Division.* When this became necessary, it was criticized.

The Panthers of the *116th Panzer Division,* the *1st Battalion, Panzer Regiment 24,* formed the right attack group in conjunction with units of the *2d Panzer Division.* It achieved the only significant success of the offensive. Under darkness it penetrated the enemy front and on the morning of 7 August, reached Le Mesnil-Adelée (four kilometers west southwest Chérencé), 14 kilometers deep in enemy territory. Strong counterattacks with tanks, supported by heavy artillery fire and by aircraft forced the combat group to retreat in the afternoon.[69] During the fighting on 7 and 8 August, two of the battalion's company commanders were killed, and the battalion commander and adjutant were wounded. *Rittmeister* Scholz assumed command. The *116th Panzer Division* recommended *Major* von Meyer, the wounded battalion commander, for the Knight's Cross, which he was awarded on 26 November.[70]

On 7 August, the unpleasant role meant for most of the *116th Panzer Division* continued. After the night attack by *Panzer-Grenadier Regiment 60* failed, the Corps urged a repeat attack during daylight, to ease the burden on the *2d Panzer Division.* This attack had to be led downhill from Perriers, which was in the enemy's view.

Panzer-Grenadier Regiment 60 commenced the attack at 1630 hours.[71] In spite of the hope that the attack by *2d Panzer Division* south of the Sée creek would have an effect on the opponent facing the *116th* in Chérencé, and in spite of combined artillery support, the attack made no major progress. The armored support was not sufficient. The *2d Battalion, Panzer-Grenadier Regiment 156* could maintain its position northeast of Chérencé and *1st Battalion, Panzer-Grenadier Regiment 60* succeeded in temporarily seizing the small villages of Le Fougeray and La Mardelle on the road to Perriers, but ultimately the attack died under the fire from fighter bombers and enemy artillery, which controlled the front of the hill. The most advanced companies of *1st Battalion, Panzer-Grenadier Regiment 60,* the *1st* and *3d,* were cut off by the enemy, and for the most part were captured.[72] *Armored Engineer Battalion 675* was therefore attached to *1st Battalion, Panzer-Grenadier Regiment 60.*

Disputes again arose with the corps commander. A phone conversation from the afternoon of 7 August, between him and the Division Commander, took a dramatic course.[73] At the end, Funck asked something like this, "Count Schwerin, if *Regiment 60* still had one spark of honor left, something like this could not have happened. When will it reach its objective? When can I count on your Division to somehow execute one of my orders?"

I cannot forget the Division Commander's answer. "General, I will not allow myself or my Division be insulted. I repeat, I will not allow myself or my Division be insulted."

All who were in my command vehicle at the Division command post, near La Georgerie northeast of Sourdeval, were shocked. They knew that with this, the rift was complete. Count Schwerin left the main command post to move to a forward CP, without divulging its location. After some time, Kluge called and ordered me to tell the Division Commander that he had been relieved of his command effective immediately and should proceed to La Roche-Guyon and report to *General* Speidel. *Oberst i.G.* Reinhard, until now Chief of Staff of *XLVII Panzer Corps,* was appointed as his successor.

Fortunately, I quickly found where Schwerin was staying and delivered the order. The change of command took place the same evening. Unlike in February in Russia, this time I remained with the Division. After his relief, the Division Commander sent a message to his subordinate commanders in the Division, which is at Appendix 7.[74]

The accusations against the Division;s leadership lacked justification regarding this subject. The extent to which the Division Commander's personal beliefs about the political and military leadership of the *Reich* affected his decisions and also the troops' is difficult to estimate. He had expressed his thoughts in his speeches to the units before the invasion. The enemy was now on the continent and trying to break out of his bridgehead. The assassination attempt of 20 July had occurred. Remembering the words of their commander, any soldier could now ask, "Is it now only about the honor of the German soldier?"

This is how the war diary of *Army Group B* depicts the events of 7 August:

> After seizing appropriate jump-off positions through surprise attacks on the night before, *7th Army* began its attack with its western wing in the early morning hours, west toward Avranches. This wing consisted of four armored divisions (*116th, 2d Panzer Division, 1st* and *2d SS-Panzer Division*s). Morning fog facilitated the attack that by noon had already gained ten kilometers of terrain. Le Mesnil-Adelée, Juvigny, Mortain were taken by storm.
>
> As the weather cleared, many hundreds of enemy aircraft continuously attacked the forward assault units. The attack collapsed in the afternoon with heavy losses in personnel and materiel. Our own fighter cover achieved nothing, because stronger enemy opposition prevented them from reaching the battle area.

The *Supreme Commander–West*, who was personally on the battlefield throughout the day, ordered the relentless continuation of the attack.[75]

This version of the events sounds heroic, but at that time awakened false hope. One did not dare report that the attack failed and could not be repeated. Everyone forced themselves to express optimism, even as the British were attacking the *5th Panzer Army* south of Caen, toward Falaise, and the danger to the deep southern flank became increasingly evident.[76]

How strong was the enemy opposing the German attack?[77] Actually, remarkably weak, as we know today. The *84th Infantry Division* stood face to face with the 9th Infantry Division. Its southern regiment, the 39th Infantry, opposed the attack of the *116th Panzer Division* near Perriers-en-Beauficel and Chérencé-le-Roussel. The regimental command post was south of the Sée sectors. Only two infantry regiments of the 30th Infantry Division defended the sector in which the rest of *XLVII Panzer Corps* attacked. The third regiment was in reserve, with two of its battalions to combat committed elsewhere. The 30th had only relieved the 1st Infantry Division on the evening of 6 August and was now in unfamiliar territory. From southeast of Mortain to Barenton was one gaping hole. Both divisions fought bravely. In the beginning, the Americans did not take the German attack seriously. But as soon as they realized the imminent danger, they quickly brought on suitable reserves; however, the divisions already on the line mastered the situation themselves, especially with the assistance of their air forces.

Preparation and conduct of this attack is not a glorious page in the annals of German military history.

Reconnaissance was insufficient. Army Group and *7th Army* did not do enough. There was no aerial reconnaissance. But with stringent effort, there would have been a chance by using the armored reconnaissance battalions of the *Panzer* divisions. The *116th Panzer Division,* which until this point had overwatched the left flank with its armored reconnaissance battalion, lost the unit on 5 August. The battalion had been attached to the *2d SS-Panzer Division* and was now deployed for defense on the Mortain-Barenton road under the *2d SS-Panzer Division.* Reconnaissance should at least have brought evidence that there was no solid front southeast of Mortain. Except for the *2d Panzer* and the *2d SS-Panzer Divisions,* the units were hastily thrown against the enemy. The troops were exhausted and reconnaissance was no longer possible. After the preceding battles, the battle strength of the German units in 1944 could not be compared to that of the summer of 1941.

Enemy artillery was reinforced very quickly and was quite flexible. On the other hand, the German artillery was not engaged at all, because our own artillery was fully occupied supporting units already committed to battle. The *Luftwaffe* did not show up over the battle area, so the enemy dominated it as it pleased. The operations journal of the *2d Battalion, Armored Artillery Regiment 146* noted on 6 August, "The extremely strong air activity of the enemy in the afternoon hours prevents the batteries from stepping up their shelling in support of the attack. The regiment orders fire missions repeatedly, even though fighter bombers were over the position."[78]

On the afternoon of 7 August, Hitler issued a new order to attack. It was far removed from reality:

> The decision of the battle in France depends on the success of the attack at the southern wing of the *7th Army*. A never-to-happen-again, unique opportunity is in the hands of *Supreme Command–West* to be able to push into an area in which the enemy is especially vulnerable, and thereby to completely reverse the situation.
>
> 1. The attack is to be carried out boldly and at all costs down to the sea. . . .
>
> 5. Most extreme boldness, determination, and imagination should give wing to the leadership all the way down to the lowest unit. Every man must believe in victory. . . . [79]

No one dared to object. One reported in the style of the daily report of *OKW* and deceived oneself. Headquarters, *7th Army* ordered the continuation of the attack "as the situation in the air allows."[80]

On the morning of 8 August, "after defending against heavy enemy attacks," the *116th*, the *1st* and *2d SS-Panzer Divisions* attacked one more time. Not one advanced. The *2d Panzer Division* was driven into defense.[81] Losses climbed. The enemy also attacked the northern front of *7th Army* and broke through south of Vire. Deep in the southern flank, the enemy entered Le Mans and thus, stood far in the rear of *Army Group B*. In the sector of *5th Panzer Army,* the allied main offensive began on both sides of the Caen–Falaise road with an attack by 600 tanks and corresponding air support. They achieved a deep breakthrough.[82]

Only after getting this news did Kluge postpone the continuation of the failed attack that was ordered for 9 August by *7th Army,* but he left the door open to possibly restart it on 10 August, with the addition of more forces.[83] On 9 August, at 0030 hours, *General der Infanterie* Buhle, who was sent to the West by Hitler, reported to *OKW* that after a realistic evaluation, he considered the forces to be too weak; thoughts of an attack were no longer feasible, even if Kluge retained the idea.[84] *Supreme Command–West*'s opinion is hardly comprehensible. In regard to Kluge, even Gersdorff, Chief of Staff of *7th Army,* failed to show consistent clarity in his evaluation of the situation. For example, on 9 August, at 1145 hours, Gersdorff wrote, "One should use the factors that were already known. Then the attack must be successful. . . . "

What he ultimately meant was that with the present forces, there was "no prospect of certain success." He was hoping for the arrival of some minor reinforcements and believed that then, "success could be guaranteed."[85]

At 1500 hours, Kluge reported to Jodl that he wanted to attack; at the earliest in the evening of 10 August. In regard to the threat from the south, he consoled himself with the words, "A trend toward the north cannot be substantiated."[86]

Meanwhile. the enemy veered to the north near Le Mans and from the south attacked the *LXXXI Corps,* which was deployed for the protection of the southern flank. On 8 August, Lieutenant General Bradley ordered Patton to advance on the line Alençon–Sées, toward the line Sées–Carrouges, and to be prepared to push further toward the flanks and rear of the enemy, in the direction of Argentan.[87] On 9 August, on the road from Vire to Sourdeval, the enemy achieved a penetration four kilometers deep. The British attack on Falaise continued.[88]

After discontinuing the last attempt at an attack on 8 August, and pulling back its left wing, the *116th Panzer Division* repelled heavy enemy attacks on the Perriers–Sées sector about 2,000 meters northeast of Chérencé (reinforced *Panzer-Grenadier Regiment 60*), and helped the *84th Infantry Division* southwest of Gathemo (*Panzer-Grenadier Regiment 156*).[89] *Armored Reconnaissance Battalion 116* continued to fight between Mortain and Barenton, mostly subordinated to the *2d SS-Panzer Division.*[90]

On the evening of 9 August, *General der Panzertruppe* Eberbach, commander of *5th Panzer Army,* arrived at *7th Army* headquarters to take charge of the counterattack; he immediately saw the situation more realistically. On the morning of 10 August, he informed Speidel and emphasized that the armored forces had been diminished. For that reason, he requested the employment of the *11th Panzer Division* as well as ammunition for anti-aircraft guns and rocket launchers.[91] He then wrote an estimate of the situation and listed the requirements necessary to dare an attack. They could not be provided, such as the request for participation of the *11th Panzer Division,* situated in southern France. Eberbach summarized:

> The *Panzer Group* believes that the directed attack can only be carried out if the above mentioned prerequisites are met. Otherwise, the attack will lead to a useless waste of the most valuable forces available for Army and Army Group. Their presence is indispensable for any further combat because the opponent has superior motorized forces available, which could not be met successfully with only infantry divisions and battle weary *Panzer* divisions.[92]

Now the situation on the southern flank developed quickly. Logistical support for *7th Army* and the supply base in Chartres became endangered. The enemy's turn toward the north was clearly recognizable. Eberbach's objections and the development of the situation persuaded Kluge to report to Jodl on the evening of 10 August that our forces would not be adequate for the protection of the southern flank. He thought "it worthwhile to consider whether a brief and boldly-led armored assault might destroy these attacking enemy spearheads, before the decisive attack toward Avranches could be resumed."[93]

At 1510 hours on 11 August, in a teletype exchange between Kluge and Jodl, the decision was reached for an attack with *Group Eberbach* from the area northwest of Alençon toward the southeast, into the flank of XV Corps. Kluge promised Eberbach three units, with a fourth to follow. He ordered that the first units were to defend Alençon. This was meant for the *116th Panzer Division.* The recently-committed French 2d Armored Division was attacking Alençon. When Kluge ordered the defense of Alençon, the enemy already stood before the town.[94]

The day before, Kluge already allowed pulling back the bend of the front northwest of Sourdeval, to enable the withdrawal of the *116th Panzer Division*.[95] This was accomplished on the night of 10/11 August. Initially, however, units of the artillery and most of the tanks and tank destroyers, as well as the armored reconnaissance battalion, were arrayed in support of the *84th Infantry Division*, with the *XLVII Corps* and *LVIII Panzer Corps*, respectively. Before its relief, *Panzer-Grenadier Regiment 60* repelled a larger attack southwest of Perriers and closed a breach with a counterattack.[96] The Division was ordered to occupy an assembly area east of Sourdeval.[97]

On the afternoon of 11 August, the Division had to prepare to intervene to the north because the enemy achieved penetrations of the *LXXXIV Corps* line. The enemy had pushed through a gap near Vengeons all the way to the assembly area. The Division had to help, but the situation was restored so that it could march off in the night of 11/12.[98] On 11 August, *Oberst* Müller arrived from *Supreme Command–West* to assume command of the Division.[99] He had been awarded the Knights Cross as a regimental commander in Africa, where he had lost an arm.

The Division suffered heavy losses during this fighting, but for conditions of that time, it was still an imposing unit. The combat strength reported by Eberbach to Army Group was: *Panzer-Grenadier Regiment 156* with 200 men; *Panzer-Grenadier Regiment 60* with 200 men including *Armored Engineer Battalion 675*; 30 *Panzer IV* tanks and assault guns. (The Panther battalion had not yet returned from the *2d Panzer Division*.)[100]

In the late afternoon of 11 August, the Division received orders to advance the following night to the area of Sées–Mortrée–Tanville, to be deployed in conjunction with *Panzer Group Eberbach* against the enemy, which advanced from the south toward Alençon.

Later on 11 August, the Division Commander was to report to *General* Eberbach at the railroad crossing, one kilometer south of Argentan on the road to Mortrée for instructions in the new task. Hardly anything was known about the enemy's or our own situation in the designated area. The armored reconnaissance battalion could not be sent ahead since it was still committed to action.

On the afternoon of 11 August, the situation near Alençon worsened very quickly. The enemy had already reached the town and pushed the defenses of the *9th Panzer Division* back toward the northwest; northeast of there, it had pushed about 20 kilometers forward to Essay and Le Mêle-sur-Sarte. The Alençon–Sées road was not defended.[101] The staff of the *116th Panzer Division* had no knowledge of any of this. It presumed the area that was to be reached would be located behind its own lines. Only the units that were already released could set out in the evening, while those still in action could only be released during the night, in spite of a request by the Division to the contrary. For this reason, one could only count on the arrival of these troops in the new area, especially the tanks, during the night of 12/13 August, or in the best case, during daylight hours on 12 August. The length of the march was about 120 kilometers on roads that at the same time served for the supply of all troops deployed in the front, and which was the preferred target of the enemy air forces, even at night. The march had to be continued during daylight. It depended on the intensity of the activities of the enemy air force for this to be feasible.

Around midnight on 11 August, the Division Commander was sent on to the command post of *LXXXI Corps*, southeast of Argentan, to be instructed by the cmmanding general, *General der Panzertruppe* Kuntzen, and *General* Eberbach, who was just arriving. Eberbach canceled the existing *LXXXI Corps* order, which had planned a position in the forest west of the Alençon–Sées road for an attack to the southeast, because the enemy was already pushing toward Sées.[102] Instead, the *116th Panzer Division* received orders to defend Sées and to eventually recapture it. Eberbach pointed out the special importance of this mission to the whole operation.

Thereafter, *Oberst* Müller, with his small command group, went to Mortrée and established a forward command post. The staff of *Armored Artillery Regiment 146* also arrived. Müller found *Panzer-Grenadier Regiment 156* on the morning of 12 August, while catching up along the road which led to Sées from the west. The group marched surprisingly rapidly. Its leader, *Oberst* Fischer, heard rumors from sidelined supply personnel of the *9th Panzer Division* about the situation and deployed reconnaissance troops from the eastern edge of the Forêt d'Écoufes toward Sées. He was on his way to the Division Commander, while the Division Commander drove toward him. They missed each other. The Division Commander met the commander of the *2d Battalion, Hauptmann* Nitsch, and ordered him to occupy Sées and defend it against the opponent, who was expected from the south.[103] He told him to add all arriving heavy weapons to the support of the Regiment. Then Müller returned to his command post, met Fischer and informed him. Fischer immediately went on to his regiment, but drove into the enemy near Sées and was captured.

Meanwhile, the commander of the artillery regiment, *Oberst* Pean, directed the first battery to arrive, consisting of four light field howitzers and one *Wespe,* to take up firing positions north of Sées and ordered the installation of an observation post south of Sées. The battery commander, *Oberleutnant* Steinmeier, was hit during the reconnaissance two kilometers south of Sées. After this, Pean moved the guns to within two kilometers of Mortrée, to use them for blocking the road against tanks.[104] Obviously, there was no time to warn *Oberst* Fischer.

A task force from the 5th Armored Division arrived in Sées around 0800 hours. It came from Essay from the southeast, and was supposed to strike toward Argentan.[105]This chased away Steinmeier. Sometime before 0900 hours, the Americans reconnoitered the road to Mortrée, but pulled back to the edge of town after one tank was destroyed by a *Wespe.* Toward 1000 hours, they launched a surprise attack with infantry and tanks, into the flank of Steinmeier's gun emplacements. The forward *Wespe* and three field howitzers were destroyed, but one got away and its crew alerted Müller and Pean in Mortrée. They deployed the remaining units of the *2d Battalion* of the artillery regiment, which had arrived in the meantime, and placed them behind Hill 209 northwest of Mortrée, with some in covered positions. In addition, another three or four Panthers of *1st Battalion, Panzer Regiment 24* arrived, and took up position by the hill. All artillery soldiers who were not absolutely needed to man guns or for fire control, were engaged in an infantry-style defense.[106] There was no sign of an attack by *Panzer-Grenadier Regiment 156,* which by now should have had its effect at Sées.

At about the same time, around 1000 hours, a task force of the French 2d Armored Division arrived in Sées from the south and caused great confusion. The French happened to be outside of their designated tactical zone. They blocked traffic through the town, as well as the approaching American fuel supply convoy, which caused a delay of the American attack by about six hours. Not until 1500 hours, after reorganizing and supplying the units, were both groups ready to attack. The Americans attacked along the main road toward Argentan; the French attacked with one group on their left, passing Mortée on the south toward Echouché, and with a second one toward the west, to Carrouges.[107]

In *Panzer-Grenadier Regiment 156*'s assigned tactical area, Müller's order to *Hauptmann* Nitsch was passed on to *1st Battalion.* In any case, both battalions attacked along both sides of the road from Carrouges toward Sées, uncoordinated and without support by artillery or tanks. The *1st Battalion* advanced first, on the right, with the *2d Battalion* to its left rear, echeloned in depth. As *1st Battalion* advanced south of the road toward the southern part of the town, *Major* Hafemeister, the commander, was about 300 meters ahead with a few messengers.[108] He came to within a few hundred meters of the town's edge and realized that it was secured by enemy armored reconnaissance vehicles. At about the same time, 30 to 40 enemy tanks carrying infantry soldiers rolled into Sées. This was most likely the French task force, which quickly moved strong defenses to the town's western edge. Under the command of *Oberleutnant* Leiding, the *3d Company* (with remnants of *1st Company,* totaling only 23 men) advanced along the road, with *2d Company* to the right of it, moving cross country. Leiding reported the following to me:

> About 250 meters in front of the town's entrance, where we could hardly find cover in the ditches near a bend in the road, the two enemy tanks at the southwest exit of Sées, opened . . . fire, but after a few shots they moved into the town. . . . Spread out and without any further enemy action, we crossed the railroad tracks and reached the town entrance. When we entered the town, advancing on both sides of the road for about 70 to 80 meters, the spearhead of a tank column with infantry riding on them appeared in front of us. As the rattle of the tracks came closer, we took cover in entranceways of houses and courtyards on the southern side of the road.

After a short exchange of fire, we observed that the infantry tried to block our return route behind the buildings. We detoured through gardens, across the railroad tracks and a remote group of buildings, probably a railroad station, toward the southwest.[109]

Early in the afternoon, Hafemeister realized that the left group of the French was preparing to attack, and ordered a withdrawal to the edge of the forest. This failed. The enemy pushed into them with tanks and infantry, and scattered the battalion. While trying to cross an open meadow with his company, Leiding was captured; only a few escaped into the forest. Hafemeister was overrun and later captured by the French.[110]

Events took a similar course in the *2d Battalion*. Reconnaissance revealed the enemy's presence in the town to *Hauptmann* Nitsch. Therefore, he deployed his battalion north of the road to the northern part of Sées and the road leading to Argentan. This proceeded without enemy contact up to within a few hundred meters of the major Alençon–Sées–Argentan road, which was busy with enemy traffic.[111] It was at this point in time that the American attack against *Battery Steinmeier,* between Sées and Motrée, may have taken place. Therefore, all companies remained in their positions and continued observing.

Communication with each other and with the battalion CP was lost. Thus, a continuation of the advance was out of the question. All companies, therefore, tried to break contact with the enemy and break through the encirclement to fight their way back to the Division, under cover of darkness if necessary. In the process, the withdrawing elements either walked into enemy fire (*7th Company*), or were surprised and dispersed (*5th* and *6th Companies*) by the enemy, who attacked in the afternoon.[112] Small groups led by the commander and company leaders could first exfiltrate and cross the Sées–Argentan road toward the north during the night, but these were apprehended one by one, mostly because French civilians pointed them out to the Americans. After two days, *Hauptmann* Nitsch and *Oberleutnant* Strackerjahn, along with the last group, were captured by the Americans, shortly before they would have reached our own front line.[113]

Oberleutnant Leiding told about his capture by the French:

> After a short interrogation by an officer and confiscation of our watches and papers, we were brought . . . along with motorized and armored convoys to Sées. A raging mob awaited us in the square in front of the town hall.
>
> For about 50 meters we had to run the gauntlet, up to the door of the town hall while being beaten the whole way. German soldiers lay already in the yard, watched by civilians wearing brassards, who in an adventurous way familiarized themselves with automatic rifles.
>
> After further questioning by an American first lieutenant, I was finally pushed into a dark cell, which was inaccessible from the yard. *Oberst* Fischer, *Leutnant* Oehlmann, and an *Oberfeldwebel* were already sitting there.[114]

A similar fate befell Baedeker, our Division's Protestant chaplain.[115]

Few escaped; for ten days, *Regiment 156* was unaccounted for. The remnants were moved back into the area east of Vimoutiers and there, together with *Armored Field Replacement Battalion 146,* established a new *Panzer-Grenadier Regiment 156.* First, *Major* Flecke assumed command, but after the retreat across the Seine, the former battalion commander, *Major* Grollmann, took over. In the beginning the regiment was, of course, only conditionally battle ready, but its cohesion quickly developed.

I did not find the *LXXXI Corps* CP at their former location, but did find *Oberst* Müller and *Oberst* Pean on the Mortrée–Argentan road northwest of Hill 209. The first reports about the catastrophe that had befallen *Panzer-Grenadier Regiment 156* arrived through the artillery liaison officer. Everyone was hoping that now more units of the Division would arrive, especially the march group of *Panzer-Grenadier Regiment 60.* By 1500 hours, only the commander of *Panzer Regiment 16,* *Major* Lueder, had arrived with one or two Panthers belonging to the staff. He was sent ahead to Hill 209 to block the road. Shortly after 1500 hours, the enemy started to attack from Sées on the road and west of it. This entailed one task force each from the 5th and 2nd French Armored Divisions, respectively. Hardly had the security forces west of Mortrée seen heavy dust develop, when their tanks and guns were taken under intense fire. The Panthers indeed destroyed a few enemy tanks, but then their commander, *Leutnant* Stetzka, received a direct hit; he was severely wounded and remained missing. Lueder's tank was also hit, and he was wounded. A forward-deployed antitank gun was lost. There was no alternative but to retreat to Argentan, under cover of the last Panthers. In the air, the enemy fighter bombers went crazy and chased every single vehicle.[116]

Since the enemy was not in hot pursuit of it, the remaining *4th Battery,* after losing one of its guns, succeeded in returning to Argentan and took up positions northeast of the town. This was the only battery out of the whole battalion that was still combat capable.[117] Luckily, it was not all alone. While I was looking for troops to employ against the enemy, I encountered *2d Battalion, Panzer Regiment 33* of the *9th Panzer Division* while crossing the Orne bridge in Argentan. Its commander, *Hauptmann* Pfannkuche, stood in the turret of the first Panther. We were members of the same year group of officers [were commissioned in the same year—*Editor*]. I subordinated the battalion to the *116th Panzer Division* and ordered Pfannkuche to immediately take up position at the southern edge of Argentan, and to defend it against the approaching enemy. The battalion had not yet been in battle and brought about 25 Panthers into combat.

The Division Commander was also fortunate. In Argentan he met the commander of *1st Battalion, Panzer Regiment 24, Rittmeister* Scholz, accompanied by a few tanks. He appointed him commander of all units in that area. Aside from that, he made contact with an anti-aircraft regiment which *General* Eberbach had ordered to protect Argentan. Under the command of *Hauptmann* Schüler, it moved a light battalion to Argentan during the night.[118] It was also subordinated to Scholz, like *2d Battalion, Panzer Regiment 33,* whose commander was wounded the following day. *Group Scholz,* reinforced later by the engineers of the Division, defended Argentan until 20 August. It contributed to a large extent to the formation and defense of a line oriented toward to the south.

Panzer Grenadier Regiment 60 was able to establish a weak security line west of Argentan. The regiment reached the area south of Ecouché by morning, established contact with the Division Commander, and established advanced outposts toward the southeast. These security positions were pushed back to Ecouché by the French, and by evening formed a line north of the Orne, from south of Montgaroult up to, but not including Argentan. The regimental motorcycle platoon repelled the advance of an enemy reconnaissance patrol and pushed them back across the Orne. The Division command post was set up in Pommainville, six kilometers northwest of Argentan. *LXXXI Corps* was informed at 2100 hours. The missing units arrived during the night and into the morning of 13 August, among them the *3d Battalion* of the artillery regiment. Aside from this, *Heavy Artillery Battalion 992* was subordinated to the Division.[119] The units were organized and wire communications were established.

The *1st SS* and *2d Panzer Divisions* came from the west and were aligned on a curve from La Ferté-Macé via Carrouges to Ecouché.[120] The situation was unclear east of Argentan. The *331st Infantry Division* moved forward from Gacé to Nonant-le-Pin, which was also approached by the enemy. There was a large gap between Argentan and the *331st* that for now could only be observed in a pathetic way by reconnaissance.[121]

The disaster that occurred on 12 August 1944 must first be attributed to insufficient reconnaissance. Neither *Group Eberbach* nor *LXXXI Corps* had enough reconnaissance forces to control the southern flank. Consequently, many of its orders were already obsolete when they were issued. The *116th Panzer Division* did not have its armored reconnaissance battalion, which is why the picture of its situation was also outdated. The second reason can be found in the absence of tanks and tank destroyers, which *7th Army* kept behind to support its front. Without them, a battle with the armored enemy had no chance of success. If the opponent had pushed further north, the Division could not have offered serious resistance, except in Argentan. Fortunately for the Division, the boundary between the English and the American army groups stretched north of Sées, and the target of the attack of the US XV Corps was Argentan. In the morning of 13 August, Patton ordered a deliberate push forward in direction of Falaise, but in the afternoon, Bradley halted any further advance to the north.[122]

While the southern front of *Army Group B* was torn open on 12 August, consideration of the conduct of the counterattack by *Group Eberbach* continued. Kluge insisted on an attack and wanted to carry it out from west to east, no longer toward the southeast. The first and only one who soberly addressed the situation on that day was the commander of *5th Panzer Army, SS-Oberstgruppenführer* Sepp Dietrich. He explained to Speidel that Eberbach's attack would come too late, and he urged a retreat of the forces west of the Orne. The next morning, he was even more precise, saying that if the retreat did not take place immediately, the Army Group could write off both armies. During the night, Hitler, however, sent a new utopian order for *Panzer Group Eberbach,* but at least allowed for a certain retreat of *7th Army.*[123] On 14 August, the Canadians attacked again from the north and achieved a deep breach, which threatened to become a breakthrough. Eberbach now pressed for a withdrawal, because an attack of his own would be impossible. In a conversation with Speidel, Kluge also felt that an attack by Eberbach could not be accomplished, and believed that a major decision had to be made. This was relayed to *OKW* on 15 August at 0100 hours.[124] A second push northeast to the Seine, below Paris, appeared in the deep flank. An allied landing in southern France was imminent.[125]

The staff of the *116th Panzer Division* did not hear anything at all about this. In any event, it was fully occupied with maintaining and strengthening its front. It shoved the beaten and the superfluous units off to the east.[126] On 13 August at 0700 hours, an enemy armored attack on Argentan was repelled and eight enemy tanks were destroyed. At 1700 hours, the anti-aircraft elements, together with engineers, pushed out a French infantry company that probably infiltrated into town with the help of local inhabitants. On 14 August, another two thrusts toward Argentan were repelled. However, on this day, Ecouché fell permanently into enemy hands.[127]

It was probably on 14 August that the Division restructured its units. *Panzerjäger Battalion 228* was deployed on the right wing, in the open terrain between Ecouché and Argentan, (exclusive of both), while *Panzer-Grenadier Regiment 60* took over the wooded sector east of Argentan with the mission of pushing the defensive line forward to the southern edge of the Forêt de Gouffern. It reached Crennes, northeast of Argentan, without a fight on the evening of 14 August, and at noon the following day encountered enemy defenses all the way to the edge of the forest, north of the Argentan–Le Bourg-St.Léonard road.[128] The forces available were not sufficient to retain control of the latter town. *Armored Reconnaissance Battalion 116* (with a strength now equal to about one company and a few squads) arrived in the meantime, and covered the town and the open flank, while it also reconnoitered toward the south, southeast, and east. The staff of *Panzer Regiment 16,* now under command of *Hauptmann* Count Brühl, and its *2d Battalion,* reinforced by some Panthers from *1st Battalion, Panzer Regiment 24,* were designated as the Division reserve in Aubry-en-Exmes. Here they were in a favorable position for action in Argentan and, with *Panzer-Grenadier Regiment 60,* could also be employed for the forthcoming required protection of the left flank. Following a suggestion by the Division staff, the anti-aircraft regiment placed another battalion in the area north of Argentan, between the roads to Falaise and Trun, disposed so that the enemy could not outflank Argentan on both sides. A third battalion was northwest of Pommainville. In those days, the *116th Panzer Division* was under immediate command of *Panzer Group Eberbach.*

Because of the inactivity of the enemy, the Division succeeded in rallying and establishing a certain defense toward the south, and to keep the passage open for the units of Army Group that were fighting west of the Orne. In the north, the enemy continued his attacks in the direction of St. Pierre-sur-Dives and Falaise. The enemy air force was dominant over the narrow corridor of only 20 kilometers' width. Nevertheless, it was possible to maintain logistical support of the divisions in the convex front line west of Argentan. On 14 August, the Division *Ib, Major i.G.* Wolf, rendered a report regarding the state of provisions:

> Ammunition and fuel allotments for the last few days could not be received, due to the clearance, that is, destruction, of supply depots, but the ammunition supply remains secured.
>
> The fuel situation is very tight.
>
> Difficulties with food supply occurred with several units because supply trucks and field kitchens were destroyed by air attacks.[129]

On 15 August, the Division was told that it would receive help for both its wings. On the right, the *9th SS-Panzer Division* was to attack Ecouché and close the gap between the *2d* and *116th Panzer Divisions.* The *2d SS-Panzer Division,* together with the *116th,* was to take Silli-en-Gouffern and Le Bourg-St. Léonard, where the enemy was emplaced, to prevent an enemy push north to Chambois.

Both *SS* divisions were controlled by *II SS-Panzer Corps,* to which *116th Panzer Division* was in this phase probably also subordinated. *General* Eberbach and the *Ia* of the *2d SS-Panzer Division* appeared at the Division command post in Pommainville in the afternoon of 15 August to discuss the combined attack.

At 1439 hours on 16 August, Kluge, whose unavailability the day before caused much excitement in the *Führer* headquarters, ordered the retreat after he finally laid out the situation to Jodl in a sober way. The order read as follows:

1. Armies move out behind the Orne in two to three nights, starting night of 16/17 August.
2. Battle to be conducted so that two divisions of *7th Army*, with direct coordination, quickly move toward *5th Panzer Army*, in the direction of Falaise.
3. Eberbach covers the withdrawal by offensive operations in the vicinity of Argentan. Then, under the control of *II SS-Panzer Corps, 2d Panzer Division* moves to the vicinity of Vimoutiers and east for disposition by Army Group.[130]

On 15 August, the enemy conducted a successful landing in southern France. The day after, *Generalleutnant* Count Schwerin wrote me a letter from the field hospital:

> Dear Guderian,
>
> We are more or less informed about the fate of the Division. Actually, I cannot be of help, I'm still on ice. . . . My greatest concern is about the leadership. The

Feldmarschall [that is, von Kluge—*Author*] does nothing to take position seriously against the completely devious orders from *OKW* that no longer fit the situation. *OKW* will probably not decide to give the only possible order for an immediate withdrawal across the Seine, and therefore, Army Group will not do so either. Things will just go on and on and the development of the situation will be completely controlled by the enemy. He is striving to close off the whole Normandy kettle, and since yesterday, he applied the next pincers with newly-arrived armored forces, by pushing via Dreux toward the Seine.

In my opinion, in the course of the developing situation, the Division will be subordinated to the *5th Panzer Army,* since Sepp Dietrich is the higher-level commander who could escape the encirclement. It seems to me that Sepp is the only man who is still capable of acting and giving orders according to the situation. Everything else has drowned in frightful apathy in regard to the *OKW.*

Keep your chin up and, if the leadership no longer functions and Eberbach remains in the cauldron, turn to Sepp Dietrich.

Your loyal old commander.[131]

In the meantime, the situation improved considerably in the vicinity of Argentan as a result of the arrival of *II SS-Panzer Corps.* On 16 August, the *9th SS-Panzer Division* attacked in the direction of Ecouché, and while it did not take the village, its appearance at the right wing of the *116th Panzer Division* brought urgently needed relief.[132] On this day, the enemy also attacked from Ecouché toward Goulet; the reinforced *Panzerjäger Battalion 228* did indeed repel the enemy who at that point lost several tanks, but for the long term, the battalion was too weak for the wide sector it was tasked to defend. The *2d SS-Panzer Division* came into action on the left wing of the *116th Panzer Division* at exactly the right time. During 15 August, after probing the weakly-defended front, the enemy succeeded in entering Le Bourg-St. Léonard. On 16 August, *SS-Panzer Regiment "Deutschland"* [of the *2d SS-Panzer Division—Editor*] recaptured the town with the support of tanks from the *116th*'s reserve and the *116th*'s artillery. The assault could not achieve more than that. On the evening of 16 August, the enemy once again gained temporary entry into the village.[133] Situated on top of the hill, the town offered the enemy a view into the Dives Valley and, therefore, remained the objective of his attack. During these battles, the *2d Battalion* of the *Panzer Regiment* lost five of its ten battleworthy tanks. On the opposite side, the 90th Infantry Division was in the sector east of Argentan, and the 5th Armored Division was pulled out to attack Dreux. The French 2d Armored Division was between Ecouché and Argentan, and was, fortunately, quite inactive. Beginning 17 August, the 80th Infantry Division was placed between the two.[134]

Due to orders by Army Group on 16 August, *II SS-Panzer Corps* was withdrawn from the front; therefore, the *116th Panzer Division* had to close the resulting gaps on both wings with their own means. On the right wing, this was not possible, since the Division did not have sufficient forces available. This left no choice but to pull back the exposed right wing, with *Panzerjäger Battalion 228,* and to hope that the *2d Panzer Division,* which was withdrawing to the Orne, would achieve a linkup from the west near Sentilly. Of greater concern was the withdrawal of *SS-Panzer Regiment "Deutschland"* from the left wing. Here again, the weakened *Armored Reconnaissance Battalion 116* was deployed, which received some support from Brühl's *Panzers. Oberfeldwebel* Pichler distinguished himself during this action, but on 17 August, Le Bourg was lost permanently.[135]

At 1800 hours, V Corps reported, "Extremely strong resistance was rendered. On numerous occasions, the town was taken and retaken. This afternoon, the Americans were thrown to the southern edge by enemy tanks that fired in the streets. They are in the process of counterattacking to restore the situation."[136]

On this day, a dangerous situation developed in the rear of the Division. The Canadians captured Falaise and pushed further southeast. On the major road to Argentan, they were brought to a halt one more time, but north of the Dives they gained ground quickly and reached the area north of Trun. With this, they came dangerously close to the Division command post that had just been moved to Tournai-sur-Dives. The Division leadership advanced a close-in security line in the direction of Magny and sent staff officers to conduct reconnaissance and establish contact with other German units fighting in that area. When news confirmed the approach of the enemy toward Trun, three tanks of the Division reserve were sent into action between Tournai and Magny. With a heavy heart, three more tanks were sent from Argentan to the road from Trun to Villedieu-les-Bailleul.[137] In this way, at least improvised protection was created in the Division rear. If the enemy advanced further, this could perhaps briefly halt the attack and allow time for other forces, taken from the retreating divisions, to be brought up.

Fortunately, from 15 to 17 August, the opponent was inactive in the vicinity of the nucleus of the defensive position, Argentan. The town, however, was constantly under artillery fire. The retreating columns of the units coming in from the west forced themselves through the barely ten-kilometer-wide corridor between Trun and Argentan, continuously exposed to low flying aircraft and the increasing fire of enemy artillery from south and north. Mostly beautiful summer weather assisted the enemy pilots in their work. Shocking scenes of destruction could be seen along the two miserable roads that were still available for the German troops' use.

Units of the *2d* and *9th SS-Panzer Divisions* were deployed toward the enemy north of Trun, as were elements of the *21st Panzer Division.* The 116th's security elements took part under the command of *Oberleutnant* Abt. Most of both *SS* divisions moved on toward the northeast in accordance with orders.

After the withdrawal of *II SS-Panzer Corps,* the *116th Panzer Division* was again directly subordinated to *Panzer Group Eberbach,* the right wing of which was *XLVII Panzer Corps.* This corps now turned back and, with the *2d Panzer Division,* established a loose connection with the *116th Panzer Division* near Moulin-sur-Orne (four kilometers northwest of Argentan). Kluge permitted the withdrawal to the Orne for the night of 17/18 August.[138] This was probably his last official act, because two hours later on 17 August at 2000 hours, *Generalfeld-marschall* Model arrived as his successor.[139] The next day, 18 August 1944, was to be a dramatic day. The 80th Infantry Division, which had been moved in near Argentan, attacked in regimental strength from southeast of Argentan and the hills north of it. All attacks were repelled by the brave defenders and the attacking regiment suffered heavy losses. A counterattack out of Argentan toward the east, assisted by effective artillery support, advanced as far as Urou. Thereafter, the enemy stopped the attack and continued it the following day with two regiments and reinforced artillery.

With very strong artillery support, the 90th Infantry Division attacked north from Le Bourg-St. Léonard. Its targets were the hills north of Bon-Ménil and southwest of Chambois, but they could only be partially reached.[140] By combining our available artillery, which was joined by a brigade of rocket launchers (*Nebelwerfer*) coming from the west, it was possible to bring the attack to a standstill again and again. The armored reconnaissance battalion, supported by a few tanks, had to turn back to Chambois. On 18 August, under the commander of the *Panzer* regiment, the weak remnants turned back an attack on Chambois. *Panzer-Grenadier Regiment 60,* situated between Crennes and Le Bourg (excluded) at the southern edge of the Forêt de Gouffern, was bypassed by this attack on its left flank. The enemy captured Fougy, the town on the northeastern stretch of the forest, and entered the forest from the east. Consequently, during the night of 18/19 August, the regiment was withdrawn to the line Crennes–Bon Menil–northern edge of the forest.

On the same night, as a result of the withdrawal of *XLVII Panzer Corps* to the Falaise–Argentan road, *Panzerjäger Battalion 228* and some combat engineers moved into the gap between the left wing of *Panzer-Grenadier Regiment 60* and Chambois, near Aubry-en-Exmes. In the north, at 1030 hours on 18 August, the enemy pushed into Trun and seized the town, house by house. Then the enemy also occupied Magny and proceeded from there southward, toward the security positions of the Division staff. There, it was repelled by tanks, but pushed further from Trun to the east and southeast. The attempt to recapture this town with elements of the *9th SS-Panzer Division* and the patrols the *116th Panzer Division*'s security forces failed, after some early successes. Even west of Trun, the enemy advanced across the Dives with weaker forces.

In the evening, the defenses of the *116th Panzer Division* thwarted several attempts of the Canadians to advance further from Trun and Magny to the south, but by now the encirclement was almost complete.[141] The only route remaining open with any kind of safety was the route through Chambois, but it was only conditionally passable during the day because the enemy controlled it with observed fire. Whatever was happening on the other side of Dives was beyond the knowledge of the Division staff. We were merely depending on rumors because we did not have any more reconnaissance forces. Today we know that the

Canadians were before St. Lambert-sur-Dives, and the Polish 1st Armored Division north of it, on the road from Trun to Vimoutiers.

On 18 August, the Division's artillery used a great deal of ammunition. The *Nebelwerfers* fired all their rockets and one could not count on resupply. There were only enough battleworthy guns for a weak artillery battalion with two batteries. For this reason, the Division decided to move the staff of the artillery regiment and all functioning vehicles—especially the ones of *Armored Signal Battalion 228*—through Chambois during the night. This was reported to *Panzer Group Eberbach* and it gave permission. All the existing artillery ammunition was turned over to the remaining batteries.

The column on which all the wounded were loaded, which included the *Nebelwerfer* brigade, was led to safety by *Oberst* Pean. He received orders to assemble all units of the Division in the vicinity of the Division trains; there, he was to organize them and restructure them into combat-capable units. He was also to pay special attention to the restructuring of *Panzer-Grenadier Regiment 156*, with the inclusion of the *Field Replacement Batallion*. Toward morning on 19 August, the Division command post was moved a little further south into a group of houses called Mont Milcent, south of Tournai, near the command post of *Panzer-Grenadier Regiment 60*. The resultant cauldron was about five to ten kilometers from north to south-and about 15 kilometers from east to west.

On the morning of 18 August, Eberbach and the Chief of Staff of *7th Army, Oberst i.G.* von Gersdorff, were ordered to the command post of *5th Panzer Army*, where Model arrived to receive an assessment of the situation. He judged it quite realistically, and subsequently calculated a retreat behind the Seine and ordered *II SS-Panzer Corps* to "first fight and free up the area of Trun to reestablish contact with *7th Army*."[142] The attack planned for 19 August had to be postponed until the next day because the required fuel did not arrive in time.[143]

On the evening of 18 August, Model rendered a sober status report to *OKW*.[144] The following morning, the enemy was before Model's command post in La Roche-Guyon, which now had to be quickly transferred to Margival.[145] Hitler had already ordered the retreat from the south of France on 16 August.[146] On 19 August, he also allowed the *7th Army* to withdraw across the Seine, "if necessary."[147] Now the fundamentals of mobile warfare—which had been declared impractical two months before—were being remembered. At this point there were no more armored units capable of an attack, and the enemy had enough forces on the continent with sufficient supplies for his offensive operations.

On the same day, Bradley ordered the First Army to advance with one corps from the area west of Dreux to the Seine and to prevent the escape of the enemy across the river. The Third Army was ordered to form and retain a bridgehead across the Seine, near Mantes, and also to push out of this area of the west bank with sufficiently strong forces toward the northwest.[148]

The cauldron was closed on 19 August. Chambois was lost to the 90th Infantry Division and the Canadians marched into St. Lambert. The 80th Infantry Division resumed its attack on Argentan from east and southeast. *Group Scholz* beat back all attacks of superior strength and even took a large number of prisoners. Only under the concealment of darkness was it possible for the Americans to sneak into a little forest on the road to Trun, northeast of Argentan. During the evening hours, the French 2d Armored Division reconnoitered from the west toward Argentan. Since the remnants of *Panzer-Grenadier Regiment 60* in the Forêt de Gouffern, between Crennes and Bon-Ménil, were pushed back further, the Division allowed the abandonment of Argentan. Early on 20 August, *Group Scholz* broke through the Americans at the Argentan–Trun road, but unfortunately suffered considerable losses of tanks and self-propelled 20mm anti-aircraft guns. With this, it went into position at the southern edge of the Forêt de Gouffern, and later in the forest up on the hill.

Throughout 19 August, the concentrated fire of strong artillery covered the cauldron. The enemy had observation posts at the northeastern edge of the Forêt de Gouffern and on the other bank of the Dives, northwest of St. Lambert, from which he could over look the whole cauldron and shoot at anything that moved. Further, artillery spotter planes continuously circled the area, also directing the artillery. Toward noon, the commanding general of *7th Army* arrived at the command post of the *116th Panzer Division,* just at the time that another sheaf of artillery rounds hit the area. After a presentation of the situation, Hausser agreed to the Division's request to break out during the following night. However, with the Division once again subordinated to his command, the commanding general of *XLVII Panzer Corps* intervened. Now, Funck told the Division Commander and me about his plans to break out of the cauldron, beginning with the *1st SS-* and the *2d Panzer Divisions* and ordered the *116th Panzer Division* to defend the southern front of the cauldron to allow the breakout of the whole army until he give orders for them to follow. Due to the unclear situation, he could not specify a time for the operation.

The commanding general of *7th Army* informed Army Group of Funck's decision to "Break through on both sides of Chambois with *XLVII Panzer Corps* and *II Parachute Corps* toward the east, and occupy the east bank of the Dives with bridgehead-like defense in order to pour the other units through."[149]

The other corps in the cauldron, namely *LXXIV* and *LXXXIV Corps,* were also to join in the attack of the two corps in front.

After the morning fog cleared, 20 August was again the picture of a beautiful August day. A peaceful state prevailed around the Division command post. In the sky however, several artillery planes circled without pause and kept the now five-by-five-kilometer cauldron under combined fire, wherever they could detect the slightest movement. The enemy fighter bombers ceased their activity over the cauldron to turn to more important targets. The Division's artillery had spent its ammunition and was silent; German aircraft were nowhere in sight.

In the morning, a duty officer sent by Funck appeared to once again remind the Division of its mission. He did not know at what time the Division was to join the breakout. *Major* Boching joined the breakout in the morning with his tank destroyers and shared decisively in its success. *Group Brühl* broke out toward the east with five tanks, two of which were lost.[150] Both acted according to the situation, but without informing the Division. The Division's eastern flank was now open.

The enemy was comparatively quiet. When no order came in from Corps by early afternoon, the Division continued reconnaissance for a possible way to break out. Under the command of *Hauptmann* Risse, Adjutant of *Panzer-Grenadier Regiment 60,* reconnaissance established that the only possibility would probably be at St. Lambert. The town was under enemy artillery fire, an indication that it was not occupied by the enemy. It would also be possible to assemble along the little Dives River, somewhat concealed by the trees.

The Division now ordered all its units to break out. By nightfall, they were to disengage from the enemy and assemble south of St. Lambert, along the Aubry-en-Exmes–St. Lambert road. All arrived there except *Group Scholz.* It turned back the pursuing enemy, and assembled afterwards near the Tertu castle, west of Miguillaume. Then, instead of driving to St. Lambert, the unit drove to Trun, directly into the enemy. Only some combat engineers under *Oberleutnant* Kuschel, who were left behind by vehicles that were speeding away too fast, found their way out of the cauldron with the help of a compass.

At dusk, the road across the Dives bridge into town was sufficiently cleared of shot-up vehicles that others could pass through. When, after a long wait, *Group Scholz* did not appear, the Division began its breakout under the concealment of darkness. There were still about 50 combat vehicles of the Division staff, the armored signal battalion, *Panzer-Grenadier Regiment 60,* and the artillery. About 60 seriously wounded men who could not be transported had to be left under the care of a physician, in the cellar of a house, where they would be captured.

For the breakout, the Division had no tanks and no assault guns. Two unknown assault guns appeared and were immediately subordinated. I ordered the lieutenant in command of the assault guns to drive in a straight line through St. Lambert, but he turned his assault gun toward Trun, even though I was riding with him and ordered him to take the other direction. After just 20 meters, the assault gun was hit. I dismounted and drove on with the second assault gun toward the northeast. The crew stopped every hundred meters, turned off the engine and listened into the night. After about one kilometer, they changed the method of advance. *Oberst* Voigtsberger and I advanced dismounted on either side of the road, the assault gun keeping pace behind us, secured on both sides by the last *Panzer-Grenadiers* of *2d Battalion, Panzer-Grenadier Regiment 60* in platoon strength.

After they covered about three kilometers in this manner, it started to rain, and the breakout seemed to be a success. Everyone climbed up on the vehicles. I ordered my radio operators in the armored command vehicle to call on all frequencies known to them. They received an answer from a station of *Group Eberbach,* which told them where the spearheads of *2d SS-Panzer Division* were located. We drove toward them. The break out route led via Mimbeville–La Cour-du-Bosq–Champosoult–La Bruyère-Fresnay–Roiville–Orville–Le Sap. Near Champosoult stood the forward defenses of the *2nd SS-Panzer Division* "Das *Reich*," which we reached at dawn on 21 August. Hundreds of dismounted men, who were staying in cellars and under cover in and around St. Lambert, joined and followed us. It was like a miracle!

How did this happen?

1. During the whole day of 20 August, the enemy did not attack the remainder of the cauldron, but was content with artillery fire. An attack would hardly have met any resistance.

2. The Canadians and Americans left a gap open between the northern part of St. Lambert and Chambois, which they could have closed easily.

3. The Polish 1st Armored Division was supposed to close the gap, but did not. On 19 August, two task forces of this division took possession of hill 262, north of Mont-Ormel. On 20 August they were hit by the diversionary attack of the *2d SS-Panzer Division.* At the same time they had to fend off the breakthrough attempts coming from St. Lambert. In the evening, fatigued, they dug in around Hill 262 and thereby freed the breakthrough route of the *116th Panzer Division,* which passed by the enemy within only a few hundred meters.[151]

The units that fled the cauldron assembled in the area east of Broglie, with other units of the Division. To the extent possible, these were consolidated under the command of *Oberst* Pean with the assistance of the *Ib, Major i.G.* Wolf.[152] The Division Commander and I reported back to the command post of *XLVII Panzer Corps* near Le Sap. There, we found *General* Eberbach, who exclaimed his joy over the escape of the Division. The greeting by *General* von Funck was, rather, one of annoyance.

The Division suffered considerable losses of men and material, but there was sufficient substance left to replenish it. The leadership and supply structures were intact. *Panzer-Grenadier Regiment 156,* the *1st Battalion, Panzer-Grenadier Regiment 60,* and *Armored Engineer Battalion 675* suffered the most. The losses of tanks and assault guns were considerable. Only a few tanks, mostly those that were in repair facilities outside of the cauldron and were in reparable condition, were still available. The Division received about twelve *Panzer IVs* from the stocks in Paris. A patrol from the *Panzer* regiment, under command of *Oberleutnant* Harder, had been sent out of the cauldron to pick them up, but were engaged by elements of Patton's army. On 17 August, they were placed under the *331st Infantry Division,* first in the area of L'Aigle, on 18 August, north of Gacé on the road to Vimoutiers, with the front facing toward west. From there, Harder joined *Panzer-Grenadier Regiment "Der Führer"* of the *2nd SS-Panzer Division* in the attack, and so contributed to the breakout of the encircled units from *116th Panzer Division*. Harder and another group of the Division which participated in the attack of *II SS-Panzer Corps* returned to the Division on 22 August.[153]

Since the reconstitution of *Panzer-Grenadier Regiment 156* from the bulk of the *Field Replacement Battalion* made good progress, it seemed possible that the Division could soon be available again with a certain combat strength. But first, all those who had been granted freedom one more time fell into a deep sleep.

Meanwhile, the next crisis was developing hardly 50 kilometers further east. On 21 August, the Americans attacked north across the line Verneuil-sur-Avre–Dreux and northwest between the Eure and Seine Rivers. Besides that, they crossed the Seine between Vernon and Mantes and established bridgeheads.[154] The remainder of the *Field Replacement Battalion,* together with the Division combat training school, were destroyed near St. Illiers-la-Ville (13 kilometers west of Mantes) by the Americans on 18 August. Only a few escaped across the Seine.[155]

On 21 August, *Generalfeldmarschall* Model evidently decided to detour toward the Seine. He offered three lines for the withdrawal. All were already obsolete at their as a result of the above mentioned advances of the enemy across their southern segments.[156] For the night 21/22 August, Army Group ordered *5th Panzer Army* to detour to the line Deauville–Lisieux–Orbec–L'Aigle.[157] With this, the Division was close behind the front without being aware of it. But there was no mishap, because the Americans attacked further east and the British could not push forward quickly enough from the west.

With the same order from Army Group came the directive to remove non-combat ready *7th Army* armored units to assembly areas in the logistical support areas near Beauvais–Senlis; they would be refurbished there under the command of *LVIII Panzer Corps*. The *5th Panzer Army* now had responsibility for the area up to the boundary with *1st Army* west of Paris. It was to attack from the vicinity of Evreux to the south with most of the armored units at its disposal. When this was ordered, the remnants of the armored units had not yet been reorganized, and the enemy was about 15 kilometers from Evreux.

On the afternoon of 21 August, the *116th Panzer Division* was subordinated to *LXXXI Corps*, and after moving all the units that were not needed across the Seine, it was to move the vicinity of Conches-en-Ouche (18 kilometers west southwest of Evreux). This order did not reach the Division, however, and on the morning of 22 August, when a brief liaison with *LXXXI Corps* was established, it was not repeated.[158]

On the afternoon of 22 August, I was called to corps headquarters to receive orders. The Division was to move to the area between the Seine and the Eure during the night of 22/23 August, and to take over that sector. The units emplaced there until now under the command of the *17th Luftwaffe Field Division* were to be subordinated to the *116th*.[159] On the return trip to our command post, a fighter bomber surprised us as we traveled in our car. The car caught fire and was destroyed. I was wounded, but after receiving first aid, I was still able to deliver the Corps' orders to the Division. After that, I was transported to the field hospital for an operation. *Major i.G.* Wolf took over my duties in my absence.

On 22 August, *Oberst* Müller issued an order of the day to the Division:

In seven days of heavy defensive battles from Argentan and during the breakthrough, the troops of the *116th Panzer Division* and attached units fought to the south and north against an enemy that was superior in numbers and material, and thereby made it possible for the *7th Army* to escape encirclement.

I express my full appreciation to the leaders and troops, especially to *Combat Group Scholz,* and expect that in the upcoming heavy battles, everyone will perform in the similar fashion. It is not only about maintaining a spotless reputation for the *116th Panzer Division,* but today more than ever, it is about the existence of our Fatherland.[160]

CHAPTER 6

Withdrawal

The order I received from *LXXXI Corps* on the afternoon of 22 August for the Division to take over the sector between the Seine and the Eure was already obsolete by the time I returned to the command post after being wounded. By that afternoon, the enemy started a new attack toward the north with more than 100 tanks between the Risle and the Eure and broke through the corps' defenses. There was fighting in Conches-en-Ouche and Evreux. The enemy pushed forward on both sides of the Eure up to Chambray (12 kilometers northeast of Evreux).[1]

At 1905 hours, *LXXXI Corps* therefore ordered the Division to move to the area east of Le Neubourg (22 kilometers northwest of Evreux). At 2252 hours, Corps apprised the Division that enemy armored spearheads had pushed into the area southeast of Le Neubourg. At 2000 hours, *Major i.G.* Wolf reported to Corps that only parts of the Division could be transferred because the promised fuel had not yet arrived.[2] Thus, the newly formed *Panzer-Grenadier Regiment 156* was ordered to march ahead to Le Neubourg. The *2nd Battalion* of *Armored Artillery Regiment 146* was also ordered to go, but because of clogged roads, it was only able to advance ten kilometers. At dawn, due to enemy air activity, this unit had to take cover in an area about eight kilometers northeast of Bernay.[3]

Early on 23 August, *Panzer-Grenadier Regiment 156,* under command of *Major* Flecke, reached the area south of Le Neubourg. *Hauptmann* von Ketteler, commanding the *1st Battalion,* wanted to occupy positions near the intersection at Les Quatres Routes. Reconnaissance showed that the enemy was already two kilometers southeast of the intersection. Very soon, enemy tanks attacked this battalion, which was not yet fully emplaced; since it had no support from heavy weapons, it had to pull back to Le Neubourg. Apparently, the *2nd Battalion,* under command of *Hauptmann* Gerke, fought on the left wing of the regiment. By counterattacking into the enemy's flank, which attacked the *1st Battalion,* it finally brought the enemy attack to a halt.[4]

In the meantime, the Division received several orders in rapid succession from the corps. At 0850 hours, the order arrived to attack via Le Neubourg toward Louviers. At noon, a previously radioed excerpt of the corps order said, "In the area east-northeast of Le Neubourg, the *116th Panzer Division*, as corps reserve, prepares to deploy at any time as a mobile reaction force, primarily in the sectors of the *344th Infantry Division* and *17th Luftwaffe Field Division.*"

These divisions were to defend along the line from southeast of Le Neubourg to the Seine southeast of Louviers, but both were just barely hanging on. At 1340 hours, *LXXXI Corps* ordered the *116th Panzer Division* to prepare a rally point for the *344th Infantry Division,* namely from the intersection south of Le Neubourg via Quittebeuf to the east, up to the boundary with the *17th Luftwaffe Field Division.* This order was also overtaken by events.[5] Toward evening, the enemy pushed the *1st Battalion* of *Panzer-Grenadier Regiment 156* out of Le Neubourg to the north, and crossed the road to Louviers northeast of it. Units of the *17th Luftwaffe Field Division* were still near Louviers. A gap developed between Le Neubourg and Louviers.[6]

On 23 August, at about 2000 hours, *Oberst* Müller received instructions at the corps command post to make contact with the *17th Luftwaffe Field Division,* but considering his minimal forces, he thought he had no hope of success. Until the morning of 14 August, the *116th Panzer Division,* with *Panzer-Grenadier Regiment 156* and the other units which were still arriving, was only able to establish a security line north of Le Neubourg on both sides of Le Troncq, "but" as *Oberst* Voigtsberger reported after the war, "because of our own weak forces, it was not continuous, but rather consisted of strongpoints allowing defense of all important terrain."[7,8]

The *331st* and remnants of the *344th Infantry Division*s returned from the west through this area. There was still a gap between the *116th Panzer* and *17th Luftwaffe Field Divisions,* through which the enemy tried to push toward Elbeuf. During the night of 23/24 August, the *21st Panzer* and the *2nd SS-Panzer Divisions* moved in from the west to reinforce the eastern wing of *5th Panzer Army* between the Seine and the Risle, and to halt the enemy advance toward the Seine crossings near Rouen. The *21st Panzer Division* was subordinated to the *116th,* while the *2nd SS-Panzer Division* received the order to block the southern edge of the forest area south and southeast of Elbeuf.[9]

The command post of the *116th Panzer Division* was in Bosguerard-de-Marcouville, southwest of Bourgtheroulde, and was then moved to Caumont, southwest of Rouen. In the morning, *Generalleutnant* Count Schwerin arrived and again assumed command of his Division, which now, together with the *21st Panzer* and the *2nd SS-Panzer Division* formed *"Group Schwerin." Oberst* Müller returned to the *Führer* Reserve. Once before, on 22 August, Model had ordered the return of Schwerin, but rescinded it and appointed him to command the units that were deployed against the American bridgehead near Mantes. *Group Schwerin's* mission near Mantes was taken over by *I SS-Panzer Corps.*[10]

The next day, 23 August, brought several violent exchanges between Model and Sepp Dietrich regarding what Model thought to be inadequate leadership during the attacks by the *Panzer* units. One result of the discussion, strongly demanded by Model, was that Schwerin should lead a coordinated attack south of the Seine. With justified concern, Model advised the headquarters of *5th Panzer Army,* "That everything must be done to reinforce the east wing, to the disadvantage of the western front of the *5th Panzer Army.* It is important that the western front be rigorously relieved, in order to strengthen the southern and eastern wings of the [*5th Panzer*] *Army* so that the creation of a second cauldron can be prevented."[11]

On the morning of 23 August, the *OKW* sent an other utopian order about the defense in the area ahead of Paris:

> The defense of the bridgehead is of decisive military and political significance. Its loss rips open the whole coastal front north of the Seine and deprives us of the basis for a long-distance battle against England.
>
> Historically, the loss of Paris has always meant the fall of all France.
>
> The *Führer*, therefore, repeats his order that Paris should be defended in front of the ring of obstacles. At the first sign of revolt inside the city, forces must intervene with the most severe military means to prevent its spread. These means include, for example, demolition of blocks of houses, public execution of ring leaders, evacuation of affected city quarters. . . . Paris must not fall into enemy hands, or if it does, only as a heap of rubble.[12]

Model obviously did not take the order very seriously. He realistically informed Jodl of the situation and reported that the *Panzer* divisions were only "torsos."[13] Surprisingly, reports of an attack by *Panzer* units appear repeatedly in the records of *5th Panzer Army* and its higher headquarters on 23 and 24 August, even though nothing of that sort happened; in fact, the enemy pushed across the Louviers–Le Neubourg road and on to the north.[14] The XIX Corps, known to the *116th Panzer Division* from the battles between Tessy and Percy, continued its attack toward Elbeuf; west of it, the British attempted an advance near Brionne and toward Montfort-sur-Risle.[15]

On the evening of 24 August, it was finally possible to establish a more or less stable line between Elbeuf and the Risle, north of Brionne. Units were deployed as follows, from left to right: *2nd SS, 116th Panzer, 21st Panzer,* and the *331st Infantry Divisions*. The sector of the *116th* ran from Les Ecameaux across the hill north of Le Thuit-Signol to Le Thuit-Simer. Under the command of *Panzer-Grenadier Regiment 60, 1st Battalion, Panzer-Grenadier Regiment 60* and *1st Battalion, Panzer-Grenadier Regiment 156* were fighting in this sector. The whole artillery, one battery of each battalion, namely the *1st, 6th,* and *9th Batteries,* were under the command of *2nd Battalion, Armored Artillery Regiment 146.*

All battleworthy tanks and assault guns—totaling about 20 at the beginning of the operation—supported this combat group.[16]

On this evening, *Generalleutnant* Gause, Chief of Staff of *5th Panzer Army,* reported that *Army Group B* had ordered Schwerin to push through to Louviers, but added right away, "At this time, the attack is not in progress, because *Panzer Group Schwerin* itself is being attacked by strong enemy tank forces."[17]

Then, Gause requested the withdrawal of the right wing toward the Risle and announced that during the course of this movement, he wanted to extricate *II SS-Panzer Corps* and the *9th SS-Panzer Division*. As the last *Panzer* division out, the

9th SS-Panzer Division was to join *Group Schwerin*; corps would then assume overall control.

An attack on the American bridgehead near Mantes on 23 August failed, and was repeated on 24 August, but was no more successful.[18] The Americans, though, started the attack on Paris, and in the night of 25/26 August, together with the French 2d Armored Division, they advanced into the city center. Near Melun, they established a bridgehead across the Seine, southeast of Paris. The spearheads of Third Army stood near Sens, at the Yonne (100 kilometers southeast of Paris).[19] On 25 August, all of Paris was lost.

The enemy decided to attack to the northeast across the Seine between Melun and the coast with three field armies, including the 21st Army Group (First Canadian and Second British Armies) and First Army, while only Patton's Third Army attacked to the east toward the Rhine between Mannheim and Koblenz. The ultimate target for the main attack to the left was the Ruhr region. British and Canadian divisions arrived at the southern wing of the *5th Panzer Army* to relieve the Americans.[20] This gave the weak German units a little time to breathe.

On the morning of 25 August, Model ordered the withdrawal across the Seine. During the night of 25/26 August, there was to be a delay behind the Risle and in the following night behind the Seine. The defense of the Seine was "to be established and reinforced with all means, so that it would stand with secure defensive forces after changing from one bank to the other." Behind the Seine, "in the area north of Rouen and Beauvais, two reaction forces were to be formed from the remaining elements of the *Panzer* divisions."

The remnants of eleven divisions of the *7th Army* were to be refurbished and employed in constructing emplacements near the Somme position.[21] The staff of *5th Panzer Army* completed the order with the directive that the bends of the Seine north of Caumont and Elbeuf should be secured by a "dead bolt," that is, should be defended. Motorized vehicles were to have precedence over horse-drawn conveyances, and combat and special vehicles were to be first in priority.

The order by *5th Panzer Army* specified the following organization for the two reaction forces: one, under *General* Count Schwerin near Beauvais, would include the *1st SS, 2nd SS, 12th SS,* and *116th Panzer Divisions*; the other, under *II SS-Panzer Corps*, would be composed of the *9th SS, 10th SS,* and *21st Panzer Divisions.*[22]

On the same day, *Army Group B* ordered new areas for replenishment of all *Panzer* and *Panzer-Grenadier* divisions east of the line Amiens–Reims–St. Dizier. There, the *General of Panzer Troops–West* would assume responsibility for the replenishment. The *116th Panzer Division* was assigned an area northeast of Reims.[23] In retrospect, one can only shake one's head about his order, because on this day it was evident that the *1st Army*, between Paris and the upper Seine, could under no circumstances offer any serious resistance; shortly, the enemy would be before of Reims. Count Schwerin did not execute this order.

To begin, all supply troops, and most importantly the repair services, were urgently needed to take in the wrecks that were coming back across the Seine. All units were assembling in the area around Beauvais; replacements and stragglers were taken there; and materiel which could be procured easily during the onset of this retreat was brought in. *Oberst* Pean, who was again in command in the rear area, sent out officers to accomplish these tasks.[24] In the repair facilities, they worked feverishly to partially equip the units again with tanks, guns, and motor vehicles. During this time, much had to be improvised, even the supply of maps for the expected large-scale movements. Michelin maps were mostly the only ones available.[25]

The line occupied on the evening of 24 August along the southern front of our own Seine bridgehead could be defended substantially until the next day. Elbeuf, which was occupied by the enemy on 24 August, was retaken by the *2nd SS-Panzer Division* in the early morning, and defended against several enemy attacks. The enemy was generally quiet on the remaining front of *Group Schwerin,* occupied by the *21st* and *116th Panzer Division*s. The *Group* only reported one enemy armored reconnaissance patrol, west of La Haye-du-Theil, which was turned back and in the course of the mission, lost two tanks and two half tracks. Moreover, the *Group* reckoned on a reinforcement of the enemy southwest of Elbeuf and expected an attack there.

The next day, 25 August, was less favorable for the right wing of *LXXXI Corps*. In the afternoon, it was caught in the right flank by an enemy tank assault from the area south of Montfort. The *9th SS-Panzer Division* was deployed as reinforcement between Montfort and Bosguerard-de-Marcouville, and was subordinated to *Group Schwerin*.[26]

All day long, enemy fighter bombers dominated the sky. Movements were hardly possible, artillery firing was impeded, and there were considerable losses in the firing positions. In the *1st Battery, Armored Artillery Regiment 146*—a self-propelled artillery battery—all of the guns were rendered useless because of damage. On the night of 26 August, the battery was pulled out and moved across the Seine.[27] During the same night, the front was moved back to the Risle, between the coast and Montfort, and then toward the east to Bosguerard-de-Marcouville–north of Le Thuit-Simer–northern edge of Elbeuf. This meant that the *116th Panzer Division* remained in its positions.[28]

On the morning of 26 August, the enemy broke through toward Bourg-theroulde, but was brought to a standstill by our tanks and artillery fire at the northern edge of the town. After the enemy was reinforced during the day, it again started to attack to the north. Since a German retreat to the Seine loop was planned for the night of 26/27 August, *Panzer-Grenadier Regiment 60* moved out under the protection of some tanks to the chord ["chord" is being used here in a mathematical sense, that is, a straight line segment across the arc formed by the loop in the Seine—*Editor*] within the Seine loop south of Moulineaux. The following were deployed in this position: *Panzer-Grenadier Regiment 60* with both battalions near Moulineaux; *2nd Battalion, Panzer-Grenadier Regiment 156* in the center in the Forêt de la Londe, and the *2nd SS-Panzer Division* on the left wing near Orival.[29]

Unpleasant events took place at the crossing sites by the Seine: The organization of the crossing was deficient, and the rules were often made by the stronger one present, which in most cases meant the units of the *Waffen-SS.* Some *Heer* units waited for days at the ferry docks and never got across.[30] In spite of that, the Division moved relatively many vehicles across the river. It was beneficial that in the evening of 26 August, together with the *2nd SS-Panzer Division,* it defended its own Seine loop, with ferries in Rouen as well as near Petit- and Grand-Couronne. It was no longer possible to operate ferries at the southern part of the Seine loop, because on the evening of 26 August, the first weak enemy forces appeared on the other bank, which is in the loop east of Elbeuf.[31]

The next day, 27 August, passed quietly. The enemy moved up slowly, and the Division's artillery resisted his efforts. The crossing site near Rouen was attacked by strong bomber units. Fighter bombers, as usual, dedicated their attention to anything that moved, and kept the ferries under their control.[32] The remaining bridgehead at the Risle was taken back on 27 August and a withdrawal to the three Seine loops, south of Caudebec-en-Caux, south of Duclair, and south of Rouen, was planned for the night 27/28 August. The armored units were to be pulled out during the night. The *331st Infantry Division* took over the loops of Duclair and Rouen.[33] The relief of the *116th Panzer Division,* which was completed on 27 August at 2225 hours, took place without a problem.

At 0720 hours the following morning, the Division Commander announced his departure to the headquarters of *LXXXI Corps.*[34] During the day, the units were moved across the Seine. Fog and rain helped these dangerous undertakings. During the night of 28/29 August and on the following day, they reached the assembly area Beauvais–St. Just-en-Chaussée–Clermont. The Division command post now was in Bulles and Monteaux, northwest of Clermont (see map 2).[35]

In the rear area, considerable parts of the Division finally reassembled, so that a combat group could be formed. Little could be found of the three SS-*Panzer* divisions; only small groups of 40 to 200 men with a few tanks and heavy weapons were discovered. All other parts of these divisions were probably moved out toward the assembly area, which had been designated for the refurbishment of the Division, east of Laon. Basically, now *Group Schwerin* was composed of the *116th Panzer Division:* At this point, the Division consisted of the following elements:

—*Panzer-Grenadier Regiment 60,* with two weak battalions

—*Panzer-Grenadier Regiment 156,* with two weak battalions

—*3d Battalion, Armored Artillery Battalion 146,* with the following attachments:

　—*Artillery Battalion 992* with four guns

　—*Parachute Nebelwerfer Battalion 21* (as of 25 August)[36]

— Two weak tank companies

—One weak *Panzerjäger* company

—One weak combat engineer company

—A relatively strong armored reconnaissance battalion (disregarding the armored car company, which had lost about half of its reconnaissance platoons)[37]

In the following days, the armored reconnaissance battalion performed outstanding service; *Major* Stephan assumed command. *Major* Grollmann took command of *Panzer-Grenadier Regiment 156. Armored Engineer Battalion 675* also received a new commander, *Hauptmann* Appel, who replaced *Hauptmann* Hossenfelder, wounded near Perriers. The recuperated *Major* von Meyer again took over *1st Battalion* of *Panzer Regiment 24.*[38]

The Division's leadership was still capable of performing its duties, as were the rear echelon services. During his absence from the Division, Count Schwerin formed a small command staff, which presented a valuable reserve for the Division staff and *Armored Signal Battalion 228*. In the far-reaching movements and totally unconnected front lines, a small reconnaissance platoon, under the command of *Oberleutnant* von Löbbecke was of special value.[39]

In the meantime, the enemy started executing his planned attacks. On 29 August, Patton's Third Army pushed east and passed north of Reims, toward the Aisne. Reims fell on 30 August. The following day, Verdun was taken and the Meuse River was crossed. At that point, the advance came to a halt for lack of fuel. This gave the German command time to build a new front with new forces at the Moselle. The First Army, under Lieutenant General Hodges, attacked on both sides of Paris. On 28 August, the VII Corps, advancing east of the town, took Soissons, and on 30 August, Laon. Coming from the bridgehead at Mantes, on 29 August, XIX Corps started to advance toward the line Compiègne–Beauvais, and reached it on 31 August. Beauvais itself had fallen on the evening of 30 August. In the center, V Corps followed from Paris and on 1 September, reached the Aisne, between Soissons and Compiègne. Montgomery's army group attacked to the left of the Americans.[40]

The British took Amiens on 31 August, unexpectedly seized *7th Army* headquarters, and captured its Commander, *General der Panzertruppe* Eberbach, who had assumed command after Hausser was wounded during the breakout from the Falaise cauldron.[41] His Chief of Staff, *Oberst i.G.* Baron von Gersdorff, was able to escape. At the same time, the guard company of the *5th Panzer Army,* comprised of personnel from the *116th Panzer Division*, was also captured, because staffs of the two armies were in the process of changing command when the British arrived. The *7th Army* was to connect with *15th Army* between Amiens and the Oise River, and *5th Panzer Army* was to assume control to the east, from the Aisne to Rethel.[42] The allied armies' main effort advancing toward the border of the *Reich* had priority of fuel supplies. The number one target was the destruction of the three aforementioned German armies, which were to be pushed back toward the coast and the mouth of the *Scheldt*.

At noon, on 28 August, Model ordered the retreat to the Somme. The front line was to be displaced rearward in stages, during the night of 1/2 September, approximately to the line Dieppe–Beauvais. On the evening of 28 August, Model contacted Jodl and requested permission to "immediately move up strong forces to the areas Metz–Luxembourg–Sedan–Maubeuge." In Model's opinion, the positions further up front were of no value for defense. The population became rebellious and could no longer be levied to assist with improvements. He considered "a strong defense supported by conscription of civilians a possibility" only for the *Westwall.* "Unlimited air dominance, similar to ours of 1940," enabled the enemy in the main effort "to push through wherever it wants."[43]

The situation developed in an alarming way on 29 August. The enemy attack across the Seine below Paris progressed to the line Rouen–Gisors–north of Pontoise. The *1st Army's LVIII Panzer Corps* was penetrated in its left wing and separated from the rest of the Army. It subordinated itself to *5th Panzer Army* and attempted to establish a line in front of the Oise, between Pontoise and just west of Soissons. Stopping before the Aisne and upper Marne was no longer an option for *1st Army.*[44] In this situation, Model accelerated the detour to the Somme. The line Dieppe–Beauvais–Creil–Senlis was to be reached during the night of 30/31 August, two nights earlier than planned. This line and its continuation (via Soissons–Aisne–Vesle to south of the line Reims–Marne–Marne Canal) was to be defended, even though it had already been breached in several locations by 29 August. The *5th Panzer Army* received the order to "quickly close the gaps in its sector through offensive activity" in the area between the Oise and Reims.[45] Only the weakened forces of *"Group Schwerin"* and *II SS-Panzer Corps*, which was not in any better condition, were available for this task. The remnants of the *9th* and *10th SS-Panzer Divisions* were subordinated to the latter. Only the combat group of the *9th* was immediately at hand, while the *10th SS-Panzer Division* was already north of the Somme, in the area designated for its refurbishment.[46]

As the last parts of the armored units, namely the *116th* and the *2nd SS-Panzer Divisions,* were just moving out from the Seine bridgehead near Rouen, *5th Panzer Army* issued the following order to the *II SS-Panzer Corps* and *Group Schwerin* on 28 August:

> Opponent advanced from the south up to Soissons. On 29 August, *II SS-Panzer Corps* and *Group Schwerin,* with all units coming from prior deployments, including small groups, immediately start formation and march to reach the area Soissons–Laon via Beauvais and Compiègne. These movements have priority over all other movements. The [*5th Panzer*] *Army* is to be continuously informed about the progress of the march.[47]

When it received the order, the *116th Panzer Division* only had *Armored Reconnaissance Battalion 116* and one battalion of *Panzer-Grenadier Regiment*

156 ready to march. To get a picture of the enemy attacking at Soissons, to recognize possible advances by the enemy against the line Creil–Compiègne at an
early stage, and to protect our own movement, *Armored Reconnaissance Battalion 116* was told to march toward the Oise. It was to reconnoiter across the line
Senlis–Crépy-en-Valois toward the Paris–Soissons road. Count Schwerin ordered
Panzer-Grenadier Regiment 156 to reach Noyon during the night, to close off the
Oise crossings there, and to reconnoiter toward Soissons.[48] Most of the Division
received orders to quickly prepare to march. The area east of Cambrai was designated as the new supply and maintenance site of the Division.[49]

During the night of 28/29 August, the reconnaissance battalion reported the
area of Senlis–Crépy-en-Valois free of the enemy, but there was light enemy traffic on the road from Paris to Soissons.

On the morning of 29 August, the Division Commander and his staff traveled
first to Noyon. There he learned that infantry were securing the Oise sector.
Furthermore it was reported that Soissons was in enemy hands, but north of
there—at the Oise-Aisne-canal near Coucy-le-Château—some of our forces were
facing an enemy which was still weak.[50]

The troops of *LVIII Panzer Corps* still found themselves in front of the Oise.
On 29 August, at 1620 hours, the *LVIII Panzer Corps* Chief of Staff, *Oberst i.G.*
Dingler, telephonically reported this to Speidel. He said that Schwerin reported
he would attack north of the Aisne from west to east. Speidel informed Dingler
that Schwerin should advance toward Reims, to establish contact with *1st Army*
and to clarify the enemy's position. Bittrich (*II SS-Panzer Corps*) would come in
north of Schwerin.[51]

Regarding the intentions of *116th Panzer Division,* this information was purely wishful thinking. Schwerin's judgment of the situation in Noyon was that the
enemy would probably advance from Soissons to the north or northeast, but not
to the northwest. Since, in his opinion, the Oise below Noyon was sufficiently
secured, he had to prepare to encounter the enemy further east. Evidently, he did
not seriously consider the higher commands' remarks about the idea to attack
toward Soissons. He hoped to be able to intercept the enemy at the Oise-Aisne
Canal north of Soissons.[52]

On the evening of 29 August, Gause informed Army Group, "*Group Schwerin,*
in its advance toward the east, has crossed the area of Compiègne. *II SS-Panzer
Corps* is also advancing into the vicinity of Soissons, and reported Laon to be free
of the enemy."[53]

Gause intended to subordinate *Group Schwerin* to the commanding general of
II SS-Panzer Corps, SS-Obergruppenführer Bittrich. In his daily report of 29
August, *Supreme Command–West* reported somewhat prematurely, "*Group
Schwerin* (subordinated to *II SS-Panzer Corps*) advancing via Compiègne to
Soissons. *Group Bittrich . . .* advances via Noyon toward Laon and from there
turns south."[54]

What was called *"Group Schwerin"* on 29 and 30 August, was only *Armored
Reconnaissance Battalion 116,* which advanced toward Soissons from the west,

and the *1st Battalion, Panzer-Grenadier Regiment 156,* which reconnoitered Soissons, probably from Noyon or Chauny. Most of the Division was still getting organized in the area east of Beauvais.

On 29 August, the defenses of *LVIII Panzer Corps* were in front of *Group Schwerin* in a line north of Damartin–Crépy-en-Valois–north of Soissons, parallel to the Paris–Soissons road.[55] Consequently, the *Group* had no enemy contact. On 30 August, however, the forces of *II SS-Panzer Corps* deployed toward Soissons encountered the enemy at the Oise-Aisne Canal. The extremely poor reports show the weak units of the *116th* in the area of Coucy-le-Château, and similarly manned elements of the *9th* and *2nd SS-Panzer Divisions* east of it, near Anizy-le-Château and northwest of Laon.[56]

The daily reports of Army Group and *Supreme Command–West* masked the conditions, "The flank attack of *Group Bittrich* was not effective. . . . The Corps was forced into the defense as a result of superior enemy force. Strong enemy took Coucy-le-Château. Laon was lost. . . . *Group Bittrich* has orders to push through to Margival and retake Laon."[57]

The last sentence points to a curious episode in those days. On 29 August, *OKW* ordered the completed command post at Margival, northeast of Soissons, to "be kept as a fortress."[58] This is where Hitler's conference with Rundstedt and Rommel took place on 17 June. This was also the destination of Headquarters, *Army Group B,* when it was chased out of La Roche-Guyon. In the meantime, it arrived in the area of Cambrai. On 30 August, *Supreme Command–West* calmed *OKW* with an Army Group report from the previous day, which stated that the defense of the site had been ordered and that a commander was appointed. It closed, "Reinforcement has been planned for 29 August by the armored *Group Schwerin.* Further reinforcement will be gained from withdrawing *5th Panzer Army* units. Name of commander will be reported later."[59]

Apparently, Schwerin heard nothing of these instructions. In the afternoon of 30 August, *II SS-Panzer Corps* rightfully considered the "execution of the attack on Margival as impossible."[60] Nevertheless, the daily report contained the quoted sentence, that *Group Bittrich* had orders "to push through to Margival," the "fate of which is not known." All this clearly shows the confusion and the continuous whitewashing. In fact, nobody lifted a finger for Margival. Nothing happened in regard to the recapture of Laon, and practically nothing could be done with the weak forces, particularly since the enemy, attacking from Laon toward northeast, took Montcornet on the Serre.[61] A combat group of the *12th SS-Panzer Division* prevented the crossing of the Serre, but most of *Army Group B* was newly threatened with being outflanked.

The *1st Army* was thrown back toward Rethel and the upper Aisne. On the evening of 30 August, Gause informed Speidel about the situation at Laon and north of it, and reported his intentions to "establish a new line of resistance" between Chauny at the Oise and Grécy on the Serre, and to assemble as combat groups "everything that was pushed back across the Oise by the advancing enemy tank force."[62]

Let us turn back to the *116th Panzer Division*. Schwerin went from Noyon to La Fère, where he met the commander of the *275th Infantry Division, General-leutnant* Schmidt. He learned that this division was prepared to defend at the Oise between La Fère and Guise, with one regiment as a combat outpost at the Serre, from La Fère east up to Crécy-sur-Serre. At noon on 30 August, he heard that Laon had been seized by the enemy. He then decided to oppose the enemy at the Serre between La Fère and Marle. For this, he moved up *1st Battalion, Panzer-Grenadier Regiment 156* and positioned it in the bridgehead east of La Fère, "to prevent a surprise enemy advance from Laon toward La Fère." He then moved *Armored Reconnaissance Battalion 116* in and guided it to Marle, to get the major Paris–Laon–Brussels road under control and to reconnoiter along the eastern flank.[63]

Most of the Division's combat units that were still reorganizing east of Beauvais were ordered to displace to the vicinity of Ham.[64] They moved out toward evening while the enemy already entered Beauvais.[65] On the evening of 29 August, the supply troops had already received orders "to immediately begin" to march into the area east of Cambrai.[66] The combat units continued their march from Ham via St.Quentin–Ribemont on the Oise toward the Serrre.[67]

On 31 August, the Division's entire combat group was deployed in the Serre sector, between La Fère (exclusive) and Marle (inclusive), as follows:

—To the right up to west of Crécy-sur-Serre: *Panzer-Grenadier Regiment 156*
—In the center on both sides of Crécy up to Erlon: *Panzer-Grenadier Regiment 60*
—To the left on both sides of Marle: *Armored Reconnaissance Battalion 116*[68]

The Division command post was transferred to Parpeville. Most of the tanks were deployed behind *Panzer-Grenadier Regiment 60*. The armored reconnaissance battalion reconnoitered to the south, southeast and east.

With this, the *116th Panzer Division* moved partially into the *275th Infantry Division* sector; after the war, the *275th's* commander wrote:

> I could not explain the reasons why this sector was occupied by a second division, but had no objections whatsoever against the reinforcement of my already weak forces that were ill-equipped with heavy arms. Of special value for me was that this arrangement now enabled motorized long-range reconnaissance. On 31 August, it discovered weak enemy forces north of Laon, which, for the time being, were biding their time.[69]

The front line between the coast and the Serre appeared to be stronger, while the situation along the boundary with *1st Army* (and in the *1st Army* itself) continued to be extremely critical. But the appearance was misleading. During the night of 30/31 August, the enemy pushed forward toward Amiens, took that town in the afternoon and continued to attack immediately toward the north and northeast. In the evening, it reached Albert and thereby stood in the rear of *LVIII Panzer Corps*. To block this dangerous enemy advance, all available reserves were brought in, including the *10th SS-Panzer Division* and the *II SS-Panzer Corps' 9th SS-Panzer Division.*[70] At 1500 hours on the afternoon of 30 August, *5th Panzer Army* ordered a withdrawal to the line Amiens–Noyon–LaFère–Marle–Montcornet–Rethel. Practically speaking, this was where the units actually were already.

At the same time, *II SS-Panzer Corps* reported that the 3d Armored Division had reached the area northwest of Laon and was advancing toward Marle and Montcornet. This is where combat groups of the *1st* and *12th SS-Panzer Divisions* were deployed, respectively, but the enemy tried to cross over in the unoccupied area between the towns.[71] In the evening, the enemy arrived south of Vervins. Forty tanks broke through our defenses east of Montcornet and reached Brunehamel. The combat groups of the *1st* and *12th SS-Panzer Divisions* retreated to the Oise, north of Vervins and south of Hirson, while other units gave ground toward Liart (25 kilometers southeast of Hirson).[72]

In the afternoon, *Obergruppenführer* Bittrich visited the *116th Panzer Division* and plainly ordered it to oppose the enemy south of Vervins, south of Landouzy-la-Ville, and north of Brunehamel. That did not succeed. On 1 September, at 1150 hours, Schwerin, therefore, reported to Bittrich from Papleux (six kilometers northwest of La Capelle).

> L.A.H. and H.J. [*1st SS-Panzer Division "Leibstandarte Adolf Hitler"* and *12th SS-Panzer Division "Hitler Jugend,"* respectively—*Editor*] no longer strong enough to resist, were this morning south of La Capelle and Hirson, therefore, order for *116th Panzer Division* near Vervins and Brunehamel superseded; they assemble in two combat groups around La Capelle and north of Hirson and prevent further enemy advance toward north.
>
> At 0900 hours, enemy in Vervins, 0930 southeast of Landouzy-la-Ville, 0830 south of Aubenton heading north.
>
> — Division Commander[73]

The armored reconnaissance battalion was again deployed on the eastern wing of the Division, southeast of Hirson, and reconnoitered to the south and southeast toward the line Montcornet–Rethel–Charleville.[74] During the night of 31 August/1 September, the rearward units of the Division were moved from the vicinity of Cambrai to the vicinity of Mons. On the following night, they moved further on to an area north of Namur–Huy.[75]

On 31 August, Bradley changed the direction of attack of the First Army from northeast to north. On the left, XIX Corps' objective was Tournai. On the right, instead of advancing from Rethel and Montcornet toward Lüttich and Namur, VII Corps was now to reach Mons via Avesnes and Maubeuge. It attacked with three divisions, with the 3d Armored Division leading on the main road via Vervins–La Capelle and via Hirson, the 9th Infantry Division to its right as flank guard, and the 1st Infantry Division to the left and behind the 3d Armored. The 3d Armored and the 9th Infantry Divisions merged near Vervins and Hirson, so that the bulk of two American divisions was attacking in this area. The broad gap between these units and the Third Army, the left wing of which was pushing through the Argonnes, was only covered by a reinforced cavalry group.[76]

On 1 September the *5th Panzer Army* fell apart. The enemy broadened his breakthrough near Amiens, seized Arras in the afternoon, and pushed further to the northeast.[77] Liaison from *5th Panzer Army* to the subordinate corps was broken, and liaison from corps to the divisions was often interrupted. If orders were not already obsolete at the time they were written, they were mostly overcome by events by the time they reached their recipient.[78]

In the afternoon, the 3d Armored Division crossed the Oise, sweeping around northwest of Vervins. It pushed into the flank of the *116th Panzer Division* near La Capelle. *Panzer-Grenadier Regiment 156,* deployed there facing south, was knocked aside, the town was lost, and the road north was open to the enemy. The *116th Panzer Division*'s mission of halting the enemy's push to north could no longer be accomplished. This led to the formation of the Mons cauldron and to the destruction of most of the *5th Panzer Army*'s infantry divisions.

The Division leadership was reproached for this in reports completed for the Americans after the war, but blame was refuted in the same media. The commanding general of *II SS-Panzer Corps* wrote, "The whereabouts of the *116th Panzer Division*, which could have been employed, could not be established. As was later determined, in contravention of its order to block the way to Mons and to keep open its route of withdrawal, it detoured toward the western edge of the Ardennes."[79]

The commander, *275th Infantry Division*, which was deployed between La Fère and Guise and became caught in the cauldron, expressed even more blame.[80] In a post-war study for the Americans, Count Schwerin justified his decision:

> In the late afternoon, suddenly, there was an emergency: enemy tanks advancing from Buironfosse toward La Capelle—shortly after, fierce tank fire at the western edge of La Capelle. Enemy pushes from west into the town. In retrospect, this surprising event could be explained to the extent that in the afternoon, enemy armored forces surprised and overran the weak Oise defenses in the neighboring sector to the west, near Marly [these were probably units of the 47th Infantry Division—*Author*[81]], and afterwards pushed forward in a quick advance via Buironfosse toward La Capelle. Although the enemy was brought to a halt there, he got tanks into the town, where wild tank firing ensued. The entire position of the Division was untenably turned upside down in one swoop. At once, *Panzer-Grenadier Regiment 156* had to carefully attempt to pull out of its position if it did not want to be attacked in the flank or from the rear or be overrun. A detour north, which would have been desirable, was no longer possible because La Capelle was blocked. The regiment, therefore, retreated on its own toward the western edge of Fourmies. There, it consolidated in the evening and dug in during the night. The Division Staff's command post, which was exactly northwest of La Capelle, had to be cleared out head over heels. The staff was reassembled in Trélon, northeast of

Fourmies. For time being, enemy remained in La Capelle. This did not change the fact that the road to Avesnes was now open for him. *Panzer-Grenadier Regiment 60* near Hirson was in contact with the enemy and had already been attacked. *Panzer-Grenadier Regiment 156* in Fourmies had to be assembled during the night. The Division had been thrown out of its position by a surprise attack: a quick regrouping of the Division in the vicinity of Avesnes was no longer possible. In the moonlit night, the enemy at once pushed with strong forces toward Avesnes and in the morning occupied the town without a fight. The Division had neither the strength nor sufficient means for a counterattack. Thus, the enemy was successful with his breakthrough. The road to Brussels was open.

For the *116th Panzer Division,* the question now was whether it should try to gain contact with friendly forces to the west, thereby becoming caught in the huge encirclement in northern France, or if it should attempt to return to German soil together with the destroyed *SS* divisions that had escaped eastward toward the border of the *Reich.* A decision about this had to be reached immediately, because the rear echelon services of the Division near Mons were exactly in the path of the enemy's advance toward Brussels. They had to be transferred right away, either to the west into the cauldron, or to the east out of the cauldron. Commander *116th Panzer Division* decided to avoid the cauldron, and to lead this Division back to the *Reich.* He therefore ordered the immediate transfer of the rear echelon to the east across the Meuse. For this case, the Division engineer and the Division ordnance officer had already reconnoitered the area of Huy, where larger rearward supply depots existed. Orders for the *116th Panzer Division* were not available from any command post. Corps, Army, and Army Group radio stations no longer answered. All higher leadership ceased for the next several days. Obviously, the higher staffs themselves tried to get out of the threatening encirclement to the east.[82]

The adjutant of *Panzer-Grenadier Regiment 156* rendered the following report about the combat at La Capelle:

> The *1st Battalion* took up positions directly east of town, on the road to La Capelle–Hirson; the *2nd Battalion* on the southern edge of town, on both sides of the major road to Vervins. At the same time, the enemy moved toward La Capelle and in the afternoon attacked from the west. He directed his armored assault toward the open right flank of the regiment and concurrently attempted to prevent any movement on the ground by employing heavy fighter bomber support.
>
> *Major* Grollmann went to the most advanced units and by quick reorganization of the regiment, he foiled the accomplishment of the enemy's intent. Scattered units were brought up and redeployed in accordance with the regimental commander's orders. This is how the strong enemy assault could be halted.[83]

During the night of 1/2 September, the *116th Panzer Division* deployed along an arc from Fourmies via the hills north of Hirson up to a point just east of the town. The Division's line was unconnected to any other unit on the right, while there were still some flank security elements of an *SS* division to the left.[84]

At 1930 hours on the evening of 1 September, the commanding generals of *LXXIV, LVIII Panzer,* and *II SS-Panzer Corps* met at the *LXXIV Corps* command post northwest of Landrecies (16 kilometers west of Avesnes). Since they no longer had contact with *5th Panzer Army, "Group Straube"* was formed under the command of the most senior of them, *General der Infanterie* Straube from *LXXIV Corps.* Considering the enemy's advance from Arras to the northeast, from southwest toward Cambrai, and from the south toward Avesnes, the danger of encirclement was evident to all. It was decided to detour to the canal between Condé on the *Scheldt* and Mons.

Even this action could no longer change the situation. The marching infantry divisions were overtaken by the enemy.

The lid on the cauldron closed on 2 September. Only some mobile units were able to escape the encirclement, among them the three corps staffs and elements of the *9th* and *10th SS-Panzer Divisions.* The staff of *II SS-Panzer Corps* was able to make its way through, along side roads west of Mons, toward the north, and together with units of the *9th SS-Panzer Division* and scattered troops, established a weak security line in the sector from Senette to west of Nivelles (south of Brussels).[85]

With its right wing still on the lower Somme, *15th Army* returned to order and secured its left flank in a line from north of Amiens to Lille.[86] It was in danger of being pushed to the coast and encircled.

According to the description by Schwerin from the morning of 2 September, the situation for the *116th Panzer Division* was not favorable. Thereafter, the opponent pushed north via Avesnes (3d Armored Division), attacked the *116th Panzer Division* near Fourmies and Hirson (9th Infantry Division), and also threatened the Division's left flank. Early on 2 September, Schwerin decided to clear the salient formed by the Division's lines. His order was to break contact with the enemy and assemble in the area near Froid Chapelle, with security positions along the forest north of Chimay.[87]

At 1000 hours, *3d Battalion, Armored Artillery Regiment 146* evacuated its positions south of Trélon and marched toward Chimay. Halfway there, it had to take up position near Macon, and, with straggling paratroopers who arrived in that area, it had to defend against an enemy tank attack from the south which lasted until afternoon.[88] There is a very vivid report about this battle:

2 September 1944, *116th Panzer Division* withdrew from superior enemy forces into the area west and south of Trélon. It was to move into a new line of defense northeast of Trélon. The Trélon–Chimay road is of vital importance for this move. The *3d Battalion, Armored Artillery Regiment 146* is positioned far ahead in the march column. The commander, *Hauptmann* Schmeermann, is sitting in the first vehicle. When the spearhead of the battalion reaches Macon, the commander's car is unexpectedly shot at from the south by enemy tanks and armored cars. It is clear that the enemy intends to cut off the march route with a quick and unexpected armored thrust.

Hauptmann Schmeermann immediately realizes the importance of keeping the road clear. He quickly makes his decision, moves the leading gun into position and hits an enemy tank, immobilizing it and forcing the others to turn back. No sooner are two more guns ready to fire when the enemy, now with tanks and infantry, attacks the road from the hills south of Macon. Under the cover of tank fire, his infantry succeeds in entering the southern part of town and moving onto the road from there. In this moment of greatest danger, *Hauptmann* Schmeermann gathers a few soldiers and charges ahead of everyone toward the enemy infantrymen. In rough and bitter close combat, he forces the superior enemy to leave Macon toward south.

Shortly thereafter, the enemy attempts his next assault against the key road with strong infantry and 12 tanks. With 30 artillerymen deployed as infantrymen and the fire of the artillery battery, this assault is repelled also, thanks to the keen and superior leadership of *Hauptmann* Schmeermann. Time and again, the enemy attacks. For three hours, *Hauptmann* Schmeermann and his handful of men keep the march route open for the Division. Only when the last vehicle has passed to the east do *Hauptmann* Schmeermann and his units move to the new line of resistance, in accordance with orders." [89]

In the afternoon, the battalion displaced to Beaumont.[90] The Division staff first moved to Chimay. From there, it went on to Clermont (22 kilometers north of Chimay).[91]

When Count Schwerin arrived in the new area, he received a radio message from an *SS-Panzer* division to immediately come to its command post for a conference with the commanding general of *I SS-Panzer Corps*. Since liaison with the *II-SS Panzer Corps* had been interrupted by the enemy attack via Avesnes toward Mons, the *116th Panzer Division* had placed itself under the commanding general of *I SS-Panzer Corps, SS-Obergruppenführer* Keppler. He asked Count Schwerin if he and his Division could take over the northern sector of the corps area near Beaumont, so that the widely scattered remnants of the *1st SS-Panzer Division* in this area could be withdrawn and reunited with the *2nd* and *12th SS-Panzer Divisions*. Schwerin accepted this new command arrangement by the evening.[92]

On the evening of 2 September, the Division, therefore, occupied positions in a line ahead of Beaumont–Froidchapelle with *Panzer-Grenadier Regiment 156* to the right and *Panzer-Grenadier Regiment 60* to the left. It seems as though *Armored Reconnaissance Battalion 116* was led from the left to the right wing, and the next day, mainly deployed for reconnaissance toward the west and north.[93] *I SS-Panzer Corps* intended to conduct a delay to the Meuse, south of Namur. One of their subordinate units, the *347th Infantry Division,* was disposed along the Sambre between Charleroi (excl.) and Namur, as well as along the Meuse up to a point just south of Namur. Another of the corps' units, the *2nd Panzer Division,* was deployed at its left wing.[94]

The enemy attacked the *116th Panzer Division* before noon on 3 September. He was repelled near Beaumont, but penetrated south of there and pushed through to Vergnies.[95] The last battleworthy tank of *1st Battalion, Panzer Regiment 24* was bombed out of action near Beaumont.[96] Continuously fighting, the Division withdrew, first toward the forests northeast of Beaumont, then toward the line Thuillies (ten kilometers northeast of Beaumont)–Fontenelle, finally across the Heure to a line from south of Charleroi to Laneffe.[97] Its opponent was the 9th Infantry Division that had turned east against *I SS-Panzer Corps.*[98] The Division command post was first moved to Tarcienne and then to St. Gérard (16 kilometers southwest of Namur).[99] Left of the *116th,* the *2nd* and *12th SS-Panzer Divisions* retreated via Philippeville to Florennes and Givet.[100]

On 3 September, *5th Panzer Army* evidently established communications with its subordinated units again, except with *LVIII Panzer Corps.* At its right wing it formed *"Group Brandenberger."* Its staff was the salvaged units of *7th Army,* under command of *General der Panzertruppe* Brandenberger. The *LXXXI* and *LXXIV Corps* were subordinated to it. *5th Panzer Army* issued an order.

1. *5th Panzer Army* with subordinated *Group Brandenberger* closes off sector Pommeroeul Canal [this is the canal from Mons west to the *Scheldt—Author*] between Mons and Charleroi–Sambre–Meuse up to Charleville inclusive
2. Main effort *II SS-Panzer Corps* near Charleroi. Here, action *116th Panzer Division.*
3. . . .[101]

The intention of *5th Panzer Army* to close off the Pommeroeul Canal was already overtaken by events, because the enemy had reached Brussels. At best, one could block the canal from Brussels to Charleroi, and most likely not even there anymore. Due to this order, the *116th Panzer Division* was again subordinated to *II SS-Panzer Corps,* which, as already mentioned, after breaking out from the cauldron of Mons, arrived east of Nivelles. It hardly had any troops left and no liaison with the *116th Panzer Division.* The boundary between *I* and *II SS-Panzer Corps* was drawn by *5th Panzer Army* in such a manner that it would cross the Sambre east of Charleroi at the right wing of *347th Infantry Division.* So, the *116th Panzer Division* was assigned responsibility for a sector north of the Sambre and east of the canal toward the north, with the area of concentration from Charleroi, at its left wing.

The order probably reached the *116th Panzer Division* via *I SS-Panzer Corps* at the command post in St. Gérard in the evening of 3 September. At this point, as the Division was withdrawing, its front line stretched south from the vicinity of Charleroi. *Armored Reconnaissance Battalion 116* and the Division Headquarters Reconnaissance Platoon reconnoitered toward Charleroi and Châtelet, which was located east of it at the south bank of the Sambre, and found out that the population was in a high uproar, expecting the Americans. The reconnaissance patrols encountered barricades everywhere and were not able to enter Charleroi.[102] Lieutenant Bargstädt, from the Division Headquarters Reconnaissance Platoon, reported about his recon mission from Tarcienne to Châtelet.

On the morning of Sunday, 3 September in Châtelet, there were no longer any German soldiers in the town. As we drove in, all houses were already decorated with black-yellow-red flags in preparation for receiving the Americans. We tore down a flag, spread it out on the hood of our *Kübelwagen* and drove through the whole town to the cheers of the populace, who took us for an American advanced echelon. Our order to reconnoiter and determine the condition of the bridges across the Sambre was fulfilled in this rare and unusual way.[103]

After questioning, Bargstädt added to his report that the Sambre bridges were intact. This was also reported by the *I SS-Panzer Corps* in its daily report from 3 September.[104]

As a precaution, Count Schwerin sent his armored engineer battalion to Namur, to keep the river crossing open if necessary. Enemy tanks appeared in Charleroi in the evening, so when he received orders to cross over to the north bank of the Sambre there, he declined. Instead, he moved the Division via Namur to the north bank of the Sambre.[105] The original order still exists:

1. Enemy attacking from Avesnes to the north toward Brussels and to the northeast toward Charleroi, Namur, and the region to the south. Increase of civil insurrection has to be counted on. The intent of opponent will be to push to the northeast to take possession of undamaged Sambre and Meuse crossings.

2. Without stopping, *II SS-Panzer Corps* withdraws on the night of 3/4 September with the *347th Infantry Division* behind the Sambre, and the combat groups of the *SS* divisions behind the Meuse. [Should read "*I SS-Panzer Corps*"— *Author*]

3. *116th Panzer Division* disengages from the enemy during the night of 3/4 September, reaches north bank of the Sambre, and with its front toward the west, delays further advances to the east by the opponent.

4. The following withdraw:

   a) *Armored Reconnaissance Battalion 116* to advance via Namur to the line Gembloux–Mazy–Onoz–Moustier.

   b) *Panzer-Grenadier Regiment 60* across eastern Sambre bridge in Namur and assembles in area Meux–Lonzée–Beuzet–St. Denis.

   c) *Panzer-Grenadier Regiment 156* (Reinforced). (with subordinated elements of *Panzer Regiment 16* and *Panzerjäger Battalion 228*) crosses western Sambre bridge in Namur and assembles in area Isnes Sauvage–Bossière–Temploux–Suarlée.

   d) *Armored Engineer Battalion 675* remains in Namur at the disposal of the Division.

   e) *Armored Artillery Regiment 146* crosses western Sambre bridge in Namur and assembles in area La Bruyère–Bovesse–Rhisnes.

   f) Division Staff and *Armored Signal Battalion 228* crosses eastern Sambre bridge in Namur and assembles in the vicinity of Villes lez Heest–Warisoulx. . .

7. Withdrawal commences 2300 hours.

8. Instructions.

a) *Armored Reconnaissance Battalion 116* secures assembly of Division along creek flowing from Gembloux into the Sambre and reconnoiters up to line Brussels–Nivelles–Charleroi.

b) *Panzer-Grenadier* regiments assemble in their areas to facilitate commencement of motorized or dismounted march to the west or northwest.

c) *Armored Artillery Regiment 146* prepares with some elements to secure the assembly of the Division, while most move out toward northwest and west.

d) *Armored Engineer Battalion 675* in cooperation with *347th Infantry Division,* if it is available in proposed area, destroys all Sambre bridges west of Namur.[106]

The transfer of the Division went smoothly. On the morning of 4 September, it was in the area northwest of Namur. There, Count Schwerin issued the order to advance to the west to establish a security line northeast of Charleroi, between Marbais and Lambousart. Reconnaissance was to be conducted toward the line Löwen–Brussels–Nivelles–Charleroi.[107]

It is not quite clear if the order was followed completely. The artillery apparently remained in the area northwest of Namur and on 5 September occupied positions near Gembloux.[108] Evidently, the most forward units of the *116th Panzer Division* advanced up to Fleurus, while the right wing remained echeloned toward the rear.[109] After the war Count Schwerin wrote:

116th Panzer Division was supposed to enter Charleroi. It was an insane idea to put a motorized division into the completely-barricaded, major factory town. As could be predicted, it did not get there, because the enemy, guided by partisans, had already pushed into the city from the west. The infantry division had to rapidly bend back its exposed wing from the eastern suburbs to Fleurus.[110]

On 4 September, the *116th Panzer Division* and the *347th Infantry Division* were subordinated to *LXXXIV Corps*, commanded by *General der Infanterie* Straube. Its right boundary followed the edge of the town of Wavre. The Division received orders from *7th Army* to establish a blocking position between Wavre and Charleroi.[111] In the Army order of 4 September, which obviously was issued before the subordination of the two divisions, were these additional instructions:

All forces in the Wavre and Charleroi sector and those arriving will be subordinated to *LXXIV Corps.*

Withdrawing units, if they have weapons, are to be halted for redeployment. A continuous barrier with strongpoints along the main roads and crossings must be built again.[112]

The *347th Infantry Division,* under the command of *Generalleutnant* Trierenberg, deployed a reserve battalion behind its right wing, south of Fleurus, because the *116th Panzer Division* did not advance into Charleroi up to the Sambre and the canal to Mons.[113] In spite of urgent warnings by Schwerin, the *347th*'s commander allowed his forward-echeloned wing stand at the Sambre, north of Châtelet.[114] The Division Headquarters Reconnaissance Platoon of the *116th* engaged in a skirmish with the Resistance near Wavre and in the evening, assumed security positions in Corbais, southeast of Wavre.[115]

The British entered Antwerp on 4 September. The *15th Army* had to fall back to a bridgehead at the mouth of the *Scheldt* to establish liaison via Vlissingen, and to continue to block the entrance to Antwerp. By order of the *Wehrmacht Commander–Netherlands*, and later of *1st Parachute Army,* a defense line was established at the Albert Canal from Antwerp to the east.[116]

On 4 September, Headquarters, *7th Army* took over the whole sector (Mecheln–Charleville) of *5th Panzer Army*, whose staff and commander, together with those of *LVIII Panzer Corps*, were pulled out for other use.[117] The staff and commander of *II SS-Panzer Corps* were also pulled out to supervise the replenishment of the *2nd* and *116th Panzer*, and *9th SS* and *10th SS-Panzer Divisions* in cooperation with the *General of Panzer Troops–West*, in the vicinity of Eindhoven. The battleworthy units of these divisions were to remain in action, while the *1st SS, 2nd SS*, and *12th SS-Panzer Divisions* were to be transferred to the *Reich* for complete restoration.[118] These plans, however, were realized slowly, at least for the *116th Panzer Division*. The operations journal of *2nd Battalion* of *Armored Artillery Regiment 146* provides a few indications.[119] To begin, on 3 September, it was announced that the *9th SS* and *116th Panzer Divisions* were to receive 30 *Panzer IVs* each, near Lüttich.[120] Two days later, the *116th Panzer Division* took possession of 15 tanks; the other 15 are said to have fallen into enemy hands in Lüttich, by fault of the *SS* officer who wanted to "organize" [the American term would be "midnight requisition"—*Editor*] them for his own division.[121,122]

On 3 September, Hitler issued a new directive for battle conduct in the west. The first sentence reads:

> Our seriously depleted forces and the impossibility of quickly procuring sufficient reinforcements do not allow the determination of a line which can be held with certainty. Therefore, it is important to gain much time to establish and bring up new units, for the completion of the West Position [that is, the *Westwall,* or in Allied parlance, the "Siegfried Line"—*Editor*], and to destroy enemy forces with individual attacks.[123]

This directive again included the idea of a counterattack deep into the flank of the opponent, this time coming from the vicinity of Lorraine. It was launched in the middle of September with insufficient forces, and had only local significance. Our *1st Battalion, Panzer Regiment 16* was involved in the attack, in concert with *Panzer Brigade 111*.[124] After being equipped with Panthers in Grafenwöhr, the *1st Battalion* was subordinated to this brigade; after the battles in Lorraine were over, it turned over its tanks to the brigade and was again transferred to Grafenwöhr, to be reequipped with other Panthers.[125]

On 3 September, the troops were warned about the Resistance, which had orders to openly rebel as of 0400 on 4 September. They were to disrupt the withdrawal of German units in the line Dunkirk–Charleroi–Lüttich, as well as along the Meuse up to Dinant. They were also to prevent the destruction of bridges.[126] On 4 September, Model issued an appeal to the soldiers of the Western Army.[127] On this day, *General* Dr. Speidel was released by *General der Infanterie* Krebs, and the following day, *Generalfeldmarschall* von Rundstedt again took over Supreme Command in the West, while Model was reduced to the command of *Army Group B*.[128] *Generalleutnant* Westphal was assigned as Chief of Staff, *Supreme Command–West.*[129]

On 4 September, while the British pushed further toward the northeast, the First Army turned right. This army's divisions attacked according to the availability of their fuel supply. The VII Corps' 9th Infantry Division continued to attack south of the Sambre toward the Meuse, on both sides of Dinant. The already mentioned reinforced cavalry group served as flank security toward Charleville. The 3d Armored Division began to attack on 4 September from the area of Mons on both sides of the Sambre, followed by the 1st Infantry Division. After refueling, XIX Corps started to move, together with the 113th Cavalry Group, the 2nd Armored, and 30th Infantry Divisions to the left, behind the 3d Armored Division, with the left wing across the battlefield from Waterloo and Wavre toward Hasselt. The V Corps was pulled over to the right wing of the First Army to close the gap with the Third Army in the direction of Luxembourg–Bastogne. All operations suffered from supply shortages. The Third Army could barely advance.[130]

It was probably the 3d Armored Division which attacked in the morning of 5 September, south of the Sambre, as well as from Charleroi and the area to the north. The attack broke through the elements of the *116th Panzer* and *347th Infantry Divisions* defending between Fleurus and the Sambre, and overran the infantry that defended the Sambre. The *347th* suffered heavy losses of its infantry, as well as parts of its artillery. The Division tried to temporarily detain the enemy at the creek sector between Mazy and the Sambre, but *LXXIV Corps* had to fall back to the line Wavre–Namur. There was no stopping here either, because the enemy who seized Gembloux pushed further to the northeast even as he also drove southeast of Gembloux, up to St. Denis and Emines. Advancing south of the Sambre, the enemy entered Namur and thereby split the *347th Infantry Division*.[131] At 2030 hours, *Patrol Bargstädt* of the Division Headquarters Reconnaissance Platoon of the *116th Panzer Division* rendered the following report from the bend in the road four kilometers northeast of Namur, "At 1945 hours, Commander, *Security Regiment 16,* issued order to evacuate city because of threat of encirclement from north." He also reported the sounds of battle and moving armored vehicles southwest of his position, namely north of Namur.[132]

The command post of the *116th Panzer Division* was relocated to Branchon; at noon, the artillery was moved from Gembloux to Grand Leez; in the evening it was taken back to Taviers.[133] According to the entries on the Division operations map, on 5 September, the Division was disposed as follows: most of the Division was northeast of Gembloux, between Perwez and St. Germain; *Armored Reconnaissance Battalion 116* was further north, at the right wing.

On the morning of 6 September, the operations map showed the *116th Panzer Division* in its sector between Jodoigne and Eghezée.[134] On the right wing, the armored reconnaissance battalion was "taken back to Jodoigne because of heavy enemy pressure from the area south of Löwen."[135] In Jodoigne it established contact with *LXXXI Corps'* newly arrived *Panzer Brigade 105* that was near Tienen. In the middle of the Division, *Panzer-Grenadier Regiment 60* was deployed between Huppaye and Ramillies–Offus. *Panzer-Grenadier Regiment 156,* with two tanks, was deployed on the left wing. These were, besides three more employed to protect the deep left flank, the only tanks to be found on the operations map.[136] The *347th Infantry Division* bordered the *116th* to the south as far as the Meuse, but its units south of Namur were fragmented.

The next day, 6 September, turned out to be a "crazy day" with "constant fighting around strongpoints."[137] Northeast of Namur, the Division Headquarters Reconnaissance Platoon ran unexpectedly into an enemy armored spearhead and sustained considerable casualties. The commander of the platoon, *Oberleutnant* von Löbbecke, was wounded and captured. *Leutnant* Bargstädt succeeded him.[138]

Reports from *Army Group B* also indicate the crisis of this day. In the north, the enemy advanced as far as Hasselt. An attack by *Panzer Brigade 105* into its flank showed no effect.[139] In the south, the *347th Infantry Division* was penetrated; their division command post was attacked by tanks. The *347th's* staff took refuge with the *116th Panzer Division,* which moved its command post back during the day via Blehen to Pousset, near Waremme.[140]

Based on the markings on the operations map, *Panzer-Grenadier Regiment 60* had to withstand the main enemy pressure. Penetrations could be discerned up to Jauche and Merdorp. *Panzer-Grenadier Regiment 156* was threatened deep in its rear by the enemy forces which broke through in the vicinity of the *347th Infantry Division*; consequently, *Regiment 156* reoriented its defenses toward the south.[141] The noon report of *Army Group B* read, "Armored units of the *116th Panzer Division* have orders to counterattack."[142] The evening report continued to spin the yarn, "Thus, counterattack by armored units of *116th Panzer Division* is under way. Some enemy tanks destroyed."[143] Even in *Supreme Command–West's* morning report of 7 September, the story of this counterattack was still floating around, although by now, the front line was already about eight kilometers further back.[144] With the few tanks available, a counterattack that would merit this attention could hardly have been carried out.

On 6 September, elements of the 3d Armored Division had advanced south of the Meuse and seized Huy with its bridges undamaged; the way to Lüttich was open. Thus, *7th Army* moved back during the night of 6/7 September to the line Hasselt–St.Truiden–Huy–Rochefort–Bouillon and intended to further yield toward the Meuse, between Maastricht and Lüttich.[145] On the morning of 7 September, the *116th Panzer Division* secured the sector between the Lüttich–Tienen railroad near Wezeren, up to about ten kilometers north of Huy. That day, according to the operations map, 16 tanks were deployed, in two groups, behind the middle sector. In mid-morning, they were ordered to the south wing, which remained opened after the collapse of the *347th Infantry Division*.[146] The *347th* again suffered badly, and no longer possessed any significant combat strength. Within two days, a newly-arrived division had been deployed under unfortunate conditions, beaten, and dispersed.

On 6 September, at 1410 hours, Gersdorff, the Chief of Staff of *7th Army*, proposed to Army Group to relieve the commander of the *116th Panzer Division*.[147] There is no reason entered in the Army Group journal. It cannot be established if the *LXXIV Corps* Commander had a complaint. After the war, Generals Brandenberger (Commander, *7th Army*) and Trierenberg (Commander, *347th Infantry Division*), complained about the behavior of the *116th Panzer Division* in their reports for the US Army Historical Division.[148] Both criticized the withdrawal of the *116th Panzer Division* during the night of 3/4 September via Namur instead of Charleroi and the positioning of the Division northeast of Charleroi, which freed the crossings over the Sambre and over the Charleroi canal to the enemy. As we have seen, Count Schwerin could bring up important reasons for his decisions. Brandenberger wrote the following in his report:

> Under its then-commander, *Generalleutnant* Count Schwerin, *116th Panzer Division* was, nevertheless, a very self-willed unit. The first proof of this was its behavior contrary to orders near Charleroi; more would follow until his relief on 14 September. . . . The . . . report of *Generalleutnant* Count Schwerin, . . . because of many untrue and biased statements, gave cause for this and also later assessments about the behavior of the *116th Panzer Division*.[149]

Almost all of these reports that were more or less written from memory unfortunately contain untrue statements, including the one Brandenberger wrote about the behavior of the *116th Panzer Division* on 5 and 6 September. They do not correlate with the events recorded on the operations maps of the *116th Panzer Division,* the journal of *Army Group B,* or the journal of *Supreme Command–West.* A quotation from Count Schwerin's report [again, written in the third person—*Editor*] may indicate the attitude with which he led his Division in those days:

> The general withdrawal across the western border of the *Reich* was in process and inevitable. Even the troops wanted to go home. To the German soldier, the war had finally become a tale of woe. He had no more hope, wanted to be led home and be done with it. The Commander, *116th Panzer Division* knew his men. His thoughts did not differ from theirs, and basically all front commanders thought this way. But the highest German leadership thought differently. They still had unbelievable illusions. The Commander, *116th Panzer Division* knew these people's way of

thinking. He knew they would continue this hopeless battle in the *Reich*'s territory. Only the front-line troops were in a position to prevent this lunacy. The Commander, *116th Panzer Division* did not intend to disappoint the instinctively-correct sentiments of his soldiers. He had no intentions of continuing the war in the *Reich*'s territory and to deliver the homeland to destruction. He was determined to act accordingly. To do this, however, he first had to lead his Division back to the *Reich*. It was part of him, and he would never allow it to be destroyed by measures of senseless leadership.[150]

The higher authorities could have sensed this opinion and it must have led to disagreements.

The collapse of the *347th Infantry Division* allowed the 3d Armored Division an almost unobstructed advance through the Meuse Valley toward Lüttich. Only a lack of fuel kept the American tanks near Huy until the afternoon of 9 September.[151] The journal of *Army Group B* describes a shocking picture of the lack of power of the German command to stop the opponent in the Meuse Valley.[152] At 1300 hours on 7 September, Krebs sent a message to Gersdorff that forbade the planned withdrawal of *7th Army* to the Meuse–Ourthe line, and required that the Meuse Valley, west of Lüttich, to be blocked effectively. An hour and a half later, Gersdorff reported to Krebs that the *347th Infantry Division* was destroyed, that the enemy had pushed forward north of Huy, and that there were no forces available to block the Meuse Valley. He added that *LXXIV Corps* had orders to stop.

At 1830 hours, Gersdorff reported enemy tanks south of Lüttich in front of Chaudfontaine and suggested removing *Panzer Brigade 105* from *LXXXI Corps,* sending it into the area south of Lüttich, and, north of the town, withdrawing to the Meuse. Model permitted the displacement of this brigade, but prohibited a withdrawal behind the Meuse. Gersdorff reported at 1850 hours that the *116th Panzer Division* had orders to fight back toward Lüttich and to establish a defensive line in front of the city, but 20 minutes later, he had to report that the Division stood between Tongern and northwest of Lüttich. He proposed establishing a defensive front with it on both sides of Lüttich, but considered the possibility of it questionable, since the enemy was already there.

The evening report of *Army Group B* from 7 September reads that the *116th Panzer Division* was "surrounded by overwhelming enemy forces from the the south and thrown back toward the line Waremme–Remicourt."[153] At 1930 hours, the Division was subordinated to *LXXXI Corps*, which, as of 4 September, was led by *Generalleutnant* Schack; it received orders to block between Tongern and Lüttich.[154] Continuing to the north from Tongern to southeast of Diepenbeek two weak combat groups of *LXXXI Corps* (*353d Infantry Division* and *Group Fiebig*) secured positions, while two more combat groups occupied the "Meuse Position" (lines along the Albert Canal, then the Meuse) between Maastricht and Lüttich. The corps was allowed to fall back to the Meuse only if forced to by the enemy.

The British forced a bridgehead across the Albert Canal north of Hasselt.[155] According to the operations map, the *116th Panzer Division* stood in a curve between Tongern (exclusive) and the Meuse, north of Lüttich. The armored reconnaissance battalion was moved from the right wing to the left wing. The Division command post was in Glons initially, and later in Loën, northwest of Viseé.[156] Upon its subordination to Headquarters *LXXXI Corps*, the battle strength of the Division was reported as follows:

Two *Panzer-Grenadier* regiments with 300 men each
A *Panzer* regiment with 12 tanks
Four light and two heavy field howitzers, one 105mm field gun
Three Russian howitzers[157]

The daily report of *Supreme Command–West* mentioned a total of 18 tanks and two heavy antitank guns.[158]

Count Schwerin sent the following written report to *LXXXI Corps* on the morning of 8 September.

116th Panzer Division and *Group Fiebig* execute exchange of river banks on 8 September until dawn. The Division takes up position on the east bank of the Meuse at the southern edge of Argenteau–southern edge of St. Remy–southern edge of Trembleu, in such a way that expected enemy attack out of Lüttich along the east bank of the Meuse can be repelled.

Reason:

1. Enemy marched with combined arms columns on both river bank roads from the south toward Lüttich and at 1800 hours the spearhead stood at the southeastern exit of town. The southern and western exits of Lüttich were reported heavily occupied by enemy. Battalion 6/66 evidently was pulled out of the city with the order to guard west and north exits.

2. A reconnaissance troop of armored combat vehicles sent to Lüttich encountered heavy enemy tank force toward 0100 hours in Rocourt, four kilometers north of Lüttich. Our armored reconnaissance troop (eight tanks) was scattered.

3. It was established that at 2300 hours all Meuse bridges between Lüttich and Maastricht (including both) were demolished. Therefore, only the Visé bridge will be available for the Division and *Group Fiebig* for change of river banks and in the course of tomorrow, the bridge will be under enemy artillery fire.

4. At 2400 hours, a duty officer sent to *Panzer Brigade 105* reported the brigade had moved out, and that at his arrival, this brigade's *Panzer-Grenadier* battalion was in process of moving out of Tongern. As a result of *Panzer Brigade 105*'s displacement, the rear of *116th Panzer Division* is totally void of battleworthy troops of our own and cannot be covered by our own forces.

5. After *Panzer Brigade 105* moved out, no combat capability can any longer be attributed to *Group Fiebig* anymore, since it was a conglomeration of stragglers.

Signed, Count von Schwerin"[159]

This report put complete facts in front of the Corps command. At 0825 hours, the corps reported via radio accordingly to *7th Army*:

> Heavy enemy tank forces on both river bank roads advancing from south toward Lüttich and unconfirmed to east toward Herve and Verviers. *116th Panzer Division* and *Group Fiebig* ahead of strong enemy push with bulk on east bank. *116th* bridgehead position Visé. All bridges in sector of corps demolished, except crossings near Visé.[160]

At 1000 hours, Gersdorff reported similarly to Army Group and further stated that the enemy was advancing south of Lüttich, but that his attempt to enter the city from the south could be parried.[161] After that, Krebs ordered to review the possibility of an attack by the *116th Panzer Division* and *Panzer Brigade 105* against the enemy advancing to the east, south of Lüttich. The brigade was now subordinated to *LXXIV Corps*, which controlled the area south of Lüttich; it reached the vicinity of Herve, but got stuck there without fuel.

When the last units of the *116th Panzer Division* had crossed the Meuse near Visé and had blown up the bridges, enemy tanks appeared on the west side.[162] Of its own accord, the Division reconnoitered east of the Meuse toward the south. At 1240 hours on 8 September, the Division reported to corps that as of 1000 hours, the line Wandre–Herve was free of the enemy, but by noon, Lüttich was encircled. The enemy received strong support from partisans and forced the battle commandant with his defenders to pull back into Fort Chartreuse.[163] At 1415 hours, the *116th Panzer Division* received orders via radio and liaison officer from *LXXXI Corps* to throw back the "enemy via Vesdre toward the south" and to establish contact with the battle commander of Lüttich. This was supposed to block the Vesdre sector.[164] The "corps order for the defense at the Meuse" (1730 hours) added that the Division was to remain in the vicinity of Battice–Herve, "so that it could prevent an advance of the opponent from the vicinity of Lüttich toward the east and northeast with an attack."[165] The *275th* and *49th Infantry Divisions* were to defend along the Meuse, from south of Maastricht to Lüttich (inclusive). The battle commandant of Lüttich, *Generalmajor* Bock von Wülfingen, was subordinated to the *49th Infantry Division*. This division had already withdrawn its left wing from Lüttich toward the north.

At 1915 hours, the armored combat group of the *116th Panzer Division* attacked to relieve the garrison under battle commander Lüttich. The *LXXXI Corps* journal reports about its assault:

> By 2056 hours it reached Beyne, four kilometers east of Lüttich. Since the Commander of the *116th Panzer Division* received a report from four military policemen that *General* von Bock broke out and was in Thimister, he suspended the attack and took the combat group back to Micheroux to secure the assembly area of the Division. The reports about the battle to free *Combat Group Lüttich* did not correspond with the facts. *General* von Bock was attacked at Fort Chartreuse from all

sides with the support of tanks and at 2125 hours, reported through *Hauptmann* Count Hardenberg in Aachen that he could no longer hold on and was negotiating surrender terms with American officers."[166]

To stop the attack based on such unconfirmed reports may have been premature, but the situation as a whole offered little prospect for success. While the armored combat group was approaching Lüttich, the commandant of the town was negotiating capitulation.[167] After the war, *Major* Stephan, leader of the armored combat group of the *116th Panzer Division* (*Armored Reconnaissance Battalion 116* reinforced by several tanks) reported about the thrust toward Lüttich:

> After thorough verbal directive by the Division Commander and corresponding organization, the combat group attacked Lüttich from Battice via Herve–Micheroux–Fléron–Beyne. The enemy was already in possession of the towns before Lüttich and allowed himself to be celebrated as liberator by the Belgian population. . . . It was growing dark, the towns we drove through were decorated with garlands. Left and right of the road were American combat vehicles adorned all over with flowers. All soldiers were ordered to open fire with all weapons if enemy resistance was encountered. Combat group had just reached the little town of Fléron when we received rifle and machine-gun fire. The tank in front answered by firing a shot. In the midst of the evening's victory frenzy in the village, the acoustical effects of this shot by themselves had such an effect that the street and the little village square looked like they were scrubbed clean. All windows were immediately closed and blacked out; the flower-decorated American combat vehicles were abandoned; and nothing moved. Only the clatter of the tank tracks and the roar of the engines interrupted the eerie silence.
>
> The spearhead of the combat group had already passed through Fléron, when the commander of the armored reconnaissance battalion received the radio message, "Cease operation, encircled German troops have broken out!" To turn around in the narrow streets of the village was not possible. In an open area, outside the village, the spearhead executed an about face, just as if it were on a parade ground. With engines at full force, we reached our starting point with only insignificant enemy resistance. As booty, the Reconnaissance Company brought back twelve flower-decked American jeeps.[168]

At 2130 hours on 8 September, immediately after his last phone conversation with Aachen, the battle commandant of Lüttich capitulated. At 0615 hours the next morning, the corps reported that the *116th Panzer Division* was moving into the area Battice–Herve. On 8 and 9 September, the Division command post was in Hagelstein near Aubel. On 9 September, it occupied an advanced command post for some time. The armored combat group of the Division remained arrayed in echelons near Micheroux, while the artillery moved into positions northeast of Battice.[169] Due to lack of fuel, *Panzer Brigade 105* was almost immobile and scattered in the area of Verviers. South of the Vesdre, two weak division combat groups of *LXXIV Corps* secured both sides of Louveigné, connecting southward along the Ourthe to the *I SS-Panzer Corps*.[170]

On 8 September, Model submitted a very candid evaluation of the *7th Army*'s situation and urgently demanded reinforcements to avoid a gap of operational consequences [that is, a gap which could effect the entire campaign—*Editor*]. Only about seven or eight battalions occupied 120 kilometers of the *Westwall* behind the *7th Army*.[171] Rundstedt forwarded Model's evaluation to Jodl. He no longer considered a battle to gain time possible and suggested a withdrawal to the *Westwall*. But Hitler decided, "The *7th Army* should fight defensively ahead of the *Westwall* and defend the Meuse and the canal west of Maastricht as long as possible. The speed of detour of *I SS-Panzer Corps* will be determined by the enemy...."[172]

He promised 20 *Luftwaffe* battalions for the *Westwall*. On the previous day, Rundstedt already sent a clear evaluation of the situation to Keitel. His evaluation of our troops is informative:

> All our forces are all involved in battle, badly bruised, partly burned out. They lack artillery and antitank weapons. No reserves worthy of the term are available. The numerical superiority of enemy tanks compared to ours is indisputable. At this time, about 100 tanks are combat ready in *Army Group B*. Enemy air force dominates the battle area and the lines of communication deep into the rear echelon. The pressure of the enemy toward Lüttich (Meuse Valley) with a clear direction of advance via Aachen toward the industrial region of Rhineland-Westphalia has developed into a serious danger. The immediate addition of strong forces (five to ten divisions), as requested several times, seems an urgent necessity to me. . . . In agreement with *Generalfeldmarschall* Model, I recognize (near Aachen) the acute danger to the rear of the *Westwall* connecting toward the south. . . . Our task is to fight with the available forces to gain time, to make the western positions and the *Westwall* completely capable for defense. . . . A time period of six weeks is forecast for the completion of the western positions. This time, therefore, has to be won through combat.[173]

On 9 September, Headquarters, *7th Army* ordered the *116th Panzer Division* to reestablish contact between the Meuse and the Ourthe positions at the confluence of the Vesdre and Ourthe, and to mop up the area north of the Vesdre, while *Panzer Brigade 105* advanced south of the Vesdre toward the Ourthe.[174] In view of the situation, this order could not be executed, especially since according to a report by Schwerin, the brigade is "scattered all over the globe" and suffered from lack of fuel.[175] The opponent took the initiative and attacked from the area south of Soumagne. At 1030 hours, about 60 tanks advanced to Grand-Rechain (three kilometers northwest Verviers), while ten armored reconnaissance vehicles entered Verviers.[176]

At 1230 hours, corps headquarters ordered the *116th Panzer Division* to prevent the enemy tank advance by attacking. *Panzer Brigade 105*, deployed for this mission, did not succeed because shortly thereafter, 20 enemy tanks had already pushed through Dison further to the northeast. The *116th Panzer Division* moved its tanks from Micheroux to the threatened east wing.[177] When the *Ia* reported this to corps headquarters at 1510 hours, he received orders "to block the roads from Verviers to Aachen with the Division and attack the enemy to prevent it from advancing further."[178] This order, on one hand to block, on the other to attack, meant an expansion of the Division up to the Verviers–Eupen road. It could only be resolved with a simultaneous subordination of *Panzer Brigade 105,* which had not been ordered. The *49th Infantry Division,* which was attacked on the road along the bank of the Meuse, received orders to hold on to the right wing at the river, and take back the front in such a way as to gain contact with the *116th Panzer Division* near Battice.[179]

At 1705 hours, the Commander of the *116th Panzer Division* reported his intent. "*Panzer-Grenadier Regiment 156* on hills south and east of Battice, *Panzer-Grenadier Regiment 60* with available armored vehicles first toward La Saute (five kilometers east of Battice) to attack from there in a general southerly direction."[180]

But even before the dispatch, the report had to be amended. "Proposed move probably already superseded by radio message 1710 hours." The radio message from 1710 hours said that enemy tanks were reported in Andrimont and Vilstain at 1600 hours. Obviously, Schwerin's plan was not realized.

The *LXXXI Corps* daily report provides an account of these battles of the *116th Panzer Division*:

> Despite strong pressures toward the east and northeast, as well as heavy deployment of fighter bombers, the continuously reinforcing opponent did not succeed in gaining ground along the road Lüttich–Aachen against combat group of *116th Panzer Division.*[181]

The daily report of the Division complemented this:

> Toward 1800 hours, the opponent, supported by 30 to 40 fighter bombers, attacked from Soumagne to the northeast with tanks and infantry. Two enemy tanks were destroyed by anti-tank guns. Attacks by fighter bombers caused heavy losses to our tanks and motorized vehicles.[182]

Panzer Brigade 105 was subordinated to the *116th Panzer Division* at 2050 hours,[183] thereby, the area of the Division's responsibility widened considerably to the south, although its exact extent cannot be determined. The Division daily report indicates that it had contact neither to the right nor to the left. Toward morning, contact with the *49th Infantry Division* on the right was reestablished. The situation on the left remained opaque, even after subordination of *Panzer Brigade 105. LXXIV Corps* consisted only of pitiful remnants and attempted to establish a "blocking position" between Pepinster and Spa, but during the night, the enemy had already pushed southeast toward the Hohe Venn, to a line west of Jalhay–Spa.[184] With this, the way to Eupen was open to the enemy. Under the command of *Oberst* Müller, commander of the *116th Panzer Division* at Argentan, a combat group from the *9th Panzer Division* came to close this gap. Neither it nor *Assault Gun Brigade 394* and its 30 assault guns (which, according to orders from noon on 9 September, the *116th Panzer Division* was supposed to "search for" in Düren and "subordinate.") were able to attack until 11 September.[185,186]

Personnel replacements arrived at the *116th Panzer Division* on 8 September. *March Battalion 524,* with 485 NCOs and enlisted men for the *Panzer-Grenadier* regiments waited in Aachen to be picked up and incorporated into the Division.[187] *Army Anti-Aircraft Battalion 960* had already been subordinated, and on 9 September, *Radio-Controlled Panzer Company 319,* which was able to fight its way out of Lüttich in time, was also subordinated. It possessed three combat-ready assault guns and 16 explosive carriers which, for the most part, were immobile.[188] These explosive carriers ("Goliaths") were later deployed during the battle of Aachen. After the war, *Oberstleutnant* Zander reported that the *2nd Battalion* of *Panzer-Grenadier Regiment 60* guided them toward the barracks (Gallwitz and Lützow Kasernes) that were being used as strongpoints by the Americans, but that no noteworthy successes were achieved.[189]

After a quiet night on 10 September, the Division adjusted its posture along the line Battice–La Saute.[190] It bent back its right wing to achieve contact with the *49th Infantry Division,* back to Froidthier. From there, the front line ran to the southeast via La Saute to Villers. The command post was moved back to Montzen.[191] Thus, the enemy could occupy the area around Battice without a fight. At 1018 hours, the following report from the *116th Panzer Division* arrived at *LXXXI Corps,* "0720 hours Chaneux [southeast Battice—*Author*], occupied by enemy. Strong tank noise west of Thimister. Expecting enemy attack today, direction Clermont."[192]

At 1230 hours, the opponent attacked La Saute, and, after heavy fighting, drove *Panzer-Grenadier Regiment 60* back by about three kilometers to Hockelbach. He also attacked *Panzer Brigade 105,* took Goé, but was repelled near Limbourg.[193] The *49th Infantry Division* was pushed back along the Meuse toward Argenteau. During the whole day, fighter bombers were very active. By the evening, *LXXXI Corps* stood along the line Meuse to Agenteau–Mortroux–Clermont–Limbourg.[194] Weak points included the areas north of Limbourg and near Goé, from whence a road through the Vesdre Valley leads to Eupen. The *116th Panzer Division* reported its observation of the enemy, "Opponent preparing in area west of Limbourg–Forêt Domaniale de Grunhault [four kilometers north-northwest of Limbourg—*Author*] for advance toward Henri Chapelle–Welkenraedt and Eupen.[195]

During the night, the Division provided warning with a follow-up report:

Continuous additions of tanks, vehicles, and infantry were observed. (Large clouds of dust). For the defense of its positions, the front units of its infantry dug in. These were secured by tanks placed in between. Enemy artillery discovered and attacked our own artillery. Our artillery forced to change position tonight. During afternoon and evening hours, the opponent adjusted fire toward all dominating points of terrain behind the sector of the Division. (The report from our artillery says that these are of a caliber up to 200mm). The whole day, fighter bomber activity, artillery, and observation aircraft activity. Division counts on supported attack as planned on 11 September.[196]

As its intention for the next day, the Division reported the closing of the roads Battice–Aachen, Limbourg–Aachen, and Eupen–Aachen.[197] The corps' order announced the engagement of the *9th Panzer Division* on 11 September. It should "be moved quickly into the vicinity of Eupen" and "by attacking, prevent an enemy advance to the northeast." *Panzer Brigade 105* was to be subordinated to it upon arrival.[198] Army Group and *Supreme Command–West* reckoned on the following, "The American army group to attempt a breakthrough in the direction of Aachen–Cologne on 11 September, as well as the English army group opposite *1st Parachute Army* wanting to gain operational freedom toward the east and north."[199]

The English attacked from the bridgehead north of Hasselt and broke through the German front in several places. Now, Army Group feared an enemy airborne landing in the Netherlands and took defensive measures. Signals intelligence indicated clues. On the evening of 10 September, when *7th Army* reported that its intention for 11 September was to push the enemy back toward Lüttich by attacking with the *116th* and *9th Panzer Divisions,* it requested the subordination of one combat group of the *9th SS-Panzer Division* that was being kept in readiness by Army Group. Model let it be known that he did not want a large attack using armored units. He would agree to smaller undertakings as a delay tactic.[200] With this, the brakes were finally applied to the illusory plans for attacks with insufficient forces.

The next day, 11 September 1944, threatened to become a critical one, even if the combat group of the *9th Panzer Division* arrived. For the time being, it only brought along a *Panzer-Grenadier* battalion, one artillery battalion, and one armored engineer company. At 0600 hours *Panzer Brigade 105* was subordinated to it, and the *9th Panzer Division* assumed control in its sector. At 0930 hours, the *Panzer-Grenadiers* occupied positions in the right sector and established contact with the *116th Panzer Division. Panzer Brigade 105* was assembled around Limbourg. In the forests south and southwest of Eupen, *Combat Group Bockhoff* was deployed to close off the roads. At 1010 hours, it reported all forest roads as impassable for all vehicles. Shortly before, the enemy started the attack on Limbourg. It advanced only timidly, so that *Panzer Brigade 105* was able to hold its position.[201] Toward noon, the enemy advanced north and south Limbourg, bypassing it. The *116th Panzer Division* rendered the following report about the northern advance, which in the end covered the whole frontline of the Division, and also included the *49th Infantry Division:*

Enemy attack at 1100 hours with strongest fighter bomber support and strong infantry and armored forces from the south toward Hockelbach, counted a total of more than 100 armored vehicles, including 30 tanks. Our own troops were thrown back toward the northern edge of Hockelbach and later toward Henri Chapelle. Opponent pushed forward with tanks from Hockelbach toward the northwest to road Clermont–Henri Chapelle and fired from elevated positions at the static units in the deep flank of *Panzer-Grenadier Regiments 60* and *156*. The Division, therefore, was withdrawn. . . . At 1615 hours, opponent attacked along the Battice–Aubel road with 12 tanks and mounted infantry toward the north, crossed the Berwinne sector and presently pushed further north. 1800 hours enemy before Aubel. Own troops were pushed back toward the north. In view of the threat to the deep flank by the enemy's penetration up to Herbesthal, *Armored Reconnaissance Battalion 116* with one company was brought into position at the intersection 1.5 kilometers southeast of Montzen with the three remaining battle worthy tanks, while Henri–Chapelle was secured by . . . *Assault Gun Brigade 394*. 1850 hours enemy advanced west of Clermont–Henri Chapelle road, passing northwest of Henri Chapelle and at present is feeling its way north of Henri Chapelle, advancing further north.[202]

At 1902 hours, there was an addition to this report, "Enemy pushes west of Henri Chapelle toward the northeast and from Lontzen toward northwest. Danger of encirclement."[203]

Since the afternoon, the command post was in Bleiberg (Plombières) and by evening was taken back to Lemiers.

South of Limbourg, in a surprise advance, the enemy reached Eupen and at 1300 hours entered the town from the south. Thus, *Panzer Brigade 105* was in danger of being surrounded in Limbourg and fell back toward the northeast. In the evening, the remainder of the combat group from *9th Panzer Division* formed a line of defense between Eynatten and Raeren.[204] In the evening, the enemy advanced through the gap between the *116th* southeast of Montzen and the *9th Panzer Division* near Eynatten, up to Hergenrath and Hauset. The *49th Infantry Division* was also driven out of its positions and forced back to the line Visé–Mortroux–west of Aubel.[205] On this 11 September, the 1st Infantry Division positioned itself to the left of the 3d Armored Division, to secure the left flank of VII Corps. In addition, the first units of XIX Corps came into view, with the 113th Cavalry Group on the right bank of the Meuse pushing north, and the 30th Infantry Division on the left river bank.[206]

LXXXI Corps reported its intention to "restructure the combat groups for defense" along the line Eijsden (on the Meuse)–Sint Martens-Voeren–Hombourg–Eynatten–Raeren, and if necessary, "to attack and seize this line at its left wing."[207]

The following order was issued to the *116th Panzer Division,* "On the night of 11/12 September, Division restructures for defense along the line Hombourg–

Montzen–Astenet (exclusive). If necessary, gain line by fighting. Main effort near main roads to Aachen."[208]

In view of the deterioration of the *116th*'s forces, but mostly due to the situation of the *9th Panzer Division,* an attack was wishful thinking. Corps, therefore, indeed sensibly requested permission at the same time to withdraw to the *Westwall.* However, this permission was not granted by *7th Army,* which found support on this issue from Army Group: At 2300 hours, Krebs informed Gersdorff that it was his opinion that forces should stay ahead of the *Westwall* for as long as possible. This was understandable since it was only on the night 9/10 September that Hitler gave the district leader of Cologne the order to evacuation Aachen and Monschau. *Supreme Command–West* was concerned that evacuation of civilians in border areas could jeopardize the logistical support of the troops.[209]

At noon of 11 September, the units stationed in the *Westwall* were alerted by *LXXXI Corps* through the staff of *353d Infantry Division,* which controlled the different units deployed at the *Westwall.* On the day before, the divisions fighting forward of the *Westwall* had already received orders to prepare to occupy positions in the *Westwall.* They were to reconnoiter the sectors of the *Westwall* in which they presumably would be deployed; for the *116th* and *9th Panzer Divisions,* this meant the sector between the Schnee-Berg and the left border of the corps near Roetgen.[210]

On the morning of 12 September, the *116th Panzer Division* once again occupied positions in front of the *Westwall,* north of the Hombourg–Moresnet railroad line, and then north of the Geul creek. The Division found that all crossings across the creek between Moresnet and Hauset had been destroyed. They searched, therefore, for the contact point with the *9th Panzer Division* north of the creek near Eynatten. At 0810 hours, the Division reported occupation of its positions to the Corps headquarters. The armored reconnaissance battalion was deployed at the left wing with its main effort near Neu-Moresnet. The Division reported further that avenues of approach for withdrawing to the *Westwall* were narrowed because of road barricades; only the road via Gemmenich to Aachen would be usable. According to a report from 1155 hours, the Division was still searching for a contact on the right with the *49th Infantry Division* and on the left to the *9th Panzer Division.*[211]

Around this time, the enemy attacked along the entire corps front, from Visé to Mouland, from Remersdaal to Epen, along the front of the *116th* near Hombourg and Neu-Moresnet, and toward the *9th Panzer Division* near Eynatten. By evening, he was able to advance along the Meuse up to Breust. Near the *49th Infantry Division,* he reached Slenaken and Epen and pushed back the *116th* to a line along the Geul creek from Moresnet to the northwest. In the evening, counterattacks by the *116th* were aimed at breakthroughs near Bleiberg and Völkerich. Eynatten and Raeren were lost in the *9th Panzer Division* sector.[212] At 1535 hours, Combat Command B of the 3d Armored Division occupied Roetgen, the first town in the *Reich,* without a fight.[213] Enemy pressure on the *LXXIV Corps* slackened.

At 1800 hours, *LXXXI Corps* issued an order to the *9th* and *116th Panzer Divisions* to "take over immediately . . . the *Westwall* positions in their sectors."[214] The changeover of responsibility for the sector was to be agreed upon at once with the *353d Infantry Division* and be reported by 2100 hours. The battalions emplaced in the position were subordinated to the Division. As late as 1000 hours, *Oberst i.G.* Wiese, *LXXXI Corps* Chief of Staff of *LXXXI* informed *Major i.G.* Wolf, "Moving into *Westwall* only by order of Corps and possibly late."[215]

At 2230 hours, Corps headquarters issued a combined "corps order for conduct of battle in the Maastricht–Aachen defensive position and the *Westwall*," in which paragraph 2 stated, "*LXXXI Corps* continues to delay the approach of the enemy toward the blocking and *Westwall* positions with strong rear guards."[216]

Orders were issued to establish the main battle line along the line Maastricht–Kanne–Margraten–Gulpen–Schnee-Berg–and on to the *Westwall*. The *275th* and *49th Infantry Divisions,* as well as *116th* and *9th Panzer Divisions,* remained committed. The two infantry divisions had to defend the obstacles between the Meuse and the *Westwall*, while the two *Panzer* divisions were only required to defend in the *Westwall*. This arrangement did not make much sense, but was necessary because of the previous unit deployments.

The mission for the *116th Panzer Division* was as follows:

> The *116th Panzer Division* defends Aachen. All units in the Aachen battle commandant's sector, including the *353d Infantry* and the *526th Reserve Division,* will be subordinated to it. The armored elements of the Division are only to be withdrawn behind the *Westwall* in the event of pressure from overwhelming enemy force. It is hereby important for the Division to ensure that special units erect obstacles in time for their immediate withdrawal toward the *Westwall*. After falling back behind the *Westwall, Assault Gun Brigade 394* is to assemble in the area of Brand and be kept in readiness as corps reserve, so that it could be deployed at any time for counterattacks in the *116th Panzer Division* sector, as well as that of the *9th Panzer Division.*

The following was also ordered:

> 5. Strong advance command posts are to be left near the enemy by all Divisions. To a large extent, they delay an enemy approach to the main battle line. Equip them with heavy weapons and antitank guns.

The advanced command posts of the *116th Panzer Division* were to remain in place between Gemmenich-West and Hauset-West; those of the *9th Panzer* in the line Hauset–Raeren-East–Roetgen-West. The orders for the artillery and the obstacles were as follows:

> 6. *Artillery Group Aachen (Artillery Regiment 116* [*sic*], *Artillery Regiment 353, Flak-Group Aachen* under commander *Artillery Regiment 116* [*sic*], *Oberst* Pean) has the mission, in close coordination with the *49th Infantry Division,* the *116th Panzer Division,* and the *9th Panzer Division* to prepare and call for block-

ing fires and combined firing ahead of the main battle line. It is very important to form concentrations for the combined firing in coordination with the antitank and barrier plans where the focus of the defense will probably be.

7. The obstacles in the main battle line are to be reinforced. Streets, roads, and lanes are to be blocked against combat vehicles with all kinds of improvised means. Barrier material may be procured from the corps engineer.

The paragraph for the artillery sounds remarkable. On a map dated 14 September, only three batteries are indicated in the sector of the *116th Panzer Division*. Near Aachen, the *Westwall* consisted of two lines: the weaker one in front ran along the *Reich*'s border, while north of Würselen, the one behind it turned toward the southeast, toward Stolberg and again joined the front line south of Losheim. The staff of the *353d Infantry Division* was in charge of the sector of *LXXXI Corps* that was in the second *Westwall* position, which was occupied by three militia training (*Landesschützenausbildungs*) battalions.

Still during the night of 12/13 September, the 1st Battalion, 16th Infantry Regiment of the 1st Infantry Division pushed through the gap between the *116th* and *9th Panzer Divisions* from the south into the Aachen town forest. It seized Bunker 161 near the Brandenberg hill in the sector of *Security Battalion 453*. A counterattack launched by the Aachen battle commandant failed. Even repeating it under control of the *116th Panzer Division* did not achieve any success.[217] Thus, the fight for the border of the *Reich* had begun; the battle for Aachen had commenced for the *116th Panzer Division*.

All in all, the situation was somewhat firmed up. The *15th Army* held its bridgehead at the mouth of the *Scheldt* and thereby closed the entrance to the important port of Antwerp until the beginning of November. At the Albert and Meuse–*Scheldt* Canal, the *1st Parachute Army* defended between Antwerp and Maastricht. The English were in possession of a bridge across the Meuse–*Scheldt* Canal, on the road from Hasselt to Eindhoven. The *LXXXI Corps* situation between the Meuse and Aachen is known. The corps of *7th Army* connecting from the south had moved into the *Westwall* or was moving in without strong enemy pressure. Further south in the *Westwall* stood *Army Group G*'s *1st Army,* opposite the Luxembourg border and along the Moselle to south of Metz. *Army Group G*'s other field army, the *19th,* made it back quite well from the Mediterranean and stood in a curve before the Burgundian Gate. [Although, in the process, *19th Army* lost 88,900 soldiers captured between the Riviera and the foothills of the Vosges—*Editor.*] West of the Vosges, the *5th Panzer Army* was assembled to push into the flank of the Third Army, which on 11 September established a loose contact near Dijon with the forces approaching from the Mediterranean and forestalled the attack of *5th Panzer Army* to the point that it broke up into individual skirmishes. Nevertheless, the formation of a continuous front ahead of the Vosges Mountains and the Gate of Burgundy up to the Swiss border was achieved.[218]

The attack of the Western Powers was exhausted.[219] The distances to the bases became too great, and the capacity of the ports was not sufficient — this is due to the success of the destruction of the harbors and the defense of several port cities as "fortresses" over a long period of time. The English and the Americans left part of their heavy artillery and anti-aircraft guns behind the Seine to be able to move the combat troops. They further brought all the available trucks together and used them to transport fuel from Normandy to the front, using one-way roads that were marked by signs with a big, red circle. About 95 percent of all supplies still traveled along the Calvados coast. At its peak, the "Red Ball Express" used 6,000 trucks in 132 convoys that were continuously on the move to get supplies to the front.

The difficulties were increased by Eisenhower's not quite energetic leadership. He did order the main effort of the offensive to be made by the English and the First Army, but he tolerated Patton's advance toward the Rhine and moved the V Corps to the right wing of First Army in the gap toward the Third Army. Consequently, the battle strength of the First Army consisted of the VII Corps and parts of XIX Corps, and they, too, were often short of fuel. The belief was that the German Army was finally defeated and one could afford such an eccentric conduct of war.

In contrast, the distances for the German Army became shorter; personnel replacements, supplies, as well as reinforcements now arrived more quickly. By using the *Westwall* and the line along the canal, it was possible to round up the troops once more, even though the *Westwall* did not at all offer the support that the returning units hoped for.[220] It had deteriorated over the past several years; the weapons had been removed; and the barbed wire obstacles taken down. Sources for electricity were partially rotted, cable ducts were flooded, and ventilation equipment was defective. The anti-tank positions were originally built for 37mm anti-tank guns, and the 75mm guns did not fit into them. The dragons' teeth were no longer sufficient as tank obstacles. Fields of fire had to be cleared. No construction staff for the fortifications was present that could hand over the installations; sometimes there were no keys. There were no maps, no diagrams, no provisions. Even records of prepared demolitions in outpost areas were not handed over. Mines were missing and several bunkers were used for other purposes. Preparations for improvements began too late. On 10 September, "167,000 workers of all kinds were working to reinforce the *Westwall* and to improve the Western Position."[221] Even though they worked with great idealism, the results were minimal due to inexperienced supervision.

A total of seven weeks were slated for the improvements, but the enemy allowed only two weeks. Despite everything, the *Westwall* gave the troops stability. It was manned by security forces that had no great battle value or heavy arms, and in the course of time were usually absorbed by the field troops that moved into their sectors. The *Westwall* also had a braking effect on the opponent, who probably overestimated it. A combination of many factors brought the enemy to a halt. "The miracle of the *Westwall*" happened. Once more, the German soldier was ready to defend his *Vaterland*. The request for an unconditional capitulation and what became known of the Morgenthau Plan strengthened his will to resist. Even the Eastern Front had consolidated. On the other hand, the almost unlimited enemy air supremacy over the battle area, as well as over the homeland, severely burdened the soldiers. It particularly troubled the numerous Rhinelanders and Westphalians of the *116th Panzer Division,* who worried greatly about their loved ones at home. Nevertheless, all in all, the hunted troops regained composure under energetic leadership, and offered increasing resistance at the *Reich*'s border against an opponent that was no longer prepared for it. German soldiers now defended an area closer to home and still hoped, in spite of many doubts, for a fortunate turn, to which they had to contribute with perseverance.

Chapter 7

Aachen

The observers from the Western Powers who evaluated the enemy's situation judged the strength of the German resistance in the West during the first days of September as poor. On 15 September, the staff of the First Army was still hoping to seize the bridges across the Rhine undamaged. On 10 September, the Army received orders from the Commander, 12th Army Group, Lieutenant General Bradley, to cross the Rhine at Koblenz, Bonn, and Cologne. Bonn was the assigned objective for VII Corps that was attacking Aachen, and Cologne was assigned to XIX Corps following to the left. Since the First Army Commander, Lieutenant General Hodges, expected increasing resistance, he wanted to replenish his ammunition supply as well as procure necessary fuel. This could not be completed before 15 September. Therefore, Hodges ordered a two-day pause, but during that time, an intensive reconnaissance was to be conducted.

The VII Corps commander, Major General Collins, was not very pleased with the order to pause, and on 11 September he asked for permission to advance combat reconnaissance elements as far as possible through the border fortifications. If that proved to be easy, Collins would first break into a limited area in the *Westwall* before replenishing his supplies. On 11 September, he ordered two combat commands of the 3d Armored Division to move across the open area south of Aachen toward Stolberg. The division still had 70 to 75 battleworthy tanks out of the original 232. The advance was to be accompanied on the right and left each by an infantry regiment of the 9th and 1st Infantry Divisions, respectively, but only with one battalion leading. If penetrating the *Westwall* turned out to be easy, the 1st Infantry Division was to take Aachen, the 3d Armored Division was to push through via Eschweiler toward Düren, and the 9th Infantry Division was to mop up the connecting forest area.

The successes of 12 September were not as great as had been hoped. It was not possible to break into the *Westwall* at any point, except for one battalion of the 1st Infantry Division in the forest south of Aachen. The immediate counterattack of 80 German soldiers at that point did not encourage a further advance during the night. Therefore, Collins decided not to take Aachen, but only the dominating hill country in front of the town, thereby protecting his left flank and tying down the German forces.

On 13 September, he continued the attack on Stolberg with "reconnaissance in force," now with the whole 3d Armored Division and with the 16th Infantry Regiment of the 1st Infantry Division echeloned to the left rear. The objective for the latter was the hills east of Aachen, while the other two regiments of the 1st

Infantry Division were to encircle Aachen from the south and southwest (minus one battalion that was attached to 3d Armored Division). The 9th Infantry Division, to the right of the 3d Armored Division, could not take part in the attack before 14 September.

Commencing 11 September, XIX Corps took part in the battles at the Meuse [called the "Maas" in the Netherlands—*Editor*], to throw back the right wing of *LXXXI Corps* across the Belgian/Dutch border to the Geul sector. The corps established bridgeheads there, and on 14 September seized Maastricht. However, due to concerns about its left flank while fighting at the Geul River, the 30th Infantry Division did not advance any further for two days.

Between its right wing near Gulpen and the left wing of VII Corps, southwest of Aachen, the 113th Cavalry Group conducted security operations without noticeable activity. Only by 16 September, when the 2d Armored Division closed up from the west, did they start to attack again and reached the *Westwall* on 17 and 18 September. The attack on the *Westwall* north of Aachen was supposed to take place on 20 September. It was, however, newly postponed out of fear of a threat to the flanks. During the British attack toward Arnhem, in conjunction with the airborne landings of 17 September, a gap developed between the British and Americans, so the attack was delayed indefinitely.

On this day, the VII Corps' attack on Stolberg was halted, about which there will be more to report. Until 26 September, only the 9th Infantry Division attempted to gain ground in the Hürtgen Forest and suffered considerable casualties. Even V Corps, which was advancing toward Koblenz, was not able to achieve any better results and basically remained stalled in front of the *Westwall*.

With this, the whole First Army came to a standstill.[1] It is from this perspective that the events in and around Aachen in the days after 12 September must be viewed. As reported, *LXXXI Corps* ordered the *9th* and *116th Panzer Division*s to occupy and assume control of their sectors in the *Westwall* on 12 September at 1800 hours, with "immediate effect," and demanded a report of completion by 2100 hours. It seems that this was not carried out, because the journal of the *9th Panzer Division* mentions that as of 0800 hours on 13 September, 0800 hours, and a report by the commander of *116th Panzer Division* names 0600 as the time of receipt of the order.[2,3]

The battle commandant of Aachen, *Oberst* von Osterroht, along with all the troops Division's sector, was subordinated to the *116th Panzer Division*. The troops he brought with him included *Infantry Training Battalion 453* (*Grenadierersatz und Ausbildungs Battalion 453*) and *Fortress-MG Battalion 34*. He divided the latter and gave it to *Battalion 453*, because it [*Bn 453*] only had two machine guns per company. The combat value of both battalions was small.[4] The battle commandant also had command of a field artillery battery, namely *3d Battery, Motorized Artillery Regiment 76*, which was subordinated to *3d Battalion, Armored Artillery Regiment 146*. The Division's own artillery thereby possessed the strength of one battalion with three batteries.[5]

On 12 September, the battle commandant received one more reinforcement: it consisted of two *Luftwaffe* fortress battalions. These battalions were assembled from all kinds of *Luftwaffe* specialists, but had no infantry training. They had no vehicles and no field kitchens. *Battalion VIII* moved to the sector of *9th Panzer Division*, and Osterroht placed *Battalion XIX* in a defensive line behind the most threatened part of the *Westwall*. As mentioned in the previous chapter, it was involved in the counterattack, which took place on the morning of 13 September against the enemy that broke in at the Branden-Berg (Hill 355). First, the attack moved forward, but later failed, because a of break in communications with the anti-aircraft artillery, which was operating as field artillery.[6] The enemy retained two bunkers (161 and 166), as well as the Pelzer tower, an observatory on the highest point of the city forest. From there, he had excellent opportunity to observe the city of Aachen. In spite of it all, the counterattacks conducted with such inadequate means achieved great success. As we learned from the opponent's view, they spoiled the Americans' plan to attack the city itself, and compelled them to push by to the south of it.

Besides these forces, there was *Anti-Aircraft Group Aachen* with several anti-aircraft units and batteries deployed as field artillery, which were to be coordinated and integrated into operations by the battle commandant. The instructions for cooperation also applied to the *116th Panzer Division,* after taking control in its sector. This cooperation did not function without friction. Therefore, on 15 September, the anti-aircraft group was subordinated to the Division.[7] In the course of 12 September, the battle commandant personally established liaison with the Commander of the *116th Panzer Division.* But it seems that clear discussions regarding how the battle would be conducted after the assumption of control by the *116th Panzer Division* did not take place. On the morning of 13 September, liaison between the Division and the battle commandant sometimes did not work out.[8]

During the night of 12/13 September, the *116th Panzer Division* conducted security operations ahead of the *Westwall,* in accordance with the instructions given to the armored units in the corps orders. At dawn, the Division was pulled out and assembled in the Richterich–Würselen area.[9] This operation cannot be considered fortunate. During the night, the Division was not in front of its future sector, but far out at the right wing. Then, along a narrow front line, it displaced back via Vaals and Vaalserquartier to an area ten kilometers behind the position that it was trusted to defend. This left the defense completely up to the battle commandant of Aachen with his inadequate forces, although the Division had already been ordered to assume responsibility for the sector commencing on the evening of 12 September or, at the latest, 0600 hours on 13 September.

The barriers that had been erected in the sector of the *Westwall* in the Aachen city forest caused the detour around the right wing of the sector. The enemy, however, found ways around them, and during the night had already broken into the *Westwall,* passing the defenses of the *116th Panzer Division* by advancing east of them through the woods. From a tactical point of view, it is difficult to understand why the Division's leadership led the whole Division so far back and did not at least position units behind their sector of the *Westwall,* where their soldiers could strengthen the occupiers' backbones. For example, artillery forward observers could certainly have rendered important assistance if they were dispatched early enough to the defending units. The artillery was emplaced north of Aachen, from whence it could operate.[10]

After the war, *Generalleutnant* Count von Schwerin substantiated his actions as follows [Still writing in the third person—*Editor*]:

> After the heavy battles of the previous days, the Commander of the *116th Panzer Division* by all means had to restructure his units; conduct maintenance of weapons and tanks; integrate replacements; and for once, give the men a chance to sleep. Additionally, the difficult conditions of the terrain within and south of the city had to be cleared up and the march route through the heavily-bombarded streets had to be determined. With permission of the corps, the Division Commander first designated an assembly area for the whole Division north of Aachen, where the troops were to reorganize on the morning of 9 September. During this time, the necessary reconnaissance was to be conducted within and south of Aachen.[11]

As reported earlier, the *9th* and *116th Panzer Divisions* had already received orders on 10 September to prepare to assume tactical control in their sectors and to reconnoiter. Surely, the heavy fighting on 11 Sepember caused some problems for such preparations, but they cannot be used as an excuse for the fact that nothing happened, since 12 September was a relatively quiet day for the *116th Panzer Division*, and it was not in such disarray that it absolutely had to be reorganized. After the war, the *7th Army* Commander, *General* Brandenberger expressed his strong criticism about *Generalleutenant* Count von Schwerin's report.[12]

At 1115 hours on 13 September, the battle commandant of Aachen reported directly to *LXXXI Corps* about the situation on his southern front. Accordingly, the enemy reinforced. With infantry and 13 tanks, the enemy stood by the captured bunkers at the Branden-Berg. An additional 25 tanks were reported advancing on the road from Bildchen to the northeast.[13] Now, corps headquarters ordered the *116th Panzer Division* to "clear out" the "penetration near Branden-Berg" using "all means."[14]

Upon receipt of this order, the units were alerted and brought forward. At 1718 hours, the *Ia* of *LXXXI Corps* conveyed to *Major i.G.* Wolf, the *Ia* of the *116th Panzer Division*, a *Führer* order with the following contents, "In the event of enemy penetration of Aachen, every house is to be defended. A withdrawal, such as from the southern edge to the northern edge of the city, will not happen."[15]

With this, the leaders in the West were tied down. Any thought of surrendering the city and falling back to the second, stronger *Westwall* line, meant disobedience.

After the war, *Generaloberst* Jodl, Chief of the *Wehrmacht* Operations Staff, wrote about the view of *OKW*.[16] Aachen did not have any special operational significance, but it was the first German city to be attacked. To the troops, the people, and the opponent, its defense to the last was to serve as a shining example of the tenacity with which we would fight for our homeland. This corresponded to Hitler's opinion in this critical situation. On 31 August 1944, he declared:

> We will defend ourselves, if necessary even at the Rhine. It is of no concern. We will, under all circumstances, fight until, as Frederick the Great once said, one of our damned opponents will get tired of fighting and until we have peace to secure the life of the German nation for the next 50 or [100] years.[17]

Unfortunately, the situation in the German *Reich* in WWII was more serious than that of Frederick the Great after he lost the battle of Kunersdorf during the Seven Years' War. After that battle, due to the death of the Russian Empress, Elisabeth, in 1762, the alliance against Prussia fell apart. After Hitler's successful campaign in France, the British rejected his peace offer. The Western Powers insisted on unconditional surrender and did not want to make peace with Hitler. Unfortunately, Hitler apparently did not make use of possibilities which were perhaps offered to reach a special peace with Russia.[18] Still, many Germans harbored similar hopes for a decay of the enemy coalition, and in spite of all setbacks, found in this hope a strengthening of their will to persevere over and over again. At that time, most people still would not believe that Hitler was playing a game of chance. In mid-September, the press exhorted the German people the following, under the headline "He who will live, fights!"

> We are confronted with a new phase of the war. In it, the enemy will learn that he will break his teeth on the Germans. This phase will also show what sacrifices of men and materiel the English and Americans are ready to make in the end, only to deliver Europe to the Soviets. The German people, with clear understanding of today's situation and the possibilities offered therein, will at this point waver for not one moment and will do everything the national fight for life requires."[19]

Anyone who today might think that such words were without effect is mistaken. They touched everyone's honor and brought inspiration for one more great effort. Any boldly-expressed doubts were dealt with in a Draconian manner, especially after realization of 20 July.

Now let's return to the Division. On 13 September, its daily report was as follows:

> Penetration into Branden-Berg on 13 September closed off by battle commandant. During the day, opponent moved new forces into this area, but remained quiet until evening. At dawn on 13 September, *116th Panzer Division* pulled out ahead of main battle line and assembled in area Richterich–Würselen, attacked point of enemy breach at 1600. Objective of the attack to mop up the attack on Branden-Berg

[should probably mean "the breach"—*Author*]. Reports about progress of attack not yet available.[20]

Further, it was reported that three *Panzer IVs,* two Panthers, and two assault guns were ready for action. At 2010 hours, *Major i.G.* Wolf reported to corps, "Enemy attacked our own counterattack. Division tries to close off along line Linzenshäuschen–Grindel–Branden-Berg. One battalion reinforced by assault guns will be positioned behind the bunkers that are no longer firing."[21]

With this, the enemy attack through the Aachen city forest widened eastward, up to the Eupen road. But at 2235 hours, the Division could report that it pushed the enemy (tanks and infantry) which advanced up to Hirtzpley (one kilometer north of the border) back to the Grenzhof; it also regained bunkers 52 and 53, which had earlier been seized by the enemy.[22] *Panzer-Grenadier Regiment 156* was deployed to the right, *Panzer-Grenadier Regiment 60* to the left. At the left wing, *Armored Reconnaissance Battalion 116* was to reconnoiter at Roetgen and maintain contact with the *9th Panzer Division.* The Aachen–Lüttich railroad marked the boundary between the two regiments.[23]

It is not all clear if stronger units of the Division had already entered the fighting on 13 September. The *2d Battalion* of *Panzer-Grenadier Regiment 60* probably fought in the city forest along the road to Eupen and were able to repel the opponent. A security post of its *8th Company* was emplaced at the "Green Oak" forester's station on the road to Lichtenbusch.[24] The *1st Battalion* reconnoitered toward Brand, found the little village free of the enemy, and left patrols. It established a strong anti-tank defense on the Aachen–Brand road (Route 258). During the night of 12/13 September and into the following day, the Division command post was in the Rahe castle, north of Aachen. Besides this, the Division had an advanced command post near the main railroad station.[25] At 1600 hours on 14 September, the Division command post was moved into the Paustenbach villa in Würselen, on Krefelder Street.[26]

On 13 September, the *9th Panzer Division,* in contact on the left, was hit by the enemy's main thrust and fell into serious trouble. The enemy pushed from Roetgen northeast toward Zweifall and in the afternoon, toward Kornelimünster. The *9th Panzer Division* destroyed 26 enemy tanks. In the evening, it received permission to fall back to the second *Westwall* position in the Stolberg–Zweifall sector. A dangerous gap developed between *116th* and *9th Panzer Divisions.* In the afternoon, the *116th* had to transfer 50 percent of *Assault Gun Brigade 394* to the *9th Panzer Division.*[27] West of Aachen, deployment of the last reserves was able to only poorly close a gap between the *275th* and *49th Infantry Divisions,* northwest of Gulpen. The Maastricht bridgehead was penetrated. Enemy tanks stood before the city and on the right bank of the Maas, they were already in behind the city. A request by *LXXXI Corps* for permission to give up the bridgehead was turned down. The city was lost during the night of 13/14 September.[28]

The *7th Army*'s evaluation of the situation in the evening of 13 September, which was sent *verbatim* via Army Group and *Supreme Command–West* to *OKW,* was worded very pessimistically. The only glimmer of hope seemed to be the

12th Infantry Division, which was due to arrive by train. If the enemy were to attack energetically along the whole corps front, then the encirclement of Aachen was hardly avoidable.[29]

As already mentioned, the 30th Infantry Division and the 113th Cavalry Group halted their attack west of Aachen on 14 September for two days. This gave the *275th* and *49th Infantry Divisions* a chance to consolidate and regroup. In the morning hours of 14 September, the enemy reconnoitered southwest and south of Aachen along the roads from Lüttich and Eupen toward Aachen. Following this, the enemy attacked across a broad front with strong infantry forces, supported by violent artillery fire. In several places, the bunker line was penetrated, and the pillboxes themselves were bypassed. In the manner of strike troops [*"Stosstruppen,"* the specially organized and trained German units employing infiltration and close assault tactics in the later stages of the First World War— *Editor*] platoons, using smoke and flamethrowers against the sides and rear of the pillboxes, they destroyed them one by one. The tanks followed the infantry to support and reinforce their attack on the bunkers. Evidently, the Americans quickly adjusted to the new conditions of combat against fortifications.

At 1340 hours, *Generalleutnant* Count Schwerin reported to Corps that all attempts to recapture the line of bunkers had failed, since armor support and effective artillery observation were impossible in the dense forest. The Division desired to maintain its current line, which ran from the right wing at the Schnee-Berg (north of Vaals) in the *Westwall* to south of Vaalserquartier, and from there along the northern edge of the forest to the road to Eupen, and further to the Beverbach, southeast of today's forest cemetery.[30,31] At 1500 hours, *Major i.G.* Wolf expressed hope to the *LXXXI Corps Ia* that the danger of a breakthrough on 14 September would be eliminated, if Linzenshäuschen, on the road to Eupen, could be held.[32]

The enemy did not break through to the town because he did not continue to attack. Nevertheless, the situation developed dramatically toward evening. The Division permitted the battle commandant and his *Infantry Training Battalion 453* to withdraw the scattered units in the first *Westwall* position in the city forest to the *Panzer-Grenadier* regiments' position prepared in depth north of the forest. This led to misunderstandings. At 2000 hours, units of this battalion and *Fortress Machine Gun Battalion 34* encountered the Commanding General of *LXXXI Corps, Generalleutnant* Schack, southeast of Würselen. *Major i.G.* Wolf reported to *LXXXI Corps* that the Commander of *Battalion 453* had believed he should fall back to the second *Westwall* position. *Generalleutnant* Schack reported to Commander *7th Army*:

> The disengagements . . . were caused by the displacement of the units in that area of *Anti-Aircraft Group Aachen.* The latter had orders to assemble at the Weiden airfield, even though the corps, in answer to a question in this case by the commander of the group, . . . explicitly ordered that the batteries were to remain in their positions, since a fall-back during the present battle situation was impossible.[33]

Far more serious than this breakdown in Aachen was the further development with the *9th Panzer Division,* as well as at the left wing of the *116th.* The whole might of the attack by the reinforced 3d Armored Division fell on the *9th.* By late morning, Kornelimünster and Breinig had already been lost; in the afternoon, the enemy pushed into the main position of the *Westwall* near Zweifall and seized four bunkers. He also succeeded in penetrating the line near Vicht, and Mausbach was attacked. South of Büsbach, however, the enemy was brought to a halt after the destruction of several tanks. Other enemy units advanced via Brand up to Eilendorf and Rothe Erde. The 16th Infantry Regiment of the 1st Infantry Division, following behind tanks to the left, marched north of what is today's *Autobahn* to the northeast toward Eilendorf.[34] The *116th Panzer Division* daily report reads, "At present, opponent marches between Bever-Bach and Lintert, three kilometers west-southwest of Brand, toward the north, into the deep flank of *Panzer-Grenadier Regiment 60. Armored Reconnaissance Battalion 116* is deployed to secure the flanks on both sides of Route 258, southeast of the forest."[35]

Moreover, the corps commander personally ordered the *Westwall* occupation units that he had encountered detouring toward Würselen to counterattack against the enemy forces that had broken through near Rothe Erde. He also ordered the anti-aircraft units, which had detoured toward Weiden, to support them. Further, at 2145 hours, he ordered all energetic officers of the *116th*'s staff to reestablish the situation there. These countermeasures succeeded in at least establishing a new front line during the night along the embankment of the Aachen—Düren railroad. Deployed in it were *Armored Reconnaissance Battalion 116,* which had been pushed back to that area, and the battle commandant's units that had been moved up by the corps commander.[36]

In the course of 14 September, the *Panzer-Grenadier* Regiments assumed control of the battle commandant's units that were still deployed in their sectors; on the right, *Panzer-Grenadier Regiment 156* occupied the sector from the Division's right boundary near the Schnee-Berg (inclusive) up to the Aachen–Lüttich railroad line. This included the following: two companies of *Infantry Training Battalion 453* in the *Westwall* from the Schnee-Berg up to south of Vaalserquartier, then, in the alternate positions of the *1st Battalion,* from about the western cemetery to Lüttich street, and *2d Battalion* up to the Ronheide railroad station. The *1st Battalion, Panzer Grenadier Regiment 60* was pulled over to the regiment's right wing. It now stood exactly south of Aachen, on both sides of Eupener street. *Regiment 60's 2d Battalion* linked up south of Burtscheid up to about Route 258. *Armored Reconnaissance Battalion 116* secured the left wing, as mentioned earlier.[37]

On the evening of 14 September, the biggest danger was at the border between the *116th* and *9th Panzer Divisions,* between Eilendorf and Stolberg. An accumulation of at least 200 vehicles of all kinds was observed in the vicinity of Kornelimünster, and the enemy was continuously reinforced.[38] At noon on 14 September, *Generalfeldmarschall* Model appeared at the corps command post and from there, telephoned Krebs. He described the situation around Aachen as dangerous and requested reinforcements, lest the loss of the city be risked.[39] Around the same time, during an evaluation at noon in the *Führer* headquarters, Hitler said, "Hold the *Westwall* or go down with the *Westwall*."[40] Rundstedt issued a corresponding order to hold the *Westwall*.[41]

At 1740 hours, *LXXXI Corps* ordered the staff of the *353d Infantry Division* to transfer the second *Westwall* position, including the militia battalions in it, to the *116th* and *9th Panzer Divisions*, respectively. The *9th* was already fighting for the second position, between Büsbach and Zweifall, and it was only a matter of time before the enemy appeared ahead of the second position, between Büsbach and Verlautenheide. The boundary between the *116th* and *9th Panzer Divisions* remained unchanged, from the northwest edge of Stolberg to the northwestern edge of Brand (both towns in the sector of the *9th Panzer Division*).[42]

Generalleutnant Count von Schwerin was relieved of his post on the evening of 14 September. *Oberst* Voigtsberger assumed command of the Division, while *Major* Zander, who just returned from the field hospital, took command of *Panzer-Grenadier Regiment 60*, and *Hauptmann* Nagel took its *1st Battalion*.[43,44] *Oberst* Bayer, the new commander of *Panzer Regiment 16*, arrived on 11 September.[45] At first, he did not have much to command. It is not clearly explicable who was responsible for that [Schwerin's] relief. It was probably arranged by Model during his visit to the corps command post.

How did this come about? To understand this development, one has to look back. We already learned in the previous chapters about Schwerin's attitude toward Hitler, toward National Socialism, and to the continuation of the war. We also covered the disagreements regarding tactical conduct of battle, which led to Schwerin's relief in Normandy, and which motivated the Commander of *7th Army* to request it anew on 6 September from Army Group. Most likely, the Division Commander would not have been removed from his troops in this critical situation if there had not been another special reason for this measure to be taken.

During the retreat through France and Belgium, Schwerin was already thinking about how he should behave if and when the war moved into the homeland. The *Ic* of the Division, *Hauptmann der Reserve* Dr. Holtermann, was a special confidant of Count Schwerin and his legal counsel. After the war he wrote:

> When, in late summer 1944, the *116th Panzer Division* approached the German border after the Seine catastrophe and during the retreat through northern France and Belgium, military defeat was sealed and the war hopelessly lost. The Division Commander, *General* Count von Schwerin, assessed the situation true to the principles of his Prussian education for the General Staff, soberly and clearly. . . .
>
> A unique brotherhood-in-arms existed between the Division Commander and his soldiers, one which was based on personal trust and which reached from the youngest *Panzer-Grenadier* to the highest-ranking commander. The soldiers of the Division knew that "their" general would not demand senseless bloodshed of them. All that mattered to him now was to preserve dignity and to see that the honor of

the German soldier remained immaculate. From many conversations, I knew that the fate of his men and the misery of the German civilians had for a long time already filled the Division Commander with burning concern.

For this reason, I was not surprised when, in the early days of September 1944, shortly after crossing into Belgium, the Division Commander told me of his decision not to continue the war on German soil, but rather to send his soldiers home when they reached the German frontier. To me, the *General* never made a secret about his thoughts regarding the war and the authorities of the Party, and that he considered the highest leadership of the *Wehrmacht* to be criminal. . . .

After revealing his decision, the *General* asked me what the commanders in the Division would say if he disclosed this decision to them. I answered that I believed that some of the commanders would accept his decision unconditionally, but that some of the others would have misgivings. Shortly thereafter, I received instructions to meet all commanders at once at their command posts and prepare them for the fact that the Division Commander would soon ask them for their opinion regarding his decision. The reaction of the commanders corresponded with my presumption: Not one of them thought for a moment to oppose the *General*'s decision, much less to betray him. The considerations raised by the commanders referred, without exception, to the serious question of whether a division commander would have the authority to relieve them from their oath. . . .

General von Schwerin was not a loyal Party follower of orders and surely not an easy-going subordinate. Although he naturally understood that obedience was a Prussian state principle, as well as the first of all military virtues, he still believed in Moltke's words, "But by us the man stands above the principle!" Count Schwerin stuck with his men—who loved him—and with his homeland, which he wanted to spare senseless sacrifices and complete destruction!

Some of the commanders raised predictable questions, in particular doubts about whether all military means to protect the homeland had been exhausted. After all, there had always been talk about the well-manned and well equipped *Westwall*, which could facilitate the build-up of an effective defensive front and the manufacture of new-style secret weapons. When I reported this to him, the *General* became pensive for a moment. He then told me that in view of the upcoming decisions, it was at this point difficult for him to even momentarily do without my presence in his immediate proximity, but that the commanders' qualms of conscience must not fade away without being heard. I was to therefore, immediately drive to Germany, taking along wireless equipment so that he could reach me any time, and find out right then and there what the *Westwall* was all about, how it was armed, equipped and manned, and what kind of secret weapons there were.

With these instructions, I left Villers lez Heest in the morning of 5 September. By 6/7 September, I was already able to report from reliable and well-informed sources.

1. The *Westwall*, neglected since 1940, was not manned at all. Two quickly-formed divisions consisting of militia and furlough battalions [literally, units comprised

of soldiers on leave who were impressed into new, *ad hoc* organizations—
Editor] were supposed to be headed to it, one of which had already been hit by
enemy air attacks during its march.

2. The *Westwall* was neither armed nor equipped. There were 2,000 anti-aircraft
   guns of an older type expected, but they had not yet reached their destinations.
3. There are new types of missiles and truly interesting weapons with promising
   effects, but there is no secret weapon of sensational or war-deciding importance.

These reports that I forwarded to the Division Commander by officer couriers
were made known in the memorable conference of the commanders, which took
place on 8 September 1944, probably either in Obsinnich Castle or in
Pietersvoeren.[46]

After the war, Count Schwerin reported about this conference [Again in the third
person—*Editor*]:

> The Commander of the *116th Panzer Division* hoped his dead-tired Division would
> get a few days of rest, protected by the wide Maas barrier. In the evening, he called
> the commanders of the Division to the Division's staff quarters for a discussion
> about the situation. . . . He wanted to calmly prepare his commanders for the task
> that would befall the Division after crossing the border of the *Reich*. . . . The rea-
> sons why the highest Army Command wanted to continue fighting in the homeland
> were explained to the officers, and it was further explained that this had led to the
> complete catastrophe and absolute destruction of our Fatherland. It was strictly up
> to the conduct of the soldier at the front if these suicidal and insane policies were
> actually to be carried out or not. The Commander of the *116th Panzer Division*
> unequivocally stated that he considered these politics criminal, that he would not
> take part in them, and that he considered his military mission completed after
> leading his Division back to the *Reich*. After that, he would only keep command
> of the Division if this could contribute to a quick ending of this hopeless war, and
> then only if this were the wish of the Division . . . Commander of *116th Panzer
> Division* . . . was, of course, fully aware that at this moment no clear opinion of the
> commanders could be expected. His intention only was to open the eyes of the sol-
> diers in time to prepare them for the decision they would have to make in a few
> days, and they should, as usual, know what their Division Commander thought
> about these fateful questions.[47]

The former commander of *Panzer-Grenadier Regiment 156*, *Major* Grollmann, reported to the author about this conference, saying that only one commander agreed with the Division Commander, while all the others unanimously
repeated the qualms already reported by Holtermann.[48]

After the war, Police *Major* (Retired) Zimmermann wrote that when the
enemy approached Aachen, its population began a voluntary evacuation, and this
evacuation increased in size as the roar of the cannon became louder.
Zimmermann further wrote that Himmler had been in Aachen on 10 September.

After a conference about the situation, he spoke to numerous citizens of the city. He told them that the enemy would not reach Aachen and that an evacuation of the city was out of the question. This quickly got around, easing the voluntary evacuation.[49]

During the night of 10/11 September, *OKW* issued the order for the evacuation of Aachen–Monschau to the *Gauleiter* (Nazi Party District Leader) of Cologne–Aachen, Josef Grohé.[50] The battle commandant received this order in the late morning, but the *Kreisleiters* [Party Area Leaders, that is, of the next smaller political subdivision—*Editor*] of Aachen-City and Aachen-Land did not receive it until evening, so the controlled evacuation could not start until 12 September.[51] This was to be accomplished using 30 trains over two days, and it also included all civil and territorial military administrations.

The *Kreisleiters* of the NSDAP [*Nationalsozialistische Deutsche Arbeiterpartei,* or The National Socialist German Workers' Party—"Nazi" Party for short—*Editor*] were responsible for the evacuation. Grohé issued an appeal to the population, which is printed as Appendix 8. At the end, it contained an evil sentence. It said, "Whoever disturbs measures of the evacuation, or tries to refuse to join the withdrawal, not only puts himself in deadly danger, but also has to be considered a traitor against the public community and dealt with accordingly."[52]

This was a free ticket for brutality and it led to it. Chaotic conditions in the city and at railroad stations had already developed on 12 September. *Major* Zimmermann reported about this:

> The official evacuation of the city was announced after the American troops reached the southern edge of the city in the evening hours of 12 September 1944. Besides the large number of people and all administration offices, the entire police, including air raid police, the fire department and medical service, with all vehicles and equipment, left the city according to higher orders and started to march toward the designated dispersal areas. On 13 September 1944, at five o'clock, I was the last police officer of the Aachen police command to leave the city, after my plea to remain with an organized body of 100 policemen was refused.[53]

Oberst von Osterroht said in his report:

> On 12 September I spoke with the *Kreisleiter* and with the police president one more time and informed them of the increasing gravity of the situation, but at the same time, told them that the line of bunkers could be held and that the evacuation could proceed as per plan. . . .
>
> It was not until 13 September that I found out that on the evening of 12 September, the area political leadership and the entire police force had left the city and that consequently, the evacuation had come to a halt. As I later found out from the *Kreisleiter,* when he heard of the takeover of the Pelzer tower by the opponent, he tried in vain to reach me. He then received confirmation from the anti-aircraft group adjutant, with the additional information that it might be still possible for

enemy tanks to enter the city that evening. This could possibly have given the impression that the tanks were already advancing into the city, since at the same time, our own tanks and assault guns rolled through town to their positions. In any case, the *Kreisleiter* received permission from the *Gauleiter* to leave the city, and the police followed. The remaining population cleared out provisions and wine supplies, but while driving through the city, I could discern that things were calm. Since I could not replace the police with a troop of military police, I instructed them to just be on guard against looting by soldiers, and to round up stragglers.[54]

On 15 September 1944, the Commanding General of *LXXXI Corps,* *Generalleutnant* Schack, reported to the commander of *7th Army* about the events of 11 and 12 September in Aachen:

On 11 September, I returned to Aachen from a trip to the command post of the *9th Panzer Division*, which was involved in heavy fighting west of Aachen. On this trip, I realized that the civilian population west of the *Westwall* was suffering severely from fighter bomber activity. Upon my return, I immediately called the *Kreisleiter* of Aachen-City, and asked him why the areas near the *Westwall* had not yet been cleared of civilians. He responded that up until now only instructions for preparations had been given, but he had not yet ordered the evacuation. I asked him to inform the *Gauleiter* in my name that in my opinion, it was high time to vacate ahead of the *Westwall*, then the population between the *Westwall* and the city, and finally, the city itself. I asked him to see to it that these measures were carried out without panic.

In the afternoon of 12 September, after visiting troops again, I found Aachen in sheer turmoil. Crying women and children wandered bewildered through the city, and old women in completely desperate conditions begged for help to get out of the city. Many explained that they had no opportunity to get out because they could no longer walk that far and there was no transportation available. I calmed down the surrounding civilians as much as possible. They all insisted that they had to leave. They said the *Gauleiter* had declared that whoever did not leave the town at once was a traitor. Obviously, they were all very afraid to be dealt with as traitors.

Right after my return, I summoned the *Kreisleiters* of Aachen-Land and Aachen-City, and related conditions of panic in Aachen. Both declared unanimously that a radical evacuation of the city was originally intended, but it turned out that in the present situation, a radical evacuation would probably no longer be possible. I asked them to see to it that the population calmed down, and that in first place, arrangements should be made to shelter women and children. Germany's future rests in their preservation. Old people, who did their life's work for the state and now wanted to remain inside their four walls, might remain in the city. Both leaders accepted this as the right thing to do.[55]

On the evening of 12 September, *Generalleutnant* Count von Schwerin drove through Aachen to his new command post, Castle Rahe. On 25 September, he wrote in a letter to the *Gauleiters* of Westphalia, north and south:

On the evening of 12 September, shortly before darkness, I drove through the city to get to my new command post. I found the population to be in a state of panic, without guidance, aimlessly and wildly fleeing the city into the night. This view— let it be understood, the first view after returning to the homeland from enemy country—made a deep and shocking impression on my officers and me. Highly respected Herr *Gauleiter*, you know that I still took measures during the night to control this panic out of consideration for the troops who would pass through the city in the morning hours.[56]

The measures taken by Count Schwerin during the night consisted of sending Division staff officers out to search for authorities who were still available, to effect reasonable control of this panicky stream of refugees. Since the officers could not find anyone in a position of responsibility, Count Schwerin ordered them to intervene and to appeal to the people not to flee, but to return home. The population accepted this directive gratefully.[57]

The next morning, at 0600 hours of 13 September, the Commander of the *116th Panzer Division* assumed command in the Aachen sector. The Battle - commandant of Aachen, who was now his subordinate, reported the American penetration of the *Westwall* at the Branden-Berg. Count Schwerin now entered the city. In the letter to the *Gauleiters* of Westphalia cited earlier, he wrote about it:

On my way there, I could see that the population calmed down, but at the same time, I found confirmation that indeed no party, government, community, or police authorities were left in the city. The people were thereby without leadership and left to their fate. This knowledge struck me again with an overwhelming effect and I began compulsively considering if I, in my capacity as military sector commander, could do anything for the people, but at the moment could not find any way of intervention. Nevertheless, in the telephone repeater station, I still found a clerk in charge. He confirmed the departure of all authorities during the previous night and connected me to the Aachen-Land *Kreisleiter* with a long-distance call. He again confirmed to me that all city services were gone. The *Kreisleiter* asked me if I were now assuming command in the city. By answering the question in the affirmative, I again became fully aware of the heavy responsibility I had to assume regarding the leaderless remaining population of Aachen. For a moment, I thought about what I could do. The military situation, as it was presented in the reports available, showed that the enemy already achieved a penetration of the bunker line south of the city. He stood at the site of the breakthrough with tanks; his infantry was advancing and was only a few kilometers away from the southern outskirts of the city. Even with the greatest of speed, my own Division could not be deployed to the area south of Aachen before late afternoon. If the enemy were to advance toward the city from the point of penetration, one would have to assume that he would appear at the southern entrances of the city and enter before my Division could get here.

Therefore, the time available was so short that it was impossible to evacuate the thousands of people who were in the city. The majority would fall into enemy hands when he pushed into the city. In this situation, I only had one thought on my mind: What can you do to help the unfortunate population, if the enemy arrives in the city ahead of time? From previous fighting in France, I knew that the American Army tried to adhere to the Geneva and Hague conventions, so it seemed possible to ease the fate of the remaining citizens by means of a purely humanitarian appeal to the American commander. I acted according to this thought. I asked the head official of the post office if one of his clerks would remain in city, even in the event of enemy occupation. He confirmed this, and said that one of his clerks was assigned to do so. Then I asked him if this man was reliable and would be able, in case of an enemy occupation, to deliver a letter to the commander of the occupation forces. The head official then summoned another clerk, consulted with him, and after thorough examination of their opinions, explained that the assigned clerk would be quite capable of carrying out such a task.

Then I wrote the famous lines openly on a piece of paper and handed it without an envelope to the head official, asking him to give it to the assigned man and to instruct him in his task, since I no longer had time for it. The head official promised to take care of the matter reliably, after I informed him about the content, which was written in English. I then left the office to go to the battle commandant's command post.

The "famous lines" were worded as follows:

To the Commanding Officer of the U.S. Forces occupying the town of Aachen:
I stopped the stupid evacuation of the civil population and ask you to give her relief. I'm the last commanding officer here.

Gerhard Count von Schwerin
13 September 44 Lt. General[58]

On the same day, at 1100 hours, a conference took place at *Army Group B* with the *Gauleiter* of its area. The *7th Army* Chief of Staff, *Oberst* Baron von Gersdorff, conveyed the following points about it at 1030 hours to the *Army Group B* Chief of Staff, General Krebs:

Cooperation totally without friction, due to combining local command posts and liaison officers. The individual field armies are depending on certain *Gauleiters*.
Evacuation of Aachen carried out last night. Generally, a zone about ten kilometers east of the *Westwall*. Men stayed back. Evacuation roads (side roads) defined. Economic evacuation occurs in mutual agreement. Destruction of industry between Rhine and *Westwall* is rejected, as is any further evacuation. A rearward position being sought.[59]

The conference with the *Gauleiters* lasted one hour. At 1450 hours, Gersdorff reported to Krebs, "that the Aachen telephone repeater station supposedly found the letter from a German General written in English, who as the last soldier entrusted the Americans with the care of the remaining population."

At 1600 hours, Gersdorff reported, "that according to an orientation by the Commanding General of *LXXXI Corps*, the evacuation of Aachen occurred in an unfriendly manner. The *Kreisleiter* issued a directive that anyone not leaving the city at once would be considered a traitor. Due to this, the civilians were chased out to the country roads without aim or control. The commanding general intervened to arrange a controlled evacuation."

Finally, at 1800 hours, Krebs informed the Chief of Staff, *Supreme Command–West, Generalleutnant* Westphal, of the following:

1. *Gauleiter* conference established: Evacuation started in part too hastily and under threat without preparation or means of transportation.
2. Schwerin's letter will be examined.

Still in the morning, Schwerin's letter reached the *Wehrmacht* commandant's office in Cologne via the *Reich*'s postal administration, and from there was forwarded to Headquarters, *LXXXI Corps*, evidently following earlier information passed by phone.[60] The original document of the *Wehrmacht* commandant's office does not indicate that it would have passed it on to another address, but party offices had probably received prior knowledge of Schwerin's letter.

By 13 September, corps headquarters requested Count Schwerin to take a position. His report was as follows:

On the night of 12 September, when I drove through the city of Aachen toward my new command post, I saw great numbers of civilians, including many women and children with handcarts and baby carriages, walking away on the roads, aimlessly and in panic. The unruly movement obstructed the mobility of the troops and caused animosity and panic even amongst the soldiers. Thus, I sent officers into the city to ask the police to stop the wild evacuation. The officers, however, found no government, party, or community authorities still in office. Therefore, according to my order, they took matters into their own hands, and told the people not to flee wildly into the night, but rather to calmly go home. On the morning of 13 September, I personally searched the city for an authority to further take care of the matter, but only found the telephone office open. From there, I spoke with the Aachen-Land *Kreisleiter*, who was at a place outside the city, informed him of the situation, and asked him to press for a halt to the panic and random wandering. The *Kreisleiter* accepted and asked how much time there would be. I answered him that I could not tell him that exactly, but that the enemy was not expected in the city before afternoon. In the afternoon, the Aachen-Land *Kreisleiter* looked for me at the command post. We discussed the situation, and agreed that the wild wandering had to be stopped, and in view of the limited availability of transportation, that armament industry workers and Hitler Youth units should be evacuated first, while the country residents should stay at home.[61]

It is obvious that the letter to the American commander was not mentioned, even if the superior authorities knew about it.

Besides the Aachen-Land *Kreisleiter,* Fried, at the Division command post, Count Schwerin was approached by Dr. Riedel, a physician from Aachen, and a farmer named Klinkenberg. Schwerin gave them the following written directive:

> In my capacity as battle commandant of the city of Aachen, I hereby order that as of now, the aimless and unorganized evacuation be stopped. The population remains in the city, and only those whose shelter, food supply and transportation are secured may leave the city.
>
> Signed, Count von Schwerin, *Generalleutnant*[62]

On the evening of 13 September, Count Schwerin counted on the continuation of the enemy attack on Aachen, as well as on both sides of the city. Regarding the significance of Aachen for further fighting in the West, he gave his opinion in his report to the Americans after the war that:

> Its possession as a most important traffic junction of the West and as a departure point of major roads toward Cologne and Düsseldorf had to be of great tactical importance to the Americans. On the other hand, the German high command requested the decisive [certainly meant "decided"—*Author*] defense of Aachen, where without a doubt, not only military reasons, but those of prestige, played a deciding role."[63]

Schwerin did not believe that Aachen could be held. He also sensed that something was brewing against him and feared that the Party wanted to label him the scapegoat for their failure. In his post-war report he wrote:

> The general [that is, Schwerin—*Author*] was of the opinion that the attack on the city, expected with certainty on the following day, would blow away all attempts of this kind and give him the freedom of action that he longed for. He thoroughly discussed the entire situation with the senior regimental commander, *Oberst* Voigtsberger of *Regiment 60.*[64]

Furthermore, Schwerin's report goes on:

> The possibilities of a successful defense were still very poor. The city would have to fall as soon as the enemy had a tight grip on it. This, however, the Commander of *116th Panzer Division* opined, will occur in very quickly. He and all the soldiers of his Division waited wholeheartedly for this moment. He would give them the chance to take the law of action into their own hands.

What Schwerin meant by "freedom of action" and "law of action" is reminiscent of the previously-reported account of the Division *Ic* and Schwerin's description of the commanders' conference of the evening of 8 September. He could also have learned from it, however, that his commanders, except for one, did not agree with his intentions. Since his troops had no knowledge at all of his plans, it is doubtful that they were waiting "wholeheartedly" for the fall of Aachen. Nevertheless, Schwerin expected his officers and soldiers to break their oath of allegiance and that they would possibly bring their comrades in the adjacent divisions into the greatest danger. Such conduct, at that time, was considered high treason by most, and today still by many, and was viewed as contrary to their honor as soldiers. It is, therefore, questionable if the Division, despite all high regard, would have obeyed its Commander unconditionally, as Count Schwerin declared with conviction after the war. In today's view, one may be inclined to accept his opinion, but one must not overlook the conflict of loyalty to which he would have subjected his subordinates.

As we already know, the night of 13/14 September passed relatively calmly. In the late morning of 14 September, the southern front of Aachen was penetrated, but was halted by the battalions of the *116th Panzer Division* that were emplaced behind the line of bunkers. At 0930 hours, Count Schwerin telephoned *Oberst i.G.* Wiese, *LXXXI Corps* Chief of Staff, and reported about complaints regarding *Luftwaffe* soldiers who ran away, and about the impudence of the anti-aircraft units, saying that "the conditions in Aachen were devastating." He added that "he ordered that as long as railroad and truck space is available, the civilian population could leave the city, otherwise any means of leaving the city would clog the roads."[65]

At 1300 hours, the Commander of the *116th Panzer Division*, reported, "Museum director and several remaining officials temporarily took over city administration. Location Quellenhof. 20,000–30,000 people still in the city."[66]

Among other things, the museum director, Dr. Kuetgens, rendered a report to Lord Mayor Jansen on 15 November 1944, as a proposal for the *Gauleiter*. It stated that on 11 September, Jansen had told him:

> In view of the enemy approach, it may become necessary for me and the officials in charge, as well as my closest staff of co-workers, to leave the city to continue administration tasks in a different location. Due to an order I have received, I am bound to leave the city under threat of impending occupation, but am to leave a person in charge behind to take care of the people and to lead an emergency administration. All officials in question are known to be in the Party or are part of the administration, and therefore cannot remain in Aachen, lest their presence lead to a confrontation with the opponent. I have therefore selected you to be my representative."[67]

After fruitless objections, Dr. Kuetgens declared himself ready to take over the task and the following day received "power of attorney according to paragraph 35,3 of the German municipal law" from the Mayor, with instructions that he was:

> To ascertain all city employees, clerks, and workers who remained in Aachen and gather the suitable ones, even if they were of the second or third ranks, for a circle of close co-workers. Thus, I would not be alone and have the most necessary help

available. Concerning technical matters, the Lord Mayor recommended the director of the *Technische Nothilfe* [Technical Emergency Service—*Editor*], Chief Section Leader Packbier, who could keep the city utilities in working order as long as the *Wehrmacht* would be in town. . . . I told the Lord Mayor that I intend to engage my brother-in-law, *Oberfeldführer* Dr. Drouven, M.D., the managing physician of the Red Cross in Aachen, especially since he is also the representative of Lord Mayor in the German Red Cross. The Lord Mayor found this quite satisfactory and ended the conversation.

To gain an overview of the population remaining in the city, Kuetgens then went to visit all 22 air-raid bunkers. There were about 25,000 people in the bunkers. Kuetgens estimated the number of otherwise remaining people in Aachen to be 5,000. He summoned the remaining members of the city administration to a conference set for 1100 hours on 14 September in the Quellenhof. He divided the tasks "as well as possible" and discussed immediate actions: measures needed to protect the city's utilities, the slaughterhouse, the food depots, bakeries, and butcher stores that were still in working order. Finally, he ordered attorney Kremer to prepare an appeal to the citizens, so that nothing would "give rise to feelings of abandonment" and to "protect them from acts of imprudence and despair." Thereafter, Dr. Kuetgens accompanied Dr. Drouven to the command post of the *116th Panzer Division* in the Berliner Hof on the railroad station street, "since it became obvious that to handle the most important questions, it was a prerequisite to know the attitude of the *Wehrmacht*."

Both men discussed the situation in the city with *Generalleutnant* Count von Schwerin. In 1944, Dr. Kuetgens wrote about him that:

> He was satisfied to hear about my efforts to establish an emergency administration to carry out the most urgent requirements for life support and protection of the citizens, and promised me all available support. However, he could not provide the guards I requested to secure the various vital establishments, and so on, but he agreed to establish a citizens' defense against looting. He had to also deny my request that the *Wehrmacht* evacuate more citizens if such became absolutely necessary. He recommended that I urge the people to stay in the bunkers for the time being, in hopes of preventing as many accidents as possible in the streets that are under fire. The general then informed us about the present military situation. He expressed his concern that the southern line of the *Westwall* in front of the city could not be held any longer than the evening of that day. During the afternoon, he would give me new information in the Quellenhof.

Upon return to the Quellenhof, Dr. Kuetgens briefed his co-workers and edited the appeal. It was signed by him, Dr. Drouven, attorney Kremer, and Chief Section Leader Packbier, and 20 to 30 typewritten copies were announced and posted in the bunkers. (Appendix 9) The appeal, like the previous announcement by Schwerin, contributed much to calm the frightened population.

The attempt to establish a citizens' defense, however, only had little success. While Dr. Kuetgens worked out measures for the safety of the provisions for the people with representatives of the bakers and butchers, Count von Schwerin reported in the Quellenhof, "that he no longer could hold the position south of the city. He would go back to the line north of the city; thereby, the city was open."

After the war, Dr. Kuetgens supplemented his report about the discussion with Count Schwerin in a declaration under oath:

> The General . . . told me what he had undertaken to help the population in recent days, since the shameful departure of the Aachen authorities. *General* Count von Schwerin was especially angry about the inhumane way the evacuation was conducted by the Aachen *Kreisleiters* who then suddenly left the town on its own. Anyone who wore a Party uniform left the city in a mad rush. . . . For me, it was a comforting and elevating feeling to see how this noble-thinking person and flawless officer, during the most difficult military situation in which he found himself, did not cease to care for the well-being of the people in the city who were in his battle sector. The general also openly discussed with me the military situation, which he considered extremely critical, if not almost hopeless. . . . He also expressed his intent that when north of Aachen, he would want to preserve the beautiful city of Charlemagne, which would by then probably be occupied by the enemy. With those explanations, my heavy heart was greatly relieved, and I thanked Count von Schwerin most sincerely for his high-mindedness.[68]

In the late morning of 15 September, instead of the Americans, *Kreisleiter* Schmeer of Aachen showed up at the Quellenhof. He believed he had "discovered some kind of a conspiracy or counter-government!" Kuetgens and his men were temporarily arrested, but released again in the afternoon.

Meanwhile, at 1120 hours on 14 September, Gersdorff reported to Krebs, "Evacuation of Aachen meanwhile somewhat more organized through intervention *LXXXI Corps* and authorities ordered by *7th Army*."[69]

In the afternoon of that day, the *Gauleiter* of Cologne/Aachen visited corps headquarters. *Generalleutnant* Schack reported about this on 15 September to the Commanding General of *7th Army*:

> In the afternoon of 14 September 1944, *Gauleiter* Grohé appeared at the corps command post unannounced, while I was up front with the troops. Among other things, he declared to the Chief of Staff, *Oberst i.G.* Wiese, that the unsuccessful evacuation of the civilians of Aachen and the chaotic conditions there are to be blamed on the fact that the *Wehrmacht* intervened unjustifiably in the progress of the evacuation. He wanted to immediately report about this to the *Führer.*[70]

It seems that Grohé drove from corps to *7th Army*, because at 2250 hours, Gersdorff reported to Krebs, "Based on discussion with *Gauleiter, Führer* order issued about enforced evacuation of Aachen."[71]

He further reported that looting was going on in Aachen and that the police would tentatively be back in Aachen by 0100 hours.

At 2345 hours on 14 September, the *116th Panzer Division* received the following orders from *LXXXI Corps,* "By order of the *Führer,* Aachen is to be evacuated, if necessary by force. The *116th Panzer Division* assists evacuation by directing traffic. For this, as of 0100 hours, police are also available."[72]

At this point in time, Count Schwerin had not been in command for several hours. The relief must have taken place in the afternoon by the commanding general, but Schwerin was still at the Division command post in Würselen.

Still on 14 September, in his capacity as Commander of the Reserve Army, using the subordinate headquarters *Wehrkreis* [Corps Administrative Area— *Editor*] VI in Münster, Himmler got busy. The *Wehrkreis VI* Chief of Staff, *Generalleutnant* Faeckenstedt, reported to Krebs at 0115 hours on 15 September that a teletype message from the *Reichsführer-SS* arrived, with the following content:

1. Commander of *Wehrkreis VI* will arrange for Aachen police to be equipped with anti-tank weapons for close combat, to destroy enemy tanks near Aachen.

2. Single tanks that broke through the *Westwall* are no reason for serious concern. Commander of *Wehrkreis VI* is personally responsible for the restoration of calm and order in Aachen.

3. Commander, *116th Panzer Division* seems to retreat with his Division as if fleeing. Location of the Division Commander, *General* Count Schwerin, is to be reported at once.[73]

Krebs explained to Faeckenstedt that he would first speak with Gersdorff and then brief him. Then Faeckenstedt reported that the commander of *Wehrkreis VI, General der Infanterie* Mattenklott, was on his way to Aachen.

Answering Krebs' question, Gersdorff reported at 0200 hours:

1. This morning, a personal discussion with *Gauleiter* Grohé took place. He was thoroughly informed about the situation and in a straightforward way about the conditions in Aachen following the early departure of the police and the *Kreisleiter,* as well the Party organizations. In a long-distance call this evening, *Gauleiter* Grohé said that the police of Aachen would be back in Aachen by midnight.

2. *General* Count Schwerin is not commanding the Division at this time. Division Commander is *Oberst* and bearer of the Oak Leaves [to the Knight's Cross— *Editor*], Voigtsberger. *General* Count Schwerin has been ordered to report to Headquarters, *7th Army* tomorrow.

3. *116th Panzer Division* presently in counterattack against enemy tanks at eastern outskirts of Aachen.

At 0200 hours, Krebs informed Faeckenstedt accordingly. Late in the morning of 15 September, Mattenklott appeared at the Division and from *LXXXI Corps,* sent the following teletype to Himmler:

The *116th Panzer Division* is still at the western and southwestern edge of Aachen. Until 1600 hours on 14 September, Division staff at the Aachen railroad station and from there, per *LXXXI Corps* order, in Würselen (six kilometers northeast of

Aachen). There, the former Division Commander, Count Schwerin, will, per orders, report to *7th Army* in Münstereifel. According to reports by Commanding General of *LXXXI Corps*, no retreats by the *116th Panzer Division* occurred. Instead, units of the security forces withdrew to the first *Westwall* position after heavy tank battle. Panic of civilians took place at a larger scale. *Generalleutnant* Schack, Commanding General of *LXXXI Corps*, reported the departure from Aachen by the police and both *Kreisleiters* during the night of 12/13 September as the reason for the panic. Close combat anti-tank weapons are neither available from the Army Group, nor from the corps.[74]

On 15 September, Count Schwerin and *Oberst* von Osterroht were ordered to corps headquarters for interrogation.[75] Count Schwerin made this report about it:

1. During the night of 12/13 September, officers of the Division staff whom I sent into the city had orders to look for a Party, government, or community authority who was still at work, to control the panic-like evacuation of civilians. They found all offices already abandoned, except for the air raid warden's, which, later that night, also stopped its activity. Only at the railroad station did some Party officials and Red Cross nurses make an effort to organize and tend to the masses of refugees gathered at the station.

2. On the morning of 13 September, I personally went into the city to seek an authority, because as of 0600 hours, I assumed command in the Aachen sector. I also did not find any of the Party, government, or community offices to be open. All buildings were abandoned. Only at the telephone office did I still find a staff of working officials. They also confirmed to me that no administrative authority was left in the city. Even the police had left.

3. The official in charge at the telephone office told me that the Aachen-Land *Kreisleiter* could most likely still be reached by phone. Then I asked to be connected with him and received the connection. In answer to my question, the *Kreisleiter* told me that he was not within the city, but in a village outside. The Aachen-Stadt *Kreisleiter* had been evacuated and was also no longer there.

   The *Kreisleiter* asked me if I assumed command of the city. . . . The *Kreisleiter* then asked me if he could also depart. I answered that this had to be his own decision. He said that he would leave during the day and asked if the command would then pass to me, which I confirmed. Then, the *Kreisleiter* bid farewell.

4. On the afternoon of 13 September, the *Kreisleiter* appeared at my command post outside Aachen, and inquired about the situation. I told him that in the afternoon my Division would go into action south of the city and that I hoped to halt the further advance of the enemy through the bunker line. I could not promise him this with certainty. We would do what we could. The *Kreisleiter* informed me that the evacuation of his area, which encompassed the greater surroundings of the city, would begin the next day. He asked me to call the *Gauleiter* in Cologne and to explain the situation to him. I answered that I had no telephone connection there and that I did not think it was up to me to do that.

5. On the late afternoon of 13 September, the regimental commander, whose command post was near the main railroad station of Aachen, reported to me that looting was going on in the city, that there were no police anywhere, and that he had sent his engineer platoon there to thwart the looting. I ordered him to pass judgment on looters by summary court-martial. This was done. Two looters were shot.

6. Until the evening of 14 September, not one administrator or person of authority had returned to the city—not even the police. I was therefore forced to bring in my military police, who were deployed elsewhere for maintenance and order in the city.

7. In the afternoon, the former museum director of Aachen appeared with a physician at my advanced command post near the main railroad station, and reported to me that he received orders from the departed mayor to organize a temporary city administration with clerks who stayed behind.[76]

In this letter, there was again no mention of the letter to the Americans. Count Schwerin had been trying to retrieve the bothersome document. In the aforementioned letter to the *Gauleiters* of Westphalia, he wrote about it on 25 September 1944:

The next morning, the military situation south of Aachen improved in our favor, since the enemy unexpectedly stopped at the point of his breach and did not advance any further toward the city. My Division, therefore, could be deployed in the late afternoon south of the city as planned; by evening, this measure had led to success. With this, the danger that the city of Aachen would fall into enemy hands was eliminated. Following this, the reason for my letter to the American commander became obsolete, since it was only written in case there would be an immediate occupation of the city by the enemy. That is why I sent an officer of my staff into the city to get the letter back. Upon his return, the officer reported to me that all officials had left the city and the letter was nowhere to be found. (The rumor that I tried to get the letter back into my hands by force of arms is as insane as the rumor that I sent the contents of the letter, or that I wanted it to be sent, to the enemy via wireless.)

I hope to have cleared up a quite unpleasant and very misunderstood matter with this truthful explanation and showed you, *Herr Gauleiter,* that it was only pure humanitarian reasons that motivated my actions.[77]

On 15 September, *Generalleutnant* Schack took responsibility for Schwerin's actions in his report to the Commander of *7th Army*. We already know the beginning of his report (see note 55). Schack ended it this way:

To summarize I state:

1. The *Gauleiter* and the *Kreisleiters* did not make contact with the troops in time. They prepared the evacuation unaware of the circumstances and were completely surprised by the actual situation.

2. In view of the surprising situation, they lost their nerve, left the city prematurely with all security services, and thereby caused panic.

3. Even when they heard about the panic, they did not return to the city to try and bring order. Only the Aachen-Land *Kreisleiter* went to see *Generalleutnant* Count von Schwerin in the afternoon of 13 September. In fullest mutual agreement, he discussed with him that in view of the situation, it would be best to first evacuate the Hitler Youth and the armament workers. The old established population that could feed itself by its own means, should, for the time being, remain and only be moved out when the situation would permit it.

Corps must defend itself with full severity against the *Gauleiter,* who wants to make the troops responsible for all the friction accompanying the evacuation and for the chaos in Aachen. Throughout those days, the troops were burdened with critical fighting of the heaviest nature in front of the city. . . .[78]

The same day, Schack sent an other report to Brandenberger, regarding the accusations by Himmler against the *116th Panzer Division*:

Rumors that the *116th Panzer Division* took evasive action to the east are totally unfounded. On neither 14 nor 15 September had the *116th Panzer Division* issued an order to any of its subordinate units to fall back toward the north or east. On the morning of 15 September, the Division also held its main battle line along the *Westwall* Vaals–Vaalserquartier–south and the eastern edge Burtscheid–following the Burtscheid–Eilendorf railroad line.[79]

In conclusion, on 15 September, Count Schwerin also sent a report directly to Himmler, and added his report to Schack. This report, with the following text, was delivered to Himmler by *Leutnant* Bischoff, duty officer for the Division *Ic*:

Herr Reichsführer! There are rumors that back in the homeland the perception exists that the *116th Panzer Division*, under my command, retreated from Aachen in full flight. This does not coincide with the facts, as the Commander of *Wehrkreis VI, General* Mattenklott, has probably already reported to you, *Herr Reichsführer.*

I am asking you dutifully, *Herr Reichsführer,* to take the enclosed service report, which I wrote today by orders of my commanding general, into consideration. It will show how the conditions in Aachen ran their course from the arrival of the Division until my relief of duty as Division Commander yesterday evening.

I hope with certainty to be able to discredit the totally absurd accusations against me, to vindicate myself and to be able to return to my troops as soon as possible. I know that they will fight to the last with all their strength.[80]

After Bischoff returned, he reported that Himmler was calmed down by the letter.[81]

This was urgently necessary, because on 16 September, Himmler still reacted to Mattenklott's report:

It seems you do not know that the evacuation of Aachen was prevented by a letter given to the Americans.

Anti-tank projectiles are to be acquired through improvisation.[82]

The last sentence is representative of Himmler's unprofessional fancy. The reports from Schack and the 2d Quartermaster (*Qu.2*) of *7th Army*, who was in charge of liaison with civil authorities, went to Army Group. *Generalfeldmarschall* Model summarized the results on 15 September, and on 16 September, *Supreme Command–West* sent this report, verbatim, to the *OKW*. It was written:

Regarding: *Generalleutnant* Count Schwerin.

Commander *Army Group B* reports:

According to reports put forward by the corps commander, the Division Commander, the battle commandant, and the *7th Army* 2d Quartermaster, the responsible Party authorities and the police—who would have been in the position to maintain peace and order during the evacuation—left the city of Aachen and attempted to control the evacuation from the outside. Due to the proclaimed warning that any citizen who excluded himself from the evacuation was to be considered a traitor, and due to the fact that no authoritative office was in contact, a panic developed which deteriorated into mindless flight and led to looting.

Based on the situation described in the city of Aachen, the Commander of the *116th Panzer Division, Generalleutnant* Count Schwerin, found it necessary to first stop the evacuation to get it under reasonable control. He worried the *Kreisleiter* of Aachen by informing him that enemy spearheads might be already approaching the city by the afternoon. He also handed a letter, written in English, to an agent of the Party who was introduced to him, in which he asked the approaching American troops to protect the people in the city. Besides, it is clearly established, that he always took all measures to defend the Aachen area, and that he led his Division with personal effort at all times, in the sense required by Higher Command.

Generalleutnant Count Schwerin has been relieved of his post as Division Commander because of the mistakes that were mentioned. An investigation pursuant to a court-martial initiated.

By immediately establishing liaison between army, corps, and Division with the corresponding Party authorities, everything is being done to control and carry out the evacuation as planned.[83]

The severity of accusations against Model in various post-war reports regarding his behavior in this matter can therefore hardly be maintained.

After the interrogation at corps headquarters on 15 September, Count Schwerin had a discussion with its Chief of Staff, *Oberst i.G.*Wiese. Both feared that this affair could have serious consequences for Schwerin. Both also counted on an early loss of Aachen, because the enemy continued his attacks against the *9th Panzer Division* and against the left wing of the *116th*. By afternoon, the enemy became active again between Aachen and the Maas. Count Schwerin asked Wiese for permission to bid farewell to his troops. With this, he hoped to gain some time in case a situation occured near Aachen which would save him the trip for a court-martial hearing at *7th Army*. Wiese granted his permission.[84]

In the afternoon of this day, at 1630 hours, the Chief of Staff of *Supreme Command–West*, Westphal, related the opinion of *OKW* to Krebs, namely that a certain disorganization of command existed and urgently required resolution. Besides, he reported that the *Führer* had ordered the defense of every house in Aachen with all means, as the Russians once did in Stalingrad.[85] At 2345 hours, Krebs opined to Westphal that if they could endure the next day (16 September), bringing in the *12th Infantry Division* would provide hope of somehow establishing a bearable equilibrium with the enemy.[86]

Count Schwerin did not harbor this hope and went to the Berensberg farmhouse owned by a certain farmer named Honnie, four kilometers north of Aachen.[87] From there, he made contact with *Panzer-Grenadier Regiments 60* and *156*. For the morning of 16 September, he scheduled a conference with the Acting Division Commander, *Oberst* Voigtsberger, and with the commander of *Armored Artillery Regiment 146*, *Oberst der Reserve* Pean, at the command post of *Panzer-Grenadier Regiment 156* in Castle Rahe. That night, when Count Schwerin returned to Hof Berensberg, he found the *Motorcycle Platoon* of *Panzer-Grenadier Regiment 60*, under the command of *Leutnant* Kleer, who, by order of the regimental commander, assumed the duty of protecting the Division Commander.

At the commanders' conference the next morning, Count Schwerin made:

> his opinion known, that he would not present himself to the court, but would remain with the troops and fight the last battle together with them. . . . The Division may be encircled or overrun in Aachen, but it will not take one step back. It would not participate in the destruction of the homeland by artificially prolonging the war. It will fight its last battle in Aachen. . . . The commanders acknowledged in serious agreement. Afterwards, details of a secret announcement to the troops of these intentions and an accordingly edited official Division order were discussed.[88]

This is what Schwerin reported to the Americans in 1945. Evidently, right after the conference, Voigtsberger issued the following daily Division order:

> On the evening of 14 September 1944, by corps order, I assumed command of the *116th Panzer Division*.
>
> I direct the commanders once more to the irrevocable *Führer* order, whereby the Division's positions south of Aachen and in the area around Aachen are to be held to the last.
>
> The honor of the Division requires that no unit withdraws and that every man remains with his commander.
>
> In this view, I find myself in complete agreement with our General.[89]

This order to the Division formally conforms to the *Führer* order and made it easier for the commanders to be available for their relieved Division commander.

At the time that Count Schwerin issued his order in Castle Rahe, *7th Army* waited in vain for his arrival. At 1045 hours, the following entry was made in the *LXXXI Corps* journal, "*General* von Schwerin not yet arrived at *7th Army*. Last news: He wanted to bid farewell to his regiments and drove around in artillery fire near Aachen. *116th* must report when and where the *General* was last seen."[90]

No corresponding Division message could be found in the Division journal. The Division staff did not divulge the whereabouts of its commander. At 1345 hours, Gersdorff reported to Krebs, "*Generalleutnant* Count Schwerin not yet arrived at Army. Whereabouts unknown since departure from Division. Investigation ongoing."[91]

In the early afternoon of 16 September, the Division's command post moved from Würselen to Mariadorf. *Major i.G.* Prinz zu Schleswig-Holstein from the staff of *7th Army* arrived on 15 September to take over as the *Ia*. *Major i.G.* Wolf took over his task as *Ib* again. The *Ib* command post was in Niederzier, eight kilometers southeast of Jülich. On 16 September, the *Ic, Hauptmann der Reserve* Dr. Holtermann returned to the Division. On the previous day, he had visited the *Gauleiter* of Westphalia-North in Münster, and by presenting Count Schwerin's report of 13 September and his letter meant for the American commander of Aachen, received *Gauleiter* Meyer's understanding for Schwerin's actions of 12 and 13 September. After considering it with *Gauleiter* Grohé, he even wanted to put a good word in for Schwerin with *Generalfeldmarschall* Model. On the way to the Division, Holtermann also went to see the *Gauleiter* of Westphalia-South in Wetter, and influenced *Stabsamtsleiter* Strube, a former officer of *116th Panzer Division,* in the same way.[92] This was quite easy with Strube, because as Holtermann reported in 1963:

> During the days in question, Strube himself was in the Aachen area for a short time, and witnessed the catastrophic failure of the Party authorities with his own eyes. He had to make the personally touching observation that the civilians who were moved from Gau Westphalia-South to the *Westwall* were treated badly and not provided for sufficiently by the Party authorities. Strube was so upset about this that he turned to the Party chancellery to file a complaint. In my description about what had happened in Aachen in the meantime, Strube found a welcome confirmation of his own complaint and he therefore promised willingly to immediately inform the party chancellery about the actual events in the Aachen area. Apparently, that's what he did.[93]

Despite his rejection of National Socialism, Count Schwerin maintained good relations with the *Gauleiters* "responsible" for his Rhine-Westphalian Division. This now paid off.

Also on 16 September, the *IIa, Major* Vogelsang, came back to the Division after his recuperation. On 18 September, he wrote in his diary:

Night before last, I arrived here at the Division. . . . On my way, by accident I met Holtermann, with whom I drove to the *Ib*. From there, we went on right away into Aachen, passing the *Ia*, to the advanced command post of *Oberst* Voigtsberger, who commanded the Division. . . . On our way, already many craters, shell holes, downed trolley wires, house rubble.[94]

Vogelsang and Holtermann then met with *Generalleutnant* Count Schwerin in his camouflaged shelter. It cannot be established with certainty if it was in Berensberg or in Aachen proper. Vogelsang's diary reports further:

According to the relevant *"Führer* order," the Division prepared itself for the defense of Aachen to the last, a task that seemed at least a bit more hopeful with the arrival of *12th Infantry Division.*

The opponent moved up plenty of artillery, primarily heavy artillery. Roars and thunders day and night. Enemy penetrations alternate with our own counterattacks. Threatening breakthroughs are haphazardly closed off by our weak forces.

It is very difficult to get used to the fact that we have to fight the war on German soil. Whole streets of Aachen, the old imperial city, fall into ruins. The population desperately clings to its hometown and can hardly be persuaded to move out, but this appears so important to avoid unnecessary loss of life. Outside of the immediate area of artillery attack, nobody thinks of leaving house or home. Everyone hopes for a sudden turn of events, for the continuously-promised new weapons and surprises. No one can or wants to accept the fact that the "enemy is on German soil!"

While Count Schwerin thought over his situation with Holtermann and asked him one more time to act calmly toward the Westphalian *Gauleiters,* corps and Army headquarters continued their effort to determine his whereabouts—without success, as two phone conversations show.[95] At 2350 hours on 16 September, Krebs remarked to the Chief of Staff of the General Inspector of *Panzer* Troops, General Thomale, that the former Commander of *116th Panzer Division* had not yet been found in spite of inquiries. During the same conversation, Krebs reported that the total number of *Army Group B* tanks and assault guns was 84, versus 1,800 to 1,900 of the enemy. Thomale could only promise *Panzer Brigades 107* and *108,* 20 fortress anti-tank companies, and 40 Panthers. That was all he could give to *Army Group B.*

The next morning, at 0900 hours, 17 September, Gersdorff reported to Krebs, "Schwerin not yet found. At 2300 hours on 15 September, he drove off from the Division command post via Geilenkirchen toward *7th Army* headquarters."

On 17 September at noon, the airborne landing by the British and the Americans began near Arnhem. Model and Krebs had to clear out from their command post in the vicinity of the city, and now had other things to do besides being occupied with the Schwerin case.[96] Yet, at 1945 hours, it was noted in the *LXXXI* journal, *"General* von Schwerin is in Kohlscheid with the *Ortsbauernführer* [Regional Agricultural Leader—*Editor*] Hommé." [Should be "Honnie"—*Author*][97]

It is not clear who discovered this. In any case, in the afternoon of 17 September, the corps commander, *Generalleutnant* Schack, searched there for Schwerin; shortly before, he [Schwerin] had gone to another hiding place in Aachen proper after a police unit appeared at Hof Berensberg. Count Schwerin was nearby, not in the house, when the police arrived. *Leutnant* Kleer reported after the war:

A police *Major* who apparently discovered the *General*'s coat somewhere requested me to lead him to the *General*. I could not blame the man for not believing my statement that I could not help him, and he became more specific. Now I believe that my answer in the presence of motorcycle troops who were armed to their teeth was still more specific.[98]

The police unit moved out. That its visit was actually meant for the *General* has not been proven, but the possibility existed. Afterwards, Kleer proposed to look for shelter near the command post of *Panzer-Grenadier Regiment 60,* in an abandoned house in a side street.

Meanwhile, the police and other authorities had moved back to Aachen. In addition, the *116th Panzer Division* reported on 17 September that two companies of police and political leaders had arrived in Aachen for the evacuation of the remaining roughly 20,000 people.[99] The conditions in the city were somewhat more orderly; a continuous procession of trucks and buses were leaving the city. The nuisance fire by the enemy was annoying. Police *Major* Zimmermann wrote after the war that on 16 September, he received orders:

to return to Aachen with a unit of the Aachen municipal police to take care of security requirements. I was especially to prevent numerous shady characters from further looting—such as had occurred during the absence of the police—of houses and businesses that had been abandoned by their owners during evacuation. The security police unit available to me consisted exclusively of policemen from Aachen. For the most part, they were police reservists and citizens of Aachen. After my arrival in the city, which was under heavy artillery fire, I immediately established a strong guard and patrol service, which quickly succeeded in reestablishing somewhat bearable conditions of police order.

On my return to Aachen, there were no units of the *SS* or *SA,* only a small group of political leaders and men from the *NSKK* [*Nationalsozialistische Kraftfahrkorps,* or Nazi Party Motor Vehicle Corps—*Editor*] who controlled the departure of the buses with people leaving the city. The railroad traffic at that point in time was almost at a complete standstill.[100]

As mentioned earlier, the temporary city administration had already been dismissed on 15 September. On 20 September, the evacuation was reported "completed" by Army Group. Still, about 6,000 people remained in the city.[101]

After the fruitless search in Berensberg, on the evening of 17 September, *Generalleutnant* Schack increased his effort to motivate Schwerin to surrender.

After the war, *Hauptmann* Risse, the adjutant of *Panzer-Grenadier Regiment 60,* said:

> Late in the evening, I got a personal call from *General* Schack, who asked me for the whereabouts of the Division Commander. Upon my answer,that I had no knowledge of where he is, and that all I could say was that the Division Commander bid farewell and might be doing the same with other units of the Division, he gave me the official order to at once do everything to determine the whereabouts of the Division Commander. After this conversation, I went to the Division Commander to report the situation.
>
> In the middle of the night, *General* Schack called again and strongly reproached me that I still had not determined the whereabouts. He asked me if I could not at least find the driver or any other man from the Division Commander's entourage. I assured him that I had done everything possible and would continue to do so to find the Division Commander, and that I would then report it at once. *General* Schack then expressed his great concern about the development of the Division Commander's personal situation and that he would be ready to visit us in Aachen for a face-to-face conference with the Division Commander.
>
> Shortly after that conversation, my brother called, who as a member of the Division for many years knew it very well and now was *Ia* with a division north of us near Alsdorf. He told me that *General* Schack called him and informed him that we in Aachen were playing a dangerous game. He was to urge me right away to tell him where the Division Commander was. Following this conversation, I conferred with the Division Commander at once. . . .[102]

Now Count Schwerin considered it correct to accept Schack's proposal. On the evening of 20 September, Vogelsang entrusted the following to his diary:

> During the night of 18 September [Vogelsang first wrote "of 19 September" by mistake—*Author*] at 0400 hours in the morning, we sent the following long-distance call to the corps commander: "I report to the corps commander that I am with the troops to guarantee the execution of the *Führer* order to hold the positions south of Aachen to the last. In view of the situation portrayed by the corps commander, I would, of course, be available for a discussion and would ask him to specify when and where this should take place. I beg him to kindly consider my promise to the Division to remain with it. If it would seem feasible and possible to the corps commander, I beg that this discussion would take place in my last quarters, to which the corps commander came earlier today to look for me."
>
> Thereafter, the corps commander declared himself willing to look up our commander at the proposed place within the Division sector. This condition had to be adhered to, since only there did his safety appear somewhat guaranteed.
>
> In the early morning, an officer took the message, but for some reason did not get through the rainy darkness and the heavy artillery fire in time, so that at the appointed hour the corps commander was left standing alone. Naturally, the expected storm did not fail to come! We had to listen to severe reproaches and found

ourselves in a ridiculous situation, because the corps commander's assumption was that this blunder had not happened by accident. In spite of everything, we could not and would not betray the *General*, and had to continue in the same fashion. Fortunately, at this moment in spite of all danger, the Division Commander drove up, clearly realizing the fact that this daring act was the only possible way to deter the looming dangers to the Division.

After a short, face-to-face exchange of words, both generals drove off together, accompanied by a small motorcycle unit of the Division. The parting words from the Commanding General were testimony to his relief and the fact that the crisis was finally resolved, and they contained a hidden message of appreciation for the unconditional cohesion within the Division.

The following day, we received *Oberst i.G.* S. von Waldenburg as our new Division Commander.[103]

After the war, *Hauptmann* Risse said that the commander of *Armored Reconnaissance Battalion 116* had an armored reconnaissance platoon follow the Division Commander with the order to stay close to him and report anything unusual, and "if necessary to prevent Count Schwerin from falling into the wrong hands."[104] On 20 September, Vogelsang noted very emotional events regarding the Division:

> The affairs of our Division Commander took a dangerous course, but then came to a relatively good ending. . . .
>
> Superior ranking authorities searched in official ways for his whereabouts. But, from the youngest private to the oldest commander, everyone in the Division kept his mouth shut. All searches remained fruitless.
>
> After several days, however, the situation came to a head. Some suspected we were concealing a defection [by Schwerin—*Editor*], others talked about a plot of the Division against the high and highest command. . . . The danger loomed that now measures would be taken against the staff and higher commanders of the Division, because of a suspected conspiracy. It was high time to end the crisis in one way or another.[105]

Generalleutnant Schack assured Count Schwerin "personal safety as well as a fair court-martial hearing." Following this, Schwerin decided "to subject himself to the court-martial hearing." In 1962, this is how Count Schwerin described his surrender.[106]

Count Schwerin drove from *LXXXI Corps* headquarters to that of *7th Army* in Münstereifel and was interrogated there. In the *Army Group B* journal entry for 1910 hours on 18 September, the following long-distance conversation between Krebs and Gersdorff, Model, and Brandenberger took part appears:

> Chief of Staff, *7th Army*, reports that *General* Count Schwerin is with the *7th Army* and is being interrogated by military judges. Up until now, it has been established that after conferring with the *LXXXI Corps* Chief of Staff, *General* Count Schwerin

bade farewell to the individual units. It seems that under the burden of the recent days he was physically run-down. There is no sign of intent to separate himself from the troops.

The Cologne *Gauleiter* asked for a report of the members of the party organizations who were to blame for the chaotic evacuation of Aachen. After consulting with the population and party offices, the Chief of the *Luftwaffe* National Socialist Guidance Staff also confirmed the interpretation of the evacuation of Aachen as represented by the *7th Army*.

The Chief of Staff, *Army Group B* emphasizes that this case is reason to again point to the trusting [*sic!—Author*] cooperation of the authorities of the *Wehrmacht* and the state.

The Commander, *7th Army* speaks up and reports that *General* Schwerin makes an impression of total lucidity, and that he did not find any significant reasons for suspicion.

The Commander, *Army Group B* emphasizes that he will not tolerate any more charades and that this craziness must strictly be put to an end. As per his order, *General* Count Schwerin is to be taken into protective custody and after interrogation by the *7th Army*, he is to be handed over to *Supreme Command–West*. Points of the hearing to be defined by Commander, *7th Army*, details to be firmed up with the Judge Advocate General, *Supreme Command–West*, also to avoid differences with the *Reichsführer-SS*.[107]

At 2140 hours, Model and Brandenberger spoke by phone one more time:

Regarding the court hearing of *General* Count Schwerin, Commander, *7th Army* reports that there is no suspicion of unauthorized absence or aiding the enemy. Commander, *Army Group B* emphasizes that in his view, the suspicion exists that Schwerin created defeatist morale and with this made the duties of the state authorities more difficult. This caused damage to the reputation of the *Wehrmacht*. Besides that, the Army Group Commander considers the three-day absence as *Köpenickiade* [a historical act of deception—*Editor*].

In this conversation, Model now also wanted the relief of the commanding general of *LXXXI Corps*, *General* Schack, even if *General* Brandenberger supported him strongly. Model announced the arrival of a successor and ordered him to so apprise Schack. In a second conversation in the morning of 19 September, Model still did not give in, and finally declared, "The relief is not based on a personal reproach, but only signifies that the difficult task requires a more robust personality."

On 21 September, *Generalleutnant* Schack was replaced by *General der Infanterie* Köchling. Schack's gallant consideration for the Commander of the *116th Panzer Division*, who was his subordinate, certainly contributed to his removal. Later on, he assumed command of another corps and was promoted to *General der Infanterie*. After the hearing with *7th Army* on 19 September, Count Schwerin was brought to *Supreme Command–West* at Vallendar near Koblenz.

In 1963, he reported [again writing in the third person—*Editor*] that his arrest was:

> done with chivalry, as the whole matter was dealt with in a gallant manner. For the continuation of his trip to *Supreme Command–West,* a *Major* was assigned as an escort to accompany the *General.* This *Major* had to bring to the *General's* attention, which he did with great style, that he had orders to make use of his weapon in case there would be an attempt to flee. To the *General's* question, if it meant that this was an arrest, the *Major* answered that it was temporary custody.[108]

On 19 September, Count Schwerin was to see the Judge Advocate General Baron von Beust. He was only responsible for the initial inquiries, because criminal cases against generals had to be deliberated according to the war court-martial order before the *Reich* war court.[109] According to the memories of Dr. Holtermann, by Model's order, the commanding general of the *7th Army,* together with the Judge General of *Supreme Command–West,* determined seven points for the interrogation:

1. Sabotage of a *Führer* order
2. Aiding and abetting the enemy
3. Undermining military effectiveness
4. Defeatism
5. Desertion
6. Unauthorized absence[110]

In a letter from 24 September 1944, Holtermann wrote to *Major i.G.* Wolf:

> The report from the Judge Advocate General concluded that the accusations brought against the *General* were legally completely without merit, and therefore no possibility exists for a court-martial. The request for it was filed by *Feldmarschall* Model, who also had arranged for the preliminary arrest of the *General.* An order to arrest the *General* was therefore not issued; to the contrary, the Judge Advocate General saw it necessary to suggest a swift cancellation of the temporary custody to *Feldmarschall* von Rundstedt. In fact, this took place immediately thereafter, and *Feldmarschall* von Rundstedt forwarded the final report of the Judge Advocate General, including his own assessment, to the *Führer* Headquarters. . . .
>
> In his assessment of the report by the Judge Advocate General, *Generalfeldmarschall* von Rundstedt expressed that the accusations against the *General,* in the view of the presiding Army Group Judge, lacked any legal grounds. Therefore, in the interest of the troops, it is urgently desired to as quickly as possible give the *General* back his rights and to reinstate him as the Commander of the Division. According to the news available at *Supreme Command–West, General* Burgdorf gave a verbal account along the same lines to the *Führer.* He was strongly supported in this, because meanwhile, numerous *Gauleiters* intervened in favor of the *General.* Due to this, and because of reports requested by him from the Party, Bormann, the leader of the Party chancellery, also came to this assessment.

The *Führer*, however, has avoided making his decision. He postponed it temporarily, indicating that similar accusations were raised once before against the General in Russia. We know from the news available in Koblenz that *Generaloberst* Guderian, together with *General* Burgdorf and *Reichsleiter* Bormann, were waiting for an appropriate moment to again deal with the subject and to provide closure for the good of the Division, according to the proposal of *Feldmarschall* von Rundstedt. Up to the time of this decision, the *General*, as per clear explanations by *Supreme Command–West*, is considered to be on leave, meaning that he is not transferred into the *Führer*-Reserve at *OKH*. *Feldmarschall* Model, who obviously does not seem to be in agreement, still asserts a certain opposition to this solution, but after his premature decision, one can understand that. He did not, however, succeed in dissuading *Feldmarschall* von Rundstedt from his positive opinion. Therefore it may be expected that the final decision will be made in concurrence with our wishes.[111]

On 24 September, *Generalleutnant* Count Schwerin went to Holtermann in Hamm, and on the next day wrote letters to both *Gauleiters,* Meyer and Hoffmann, which were quoted several times. He then visited them to thank them for their assistance. Afterwards, Count Schwerin went to the Division's quarters for non-essential personnel east of Cologne," to Grimberg near Altenberg, and from there to his family at the Tegernsee.[112] Holtermann's eager activity, which in October also led him to the personnel office in Lübben and to the *Reich* War Court in Torgau, bore fruit.[113] On 16 October, the leader of the Party chancellery, Martin Bormann, wrote to the *Gauleiter,* Dr. Meyer in Münster:

Regarding: *Generalleutnant* Count Schwerin

Dear Party Comrade, Dr. Meyer!

About *General* Count Schwerin, the *Führer* repeatedly received reports, the situation is unobjectionably clear. As *General* Burgdorf explained to me a few days ago, *General* von Schwerin will be transferred to another unit.

On 27 October, Meyer forwarded the letter with the following additions to Schwerin:

Honorable *General!*

With the enclosed I would like to inform you of the letter from *Reichsleader* Bormann from 16 September. I beg you to treat the letter confidentially. Even if you no longer have your old, proud Westphalian *Panzer* Division to lead, it gives me great pleasure to know that you will be able to serve the *Führer* and Greater Germany as the head of another unit and a proven commander in such a decisive time.

I send you the most heartfelt wishes for your personal and military future.[114]

Nevertheless, Count Schwerin still hoped to be able to take over his old Division again.[115] Even Sepp Dietrich tried to influence Hitler to permit Count

Schwerin to remain with the *116th Panzer Division.* Holtermann informed
Schwerin on 15 November, "that *Oberstleutnant* Guderian has in the meantime
returned to the Division and the General [Schwerin—*Editor*] should report to
Führer Headquarters, after Sepp Dietrich again spoke to the *Führer* in favor of
the *General.* First, however, the *General* was to report to *Generaloberst* Guderian
for instruction."[116]

But Count Schwerin did not drive to the *Führer* Headquarters, which saddened
Holtermann to some extent. Holternann then wrote on 28 November:

> I truly hoped and wished that the *General,* after receiving my news about Sepp
> Dietrich's intervention, would have driven to the *Führer* Headquarters to be
> installed there in his former position, and again be given command of the Division.
> Since several weeks have passed, I am very afraid that this will no longer happen.
> In any case, I doubt that the P.A. [Army Personnel Office—*Author*] would, after
> such a long time, make a decision for a new change of the Division command. This
> is true especially since Model recently did not consider that as desirable, because
> the troops—and mainly he himself—had become used to the new Division
> Commander, and got along well with him.[117]

Already by 15 November Holtermann had reported, "that the Division is *per-
sona grata* with Model. It has indeed accomplished outstanding achievements,
but is now totally exhausted. Our own losses are very high. . . ."[118]

To be sure, Holtermann asked the most important commanders and officers of
the Division staff "individually" for their opinion about a return of Schwerin to
the Division. He reported:

> What also worries me is that the commanders only look forward to the *General's*
> return with unanimous pleasure if this were to be accompanied by something other
> than his former attitude toward the war. . . . Otherwise, they feared that sooner or
> later there would be new complications that could then easily lead to a tragic out-
> come. If the *General* would acknowledge the opinion desired by the commanders
> and then return to the Division, all requirements for a new lift in morale would be
> fulfilled and the Division would, under command of the *General,* again be capable
> of great achievements.[119]

Toward the end of the letter, Holtermann writes, "In retrospect, we are happy
that Guderian is back! And the joy would be unimaginable if in the end the
General would show up here."

All superiors and Party officials, with feelings of guilt due to their failure in
Aachen, supported Schwerin as one can see, since no one knew of his secret
plans. His return after such a long absence probably failed because of Model's not
quite unjustified skepticism. The following part of Holtermann's letter may show
how well it worked to sway the Party to Count Schwerin's side:

> I just received word from *Oberst* Lattmann that during a recent visit to the front,
> *General* Burgdorf discussed returning command of the Division to the *General* with

Feldmarschall Model. The *Feldmarschall* opined that the *General* should rather not get the Division, because the matter of Aachen, at that time, created much attention. *General* Burgdorf was supposed to have answered that, by all means, the Party wants it! As a humble person, I can only add that with God's help, it may have a good outcome: *Quod deus bene vertat.*[120]

As can be seen from a letter of 9 December to the Commander-in-Chief, Southwest, *Army Group C* in Italy, *Generalfeldmarschall* Kesselring, the *Reichs* War Tribunal decided the following on 13 November:

> The trial ordered against *Generalleutnant* Count von Schwerin for insubordination in the field and undermining military effectiveness was dismissed on 13 November 1944 by the *Reichs* War Tribunal.
>
> In connection with the evacuation of Aachen, *Generalleutnant* Count von Schwerin intervened without prior agreement with his higher headquarters, as well as without permission, in the process of evacuation. In this context he composed a letter on his own to the commander of the American forces, in which he asked for protection and assistance for the civilians of the city.
>
> Only in view of the special merits in the command of his Division, his personal bravery, and because *Generalleutnant* Count von Schwerin was in an understandable and justified state of agitation about the conditions of Aachen, the *Führer* dispensed with more serious consequences.
>
> *Generalleutnant* Count von Schwerin will be served a warning. This has to be made known to *Generalleutnant* Count von Schwerin.[121]

From this letter, it is evident that Count Schwerin was given command of another Division by the personnel office. On 4 December, he wrote about it to Holtermann:

> I am thankful to the P.A. for the decision it reached. As time went by, it became more and more clear to me that my return to the Division would not be practical— for all involved. Your letter of 28 November finally made it clear to me. In time, one even has to be able to part with that which one loves. "Count von Schwerin and his Division" were an institution in the Army.
>
> It found its shining conclusion. Every attempt to have the star that fell with the lucky return of the Division to German soil shine again would have been in vain. It would only have become a dim reflection of past beauty to the disappointment of everyone. The way this was solved, dear Holtermann, leaves an inextinguishable memory of a great time to all of us, of a great common experience, and a spotless, unblemished, and in a decisive aspect, a successful ending to this time. . . .
>
> The *90th Panzer-Grenadier Division* that is now entrusted to me is fighting in Italy, which will make my heartfelt desire to help defend the South Tyrol apparently come true in a marvelous way. This battle will be easy for me. I will dedicate myself to it wholeheartedly.[122]

On 5 December, Count Schwerin sent a parting letter to the *116th Panzer Division*, which was made public by his successor:

> As per orders of Army Headquarters, on 10 December, I will assume command of the *90th Panzer-Grenadier Division.* With this, a chapter of the *116th Panzer Division* comes to a close, one that will probably never be found in the history of any Division again. Filled with pride and love, I look back to the two years in which I saw this Division at the highest heights of success at arms, of glory and honor, but also in the deepest depths of the most difficult soldierly experiences. Yet always it retained unshakable courage, a tenacious zest for battle, and a strong will for self-preservation. It was full of confidence and as I truly know, also full of affection for me. The old soldiers and fighters from the Kalmuk steppe, from the Don, from the Mius, from Cuibishevo, from the Donets, from Zaporozhe and Krivoi Rog, from Normandy and from the Seine, those quick, tenacious, brave and proud Greyhounds, know how to tell it to those who only later came to the Division, but were so quickly trained by it to become tough fighters. With thanks in my heart I want to say to everyone: To have owned the trust and love of my soldiers has been the most beautiful reward. It gave me deepest inner satisfaction to finally bring the brave Division, unbroken and battle-strong, out of the cauldron of France and happily back to German soil near Aachen.[123]

After he transferred command to *Oberst* von Waldenburg, *Oberst* Voigtsberger also left the Division. He was under suspicion as an accessory in the prevention of Schwerin's arrest, and had to be prepared for the impending trial of Schwerin.[124] After completing the course for division commanders, Voigtsberger was installed as commander of the *309th Infantry Division* on the Eastern Front; on 1 February 1945, he was promoted to *Generalmajor.* On 19 September, he issued the following parting order to *Panzer-Grenadier Regiment 60*:

> To my brave and loyal regiment!
> After a brief command of the Division through fateful days and in the fight to keep our beloved *General,* and after transfer of command of the Division to your new Division commander, I leave you without knowing if I will ever come back to you.
> For 20 months I stood with you as your commander in difficult, heavy combat on the Eastern Front and in the West. Many dear comrades were torn out of our ranks and died as soldiers, and you know that I mourned each one.
> In the fateful, bloody battles of the last months, after crossing the Seine I made it my task to lead a firm and united regiment, fighting the enemy, to the Homeland. This was possible up to the border of the *Reich,* but the war must be continued inside the *Reich.*
> I beg all of you to do your duty under my successor also and to maintain the honor of the regiment pure and untainted. . . .
> I thank all of you for the trust you have given me, your obedience, your performance of duty, and your very unique camraderie. . . .[125]

Generalleutnant Count Schwerin and *Oberst* Voigtsberger left the Division as the most recognized commanders of their great time in the East. In 1957, the city of Aachen honored Count Schwerin with a ceremony and in 1975 they named a street after him.

Unfortunately, Count Schwerin clouded his image with the epilogue in his report to the Americans in 1945. He wrote:

> *General* von Waldenburg assumed command of the *116th Panzer Division*. Under him, the Division fought for some time in a hit-or-miss fashion. It still participated with distinction in the Ardennes offensive. In general, its achievements declined considerably. Its backbone was broken.
>
> Mysterious forces had inspired the Division for years, sometimes carrying it beyond normal capability. These forces, based on a perfect, trusting harmony of thought, sentiment, and action between the simple combat soldier and his leaders, had faded away.[126]

The following chapters will show that this judgment is false. Count Schwerin could not judge the achievements of the Division from far away. Surely the game of chance played with the Division from 12 to 18 September did not strengthen its fighting spirit. As the commanders rightfully expressed, Count Schwerin's attitude, at least since the mud catastrophe in the beginning of February 1944, carried a steady danger of complications. It lamed the Division. Since then, Count Schwerin was relieved of his post three times. For the officers around him, each time meant a "Ride across Lake Konstanz." [This is a saga of an equestrian rider who, on his way to the lake, went far beyond to the other side, not aware that he was riding on the frozen lake When informed of the danger he had faced, he became so scared that he dropped dead—*Translator*]

It was a wonder that it happened three times without evil consequences. Over and over again, well meaning advocates stood up for him. They were impressed by Schwerin's achievements in the battles in the Kalmuk steppe, on the Mius, and near Zaporozhe. They were also misled about his true intentions by his cunningly edited writings, such as the 1943 letters to Hitler and his adjutant, *Major* Engel.[127] Schwerin's last sentence displays another—mostly hidden—side of his character, which tripped him up several times during his life. He was no stranger to vanity, and on occasions overestimated himself and his capabilities. With his conceited statements, he sometimes caused himself aggravation and tarnished the image of an extraordinary personality. But let us follow the obituary written by Dr. Holtermann in the magazine *Der Windhund,* March 1981, who quoted Shakespeare, "He was a man, take him for all in all, I shall not look upon his like again" (*Hamlet,* Act I, Scene V):

> We have advanced far beyond the events of the front before Aachen and now we go back there again.[128]

On the evening of 14 September, the enemy stood in Rothe Erde and in front Eilendorf. The report that he entered Eilendorf was wrong; at dusk, the American tanks withdrew from the outskirts toward Brand.[129]

At 0815 hours on 15 September, 25 enemy tanks and numerous personnel carriers attacked from Brand toward Eilendorf, but turned east to Stolberg toward the *9th Panzer Division.* Before noon, the enemy forced his way into Eilendorf with tanks and infantry, and pushed the defenses of the *Armored Reconnaissance Battalion* back to the railroad line. *Oberst* Voigtsberger drove ahead to clarify the situation. At 1700 hours, the enemy attacked with tanks and infantry, after *Panzer-Grenadier Regiment 60* had just been emplaced, south of Burtscheid. It was turned back. The massing of the enemy in the area Eilendorf–Brand increased during the whole day. At 1700 hours, these forces started to attack toward the northeast at Geisberg, west of Stolberg, and at 1830 hours, they also attacked with 30 tanks from Eilendorf toward the north. Concentrated artillery fire immobilized them, however.[130] This was a grand success for the *3d Battalion* of the *Artillery Regiment,* which engaged the tank concentration in the vicinity of Eilendorf with 1,250 rounds.[131] Six NCO forward observers from *2d Battalion,* which was not deployed, were called up as a real necessity.[132] The staff of *1st Battalion* was also ordered to march to Aachen; subordinated to it were two heavy batteries with 152mm howitzers [captured Soviet weapons—*Editor*], namely the *2d Battery, Artillery Battalion 992* and the *3d Battery, Artillery Battalion 997.*[133] The rest of the front of *116th Panzer Division* in the west and south remained quiet.

It was again a very critical day for the *9th Panzer Division.* On 15 September, after the division succeeded during the night in regaining all but two bunkers of the *Westwall* position by Mausbach, the enemy, reaching around to the north, pushed into the village. He was brought to a halt in front of Gressenich. The *9th Panzer Division* shot up 42 enemy tanks and the *116th* destroyed two. The front line of both Divisions ran from Schnee-Berg in the first *Westwall* position to Bunker 10, near Vaalserquartier. From there it ran east and south in an arc to the Ronheide railroad station, then south of Steinebrück–south of Burtscheid to the Aachen– Eschweiler railroad line. After that, it was almost in line with this up to the tunnel entrance northeast of Eilendorf, and from there it ran to the *9th Panzer Division*'s sector of the *Westwall,* except for the deep breach near Mausbach and a second one at the right wing.[134]

In the afternoon, the enemy got busy again between the Maas and Aachen. An attack could be counted on for 16 September. The enemy entered Monschau in the sector of the unit on the left, *LXXIV Corps.* A continuation of the attack against the *9th Panzer Division* and against the left wing of the *116th* had to be expected with certainty, especially since in addition to the 3d Armored and the 1st Infantry Divisions in front of Gressenich, the presence of the 9th Infantry Division had also been revealed by prisoners.[135] The *116th Panzer Division* reported the following evaluation of the enemy:

During the day, south of Eilendorf, the enemy was reinforced to about the size of one *Panzer* Division . . . south of Aachen, the arrival and adjustment of fire by enemy artillery disclose the preparation of at least one infantry division.

Attack on Aachen toward the north is to be expected on 16 September, after corresponding support by artillery and air force.[136]

With this situation report, the Division made it look worse than it was. American historical material expresses the following:

Because the *116th Panzer Division* assumed that a complete US infantry division was assembled south of Aachen and almost a full armored division near Eilendorf, *General* Schack hesitated to pull the *116th Panzer Division* from Aachen into the Stolberg corridor. Almost uninterrupted bombardment by American artillery strengthened the belief that the city would be hit by an attack of great dimensions on 16 September. Thus, the German defense remained scattered.[137]

The *116th Panzer Division* reported its intentions for 16 September, "As per *Führer* order," new units had been subordinated: *Anti-Aircraft Group Aachen* and *Militia Training Battalion II/6,* deployed in the second *Westwall* position. A diagram of the structure of the Division from 15 September is shown as Appendix 10. It clearly shows the low strength of and the few weapons available to the Division, as well as the subordinated units. *Anti-Aircraft Group Aachen,* with its considerable weaponry, stands out: 14 8.8cm, 15 3.7cm, and 100 2cm guns. The Commanding General arrayed *Machine Gun Battalion 34* near Eilendorf behind *Combat Group Berger,* along with stragglers, and elements of *Militia Training Battalion II/6.*[138]

The weekly status report of 16 September completes the picture of the Division.[139] According to this, it consisted of the following battalions:

1 Average strength
2 Medium strength
1 Weak

Besides this, it had four strong attached battalions:

Luftwaffe Fortress Battalion XIX (Neubert).
Infantry Training Battalion 453
Battalion Kühne (a parachute infantry unit)
Battalion Berger (Now probably *Militia Training Battalion II/6* with *Machine Gun Battalion 34*)

Armored, anti-tank, and artillery included:

3 *Panzer IVs*
1 *Panzer V*
1 Assault Gun
8 7.5cm towed anti-tank guns

1 self-propelled 7.5cm anti-tank gun

In addition to organic artillery (see schematic), 2 additional heavy batteries, that is,

2d Battery, Artillery Battalion 992 and *3d Battery, Artillery Battalion 997*

The Division reported a mobility factor of 40 percent, and its battle value the incomprehensibly high level of "II." As of 17 September, the Division status report indicated two more *Panzer IVs* and also mentioned 65 armored personnel carriers and 12 armored reconnaissance vehicles (8-wheel). On 16 September, corps staff intended to install the staff of *353d Infantry Division* in command of the *9th Panzer Division*'s left sector, from north of Zweifall to the south. On that morning, the first units of the *12th Infantry Division* were expected in Jülich and Düren, and were to be moved up in convoys provided by corps.[140] On 15 September, *Army Group B* complained, "The absence of mobile heavy anti-tank weapons definitely apparent. The provision of tank or assault gun brigades is an urgent requirement."[141]

LXXXI Corps experienced another disturbing day on 16 September.[142] From 1000 hours on, the enemy attacked the inner wings of the *275th* and *49th Infantry Divisions*. While the *275th* was able to hold its position, the *49th* was pushed back to Ubachsberg and Simpelveld. A gaping hole west of Ubachsberg developed between the divisions. The attack on the *49th Infantry Division* also had ramifications on the right wing of the *116th Panzer Division*. This was in the sector of *Panzer-Grenadier Regiment 156* and the unit to its right, *Luftwaffe Fortress Battalion XIX,* which was deployed in the *Westwall* and evidently attached to *Infantry Training Battalion 453*. The enemy succeeded in penetrating the sector held by *2d Battalion, Panzer-Grenadier Regiment 156,* but this was mopped up. *Panzer-Grenadier Regiment 60*—most likely the *1st Battalion*—parried an enemy tank attack south of Steinebrück. At 2350 hours, the Division reported, "All attacks on the southern edge of Aachen turned back. Breach mopped up. *Infantry Training Battalion 453* regained two bunkers in counterattack." These bunkers were in the vicinity of Vaalserquartier.[143]

As expected, the situation on the Division's left wing became much worse, as it did for the *9th Panzer* and *353d Infantry Divisions*. By 0545 hours, the *116th Panzer Division* had already reported:

> Increasing nuisance fire, including heavy calibers. Strike troop platoons infiltrated through, remaining near bunkers south of Verlautenheide. Militia and scattered troops deployed in the *Westwall* are not combat effective. *Division Reconnaissance Platoon* deployed for reconnaissance and security toward Verlautenheide.[144]

At the same time, the *9th Panzer Division* reported an enemy attack on Atsch, which was situated southeast of the Division. It moved *Training Battalion 473* into the gap that developed in that area. The fighting in the vicinity of the breach south and southeast of Stolberg continued. An attack planned to regain Mausbach had to be canceled because in the morning, the enemy was able to overcome the *Westwall* in the forest southeast of Zweifall almost without a fight and entered

Schevenhütte at 1810 hours. The commander of the *353d Infantry Division,* who had assumed command there, had to report that by 1025 hours the militia had left the second *Westwall* position, south of Zweifall. The *9th Panzer Division* did get the order to secure the five-kilometer-wide gap through reconnaissance, but could not prevent tragedy. The Division had to bend its left wing north of Schevenhütte. The left wing of the *353d Infantry Division* was ascertained west of Hürtgen.[145]

Now, the first regiment of the *12th Infantry Division, Füsilier Regiment 27 (Reinforced),* attacked at the boundary between the *116th* and *9th Panzer Divisions.* It attacked with one battalion each via Verlautenheide and Atsch, respectively, and threw the enemy back to the *Westwall.* Verlautenheide and Atsch were retaken. Further advances were halted by heavy artillery fire.[146] Earlier, Verlautenheide was cleared of weak enemy units by the Division reserve, *2d Company, Panzer-Grenadier Regiment 156,* under the command of *Oberleutnant* Triantaphylides. Then, the company linked up with *Füsilier Regiment 27* at its right wing, joined it in its attack and seized three bunkers. The *2d Company* remained there, at the boundary with the *12th Infantry Division* at the left wing of *Combat Group Berger,* until 21 September.[147]

The *Army Group B* journal greeted the intervention of the *12th Infantry Division* with the following, "The units of the *12th Infantry Division* that arrived on the battlefield today led a successful counterattack east of Aachen. The fact that strong new, units appear has encouraging effects on troops and the populace."[148]

At 2000 hours, the *Ia* of the *12th Infantry Division* arrived at the command post of the *9th Panzer Division* to coordinate the transfer of command in the *9th's* sector and to discuss the attack by the 12th on Mausbach.[149]

On 16 September, *Supreme Command–West* issued an order for the defense of the West pursuant to an *OKW* directive of the same day:

> The fighting in the West has reached across the border to the German homeland in broad sectors.
>
> German towns and villages become battle areas. This fact must bring fanaticism to the way we fight, and it has to heighten our strength by deploying every able-bodied man in the battle area to the fullest. Every bunker, every block of houses in a German city, every German village must become a fortress before which the enemy either bleeds to death or is buried beneath in man-on-man fighting. There is no more large-scale maneuver, only defending the position or destruction. Leaders of every rank are responsible for awakening this fanaticism amongst the troops and population, to continuously increase it, and to use it as a weapon against the invaders on German soil. Anyone indifferent, whether leader or simple soldier, who is not aware of the important and decisive obligation of the hour and does not do his duty with mortal dedication is to be removed and held responsible.[150]

The *7th Army* also issued an order for conduct of battle and organization in the *Westwall.* The first two paragraphs and the mission for *LXXXI Corps* follow:

1. Enemy main effort will still be in the vicinity of the penetration east of Aachen. Further strong efforts are on the front west of Aachen, where the opponent will try to break through the obstacles between the Maas and *Westwall* toward the north or northeast. Others will be directed toward the southern flank of the Army, where the opponent penetrated the northern wing of *1st Army* with strong forces toward Bitburg. A change of direction by these forces is possible at any time. At this time, seven infantry divisions nd three armored divisions can be counted along the total front of the Army.

2. *7th Army* defends the position northeast of Maastricht–Aachen and the *Westwall* to the last man and to the last round. The breaches achieved by the enemy are to be mopped up.

...

4. a. *LXXXI Corps* defends the position northeast of Maastricht–Aachen and the *Westwall*. First, it mops up the breaches in the second *Westwall* line east of Aachen, then counterattacks to throw the enemy out of the area east of Aachen and back across the forward *Westwall* line and secures the retaken position.

   For this, the *12th Infantry Division* will be subordinated to the corps. Besides, as of 18 September, a *Panzer* brigade will be moved up into the vicinity of Düren and subordinated to the Corps. The intention regarding the *183d Infantry Division,* arriving as of 18 September in the Vettweiss–Zülpich–Euskirchen area, is to deploy it at the right wing of the corps.[151]

In the order, the *353d Infantry Division* was detached to *LXXIV Corps,* and the boundary between it and *LXXXI Corps* was changed so that Zweifall was still in the sector of *LXXXI Corps.* Furthermore, *LXXXI Corps* received orders, "to pull out the *116th Panzer Division* after the *12th Infantry Division* goes into action, and to keep it in readiness as corps reserve in the vicinity of Eschweiler. The *Panzer* brigade appropriated to the corps on 18 September is to be incorporated into the *116th Panzer Division.*"

Both moves were delayed. First, the *9th Panzer Division* was pulled out. *Panzer Brigade 105* was incorporated to it.

"The Corps Order for the Defense of the *Westwall*" from 2000 hours on 16 September contained the following paragraphs:

1. Corps counts on the enemy to mass its armored forces on 17 September to strive for a penetration on both sides of Aachen.

2. *LXXXI Corps*, to which *12th Infantry Division* was incorporated and subordinated via rail trainsport, continues to defend the sinew position and in the *Westwall*.

3. Combat Missions: . . .

   116th Panzer Division holds present main battle line, seeks link up with the forces of the *12th Infantry Division* that were deployed near Verlautenheide and toward east. It establishes a mobile armored reserve, to counterattack the expected tank attack by the opponent on 17 September.

The artillery of the *116th Panzer Division* is to be employed in close cooperation with the *49th Infantry Division* and *12th Infantry Division* not only for
defense against enemy attacks in front of our own front, but also for support of
the *49th Infantry Division.* Combined fire is to be especially assured at identified enemy main efforts in cooperation with the *12th Infantry Division* and
Combat Group 9th Panzer Division.

12th Infantry Division. Effective 2000 hours on 16 September, the former *9th
Panzer Division* with all subordinated and incorporated units will be subordinated to the *12th Infantry Division.* Using a strong combination of all armored
forces in *Combat Group Sperling* [*9th Panzer Division—Editor*], the *12th
Infantry Division* attacks from the vicinity of Eschweiler–Wenau–Merode to
seize the *Westwall* in the Geisberg–Zweifall sector, and repels the opponent that
advanced across the *Westwall* toward the east and northeast. Further, through
active reconnaissance in the Zweifall–Lammersdorf–Hürtgen sector, the *12th
Infantry Division* links up with the northern wing of the *353d Infantry Division*
in the vicinity of Drei-Kaiser-Eichen.

4. Without consideration for weakening units at the front which are not under
   attack, all divisions must designate reserves and keep them in readiness for
   deployment at points under attack, so that they may be deployed in a timely fashion on short notice.[152]

The boundary between the *116th Panzer* and *49th Infantry Divisions* now ran
from Schnee-Berg (belonging to the *116th*) along the *Westwall* toward the northeast to Bardenberg (along in the *116th*'s sector). This was an astonishing measure, because by doing so, the defense of this part of the *Westwall* remained
uncertain. The boundary with the *12th Infantry Division* assigned Eilendorf to the
116th. At 1510 hours on 17 September, the Verlautenheide–Eilendorf road was
designated as the boundary, with the *12th Infantry Division* being assigned
responsibility for the road.

This day brought a new crisis to the Western Front. The daily report of
Supreme Command–West reported the following about the situation of *Army
Group B*:

17 September was marked by large enemy air landings in the area between
Eindhoven and Arnhem. With two to three divisions, the enemy tried to gain possession of all essential crossing points, to keep the roads across canals and rivers
open for the English Second Army, which started to attack toward the north during
the afternoon. From all sides, countermeasures by training and supply units of all
parts of the *Wehrmacht* are in process. According to recent news, the enemy could
only achieve his objectives at some points. Continuation of the landings during the
night must be expected. The absence of mobile, robust reaction reserves increases
the difficulty of this battle, to which the opponent evidently attributes decisive
importance. . . .

On the right wing of *7th Army*, the enemy also threw back units of *LXXXI Corps* to the north. Our own counterattacks east of Aachen are progressing slowly. The fluctuating battles at the Eifel front of *I SS-Panzer Corps* continue. Several enemy breaches could not be cleared. The overall condition of the extremely strained *Army Group B* is again critical. . . .[153]

The addition of more units with heavy, mobile anti-tank capabilities was then requested and complaints were made regarding lack of fuel. The complete absence of air and ground counteraction against the airborne landing prevented countermeasures. Originally, the enemy airborne landing had the Ruhr area as its ultimate objective and was supposed to be via Venlo to Wesel, but on 8 September, when the first V-2s were launched from western Holland and landed on London, Montgomery decided to direct the operation toward Arnhem. This operation was code-named MARKET GARDEN.[154]

On 17 September, northwest of Aachen, the *275th* and *49th Infantry Divisions* were thrown back to a line along the Nuth–Heerlen railroad, to the southern edge of Kerkarde, and then merged with the *Westwall*. On the left wing of the *49th,* in front of the right wing of the *116th Panzer Division*, the towns of Horbach, Bochholtz, and Orsbach were lost. At 1420 hours, the boundary between the *49th Infantry Division* and *116th Panzer Division* was moved to the north up to Orsbach. With this, clear conditions were established. During the night of 16/17 September, the *116th* had already deployed reconnaissance patrols from the *Armored Reconnaissance Battalion* forward of its right wing to monitor the enemy's advance. They discovered, thereby, a parachute unit with three companies in the area of Orsbach. This was subordinated to the Division for deployment in the *Westwall*, between Schnee-Berg and Vetschau. The *1st Company* of *Security Battalion 302* was already deployed between Vetschau and Horbach, and was also subordinated to the *116th Panzer Division*.

To assume control of the additional sector on the Division's right, the staff of *Armored Reconnaissance Battalion 116* was brought over from the left wing. Its remaining units near Rothe Erde were subordinated to *Panzer-Grenadier Regiment 60. Combat Group Berger* linked up at the very tip of the Division's left wing. Aside from the named units, the Division received ten assault tanks from *Assault Tank Battalion (Sturmpanzerabteilung) 217* for the defense of the newly assigned *Westwall* sector. [These "assault tanks" were fully-armored 15cm howitzers used for fire support missions, as opposed to the multi-role, 7.5cm "assault guns" found in *"Sturmgeschütz"* battalions—*Editor*] They were in Düren and were initially ordered up to Broichheiden, south of Mariadorf.[155] Further, *Luftwaffe Fortress Battalion XIII* was also subordinated to the Division. It was to be picked up in Jülich. Vogelsang noted:

> The first replacements for the Division arrived. Yesterday, we received a so-called *Luftwaffe* fortress battalion, which was put together hastily from dissolved bomber squadrons and ground units, and was comprised almost exclusively of important

specialists of all kinds. The overall impression of the personnel is excellent, only fresh young men, in a condition we have not seen in a long time.

Due to the lack of anything resembling infantry experience and training of the men, the planned deployment of the battalion as an integral unit seemed irresponsible. This is why we distributed the personnel according to capability and preparatory training to all types of weapons of the Division. The best place for them was there, amongst experienced, old *Landsers* [infantrymen—*Editor*] and commanders.

At the same time, a march battalion from our own replacement units arrived, 20 officers and 380 men strong, half of them being recovering Division veterans, returning as convalescents.[156]

On 17 September, the *49th Infantry Division* deployed the newly-arrived *Fortress Machine Gun Battalion 47* in the gap existing between Herzogenrath and Kohlscheid.

By these measures, the imminent danger of an American breakthrough north of Aachen was averted for the time being. At 2215 hours, Horbach was again found to be free of the enemy. Enemy advances were repelled south of Aachen, near *2d Battalion, Panzer-Grenadier Regiment 156,* and near *2d Battalion, Panzer-Grenadier Regiment 60.* Division artillery supported the attack of *Füsilier Regiment 27* of the *12th Infantry Division* near Eilendorf with combined fires. The attack, however, was stifled due to heavy enemy artillery fire.

At 1200 hours on 17 September, the second infantry regiment of the *12th Infantry Division* and the combat group of the *9th Panzer Division* that arrived in the meantime attacked Mausbach. This brought some initial success, but the attack did not reach its objective and was to be continued the next morning. Our own attack troops suffered heavy losses. Toward midnight, the enemy attacked from the southeast toward Stolberg, turned the flank of the bunker position up to Binsfeldhammer, and seized the Hammer-Berg. The *12th Infantry Division* now stopped the attack on Mausbach and with permission from Corps regrouped its forces in such a way that it could push into the flank of the enemy. This attack, which was initiated the next morning, also only brought modest success.

The attack by a battalion from the left flank of the *12th Infantry Division* toward Schevenhütte in the night of 16/17 September failed.[157] Thus, the *12th* arrived at the proper moment to foil the breakthrough, but it did not succeed in retaking the *Westwall* because it had to be deployed hurriedly and in a piecemeal fashion.

Headquarters, *LXXXI Corps* reported its intention for 18 September to be, "Holding of blocking position and the city of Aachen, and retaking the *Westwall* position, initially between Eilendorf and Zweifall."[158]

The *49th Infantry Division* detected enemy assembly areas with tanks near Heerlen and Terwinselen. Here, as with the *275th Infantry Division,* the enemy continued his attacks during the day on 18 September. In the evening, both divisions stood along the line Brunssum–Nieuwenhagen–Kerkrade–*Westwall*, up to the contact point near Horbach.

On 18 September, the *116th Panzer Division* reported the following: Advances toward the Schnee-Berg east of Vaalserquartier and north of Rothe Erde were repelled. The armored strength of the Division was raised considerably. Besides the seven tanks and twelve armored reconnaissance vehicles reported on 17 September, it now also had ten assault tanks mounting 15cm guns from *Assault Tank Battalion 217* at its disposal, as well as fifteen assault guns from *Assault Gun Brigade 394*. It also had a captured American reconnaissance vehicle, brought by a soldier when he escaped from captivity. On the afternoon of 18 September, the assault tanks stood east of Herzogenrath, already behind the left wing of *49th Infantry Division.*

The *12th Infantry Division* was pushed into the defense and turned back enemy attacks on Verlautenheide, Stolberg, and Gressenich.[159]

On the morning of 18 September, Gersdorff reported to Krebs, "southeast of Aachen situation calm; succeeded in establishing front. . . . Artillery fire in previously unknown strength."[160]

At 1910 hours, Gersdorff reported, "that the *275th* and *49th Infantry Divisions* have no long-term defensive power. By deploying *183d Infantry Division* one believes to remain master of the situation."

Krebs emphasized, "that the *183d Infantry Division,* as Army Group reserve, can only be deployed independently in response to the most serious threat."

The 18 September daily report from *Army Group B* stated:

> After a noticeable reduction in the air during the morning, the enemy continued its airborne landing during the afternoon, with the bulk into yesterday's areas, north of Eindhoven near Nijmegen and west of Arnhem. It is estimated that three divisions have landed. Our countermeasures, so far, have had only partial success. . . .
>
> The opponent continued his attacks with local successes on the inner wings of *1st Parachute Army* and the *7th Army*. The focal point of heavy fighting was the area east of Aachen, where the attack of the *12th Infantry Division* coincided with strong enemy attacks. Considerable enemy artillery effects caused heavy losses to our troops. The attack to achieve a line favorable for defense will be continued on 19 September in the manner of strike troops.
>
> There were no changes on the remainder of the *7th Army* front.[161]

The formula to continue the attack in a "strike troop manner" came from reaching the conclusion that the Americans had materiel superiority regarding artillery, air power, and tanks.

The situation of *Army Group B* continued to be critical. The bridgehead across the Western *Scheldt* near Terneuzen was attacked by strong forces of the Canadian First Army, including 200 tanks. It had to be narrowed. Regarding the airborne landings and the situation of the *7th Army, Supreme Command–West* reported that the English units, advancing north via Eindhoven, linked up with the American airborne southwest of Nijmegen and were now advancing toward the Maas near Nijmegen.[162] Our counterattack from the southeast toward Nijmegen did not get a good start. The counterattack against the English who landed west of Arnhem, however, made good progress. The situation along the boundary between the *1st Parachute Army* and the *7th Army,* southwest of Heins, caused concern to *Supreme Command–West.*

The gap between *1st Parachute* and *7th Armies* in the Selfkant actually invited the enemy to break through toward Heinsberg and separate the armies. But *XIX Corps* omitted, as we heard earlier, the scheduled attack for 20 September, out of concern for its northern flank. Thus, the fresh *183d Infantry Division* could be brought on and emplaced in the *Westwall* on both sides of Geilenkirchen. Through an attack on 20 September it managed to reestablish a connection with the *1st Parachute Army* northwest of Geilenkirchen.[163] During a long-distance call on the morning of 19 September, Model announced to Brandenberger that the *180th* and *190th Infantry Divisions* were on the way. The *246th Volks-Grenadier Division* was also approaching as of 21 September, while another one could be expected as of 24 September.[164]

He furthermore ordered that, "The curved frontline at Aachen is to be held, regardless of how many forces it may cost."

The other divisions of *LXXXI Corps* (*49th Infantry Division, 116th Panzer Division, 12th Infantry Division* with the *9th Panzer Division*) were in the same positions in the *Westwall* on 19 September as they had been on the previous day. Heavy fighting took place only in the sector of the *12th Infantry Division,* and there mainly around Stolberg, where the *9th Panzer Division* combat group was assembled. The still-undecided state of the left wing near Schevenhütte troubled the Corps staff. It again reported its intentions for 20 September, "*12th Infantry Division* to attack, clear up *Westwall* position up to Zweifall."[165]

On 19 September, *Oberst* von Waldenburg assumed command of the *116th Panzer Division* from *Oberst* Voigtsberger at the command post in Mariadorf. After an in-briefing at corps headquarters, he confided in his pocket calendar, "Predecessor apparently had nervous breakdown."[166] After assuming command he wrote, "Difficult conditions and . . . materiel superiority of the Americans." The following day, the new Division Commander recorded, "Moved in and getting to know staff, some things have to change! Division seems to be quite all right, but all somehow like a *Freikorps*!!" [*Freikorps* were groups of irregulars which formed from dissolving Imperial Army units during the chaos in Germany which followed the November 1918 armistice—*Editor.*]

After all that had happened, at this point, he was probably not all wrong.

The Division received the new man with some suspicion, fearing that he was sent as an observer who was told to pry. Since this was not the case, the reservations of most were quickly cast aside. After almost exclusive service in the General Staff, *Oberst* von Waldenburg participated in a course for Division commanders in February 1944, and led the *24th Panzer Division*'s *Panzer-Grenadier Regiment 26* in the East from April until August, where he gained combat experience as a troop commander. After he led the *25th Panzer-Grenadier Division* during its restructuring at the training area Grafenwöhr for five days, on 17 September, Waldenburg was ordered to the West to assume command of the *116th Panzer Division.* Unlike his predecessor, Waldenburg was not an extraordinary personality. However, this was good for the Division. It was led with expert knowledge during very difficult times. The time of surprising decisions was over. All who became closer to Waldenburg learned to appreciate him. He was personally brave and humble, always stood up for his subordinates, and allowed them freedom of action.

On 21 September, Waldenburg issued the following Division order:

> On 14 September 1944, the Commander, *Generalleutnant* Count von Schwerin, was called away for a different assignment. For almost two years of battles and deployments that were mostly very difficult, he led the Division from success to success; he had his soldiers' deepest trust, reverence, and willingness to fight, and gave special meaning to the name of the Division.
>
> On 19 September 1944, I assumed command of the Division from the Acting Division Commander, *Oberst* Voigtsberger.
>
> I will continue to lead the Division in the old spirit and I expect that all officers, NCOs, and troops will afford me their full trust, as they did to their old commander. During the most difficult hour, all our people are in the hardest fight, we soldiers in heavy battles at the borders of the *Reich.* The great struggle requires the extreme dedication of every sold.ier until final victory is achieved. This holy battle for the existence of our *Reich* has to be, now more than ever, in every soldier's consciousness! . . .[167]

The daily report by *Supreme Command–West* on 20 September contained:

> The English Second Army was able to considerably widen its successful breakthrough with its XXX Corps toward the north. With heavy tank and artillery support, with smoke and white phosphorus, the opponent was able to overwhelm the defenders of the Nijmegen bridgehead and to seize the railroad bridge across the Waal. The road bridge was still being fought over in the evening. . . . The danger exists of further advances on Arnhem by the superior enemy, in connection with possible new airborne landings in this area. The attack from the southeast toward Nijmegen made only minor progress. The battles to destroy the British 1st Airborne Division west of Arnhem are still ongoing. The number of prisoners, including the Division Commander, has risen to 1,800. [*sic*—Major General Roy Urquhart, the commander of the British 1st Airborne Division, was not captured—*Editor.*] About 1,000 Englishmen are encircled and are defending themselves vehemently. The attempts of *1st Parachute Army* to cut off the enemy supply road . . . north of Eindhoven did not lead . . . to the desired result. . . . In the *7th Army* area, the day generally passed successfully. The link up with *1st Parachute Army* was . . . completed. Small successes in defense and attacks were achieved east of Aachen, as well as by *LXXIV Corps* and *I SS-Panzer Corps.*

The enemy's breakthrough southwest of Bitburg could almost be cleared. Making good progress, offensive operations there are not yet finished. For 21 September, the recommencement of stronger, concentric attacks in the area around Aachen must be reckoned with. The absence of sufficient, mobile, heavy anti-tank weapons (tanks and assault guns) today again had a decisive influence on the battles.[168]

Near the *116th Panzer Division,* south of Burtscheid, a strong enemey reconnaissance patrol was turned back by *Panzer-Grenadier Regiment 60* at 0800 hours. Using combined fires, the Division's artillery duelled with enemy mortar and artillery positions, as well as assembled armored formations northeast of Brand. In the evening hours, an enemy reconnaissance advance was turned back by *2d Battalion, Panzer-Grenadier Regiment 156* with bloody losses for the enemy.

There was heavy fighting in the *12th Infantry* and *9th Panzer Division* sectors. During the day, the enemy's local attacks, mainly against the dominating hills southeast of Stolberg, were repelled or beaten back by counterattack. At 1455 hours, the *116th Panzer Division* received orders to transfer control of *Security Battalion 302*'s sector to the *49th Infantry Division* and to shorten the protruding salient of the main battle line south of Aachen, while leaving strong defenses in the old position. The as yet unsecure salient was in the *Panzer-Grenadier Regiment 156* sector, southwest of the city, on both sides of the road to Lüttich. At 2300 hours, the Division was instructed to prepare to assume responsibility for a battalion sector at the left wing. This was done during the night of 21/22 September.[169]

On 20 September, the Division requested the addition of its anti-aircraft battalion, which had been left without guns since its organization in France, and been split up during the withdrawal into the Saar area.[170] The request was granted. In the meantime, the battalion had received guns and returned to the Division about five weeks later.

At midnight on 20 September, Vogelsang noted:

> The enemy artillery was unpleasantly active. Day and night, rounds and nuisance fire of all calibers crashed into Aachen, Stolberg, Eschweiler, and Würselen. No village near the front was spared, today, even Mariadorf received its first heavy packages. We are actually afraid for the evacuation trains, which often wait for hours at the railroad station for their departure and are jammed full of women and children!
>
> The positions of the Division could all be held, whereby the subordinated non-organic units such as militia, training units, scattered elements, and reaction forces which, contrary to expectations, fended for themselves quite well. In heavy fighting, the *12th Infantry Division* succeeded in slowly pushing the opponent out of the point of breach near Eschweiler.
>
> Near the right neighbor, the American, nevertheless, surpisingly broke through to the *Westwall*. . . . The evacuation of Aachen comes to its end in relative order.[171]

We can learn from Vogelsang's observations about the achievements of the non-organic units that it is irresponsible to throw such pitiful units abruptly into a big battle, as happened in the beginning of the battle of Aachen. They lacked everything required to endure. But incorporated in an organized major unit, which can afford support with heavy weapons, with tanks to help if necessary, and which can secure dependable logistical support, the soldiers quickly find their place and pull their weight. The effect produced by the presence of an artillery forward observer, the emplacement of an anti-tank gun, or the regular appearance of a field kitchen can only be appreciated by someone who had to make do without all that assistance. The initial complaints of the superiors about such units running away were actually true to the facts, but highly unjust and in part their own fault.

The night of 21 September passed for all Divisions of the corps without any significant events. In accordance with orders, in the morning, *116th Panzer Division* moved the main battle line back southwest of Aachen to a "sinew" as follows: a farm house, approximately 500 meters southwest of the railroad bridge, across the road to Vaals, to the railroad line almost two kilometers southwest of the main railroad station.[172] [See p. 266 for a sketch of a "sinew."]

The situation became extremely unfortunate near Nijmegen during the night of 21 September. The enemy crossed the Waal during the afternoon of 20 September. Nevertheless, Army Group did not permit blowing up the road bridge at 1930 hours. At 2330 hours, *II SS-Panzer Corps,* which was responsible for that sector, reported that the demolition of the bridge would no longer be possible. Our attack from the southeast toward Nijmegen failed. On the afternoon of 21 September, Krebs discussed the loss of the bridge with *Supreme Command–West* and *OKW*. He admitted that it would have been better to blow it up, but referred to Arnhem, where it was good to have not done so. There, the bridge was back in our hands and the traffic moved south, to establish a blocking position north of Nijmegen.[173]

The battles of *LXXXI Corps* on 21 September were not mentioned at all in the Army Group daily report. Nevertheless, things were not so quiet, especially not in the sectors of the *12th Infantry* and *9th Panzer Divisions*.[174] The *9th Panzer Division* journal reports heavy battles at Stolberg and the hills east of it, the Hammer and Donner Berg.[175]

The report by Army Group was true for *116th Panzer Division. Oberst* von Waldenburg wrote on 21 September, "Morning with *Regiments 156* and *60* in Aachen, make good impression. Quite calm at the front. Enemy attempts to bypass us on both wings."[176]

During the night of 22 September, the *116th Panzer Division* carried out a reorganization of its defenses. In the right sector, *Panzer-Grenadier Regiment 156* assumed control from Vetschau to the Aachen–Lüttich railroad line. In accordance with the situation of 24 September, four battalions were deployed. *Battalion Kühne* (the parachute infantry unit) was on the right wing; *Infantry Training Battalion 453* was withdrawn, handing over control of its sector to *Luftwaffe*

Fortress Battalion XIX, separately deployed; and the remainder of the sector was defended by both battalions of *Panzer-Grenadier Regiment 156. Panzer-Grenadier Regiment 60* commanded both its battalions in the south and southeast sector in front of Aachen without change. Adjacent to and in contact with *Panzer-Grenadier Regiment 60* was *Armored Reconnaissance Battalion 116,* whose staff transferred the command in the right sector of the Division to the Commander, *Panzer-Grenadier Regiment 156. Machine Gun Battalion 34* and *Combat Group Berger* were deployed near Verlautenheide. At the left wing, east of Eilendorf, *Infantry Training Battalion 453* took over the sector of a battalion of *Füsilier Regiment 27.* The left wing of the Division was now at the large Schwarzenbruch farm house, in contact with the *9th Panzer Division* combat group.[177]

On 21 September, Rundstedt rendered a situation report to Jodl, the final sentences of which were:

> The need to *hold, under all circumstances,* and not to give up even one foot of land for any tactical or operational reason, will lead to a continuous consumption of strength and wear and tear of materiel.
>
> It will be necessary to
>
> a) continuousely feed the front with personnel and materiel and
>
> b) to prepare and move up forces *behind* endangered portions of the front in sufficient strength so that under no circumstances can the line be torn up or penetrated.
>
> This consideration repeatedly leads to the request for *strong* new forces, amounting to at least twelve infantry divisions and three to four combat-proven armored units, to be maintained in readiness as command reserves capable of attacking to catch and destroy any enemy which may break through. . . .
>
> In the *near future* it is important for *Supreme Command–West* to *gain time* in tense battle. With this time, wherever still possible, it must complete positions in the West and the *Westwall* to make them capable of defense and of lasting until the various new armaments being prepared by the High Command can be brought to bear. If this succeeds, the enemy will be forced into static warfare with increasing daily losses, and would only have limited use of the full mobility which affords him so many advantages.
>
> In my view, the *final objective* for the conduct of the battle in the West should be to *attack* and *defeat* the enemy *decisively* at a later point in time in *one* place. Only in this way can the threat against German soil be eliminated and above all, the bases of the enemy air force be pushed back.[178]

On the afternoon of 22 September, the troops attacking from west and east against the English who broke through toward Nijmegen were able to temporarily interdict the enemy's route of advance between Eindhoven and Nijmegen. In view of the weakness of these troops, this was a considerable achievement. During the night of 25 September, another interdiction of the road was achieved. The English attempt to break through from Nijmegen to Arnhem was averted with difficulty. The battle with the surrounded English paratroopers west of Arnhem was still going on.[179]

The events of 22 September in the *7th Army* sector were reported in the daily report of *Supreme Command–West* as follows, "By the evening, with a heavy attack, *7th Army* was able to throw the enemy that advanced east of Stolberg back to its original position. Thereby, under its commander, *Oberst* Engel, *12th Infantry Division* distinguished itself again by especial steadfastness."[180]

The *116th Panzer Division* sent seven assault guns and two *Panzer IVs* to support the battle, and joined in the battle for Stolberg with its artillery. It had no other tanks available, partly because of a fuel shortage. Already, the Division had to report to the corps during the night that its tanks were immobile and that repaired ones could not be brought up, since there were only 0.3 fuel quotas available [enough fuel to move only 30 percent of the Division's vehicles—*Editor*]. Nevertheless, the Division had the following ready for action:

11 *Panzer IV*
1 *Panzer V*
2 Assault guns
2 Self-propelled 7.5cm anti-tank guns
20 Towed 7.5cm anti-tank guns
Subordinated *Assault Gun Brigade 394* had 16 assault guns ready for action.[181]

The next day, 23 September, passed relatively calmly in the whole *LXXXI Corps* sector.[182] At 1250 hours, it was announced to *7th Army* that the *246th Volks-Grenadier Division* was to relieve the *9th* and *116th Panzer Divisions*. First, it should be assembled in the vicinity of Düren at the disposal of *Army Group B*.[183] The relief of *9th Panzer Division* was ordered without waiting for the *246th Volks-Grenadier Division* and it was to be completed by the night of 24 September, except for armored artillery and anti-tank guns.[184] Along with his staff, *Major* Bochnig, commander of *Panzerjäger Battalion 228*, assumed responsibility for the sector of former *Combat Group Berger* at the left wing of the *116th Panzer Division*. Deployed under his command were *Machine Gun Battalion 34, Militia Training Battalion II/6, Infantry Training Battalion 453*, two scattered companies, and one infantry company formed by the *Panzerjäger* battalion, as well as two batteries of *Assault Gun Brigade 394*.[185] Twenty of the sixty tanks received by *Army Group B* were to be delivered to the *116th Panzer Division*.[186]

The weather over Holland improved during the afternoon of 23 September and strong airborne landings resumed, but they were the last ones in this area.[187] They caused zealous considerations at *Supreme Command–West* and Army Group regarding what should be done. These thoughts were reflected in the unit journals of 24 September.

On this day, Rundstedt delivered a new status report to *OKW*. It tied in with the one from 21 September, and suggested shifting the main effort from *Army Group G* to the right wing of *Army Group B*, especially since *Supreme Command–West* was not expecting any success from the continuation of its own attacks in Lorraine. At 1235 hours, Westphal and Krebs discussed these thoughts. Earlier already, Model ordered Brandenberger to withdraw the mobile units from the front, including *116th Panzer Division,* without waiting for the *246th Volks-Grenadier Division.* Model considered an attack from the area west of Venlo toward the northwest and required the supply of new forces.[188]

At 1720 hours, *Supreme Command–West* relayed to Army Group Hitler's rejection of his proposal of transferring the main effort from Lorraine to Holland, and emphasized the necessity of withdrawing the *9th* and *116th Panzer Divisions.*[189] At 2030 hours, the *Supreme Command–West* corollary order went out to Army Group. Both divisions were to be deployed south of Nijmegen.[190] At 2250 hours, a conversation between Westphal and Krebs followed, regarding the replenishment of both divisions. For the *116th,* Army Group requested ten Panthers, besides the ones already on the way, a light artillery battalion, and 250 tons of cargo space.[191] This remained wishful thinking.

At 1300 hours on 25 September, Rundstedt and Model met at *7th Army* headquarters to discuss conduct of impending battles. *OKW* demanded the destruction of the deep thrust toward Arnhem by attacking from west and east, in other words, a repetition of previous attempts. The *9th* and *116th Panzer Divisions* were selected for this, along with *Panzer Brigade 108.* This was certainly the correct operational solution. It might have been successful if the attack had taken place at the proper time with sufficient forces. In principle, Rundstedt and Model shared *OKW*'s opinion and reported accordingly. However, *1st Parachute Army* had a different view, and prevailed.

The next morning, after Krebs argued with the Chief of Staff of *1st Parachute Army* over whether the attack should be south or north of the Maas—Krebs pleaded for south, *1st Parachute Army* for north, since a more favorable balance of forces could be achieved there—Model decided to attack first with the *9th Panzer Division* near Arnhem, and then to attack Venlo from the bridgehead. At 1555 hours, *7th Army* received orders to immediately dispatch the *9th Panzer Division* to the area northeast of Arnhem and—on the evening of 27 September, beginning with one combat group—to have the *116th* follow in the area of Zevenaar and southwest of it.[192]

Model's decision contained conflicts. With the objective being Zevenaar, only twelve kilometers southeast of Arnhem, he also committed the *116th Panzer Division* for deployment near Arnhem. This took place, even though the English near Arnhem surrendered on this day. The daily report read as follows:

> On 26 September, after almost ten days of heavy fighting, the English airborne Division west of Arnhem was finally destroyed. . . .
>
> On the afternoon of 26 September, in the vicinity of *1st Parachute Army,* the opponent started a heavy attack north of Nijmegen and was turned back. Our own attack in the Arnhem-Nijmegen vicinity was delayed due to regrouping and the

delivery of reinforcements and ammunition. On 27 September, by deploying strike troops, the front between the Lower Rhine and Waal will be closed and the situation at its north wing improved. The unified attack for the destruction of the opponent between the Lower Rhine and Waal has been planned for 30 September by deploying combat groups of the *9th* and *116th Panzer Divisions,* whose replenishment was delayed, according to the latest reports. By *7th Army,* no major changes. There are no indications of the immediate, impending attack expected in the Aachen area.[193]

At 0030 hours on 27 September, contrary to Hitler's order, *Army Group B* issued an order to destroy the enemy between the Lower Rhine and Waal.[194] At 1600 hours, Westphal relayed to Army Group Hitler's opinion that the attack against the Veghel–Eindhoven line should be carried out, but in bad weather. Model replied that he had considered doing the same thing, but the paucity of forces did not permit this solution.[195]

With this, the die was cast for an attack to be conducted in a manner that was difficult to understand. The terrain between Arnhem and Nijmegen was extremely unfavorable for the deployment of tanks, as the English already found out. To conduct a frontal tank attack here against the continuously reinforcing enemy spearhead was a hopeless undertaking. It is difficult to understand Model's acceptance of the plans of *1st Parachute Army,* which certainly had little experience in dealing with tanks. And where was there an operational objective that would have warranted the attack? Even if pushing through to Nijmegen was successful, what would have been gained? Did this justify the expense? Nevertheless, the front in Aachen was stripped of its defense, even though the Americans could be counted on to resume their offensive. The distance from the vicinity of Cologne–Aachen to Arnhem was about twice as far as to Venlo. First, this meant a large consumption of fuel, a scarce commodity at this time. Second, it was a much greater distance to get back to the Aachen area in the event that the situation there worsened.

The Commanding General of *II SS-Panzer Corps, Obergruppenführer* Bittrich, who was supposed to lead the attack, expressed his concern when he heard of this plan. He suggested omitting the attack if better preparations could not be made. Model declined.[196] On 28 September, Hitler finally backed away from the request to attack south of the Maas.[197]

We want to return to Aachen. Nothing much of importance happened there after 23 September. On 24 September, *7th Army* issued the following order to *LXXXI Corps,* "to attempt to pull out and refresh as many strong units of *116th Panzer Division* as possible, but immediately behind Aachen, so that deployment would be possible toward Aachen as well as Stolberg."[198]

As of 0600 hours on 24 September, the *116th Panzer Division* issued a report of strength and an organization plan, which is included at Appendix 11.[199] The plan shows clearly how the Division had grown in the meantime, especially in personnel. Much of the credit for this goes to staff sections *IIa* and *IIb,* Major

Vogelsang and *Hauptmann der Reserve* Stukenberg. The plan also indicates which units were subordinated to the Division. The report of strength contained the following data:

1. Battalions: 2 strong, 2 medium-strong, 1 average and 1 weak combat engineer battalion; field replacement battalion being formed. Attached: 2 strong, 2 medium strong, 1 battle-fatigued.
2. a) Anti-tank guns: 20 towed, 1 self-propelled
   c) *Panzer IV:* 11
   d) *Panzer V:* 5
3. Artillery
   a) 1 light battery
   b) 2 heavy batteries
4. Mobility: 40%
5. Total rating: III

The attached supporting artillery is not listed here. It was four batteries strong, with two light and two heavy. Regarding our organic artillery, the organization plan contains only one light (*6th Battery, Armored Artillery Regiment 146*) and one heavy (*3d Battery, Motorized Artillery Regiment 76*) battery. Apparently, *7th Battery, Armored Artillery Regiment 146* was out of action during the night of 24 September. A fourth one, the 8.8cm battery, was evidently added to *Anti-Aircraft Group Aachen* (Staff, *Anti-Aircraft Battalion 514*). Only 36 of the 2cm guns available on 15 September were still in action.

On 24 September, Waldenburg wrote, "Very uneasy day. Heavy artillery fire to front and rearward areas during the night. Several reconnaissance thrusts repelled. Afternoon in field and with artillery commander. . . ."[200]

At 1900 hours on 24 September, Vogelsang noted in his diary in Langweiler (whence the Division staff had moved in the meantime):

Meanwhile we moved to this smaller and less conspicuous village. Near Stolberg, the Americans attacked again heavily and achieved a breach. A counterattack, supported by our last tanks, was able to avoid an impending breakthrough.

Enemy pressure has increased along the whole front of our Division. The severity of the artillery fire increases steadily and is escalated by the hour to a drumfire. With long-range batteries, the enemy holds the whole rear echelon all the way to Aldenhoven under a tight net of nuisance fire directed against roads, intersections, and towns. The villages near the front are already quite shot up.

The night before yesterday, a rumor reached a higher headquarters that a large number of men from a replacement company, subordinated to us, surrendered to the enemy. Together with Stukenberg, I received the order to investigate the matter.

In a pitch-dark night we sped down the Mariadorf–Weiden road using partly blacked-out headlights. From the relentless flashes of gunfire, the whole western horizon looked like it was sprinkled with sugar and dipped into the dim red of the smoldering fires. In front of us, behind us, and on either side, heavy projectiles burst

in an insidious blue. We carefully rolled along the rubble-covered road of Verlautenheide and reached the command post of the battalion in question, which moved into
one of the strong *Westwall* bunkers near the village.

A battalion messenger led us to the accused replacement company. We carefully walked in a ditch next to the road to the hills of Haaren, then left the road and,
closely together, sneaked quietly through the Stygian darkness, trying not to lose
contact and avoiding enemy reconnaissance. We went through a gap in the front
near the railroad tunnel at the forester's house. We stumbled through shell craters
and across torn off branches and shattered trees, straight into a *Westwall* bunker,
when several rounds of artillery splintered the crowns of the old beech trees with
ear-splitting noise.

Here we found the company command post, 100–150 meters away from the
Americans, who had settled in a neighboring bunker further up on the hill. As so
often happens, it became clear that it was just talk. The platoon in question was cut
off and overrun in battle by the Americans. Any thought of defecting was out of the
question!

The company staff and bunker crew made a thoroughly good impression. The
company commander was a veteran wounded in Russia, his presentation as well as
that of his people seemed fully believable. It took us several hours to conduct the
necessary questioning. The initial anger of the men was soon subdued with the cigarettes we brought.[201]

This occured on the night of 23 September at the positions of *Infantry Training
Battalion 453.* The company command post seems to have been near the
Schwarzenbruch forester's station near the tunnel exit of the Aachen–Eschweiler
railroad. On 23 September, Vogelsang was driven to the training battalion on the
east bank of the Rhine and wrote about it on 24 September:

A Division staff *Escort Company,* so far non-existent in our unit, shall be newly created. Since we considered a *Leibgarde* [personal body guard—*Editor*] for the staff
superfluous, and, under the tense situation, unjustifiable, it was decided that if an
elite unit were to be established at all, it would be one to use as Division reserve for
special cases and tasks.

For this reason, we carefully selected the personnel from the *Field Replacement
Battalion* and formed a cadre of combat-experienced leaders and men, and manned
it with volunteers from the recently assigned *Luftwaffe* units.

Already this evening, the overstrength company stood ready with two rifle platoons, and one each 2cm automatic anti-aircraft cannon platoon, a heavy platoon
(with heavy machine guns and mortars), a scout platoon, and an anti-tank platoon
(initially equipped with Teller mines and *Panzerfausts,* and later 7.5cm anti-tank
guns, plus several engineers).

On 25 September, Waldenburg wrote in his pocket calendar, "Quiet day, no airplanes. . . . Artillery activity somewhat diminished, in the evening again very
active. Relief of the Division should take place anyway.[202]

During this time, the *Ib* command post moved from Niederzier to the same location in which corps had established its in Niedermerz, as a neighbor of the *Ia*.

The *7th Army* reported to corps that the *246th Volks-Grenadier Division* was brought in to enable the rapid withdrawal of the *116th Panzer Division,* which was to be promptly resupplied. Six stationary anti-tank guns without tractors were to be given to the relieving Division.[203] According to a directive from corps headquarters, the *116th Panzer Division* issued an "order for establishing a battle commandant for the city of Aachen" (see Appendix 12).[204]

The *Ia* of the *116th Panzer Division* at that time, *Major i.G.* Prince Holstein, reported to corps that two *Hummel* batteries (self-propelled 15cm howitzers) were in the rear echelon and could not be moved up due to lack of fuel.[205] The artillery rear echelon had been in the vicinity of Raesfeld since 11 September, but during the night of 18 September, they were moved to an area east of Düsseldorf. Assigned guns and *Maultiere* ("Mules," trucks with tracks instead of rear wheels—*Author*] as tractors could not be obtained in Arnhem because of the fuel shortage. Temporarily, the guns fell into enemy hands, while the *Maultiere* got away. On 22 September, the guns finally arrived, but showed considerable damage. On 22 and 23 September, personnel replacements also arrived, but they were without training, and therefore they had to be instructed. On 25 September, the commander of *2d Battalion, Armored Artillery Regiment 146, Hauptmann* Müller, who had been wounded in Normandy, returned and resumed command of his battalion and, at the same time, the rear echelon units of the whole regiment. For the upcoming transfer of the Division toward Arnhem, the *Hummel* batteries were situated quite favorably.[206]

On the evening of 25 September, the enemy's activities in the Division sector came to life again.[207] In Waldenburg's calendar it says on 26 September, "Again a very uneasy night. Heavy artillery fire on main battle line and rear area. Repelled three advances against Aachen (*Grenadier Regiment 60*). . . ."[208]

At 0900 hours, *7th Army* urged Headquarters *LXXXI Corps*, "to instantly withdraw" the *116th Panzer Division.* At 0930 hours, a conference with the Division *Ia* took place at corps. The *116th Panzer Division* was ordered to only take its own artillery, to transfer *Radio-Controlled Tank Company 319* to the *246th Volks-Grenadier Division,* and to carry out the release of the anti-tank guns with "utmost security." The Division was allowed to take along *Army Anti-Aircraft Battalion 960.* Transportation notices for units with tracked vehicles had to be presented. The "corps order to pull out *116th Panzer Division*" is included as Appendix 13, as is the corresponding Division order (Appendix 14). [209,210]

At 1855 hours, Gersdorff pried to see if everything went smoothly.[211]

At the same time, *116th Panzer Division* received the following order from *LXXXI Corps*:

116th Panzer Division transfers on 27 September after relief by *246th Infantry Division*:

　　1 *Grenadier* regiment of two battalions with staff
　　1 artillery battalion
　　1 *Panzerjäger* company
　　1 combat engineer company

into the vicinity of Zevenaar (northwest of Emmerich)—commander ahead to *1st Parachute Army* in Terborg.[212]

This order called for speed and practically cancelled the paragraph of the corps order by which the artillery and all tanks and anti-tank guns were to "temporarily be left in the sector" because the Division only had one artillery batallion and one battleworthy *Panzerjäger* company.

This way of issuing orders offers a vivid example of how it should not be done. Without consideration of the situation at the front near Aachen, Army Group pressed for a release; *7th Army* passed on the pressure, probably reluctantly. Corps headquarters tried to slow it down, without much success. The Division received the order, which "for now" pinned down its most important units, and then was driven to utmost speed by hasty instructions.

At 0700 hours on 27 September, the Division reported that *Panzer-Grenadier Regiment 156* would be released with all units by 0800 hours and *Assault Gun Brigade 394* would be transferred to the *12th Infantry Division*.[213] Commencing at 1000 hours, *Panzer-Grenadier Regiment 156* rolled in loose march formation with individual vehicles into the assembly area east of Jülich (Stetternich—Steinstrass). At 1845 hours, *7th Army* renewed the order for a speedy release of the *116th Panzer Division* to set off into the vicinity of Zevenaar. At 1921 hours, this order was transmitted to the Division.[214] In the course of 27 and 28 September, there was some confusion about the execution of the transfer, that is, if the artillery should be towed behind trucks or be loaded onto trains; about the provision by higher headquarters of truck convoys to assist the march; and also about the tempo of the release by the *246th Volks-Grenadier Division*.[215] Finally, during the night of 28 September, *Panzer-Grenadier Regiment 156* marched via Neuss and Wesel, into the new area of the Division southeast of Arnhem. On the morning of 28 September it reached the region of Dinslaken, and early on 30 September, the objective area.

On the night of 28 September, the staff and *2d Battalion* of *Panzer-Grenadier Regiment 60* were relieved, while the *1st Battalion* was only relieved during the night of 29 September. After that, the regiment marched behind *Panzer-Grenadier Regiment 156*. The tracked units were entrained. The *3d Battalion, Armored Artillery Regiment 146*, with its two batteries (*6th Battery, Regiment 146* and *3d Battery, Motorized Artillery Regiment 76*) was, after some back and forth, pulled out on 28 September due to an urgent Army order. They were transferred to Garzweiler (southwest of Grevenbroich) and in the evening had to follow *Panzer-Grenadier Regiment 156*. A company of *Armored Engineer Battalion 675* was also assigned to *Panzer-Grenadier Regiment 156*. *Armored Reconnaissance*

Battalion 116 was relieved on the night of 28 September, and on that day, with the Reconnaissance Company ahead, set off for Arnhem. On the morning of 28 September, *Panzer Regiment 16* assembled in area east of Jülich. The tracked units were to be entrained between 0515 hours on 29 September and 1000 hours on the next day at the following railroad stations: Jülich, Ameln, Vedburg, and Elsdorf. Entrainment was also to occur from 1900 hours on 30 September through 0500 hours on 1 October in Cologne-Nippes, Bergisch-Gladbach, Elsdorf, Jülich, and Bedburg.

On the evening of 30 September, twelve of the seventeen scheduled trains had left, and three were loading. The last two were to be entrained early on 1 October. It was astonishing that trains were indeed moving, since there was a lack of empty freight cars, and since air attacks caused delays at Cologne and Euskirchen, as well as on the Jülich–Mönchen-Gladbach line. Sometimes, a road march by all units was considered, but there was no fuel for this.

The *246th Volks-Grenadier Division* assumed control in the former sector of the *116th Panzer Division* at 0600 hours on 28 September and also took on responsibility for the missions of the battle commandant of Aachen. The corresponding orders were to be turned over.[216]

While the *9th Panzer Division* was granted a short rest period, the *116th* marched directly from the front forward of Aachen into the next battle.[217] In spite of all efforts by the Division command, there was no day of rest for most of the Division. The numerous replacements that arrived, among them as mentioned *Luftwaffe Fortress Battalion XIII,* had been incorporated into the units of the Division, but a few days of rest would have considerably helped the men get acquainted. Better acquaintance between leaders and followers would thereby have raised the cohesion and the battle value of the troops.

The troops' attitude was affected by various feelings. After the depressing retreat through France and Belgium and the relief of the revered Division Commander, the successful defense against the enemy attack on Aachen in a secured and relatively quiet position restored the soldiers' confidence in their own accomplishments. In contrast, fighting on the soil of the homeland and the overwhelming materiel superiority of the opponent, especially in the air, was weighing heavily on everyone's souls. At that time, *Oberst* von Waldenburg wrote:

> The mood of the troops is not good. Everybody here must have recognized the serious situation in the East and the hopelessness of a continuation of the fight here, in addition to the absolute air superiority of the opponent with its brutal air war against the homeland. Even the situation of my predecessor, Count von Schwerin, inflicts stress. I will still have some problems with this, but I knowingly stay out of these things and hope to soon gain the full confidence of the commanders. Work with the staff is good, as is the camaraderie, and after all, we will try to correctly do our almost inhumanly difficult duty.[218]

Chapter 8

Autumn Battles

Part 1: Arnhem

The previous chapter described the development of the battle against the enemy that arrived by airborne landings and also the penetrations in the Nijmegen–Arnhem vicinity. The *9th* and *116th Panzer Divisions* were brought in to finally eliminate the danger of an imminent breakthrough. The unfortunate plan of their deployment was also mentioned before. Objections preferred to the commanding general of *II SS-Panzer Corps*, *Obergruppenführer* Bittrich, who commanded the attack, fell on deaf ears.

The march of both divisions proceeded at a slow pace.[1] While the units which conducted a road march moved up relatively well, those moved by rail trickled in with considerable delays, even though they were soon unloaded again, that is, *2d Battalion, Panzer Regiment 16* in Duisburg and *Armored Engineer Battalion 675* in Bocholt.[2,3] The last trains were unloaded on 2 October and reached the Arnhem area on the next day.[4]

On 30 September, most of the *9th Panzer Division* was assembled at the bridgehead south of Arnhem and prepared for the attack.[5] Only the staff, *Armored Reconnaissance Battalion 116,* and *Regimental Group 156* arrived in the Arnhem–Zevenaar area on this day. *Panzer-Grenadier Regiment 60* and the tanks were still missing.[6]

Regarding the transfer of the Division to Arnhem, on the evening of 30 September Vogelsang stated:

Hurry, hurry! The bulk of the Division, except for *Panzer-Grenadier Regiment 60,* had already been relieved by the *28th. Panzer-Grenadier Regiment 156* was already marching north, units of the artillery followed. Everything else has to be shipped by train because of the chronic shortage of fuel.

On 28 September, the Division Staff, together with the *Escort Company,* split up into small groups, and marched off. . . .

The following morning, we reached the release point in Zevenaar and after consultation with the Division Commander, proceeded to Arnhem to determine a location for the command post. . . . The rapid arrival of the different divisions and the distribution and assignment of quarters was organized hastily. The units whirled about amongst one another in the constricted area. . . .

This morning, after a visit by *Feldmarschall* Model with more detailed instructions about the sectors to which we were supposed to move, we looked for hours northwest of Arnhem for a suitable site. In the end, against tactical considerations and other habits, we settled in the northwest part of the city. . . .

With the help of a civilian whom we met by accident, we were able to get the keys to the house from the people who had been evacuated to the north, and thus were able to prevent damages. A security patrol saw to it that the houses were kept clean and that the furnishings remained accounted for.[7]

After Vogelsang raved about the friendliness and cleanliness of Holland, he wrote:

But sadly, the war also rages across this idyllic place. The Tommies and the Poles fire into the town. Mid-size shells are howling over us or burst in the southern part of the city, and like pesky insects, the planes give us no peace.

In many parts of the nearby surroundings, wrecks of the English 1st Airborne Division are strewn about—shattered gliders, aircraft parts, weapons, and equipment in large quantities.

On the same day, Staff Paymaster Wolff-Boenisch noted, "The population here in Holland is also friendly."[8]

The attack by *II SS-Panzer Corps* was postponed from 30 September to 1 October due to the delays in the conduct of the march.[9] Further postponement was not permitted. Army Group feared an all encompassing attack against *15th Army* and saw signs indicating a renewal of the enemy attacks near Aachen. One also wanted to take advantage of the dreary weather.[10]

The first objective for *II SS-Panzer Corps* was Elst, halfway between Arnhem and Nijmegen, Nijmegen being known as the "ultimate objective" of *Army Group B*. On 30 September at 1100 hours, Army Group reported to *Supreme Command–West*:

The intended attack consists of the following three phases:

a) Phase 1: Establishment of the line of departure in separate sectors. Attack against Driel and Elst at the same time.

b) Phase 2: The actual strike. The aim is to reach the targeted bridges in Nijmegen with greatest speed, by forming of quickly changing main efforts (right, center, left).

c) Phase 3: Simultaneously or separately from Phase 2—link up and close up the flanks. Thereby, the attack of the *XII SS-Corps* and *II Parachute Corps* will be orchestrated to pull strong enemy forces away from the actual point of decision.[11]

The following units were to attack:

To the right, *116th Panzer Division*
In the center, *9th Panzer Division*
To the left, *10th SS-Panzer Division*

At the same time, to divert the enemy, *XII SS-Corps* units were to cross the Rhine southeast of Doorwerth (eight kilometers west-southwest of Arnhem) and push toward Driel. Besides that, *363d Infantry Division* was moved to the isthmus between the Lower Rhine and the Waal, southwest of Wageningen, to tie up the enemy from the west. However, it could not become effective immediately.[12]

The main effort of the attack was to be at the inner wings of the *116th* and *9th Panzer Divisions*. But since the attack had to be started in the early morning of 1 October, by which time nothing of the *116th* was in place, initially, the *9th Panzer Division* had to bear the brunt of the attack almost alone. The *10th SS-Panzer Division* was supposed to tie up the enemy at Bemmel with only a limited objective attack.[13]

Before the attack, the frontline of the Arnhem bridgehead ran first from the railroad bridge west of Arnhem along a stretch of the railroad embankment southeast toward Rijkerswoerd, from there to the Linge River, about one kilometer southeast of Aamsche-Brücke, then along the Linge and finally south toward Haalderen on the Waal.[14]

The units already deployed in the *116th* and *9th Panzer Division* sectors of the bridgehead were subordinated to both divisions when the change of command took place. The *116th* took over *"Blocking Unit ("Sperrverband") Harzer,"* which consisted of heterogeneous, hastily assembled units from the *9th SS-Panzer Division.* Included in this were *Naval Training Battalion 14* [*Schiffsstammabteilung 14*] in the sector south of the Lower Rhine; *Fortress Machine Gun Battalions 37* and *41*; as well as *Luftwaffe* emergency reaction units, adjacent to the south. The *9th Panzer Division* took over *Battalions Knaust* and *Bruns* that were comprised of *Wehrkreis VI* replacement-and training units, and which had fought bravely in previous battles. Further, *Panzer Battalion 506* (Tiger) was attached to the *9th.*[15] An emergency reaction battalion formed from *Panzer-Grenadier Replacement Battalion 60* from Rheine, under the command of *Hauptmann* Schörken, was also in that area. Early on 21 September, it took up position south of Elden. On the evening of that day during an advance, the commander of this battalion's *2d Company, Leutnant* Beckmann, captured a Polish officer-cadet who said that a Polish parachute infantry regiment had jumped in the afternoon. Through a counterattack, Beckmann regained a lost piece of the railroad embankment on 24 September. On 27 September, the naval troops took over the position at the embankment, and Battalion Schörken went into reserve southeast of Arnhem.[16]

Armored Reconnaissance Battalion 116, which arrived at Arnhem ahead of the Division staff, was deployed by the staff of *II SS-Panzer Corps* to immediately mop up remnants of scattered groups of the English 1st Airborne Division in the area north of the Rhine. With respect to personnel and materiel, the battalion was again fully combat-ready.[17]

For *Regimental Group 156,* 30 September became a well-deserved day of rest. The commanders, however, found no peace, and used the day for reconnaissance.

The Division staff and the artillery commanders also reconnoitered. Fire support plans were worked out in cooperation with the adjacent *9th Panzer Division. Armored Signal Battalion 228* had already laid the necessary wire connections, while *Armored Engineer Battalion 675* had orders to secure any gear they could find for river crossings, a measure that later, when the Arnhem bridge was destroyed, proved to be very useful. An advanced command post was established in a brickyard on the south bank, about one kilometer northwest of the bridge.[18] After the war, *Oberst* von Waldenburg wrote about the result of the reconnaissance:

> The results of the reconnaissance available that evening offered quite an unfavorable picture for the planned attack!
>
> The terrain south of Arnhem is as flat as a table. Numerous deep-water ditches and small canals criss-cross this sector; hedges, rows of trees, and sometimes the very high railroad embankment block every view. There are not observation posts for infantry heavy weapons, much less for the artillery; for the latter, there are some possibilities on the north bank of the Rhine. Deployment of tanks is impossible in this terrain. This conclusion is still being presented to *II SS-Corps* during this night, but the order remains in effect with reference to an obviously not very strong and relatively idle opponent.[19]

The *9th Panzer Division* commenced the attack at 0600 hours on 1 October. A night assault by the attached *Battalion Knaust* from division's right wing across the Linge River against Aamsche-Brücke failed. By noon, the division's attack achieved only modest success against tough resistance. Het Nieuwslag and Heuvel were seized in heavy fighting, but Aam and Vergert remained in enemy hands. The opponent flanked the attack from both sides, in the north from Aamsche-Brücke, in the south from the vicinity of Baal. To block the effect, the *9th Panzer Division* started another assault against the bridge. It failed again. In the south, the *10th SS-Panzer Division* advanced its position so far forward that the flanking fire diminished. By evening, eight of the supporting Tigers had been rendered useless by mines, anti-tank guns, or artillery.

As soon as the weather cleared up in the afternoon, enemy air activity increased. Artillery fire also increased. Our own losses accumulated, and digging in was almost impossible in the wet terrain, mainly due to the high water table.[20] Now corps ordered that the available units of the *116th Panzer Division,* in other words, *Panzer-Grenadier Regiment 156 (Reinforced),* mount the attack as soon as possible on both sides of the Arnhem–Elst road.

The most important paragraphs of the order for the *116th Panzer Division* on 1 October 1944 follow:

> 2. *II SS-Panzer Corps,* with *116th, 9th,* and *10th SS-Panzer Divisions,* destroys enemy forces between the Waal and Lower Rhine by attacking from the Elden–Haalderen bridgehead with a strong right wing via Driel–Elst.

3. For this, after assembling in the vicinity of Rijkerswoerd and the area to the north, reinforced *Panzer-Grenadier Regiment 156* (reinforced by *1st Company, Armored Engineer Battalion 675*; *3d Battalion, Armored Artillery Regiment 146*) seizes the area around Snodenhoek. Occupy the assembly area by 1500 hours.

4. Attachments at the commencement of the attack:

   Five Tigers of *Tiger Battalion 506*

   Four Panthers of the *9th SS-Panzer Division.* . .

   After removal from Elst:

   Battalion Bruns (currently with the *9th Panzer Division*)

   Continue the attack from Snodenhoek toward the northwest:

   M.G. Btl. 37. . .

5. Boundaries:

   To *9th SS-Panzer Division*: Malburgen (*9th SS*)–de Laar (*116th*)–

   Vlot (*116th*)–School, north of Driel (*9th SS*)– . . .

   Left boundary to *9th Panzer Division*: Rijkerswoerd (*116th*)–Elst (*9th*)–

   Lienden (*9th*). . .

6. Order of Battle:

   Reinforced *Panzer-Grenadier Regiment 156* occupies assembly area in the vicinity of Rijkerswoerd and reaches Snodenhoek as first objective, to presumably attack Driel on 2 October. . .

7. *Armored Artillery Regiment 146* supports the attack with *3d Battalion, Armored Artillery Regiment 146* and *Artillery Regiment 191.* . . . It is important to keep enemy in check at railroad embankment and to prevent a counterattack from west and south.[21]

Snodenhoek is exactly northwest, Rijkerswoerd three kilometers northeast of Elst.

II SS-Panzer Corps intended to use the attack by *Panzer-Grenadier Regiment 156* to restore the right flank of the *9th Panzer Division,* and thus to get it moving again.[22] In the early afternoon, the regimental group, with *Major* Grollmann in command, advanced across the Rhine into the assembly areas southwest and south of Elden. It attacked during the evening. The *Supreme Command–West* daily report carries the following entry:

> In its attack that started in the evening hours, the *116th Panzer Division* gained the intersection 2.5 kilometers north-northeast of Elst and the intersection two kilometers northeast of Elst at 0200 hours in battle against a tenaciously defending opponent.[23]

The *Army Group B* morning report of 2 October states:

> The *116th Panzer Division* reached the railroad embankment west of De Gouden Klomp, two kilometers north of Elst. One company entered Aamsche-Brücke and

Aam [probably a single group of houses, south of the bridge, north of the town—*Author*]. House-to-house fighting against tough enemy resistance.[24]

At noon, Army Group reported, "2.5 kilometers north of Elst, *Combat Group* of the *116th Panzer Division* 500 meters west of railroad embankment in heavy fighting with counterattacking enemy."

The plans for linking up the *9th Panzer Division* with *Panzer-Grenadier Regiment 156* for the attack were dropped, because the enemy began counterattacking against the *9th*.[25] If one compares the post-war report that Grollmann wrote from memory to those more or less certain facts, one can establish approximately the following course of attack of his *Panzer-Grenadier Regiment 156*.[26] The regiment still commenced the attack on the evening of 1 October, with *2d Battalion* south of the Arnhem–Elst road attacking via Rijkerswoerd on the left (where the regimental command post was also established), while, after an interval, *1st Battalion* attacked toward the west, north of the road and across the railroad embankment northwest of the De Gouden Klomp intersection. The main effort was in the *2d Battalion* zone, where the attached tanks and combat engineers were. During the night, *2d Battalion* slowly gained ground against a tenaciously defending opponent to about the Linge River, between Aamsche-Brücke and the Arnhem–Elst road. On the morning hours, under the command of *Leutnant* Junge, *7th Company* succeeded in seizing Aamsche-Brücke and the group of houses south of it.[27] After crossing the railroad embankment northwest of de Gouden Klomp, *1st Battalion* remained stuck in the completely level terrain for the time being. At dawn, however, it succeeded in pushing the enemy to the south of the De Laar farm houses and occupied positions in some of the houses. North of there, after crossing an area without cover, they reached a wide water-filled ditch, bordered by poplars. Under heavy enemy defensive fire, it proved impossible to cross it. During the attack on De Laar, the commander of the *1st Company, Oberleutnant der Reserve* Heiberger particularly distinguished himself.[28]

The enemy began counterattacking during the morning of 2 October, and tried to throw the *1st Battalion* back across the railroad line.[29] A heavy enemy concentration along the boundary between *9th Panzer* and *10th SS-Panzer Divisions* was dispersed by artillery fire.[30] At 1510 hours, supported by tanks, the enemy attacked along the Elst–Arnhem road. The attack was repelled and the intersection about two kilometers northeast of Elst was retained by *Panzer-Grenadier Regiment 156*.[31] The *9th Panzer Division* deflected a counterattack supported by 30 tanks from the towns of Aam and Vergert.[32] With continuing improvement of the weather, enemy air activity was vigorous throughout the whole day. At 1115 hours, about 100 of our fighters appeared over the battlefield, but apparently without much effect.[33] The supporting attack of 1 October across the Lower Rhine, southeast of Doorwerth, created a small bridgehead on the southern bank, about 750 meters wide and 250 meters deep, but this did not provide noticeable relief.[34] The enemy moved forces across the bridge at Nijmegen.[35]

The success of our attack on 1 and 2 October was insignificant, and the enemy had already gone over to the offensive, conducting dangerous counterattacks. It could be seen that a continuation of the attack would hardly be beneficial. Nevertheless, Army Group stuck to its attack and specified Driel as its next objective. Army Group reported that for the time being, energetic participation by the *Parachute Corps* south of the Waal toward Nijmegen was out of the question. The Americans initiated a new offensive near Aachen. From experience, Army Group reported that night attacks on a larger scale would fail because of insufficient training.[36] One worried needlessly about new airborne landings by the opponent north of the Lower Rhine, but units of the *9th Panzer Division* were held back for this reason anyway. During the night of 1/2 October, all rear echelon units were alerted, and continued in this status for the next few days.[37] *Major* Vogelsang noted the following in his diary on the evening of 2 October:

> The fighting is extraordinarily hard. The Tommies had laid mines carefully in front of their positions and defend every house and every ditch with dogged obstinacy. Against uninterrupted counterattacks by the enemy, the attack gains very little ground. Enemy bombers and fighter bombers severely disturb the attacking units, artillery, and supply columns.
>
> *156* already reported 100 casualties, the commander of *3d Artillery Battalion* was wounded by a bomb in his command post.[38]

To replace *Hauptmann* Schmeermann, *Hauptmann* Kusenberg took command of *3d Battalion* of the *Artillery Regiment*. On 2 October, Vogelsang further noted, "By accident we learned that somewhere in this area, a battalion was in action which had been formed in Rheine from our Division's veterans assigned to our replacement regiment. We are searching with all available means."

At least some elements from *Battalion Schörken* were again deployed near Elden from 1 to 3 October. *Company Beckmann* was deployed at the railroad embankment in the sector of *116th Panzer Division,* apparently within the framework of the *Naval Training Battalion.*[39]

About twenty new Panthers arrived at *Panzer Regiment 16* for issue to the *1st Battalion* of *Panzer Regiment 24,* so on 2 October, the subordination of the few battleworthy tanks of this battalion to *2d Battalion, Panzer Regiment 16* could be cancelled. The latter unit had nine battleworthy *Panzer IVs,* while six were being repaired.[40] On the night of 2/3 October, *9th Panzer Division* took over from the *116th* the sector along the Linge from Aamsche-Brücke to the bend of the Rijkerswoerdschen Path, directly east of the Elst–Arnhem road. By 0600, the *9th Panzer* released the elements of the *2d Battalion, Panzer-Grenadier Regiment 156* that were deployed there.[41] It tried to further advance against Elst on the wide road, and initially even had some success before becoming bogged down. The reports of *Supreme Command–West* provided an account of this.[42] On the morning report of 3 October, it included, "In heavy combat, the attack by the *116th Panzer Division* reached the road fork directly east of the Arnhem–Elst road, 1.5

kilometers north-northeast of Elst. Heavy enemy artillery fire in the whole corps sector."

At noon, the report recorded, "Bitter fighting in area northeast of Elst, where enemy defends every house."

The evening report states, "Strong enemy attack in progress since 1530 hours from area two kilometers southeast of Driel toward the east. Fighting continues northeast of Elst."

The daily report summarized, "Enemy counterattack from area three kilometers southeast of Driel, supported by very heavy artillery and tanks, was able to reach the railroad crossing 2.5 kilometers north of Elst after severe alternating battles, while it was beaten bloody to the north and south. Counterattack is in progress. Renewed enemy positions, west of the railroad, attacked effectively with artillery fire."

The commander of *2d Company, Panzer-Grenadier Regiment 156, Oberleutnant* Triantaphylides, portrayed the *1st Battalion's* activity during the afternoon of 3 October in his diary:

> Attack by tanks from Elst to the north and in broad front across the railroad embankment to the east. *Platoon Warnke* is being destroyed. Coordinating artillery blocking fires through the regimental CP. Simultaneously, enemy attacks from De Laar forward of Heiberger. *3d Company* positioned in between is cut off and destroyed, remnants captured. . . . Enemy attack breaks down in artillery fire. Three assault guns push forward. Two are destroyed.[43]

On the evening, Vogelsang wrote down the following:

> In bright moonlight, our attack last night advanced further. *Panzer-Grenadier Regiment 156* was able to gain two kilometers of ground and wrest two important positions from the opponent's front. The battles, especially against an English Guard Division, are unbelievably hard. Literally, each house and each cellar must be taken with *Panzerfaust* and flamethrower. Despite many losses, our people fight outstandingly. (*Regiment 156* reported 23 dead and more than 100 wounded.)
>
> This afternoon, the Tommies suddenly commenced a drumfire barrage and mounted a counterattack soon thereafter. *Regiment 156* was pushed back a few hundred meters, but could contain the enemy advance.
>
> Tomorrow morning, our attack should continue—now directly along the Rhine bank supported from the north bank by fire of 30 assault guns and tanks.[44]

On 4 October, he added:

> The fighting continues with unrelenting severity. The losses of *Regiment 156* are very high. The *1st Battalion* took the railroad line, and with the *3d Company* pushed to Laar, but clashed there with a counterattack by the English Guards. But toughly and tenaciously, the *Grenadiers* [German infantrymen—*Editor*] held on to the terrain gained and beat the attack back. Now, however, the company consists of only a handful of men.

The *9th Panzer Division* remained in place on 3 October. During the night, the *10th SS-Panzer Division* conducted an attack to relieve the *9th* at the intersection southeast of Heuvel. Despite successes at the outset, the effect remained minor.[45] Apparently, *Oberst* von Waldenburg summed up the events in a note in his pocket calendar on 3 October:

> Heavy fighting with 43d English Division in defense and attack. Extremely difficult terrain. Tanks were barely effective, since they could only move on the few dams and roads! After initial success, our own attacks had no effect! The English have magnificent manpower. We, being fatigued, sometimes have superiority on the ground, however, the English have absolute air dominance. Unfortunately, German airplanes are no longer seen, a heavy burden for our troops. . . . In part, bitter fighting, unfortunately also high casualties![46]

Originally, the Division had planned to have *Panzer-Grenadier Regiment 60* attack on the right at noon on 3 October, adjacent to *Panzer-Grenadier Regiment 156*. The scheduled operation was postponed until early on 4 October because not everything had arrived in time.[47] *Panzer-Grenadier Regiment 60* was to attack toward the west on the Division's right wing, with its right shoulder on the Rhine. It was to seize the town of Driel. From there, it was to establish a linkup with the units of *II SS-Panzer Corps* that were attacking from Doorwerth bridgehead to the southeast. Then, one hoped, *Panzer-Grenadier Regiment 156* would be able to attack, perhaps in concert with the *9th Panzer Division.*[48]

The artillery support for the attack is described in the journal of *2d Battalion, Panzer Regiment 16*:

> At 0630, the following units were to take part in a barrage designed to cover unobserved enemy terrain:
> Batteries of the naval artillery; Army heavy artillery; the complete Division artillery with units of other divisions; the regiments of the Division, using all heavy weapons; as well as the regiment's *Panzer Vs*, to be deployed as artillery. The regiment's anti-aircraft platoon, under *Leutnant* Kabitz, takes over part of air defense.[49]

The *1st Battalion, Panzer Regiment 24,* in position south and southwest of Oosterbeek with its 26 Panthers, was now commanded by *Rittmeister* Böke.[50] *Rittmeister* Weidemann portrays that attack as follows:

> At 0627 hours, three minutes before attack starts, the battalion fires a barrage of 500 high explosive shells at the assigned targets, which soon disappear in fire and smoke. . . . In spite of running fans and open turret hatches, the effect from the smoke of spent ammunition shells is so dense in the battle area that several crew members in this "new type of deployment" temporarily had to leave the area! Ground fog made it difficult if not impossible for any further observation or fire guidance; thus, the achieved effect of the weapons was not in proportion to ammunition expended. The attack by our *Grenadiers* only gains ground slowly.[51]

During the night of 3/4 October, *Panzer-Grenadier Regiment 60,* commanded by *Major* Zander, was placed in readiness in the vicinity south of Elderhof. *Naval Training Battalion 14,* deployed in that sector, was subordinated to it. It received orders that after *Panzer-Grenadier Regiment 60* attacked beyond its frontline, in conjunction with the regimental engineer company, it was to expand its former position into a receiving area.

At 0700 hours, the attack commenced as follows: *1st Battalion, Panzer-Grenadier Regiment 60* on the right, along the Rhine; *2d Battalion* left of it adjacent to the right wing of *Panzer-Grenadier Regiment 156,* about 1.5 kilometers northeast of De Laar.[52] The journal of *2d Battalion, Panzer Regiment 16* noted the following:

> At 1045 hours, the commander comes back from the front. First, the opponent was surprised, but returned fire very soon. The *Grenadiers'* attack nevertheless advanced very well, so that in some places the opponent had to beat a hasty retreat. But very soon he was able to size up the situation and mount counterattacks.[53]

Obergefreiter Schäfer wrote in his diary about the attack by *2d Battalion, Panzer-Grenadier Regiment 60:*

> 0630 hours: After three minutes of preparatory artillery fire, *6th* and *7th Companies* attack across the railroad embankment. The *6th Company,* under the command of *Oberleutnant* Tzschentke, advances well. On the other hand, *7th Company* remains stuck in enemy fire. Therefore, *5th Company* should attack in the afternoon . . . toward the south.[54]

About 200 meters after crossing the railroad embankment, Tzschentke was wounded and put out of action.[55]

The *Supreme Command–West* journal states that the attack by *Panzer-Grenadier Regiment 60* at 1100 hours gained about one kilometer of ground west of the railroad, but that our attacking spearhead was attacked by the enemy from the southwest. *Supreme Command–West's* daily report says, "Attack by *116th Panzer Division,* effectively supported by its own artillery, reached north–south road south of the Lower Rhine, 1.2 kilometers west of railroad embankment.[56]

The bridgehead south of Doorwerth could also be enlarged somewhat, and the *363d Infantry Division* assumed control between the Waal and Lower Rhine, to attack on 5 October toward the east, near Opheusden.

But the enemy already began to attack at about noon on 4 October, after an artillery barrage and smokescreen against the *9th Panzer* and *10th SS-Panzer Divisions.* He did the same at 1430 hours against the left wing of the *116th* along the Elst–Arnhem road. While *Panzer-Grenadier Regiment 156* was able to beat back the attack, the opponent achieved a breach at the boundary between the two other divisions. Baal and Haalderen were lost in the *10th SS-Panzer Division* sector, and Heuvel was lost in the *9th Panzer Division's* area. Both sides suffered heavy losses. During the night, the main battle line of *9th Panzer Division* was taken back everywhere behind the Linge, to again afford contact with the unit on the left.[57]

By order of the *116th Panzer Division,* in the afternoon, the battleworthy tanks of the *2d Battalion, Panzer Regiment 16* were set to march across the Rhine to *Panzer-Grenadier Regiment 156,* probably because of the impact of these counterattacks. They took up positions at the southwest fringe of Elden. *Oberleutnants* Adam and Janske-Drost were in command. On the evening, the anti-aircraft platoon, with five guns, followed to the eastern edge of Elden.[58]

II SS-Panzer Corps ordered the following for 5 October:

1. Enemy mounted counterattack against corps' south wing with strong forces and took Haalderen, Baal, and Heuvel. Advances against other fronts were repelled. . . .

3. *II SS-Panzer Corps* defends main battle line and proceeds with advance at north wing to seize Driel. . . .

6. *9th Panzer Division* and *Combat Group Harmel* [*10th SS-Panzer Division—Author*] defend Linge. . . .

7. *Armored Reconnaissance Battalion 116* and one company of the *Panzer* regiment [of the *9th Panzer Division—Author*] in corps reserve in Angeren prepares for action to the south and west.[59]

Unfortunately, only these fragments of the order are available. The order for the *116th Panzer Division* is missing, but one can derive it from the order to the corps.

On the evening of 4 October, Vogelsang found time for a notation:

Early this morning, *Panzer-Grenadier Regiment 60* attacked from the right wing after violent preparatory artillery bombardment with 2,000 shells. Despite tough resistance by the English and Poles, the attack went quite well, so that one can count on more overall success tomorrow. . . .

Today, I was again in the advanced command post for a conference. The command element is hidden, quite well protected and camouflaged in its brickyard kiln . . . In the evening, a small circle of us found a short respite in our quarters with one of the bottles of Burgundy donated to us by the Dutch in return for maintaining their homes well.[60]

On 5 October, Vogelsang noted:

During the night and in the morning, in tense and unrelenting thrust forward, *Panzer-Grenadier Regiment 60* was able to penetrate a considerable distance toward Driel.

A strong English attack in the afternoon, however, brought a heavy setback. There were very heavy losses—five company commanders in *Panzer-Grenadier Regiment 60*. Replacements must be urgently found.

The first heavy shells burst between our fragile villas and caused much harm. Our idyllic time seems to have ended.

Supreme Command–West reported similar incidents, such as, "1700 hours, enemy with tanks advanced to railroad embankment from vicinity east of Driel in bitter and close combat. Fighting still in process. One enemy tank destroyed."[61] In his post-war report, *Major* Zander relates that during the continuation of the attack on the morning of 5 October, the *3d* and *7th Companies,* advancing in the middle of the regiment, were especially able to advance and enter the forests [probably along the road south of Vogelenzang—*Author*].[62]

On the right wing of the *1st Battalion, Panzer-Grenadier Regiment 60, 2d Company* gained about one kilometer of ground along the Rhine, while on the left wing, the *5th* and *6th Companies* of *2d Battalion* had the task of shielding the attack toward the southwest. Zander further reported how in the afternoon a strong English counterattack from the southwest broke into the spearhead of the regiment. Thereby, the *3d* and *7th Companies* were cut off and most of their members were captured. On the night of 5/6 October, the commander of the *7th Company, Oberleutnant* Weiss, along with a man from his company, was able to break through to our lines, which again were at the railroad embankment. Only the *2d Company* on the right wing still stood forward of the railroad, for the time being. A diversionary counterattack with assault guns failed after the first vehicle was destroyed in a railroad underpass. The *2d Company* was thereafter also withdrawn to the railroad embankment. On the evening of 5 October, *Oberst* von Waldenberg wrote, "Changing to defensive. *Armored Reconnaissance Battalion* available to corps. Both regiments deployed. Engineers available. Building main battle line, unfortunately have to give back previously gained area."[63]

The 5 October daily report of *Supreme Command–West* stated that our De Laar strongpoint had been reinforced.[64] That was completely out of date. The events around De Laar took the following course: during the night of 3/4 October, *2d Battalion* of *Panzer-Grenadier Regiment 156* relieved *1st Battalion* and took De Laar. *Oberleutnant* Triantaphylides, Commander of *2d Company, Regiment 156,* wrote in his diary:

> Relief during the night of 3/4 October. In reserve behind Heiberger. Toward noon on 4 October, I receive order to deploy toward De Laar to *2d Battalion,* which took possession of the southeast part of the village during the night. During the day, there is no way to get from the railroad embankment to the village. Crawling with Jakob. The company follows in darkness. At night, the regimental commander comes up to us and discusses the situation. It is a clear, cold, moonlit night. Reorganization, which will thereby weaken the position.[65]

Major Grollman feared that the *2d Battalion, Panzer-Grenadier Regiment 156* would be cut off by the enemy in De Laar because it could not be reached from the embankment during the day. For this reason, he wanted to extend both wings of the battalion to the railroad embankment. Since he was concerned that the very fatigued troops could not raise the requisite strength, he went to De Laar during the night and convinced the completely exhausted men of the necessity to occupy and complete the new positions during this night.[66] But not even that could stop the misfortune. Regarding 5 October, Triantaphylides recalled:

> Late morning, little mortar fire. Early afternoon, barrage with very quick advance. Breakthrough by opponent . . . in company strength. Takes up position left and right of a haystack. I hide with *Feldwebel* Klein for about an hour, because escape across the open fields to railroad embankment impossible. We are being discovered. Taken prisoner.[67]

On the afternoon of 5 October, the journal of *2d Battalion, Panzer Regiment 16* includes, "In sector of *Panzer-Grenadier Regiment 156* near De Laar, pushing along the railroad embankment from the north, the opponent cut off *2d Battalion* and raked in most of it."[68]

Thereby, after high losses by both *Panzer-Grenadier* Regiments and in spite of all the action, the whole front of *116th Panzer Division* was again thrown back to the railroad embankment. The attack by *II SS-Panzer Corps,* as a whole, had failed. For the other two divisions of *II SS-Panzer Corps,* October 5 passed quietly. An advance from the Doorwerth bridgehead, east along the Rhine toward the area north of Driel, was successful. A second, smaller bridgehead was established near Renkum, west of Doorwerth. The *363d Infantry Division* mounted an attack south of Opheusden toward the east. All this had little impact on the opponent near the Arnhem bridgehead, but inspired *Army Group B* and *Supreme Command–West* to report, "The concentric attack against the opponent west of Elst will be continued on 6 October."[69]

This was a remarkable intention in view of the actual situation near Arnhem! *Obergruppenführer* Bittrich requested the suspension of the attack, but was not able to convince Army Group, as evidenced by its persistence with its attack plans.[70] At 1200 hours on 6 October, Krebs provided an evaluation of the situation to *Supreme Command–West.*[71] He was of the opinion that our attack south of Arnhem had pushed into an enemy assembly area and prevented an enemy breakthrough toward the north; it should be continued to relieve *15th Army.* By order of *OKW*, this was to block the *Scheldt* for as long as possible, to deny the enemy supply line access to the port of Antwerp. Therefore, it had to endure a long wait south of the Maas and Waal. Krebs reported further that the attack by the *363d Infantry Division* got under way again, but that the *116th Panzer Division,* "after the setback of 5 October, was not yet back in shape." At noon, Army Group reported that the attack by the *116th* was to be continued in the fashion of strike troops.[72] There was no way this could be done. The *116th Panzer Division* was no longer capable of attacking.

The corps expected an enemy attack on 7 October, since more enemy units were detected at the boundary between the *9th Panzer* and *10th SS-Panzer Divisions* (the 157th Brigade of the British 52d Division and units of the 502d Parachute Infantry Regiment of the 101st Airborne Division).[73] The fear of a renewed enemy airborne landing north of the Rhine was growing.[74] Later, at 1155 hours on 6 October, an enemy air attack flown by 25 twin-engine bombers severely damaged the bridge in Arnhem.[75] By midnight, it was repaired for vehicles of up to eight tons.[76] The engineer platoons of both battalions of the *Panzer Regiment* took part in the repair.[77] Heavy vehicles could only be brought across the Rhine on ferries. The attack on the bridge hardly justified the conclusion of a planned airborne landing by the enemy north of the Rhine.

On 6 October, the *116th Panzer Division* still had to defend itself against another enemy advance at the railroad, two kilometers north of Elst. The *10th SS-Panzer Division* succeeded in beating back an attack east of Haalderen.[78] In his post-war report, *Major* Stephan opined that *Armored Reconnaissance Battalion 116* was, at times, deployed there for defense.[79] In any case, except for some small units, it was withdrawn from the Division and did not return until noon of 8 October.[80] Our bridgehead at Doorwerth was widened by 800 meters toward the east. The *363d Infantry Division* encountered strong enemy forces, but was to attack further toward the east on 7 October.[81]

On 7 October, in answer to the *OKW*, Rundstedt was in agreement with Army Group regarding the attack at Arnhem: it had prevented a planned attack by the enemy.[82] His main concern, however, was the area around Aachen, where the enemy was preparing a "starting point" for a major assault toward Cologne. He expressed his intentions to release the *116th Panzer Division* from Arnhem to place it in readiness northeast of Aachen, together with the *3d Panzer-Grenadier Division,* under the command of *I SS-Panzer Corps* as the *Supreme Command– West* reserve. Besides this, he requested the release of more forces for his front. The *3d Panzer-Grenadier Division* came from *Army Group G* in Lorraine.

In the meantime, the commander and staff at *Army Group B* also had a change of mind. At 0850 hours on 7 October, they ordered *1st Parachute Army* to cease the attack near Arnhem and at once to release a reinforced regimental group of the *116th Panzer Division* to assemble east of the city. This group was to prepare for a 150-kilometer march during the night of 8/9 October. The rest of the *116th* was to be released during the evening of 8 October.[83]

At 1345 hours, bombs totally destroyed the Arnhem bridge.[84] All the troops in the bridgehead therefore depended on ferries that were not very efficient. *Armored Engineer Battalion 675,* the engineer companies of the *Panzer-Grenadier* regiments, and the engineer platoons of the *Panzer* regiment were deployed for the construction and operation of ferries and auxiliary crossing craft.[85]

On the afternoon of 7 October, the corps order arrived to release the *116th Panzer Division.*[86] During the night of 7/8 October, a battalion sector on the left wing of the *116th* was taken over by the *Division Escort Company* of the *9th Panzer Division.*[87] The position of *Panzer-Grenadier Regiment 60* was taken over by the already-emplaced *Naval Training Battalion 14.* During the night of 8/9 October, *Panzer-Grenadier Regiment 156* and its subordinated tanks from the *2d Battalion, Panzer Regiment 16* were to follow.

On the evening of 7 October, *Oberst* von Waldenburg wrote, "Received orders to move out of Arnhem area with the Division. *Panzer-Grenadier Regiment 60*, [the Division's] Panthers and units of the artillery will be released tonight. Destination still unknown."[88]

The day after, Waldenburg added, "Preparation for transfer. . . . Most likely deployment against expected new airborne landings!"

The *II SS-Panzer Corps* now ultimately went into the defense, namely along the line from the railroad embankment–west of De Gouden Klomp–Linge River–east of Haalderen–Waal, southeast of the town.[89] The *363d Infantry Division* also ceased its attack.[90] On 8 October, at 1145 hours, *1st Parachute Army* received orders from Army Group to prepare *116th Panzer Division* in the vicinity of Geldern–Kempen in such a way that a quick transfer to either the north or south would be possible.[91] Therefore, the already released regimental group was transferred into the new area during the night of 8/9 October. The remaining units were to be released by the morning of 9 October and transferred to the same area during the following night.

Supreme Command–West reported to *OKW* that a reinforced regiment of the *116th Panzer Division* was being prepared near Arnhem, and that its transfer to Aachen was planned for the night of 8/9 October.[92] This regimental group, commanded by *Oberst* Bayer, Commander of *Panzer Regiment 16,* consisted of the following:

Panzer Regiment 16 staff
1st Battalion, Panzer Regiment 24
Panzer-Grenadier Regiment 60
1st Battalion, Armored Artillery Regiment 146 (with the staff, *2d* and *7th Batteries*)
Elements of *Armored Engineer Battalion 675.*[93]

In Vogelsang's diary, the following entry is found for 7 October:

Considering the situation of replacements, a trip to *Field Replacment Battalion* was necessary yesterday. . . .

A loss of over 800 men had to be compensated for, but at best, not more than four officers and 180 men could be obtained from the *Field Replacement Battalion.* It is just enough to bring, at most, four companies back to combat strength.

Further replacements have to be gained by exchanges in personnel between old and young and by reductions of communication troops, supply, and so on. 100 naval ratings, who had just arrived, first had to be retrained; their immediate deployment at the front would not be justifiable.

The attack at the bridgehead had to be stopped. The opponent has become too strong and the losses suffered already are not proportionate with the success achieved. Most of all, the enemy's artillery intensified considerably. Disregarding the immediate front, today various parts of town, the banks of the Rhine and rearward areas, were under uninterrupted fire from heavy guns. Our lightly built houses

swayed and trembled without pause. A battery behind us sustained hits. Getting
supplies across the Rhine is becoming more and more difficult, especially now,
since 50 bombers entirely destroyed the Rhine bridge.

1,800 heavy bombers flying across our area made us all feel uneasy. What good
is it if two are downed? Where in the homeland will they unload their deadly cargo?
And this, with most of our men's homes in Rhineland-Westphalia.[94]

The replenishment of the *Panzer-Grenadier* Regiments with replacements
progressed better than anticipated. Since 21 September, after all, *Battalion
Schörken* was in the Arnhem area. Vogelsang put all wheels in motion to obtain
it for the Division, and on 7 October, Army Group ordered the battalion to be
incorporated into the *116th Panzer Division*.[95] On this day, Vogelsang therefore
added, "Against expectations, we succeeded in nabbing the afore-mentioned battle battalion of our *Replacement Regiment*. With its 600 men, we are in the position to raise the battle strength of the regiments to a useable level."

A member of this battalion, the then-17-year-old recruit Strickhausen, told the
author that on the evening of 19 September, he moved out with *2d Company* from
Rheine and was deployed to secure Elden.[96] While the older men were incorporated into the *Panzer-Grenadier* regiments at the onset of the Division's march,
most of them went to *Armored Field Replacement Battalion 146*, which was first
stationed in the area of Borken, and as of mid-October, east of Düsseldorf. On 19
November, Strickhausen was transferred to the *2d Company* of *Panzer-Grenadier
Regiment 60. Hauptmann* Schörken was assigned to *Armored Field Replacement
Battalion 146* as commander of the Division NCO combat training school.

On 14 October, Vogelsang visited the *Armored Field Replacement Battalion*:

Reorganization is urgently required. Due to a lack of sufficient training opportunities in the homeland, the arriving replacements in no way comply with the minimum requirements. We have to help here with three- to four-week courses.

In addition to the former five cadre companies for riflemen, the following were
established: a sixth one for the advanced junior enlisted and NCOs; a seventh one
for tank, tank destroyer, and armored reconnaissance crewmen; an eighth for
artillery; and a reinforced communication platoon for telephone and radio training.
The training on heavy infantry weapons will be combined with one of the riflemen
companies. The Division's combat-experienced officers and NCOs who can no
longer play an active part at the front will take command and provide the leadership, strengthened by instructors from the regiments. Section *Ib* of the Division staff
provides equipment, fuel, and live ammunition for close combat training—this is
what replacements need most.

29 officers have arrived. They make a good impression and are immediately
assigned to units. The biggest worry was the lack of much-needed NCOs (15
October 1944).[97]

In spite of all these efforts, the combat companies of the *Panzer-Grenadiers*
were for now still quite weak and, of course, not broken in. But at least the

Division was able to close ranks again and could form reserves for expected losses in its *Field Training Battalion.*

Now back to Arnhem. During the night of 8/9 October, the whole Division was withdrawn from the bridgehead.[98] The relief and transfer went smoothly. The tanks were transported across the river by the only capable ferry, at Pannerden (13 kilometers southeast of Arnhem).[99] In the remaining sector of *Panzer-Grenadier Regiment 156*, *Luftwaffe* emergency reaction units took over the positions. Command in the whole sector of the *116th* went to the *9th Panzer Division.*[100] The transfer order for most of the Division to the area southeast of Geldern arrived during the night of 8/9 October.[101] *Group Bayer* had already marched ahead to the Wesel–Geldern area during the night of 8/9 October. At 1230 on 9 October, Army Group delivered this order to *1st Parachute Army*, "*116th Panzer Division* continues march toward the south in two march groups."[102]

At 1900 hours on 9 October, *Group Bayer* was to start its march via Süchteln–Dülken–Rheindahlen–Erkelenz and reach the area southeast of Aldenhoven by 0700 hours on 10 October. The commander was to report ahead to *LXXXI Corps.* The second march group was to follow 24 hours later to the Kempen–Aldekerk area and prepare for the continuation of the march from there at 1900 hours. Most likely, units of *Group Bayer* were going to have to march during the day. Fortunately, all Division moves were helped by dreary weather from the time of the release of the order on 7 October right up to 11 October.[103]

Waldenburg took notes on 10 October, "At night with Army Group *Feldmarschall* Model in Krefeld. Again, night marches to the vicinity of Aachen! All around us air attacks with heavy bombardments!"[104]

In his post-war report, Waldenburg describes his visit to Army Group Headquarters as follows:

A short report of the experiences during the battles near Arnhem and a status report of the Division were compiled hastily. Again, this opportunity is used to suggest and urgently request giving the Division a few days' rest, especially to integrate the replacements and to effect required maintenance and repairs. With reference to the experiences at Arnhem, it was asked to only employ the Division as an integral whole in its next mission. Even on these long marches, when the chronic lack of fuel and the uninterrupted threat from the air bring about delays, such an arrangement would be the prerequisite for success.

The *Feldmarschall* was not opposed to all these wishes, expressed his special praise for the Division, but referred to the very serious situation at Aachen, which required the Division's immediate employment. A new enemy air attack behind the German front in combination with the attack on Aachen is a possibility to be considered.

The following consultation with several expert advisors of the Army Group resulted in a far reaching and favorable consideration for the Division, at least regarding materiel.

Thus, in spite of all expectations, the tired and badly battered Division had no other choice but to fulfill its obligation anew without the much needed rest, and once play the role of "fire department."[105]

On 10 October, *Group Bayer* was subordinated to *LXXXI Corps* and during the night of 10/11 October, it moved forward to the vicinity of Vorweiden (eight kilometers northeast of Aachen) to be deployed according to the developing situation north or east of Aachen.[106] During the afternoon of 10 October, the remaining units of the Division started to march from the Aldekerk–Kempen area further into the vicinity of Jülich. The *2d Battalion, Panzer Regiment 16* moved into Barmen (five kilometers northwest of Jülich). At its arrival, it had three battleworthy *Panzer IVs.*[107]

The *5th Company* of *Panzer-Grenadier Regiment 156,* commanded by *Oberleutnant* Löffler, also moved into Barmen. After the war, he reported:

The population receives us as if we were their own sons and gives us anything they can. A feeling of solidarity as I have rarely seen before develops between the civilians and the soldiers of the *Greyhound Division.* After all, we came to defend the land between the Roer and the *Reich*'s border, and to keep the opponent away from their homes and fields. And some obviously still believed in this. . . .

We receive about 20 men as replacements, amongst them a few old 156ers who had already fought in Russia or in the West with our Regiment, and distinguished themselves there. Several members of the company came back from our field hospital, where their wounds had healed. I will never forget a group of six 18-year-old boys—all Hitler Youth Leaders—who, after finishing their training, reported to me as volunteers for their first deployment at the front. With trusting eyes they joined the company's ranks and quickly won the hearts and the respect of the older combat soldiers.

At this point in time, they still believed in a turn for the better and in the following battles at Würselen, later in Vossenack, and in the Ardennes offensive, they gave their all. In Würselen, Volunteer Schirmer already received the Iron Cross II for bravery. Several others gave their lives for us and for the defense of German soil.[108]

On 9 October, *Supreme Command–West* forwarded the request to abandon the Arnhem bridgehead, which was permitted at once by the *OKW.* However, the isthmus between Lower Rhine and Waal, south of Wageningen (*363d Infantry Division*) had to be held to secure the flank of *15th Army.*[109] During the night of 13/14 October, with the release of the *9th Panzer Division*, the bridgehead was moved back to smaller bridgeheads south of Arnhem and opposite Pannerden, and was completely abandoned during the following night.[110]

The *15th Army* was able to block off the entrance to the *Scheldt* until the beginning of November. Then the Breskens bridgehead, south of the *Scheldt*, and the islands South-Beveland, Walcheren, and North-Beveland were lost. Finally, on 9 November, *15th Army* everywhere withdrew behind the Maas. Northeast of 's-Hertogenbosch, the front fell back to the Waal, and south of Wageningen to the Lower Rhine, until it moved southeast of Nijmegen toward the Maas again. A large bridgehead across the Maas was still held west of Venlo and Roermond. Near Geilenkirchen, the front then reached the *Westwall* in the vicinity of Aachen, where a fierce battle had been raging since 2 October and whence *116th Panzer Division* had now to return.

The failure of the German attack south of Arnhem was in accord with the previously mentioned fears. It remains incomprehensible how *1st Parachute Army* and *Army Group B* could have fallen for this plan. In an estimate of the situation forwarded by Model to *Supreme Command–West* on 3 October, the not very successful attack at Arnhem and its "continuation in sectors" was next justified.[111] It was supposed to have been necessary to keep up pressure against the British. Model rejected a change of main effort, because the opponent might have taken advantage of the consequent weakness near Arnhem. He wanted to keep the two *Panzer* divisions there until they could occupy the strong line Waal–Maas-Waal Canal. Then, astonishingly, he continued:

> Hereby once again must be mentioned the unique operational opportunity to take advantage of what is, even for the enemy, a very unfavorable front line, and to deal a promising blow to the deep flanks of the enemy's penetration area (corridor). For this task, two full *Panzer* divisions and two infantry divisions would have been sufficient, if they could have attacked by 12 October.

This was a correct concept, but it was of no value. Against Model's original intentions, the *9th* and *116th Panzer Divisions* were tied down in Arnhem by his actions and were wearing out. Whence four new divisions could come from so quickly remains unknown. To the many hypothetical issues that put success in question from the beginning—frontal confrontation with the spearhead of the opponent, in completely unsuitable terrain, in an area too narrow, with the opponent ruling the air—Army Group added the burden of the totally piecemeal deployment of the units.

The only benefit to be derived from the sacrifice of the divisions of *II SS-Panzer Corps* may have been a certain relief for the *15th Army.* For the two *Panzer-Grenadier* Regiments of the *116th Panzer Division,* which, after the retreat from France, had just regrouped and fought bravely, this meant a severe setback that again weakened confidence in their leadership.

Part 2: Aachen Once Again

After a short rest period, the First Army intended to push ahead toward the Rhine, between Bonn and Düsseldorf. The first mission was to seize Aachen, then to reach the Roer. To do this, IX Corps with the 30th Infantry Division, was to attack eastward across the Wurm River south of Geilenkirchen, penetrate the *Westwall*, and turn south. Their objective was Würselen, where they were to link up with the VII Corps' 1st Infantry Division, which was to attack later from the south. The 2d Armored Division of XIX Corps received orders to follow the 30th Infantry Division across the Wurm and secure the flanks and rear of the 30th by advancing to the east and north. The 29th Infantry Division was to secure the deep left flank of XIX Corps between Geilenkirchen and the Maas.

After careful reconnaissance and several days of artillery preparatory fires, on 2 October, the 30th Infantry Division attacked on both sides of Rimburg Castle. After a violent air attack on the German *Westwall* position, and with the support of 26 artillery battalions, which together with the infantry's mortars fired 19,000 rounds within twelve hours, two infantry regiments attacked across the Wurm. The effect of the firing was disappointing, and the success was modest until the evening of the second day of attack. Two small bridgeheads were formed, into which at least one combat command of the 2d Armored Division could be advanced across the Wurm.[1]

On the evening of 3 October, the German side attributed only local significance to the attack and was not clear about its purpose and direction. It was feared, however, that it represented the prelude to a larger operation. Three thousand sorties by the enemy air force were counted. Our own flew 170. The attack hit the boundary between the *183d Volks-Grenadier Division* and the *49th Infantry Division.* The counterattack during the night of 2/3 October by a battalion of the *183d Volks-Grenadier Division,* reinforced by assault guns, was delayed by enemy artillery and did not succeed.[2] Diversionary attacks by the 29th Infantry Division and the appearance of the 7th Armored Division in front of the bridgehead of Venlo increased German insecurity.[3] On 4 October, on the German side, the situation was already considered critical. Reinforcements were brought in, first from the area of *LXXXI Corps*, then also from the remaining area of *7th Army*. On 5 October, *Supreme Command–West* ordered *Army Group G* to set the *3d Panzer-Grenadier Division* in motion toward Aachen.[4]

Obviously, *Army Group B* did not consider the situation as particularly terrifying. On 5 October, it ordered *7th Army* to defend the corners in the north and south, to close off the breach, and to prepare to counterattack on 7 October with the forces that had been brought up. At the same time, as mentioned in the previous chapter, it ordered the continuation of the attack at Arnhem to connect the bridgeheads south of the Lower Rhine.[5]

The counterattacks against Übach by the reserves brought up from *LXXXI Corps* failed, as did those to the southeast of Rimburg on 4 October. At the same time, the 2d Armored Division gained ground toward the north and advanced its second combat command. On 5, 6, and 7 October, this division extended its successful attacks to the north, east, and southeast, up to south of Geilenkirchen–east of Beggendorf–west of Oidtweiler. The 30th Infantry Division could now breathe more easily and on 6 and 7 October, reached the line Merkstein–Alsdorf. They took 1,000 German prisoners. The 2d Armored Division was called to a halt and received orders to secure the rear and flank of the 30th Infantry Division as it attacked toward the north and east. The latter was reinforced by a regiment from the 29th Infantry Division and its leadership thought it would be easy to reach its objective, Würselen, and link up there with the 1st Infantry Division that was to attack from south on 8 October.[6]

On 7 October, the German side took the situation very seriously. *Supreme Command–West* expected an attack against the *12th Infantry Division* southeast of Aachen and feared a heavy attack toward Cologne. The decision was made to move up the *116th Panzer Division* and the staff of *I SS-Panzer Corps*. Under its command, the *116th Panzer* and *3d Panzer-Grenadier Divisions* were to be deployed combined.[7] But this did not work out. Both divisions were thrown in piecemeal, just as the local reserves had been in the past.

While it was still dark on 8 October, a regiment of the 1st Infantry Division attacked from the south to link up with the 30th Infantry Division near Würselen and to encircle Aachen. Taking advantage of the surprise, the regiment took Verlautenheide and in the afternoon, the dominant Hill 293, the Haarener Steinkreuz; during the next few days, it also seized Hill 231, between Haaren and Würselen (Ravelsberg), as well as Haaren itself. Aachen was encircled except for a narrow corridor. All attempts by the German side to widen the corridor failed. The Americans could not be driven off the heights northeast of the city, despite massive fire—which caused inflicted considerable casualties upon them—and in spite of all counterattacks.[8]

On 8 October, the 30th Infantry Division, now with all three regiments, also mounted an attack. The left regiment attacked Mariadorf, the one in the middle attacked toward the area northeast of Würselen, and the rightmost regiment attacked Würselen itself.[9] The attack near Mariadorf encountered the newly-arrived *Mobile Regiment von Fritzschen,* which was reinforced by tanks; the latter's northern attack group succeeded in attacking up to Alsdorf via Schaufenberg and pushed into the rear of the attacking Americans. There, however, this group met strong resistance and could not hold on. On 9 October, it also lost Schaufenberg, but the American attack had been brought to a standstill.[10]

On this day, the middle regiment of the 30th Infantry Division attacked via Birk and Euchen to gain the hills northeast of Würselen, while the regiment on the right pushed via Bardenberg toward Würselen-North.[11] Crosswise to this advance, an attack group from the *246th Volks-Grenadier Division,* the main force of which was built around *Panzer Brigade 108,* pushed from the east toward Bardenberg. In Euchen and Birk it met the spearhead of the middle American regiment, repulsed it, and advanced through to Bardenberg, cutting off the spearhead battalions of the rightmost American regiment in Würselen-North. The strength of these attack groups was not sufficient to hold on to their gains nor to achieve full success by destroying the two American battalions in Würselen.[12] On 10 October, the spearhead of *Panzer Brigade 108,* the reinforced *Panzer-Grenadier Battalion 2108,* was itself cut off in Bardenberg, after the Americans overwhelmed German security elements that were asleep in Birk. For more than two days—until the evening of 11 October—Bardenberg was held against several attacks. A counterattack on the afternoon of 10 October by the *246th Volks-Grenadier Division's Grenadier Regiment 404,* supported by several tanks from *Panzer Brigade 108,* had failed. In the afternoon of 11 October, when the weather cleared up and the enemy air forces reappeared in the sky, the resistance weakened, and collapsed by evening. A counterattack by the *12th Infantry Division* against Haarener Steinkreuz and Verlautenheide suffered the same fate.[13]

The Americans demanded the surrender of Aachen on the morning of 10 October. The battle commandant declined. About the same time, *LXXXI Corps* received an order from Model to defend every square meter of ground in the Aachen corridor to the end, and to widen the corridor by well-prepared attacks, even with partial units, step by step.[14] A *Führer* directive from 9 October was the basis for this order, whereby a breakthrough into the industrial area of Aachen west of the Rhine was to be prevented, and the city itself was to be defended to the last heap of rubble.[15] The 10 October written order from *Army Group B* to *7th Army,* demanded:

1. Preparation for the 12 October attack by *I SS-Panzer Corps* with *3d Panzer-Grenadier* and *116th Panzer Divisions,* reinforced by *Tiger Battalion 506* and *Heavy Tank Destroyer Battalion 519.*
2. Until then, prevention of encirclement of Aachen, if necessary with units from the *116th Panzer Division.*
3. Defense of Aachen to the last man.[16]

A piecemeal deployment was preprogrammed through point #2. Krebs then reported to *Supreme Command–West* that the situation near Bardenberg had become critical and that the enemy had achieved a deep penetration in the vicinity of Würselen.[17] He requested permission to move up a reinforced regimental group of the *116th Panzer Division* to continue the attack on 11 October. *Supreme Command–West* granted permission. Thereby, all the good intentions of holding the forces together and to mounting a combined attack under the command of *I SS-Panzer Corps* were abandoned, even before the first regiment arrived in the Aachen sector. However, the Army Group daily report for 10 October still read, "*Panzer-Grenadier Regiment 60* will be placed in readiness by the morning of 11 October in the vicinity of Vorweiden [2.5 kilometers northeast of Würselen—*Author*]. Deployment according to development of situation.[18]

At 2030 hours, the Chief of Staff of *7th Army,* Gersdorff, informed *LXXXI Corps* that to execute the attacks near Bardenberg and south of Haaren, the corps would have at its disposal, "Reinforced *Panzer-Grenadier Regiment 60* and *Combat Group Diefenthal* (from the *I SS-Panzer Corps* area, coming from *1st SS-* and *2d Panzer Divisions*).[19]

At 2110 hours, *LXXXI Corps* gave its orders to *246th Volks-Grenadier Division* and the *12th Infantry Division.*[20] The former received orders to attack the enemy in the area Würselen on 11 October and to close the gap between Euchen and Kohlscheid. For this, the following were subordinated to it:

Elements of the *116th Panzer Division*
Elements of *Group Diefenthal*
Elements of *Panzer Brigade 108*
Elements of *Heavy Tank Battalion 506*
Assault Gun-Brigade 394
Assault Gun-Brigade 902

From this list, one can see that the use of the word "elements" makes it look grander than the reality.

The *12th Infantry Division* assumed control in the sector east of Aachen from the *246th Volks-Grenadier Division.* With the fighting troops of the latter in that area, as well as units from *Group Diefenthal* and an assault engineer battalion, it was to mop up the breach near Verlautenheide–Haaren.

During these days, *LXXXI Corps* received three orders to withstand, one each from Rundstedt and Model, and one without signature, probably from Brandenberger.[21] Model's order is included as Appendix 15.

At 2310 on 10 October at the *LXXXI Corps* command post in Niederzier, *Oberst* Bayer, the Commander of *Panzer Regiment 16,* reported the arrival of his regimental group in the assigned area southwest of Jülich.[22] *Group Bayer* was attached to the *246th Volks-Grenadier Division,* which evidently combined all units taking part in this attack under the command of Bayer, designating it as *"Attack Group North."* The following units were assigned to it:

1. *Group Bayer* with
   Panzer-Grenadier Regiment 60 (two weak battalions, 650 men)
   1st Battalion, Panzer Regiment 24 (nine battleworthy Panthers)
   1st Battalion, Armored Artillery Regiment 146 (four *Hummels*)
2. *Battalion Rink* from *1st SS-Panzer Division* (three *Panzer-Grenadier* companies, one anti-aircraft platoon)
3. *Assault Gun Brigade 902* (eighteen guns)
4. Remnants of *Panzer Brigade 108* (five Panthers, as well as three Tigers of *Heavy Panzer Battalion 506*)[23]

Attack Group North prepared for operations in the vicinity of Kinzweiler–Broichweiden and mounted the attack on Bardenberg at 1205 hours on 11

October. Thereby, the front between Euchen and Kohlscheid was to be reestablished and the encircled *Panzer-Grenadier* battalion of *Panzer Brigade 108* in Bardenberg relieved. At 1450 hours, the *246th Volks-Grenadier Division* reported, "Attack proceeds as planned, but very slowly. At this time, reached Birk–Aachen road." [*Reich* Route 57—*Author*][24]

According to the daily report of *Army Group B* and *Supreme Command–West,* by 1600 hours on 11 October, the attack had reached the Würselen-North railroad station. They state that in heavy house-to-house fighting, the opponent still held the Gouley mine (northwest of the railroad station) and that the attack against it was continued in close combat.[25] *Panzer-Grenadier Regiment 60* had deployed its *1st Battalion* on the right. Supported by the Panthers of *1st Battalion, Panzer Regiment 24,* it seized the Würselen-North railroad station. To the left, *Battalion Rink* attacked and seized the settlement south of the Gouley mine. For the time being, *2d Battalion, Panzer-Grenadier Regiment 60* remained in reserve.[26] At the Würselen railroad station, the attacking regiment found some friendly units. *Armored Engineer Company 2108* of *Panzer Brigade 108* had been fighting there since 9 October. It took part in the brigade's attack on Bardenberg at the left wing, advanced to the railroad station, and repulsed several enemy attacks. On 11 October, the company commander, *Hauptmann* Albert, wrote in his diary, "As of 1300 hours, sporadic infantry fire left rearward; mortar fire; the hits are almost in my positions. Toward 1700 hours, *Grenadiers* [*Panzer-Grenadier Regiment*] arrive at our positions from south. Immense astonishment to find us here. Target of attack: Pass west of the Würselen church, advance to Bardenberg."[27]

From then on until 20 October, Albert's company fought alongside *Panzer-Grenadier Regiment 60* near the Würselen railroad station and defended its positions against numerous attacks. After its relief, it was incorporated into the *116th Panzer Division.* The corps order from 2400 hours on 11 October credited the attack of *Group North* as follows, "In a keen attack, *246th Volks-Grenadier Division,* with the attached combat group of the *116th Panzer Division,* threw back the opponent beyond the north edge of Würselen."[28]

The attack by *Attack Group South* was not addressed in the order. It should have started by 1500 hours, but did not. To the contrary, the enemy was able to expand his already dominant position and now closed the main access roads into the city of Aachen.[29] The only road still passable there ran from the center of Würselen to the west, via Teuterhof to Kohlscheid-South, then south via Soers to Aachen.

The keen beginning of the corps order, however, could not hide the fact that the attack by *Group North* also came to a standstill. The report of Army Group gave a somewhat strange reason for throwing *Group Bayer* into the battle of Würselen at such an early stage: The withdrawal of our defenses to the vicinity of Haaren had forced the deployment of units of the *116th Panzer Division* toward the west and northwest, to prevent the complete encirclement of Aachen.[30] These attacks directed toward Bardenberg would have to be continued on 12

October by the entire *116th Panzer Division,* while the breach near Haaren was to be closed off by other units.

During the night of 10/11 October, at 0130 hours, the whole *116th Panzer Division* was already subordinated to *LXXXI Corps* and received orders to advance still during this night into the vicinity of Kinzweiler–Broichweiden. This could not be done. Most of the Division just moved into the vicinity of Linnich–Jülich. It did not get any rest there, because at 0710 hours *LXXXI Corps* alerted the Division and ordered it to occupy an assembly area in the vicinity of Aldenhoven–Pattern–Lohn (southwest of Jülich) in preparation for an attack. As soon as it arrived there, the Division received orders to immediately advance further into the vicinity of Broichweiden–St. Jöris–Kinzweiler by 1300 hours.[31] The tanks of *2d Battalion, Panzer Regiment 16* were to support *Panzer-Grenadier Regiment 156* and conducted preparations near Lürken.[32] The Division advanced command post was established in Erberich, while the main command post went to Altdorf on the Inde River.[33] In the *LXXXI Corps* journal, the following summary about this *"2d Group, 116th Panzer Division"* is recorded [obvious mistakes corrected—*Author*]:

> *Panzer-Grenadier Regiment 156*
> *2d Battalion, Panzer Regiment 16* (six *Panzer IVs*)
> *Armored Reconnaissance Battalion 116* (two 7.5cm anti-tank guns)
> *Armored Engineer Battalion 675* (two weak companies, total 150 men)
> *3d Battalion, Armored Artillery Regiment 146* (six light field howitzers)
> *Panzerjäger Battalion 228* (nine assault guns)[34]

Then, at 1235 hours, *7th Army* ordered *LXXXI Corps* that the *116th Panzer Division* was to take control of *Attack Group North.*[35] Obviously, this did not take place before the evening of 11 October.

At 1045 hours, Model had already informed *Supreme Command–West* that the situation near Aachen had worsened and the corridor was only three kilometers wide.[36] As a reason for the unfortunate development he mentioned the burn-out of the divisions and requested replacements. Rundstedt forwarded Model's request to *OKW.* At 1135 hours, he ordered the subordination of *Supreme Command–West* Reserve, *I SS-Panzer Corps,* and the *3d Panzer-Grenadier Division* to *Army Group B.* At the same time, he requested the "most combined deployment possible" of the *3d Panzer-Grenadier* and *116th Panzer Divisions.*[37]

At 2100 hours on 11 October, *I-SS-Panzer Corps* assumed control of the *183d Volks-Grenadier, 49th Infantry,* and *116th Panzer Divisions.* It received orders from *7th Army* to first establish a secure link-up with the *116th Panzer Division* between Würselen and Bardenberg. Obviously, it was not yet known at corps that in the meantime, the resistance of *Panzer-Grenadier Battalion 2108* in Bardenberg had been extinguished. As a second objective, *I SS-Panzer Corps*—that is, the *116th Panzer Division*—was ordered to establish contact between Euchen and Bardenberg. The third objective was to be—"if necessary by deployment of *3d Panzer-Grenadier Division"*—the seizure of the line Kellersberg–Herzogenrath.[38] In consideration of the development of the situation and in view of the available forces, this was a very far-reaching objective for a frontal attack against the enemy spearheads. One could not actually expect that the enemy would further tie down its strongest attack unit, the 2d Armored Division, in the protection of its attack to the north and east. Surprisingly, however, this is what he did.

The boundary between *I SS-Panzer Corps* (*116th Panzer Division*) and *LXXXI Corps* (*246th Volks-Grenadier Division*) was determined as follows: Warden–southern edge Neusen–southern edge Broichweiden–Würselen (to *I SS-Panzer Corps*)–eastern edge Kohlscheid–eastern edge Herzogenrath.[39]

The reinforced *116th Panzer Division* received orders for 12 October to attack Bardenberg, and thereby to restore the front between Euchen and Kohlscheid.[40] Simultaneously, *Grenadier Regiment 404,* still emplaced in Würselen, was to be released and prepared at the south edge of Würselen so that it could be deployed by the *246th Volks-Grenadier Division* against the enemy at the Ravelsberg.[41] The Division attacked at 0700.[42] By 0900 hours, the right attack group, *Panzer-Grenadier Regiment 156 (Reinforced)* with the tanks of the *2d Battalion, Panzer Regiment 16* stood before Birk. There were strong enemy defenses. The left attack group, reinforced *Panzer-Grenadier Regiment 60,* seized a group of *Westwall* bunkers, 800 meters west of the Gouley mine and was fighting for the mine itself. But at 1020 hours, the attack there came to a standstill because the enemy artillery fire and attacks by fighter bombers became too intense. The right attack group also suffered so strongly under this burden that it had to retire to the Euchen–Würselen railroad line.[43]

The journal of *2d Battalion, Panzer Regiment 16,* includes the following about the attack on the right:

> After preparatory fire by our artillery, our tanks attacked from the positions northeast of Würselen. The opponent very quickly detected the attack and laid strong artillery fire on our positions. From the vicinity of the intersection 1.5 kilometers north of Würselen [Birk—*Author*], violent anti-tank fire. Since our infantry is still not here, but the opponent continuously increases his fire, the tanks were finally pulled back to Weiden.
>
> Enemy bombers circling throughout the whole morning over the battle area are being effectively fought by our anti-aircraft guns. Our four barrel guns . . . are involved in shooting down two enemy bombers. 1000 hours . . . the infantry attack that began in the meantime, gains some ground. . . .
>
> During the afternoon, our tanks were incorporated into the main battle line for the defense near the Würselen area and have little enemy contact.[44]

The commander of the six tanks was *Oberleutnant* Erdmann. One anti-tank gun was destroyed near Birk. The daily reports of Army Group and *Supreme Command–West* included entries about bitter battles in the vicinity of Aachen.[45]

About the *116th Panzer Division,* it said that its counterattack during strongest artillery fire by the enemy and growing attacks by fighter bombers had by 2130 hours reached the line from the southwestern exit of Euchen–northern edge Würselen–Würselen-North railroad station; fighting for the Gouley mine was still going on, and west of it, the captured group of bunkers was in friendly hands. The link-up toward Kohlscheid to the right wing of the *246th Volks-Grenadier Division* was to be established by reconnaissance patrols. Continuation of the attack from Euchen to Birk and from the vicinity west of Würselen toward Bardenberg was planned during the night or on 13 October.

The enemy forces facing the *116th Panzer Division* were not very strong, but they fought bravely and benefited from the help of strong artillery and an over-whelming air force, which operated almost undisturbed. Near Birk, the Division encountered units of the 120th Infantry Regiment, and in Würselen, elements of the 119th Infantry Regiment, both parts of the 30th Infantry Division. Both regiments were weakened and tired by the battles that had gone on for days. The appearance of the *116th Panzer Division* and—because of the presence of *Combat Group Rink,* possibly the *1st SS-Panzer Division*—created some worry in the heads of the American leaders. Nevertheless the Commander of First Army insisted on continuing the attack on Aachen. To reinforce the 30th Infantry Division, XIX Corps moved up a tank battalion from the 2d Armored Division and the fresh 116th Infantry Regiment (minus one battalion) of the 29th Infantry Division. These forces now became the main opponents of *116th Panzer Division* near Würselen.[46]

In Aachen, the commander of the *246th Volks-Grenadier Division, Oberst* Wilck, was appointed battle commandant of the city. On October 11, he attempt-ed in vain to convince Model to give up Aachen.[47]

To strengthen the defense of the city, the *116th Panzer Division* was to release *Battalion Rink* during the night of 12/13 October, and move it toward Aachen; this order was hard to understand, because the Division was supposed to contin-ue to attack.[48] This did not happen. The enemy, the 116th Infantry Regiment (Reinforced) conducted to attack, and Rink could not commence his march to Aachen. There was just enough time for its relief by *Armored Engineer Battalion 675.* Therefore, on the morning of 13 October, the forces were deployed as follows:

> On the right: *Panzer-Grenadier Regiment 156* between Euchen and the northern edge of Würselen.
>
> In the center: *Panzer-Grenadier Regiment 60* with *1st Battalion, Armored Engi-neer Battalion 675,* its own *2d Battalion,* and most likely, at the regiment's right wing, *Armored Engineer Company 2108.*
>
> On the left: *Armored Reconnaissance Battalion 116,* approximately between Würselen and Teuterhof. Here, the forward line ran along the second *Westwall* position.

At 0050 hours, the *Ia* of the *116th Panzer Division,* Prince Holstein, already reported to the *LXXXI Corps* Commander that *Battalion Rink* was being relieved at this time, presumably with great losses, due to the hours-long drumfire artillery bombardment they had sustained.[49] The battle report of *Combat Group Rink* from 22 October 1944 includes the following about its relief by the Division's combat engineers:

> In the late evening hours [of 12 October], the enemy continuously reinforces in front of our sector with infantry as well as with tanks. In all, ten Shermans were clearly recognized and identified.
>
> The space between the two forward lines . . . was only a few meters, generally 30 to 40 meters. At about 2240 hours, the order for the relief reaches the combat group via *Panzer-Grenadier Regiment 60.* . . . At about 0230 hours, the last parts of the relieving unit were in place. In their approach to the sector, they had already sustained considerable casualties due to enemy artillery fire. . . . According to orders, the relief was completed by about 0700 hours. At 0800 . . . the battalion commander of *Armored Engineer Battalion 675* was informed by his company commander that the enemy had sent intermediaries who demanded surrender, because they, the enemy, had become aware of the relief. After declining, the enemy broke into the right and left of the *Armored Engineer Battalion* position with tanks and infantry, and dispersed it. This developed an extremely dangerous threat to the flank of *2d Battalion, Panzer-Grenadier Regiment 60,* which was adjacent to the left. *Hauptmann* Appel, commander, *Armored Engineer Battalion 675,* personally threw himself and his few reserves toward the enemy breach and thereby found a hero's death. Both company commanders were severely wounded. At this point in time, 20 to 30 men were left, everything else could be considered destroyed, that is, dispersed. I called *Majors* Zander and Carstensen by phone and told them of my decision to at once mount a counterattack, since they had urgently asked me to do so. In the following counterattack, the combat group succeeded in throwing the enemy out of the western part of Würselen and in regaining half of the village. These positions were then held in the course of 13 October. Thereby, one, possibly two, Shermans were destroyed by *Panzerfausts.* [Obvious mistakes corrected—*Author*][50]

During the following night (13/14 October) *Battalion Rink* was relieved by *Panzer-Grenadier Regiment 60,* whereby both of its battalions took charge of a half of the sector.

Staff Paymaster Wolff-Boenisch sadly commented in his diary on 13 October:

> This a is black day for the Engineer Battalion; *Oberleutnant* Dieckmann, *Leutnant* Leufen, and *Leutnant* Müller wounded, our Commander, *Hauptmann* Appel killed at Robert-Ley village near Würselen. This is how they leave us, one by one. I felt really badly about the commander. . . . I believe, there was no man more decent, unselfish, and humble than he. *Leutnant* Varnholt has again taken over command of *1st Company.*[51]

The daily Army Group report summed up the battles at Aachen of 13 October, about as follows: In the area of Aachen the large-scale battle continued with increasing deployment of equipment.[52] More and more, the battle takes on the character of static warfare with especially high losses. The enemy was able to narrow the entrance to the city again. While a breakthrough by the enemy from Bardenberg to the south was prevented by a counterattack by the *116th Panzer Division,* the enemy succeeded at the eastern front of Aachen in breaking through up to the vicinity of the northern railroad station.

On 13 October, Headquarters, *7th Army* described the situation as follows:

> The opponent unalterably maintains the intention of encircling Aachen. In reaction to the attacks of the *116th Panzer Division,* he has considerably reinforced his forces in the vicinity of the breach area north of Aachen, mostly with artillery (according to the artillery reconnaissance report, a total of 148 batteries). Action by the reinforced *116th Panzer Division* seems to have secured the seal toward the north. The *[7th] Army's* objective is still to advance its front here to the line Euchen–Bardenberg. The *116th Panzer Division* has orders, after regrouping, to renew the attack on 14 October with the main effort on the left. . . . In the breach near Haaren, the opponent has a favorable basis for further operations against the city area, as well as against the Würselen corridor. Therefore, considering the development of the situation, the Army's position is that a mop-up of this breach has become urgent. Under its direct control, the Army intends to use the *3d Panzer-Grenadier Division,* reinforced by *Tiger Battalion 506* and supported by reinforcing artillery, to attack over and across the right wing of the *12th Infantry Division.* The objective of this limited attack is the line from the slaughterhouse (in the northeast of Aachen at the Jülicher street)–southern edge Haaren–Verlautenheide.[53]

Soon thereafter, a corresponding Army order was issued.[54] It determined the time for the *3d Panzer-Grenadier Division's* attack to be late afternoon on 14 October. The intention of *7th Army* to take over control of the *3d Panzer-Grenadier Division* itself was an astonishing interference with the command of *LXXXI Corps.* This Corps had been in control in the vicinity of Aachen from the beginning; its leadership knew the conditions there as no one else and it also proved itself. The deployment of the *I SS-Panzer Corps* in this unfamiliar area was already a doubtful start, and would only have made sense if indeed there would have been a combined attack by both mobile forces. Now, however, three higher staffs now operated in the former sector of *LXXX I Corps*: *I SS-Panzer Corps* controlled it from northwest of Geilenkirchen up to Würselen, then *LXXXI Corps* controlled it up to southeast of Eschweiler, and finally, in the middle of the sector of *LXXXI Corps, 7th Army* directly controlled the attack of a single Division. After all that had happened over the past three days, the intention of attacking with the *116th Panzer Division* also creates amazement. On 14 October, there was no attack by the *116th.*

The enemy was reinforced at the Gouley mine during the night of 13/14 October. At 0730 hours, it mounted an attack toward the south and southeast against the settlement south of the mine. The enemy succeeded in penetrating and in slightly pushing back the front line, but finally, all attacks were repulsed in heavy fighting. After preparatory aerial bombardment at 1700 hours, an attack supported by tanks toward the north edge of Würselen was also repulsed; four enemy tanks were destroyed. Both sides suffered heavy losses. *I SS-Panzer Corps* reported that the infantry battle strength of the *116th Panzer Division* had dropped considerably. Between Würselen and Holscheid, the *Armored Reconnaissance Battalion* maintained contact and dispatched reconnaissance patrols.[55] *Panzer-Grenadier Regiment 60* carried the main burden of the fighting on this day. During the night of 14/15 October, *1st Battalion, Panzer-Grenadier Regiment 156* was relieved by *Volks-Grenadiers* and put into readiness as the Division attack reserve.[56]

The situation became a little more stable in Aachen. The opponent, who entered the city from the east, advanced further toward the area of the spa, but was beaten back after seven of his tanks were destroyed. On 14 October, eight assault guns reached the city and in the night of 14/15 October, *Battalion Rink* also made its way there. Even 15 trucks with supplies arrived in Aachen during the night. The *3d Panzer-Grenadier Division*'s attack had probably been effective. It attacked from the area southwest of Eschweiler at 1830 hours on 14 October, and by 2000 hours had crossed our main battle line.[57] Even if the night attack conducted by strike troops did not achieve a major gain in terrain, it still compelled the 1st Infantry Division to temporarily suspend the attack on Aachen.[58]

The battles in the vicinity of Würselen flared up again with heightened intensity on 15 October. The 116th Infantry Regiment, supported by 2d Armored Division tanks, attacked the road-railroad intersection near the eastern edge of town, as well as the settlement in the western part. While the enemy was repulsed at the northern edge of Würselen, he was able to penetrate deeply into the western part, up to 600 meters south of the settlement. A counterattack by *Armored Reconnaissance Battalion 116* and the Division reserve, *1st Battalion of Regiment 156* supported by six *Jagdpanthers* ["Hunting Panthers," the heavily-armored, turretless, 88mm gun-equipped version of the Panther—*Editor*] threw the enemy back to the settlement.[59] Five enemy tanks were destroyed. In these battles, the Commander of *1st Company, Panzer-Grenadier Regiment 156, Oberleutnant* Heiberger, and *Oberfeldwebel* Orb of *3d Company, Armored Reconnaissance Battalion 116* distinguished themselves. In a counterattack, Orb and his platoon rescued the command post of *2d Company*; it had been surrounded in the Scherberg schoolhouse. They brought four comrades back to freedom and captured 15 Americans.[60]

Supported by the few Tigers of *Heavy Tank Battalion 506*, the *3d Panzer-Grenadier Division* attacked again on 15 October, and again, they were denied a major success in their attack. In Aachen, the enemy had advanced to the city gardens, but was thrown back. *LXXXI Corps* ordered that no new forces were to be moved into Aachen. It was believed that the attack by the *3d Panzer-Grenadier Division* would bring relief to the troops in the city.[61] That was indeed true, but only for a short time. The Division lacked the endurance necessary for protracted combat, and the Americans quickly detected this.

Army Group reported that on the thirteenth day of fighting, the battle for Aachen continued with unrelenting severity.[62] In a report to Rundstedt, Model related our losses from 2 to 11 October as 600 to 700 dead with 4,500 wounded or missing; 355 Americans had been captured and 128 enemy tanks were destroyed.[63] On the evening of 15 October, *7th Army* issued a new order: For the continued battle for Aachen, it was of decisive importance that the corridor be maintained with sufficient width to allow use of the supply route.[64] For this, *I SS-Panzer Corps* was to gain and hold a main battle line at least at the southern edge of the settlement, south of the Gouley mine. *LXXXI Corps* was to secure the area south of Würselen and east of Soers, until the attack by *3d Panzer-Grenadier Division* to establish a new defensive line had taken effect. The first task for this division was to establish a strong defense along the line, and the second was to seize the Haarener Steinkreuz hill mass. It was believed that after seizing the key positions on the heights between Haarener Steinkreuz and Verlautenheide, the attack could be continued toward Haaren and to the west toward the Ravelsberg. Besides this, after gaining some relief from the attack of *3d Panzer-Grenadier Division, LXXXI Corps* was ordered to use mobility tactics to push the enemy back in the northeastern part of Aachen.

In his elaboration after the war, the Commanding General of *I SS-Panzer Corps* credited the achievement of *116th Panzer Division* of 15 October, "The day was marked by constantly renewed defensive battles and counterattacks, both of the toughest type. In spite of the oppressive enemy superiority, it is solely the merit of the brave and steadfast *116th Panzer Division* that denied the opponent the success he wanted to achieve. Encirclement of Aachen failed."[65]

General Hodges, Commander of the First Army, was quite disturbed by the minor achievements of 30th Infantry Division and wanted to have the division commander relieved because "he could not advance an inch in four days." Pressured by his superiors, on 16 October, he made the decision to attack with the 119th Infantry Regiment on both sides of the Wurm River, to seize Kohlscheid, and to push through to Hill 194 (southwest of Würselen, about one kilometer northwest of the Ravelsberg). Simultaneously, the 116th Infantry Regiment and one battalion of the 120th Infantry Regiment were to continue the attack on Würselen. The 117th and 120th Infantry Regiments, at the eastern flank of the 30th Infantry Division, were ordered to conduct diversionary operations. They were ordered to feign attacks with fire and by assaults in company strength.

The intention of the 30th Infantry Division now to bring the attack to the south to a close with the encirclement of Aachen gave the battles of 16 October their character. They surpassed the battles of 15 October in tenacity. Fortunately, it was overcast and rainy weather, which diminished the threat from the air. Still before daybreak, two battalions of the 119th Infantry Regiment crossed the Wurm and seized Kohlscheid.

In heavy fighting with *Militia Training Battalion II/6,* the 2d Battalion, 119th Infantry Regiment penetrated the line of bunkers due east of the Wurm. Supported by fire from the west bank of the Wurm, the 119th seized a hill southwest of Würselen, halfway to the objective, Hill 194. Here, the attack ground to a halt in the face of German artillery fire. However, when the German artillery had to move its fire over toward the American attacks against Würselen and the area northeast of it, the 2d Battalion, 119th Infantry Regiment caught its breath again, and took Hill 194 during the afternoon. On top of the Ravelsburg, the Americans reported that they could see their comrades on Hill 194. At 1615 hours, a reconnaissance patrol coming from Hill 194 reached the Ravelsberg. The link-up was established.[66]

The *Army Group B* report from the morning of 16 October states that after repelling several enemy advances south of the settlement and west of Würselen, units of the *116th Panzer Division* were locked in vicious battles in forward areas.[67] But at 0730, the enemy had already mounted an attack from the development toward the southeast against the left wing of *Panzer-Grenadier Regiment 60.* It encountered mostly *Armored Reconnaissance Battalion 116,* and it gained ground up to the Scherberger street. The school in Scherberg was encircled, and the counterattack to free those locked inside failed.[68] *Leutnant* Beckmann, duty officer with *1st Battalion, Panzer-Grenadier Regiment 156,* wrote in his diary about the battalion's attack:

> In the meantime, night set in. For orientation on the situation, I am being sent to *2d* and *3d Companies.* Both companies are positioned close to the school, which is defended tenaciously by the Americans. Earlier, five German officers and men of the *Armored Reconnaissance Battalion* were captured. A reconnaissance patrol sent to the school was captured as well. I reported this to the commander and later returned to the school. The two companies did not advance any further. Meanwhile, a man of the just-mentioned reconnaissance platoon showed up. . . . Questioning was sufficient to determine the layout of the school and everything else around it. . . . Thus, I worked myself into the school's cellar entrance and asked the inhabitants to surrender.[69]

Beckmann captured twelve Americans this way, but the school was not recaptured. The forward line basically followed the Aachener street (*Reich* Route 57), between the road-railroad crossing via the bend in road near Hill 182.0 toward Kaisersruh. The intersection with the Scherberger street remained in enemy hands for the time being.

Further west, the enemy, consisting of the aforementioned 2d Battalion, 119th Infantry Regiment, broke through the German position on both sides of the boundary between the *116th Panzer Division* and the *246th Volks-Grenadier Division*. There, three bunkers were lost and with them, communication with the units of the *246th*, which detoured from Kohlscheid to Richterich. The road to Hill 194 was therefore open to the enemy. Only the bunkers southwest of the Kaisersruh station now formed a barrier.

On the evening of 16 October, Vogelsang wrote in his diary:

> After a heavy barrage, the Americans attacked the *Armored Reconnaissance Battalion* today. Bitter fighting developed, the *3d Company* was encircled in the Würselen school [part of Scherberg—*Author*] and defended itself desperately. There was telephonic connection with it via the underground net connecting the pillboxes until the last moment. Dramatic conversations developed, but outside help could no longer be offered. Besides the *3d Company*, in addition to a large number of NCOs and men, four officers became casualties.[70]

On 17 October, Vogelsang added:

> The attack finally ran aground. The Division went over to the defensive. All positions could be held without exception against heavy pressure by a superior opponent. The unit fights in an exemplary fashion, in spite of all materiel and numerical inferiority. Yesterday, the *2d Battalion, Panzer-Grenadier Regiment 60* alone repelled the attacks of two regiments. Even the heavily-battered *Armored Reconnaissance Battalion* held its position against all attempts to break through it, despite heavy losses and extremely unclear conditions. Two of the recently organized and equipped sniper platoons shot down more than 50 opponents. Twenty tanks were put out of action within the Division sector.
>
> The artillery fire roars without pause. Our batteries attempt to compensate for the mass fires of the enemy with precision fires of their own. This morning, with concentrated fire, the *Artillery Regiment* already succeeded in destroying an enemy unit while it was still in its assembly area.
>
> The attitude of the Americans has sunken considerably. The prisoners being brought in look tattered and run down. All of them wish that this damned war would finally come to an end. The unexpected halt and the hard battles at the German border have destroyed many high hopes.

On 16 October, in the Euchen–Würselen sector, the 30th Infantry Division's attack also hit *Panzer-Grenadier Regiment 156*, which up until now had been largely spared. The main effort aimed for the road-railroad intersection at the northern fringe of Würselen. During heavy fighting, the regiment was able to repel three attacks supported by tanks.[71] In this action, as usual, *Panzer-Grenadier Regiment 156* was supported by the *2d Battalion, Panzer Regiment 16*. The latter's journal includes the following about the battle:

> After heavy, concentrated artillery fire, the opponent attacks in the morning with tank support. From the vicinity of Bardenberg, he attempts to advance via Euchen

to take Würselen. He achieves penetrations at the northwestern and western edges of town.

The northern breach can immediately be sealed off, while fighting lasts all day in the vicinity of the other breach.[72]

Oberleutnant Löffler, Commander of *5th Company, Panzer-Grenadier Regiment 156,* was with his company in the middle of his battalion's position on the northern edge of Würselen. He reported the following to me about the action on 16 October:

> After a massive barrage, an attack by the opponent with tank support. At the right wing of the company, the opponent comes to a halt, closely in front of the main battle line. Taking along the wounded, he pulls back during the night. The Americans achieved a breach on the left wing, at the northwestern edge of Würselen. With support from our tanks and with the participation of *2d Platoon, 5th Company,* the opponent is thrown back in a counterattack. Our *Panzer IVs* destroyed two Sherman tanks.[73]

The diversionary attacks by the enemy north of Euchen were reported as repulsed. However, together with the attacks against the *116th Panzer Division,* they captured German attention and weakened the German defense between Würselen and Kohlscheid. Thus, the Americans succeeded in the decisive breakthrough for the encirclement of Aachen.

Success was denied to the attack conducted by the *3d Panzer-Grenadier Division* during the night of 16/17 October and throughout the following day.

During the afternoon, an assault by the enemy from the Ravelsberg to the north was smashed with combined fire by the *12th Infantry Division.*[74] This unit was renamed the *12th Volks-Grenadier Division* the same day. *Supreme Command–West* reported that the corridor into Aachen was still 300 meters wide.[75] In fact, it was interrupted. *Oberst* von Waldenberg confided in his calendar:

> Defense and counterattacks alternate. It is very, very tough fighting, and the casualties are accordingly high. Contrary to expectations, the American fights well. My people perform splendidly. They are under uninterrupted fire. The Americans succeed in the encirclement of Aachen; they broke through the *246th Division.* My front held its own. Even the deployment of *3d Panzer-Grenadier Division* could not change anything. Nothing helps anymore, enemy fire is too strong.[76]

On 17 October, we had a day of relative calm.[77] For once, both parties had to catch their breath. The Americans tried to expand their success and reinforce the encirclement of the city. The 1st Infantry Division continued its attack in the inner city and pushed forward north of the Ravelsberg and at Verlautenheide. The 99th Infantry Battalion [a separate unit consisting of Norwegian-Americans originally intended for the invasion of Norway—*Editor*] was deployed as part of the 116th Infantry Regiment, opposite the left wing of the *116th Panzer Division,* and tried to close off the Würselen–Aachen road near the Kaisersruh station.[78]

On the German side, after being released from the front, the *3d Panzer-Grenadier Division* was subordinated to *I SS-Panzer Corps*. This unit had the mission of reestablishing contact with Aachen on 18 October through attacks by the *3d Panzer-Grenadier Division* and strong units from the *116th Panzer Division*. As ordered by *7th Army*, the first task was the seizure of the Ravelsberg and the group of bunkers south of it in surprise attacks. Afterwards, all available forces were to be used to attack further west and reopen access to Aachen.[79] Even if this would have worked, the corridor would only have been about one kilometer wide, without any usable road connection.

The prerequisites for this plan worsened noticeably. During the afternoon of 17 October, the *246th Volks-Grenadier Division* lost the bunkers on both sides of the Würselen–Aachen road, south of the Kaisersruh station. They were the key to opening the corridor.[80]

On 17 October, new forces were evidently brought in to the *116th Panzer Division* to strengthen the Division's weakened units, or to free them for the attack on 18 October. "In the vicinity of Euchen" were, according to a report at 1850 hours by the Division *Ia* to *LXXXI Corps, 2d Battalion, Grenadier Regiment 689* and *Engineer Battalion 246* of the *246th Volks-Grenadier Division*. Most likely, *Armored Reconnaissance Battalion 116,* at the Division's left wing, was relieved by *Battalion Trier.*[81]

The last attempt was made to gain to access to Aachen on 18 October. Unfortunately, an integrated attack was not conducted. At 0510 hours, *3d Panzer-Grenadier Division* attacked the Ravelsberg. The *116th Panzer Division* could not finish its reconsolidation in time for the attack and in the late morning was itself attacked on the northern edge of Würselen. Its attack group did not follow along the Würselen–Aachen road until 1400 hours. In the evening, the *3d Panzer-Grenadier Division* seized the group of bunkers at the Ravelsberg against violent resistance. Because of its narrowly structured attack, though, it was outflanked on both sides in the attack to right of the Kaisersruh station. This is also the location of the bunkers that were lost in the afternoon of 17 October. In the late evening hours, however, during very severe fighting, the attack group of the *116th Panzer Division* succeeded in seizing one block of houses northwest of the station and the bunkers east of the road to Aachen (Bunkers 110, 111, 113, and 118). This afforded some respite to the *3d Panzer-Grenadiers,* but its attack could not get going again.[82] Other units of the *116th,* namely the *1st Battalion, Panzer-Grenadier Regiment 156,* attacked the intersection in Scherberg (500 meters northeast of Hill 182.0) which was lost on 16 October, and retook it.[83] The *116th's* attack along the road to Aachen was renewed on 19 October, but was not successful. On the morning of 19 October, the *3d Panzer-Grenadier Division* lost all of its laboriously-conquered bunkers to an enemy surprise attack. The attempt to recapture them in the afternoon failed. The daily report of *Supreme Command–West* admitted that the attack by *I SS-Panzer Corps* would have to be discontinued.[84]

During the battles near Kaisersruh, the *116th*'s combat group was commanded by *Oberstleutnant* Musculus, the Commander of *Panzer Brigade 108*. The following units were assigned to it:

Staff of *Panzer Brigade 108*

Remnants of *Panzer Brigade 108* (*4th Company* of the tank battalion and some
Panzer-Grenadiers)

Armored Reconnaissance Battalion 116 (already very weakened by the battles near
Würselen)

Elements of *Heavy Tank Destroyer Battalion 519* (Hunting Panthers)

Engineer Battalion 246 of the *246th Volks-Grenadier Division* with apparently one
company from *Battalion Trier* attached.[85]

A member of *Group Musculus'* staff, Rolf Alsleben, made the following entry
in his diary on 18 October:

At 1400 hours attack with heavy barrage, advance quite well, the *"Kanacken"* [A
soldiers' nickname for the opponent—*Author*] trembling and pale near the houses.
Enemy artillery and mortar fire strengthening. We have heavy losses, later up to 50
percent, we have to return, because we have no infantry, what a pity, we would have
chased them! Two Shermans and two anti-tank guns are destroyed, took 40 prisoners. Our losses, three tanks, in addition many technical failures. Bunkers 110 and
113 are back in our hands. We are sitting on the roof of 111, the *"Kanacken"* are
inside beneath us.[86]

On the evening of 18 October, at 2045 hours, the *Ia* of the *116th Panzer
Division* quite optimistically issued an order to *Combat Group Musculus,*
"Continue attack with deployment of all forces. After taking bunker line 100, 113
objective Wurm sector. Move up mortar men."

Panzer Regiment 16 and *Panzer-Grenadier Regiment 60* received orders to
support *Musculus*.[87]

On 19 October, Alsleben's diary includes the following:

Bunker 118 is lost again in the early morning hours. . . . At 1400 hours, a two-hour-
long barrage hits our part of town. . . . After the barrage, the American attacks along
the whole line, breaks through the adjacent unit on the left and comes close to our
hides. Tank position around the command post for a last defense, the infantry comes
back, MG bursts whistle along the streets. By 1800 hours, the *Kanacken* to our right
were chased out. Bunker 118 back in our hands. It is a constant back and forth!
Ravelsberg, with all its bunkers is being lost.

Vogelsang's diary includes the following entry on the evening of 19 October:

Fighting went back and forth for every bunker, house, cellar, and for every meter of
ground.

Thirty prisoners arrived here for interrogation. They were not in a very good
mood either. They thought our way of fighting in Würselen was unfair. There, after

artillery preparation, a combat group of infantry, engineers, and tank crewmen with a few Hunting Panthers cleaned out a street. Just because for once there was materiel equality in limited space does not mean it is unfair! What should our men say every day![88]

On the afternoon of 19 October, all American attacks northeast and north of Würselen were beaten back in tenacious fighting, while a local breach southeast of the road–railroad intersection was mopped up with a counterattack.[89] These battles were mainly fought by *Panzer-Grenadier Regiment 156.* They don't seem to have been too serious, since Sandkuhl took note of only one small enemy attack, and *Oberleutnant* Löffler reports on 19 October from *5th Company* at the north edge of Würselen:

Dismal weather, raining the whole day. Our *Panzer-Grenadiers* are completely soaked and overly tired. I take a few groups at a time so they can get some sleep and dry their uniforms. . . . An American strike force stalled by fire in front of *2d Platoon* and leaves three dead.[90,91]

On 18 and 19 October, the situation in Aachen itself worsened. The war diary of LXXXI Corps portrays the events impressively. On 18 October, at 1300 hours, battle commandant *Oberst* Wilck reports:

Strong enemy breaches in Aachen and at Laurensberg. Quellenhof, city center, and Laurensberg occupied by enemy. Last defense takes place at Lousberg. Directed counterattack only possible as break-out. Decision requested. Battle strength about 1,200 men. Battle value insufficient because of continuous demands. Wilck.[92]

At 1550 hours, *Oberst* Wilck warned, "Situation in Aachen such that last resistance probably coming to an end on 19 October. Breakout via Soers tonight still possible. Request decision soon. Wilck."

From the reports of *LXXXI Corps,* it was clear that the forces were deteriorating. There were no longer any prospects of again freeing the city for the purposes of holding on to it. Nevertheless, on 18 October, *7th Army* issued an order for the continuation of the counterattack by *I SS-Panzer Corps* "from Würselen via the area both sides of Soers to the southwest." The *246th Volks-Grenadier Division* was tasked as follows:

Main task of *246th Infantry* [sic] *Division* remains the defense of Aachen to the last man. The forces have to be combined according to the situation. Furthermore, the Division has to be ordered to maintain a mobile force (*Combat Group Diefenthal, Assault Gun Brigade 341*) in the area north of Aachen prepared to link up with the *SS-Panzer Corps* as its attack progresses in the general direction of Soers. Preparations to be made to evacuate the wounded.[93]

In addition, on the evening of 18 October, with an emphatic warning by *Supreme Command–West*, the battle commandant received Model's order to persevere, to defend the city to the last man and the last shell, and, if necessary, to be buried under its rubble.[94] On 19 October, the Germans occupying Aachen were pushed back to the northwest part of the city. *LXXXI Corps* reckoned with the end of Aachen and expressed this in the daily report.[95] On 20 October, the Americans continued their attacks against the encircled troops, and on the morning of 21 October, advanced to the battle commandant's command post in the air-raid bunker at the foot of the Lousberg. *Oberst* Wilck capitulated.[96] In the *OKW* journal it was noted:

> This several-week-long fight for the old imperial city not only gave the opponent, basking in previous successes, an idea of the tough combat awaiting him on German soil, but also gained time for finishing the construction of fortifications and replenishing units.[97]

Now let us turn back to the fighting outside the city. On 20 October, *LXXXI Corps* also assumed control of the *49th Infantry, 116th Panzer,* and *3d Panzer-Grenadier Divisions.* The staff of *I SS-Panzer Corps* was pulled out.[98]

During the night of 19/20 October, the enemy advanced from the Ravelsberg northwest against the left wing of the *116th Panzer Division, Group Musculus.* The most forward, Bunker 118, had to be given up since it was surrounded by the enemy. The situation of the bunkers left of it was unclear at first. A reconnaissance patrol of *Engineer Battalion 246* encountered a heavy enemy concentration there and was destroyed, except for one man. Thereafter, *Group Musculus* withdrew its forces to their starting position and formed a new main battle line in the old line from Hill 182.0 to the Würselen–Aachen road toward Bunkers 127 and 128 at the extreme left wing. The last infantry units of *Armored Reconnaissance Battalion 116* were employed in this sector. *Battalion Trier* defended the area adjacent to the right, up to the road intersection 500 meters north of Hill 182.0. Then followed *1st Battalion, Panzer-Grenadier Regiment 156*, which was subordinated to *Panzer-Grenadier Regiment 60.* The *1st* and *2d Battalions* of *Panzer-Grenadier Regiment 60,* as well as *Armored Engineer Company 2108,* with its front facing northwest, were fighting in Würselen. *Regiment 156* controlled the sector from the northern edge of Würselen along the railroad to Euchen. Subordinated to it were *2d Battalion, Panzer-Grenadier Regiment 156, Militia Battalion 771,* and the *2d Battalion, Grenadier Regiment 689* of the *246th Volks-Grenadier Division.*

Besides the attack on *Group Musculus,* on the morning hours of 20 October, after a violent barrage, the enemy made several thrusts along the boundary between the *1st* and *2d Battalions* of *Panzer-Grenadier Regiment 60.* The enemy was repelled in house-to-house fighting. The main battle line remained in our hands. Starting at 1345 hours, the enemy again started assaults against the *Panzer-Grenadier Regiment 60* sector near the athletic field in Würselen, 600 meters southwest of the road–railroad intersection. Enemy artillery activity also came to life again. The assaults were repelled.[99]

After a discussion at corps headquarters among the 1st General Staff Officers of the divisions, at 2400 hours on 20 October, a corps order was issued for the defense, the organization of the units, and the release of *116th Panzer Division.* The paragraph for the *116th Panzer Division* read, "After its release, *116th Panzer Division* occupies an assembly area in the vicinity west and southwest of Jülich, so that the Division can be deployed at any time in the corps sector."[100]

Besides this, the absorption of *Panzer Brigade 108* into the Division was ordered. In the same night, *Combat Group Musculus* was relieved by the *3d Panzer-Grenadier Division*; the *1st Battalion, Panzer-Grenadier Regiment 60,* along with *Armored Engineer Company 2108,* was relieved by *Füsilier Battalion 246.* Neither operation proceeded smoothly. The *116th Panzer Division* reported about the night of 20/21 October, "During the night, artillery nuisance fire and barrages of heavy-caliber shells and delayed-action fuses throughout the whole Division sector. Enemy thrusts toward the right wing of *Panzer-Grenadier Regiment 60* were repulsed. The relief of *Group Musculus* [proceeded] as planned."[101]

However, the *3d Panzer-Grenadier Division* complained in its evening report. Its report said that units from *Group Musculus* did not depart from their positions in an orderly fashion, and that in some places, the enemy followed and took Hill 182.0 as well as the intersections to the north. The units assigned for the relief of *1st Battalion, Panzer-Grenadier Regiment 156,* bordering *Group Musculus* to the right, had mounted a counterattack. The first attack failed, but the second one was reported a success on the morning of 22 October.[102]

The events of 21 October developed much more critically for *Panzer-Grenadier Regiment 60.* The relief of its *1st Battalion* and *Armored Engineer Company 2108* by the *Füsiliers* of the *246th Volks-Grenadier Division* was indeed concluded by 0600 hours; however, at 0800 hours, the enemy attacked in battalion strength by using smoke against *5th Company, Regiment 156,* the unit to the right. [The *Füsilier* unit of a *Volks-Grenadier Division* was the division's elite light infantry outfit, meant to be employed for classic light infantry missions such as reconnaissance and other patrolling. Some *Volks-Grenadier* divisions had only a company, while others, such as the *246th,* had an entire *Füsilier* battalion—*Editor.*] The attack followed the railroad toward the Würselen train station, dispersed *1st Company, Füsilier Battalion 246,* and came out of the smoke to destroy the leftmost platoon of *5th Company* from the left. The Hammer-Halde hillside (named so, probably because of the symbols on the map), 750 meters northwest of the railroad station, fell into enemy hands. The commander of *2d Battalion, Panzer-Grenadier Regiment 156, Hauptmann* Gerke, intervened with the *6th Company* to restore the situation at the left wing of his battalion. The *116th Panzer Division* immediately deployed its reserve for a counterattack. These were the *Combat Engineer Company* of *Panzer-Grenadier Regiment 156* and the *Division Escort Company,* supported by the tanks attached to *Panzer-Grenadier Regiment 156.* The leadership of *Panzer-Grenadier Regiment 156* was entrusted with the control of the attack. The recently-relieved *1st Battalion,*

Panzer-Grenadier Regiment 60 was alerted and ordered to prepare for action. The interim report of the Division from 21 October stated:

> At left wing of *Panzer-Grenadier Regiment 156,* the Division reserve attacked and re-took the southeastern edge Hammer-Halde and area east. Three Shermans destroyed. Most of *Füsilier Battalion 246* beaten. Freed 40 men without weapons from American captivity. Took eight prisoners. *Füsilier Battalion 246* at present usable, with limitations, for defense with only one company. As of 1700 continuation of attack to regain Hammer-Halde. Enemy assault at left wing of *Panzer-Grenadier Regiment 60* repelled.[103]

The *1st Battalion, Panzer-Grenadier Regiment 60,* which was standing by, was also deployed; its attack regained the lost terrain. Thereby, more prisoners were brought in, for a total of 61 on this day. The company of *Füsilier Battalion 246* that was still intact joined the attack at the left wing and won back the houses on route 57 (300 meters southwest of the hillside). The *Division Escort Company* proved itself in its first deployment after it overcame initial problems, under the good leadership of *Hauptmann* von Linde-Suden. It was again relieved during the night and put placed on standby as reserve. Hammer-Halde was mopped up of enemy remnants during the night of 21/22 October. There were 57 dead enemy soldiers left behind.[104]

These battles are portrayed in the journal of the *2d Battalion* of *Panzer Regiment 16*:

> During the day, after artillery preparation, the enemy attacks under cover of smoke and works his way toward our defenses. Since there is no longer any visibility, our tanks have to withdraw to the first houses. The opponent sneaks into our position from the northwest toward the Würselen railroad station.
>
> A briskly-led counterattack by our units with tank support is successful. The old lines are reached again; besides that, the hillside at the northwestern edge is taken. Prisoners are taken and about 50 German prisoners are freed. After this, the afternoon and night are relatively quiet.
>
> The Division Commander expresses his full appreciation to the regiment for its counterattack.[105]

Further, as a note for experience, it stated, "Our counterattack was fully successful because it was led promptly and by unit commanders of the lowest ranks (Platoon leaders, and so on)."

A note in the *2d Battalion, Panzer Regiment 16* journal shows how much the lack of fuel hindered the German conduct of battle. On the morning of 21 October, when the order came to send all battleworthy tanks forward immediately, two of the five repaired tanks of the battalion could not roll out due to insufficient fuel. On this day, the commander of *7th Army* visited the Division and expressed his special appreciation. He bid his farewell, since *7th Army* was to turn over the control of *LXXXI Corps* and *XII SS-Corps* north of it to *5th Panzer Army,* coming from Lorraine.[106]

As already reported, resistance in Aachen was extinguished on 21 October.

In the journal of *Supreme Command–West,* it stated that with this, the enemy achieved his first objective toward the attack on Cologne and that the continuation of the attack had to be expected within a reasonable time.[107] As a consequence of this thought, *Army Group B* was told that it was important to relieve the mobile units to be used as reaction forces. On the previous day, *Supreme Command–West* related his status report to *OKW* and requested new forces.[108] His special concerns were the increasing destruction of the Rhine bridges and the railroad installations by the enemy air forces. *Supreme Command–West* feared that fresh units, such as the divisions of *6th Panzer Army,* could not be brought across the Rhine in time.

At 1300 hours on 22 October, the opponent attacked in battalion strength at the boundary between *Panzer-Grenadier Regiments 156* and *60* and infiltrated near the left wing of *1st Battalion, Panzer-Grenadier Regiment 60* where the company of *Füsilier Battalion 246* was deployed at the Hammer-Halde. The attack was repulsed and with a tank-supported counterattack by *1st Battalion, Panzer-Grenadier Regiment 60,* the infiltrating enemy was thrown back. By 2010 hours, *Oberst* von Waldenburg was able to report that the entire main battle line was again in our hands. The corps commander expressed his special appreciation to him. At 2205 hours, *7th Army* requested supporting documents from *LXXXI Corps* to support mentioning the *116th Panzer Division* in the *OKW* report.[109]

During the night of 22/23 October, the staff of *Panzer-Grenadier Regiment 156,* the regimental engineer company, and its *2d Battalion* were relieved by units from the *246th Volks-Grenadier Division.* The *116th*'s tanks that were deployed there remained in place for another 24 hours.[110] The consolidated report of the *116th Panzer Division* regarding the battles near Würselen was forwarded to *LXXXI Corps* and served *Supreme Command–West* as support for the proposal of mentioning the Division in the *OKW*'s report:

On 10 November 1944, after eight days of heavy offensive and defensive battles in the vicinity of Nijmegen–Arnhem, and after a roughly 200-kilometer march to the Aachen area of operations, the *116th Panzer Division* was deployed against the enemy that was attacking from the northwest to cut off the city of Aachen. In 12 days of uninterrupted, heavy offensive and defensive battles, under the heaviest enemy artillery fire and enemy air domination, near Würselen, the *116th Panzer Division* prevented all enemy attempts at penetrating the Division's sector. Some of the fighting included close combat in the rubble of the city. Enemy penetrations were always cleared up by immediate counter advances or counterattacks. Under considerable personnel losses of our own, by ruthless use of rocket-propelled grenades and close-combat weapons by our troops, the enemy suffered very high, bloody losses in house-to-house fighting. This made it necessary to employ young, inexperienced replacements.

Between 11 and 20 October 1944, the following were shot, that is, destroyed:

11 enemy heavy anti-tank guns

29 enemy tanks

1 enemy tank heavily damaged

1 fighter-bomber, 2 bombers

1 fighter-bomber up in flames

There were 120 prisoners were taken. The number of dead is four times higher (In one day, 53 Americans were finished by two snipers with single shots, and at a different place, 75 dead were counted). Statements by prisoners confirmed the high, bloody losses.[111]

According to the weekly report from 21 October, the Division was in possession of two medium strength, two average, and one weak battalion; additionally, the weakened *Füsilier Battalion 246* was attached.[112] Battleworthy anti-tank guns and tanks included the following:

8 anti-tank guns

8 organic tank and 19 attached tank destroyers and assault guns

6 *Panzer IVs*

18 organic and 6 attached Panthers and Hunting Panthers.

On 22 October, the artillery had:

3 light and

2 heavy batteries with a total of only 18 tubes.[113]

The attached tanks and tank destroyers probably belonged to *Assault Gun Brigade 902,* to *Heavy Tank Destroyer Battalion 519,* and to *Panzer Brigade 108.* All together, the Division still had more than 57 tanks available. On 22 October, the arrival of *March Battalion 619* with replacements was announced to the Division.[114] On that evening, Vogelsang wrote the following in his diary:

To compensate for our high losses, *Panzer Brigade 108* was assigned to us for assimilation. . . . In respect to materiel and personnel we are, thereby, in better shape now than we have been in a long time.

The *Field Replacement Battalion* has received replacements the normal way. There we now have a leader reserve of 46 officers. Now the training of the replacements from the homeland can be done effectively, according to plan, so that for some foreseeable time we are not forced to hastily release them to the combat units. With *Hauptmann* Baumgarten, the bearer of the Knight's Cross with Oakleaves from *156* as the commander, and the combat-experienced *Hauptmann* Schörken as leader of the NCO combat school, this important project is in the best hands.

Besides pure battle training, the spiritual care and structure of leisure time are managed most carefully under *Oberleutnant* Inboden, the adjutant. A Division band, as well as a theater group, provide essential relaxation from the stressful days. A daily hour-long lesson about the Division's history takes care of the required introduction to the special mentality of our unit. After successful completion of his training, every man receives the Greyhound emblem in a ceremony before his release to the front.

The cooperation with the population and the authorities in Neviges is exemplary. *BDM* girls [*Bund Deutscher Mädchen,* or the "Union of German Girls," the Nazi Party group for girls 14–18 years old—*Editor*] help in the kitchen, the Red Cross helps take care of the sick and wounded, and in exchange, the band plays music for the town.[115]

On 23 October, *LXXXI Corps* reported its intentions as follows, "*116th Panzer Division* is presently being released to stand by as corps mobile reserve in the area west of Jülich, so that it can be deployed against the expected enemy attack from the vicinity of Alsdorf, as well as against Stolberg."[116]

The new field army commander, General der *Panzer* Truppen von Manteuffel, visited the Division and had a lengthy discussion with *Oberst* von Waldenburg.[117] During the night of 23/24 October, 1st Battalion, *Panzer-Grenadier Regiment 156* was relieved by the *3d Panzer-Grenadier Division.*[118]

The tanks of *2d Battalion, Panzer Regiment 16* were also pulled out and attached to *1st Battalion, Panzer Regiment 24.* The *2d Battalion, Panzer Regiment 16* by itself—without its battleworthy tanks—moved into the vicinity of Rath (northeast of Erkelenz) and there, started intensive training at once.[119] *Panzer-Grenadier Regiment 156* moved into quarters in the area northwest of Jülich. The planned relief of *Panzer-Grenadier Regiment 60* for the coming night (24/25 October) was postponed by 24 hours. Calm prevailed at the front. Thus, during the night of 24/25 October, it was possible to withdraw *Panzerjäger Battalion 228*; all of *Heavy Tank Destroyer Battalion 519* was therefore deployed in the sector of *Panzer-Grenadier Regiment 60.* On 25 October, not much was happening at the front. On this day, the *116th Panzer Division* transferred the sector of *Grenadier Regiment 352* (formerly the sector of *Panzer-Grenadier Regiment 156*) to the *246th Volks-Grenadier Division.* In the evening, the relief of *Panzer-Grenadier Regiment 60* by the *3d Panzer-Grenadier Division* began. *Heavy Tank Destroyer Battalion 519* was also pulled out. By the morning of 26 October, the whole Division was finally relieved; it became Army Reserve in the vicinity of Linnich–Titz–Steinstrass–Hambach–Schophoven–Pattern–Bourheim. The unarmored units were to move in west of Jülich and the armored units east of the town. The Division staff moved together to Altdorf. The staff of *Artillery Regiment 146* was there also.[120]

Still on 25 October, *Generalfeldmarschall* Model visited the Division and listened intently to the details about the battles, the losses, the condition of the Division, and about the behavior of the enemy. He also expressed his special appreciation for the achievements of the Division and promised help for the planned replenishment. But he pointed out that it was the Division's task to again become combat ready as quickly as possible, because this is what the situation simply demands.[121] The units of the Division had not yet reached their newly assigned areas when they were already called for. The *5th Panzer Army* granted the *LXXXI Corps* request to deploy a battalion of *Panzer-Grenadier Regiment 156* with the *246th Volks-Grenadier Division* in the evening of 26 October, so that two battered regiments could be combined into one. From the evening of 26 October up to the morning of 28 October, *1st Battalion, Panzer-Grenadier Regiment 156* was put at the disposal of *246th Volks-Grenadier Division*.[122]

It was a gratifying event when *Army Anti-Aircraft Battalion 281* returned to the Division on 26 October.[123] Now the Division again had all the units that belonged to it. The staff of *2d Battalion, Armored Artillery Regiment 146* came back from the rear echelon with the *5th Battery,* which was finally equipped again with guns and prime movers. With this, it again had its three batteries. However, the *1st* and *3d Battalions* of the *Artillery Regiment* were still very weak.[124] *Hauptmann* Hossenfelder, former commander of *Armored Engineer Battalion 675,* had recovered from his wounds and had again assumed command.[125] *Armored Signal Battalion 228* received a new commander, since *Major* Kleckel had been transferred. In the meantime, *Hauptmann der Reserve* Agne had commanded the battalion. Now, *Hauptmann* Bartels took over.[126]

In the afternoon of 28 October, all of the Division's commanders attended a conference. In his diary that evening, Vogelsang wrote, "It happens so rarely that everyone can get together."[127]

On this day, the report of the *OKW* included this supplement, "*116th Panzer Division,* under command of *Oberst* von Waldenburg, in heavy fighting in the area north of Aachen, destroyed all break-through attempts by the enemy, and in brave and skilled counterattacks, inflicted great losses on the enemy."[128]

Part 3: The Hürtgen Forest

On 27 October, *Oberst* von Waldenburg had already written in his calendar, "Calm does not last long. Should get transferred again."[1] On this day, the *XLVII Panzer Corps,* together with the *9th Panzer Division* coming from the Maas bridgehead of Venlo, mounted a limited objective attack toward Asten (20 kilometers southeast of Eindhoven). On the next day, the *15th Panzer-Grenadier Division* took part in the action. On the same day, *Army Group B* requested permission from *Supreme Command–West* to also pull up the *116th Panzer Division;* it was permitted.[2] On the evening of 28 October, the *116th Panzer Division* received orders to reach the Erkelenz–Wegberg–Krüchten area during the night of 28/29 October.[3]

Earlier, on 17 October, *XII SS-Corps* took over the sector on both sides of Geilenkirchen with the *176th Infantry* and *183d Volks-Grenadier Divisions.* In the beginning of the attack, on 27 October, *XLVII Panzer Corps* controlled the southern part of the Venlo bridgehead, with *LXXXVI Corps* being restricted to the northern part. The attack by *XLVII Panzer Corps* also lacked determination, as it was with the *II SS-Panzer Corps* at Arnhem and with the *I SS-Panzer Corps* at Würselen. The *9th Panzer Division* attacked first and because they were able to surprise the enemy, they were successful. By the time the *15th Panzer-Grenadier Division* joined in the attack, the momentum of the surprise had petered out.[4] The enemy's resistance stiffened.

On 29 October, therefore, *Supreme Command–West* ordered a halt to the attack, since it no longer promised success and the deployed divisions were in danger of suffering losses that could not be replaced promptly. Army Group insisted on a continuation; *Supreme Command–West* relented and allowed it to continue up to the evening of 30 October, but the attack no longer produced results and was stopped. On 3 November, the two mobile divisions were released, as well as *XLVII Panzer Corps.*[5] On 29 October, *5th Panzer Army* also assumed control of *XLVII Panzer* and *LXXXVI Army Corps. Army Group B* turned over its entire front in the Netherlands, from Nijmegen to Walcheren, to the newly established *"Army Group Student,"* which later became *Army Group H.*[6]

The order of 28 October for the transfer into the area northwest Erkelenz includes the following instructions for the *116th Panzer Division*:

From this assembly area, prepare for contingencies as follows:

a) In the sector of *176th Infantry Division.*

b) In the sector of *LXXXVI Corps,* particularly an advance via Venlo into the vicinity of Horst and the southeast.

As of 2400 hours on 29 October, the Division will be Army Group Reserve. Continue under *5th Panzer Army* for troop matters and supply.[7]

The Division staff moved to Niederkrüchten. Near the town and south of it was *Panzer-Grenadier Regiment 156* with *2d Battalion, Armored Artillery Regiment*

146; Panzer-Grenadier Regiment 60 was in the vicinity of Wegberg. *Panzer Regiment 16* with *Panzerjäger Battalion 228* and *1st Battalion, Armored Artillery Regiment 146* was positioned between Erkelenz and Wegberg; the battleworthy tanks of both tank battalions moved into Berg. They were commanded by *Rittmeister* Böke, the commander of *1st Battalion, Panzer Regiment 24.*[8]

Upon his departure from *LXXXI Corps, Oberst* von Waldenburg again received appreciation for the Division.

After his arrival in the new area on 31 October, he wrote "Quiet day! We hope for two weeks of calm!? Issue training order. Outside dense fog, therefore no enemy aircraft. Not a shot to be heard, what a rarity and what comfort."[9]

The entry in the journal of *2d Battalion, Armored Artillery Regiment 146* for this day includes the following:

> *116th Panzer Division* will shortly be refurbished in present area as Army Group Reserve, and, after refurbishing is complete, will be available to mount counterattacks as a standard *Panzer* division.
>
> A reaction force will be assembled and put on two-hour alert under the leadership of the Commander, *Panzer-Grenadier Regiment 156, Major* Grollmann, with reinforced *Panzer-Grenadier Regiment 156* and *2d Battalion, Armored Artillery Regiment 146.*
>
> Within the framework of this two-hour alert requirement, training by the batteries will continue.[10]

The remaining units of the Division were standing by on eight-hours' notice. In addition, a company of *Armored Engineer Battalion 675* and a mixed company of *Panzer Regiment 16* (15 *Panzer Vs* and five *Panzer IVs*) also belonged to the reaction force, and were placed on two-hour alert.

The *2d Battalion, Panzer Regiment 16* had to give up ten percent of its personnel, about 40 to 50 men, to the *Field Replacement Battalion* for retraining as infantrymen.[11]

On 2 November at 1200 hours, the announcement arrived at *2d Battalion, Armored Artillery Regiment 146* that the reaction force had to expect marching off and a subsequent deployment on 2 or 3 November. In the evening, the order came to depart for the area south of Düren.[12] On this day, Vogelsang noted in his diary:

> A few days of rest for the troops, the first in a long time! Everyone is either sleeping, cleaning, or writing. Only in the staffs does the paper war continue to rage. Prospects for deployment for defense toward the southwest, for attacks toward the west and northwest are being explored.
>
> As replacements, one and a half more march battalions arrived for training with the *Field Replacement Battalion*. Once again, the personnel reserve has been replenished. . . . The Division Commander conducted his first training inspection of the F. R. B. It had a thoroughly good result. Stukenberg magically came up with a

movie—light opera 'A Night in Venice'—a pleasing loosening of the mood and new melodies to whistle daily "around the house"![13]

From other supporting documents, it can also be seen that it was possible to replenish the Division personnel as well as some materiel, in a short time. Thereby, *2d Battalion, Armored Artillery Regiment 146* had 12 fully mobile guns and could pack 8,000 rounds of ammunition. *Panzer-Grenadier Regiment 60* now again had all its companies. Even *Armored Engineer Battalion 675* almost reached full strength. The incorporation of *Panzer Brigade 108,* as already reported, contributed much to the reconstruction of the Division.[14]

Vogelsang closed his entries on 2 November, "But, 'The Fireman's Fate'! The rest period obviously already lasted too long! The Americans broke through southeast of Aachen. The reinforced *Panzer-Grenadier Regiment 156* is again on its way. Everything else is to remain. However, we fear it won't be for long!"

On 3 November, he remarked with grim humor, "On 3 November, Stukenberg's cinema showed 'Circus Renz'—right after this, the circus started all over. All men to the Hürtgen Forest! The Americans broke through south of Stolberg."

The Americans were attacking from a small breach near Germeter toward the north, east, and south. This is where the 9th Infantry Division had attacked from 6 to 16 October with only little success. It was supposed to take the village of Schmidt and thereby secure the right flank of the attack on both sides of Aachen. After heavy losses, the 9th Infantry Division was relieved by the 28th and the sector taken over by V Corps, with the left boundary north of Hürtgen. Since the leadership of the First Army continued to fear that its attack planned for 5 November from the vicinity of Aachen toward the Roer could be threatened from the obscure forest area near Hürtgen, it again ordered the attack on Schmidt. The 28th Infantry Division was to attack on 2 November.

Besides the usual reinforcements of one tank- and one self-propelled tank destroyer battalion, the 28th Infantry Division also received one engineer group (three battalions), one tank destroyer battalion, a chemical mortar battalion, eight artillery battalions, and one separate battery. Six more artillery battalions of the adjacent VII Corps to the left joined in the preparatory fire, and five squadrons of fighter bombers and one squadron of night fighters were provided for support of the attack, mainly for sealing off the battle area. The mortar battalion, originally designed for delivering chemical munitions such as gas shells, fired high explosive, smoke, and white phosphorus rounds. A battalion with 47 "Weasels," small tracked vehicles, was assigned to the division to facilitate supply in the difficult wooded area.

The 28th Infantry Division received binding instructions for the conduct of its attack. One regiment had to attack from Germeter north toward Hürtgen to secure the left flank of the attack. One regiment had to push from Germeter to the south to open the way for an attack group of 5th Armored Division, which later was to attack Schmidt from Monschau. Only one regiment remained for the attack on the objective, Schmidt. This intervention in the division leadership's prerogatives is an example of the opposite of mission-based operations.

The First Army retained 2 November as the day of attack, even though the main attack on Aachen was postponed for five days and the weather on the morning of the 2 November precluded air support. The Army leadership hoped for a withdrawal by the German reserve from the front east of Aachen. Thus, the 28th Infantry Division attacked along the whole front between Roermond and Metz by itself.

The terrain favored the defender. Both attacks, the one to the north, as well as the one to the south, had to be carried out in the dense forest. Only the center, the ridge of hills from Germeter to Vossenack, offered a small, hard strip that allowed deployment of tanks. In front of the hills of Schmidt, which were the division's attack objective, was the deeply-carved Kallgrund, crossed only by a scant path with a bridge near the Mestrenger Mill. Lines of communication from the rear were also modest. Everything had to be brought to Germeter through the dense forest on narrow dirt roads. Soon, these dirt roads gave way and had to constantly be repaired by engineers.

The attack by the 28th Infantry Division began on the morning of 2 November. The artillery fired a 12,000-round preparation, but because of the fog, the effect of the rounds was unobserved. There was no air cover. Not until the afternoon did parts of the planned units attempt to join in, but without major effect.

By the evening of 3 November, the 109th Infantry Regiment on the left achieved a penetration with its 1st Battalion, west of the road up to the edge of the forest, southwest of Hürtgen. The 3d Battalion, attacking to the right of 1st Battalion and east of the road, came to a halt in front the "*Wilde Sau*" ["Wild Sow"—*Translator*] minefield, which was laid in the forest north of the Wittscheidt forester's station on both sides of the road. It was not possible to eject the German soldiers who occupied the Weisser Wehbach valley. Despite several attempts to attack, for some time, the regiment stayed in the same place, but it accomplished its task of protecting the flank to the north.

From the middle unit, the 112th Infantry Regiment, at first only the 2d Battalion mounted an attack, supported by one company of tanks. The remaining tanks and tank destroyers took part in the artillery preparation. With the help of the tank support possible here, the 2d Battalion reached its objective, Vossenack, relatively quickly and without major losses.

In the afternoon, the remaining two battalions of the 112th Infantry Regiment attacked from Germeter southeast toward the Kall sector, with their objective being Schmidt. Very soon, this main effort came to a halt under fire. It was stopped and restarted on 3 November via Vossenack–Mestrenger Mill. It was successful there. At 1430 hours, Schmidt, the target of the attack, was seized by 3d Battalion, the most forward one. The following 1st Battalion occupied positions in the vicinity of Kommerscheidt. Both battalions prepared to defend in the captured villages. During the night of 3/4 November, three Weasels brought 60 mines to Schmidt, which were openly placed on the four roads leading into Schmidt. Except for the bazookas, this was all that was available for defense against tanks. Reconnaissance was not employed.

On 2 and 3 November, without tank support, the 110th Infantry Regiment on the right (without one battalion, being held as division reserve), could not advance one step. Only the deployment of the 3d Battalion from Vossenack to the south enabled the seizure of Simonskall on 4 November, but the German corner pillar near Raffelsbrand in its *Westwall* bunkers held the position against the two other battalions.

Now everything had to be done to get the tanks across the Kall sector to Schmidt. At first, this failed, as the trail across the Mestrenger Mill was too narrow. Engineers had to come, but due to inadequate organization, they did not achieve much. Several tanks slid down, threw tracks, and became stuck. Not before the morning of 4 November did three tanks reach Kommerscheidt. Others blocked the way, so that supplies could only slowly move up across the Kall sector. Still other tanks waited in Vossenack to be called and their crews did not show much initiative about moving forward. The engineers who were working on the trail were also put in charge of securing the Kall road, but not much was happening. The forces, about one-and-one-half companies of the 20th Engineer Combat Battalion, were already too weak for the task to make the trail passable and to maintain it. Only local defenses were established, and neither the division leadership, nor that of the engineer group, nor that of the 112th Infantry Regiment, intervened.[15]

Now we want to turn to the German side. The American attack hit the *275th Infantry Division.* This unit contained the remnants of three divisions (*275th, 347th,* and *353d Infantry Divisions*) and a series of individual troop elements from the most varied origins. The division had not yet grown to be a cohesive unit, but was able to withstand the attack by the 9th Infantry Division in October. Now, however, a breach developed which their forces could not close off, let alone remove. This could already be discerned on 2 November, but was obvious by the next day. The *275th Infantry Division* was controlled by *LXXXIV Corps,* which in turn was under the command of the *7th Army.* The division's right boundary with the *12th Volks-Grenadier Division* by Schevenhütte also formed the boundary with the *5th Panzer Army.*[16]

To address the problems along the boundary between *5th Panzer* and *7th Army,* by a directive of *Army Group B* on 2 November, a game plan was worked out under the direction of the *5th Panzer Army* commander, *General der Panzer-truppe* von Manteuffel. Model was present and Brandenberger took part in it. The Americans' attack at Germeter was announced during the planning. Now, the game became reality, and measures were taken immediately.[17] The first reinforcements were ordered: assault guns, army engineers, artillery and mortars. At noon, the reaction force of the *116th Panzer Division* received orders to be ready to march within two hours and to prepare for deployment on 2 or 3 November.

On the evening of 2 November, it set off for the area southeast of Niederzier (north of Düren), and arrived there on at 0830 hours on the next day. The reaction force now consisted of the following:

—*Panzer-Grenadier Regiment 156*
—*2d Battalion, Armored Artillery Regiment 146*
—One company of *Armored Engineer Battalion 675*
—One company of *Panzerjäger Battalion 228*
—Attached: *Assault Gun Brigade 341*[18]

Charles B. MacDonald remarks in his book, *The Siegfried Line Campaign,* "A *Kampfgruppe* of the old warhorse, the *116th Panzer Division,* was to leave immediately to assist local reserves in a counterattack against the 109th Infantry's penetration north of Germeter."[19]

At 1132 hours, *5th Panzer Army* again ordered march readiness and announced the transfer of the reaction force to the *275th Infantry Division.* One hour later, orders came for it to march off into the vicinity of Birgel–Strass–Gey, and for the commander (*Major* Grollmann) to proceed to the command post of the *275th Division* in Winden. The combat group was to at once set off and march in loose formation. At 1310 hours, *5th Panzer Army* announced that the entire *116th Panzer Division* was to follow the combat group.[20] At 1520 hours, *LXXXI Corps* received a combined order from *5th Panzer Army.*[21] Paragraph 2 directed "Bulk of the *116th Panzer Division* also subordinated to *7th Army* marches as soon as possible to attack in the area Düren–Gey. . . . It is important that the march gets under way with greatest possible speed so that the Division will be ready to attack on the morning of 4 November."

The Division marched from the area northwest of Erkelenz in two march groups on two roads. On the right, *Panzer-Grenadier Regiment 60,* with 3d *Battalion* of *Armored Artillery Regiment 146,* proceeded via Hückelhoven–Lövenich–Mersch–Steinstrass–Ellen, while to the left, *Panzer Regiment 16,* with the *1st Battalion, Armored Artillery Regiment 146,* the *Panzerjäger* and the engineers (without the units assigned to the reaction force) marched via Erkelenz–Jackerath–Elsdorf–Buir.

Armored Reconnaissance Battalion 116 marched ahead to Kufferath. The advanced units were ordered to the Division release point, which was established in Stockheim. There, the march groups were apprised of their next march objectives.[22]

The Army Group leadership decided to move up the entire *116th Panzer Division* when they discerned the enemy attack toward Schmidt from Vossenack (which was taken on the first day of attack) via the Mestrenger Mill.[23] Simultaneously, the *89th Infantry Division* was able to be deployed against the breach. To be replenished, it had just been relieved in the sector adjacent to the *275th* on the left by the *272d Volks-Grenadier Division.* One regimental group (*1055*) was already marching via Schmidt to Nideggen, while the second one

(*1056*) was still in the old sector. The *3d Battalion, Grenadier Regiment 1055* turned around and on 3 November at 1600 hours approached Schmidt, which was now occupied by the enemy, from the northeast. The battalion reached Harscheidt, reconnoitered Schmidt, and prepared to attack on the following morning. *Assault Gun Brigade 341,* which marched along with *Group Groll-mann,* probably arrived at *Grenadier Regiment 1055* during the night. The *1st Battalion, Grenadier Regiment 1055* followed the *3d Battalion,* while the *2d,* which had not yet passed Schmidt, occupied positions west of the town.

Additionally, *3d Battalion, Grenadier Regiment 860* of the *275th Infantry Division* was brought up toward Schmidt from the south.[24]

Southwest of Hürtgen, a counterattack was also under way on 3 November.

Here, *Engineer Battalion 253,* under the command of *Hauptmann* Brückner, pushed into the attack by the 109th Infantry Regiment and inflicted great confusion on the enemy. *Battalion 253* then pushed up to about three kilometers into the forest southwest of Hürtgen and also regained the position west of the Weisser Wehbach, near Point 312. By this, contact was reestablished with the as-yet-unengaged units of the *275th Infantry Division* to the south, west of the Wehbach. The 21 prisoners taken were proof of the success. However, the enemy was able to hold its ever-so-narrow breach in the forest west of the Germeter–Hürtgen road, and thus threatened the bend that had been regained in the front line that jutted into the valley of the Weisser Wehbach. In the ensuing days, all American attempts to eliminate the German salient failed in the same way the German ones failed against the American breach.[25]

On the evening of 3 November, the forward line ran from the bridge across the Weisser Wehbach near point 312, toward the northeast to the road bend southwest of Hürtgen; from there it ran south to the Wittscheidt forester's station, further along the edge of the forest, north of Vossenack, into the valley of the Tiefenbach, and along the valley via the Lukas Mill up to the Kall, northwest of Zweifalls-hammer. From there, it climbed up the hill south toward the western edge of Harscheidt. Ultimately, our units stood due east and west of Schmidt.[26] One should, however, not picture a continuously-occupied line. There were only a few defenses in the sectors between the Wittscheidt forester's station and Harscheidt. There was a gap between Schmidt and Simonskall.

The *116th Panzer Division* marched on 3 November and moved into its assembly areas on the night of 3/4 November. At 0220 on 4 November, the *01* of the *116th Panzer Division,* by now *Hauptmann der Reserve* Küpper, reported the status of the move to *LXXXI Corps. Armored Reconnaissance Battalion 116* had reached the area north of Brandenberg, and *Panzer Regiment 16* had arrived in Winden. *Combat Group Grollmann* occupied the assigned assembly area around Kleinhau. *Panzer-Grenadier Regiment 60* was "with its bulk in the assembly area west of the Roer."[27] It can no longer be determined where that was; however, the regiment was not, under any circumstances, able to be ready for an attack in the morning.

LXXIV Corps pressed for immediate deployment, without allowing time for sufficient reconnaissance or for preparing the artillery to fire. *Oberst* von Waldenburg could not prevail with his objections.[28] He relocated his command post to a bunker due east of Grosshau, and the majority of the Division staff moved to Kreuzau. The *275th Infantry Division* was subordinated to the *116th Panzer Division.*[29]

The reinforced *Panzer-Grenadier Regiment 156* deployed with *1st Battalion* in the forest south of Hürtgen, arrayed to attack Vossenack from the north through the forest. A passage through the forest had be improved to facilitate support this attack by tank destroyers. The *1st Company* of *Armored Engineer Battalion 675,* which was subordinated to the regiment, received orders to clear the mines laid by our own troops and to create a lane. The *2d Battalion, Panzer-Grenadier Regiment 156* advanced dismounted from Grosshau via Kleinhau into the valley of the Tiefenbach and prepared for the attack at the forest's edge northeast of Vossenack. To supply the battalion through the steep forest, void of paths, on both sides of the Tiefenbach, caused great difficulties.[30]

The reports about the attack on Vossenack on 4 November by the *116th Panzer Division* differ widely. In any case, in the morning only *Panzer-Grenadier Regiment 156* and perhaps *Armored Reconnaissance Battalion 116* went into action. The attack by *Panzer-Grenadier Regiment 156* was to start at 0650 hours, but did not get under way until 0800. The journal of *2d Battalion, Armored Artillery Regiment 146* reports, "After good artillery preparation by the whole emplaced artillery the attack first makes good progress, but comes to a halt in the midday hours due to strong enemy defensive fire. Toward 1700 hours, our infantry is withdrawn to its line of departure."[31]

The daily report by *Supreme Command–West* summed up, "Attack *116th Panzer Division* gained insignificant ground north of Vossenack and because of strong flanking . . . came to a standstill. Enemy counterattack with tanks northeast of Vossenack pushed Division's left wing back toward edge of forest, northeast of Vossenack."[32]

If the sparse reports from the ranks of the Division are compared with the above mentioned, one gets the following impression. The *1st Battalion, Panzer-Grenadier Regiment 156,* commanded by *Hauptmann* Winter, advanced from the north through the forest up to its edge, north of Vossenack, supported by the assault platoon of the *1st Company* of *Armored Engineer Battalion 675* with flamethrowers under command of *Leutnant* Eisen.[33] The other two platoons of the engineer company were deployed to create lanes through the forest. Their commander, *Leutnant* Varnholt, reported, "An inquiry revealed that there was no sketch of the mines that had been laid and that clearing the obstacles would take much too much time and would also be dangerous. Therefore, I decided to simply go around the marked minefields by cutting new lanes."[34]

Panzerjäger Battalion 228 remained near Hürtgen and supported the forces of the *275th Infantry Division,* deployed on both sides of the road Hürtgen–

Germeter. These were two battalions of *Regiment Wegelein,* a unit that had been quickly put together from different units and whose commander had been killed during the battles in October; it was now under command of *Major* Weinen. There was also a battalion of *Infantry Regiment 985.* All three only had little combat effectiveness.[35] Here, the enemy seized the Hürtgen forester's house, situated at the forest's edge, west of the road; attacks against the Wittscheidt forester's station were turned back.[36]

The *2d Battalion, Panzer-Grenadier Regiment 156* attempted to approach Vossenack from the northeast out of the Tiefenbach valley. As reported by the commanders of *5th* and *6th Companies, Oberleutnants* Löffler and Noltensmeyer, respectively, an assault platoon from the *6th Company* worked its way toward the American hill position in front of Vossenack during the night. The Americans were alert, however, and the assault platoon was thrown back and suffered losses. The *5th Company* provided covering fire to the *6th* to bring in the wounded. Neither officer mentioned anything about any further attacks by these companies on 4 November.[37]

On the morning of 4 November, the *Panzer-Grenadiers* from *Regiment 60* left their vehicles in Untermaubach and reached the Tiefenbach valley on foot via Brandenberg. Evidently, in the afternoon of 4 November, only parts of *1st Battalion* mounted close combat assaults from the valley against the enemy in the hills ahead of Vossenack and hardly any came out of the forest. The *2d Battalion* followed *1st Battalion* via Brandenberg to Lukas Mill, where the *1st Battalion* command post and aid station (which also serviced the *2d Battalion, Panzer-Grenadier Battalion 156*) were set up.[38]

Armored Reconnaissance Battalion 116 received orders to seize the Mestrenger Mill in the Kall Valley, to interdict the enemy advance route, and to cut off the enemy units that had pushed forward beyond the Kall. It advanced in the valley, as well as parallel to it up the rising hillside toward Vossenack. In the evening, its spearhead reached the path that leads from Vossenack south to the Mestrenger Mill, but the action by *Armored Reconnaissance Battalion* on 4 November did not yet show that it had any effect on the enemy.[39] In any case, there is no mention of it in MacDonald's very explicit work. Therein it says the following about the 2d Battalion, 112th Infantry Regiment, which defended Vossenack on 4 November:

> An enemy patrol in force hit Company F [which defended the southern half of Vossenack, while Company G held the northern half—*Author*] at approximately 0630, but was beaten off with small arms fire and artillery support on call from the 229th Field Artillery Battalion. When daylight came, the defenders had to steel their nerves against relentless enemy shelling. It seemed to the soldiers forward of Vossenack that the enemy concentrated his fire on each foxhole until he believed its occupants knocked out, then moved on. The shelling forced the 2d Battalion to move its command post during the day to an air raid shelter about a hundred yards west of the church on the north side of the street. The companies initiated a practice

of bringing as many men as possible into the houses during daylight, leaving only a skeleton force on the ridge.[40]

The direct fire by German tanks and assault guns, in position on the ridge of Brandenberg was considered especially unpleasant. Even tanks abandoned the open field around Vossenack and their crews sought protection behind the houses.

Irrespective of the fire by the artillery and assault guns, it is obvious from all this that the actions by the *116th Panzer Division* against Vossenack on 4 November did not produce any lasting impact. Besides *Armored Artillery Regiment 146*, many batteries took part, among them, the artillery of the *275th Infantry Division*, units from *Volks-Artillery Corps (Motorized) 766*, *Artillery Battalion (Motorized) 628* with 21cm mortars, and *Assault Gun Brigade 394*, which was known to the Division from the days at Aachen.

As of 5 November, Panthers from *1st Battalion, Panzer Regiment 24* and probably also units from *Heavy Tank Destroyer Battalion 519* with Hunting Panthers took part in the shelling of Vossenack; possibly also participating were *Heavy Tank Destroyer Battalion 682* with 27 8.8 cm anti-tank guns, as well as *Artillery Battalion (Motorized) 992*, which had already fought alongside the Division near Argentan and Aachen.[41]

While there were no noticeable results achieved around Vossenack, the retaking of Schmidt and the destruction of 3d Battalion, 112th Infantry Regiment were a success. Luckily, the full *Grenadier Regiment 1055* from the *89th Infantry Division* was available at the right time in the right place. Early on 4 November, after artillery preparation, it attacked with two battalions (*1st*, *3d*) from Harscheidt in the northeast, with the *2d* from west, and with the *3d Battalion, Grenadier Regiment 860* from the southeast toward Schmidt. The *3d Battalion, Grenadier Regiment 1055*, effectively supported by *Assault Gun Brigade 341*, took the northern and western parts of Schmidt at 1045 hours.[42] The enemy was overrun and abandoned the town.[43]

On the afternoon of 4 November, the tanks of *2d Battalion, Panzer Regiment 16* joined the battles of Schmidt and Kommerscheidt. At 0900 hours, nine *Panzer IVs*, under the command of *Oberleutnant* Adam, arrived west of Nideggen. They were subordinated to *Grenadier Regiment 1055*. Around 1250 hours, Adam received the following order at the regimental command post:

1. Situation.
   Enemy still in possession of Vossenack, Kommerscheidt, and eastern part of Schmidt. In the morning he attempted to advance further east, but was repulsed.
2. Units of the *116th Panzer Division* are in the attack from the north out of Hürtgen to Vossenack, and by noon, reached the edge of the forest north of Vossenack without major enemy resistance.
3. *3d Battalion, Grenadier Regiment 1055*, with support from assault guns, attacked Schmidt in the morning, seized the northern and western parts and is

staying in place. The *3d Battalion, Grenadier Regiment 860,* adjacent to the left, remained stuck in the morning at the southeastern edge of Schmidt.

4. The attack on Kommerscheidt to gain the hills north of Kommerscheidt, will be continued at 1400 hours.

5. This will include: *1st* and *2d Battalions, Grenadier Regiment 1055; 10th Company, Grenadier Regiment 1055; 3d Battalion, Grenadier Regiment 860; Company Adam* with eight battleworthy *Panzer IVs.*

6. Preparation for the attack by artillery barrage on Mausbach, Froitscheidt, and afterwards on Kommerscheidt.

7. Planned course: By onset of barrage, the infantry units mount attack toward the west on Mausbach and Schmidt, and continue westward. Simultaniously, the tanks attack Schmidt from the assembly area, support *3d Battalion, Grenadier Regiment 860,* which was left there during the attack on the southeast part of Schmidt, then turn toward Kommerscheidt and take Kommerscheidt with the infantry units. After taking the town and the hills, all units occupy positions.[44]

The battalion journal provides the following report about the battles on 4 November:

Our tanks attacked at 1400 hours. During the whole attack there is no sign of artillery preparation or support. Even the infantry did not advance. Thereby, the attack's success is substantially put into question.

In spite of this and brisk activity by fighter bombers, *Oberleutnant* Adam attacks Schmidt from the east in a swift dash with one platoon and with the other one, passes by north of Schmidt. The complete seizure of Schmidt goes as planned within a few minutes. Both platoons then started to attack Kommerscheidt from the northwestern edge of Schmidt. Immediately after starting the attack, the absence of infantry and of preparation for the attack became decisively noticeable. Nevertheless, *Oberleutnant* Adam decided to continue the attack without support. *Leutnant* Schaller's tank at once received heavy infantry and anti-tank gun fire from the forest and outside of the town. With several hits, the vehicle comes to a halt and burns. *Leutnant* Schaller is seriously wounded, part of the crew is killed. *Oberleutnant* Adam now establishes covering fire attacks with the tanks of *Oberfeldwebel* Pichler and *Feldwebel* Dolezal, and continues the attack. The tanks that are providing covering fire are being shot at when they change positions, and two more tanks are lost. A third one got stuck in the swamp.

With three tanks, including his vehicle, at 1450 hours the attack pushes into town. Two anti-tank guns are destroyed there. In a quick dash, the hills north of Kommerscheidt are taken. After *Oberleutnant* Adam occupied positions with his two tanks for quite a long time and again waited in vain for support by the infantry, he had to retreat from the hill head over heels. The enemy who was in hiding during the attack through Kommerscheidt now assembled for renewed resistance. Besides, low-flying enemy aircraft discovered our tanks. During the scrambling retreat, three Shermans now come out of the woods northwest of Kommerscheidt and fire at *Feldwebel* Dolezal's tank, which immediately returns fire, but *Feldwebel* Dolezal and part of his crew are killed, while the tank burns. *Oberfeldwebel* Pichler, who, with his tank rushes to help the remaining crew, takes up the fight, shoots and destroys a Sherman at a range of more than 1,000 meters. The opponent becomes aware of our retreat and now engages the tanks that took over the covering fire with several anti-tank guns which had thus far remained silent to avoid detection. With this, two more tanks were hit and immobilized.

Now *Oberleutnant* Adam orders the remaining units to withdraw to the northern edge of Schmidt. The tank that got stuck in the swamp receives a direct hit from artillery and also burns out.

After reaching Schmidt, *Oberleutnant* Adam guides the remaining tanks into a secure position and has the rescued wounded transported out. After reporting about the course of the attack to the command post of *Regiment 1055*, he pulls his tanks back into the starting position. [Between Kommerscheidt and Schmidt, according report Adam—*Author*]

The attack led with exceptional bravery was denied success only because it was not sufficiently prepared and was conducted without infantry.

After this attack, still battleworthy in the evening are: five *Panzer IVs*, two twin-barrel anti-aircraft vehicles, the engineer platoon, and medical detachment.

This sounds very one-sided. The somewhat propagandistically-produced "Division Mirror" of the *89th Infantry Division* does not mention the attack on Kommerscheidt at all.[45] The activities of *Assault Gun Brigade 341*, which was so successful in the morning, cannot be established. The journal of the *2d Battalion, Panzer Regiment 16* notes the experience:

The attack . . . is completely insufficiently prepared . . . ordered with little time and already for this reason could not work, because the urgently necessary dialogue about battle conduct . . . before the attack is missing. The omission of precise planning . . . by the appropriate command leads to the failure of the attack, which, with the unprecedented bravery and fortitude of our tankers could have led to the fullest success.

On 28 November, in the honor roll of the *116th Panzer Division, Oberst* von Waldenburg expressed his special recognition of the outstanding bravery in the action by *Oberfeldwebel* Pichler and *Feldwebel* Dolezal and their crews near Kommerscheidt on 4 November 1944.[46]

In the memory of the Americans, the battle of Kommerscheidt on 4 November played out as follows:

Then, about 1400, at least five enemy tanks, accompanied by a small force of infantry, attacked from the wooded draw on the southeast. . . . The enemy tanks, *Mark IVs* and *Vs,* imitated the tactics they had used so effectively earlier in the day in Schmidt, standing out of effective bazooka range and firing round after round into the foxholes and battle-scarred buildings. Artillery observers with the defenders called for numerous concentrations against the attack, but the German tanks did not stop. From Schmidt, other German direct-fire weapons, possibly including tanks, supported the assault.[47]

The three tanks of Company A of the 707th Tank Battalion under Lieutenant Fleig, situated near Kommerscheidt, saved the situation. They were

in a slight draw in the open just northwest of Kommerscheidt near the western woods line. The tank men pulled their Shermans up on a slight rise and fired at the enemy tanks, Fleig claiming two of the attackers knocked out and his companions a third. Noticing that the infantry was retreating from the left flank of the town, Fleig moved in that direction into a sparse orchard, just in time to see a *Mark V* Panther coming into position at a range of 200 to 300 yards, Fleig fired, hitting the German tank twice; but he was using high-explosive ammunition, and the Panther's tough hide was not damaged. The lieutenant discovered then that he had no armor-piercing ammunition available, all of it being outside in the sponson rack. When the German crewmen, evidently frightened by the high-explosive hits, jumped out of their tank, Fleig ceased firing and turned his turret to get at his rack and the armor-piercing ammunition. The Germans seized the opportunity to re-enter their tank and open fire, but their first round was a miss. Working feverishly, Lieutenant Fleig and his crew obtained the armor-piercing ammunition and returned the fire. Their first round cut the barrel of the German gun. Three more rounds in quick succession tore into the left side of the Panther's hull, setting the tank afire and killing all its crew.

This could have been the destruction of *Feldwebel* Dolezal's tank. Now the fighter bombers joined the battle. They immobilized one German tank with bombs, and this tank later fell victim to a bazooka. The American report concludes:

With the arrival of air support and the continued hammering by the artillery, mortars, small arms, and the three tanks, the German assault was stopped around 1600. The defenders had sustained numerous personnel casualties, but in the process they had knocked out at least five German tanks without losing one of their own three. Just how big a role a small number of tanks might have played had they been available for the earlier defense of Schmidt was clearly illustrated by the temporary success at Kommerscheidt.

In the course of 4 November and during the night to 5 November, no other American tank made it across the Kall; only a small supply group of the 707th Tank Battalion could force its way to Lieutenant Fleig. Ready to cross the Kall Valley, the remainder of Company A, 707th Tank Battalion and a company of tank destroyers (Company C, 893d Tank Destroyer Battalion) were waiting in and around Vossenack. The defense of the bridge across the Kall at the Mestrenger Mill was still in the hands of the engineers who were working along the path and only had four men at the bridge.[48]

On 4 November, while the 110th Infantry Regiment with two battalions could again not advance one step toward the German corner pillar, its 3d Battalion, as already mentioned, was able to take Simonskall by attacking southwest from Vossenack.[49] With this, the Kall Valley, between Simonskall and the Mestrenger Mill, was in the hands of the Americans. The German position on the hill near Raffelsbrand became exposed, but remained in German hands until the conclusion of the battles of the year 1944. The third regiment of the 28th Infantry Division, south of Hürtgen, also did not make any more progress on 4 November. In the forest, southwest of Hürtgen, a German group, probably from *Army Engineer Battalion 253,* infiltrated and captured a battalion command post.[50]

No extradordinary successes occurred for either side on 5 November, but the scale started to tip slowly toward the Germans. *Armored Reconnaissance Battalion 116* succeeded in gaining ground on the northern slope of the Kall Valley and in the valley itself. It reached the American supply line between Vossenack and the Kall, its spearhead crossed it up to Kradenberg, it took the Mestrenger Mill, and in the evening was able to establish contact with the *2d Battalion* of *Grenadier Regiment 1055,* which was pushing by Kommerscheidt from the south.[51] This cut off the enemy in Kommerscheidt from contact with the rear. Yet, the cut-off was very weak and had hardly any impact on the Americans on 5 November. In the following two days, the Mestrenger Mill changed owners several times, so that the enemy could bring units across the Kall again and again. For his personal leadership in the battle for the mill, *Major* Stephan was recommended for the Knight's Cross, but the army personnel office only permitted mentioning his name in the Army honor roll.[52] Stephan reports that his *3d Company,* under the command of *Oberleutnant* Sesterhenn, especially distinguished itself.

The second regiment of the *89th Infantry Division, Grenadier Regiment 1056,* which in the meantime had been relieved by the *272d Volks-Grenadier Division,* started to move from the south into the Kall sector on 5 November. It moved between the Mestrenger Mill and Simonskall, to avert the danger of the enemy pushing further from Simonskall across the sector.[53] On 5 November, heavy battles raged around Kommerscheidt. Numerous attacks by the reinforced *Grenadier Regiment 1055,* in which the tanks under *Oberleutnant* Adam took part, were not effective.[54] But the ring around Kommerscheidt was tightened and the enemy in the town was worn down by the fire and attacks. Considering this situation, an order by the *28th Infantry Division* to recapture Schmidt remained without effect. However, the Americans in Kommerscheidt received reinforcements. Seven tank destroyers and five tanks arrived by noon; Company D from the 112th Infantry Regiment, which had been left back, arrived later in the evening.[55]

The main effort of the battles of the *116th Panzer Division* was near Vossenack. The journal of *2d Battalion, Armored Artillery Regiment 146* offers the following report about 5 November:

Entire Division arrived, and attack on Vossenack and Kommerscheidt is planned for this morning. Our strong drumfire barrage initiates the attack. Infantry advances quite well, an hour later is in the positions that were taken the day before.

After the battalion takes down several tanks and anti-tank gun positions near the edge of Vossenack, the attack was moved forward and by 1200 hours, the infantry spearhead had pushed up to the church. Half of the town is in our hands.

At the left wing by the *Armored Reconnaissance Battalion* . . . successes were also achieved. Heavy fighting flared up around the Mestrenger Mill. It changes owners several times.

By 1400 hours, enemy starts counterattack with tanks. Reinforced, its artillery sprays heavy nuisance fire in the whole sector and pushes infantry out of Vossenack. For the night, withdrawing the front to the line of departure was ordered.[56]

Similar descriptions were recorded in the journal of *Supreme Command–West*. According to them, the attack by the Division had advanced to within 200 meters of the northern edge of Vossenack and into the eastern tip of town. The *Armored Reconnaissance Battalion* supposedly even brought four tanks up the hill 500 meters southeast of the church in Vossenack. In *Supreme Command–West*'s daily report, it mentioned numerous enemy counterattacks in the northeastern part of Vossenack that were turned back.[57] Comparing these reports to the available single reports and to the American version of the events at Vossenack on 5 November, one reaches a much more humble result. The *1st Battalion, Panzer-Grenadier Regiment 156,* with the attached assault platoon from *1st Company, Armored Engineer Battalion 675,* may again have advanced through the forest from the north toward Vossenack. It already suffered casualties from enemy artillery fire while in its attack position. The commander of *3d Company, Panzer-Grenadier Regiment 156, Leutnant* Bargstädt, was seriously wounded.[58] A noticeable effect on Vossenack by the battalion may hardly have taken place. Two platoons of the *1st Company, Armored Engineer Battalion 675* continued to work on the forest lane for the tank destroyers.[59] *Panzerjäger Battalion 228* supported the battalions of the *275th Infantry Division* near the Hürtgen forester's station.[60]

Still during the night, the *2d Battalion* of *Panzer-Grenadier Regiment 156* attempted a surprise attack on Vossenack. The *1st Platoon* of the *5th Company,* under *Leutnant* Kunstmann, worked its way toward the town, but soon got stuck in the Americans' fire. Kunstmann and more than half of the men of the platoon were wounded. Three severely wounded men died during the difficult trip to the aid station at Lukas Mill. Also during the night, a second assault by *10th Company, Panzer-Grenadier Regiment 156,* the regimental combat engineer company, mounted from the positions of *5th Company,* failed in spite of supporting fires by the *5th* and *6th Companies.*[61]

During the night of 4/5 November, *Panzer-Grenadier Regiment 60* pulled *2d Battalion,* which had not yet been deployed, out of the Tiefenbach Valley into the Kall Valley. On the morning of 5 November, it attacked with the *1st Battalion* from the east and with the *2d Battalion* from the south toward the eastern part of Vossenack. The attack was repulsed.[62] After the war, *Obergefreiter* Palm reported about the attack by *6th Company* of *Panzer-Grenadier Regiment 60.* He attacked his own village and he knew every street corner there. After the war, he became mayor of the village. According to Palm's account, *6th Company* was to advance on the trail coming from the Kall Valley northwest, passing Point 371, which led to the eastern part of Vossenack. To the right of the *6th,* the *5th* and *7th Companies* attacked. Palm writes:

> The order for attack arrived: 0630 sharp, surprise attack into the village. . . . After hardly the first 100 meters ahead, got to the bend in the path, which was in full view of the village, when they were received by a raging barrage. Four dead. Exactly the first four that could be seen by the enemy were hit. Luckily, our platoon leader was not among those four, otherwise the platoon's leadership would have been in question. All the "*Landsers*" rushed back and looked for cover because of the suddenly exploding grenades. Damned, the American was on the ball. Without a doubt, the first attack in this place went to pieces. Nobody will ever pass this place again, where just now those four became bait for machine gun fire and high-explosive shells and rolled in their blood. The *5th* and *7th Companies* were also smeared.[63]

The attack was repeated in the afternoon. On the evening of 5 November, Vogelsang said, "*Panzer-Grenadier Regiment 60* slipped by . . . Vossenack and at 1400 hours, supported by the *Panzer Regiment,* attacked Vossenack from the south."[64]

The *Panzer* Regiment could only provide support by fire from the hills near Brandenberg and Bergstein. It also put four Panthers into position in the Kall Valley. They had the task of blocking off the valley just in case the opponent was able to overrun or bypass the *Armored Reconnaissance Battalion* and thereby push into the flank of *Panzer-Grenadier Regiment 60.*[65] These four tanks may have been the same that according to the report by *Supreme Command–West,* supposedly were moved up to the hills south of Vossenack.

The attack in the afternoon had no success either.

This is how Palm describes it:

> The order to attack came again. This time, 500 meters further west, to enter into the middle of the lower village. The company passed by the forest about 500 meters toward the west. The artillery fire calmed down. Slowly, always running one at a time, we worked ourselves forward. The Americans who were in position directly by the houses still could not see us. But it was clear to all of us that they constantly were on the alert. Slowly, always closer to the village, the company worked itself forward, spread out over a wide area. Another 100 meters, and I was in our field and found favorable cover in a bomb crater. The artillery continuously fired nuisance fire. Here I was laying on the soil of the homeland, on mother earth. Hundreds of times, I had worked in this field, spent many carefree, beautiful hours guarding the

cattle. . . . At the same moment that I took cover in one of the countless craters, again another barrage against the attacking company. Like a hail of fire from innumerable barrels the shells sputter between and above us. Every attack comes to a halt, or it became an assault into death without any success. . . .

From crater to crater, from man to man, the company commander's order was passed on, "Withdraw one by one and return to the starting position!"[66]

Major Sandkuhl summed up the distressing result of 5 November in his diary, "Our attacks on Vossenack without success. Strong enemy defense."[67]

The portrayal of the events in Vossenack from the American point of view presents the following picture:

Occasional enemy patrols hit the exposed forward position of the Vossenack ridge, and shattered nerves gave rise to many reports of enemy counterattacks, which did not actually develop.

Early in the morning, the 2d Squad of the 1st Platoon, Company F, under Staff Sergeant Charles W. Cascarano, in position at the head of a shallow wooded draw leading into the positions in the east, saw about 20 Germans moving in a column of twos through the wooded draw toward its positions. The squad's automatic rifleman sprayed the Germans with fire, wounding nine, killing four, and putting the rest to flight. The wounded Germans lay where they had fallen for about four or five hours, moaning and crying, before five German medics with a cart picked them up.[68]

Nevertheless, on the evening of 5 November the situation with the Americans was very tense. It is said:

At Vossenack the situation was perhaps the worst of all, though its seriousness was perhaps not so readily apparent. Remnants of the 2d Battalion, 112th Infantry still held the town but they had been subjected to three days and four nights [On the morning of 6 November—*Author*] of murderous fire from German artillery, self-propelled guns, and mortars. The men had undergone about all they could stand. The company commanders knew the situation in Vossenack, and the battalion staff knew it (the staff had a combat exhaustion case of its own in its battalion commander), but neither Regiment nor Division seemed to appreciate the situation fully.[69]

On the evening of 5 November, except for two platoons, the American tanks and tank destroyers were taken back to Germeter and Richelskaul. They had to sustain a large number of hits and "found the area provided with ample artillery and mortar fire."[70] During the night from 5 to 6 November, *Armored Reconnaissance Battalion 116* had an effect on the supply route between Vossenack and Kommerscheidt. At its right wing, on the path south of Vossenack, the *Division Escort Company* was now deployed. MacDonald writes:

In the Kall Gorge, the Germans had gained the upper hand. They had infiltrated the main supply route and had mined the trail. . . . The combined 1st-3d Battalion, 112th Infantry, aid station still functioned in the log dugout in the Kall Gorge, although the Germans were all over the area. No vehicle that had tried to use the supply route since about 0200 (6 November) had been able to get through, not even medical jeeps and Weasels.[71]

No measures were taken to fight to clear the path.

On 5 and 6 November, the battle of Vossenack and Kommerscheidt reached its climax. Let us remain in Vossenack. *Supreme Command–West*'s morning report said, "*116th Panzer Division* at 0400 mounted attack in east part."[72]

At midday, it was reported that the attack reached the church in Vossenack, that an enemy counterattack with two tanks was turned back by destroying both tanks, and that the attempt by the enemy to bring up more tanks was smashed by concentrated artillery fire.[73] The seizure of Vossenack and the isolation of the Americans in Kommerscheidt was brought up in the midday briefing in Hitler's headquarters.[74] However, in the afternoon *Supreme Command–West* had to mention an unpleasant set-back for *Armored Reconnaissance Battalion 116*.[75] It was pushed back by an enemy tank attack from the Kradenberg to the path from Vossenack into the Kall Valley and later from there to the edge of the forest, east of it, and also had lost the Mestrenger mill.

The journal of *2d Battalion, Armored Artillery Regiment 146* recorded the following on 6 November:

> Except for very heavy enemy artillery fire, the night passes without incidence. During the night, the opponent fires approximately 3,000 to 4,000 rounds.
>
> 0400 hours. Under cover of night, Vossenack is attacked without heavy artillery fire and is to be taken in a surprise attack.
>
> Attack advances well and with the first assault, our own infantry occupies the eastern part of town.
>
> Enemy counterattacks with tanks that are fired on by the battalion.
>
> Batteries continue to fight enemy groups and movements in the area around the church of Vossenack and fire the barrages ordered by Artillery Command. . . .
>
> During the whole day, the plentiful supply of ammunition permits firing heavy barrages and continuous nuisance fire on the west part of Vossenack and Germeter, and thwart reinforcement of the opponent in Vossenack.
>
> By noon, the designated line 370.0 [at the forest corner 500 meters northwest of the Vossenack church—*Author*]–Vossenack church . . . has essentially been reached and so far has been held against all counterattacks.
>
> Continuous nuisance fire from enemy artillery. The towns of Hürtgen, Kleinhau, and Grosshau are under constant fire. Heavy barrages fall on our rear area. . . .
>
> Enemy fires approximately 4,000 to 5,000 rounds. Due to bad weather, very little enemy fighter bomber activity. Rounds fired: 901 from light field howitzers.[76]

If one estimates a similar high usage for the other artillery battalions, the fire on both sides is about equal. There are also different reports about the activity of fighter bombers in the afternoon. Sandkuhl remarked, "Heavy enemy airplane activity. Dropping of incendiary bombs."[77] Vogelsang also got acquainted with enemy planes and on the evening of 6 November, amongst other things, wrote:

> In extremely heavy battles, the curve of the enemy breach was narrowed down further. Half of Vossenack was recaptured. An American battalion with nine tanks is encircled north of Schmidt. Five tanks were destroyed, one by a *Leutnant* from *Panzer-Grenadier Regiment 156* with close combat weapons. Three tanks and many vehicles with 30 prisoners were brought in.
>
> Our losses, unfortunately are also very high. In the few days of fighting here, we again have heavy casualties, 11 officers and 350 men.[78]

With its anti-aircraft weapons, on this day the *116th Panzer Division* shot down seven Lightnings.[79] MacDonald also reports about the action of the American air forces, which appeared over Vossenack in the afternoon, attacked the east part of the town, and then for the first time in this battle, temporarily silenced the German artillery.[80] So much for the reports that give an overview of the events around Vossenack. They will be supplemented with individual reports.

The *1st Battalion* of *Panzer-Grenadier Regiment 156* again had the task of pushing from the north toward Vosssenack. Tank destroyers from *Panzerjäger Battalion 228* were to support this by advancing through the lanes cleared by the engineers. The plan failed. *Leutnant* Varnholt, commander of the engineer battalion's *1st Company,* personally received orders from *Oberst* von Waldenburg to advance the tank destroyers through the forest, so they could attack Vossenack at dawn together with the *Panzer-Grenadiers.* After about one kilometer, however, the first tank destroyer got stuck with damage to its clutch, exactly in a narrow path and it could not be started up again.

This caused the attempt to deploy tanks near Vossenack to fail. The *1st Battalion* reached the edge of the forest north and northwest of Vossenack. From there, they supported the other battalion's attack with fire, and protected it in the northern part of Germeter against the enemy, whose flanking effect was already found to be unpleasant during the previous days.[81]

From the forest fringe, *2d Battalion* of *Panzer-Grenadier Regiment 156* attacked Kreuzheck and south from there toward Vossenack.[82] The *6th Company* (left) attacked Vossenack from the gorge that ran toward the town from the east and *5th Company* attacked frontally to the right from the old positions near the forest. At the same time, *7th Company* (until now kept in reserve) under *Leutnant* Junge, flanked the enemy position from the north and rolled over it. All three companies then pushed through the elongated town west toward the church. An enemy counterattack with three tanks was repulsed with *Panzerfausts* by *6th Company.* Its commander, *Oberleutnant* Noltensmeyer, was wounded at the T-intersection of the church and had to leave his company. Finally, the companies of *2d Battalion, Panzer-Grenadier Regiment 156* advanced to the church and for the night moved into a position that ran from north to south, more or less in line with the church. In the attack on Vossenack, *Oberfeldwebel* Lauer from *7th*

Company distinguished himself in particular. The recommendation for awarding the German Cross to him includes, "He had the mission of rolling over the enemy's especially favorable field positions and securing and defending the right flank of the troops that were deployed against the town itself."[83]

On the left, next to the *2d Battalion, Panzer-Grenadier Regiment 156, 1st Battalion* of *Panzer-Grenadier Regiment 60* attacked Vossenack, probably only with the *1st* and *3d Companies,* while *2d Company* seems to have been attached to *Panzer Regiment 16.* Reports are only available from *3d Company.* After the war, the attack by this company in the Tiefenbach Valley near the Lukas Mill was described by *Panzer-Grenadier* Otten:

> At 0500 it was, "Prepare for attack." Move forward to initial position. We proceeded close to the town's entrance and waited for the signal to attack. We remained there in the pouring rain until about 0700. Then the signal for attack sounded. By the light of dawn, we ran toward the American positions that were directly in front of us. We had the disadvantage. Our clothes were heavy from the rain and our limbs were stiff, besides that we had run uphill, burdened by ammunition cases and machine guns. . . . When crossing the fields we had no cover, and many comrades already fell there. . . . At the mill [Halmes Mill, in the eastern part of town—*Author*] we took the first prisoners. They were completely surprised by our attack. We blew up a jeep and crippled a tank. This discouraged the American soldiers and gave us courage and confidence. Up to now, our losses must have been considerable, because only a handful of men, including a *Feldwebel* and I, received orders to comb through Vossenack up to the church. For today, the attack was to be stopped at the church. . . . With another comrade, we combed the row of houses on the left side of the street. First, we thoroughly observed every house, then one of us ran over to it, while the others covered him. . . . Around 1100 hours, we reached the parsonage and church. The church already showed many signs of the war. . . . I felt my way through the rubble to the door, where I was to take up position. About 40 meters in front of the door was an American tank with its commander looking out, Americans were all over the street, as though they just came from the chow line.[84]

A *Feldwebel* attempted to destroy the tank with a *Panzerfaust.* That failed. The *Feldwebel* was killed. More from Otten:

> Automatically, firing started from machine guns and tank cannons. I crouched behind the right support wall of the tower, hoping to be in the safest place, while the tank shells buzzed close above me to the altar and ripped it to bits in front of my eyes. . . . After some time, the shooting stopped. I used this break to quickly report the events to the parsonage. I was relieved by the door and told to first go to the cellar of the vestry and rest. I immediately fell asleep and did not wake up until I heard the moans of a wounded soldier and the rustle of weapons. The Americans actually went around my successor at the post "in front," took him out of action by shooting him in the knee, and were now standing at the top of the cellar entrance. We sat in a trap. We were disarmed and brought into the Wehe Valley for questioning.

The commander of *1st Battalion, Panzer-Grenadier Regiment 60, Hauptmann* Nagel came up front and in the night deployed an assault platoon to take back the church.[85] He was successful. The *2d Battalion* of *Panzer-Grenadier Regiment 60* also took part in the attack, again from the south out of the Kall Valley, with the *6th Company* out of the gorge from the southeast toward the southern tip of Vossenack. Unfortunately, nothing is known about the battalion's other companies. Apparently, members from different units spent at least some time at the church. It seemed to have had a magnetic power of attraction. Evidently, there was no uniformly strict leadership on the objective of the attack. The boundary between the two regiments and the one between the two battalions of *Panzer-Grenadier Regiment 60* crossed in the area of the church. This had an unfortunate effect and plainly called for the appointment of a responsible leader for further conduct of the battle in Vossenack; the commander of *1st Battalion, Panzer-Grenadier Regiment 60,* for example, who was probably the only one at the site of the action.

The night of 6/7 November went by relatively quietly, with little firing or enemy reconnaissance. Ammunition and food supply arrived, and the wounded could be transported back.[86]

While the Division's two *Panzer-Grenadier* Regiments fought for Vossenack, on the path to the Kall Valley and the Mestrenger Mill *Armored Reconnaissance Battalion 116* suffered the setback already described. It had been brought on by a battalion of the 110th Infantry Regiment, which together with tanks and tank destroyers were to attempt to recapture Schmidt. The battalion did not advance to the Kall Valley via the supply route, but rather, south of the church, turned south onto a trail on the Kradenberg. There, it came upon the most forward units of the *Armored Reconnaissance Battalion* and had to fight hard against them to clear their way to the Mestrenger Mill and across the Kall. Toward noon of 6 November, the battalion did reach the forest fringe ahead of Kommerscheidt, but no attack on Schmidt took place. The battalion reinforced the Kommerscheidt defense in depth.[87]

A platoon of tank destroyers, which on the morning of 6 November was also supposed to advance to Kommerscheidt, encountered a German group south of Vossenack. Therefore, and because engineers said that the path was impassable, the platoon remained idle at the fringe of the forest and drove back to Germeter in the evening.[88] In the battles against the Americans who advanced toward the Mestrenger Mill, *Leutnant* Lutz from the *Division Escort Company* distinguished himself especially and received the Knight's Cross.[89]

How did the Americans portray the loss of Vossenack? The major blame was placed on the crushing fire of the artillery and the direct fire of the tanks and assault guns from the high ridge near Brandenberg.[90] On the evening of 5 November, the soldiers of the 2d Battalion, 112th Infantry Regiment were already so much at the end of their strength that they coud barely endure in their exposed positions around the eastern part of Vossenack. By daybreak on 6 November, they were waiting for the continuation of the fiery storm. This did not occur, but an eerie calm prevailed during rain and bad visibility. Suddenly, the fire from German automatic weapons fell silent, and a piercing scream could be heard. Then it was quiet again. After some time, the German artillery fire began, probably the mission for the protection of the German breach area. This shattered the nerves of the American soldiers lying in the open field, northeast of Vossenack, and they ran toward the rear in panic and fear. All of Company G were seized by panic. The commander of Company F, in the southeastern part of town, gave orders to pull back to the edge of town. As his platoons withdrew, they, too, were overtaken by panic. "Although no one professed to have seen any enemy soldiers, the troops of both Company G and Company F were convinced the German were attacking."

The reserve company, Company E, was caught in the whirlpool in the middle of town, as were the heavy weapons of Company H and the mortars. Just as they reached the line of the battalion command post, about 100 meters west of the church, some courageous officers from the battalion staff succeeded in halting a few groups and got them into position in a thinly-manned line. By 1030 hours, they had gathered about 70 men. The bulk of the battalion rushed back to Germeter.

The American tanks and tank destroyers played a role that was not particularly praiseworthy.[91] This had less to do with a lack of bravery than with a lack of leadership and insufficient cooperation with each other and the infantry. The individual platoons of two tank and one tank destroyer companies conducted their battles more or less independently. Neither the battalion commander nor the company commander from the tank destroyers were to be found. They were busy far in the rear, but were acting more like brakemen than like the engineers of a train. The tank battalion commander was assigned by the Division commander to command the counterattack on Schmidt; one company commander was killed, the second one tried to command, but with only little success. Out of six platoons, there were never more than three in battle at the same time. The rest, like the bulk of the tank destroyers, stood around in Germeter and Richelskaul, or drove back and forth between Vossenack and the rear. During the German attack through Vossenack, all tanks and tank destroyers went into the town's western part to get out of the way, without having been forced to do so by any immediate threat, except for the unpleasant fire by the German artillery and armored vehicles from the hill near Brandenberg. Yet, there was no more American infantry around to protect the tanks. There was no orderly counterattack of any kind by the tanks and tank destroyers to speak of against the German attack on 6 November.

Meanwhile, the *Panzer-Grenadiers* of the *116th Panzer Division* did not even have tanks or anti-tank guns. All they had were *Panzerfausts*. The loss of tanks on the American side, therefore, was small, and the German figures of destruction were exaggerated. What the Germans reported as counterattacks with tanks were really only chance events.

To restore the situation in Vossenack, all available combat engineers under the leadership of commander of the 1171th Engineer Combat Group were deployed by the acting commander of the 28th Infantry Division, Brigadier General Davis, who had just arrived at the front. He passed the command to one battalion commander in Vossenack and to another one at the Kall bridge.[92] The main merit belongs to Company A of the 146th Engineer Combat Battalion which was brought in from road construction with many men still wearing their galoshes. Nobody knew anything about the situation when the company mounted the attack from Germeter with the order to throw the enemy out of Vossenack. One platoon each advanced north and south of the road and the third one followed as reserve. At the elevation of the 2d Battalion, 112th Infantry Regiment command post, about 100 meters west of the church, the forwardmost were fired on. The American report reads:

> The 1st Platoon on the right (south) using "run and duck" tactics which involved advancing in short rushes singly or in pairs, reached the crossroads and captured the church, taking eight or ten German prisoners at the cost of approximately five engineers wounded. Other men of the platoon took a building on the right of the church. By nightfall the company had established itself completely in everything west of the church. It held the church as well, one house beside it on the south, and three houses on the west side of the street leaving from the church toward the Kall Gorge.[93]

In the evening, Company C took over these positions.

It lost the church during the night. The American portrayal reads:

> About 0200 a machine gun position of this platoon slightly southwest of the church was hit by a German hand grenade, and the machine gunners withdrew to a nearby alternate position from which they could still cover their assigned target area. Taking advantage of the darkness, the Germans about the same time infiltrated into the east portion of the church and opened fire with burp guns on the 3d Platoon men in the other side of the church. One engineer was killed, the others withdrew, and the much-disputed church once again changed hands.[94]

While these events of the night of 6/7 November took place in and around Vossenack, *Armored Reconnaissance Battalion 116* retook the Mestrenger Mill, but with considerable losses.[95] After the war, *Major* Stephan said that the casualties were mainly caused by our own preparatory artillery fire, which was not firing far enough.[96] An enemy counterattack on the mill was repulsed. In these battles, *Oberfeldwebel* Orb particularly distinguished himself. He and his platoon stormed the bridge. After the company commander fell and the bridge was back in enemy hands, Orb took it again and defended it, inspite of being wounded, until he was relieved.[97] McDonald described the events of the night of 6/7 November as follows:

> Later, about 2330, a particularly heavy concentration showered the area. Close on its heels came a group of about 25 Germans, following the artillery so closely that

they were almost atop the 2d Platoon position on the west bank when the shelling lifted. They opened fire with burp guns, machine guns, and grenades. . . .

For the rest of the night, the Germans again roamed the Kall Gorge almost at will. . . . By daylight on 7 November, the situation at the Kall Trail was something of a paradox. The Germans claimed that despite "considerable losses," the *116th Panzer Reconnaissance Battalion* again had cut the trail and established contact with the *89th Infantry Division* in the woods to the south. Yet an American supply column had crossed and recrossed the Kall during the night. The Americans thought their engineers controlled the trail, but by mid-morning of 7 November, the only force in position to do so . . . was down to the company commander and five men. The rest of the engineers had melted away into the woods.[98]

On 6 November, the ring around Kommerscheidt was pulled more tightly. The reinforced *Grenadier Regiment 1055* had entered the town with some units; it was thereby supported by the tanks of *2d Battalion, Panzer Regiment 16*.[99] *Oberleutnant* Adam was wounded, *Oberfeldwebel* Pichler took command of the three still-operational tanks. The battalion journal recounts the following:

> In the morning, *Oberleutnant* Adam again receives orders to attack Kommerscheidt, this time from the southwest, and to establish defenses at the edge of town and toward the northwest. This attack is also carried out without our infantry, since our units are already supposed to be in the east part of K[ommerscheidt].
>
> 0845 hours, after light artillery preparation, Adam attacks. He receives heavy anti-tank fire from the edge of town and from the forest edge, northwest of K[ommerscheidt]. Thereby, the command vehicle and one more tank were hit and immobilized. *Oberleutnant* Adam is wounded, but continues the attack anyway. A defense was successfully established and some of our prisoners were freed. During the afternoon, fighter-bomber attacks and artillery barrages cover the defense positions.
>
> *Oberleutnant* Adam did not go to the aid station until all the wounded were transported out.[100]

On the evening of 6 November, the commander of the *89th Infantry Division, Generalmajor* Bruns, gave orders for the destruction of the enemy forces encircled at Kommerscheidt.[101] For this, *Group Bayer* was established under the command of *Panzer Regiment 16*. Together with *Grenadier Regiment 1055,* it was to capture Kommerscheidt on 7 November, while *Regiment 1056* and *Armored Reconnaissance Battalion 116* were to continue to interrupt communication between the bulk of the enemy north of the Kall and the encircled enemy units.

Group Bayer consisted of the following:

— *1st Battalion, Panzer Regiment 24*
— *3d Company, Armored Engineer Battalion 675*
— *Heavy Tank Destroyer Battalion 519*
— *Assault Gun Brigade 341*

— *3d Company, Luftwaffe Fortress Battalion V,* and probably *2d Company, Panzer-Grenadier Regiment 60.*

The bulk of *Regiment 1055* attacked Kommerscheidt from the east, while *Group Bayer* attacked from the south. At the same time, the *2d Battalion, Grenadier Regiment 1055* advanced from the west toward the town, and with it, the last four tanks of the *2d Battalion, Panzer Regiment 16,* under *Oberfeldwebel* Pichler. Only the *4th Company* of the *1st Battalion, Panzer Regiment 24,* under *Rittmeister* Weidemann, took part in the attack; the *2d* followed, and at this time, *1st* and *3d Companies* were attached to other units.[102]

The journal of *2d Battalion, Panzer Regiment 16* includes this about the 7 November attack on Kommerscheidt:

> In the morning at 0630 hours, after a barrage by our artillery, a new attack begins on Kommerscheidt in which four of our *Panzer IVs* take part. Our tanks have the mission of facilitating the penetration into the western part of Kommerscheidt for a platoon of *Grenadier Regiment 1055.* During the same time, other combat groups with tank support are to enter the town from south and east. This attack slowly gains ground. After four hours of hard fighting with the infantry, our four tanks gain entry into the western part of town. Since the opponent's resistance stiffens in the northern part during the advance of the other tank groups, and the attack threatens to falter, two of our tanks, together with the infantry, fight from house to house. One tank hits a mine and becomes immobilized.
>
> In cooperation with units from *1st Battalion, Panzer Regiment 24,* Kommerscheidt falls entirely in to our hands in the afternoon. Our three still battleworthy tanks are then ordered to secure the edge of the forest west of hill 469 in direction Vossenack.[103]

Movements into or out of Vossenack were engaged from this position. Three of the four American armored vehicles that drove from the town into the Kall Valley were destroyed, and the fourth one went over the side and crashed. These were a platoon of tank destroyers that on orders from General Davis began to attack at 1500 hours and were to cross the Kall, so that together with a battalion from the 109th Infantry Regiment, they could replace the forces in Kommerscheidt and retake Schmidt. This undertaking, however, came too late to save Kommerscheidt and already failed in the early stages. On 7 November, the 109th Infantry Regiment had been relieved by the 4th Infantry Division's 12th Infantry Regiment. Its 3d Battalion, like the tank destroyers around 1500 hours, started the attack from the forest west of Germeter to take over the defense at the Kall bridge. However, it lost its way and, far from its objective, dug in southwest of Richelskaul; its leaders believed that the battalion was at the bridge across the Kall, near the Mestrenger Mill. Not before the afternoon of 8 November did the battalion reach the Mestrenger Mill.[104]

The *"Division-Spiegel"* of the *89th Infantry Division* celebrated the success of 7 November in Kommerscheidt:

At 1500 hours, the report traveled through the wire: The battle of Kommerscheidt has ended successfully. On this last day, 260 prisoners were taken; so far 100 dead have been counted, 11 tanks destroyed, probably two more, and another two surrendered. Only individual small combat groups are still putting up some resistance. The combing of the cauldron against these nests of resistance continues. *Oberst* Bayer and his tanks along with our *Grenadiers,* who hardly got an hour of sleep during those days and nights and fighting without interruption, continue to face the enemy to destroy the last remnants of the encircled, and to finally close the gap in the front.[105]

After taking Kommerscheidt, *1st Battalion, Panzer Regiment 24* advanced further to the point where the trail to the Kall bridge disappears in the forest. *Rittmeister* Böke, the battalion commander, distinguished himself there.[106] On 8 November, the mop-up around Kommerscheidt continued. A group of Americans scattered in the area southwest of Schmidt since since 4 November surrendered. At the Mestrenger Mill, *Grenadier Regiment 1056* fought back and forth with the American engineers who were sent there and by the afternoon also fought with 3d Battalion, 109th Infantry Regiment, but repelled all attacks.[107]

The tanks of the *116th Panzer Division* remained with the *89th Infantry Division* around Schmidt until 14 November. On that day, *Generalleutnant* Thomale from the office of the Inspector General of *Panzer* Troops visited the *Panzer* Regiment to discuss its replenishment and perhaps also the exchange of the *1st Battalion, Panzer Regiment 24* with the *1st Battalion, Panzer Regiment 16.* The return of *1st Battalion, Panzer Regiment 16* to the Division was finally announced. In September, the battalion fought in Lorraine, and after its relief was replenished for the second time in Grafenwöhr; it was now approaching. On 15 November, *Generalfeldmarshall* Model went to see the regiment.[108] At his parting, the commander of the *89th Infantry Division* gave his thanks to *Panzer Regiment 16* with the following letter of appreciation:

> In the attack conducted with ardor on Kommerscheidt, the regiment played a decisive part in the division's successes, which led to the recapture of Kommerscheidt, the town mentioned in the report of *Wehrmacht* Headquarters. Due to the brave action of *Panzer Regiment 16,* the division succeeded in repulsing the enemy and in defending the position against further enemy attacks.[109]

MacDonald's portrayal of the battles for Kommerscheidt is basically congruent with the one above.[110] According to it, the German artillery preparatory fires were the heaviest ever encountered by the men in Kommerscheidt. When the artillery stopped after a 30-minute barrage, the German tanks appeared so closely behind the last detonations that they were not noticed until they opened fire. At 0830 hours, the Americans were so startled that many turned to flee. However, it was possible for them to destroy several German tanks. After the loss of two tanks and three tank destroyers, the remaining American tanks retreated north to the edge of the forest. Two more tanks were lost in the process. Now the situation in the town became unbearable for the infantry. Some of them also tried to withdraw, but suffered heavy losses; the others surrendered. The loss of Kommerscheidt was reported to the 28th Infantry Division at 1125 hours. A German attack toward the forest edge north of Kommerscheidt, mounted by four tanks and infantry at 1830 hours, was able to be repulsed. That might have been Böke.

In accordance with orders, on the evening of 8 November the remnants of three American battalions, one tank company, and one tank destroyer company moved back across the Kall, leaving heavy equipment behind.[111] A column of wounded used the trail and the Germans allowed it to pass.[112] The others beat their way further west, cross country and across the Kall, toward the positions of the 3d Battalion, 109th Infantry Regiment, which as earlier reported, relieved the engineers on 8 November. Of more than 2,200 men who crossed the Kall, about 300 came back in formation. The aid station on the Kall Trail, between the front lines, could not be evacuated until 11 November.[113]

The situation of the retreating Americans was eased by the retaking of Vossenack on 7 November. *Armored Engineer Battalion 675,* which saved the situation on the day before, received orders to recapture the eastern part of the town with tank support on the morning of 7 November. For this, it had two companies, as its third one was in action elsewhere. It only received one platoon of tanks, even though two companies were available in the vicinity of Germeter–Vossenack. One platoon that remained overnight in Vossenack was even brought back to Germeter on the morning of 7 November.

After 30 minutes of artillery preparation, the attack was to get under way by 0800 hours, with one company each north and south of the road. The tank platoon was ordered to support the attack from the south side of town by firing on every house that was to be taken. Because of the hasty deployment the day before, the engineers lacked communication equipment, and did not possess hand grenades. Artillery fire hit its targets. The attack, however, was delayed by fifteen minutes, until 0815 hours. When the American artillery became silent, the German artillery commenced firing at 0800 hours. The left attack company suffered losses from the shelling. At 0815, the company on the right attacked, took the church and the cemetery in its first assault, and took 16 prisoners. Under cover of fire by the right company, the left company then advanced further from the cemetery, seized the first few houses, and thereby took 20 prisoners. While the right company continued to occupy the church, the left now also advanced on the right side of the road eastward from house to house, and thereby took another 20 German prisoners. Around 1500 hours, it reached the eastern edge of Vossenack. When the tank platoon also appeared there, it received heavy fire from the hills near Brandenberg. After this, air support was requested, and the aircraft attacked with bombs and machine guns. The tank platoon lost one vehicle to a *Panzerfaust* and one to a mine. A total of 150 German dead and wounded were reported.

After dark, the 2d Battalion, 109th Infantry Regiment relieved the brave engineers. During the night, the tanks were withdrawn to Germeter. This battalion no longer occupied the exposed positions on the hills around Vossenack, but remained in town, where most of the men sought cover in houses and cellars. This minimized the losses caused by the continuing heavy German artillery fire on 8 November. On the evening of this day, the 109th's 1st Battalion moved into a second position near Germeter and moved one company forward to Vossenack-West.[114]

Now let us again turn to the fighters of the *116th Panzer Division* at Vossenack. On the evening of 6 November, the following were deployed there:

— *1st Battalion, Panzer-Grenadier Regiment 156* at edge of forest north of Vossenack, opposite Bosselbach and the center of Vossenack.

— *2d Battalion, Panzer-Grenadier Regiment 156* in the center of Vossenack, north of the main street.

— *1st Battalion, Panzer-Grenadier Regiment 60* linking up to the left, around the church, south of the main street.

— *2d Battalion, Panzer-Grenadier Regiment 60* left of it, in the southern outskirts of the town.

As already reported, the *Armored Reconnaissance Battalion* with the attached *Division Escort Company* was fighting between Vossenack and the Mestrenger Mill on the Kall Trail. Apparently, the aforementioned four tanks of the *1st Battalion, Panzer Regiment 24* attached to it as a back-up for closing off the trail in the Kall Valley. Besides this, during the night of 6/7 November, the bulk of *1st Company, Armored Engineer Battalion 675* was brought in to strengthen the defense and to prepare mined obstacles in the Kall Valley. After carefully weighing all reports, some of them quite contradictory, this is the picture one gets.[115]

Panzerjäger Battalion 228 continued to support the units of the *275th Infantry Division,* deployed near Hürtgen, and sometimes joined in the attacks by fire against Vossenack from the hills near Brandenberg.[116] On 6 November, the fighting for the Hürtgen forester's house started anew. It again fell into enemy hands.[117] *Hauptmann* Brückner, commander of *Engineer Battalion 253,* had landmines brought in from Westphalia to give his position in the forest more backbone. Its transfer began on 7 November; the mines had an extraordinary effect. The enemy suffered such high losses that he gave up attacking the battalion positions. Scattered mock minefields looked similar to the real ones and had the same effect.[118]

After retaking the church in Vossenack on the evening of 6 November, calmness temporarily prevailed. *Oberleutnant* Löffler, who combined the *5th* and *6th Companies* of *Panzer-Grenadier Regiment 156,* reported after the war, "At dawn, we beat back some American reconnaissance strike troops. Then, very heavy artillery fire starts, which covers the center of Vossenack completely. The fire is so dense that almost nothing can be recognized. Visibility in some places is only 30 to 50 meters."[119]

Coming out of the fire, the Americans attacked and rolled over the most forward positions of the *116th Panzer Division.*

Löffler continues to write:

> I keep the *Panzer-Grenadiers* of *5th* and *6th Companies* together and we are able to hold a line 250 meters east of the church for about 2 hours. An attack, mounted by approximately 80 American infantrymen with tank support collapses, because a group from *5th Company* and my company almost simultaneously fire 15 *Panzerfausts,* which we found at the corner of a house by accident, into the spearhead. One Sherman is destroyed. The infantrymen are totally surprised by this improvised "barrage" and retreat about 100 meters. But we lack heavy weapons and at this point, both companies only have five operational machine guns. By noon, the communication links are completely broken off. . . . We assume that nobody really knows where the fighting units are.
>
> Our own artillery now shells the sector held by us and covers us fully. By 1230, heavy fire (15cm and 17cm) is laid over the remnants of *5th* and *6th Companies.* I am crouching in the entrance of a house which receives a direct hit. The company troop commander and two *Panzer-Grenadiers* are killed. Together with an *Obergefreiter,* I am buried in rubble and am freed by my men.
>
> In one of the last houses at the eastern edge of Vossenack, I wake up and along with 40 wounded who were laying there already, I am driven to the aid station. . . . From the Breuersberg, southwest of Brandenberg, I glance at Vossenack for the last time. Here they are . . . tanks and assault guns, which were employed as artillery support.

Assigning blame is senseless. Unfortunately, it happened that the infantry was hit by our own fire. This can only be prevented by employing sufficient forward observers, with good communication equipment, and also by strict fire control within the Division. In any case, this was excellently mastered by the staff of our *Artillery Regiment* under the leadership of *Oberst* Dr. Pean.

The *1st* and *2d Battalions* of *Panzer-Grenadier Regiment 60* had an experience similar to *2d Battalion, Panzer-Grenadier Regiment 156. Oberfeldwebel* Dreiling noted in his diary about the events of the *3d Company,* "The following morning, opponent attacks, we lose ground and in the end have to clear out of the village. Things go crazy. The companies assemble; the losses are considerable, including materiel. The *3d Company, Panzer-Grenadier Regiment 60* consists of only 11 men."[120]

On 7 November, while in his advanced command post in Vossenack, the *1st Battalion* Commander, *Hauptmann* Nagel, was wounded. With him, the most important commander in Vossenack was lost. Later, *Hauptmann* Kroll assumed command of *1st Battalion, Panzer-Grenadier Regiment 60.* There is a recommendation for an award in connection with the events concerning the *6th Company* of *2d Battalion, Panzer-Grenadier Regiment 60.*[121] According to this,

Feldwebel Gaiser, who had already distinguished himself during the attack on the previous day, deserves the main credit for defending the houses in the southern part of Vossenack against attacking tanks and infantry, until the order came to withdraw. The *1st Battalion* and elements of the *7th Company, 2d Battalion, Panzer-Grenadier Regiment 156*–north of Vossenack–were not directly affected by the accident in the town. Their fire facilitated the withdrawal of the others. Thereby, *Oberfeldwebel* Lauer from *7th Company, Panzer-Grenadier Regiment 156* distinguished himself again.[122]

The journal of the *2d Battalion* of the *Artillery Regiment* for 7 November records the following:

> In general, the night passes quietly. Very little enemy artillery fire.
>
> In late morning, enemy artillery fire intensifies, mainly in the vicinity of Vossenack. Under pressure of the heavy fire, our infantry leaves Vossenack and in the late afternoon hours withdraws to the old line of departure.
>
> Both infantry battalions of *Panzer-Grenadier Battalion 156* are badly hit and consist of very few people. . . . With single shots, the battalion fights enemy tanks trying to launch an attack on the northern side of Vossenack and forces them back. Enemy concentrations by the swimming pool and in the central and western part are successfully engaged.
>
> Enemy air force more active than on previous day. Targets in area Gross and Kleinhau are attacked by bombs and machine guns. Some fighter bombers drop bombs with incendiary oil [Napalm—*Editor*].
>
> Rounds expended: 1,414 from light field howitzers.[123]

It is evident that the events look quite different from the command post of an artillery battalion stationed somewhere in the rear than they do at the front line. In the journal of *Supreme Command–West* for 7 November, one can read in the noon report, "Enemy attack against Vossenack church with support of four tanks."[124]

In the daily report it then said, "Attack on Vossenack with unusually heavy fighter-bomber activity (bombs, machine guns, phosphorus cannisters) stopped after heavy fighting at eastern edge. Our losses considerable."[125]

The "Division order for the course of action on 8 November 1944" on the evening of 7 November had the Division change "to defense in the vicinity of Vossenack."[126] During the night, *Armored Reconnaissance Battalion 116* was to be relieved by *2d Battalion, Grenadier Regiment 1056* and to stand by as Division reserve in the area of Zweifallshammer. The *2d Battalion, Grenadier Regiment 1056* was attached to *Panzer-Grenadier Regiment 60*. The *89th Infantry Division* assumed responsibility for the Mestrenger Mill.

Disregarding busy fighter and fighter bomber activity, calm prevailed on 8 November in the Hürtgen–Vossenack–Kommerscheidt area. The combat with the Americans who retreated across the Kall near the Mestrenger Mill and the mop-up in the woods of the Americans who bypassed that area southwest of Schmidt has already been portrayed. The relief of the *Panzer-Grenadier* Regiments of *116th Panzer Division* by the *89th Infantry Division* was ordered, and was essentially completed during the night of 8/9 November.[127] Both regiments, the *Armored Reconnaissance Battalion*, and the *Armored Engineer Battalion* moved into the villages south and southwest of Düren. The entry for 8 November in the journal of *2d Battalion, Armored Artillery Regiment 146,* from 8 November, states the following:

> *Panzer-Grenadier Regiment 156* is being relieved for replenishment. . . .
>
> *Panzer-Grenadier Regiment 156* is very weakend by the heavy battles in the forest and the continuous bad weather. Only the heavy companies are still present. Battle strength of the other companies is one NCO, ten men; one NCO, three men; and so on. After replenishing the regiment, the penetration near Hürtgen is to be cleared. *Armored Artillery Regiment 146,* therefore, remains in position and has instructions for cooperation with *Grenadier Regiment 1055.*[128]

As will be seen, there was unfortunately no replenishment. On 10 November, *Supreme Command–West* issued a summarized report:

> During the period from 4 to 8 November 1944, the *116th* and the *89th,* with subordinated units, have achieved success in heavy battles against the US 28th Infantry Division and units of the US 9th Infantry Division (reinforced by one army engineer battalion) in the Schmidt–Kommerscheidt and Vossenack area: two battalions, one tank battalion, and elements of one engineer battalion were enveloped and destroyed.
>
> In detail: 641 prisoners brought in, 53 tanks destroyed, seven hit and immobilized. 22 aircraft destroyed by the Division's anti-aircraft elements.
>
> Captured materiel: two tanks, one armored ambulance, two armored personnel carriers, four trucks, twelve Jeeps, one anti-tank gun, numerous small arms. Two other tanks surrendered.[129]

In his diary, Vogelsang noted:

> The bend of the penetration is now ironed out for the most part, the danger of a threatening breakthrough has been eliminated. Both sides suffered heavy losses, but the opponent more than us. . . . The new *Escort Company* has proven itself outstandingly next to the old units of the Division. . . . The troops are now extremely exhausted. The uninterrupted fire; the hard, alternating fighting; the rain, the dampness, mud and cold all did their part.[130]

MacDonald declares 6,814 casualties for the 28th Infantry Division and estimates the German casualties to be about half this number. The unit which sustained the brunt of the effects, the 112th Infantry Regiment, alone lost 2,093 men: 167 killed, 719 wounded, 232 captured, 431 missing, and 544 non-battle casualties.[131] The Americans did not reach their objective to improve the protection of the southern flank for the planned offensive toward the Ruhr. They did, however, make it impossible for the *116th Panzer Division* to be replenished, so that it was not available as a mobile reserve in the upcoming main battle.

This time, the Roer Valley dams were not yet the Americans' targets. Even if *Supreme Command–West*, in its evening report of 6 November, questioned if the enemy wanted to gain the eastern exits of the Eifel and the dams, the author could not find any documents from that time of either side that showed the military significance of the dams to be of great importance.[132] The economic importance—the supply of electricity for the industry in the area north of the Eifel—seemed to have been rated more highly by the Germans.

Whatever the case may be, the *116th Panzer Division* was not allowed to be replenished, but was held to eliminate the enemy salient protruding toward Hürtgen.

To clean up this local blemish, a *Panzer* division had to remain in action, even if its infantry battle strength was bled to death, even if there were signs of preparation for a large offensive near Aachen, and even if the enemy had already started one near Metz.[133]

The appearance of the 12th Infantry Regiment near Hürtgen did its part to again cause deployment of the *116th*, but this time in a fight entirely in the forest.[134] This intention already made its mark in the *2d Battalion, Armored Artillery Battalion 146* journal note of 8 November. On 9 November, Waldenburg noted "Relief for units carried out. Preparation for local operation. Evening commanders' conference in my bunker for Operation Grollmann. The first snowfall!"[135]

The opposing side also did not want to take its fingers off Hürtgen, but instead ordered a new attack for the improvement of the position opposite Hürtgen. For this were deployed the 12th Infantry Regiment near Hürtgen in the old zone of the 109th Infantry Regiment and the 1st Battalion, 109th Infantry Regiment, which was replenished with replacements north of Vossenack approximately at the boundary between the *89th Infantry Division* and the units of the *275th Infantry Division* that remained in position southeast of Wittscheidt. Near Raffelsbrand, the Americans also wanted to gain ground one more time, but continued to fail.[136]

On 9 November, the broken pieces of both *Panzer-Grenadier* Regiments of *Armored Reconnaissance Battalion 116,* and the bulk of *Armored Engineer Battalion 675* were withdrawn from the front. Artillery and anti-aircraft elements remained in position, as did *Group Bayer* with the *89th Infantry Division* and *Panzerjäger Battalion 228* near Hürtgen.[137] In the evening, *Group Grollman* was formed. Under command of *Major* Grollmann, it consisted of the following:

— *Panzer-Grenadier Regiment 156*—actually, the remnants of the *Panzer-Grenadier* companies and the regiment's heavy weapons.
— The *Division Escort Company*
—*Panzerjäger Battalion 228*
—Flame throwers and mine sweepers of *Armored Engineer Battalion 675*

Two attack groups were formed, one under the command of *Hauptmann* Winter, commander of *1st Battalion, Panzer-Grenadier Regiment 156.* The second consisted of the *Division Escort Company.*[138] After the pouring rain, the paths had eroded, and after the firestorm from both sides it was almost impossible to penetrate the forest. For the *116th Panzer Division,* the battle in the Hürtgen Forest only now commenced.

First, however, the enemy attacked. On the morning of 10 November, the 12th Infantry Regiment attacked on both sides of the Weisser Wehbach, as well as in the forest southwest of Hürtgen and north of the Wittscheidt forester's station. Two breaches along the west bank of the creek in tracts 181 and 177 were mopped up, as well as a breach near the Schneisenkreuz near Hill 408.7 (one kilometer west of the Hürtgen forester's station). But between it and the Germeter–Hürtgen road, enemy units—two companies—pushed north up to tracts 91 and 92 west of Hürtgen. The resulting gap could not be closed up for the time being. In contrast, the American thrust near Wittscheidt was not successful.[139]

Near Bosselbach, the 1st Battalion, 109th Infantry Regiment did not have luck on its side: One company was destroyed by German artillery fire, a second one became lost in the forest, and the third one arrived way back behind the German front, up to tract 52 (one kilometer south of Hürtgen), and enjoyed three days of "great solitude" there until it was discovered.[140] At noon, *Combat Group Grollmann* attacked the American breach southwest of Hürtgen. The journal of *2d Battalion, Armored Artillery Regiment 146* from 10 November, reports the following:

> Preparation area for the attack is in the forest northwest of breach. All heavy weapons of the *Panzer-Grenadier Regiment* are combined under *Schwiko* (*Schwere Infantrie Waffen Kommandeur*—infantry heavy weapons commander) *Hauptmann* Gerke, and units from *Assault Gun Battalion Bochnig* (Commander, *Panzerjäger Battalion 228*) are in Hürtgen area to support our attack with direct fire.[141]

The journal then deals with questions regarding artillery, such as regrouping observation posts, as well as difficulties with observation in the high forest. It continues:

> In a 25-minute preparation, *Artillery Regiments 275, 1020,* and *Armored Artillery Regiment 146,* spray the heaviest barrage on the area to be cleared, and after the attack by the infantry, shift fire toward targets in Wittscheidt, Germeter, und Vossenack.
>
> Further firing orders will be given by artillery commander (of *LXXXIV Corps*).
>
> 1230 hours commencement of our barrage. Infantry attack as per orders at 1300 hours.
>
> Since observation of the advancing infantry is not possible, during the whole afternoon strong artillery fire will be directed only by request of *Arko* (artillery commander) into the rearward area of the breach near Hürtgen.

At 1900 hours, one learns about the situation:

The southern strike group breaks through half of the forest. Meets heavy resistance, comes to a halt.

The northern strike group reached the Hürtgen forester's house and then turned north.

There are three fresh [American] battalions in the sector. . . . Elements of them are cut off in the forest and in heavy fighting with our infantry. . . .

Rounds expended: 1,676 light howitzer. . . .

Weather: Driving snow, rain.

From the journal of *Supreme Command–West* from 10 November, it can be established that *Combat Group Grollmann* attacked from the area south of the Rondsberg southeast to the road bend south of the forester's house and to the Schneisenkreuz, Hill 417.0 (500m southwest of it), and reached both objectives despite strong enemy resistance.[142] The "Division order for the course of action on 11 November 1944" directed *Combat Group Grollmann* to destroy the units of the 12th Infantry Regiment which were encircled in tracts 91 and 92, by attacking them from behind out of a line from Hill 408.7 (Schneisenkreuz) to the road bend.[143] *Armored Reconnaissance Battalion 116*, which was also moved up, attacked the enemy from the north. Advancing southward together, both groups were to gain the line Hill 408.7–Hill 417.0–northwest corner of the "Wild Sow" minefield as their main battle line. Afterward, they were to hand it over for defense to *Engineer Battalion 253*. This battalion already took part in the attack with one company.[144]

Despite the new deployment of forces, the battle against the encircled enemy on 11 November did not succeed. However, between Hill 408.7 and the road bend, the front toward the south, as well as the ring of encirclement with its front toward north, could be held. A new, shorter, main battle line was established behind the protruding bend in the front line of the *275th Infantry Division* near Hill 312, along the "sinew" from Hill 408.7 to the northwest across the Weisser Wehbach. The protruding bend remained occupied by combat outposts.[145]

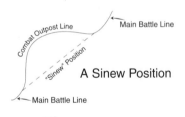

A Sinew Position

Since the gap between the *275th* and *89th Infantry Divisions* near Bosselbach, north of Vossenack, could not be closed by these divisions, *LXXIV Corps* ordered the *116th Panzer Division* to again also take over this sector up to one kilometer north of Vossenack. For this reason, during the night of 10 November, *Major* Zander, his staff, and the rest of *Panzer-Grenadier Regiment 60* under the command of *Hauptmann* Kroll, as well as the *Assault Platoon* of *1st Company, Armored Engineer Battalion 675* were brought up. The troops of the *275th Infantry Division* that were deployed there were subordinated to him. In conjunction with the *89th Infantry Division, Group Zander* was to close the gap to prevent an enemy breakthrough from tracts 52 and 53 north toward Hürtgen, and finally to destroy the enemy.[146] The reconnaissance employed against this enemy group could not locate the Americans. However, in the frontline near the forest edge, reconnaissance patrols established contact between the *116th Panzer* and *89th Infantry Divisions.*[147] *Panzerjäger Battalion 228* with subordinated *Assault Gun Brigade 394,* depending on cooperation with both *Panzer-Grenadier* Regiments, stood in the Hürtgen–Kleinhau area, to avert an enemy breakthrough from the southwest, as well as from the forest south of Hürtgen.[148]

The daily report by *Supreme Command–West* from 11 November saw the enemy approaching destruction southwest of Hürtgen and a strong front also being established. This was a little premature.[149] On this evening, Waldenburg wrote, "Heavy fighting in area southwest of Hürtgen. Have encircled a small enemy group, but am too weak to destroy it. The exhaustion of the troops is immense, as are the casualties. Very bad weather; for days, the people outside are laying in dampness!"[150]

During the night of 11/12 November, the Americans penetrated the just-established main battle line between Hill 408.7 and the road bend, and reinforced the units that broke through by two more companies. The Hürtgen forester's house was once again lost. Toward 0900 hours, the situation was restored by a counterattack with the support of *Panzerjäger Battalion 228.*[151] The *Division Escort Company* was substantially involved in this.

In a report it says:

Acting as quickly as lightning, *Hauptmann* von Linde-Suden gathered the remnants of the *Division Escort Company* and all other units in the area, and closed off the front to the southwest. Thus, the enemy could not succeed in entering the second hunter's lodge and the Hürtgen village. With a reconnaissance patrol, *Hauptmann* von Linde-Suden again established connection with the former adjacent units. He stormed forward at the front of the company, broke the enemy's resistance, and again occupied the previous main battle line, as well as the forester's house.[152]

In the afternoon of 12 November, the enemy attacked near Wittscheidt. The journal of the *2d Battalion, Armored Artillery Regiment 146* recorded, "In the afternoon hours, the enemy again mounted an attack in the vicinity of Wittscheidt. Good visibility enables engaging the attack with artillery. The attack, mounted by two strong companies, is broken up as it unfolds."[153]

Earlier, the writer of the diary complained about the battles southwest of Hürtgen, "Artillery support can hardly be given to the fighting infantry because observation in the impenetrable forest is impossible."

The *116th Panzer* and *89th Infantry Divisions* strengthened contact along the boundary. Suprisingly, the eastern part of Vossenack was observed to be free of the enemy. It was occupied by the *89th* with a line of separate, individual positions, but given up again on 14 November.[154] On 12 November, the journal of the *2d Battalion, Armored Artillery Regiment 146* records about the enemy group in the forest south of Hürtgen that, "The enemy group in the rearward area of the front in tract 52 has been reinforced further and is now continuously being attacked by our weaker forces."[155]

On the evening of 12 November, Waldenburg noted, "Again, heavy enemy attacks. It succeeded in linking-up with its encircled group."[156]

Further, he noted, "Prince Holstein, who has been my *Ia,* is relieved by *Oberstleutnant* Guderian."

Vogelsang remarked, "Today, to everyone's joy, our old *Ia, Oberstleutnant* Guderian returned to us after recuperating from his serious wounds. Prince zu Holstein, who got used to us and acclimated himself quite well, takes over a regiment on the Eastern Front."[157]

Earlier, Vogelsang wrote:

> The battles sway back and forth in uninterrupted severity. It is raining, wet patches of fog or clouds of snow sweep across the muddy land filled with puddles. The *Landsers* wading, lying, or fighting in mud and water are close to complete physical exhaustion. The reported battle strengths fall shocklingly. The artillery battle rolls on without surcease.

Leutnant Schwörer, keeper of the journal of *2d Battalion, Armored Artillery Regiment 146,* once again had a chance to make an entry in his private diary:

> Inside the forest it looks quite wild. Due to continuous fire, the trees lay in all directions, the trails are completely soaked and ankle-deep water is everywhere. The infantry soldiers look like pigs. No peace, already for more than a week, and not a dry thread on the body; it is always raining and there is always fog. It is a jungle war, man against man with tremendous strain on the individual.
>
> No vehicle can make it through the forest. Everything is too muddy and dirty. Only half-tracked motorcycles and armored personnel carriers can still get through. The infantry of the Division is completely finished. There are only staffs left and very few men. Even men, who under threat of a pistol would not move forward, were among them.
>
> We from the artillery can still handle it. All we are lacking are overcoats. The butcher company has to give up all of theirs. It is a sad operation.[158]

On 13 November, the attack continued against the encircled Americans in tracts 91 and 92. Units from *Engineer Battalion 253* pressed on from the north. The small cauldron was mopped up, but most of the Americans escaped to their own lines. Only 27 prisoners were taken.[159]

The forward line now ran from the western edge of tract 181 to the west bank of the Weisser Wehbach via Elevation 408.7 to the northwest corner of the "Wild Sow" minefield, and from there southeast to the boundary with the *89th Infantry Division.* On the evening of 13 November, the Division ordered the point of link-up between *Groups Grollmann* and *Zander* to be the Schneisenkreuz, 250 meters southwest of the road bend.[160] Both groups now had to prepare themselves for defense and complete their positions in the newly established main battle line. Each was to designate a reaction force. *Armored Reconnaissance Battalion 116* and the *Division Escort Company* were relieved. The Division ordered the rein- forced *Panzerjäger Battalion 228,* which was depending on cooperation with both regimental groups, "to deploy elements for defense at the southwestern forester's station (at the road bend) and, using all means, prevent repossession of it by the enemy."

The journal entry of the *2d Battalion, Armored Artillery Regiment 146* from 13 November records, "Toward evening in the forest,which was almost impassible from artillery hits, some of our reconnaissance patrols find the positions of the opponent empty. New main battle line along the trail firmly in our hands."[161]

Oberstleutnant Grollmann, promoted on 9 November, congratulated *Haupt- mann* Brückner from *Engineer Battalion 253* for his success.[162] Everyone was happy about the clean-up of the situation and the strengthening of the front. MacDonald, however, reaches the following conclusion about the deployment of the 12th Infantry Regiment, "In nine days of bitter combat, the 12th Infantry had lost rather than gained ground. A thousand men had fallen victim either to enemy fire or to combat exhaustion, trenchfoot, or respiratory diseases."[163]

The result was that during the main offensive on 16 November, the regiment again could not fulfill its task.

On the evening of 13 November, *Feldmarschall* Model visited the staff of the *116th Panzer Division* in the bunker near Grosshau. Now the Division was, indeed, to be pulled out.

Waldenburg noted on 16 November, "Relief of the Division finally ordered. It is high time, severely battered and exhausted."[164]

The Commander in Chief of the *7th Army, General* Brandenberger, visited the Division on 14 November and expressed his appreciation for its achievements. The relief of the Division was carried out during the night of 14/15 November, but again only halfway. The staff of *Panzer-Grenadier Regiment 60,* as well as *Combat Group Winter,* established from units of both *Panzer-Grenadier* regi- ments and the engineers, remained temporarily deployed to destroy the enemy in tract 52. Besides this, the entire *Armored Artillery Regiment 146* and *Army Anti- Aircraft Battalion 281* remained with the *275th Infantry Division,* which again took over control at the front between Schevenhütte and Bosselbach, connecting with the *89th Infantry Division* near Bosselbach. On 15 November, at 0600 hours, the *275th Infantry Division* was in charge, while the staff of the *116th* with the staff of *Panzer-Grenadier Regiment 60, Major* Zander, continued the fight for tract 52.

No clear success came his way, especially since the front near Bosselbach was still quite porous. Again it came to the earlier-mentioned tough battles in the for- est. The encircled Americans from the 1st Battalion, 109th Infantry Regiment did not give in. Without having completed the operation, the Division staff left the battlefield. Staff Zander and his combat group followed later; the exact time cannot be established. On 16 November, in any case, they were still in action. The relieved units, if they were battle ready, had to be ready to march within two hours.[165]

Only 33 of the cut-off Americans returned to their regiment.[166] Like their comrades in the forest near Hürtgen, they proved to be brave and tough fighters and deserve the highest respect. In the daily report by *Supreme Command–West* from 15 November, it is recorded, lightly embellished, that the *116th Panzer Division* (without artillery) was out, to assemble in the area east of Düren.[167] On 16 November, the Division staff was still in Kreuzau.

With this, the heavy battles around Vossenack and Schmidt, as well as in the Hürtgen Forest, were concluded for most of the Division. The description of its course may have conveyed some of the harshness that marked these fights. The soldier not only fought his opponents, but also the terrain and the weather. However, as much as weather and terrain hindered the fighting man, they favored the defender and contributed to its success. The *116th Panzer Division* mainly fought in the attack mode, without being able to bring to bear the full effect of its strength, the tanks. In this terrain, it was misplaced. On the other hand, the Americans could not take full advantage of their superiority. Neither tanks nor airpower were able to play their accustomed roles. They had totally new experiences. Legends were created. One says that the church in Vossenack changed owners 28 times. In fact, it changed over five times or at the most, seven times. It was also said that this battle was "the Verdun of WWII."[168] This is surely exaggerated, but the 28th Infantry Division suffered higher losses than practically any other American division.

The *116th Panzer Division* also had high casualties. On 16 November, Vogelsang noted:

> The Division's task in the Hürtgen Forest was entirely resolved with success, but it led to very high losses. The battle strengths of the companies dropped to an average of 25 men or less. Again we have a need for 1,800 men to fill the gaps. Where are we get all these replacements?[169]

It is, therefore, with good reason that the Division erected the memorial to its fallen comrades near Vossenack. There, it commemorates all the dead of the great fight, no matter how they gave their lives. Yet those who were left behind in November 1944 will of course always remain in the hearts and minds of the living.

Part 4: Scattered

At 1200 hours on 16 November, while in Kreuzau, *Major* Vogelsang wrote in his diary:

> Once again, outside all hell breaks loose! For the last hour, an endless stream of heavy bombers is flooding the country. "Christmas trees" (flares on little parachutes) to mark targets came down all over the area followed by tight carpets of heavy bombs, which sank whole regions into fire and smoke with thunder and rattle. The worst is in Stolberg–Eschweiler Valley. The ground is shaking and the windows clink without let-up. Road crossings, villages, all more or less prominent points are under fierce artillery fire. The front itself is a roaring hell. . . . Everything points to a major offensive in the Stolberg area. It is, therefore, calming to learn, that *SS-Panzer Army Sepp Dietrich* is supposed to be approaching!
>
> Even if our original task here is completed and the command has already been transferred, we have a foreboding of evil.[1]

In the evening, Vogelsang completed his notes:

> What a firestorm today! Literally thousands of planes bustled in the air above roaring bombardments. By noon, the pack lunged toward the Eschweiler–Stolberg area. It was Düren's turn for an hour starting at 1500 hours. Wave upon wave came thundering at an altitude of only 2,000 meters. Sparkling Christmas trees were gliding toward the unfortunate town, followed by the densest, howling carpet-bombing of the heaviest calibers.
>
> Within a few minutes, in place of the town, there was an immense, quivering, black bubbling cloud, permeated by a red glow. Even now, Düren is still one single huge fireball. All attempts to enter the town failed because of rubble and fires blocking the roads.
>
> We were standing in the gardens next to our foxholes and looked at this devilish inferno with uneasiness, fearing that any second it would be our turn. All sorts of anti-aircraft fire was feverishly shot off. Our battalion shot down five and *Panzer-Grenadier Regiment 156* shot down two bombers of the endless bomber stream. . . . A drop in the bucket with more than a thousand of these birds!
>
> What will follow after all this on the ground, after this tremendous preparation! . . . An order arrived to immediately prepare a combat group from the staff of the *Panzer* Regiment, the Panther Battalion, one battalion of armored vehicles, one engineer company, and one battery.
>
> Even in our "resting areas" we had losses. An officer replacement center was hit, the staff of the *1st Battalion, Panzer-Grenadier Regiment 156* was bombed out, the regimental staff of *Regiment 156* had the house shot to pieces above their heads, supply units and repair installations in Düren were taken.

On the morning of 18 November, in Jakobwüllesheim, where the Division staff relocated on 17 November, Vogelsang noted:

Yesterday we had to give up our nice quarters in Kreuzau for a terrible small place. If the Americans ever drop their bombs on these over-crowded, confining villages that are spread out in the plains without cover—all the best!

With our empty truck columns we now send families with their most essential belongings from the Roer Valley back across the Rhine.

The situation is not entirely clear yet. Between Geilenkirchen and Schevenhütte, south of Eschweiler, the opponent has mounted the expected major offensive across a broad front. It is hard to believe that anything remained in one piece during the fireworks! But the *Landsers* came out of their holes and hideouts everywhere and again went into positions to defend themselves tenaciously and doggedly. Until now, the opponent has only been able to achieve a few penetrations.

So much for the "calm!" In groups, the Division has to close gaps. Only yesterday, *Oberst* Bayer, with *1st Battalion, Panzer Regiment 24* and the *Armored Reconnaissance Battalion* (battle strength still 30 men) was deployed . . . with *LXXXI Corps*, the commander of *Panzer-Grenadier Regiment 156,* with remnants of his regiment and a battalion made up of leftovers from *Panzer-Grenadier Regiment 60,* is inserted into the right wing of the *275th Infantry Division,* southeast of Stolberg. The artillery is firing in the sector of the *275th Infantry Division* from its positions near Winden.

Thus, luckily, the whole unit is ripped apart and we are sitting here alone with the Division staff and a few more people. Now, after all previous losses, the framework for reconstitution also seems to be lost!"

Vogelsang's descriptions provide a true picture of the situation of the *116th Panzer Division* during those November days. No sooner did the staff arrive in Kreuzau from its bunker near Grosshau, than the depicted major offensive by the Americans began. Two American field armies were attacking, the Ninth to the left, between Geilenkirchen and Würselen, the First on the right, between Würselen and Hürtgen. At the onset, however, only the two corps at the inner wings of the armies took part, the XIX in the north and the VII in the south. The objective of the offensive was the Rhine on both sides of Cologne, with the intermediate objective the Roer between Düren and Linnich.

The battles of the 28th Infantry Division near Schmidt and Vossenack initiated the offensive and had to protect its right flank. As we saw, they were not successful. The main attack was postponed several times mostly due to bad weather. At the latest, the attack was to take place on 16 November, if necessary, even without support from the air. The strongest air support of the whole war was planned. Two thousand, four hundred American and British heavy bombers were to attack the areas of Eschweiler–Weisweiler, Langerwehe–Jüngersdorf and the towns Düren, Jülich, and Heinsberg. More than 600 medium bombers were assigned to targets in the vicinty of Linnich and Aldenhoven, as well as some villages northwest of Düren, where command posts were suspected. Besides this, 750 fighter bombers were to assist the fighting on the ground. Eight hundred fighters were planned as escorts. Approximately 1,250 guns were to initiate the attack with 50,000 rounds. Added to this was the fire by the mortars, as well as the fires from tanks and tank destroyers. Three hundred tanks and tank destroyers were ready to attack.

When the order finally came to start the attack on 16 November, it was not clear if the air corps could take part. However, despite the clouds, the 2,400 heavy bombers were able to take off. They dropped about 10,000 tons of bombs on the planned targets, about 2,800 on Düren alone. From the medium bombers, only 80 made it into the air; the planned number of fighter bombers could not take off as scheduled either, but they still flew about 350 sorties. The escorts were all in the air, but saw only four German aircraft. All together, about 4,000 sorties were flown. Only 12 planes were shot down by German anti-aircraft guns.

The air attacks started at 1130 hours and the ground troops attacked at 1245, between Geilenkirchen and Hürtgen.[2] The opponent also attacked on the rest of the Western Front, the British against the Maas bridgehead at Venlo, and the Americans near Metz, as well as north, south, and through the Vosges Mountains.[3] The battle erupted more or less along the whole front, between Venlo and the Swiss border. Metz and Strasbourg were lost, and the troops west of the upper Rhine were pushed back into a bridgehead near Colmar.[4]

In spite of the immense fire preparation, the American attack on boths sides of Aachen achieved only minor success.[5] A breach east of Geilenkirchen was most unpleasant. To eliminate the danger, *Supreme Command–West* released *XLVII Panzer Corps* with the *9th Panzer* and *15th Panzer-Grenadier Divisions.*[6] An attack on 17 November east of Geilenkirchen conducted by only the *9th Panzer Division* could not get through.[7] Nevertheless, the deployment of the Corps on both sides of this town prevented the American penetration toward Linnich.[8]

The *116th Panzer Division* already received orders on the evening of 15 November to keep its battleworthy units prepared to march as reaction forces.

The paragraph referring to the enemy in the corresponding Division order was as follows:

Heavy enemy bomb attacks in the vicinity of Stolberg–Eschweiler–Weisweiler, reinforced enemy artillery fire along the whole front up to the Kommerscheidt–Schmidt area, and according to a reliable source, detected pairing of close air support squadrons with certain armored and infantry divisions, lead to expect the beginning of the enemy's major offensive in the vicinity of Aachen.[9]

The next evening, the first reaction force was called up. *"Group von Manteuffel,"* the codename for the *15th Army,* took over the sector of *5th Panzer Army* on 15 November. On the next day, at 1905 hours, it made a combat group of the *116th Panzer Division* available to *LXXXI Corps.*[10] It was to consist of one tank battalion, one armored personnel carrier-borne infantry battalion, one artillery battery, and one engineer company.[11] Under the command of *Oberst* Bayer, the Division sent the *1st Battalion, Panzer Regiment 24* (19 Panthers), the depleted *Armored Reconnaissance Battalion 116* (without reconnaissance units), but reinforced with combat-ready units from *1st Battalion* of *Panzer-Grenadier Regiment 60,* the *5th Battery* of *Armored Artillery Regiment 146,* and the *3d Company* of *Armored Engineer Battalion 675,* its armored personnel carrier-borne company. *Oberst* Bayer was to report to the command post of the *12th Volks-Grenadier Division* in Lamersdorf. His combat group was ordered to march to Langerwehe, to be prepared to defend there against the enemy that attacked Hastenrath and Hamich.[12]

The 16th Infantry Regiment of the 1st Infantry Division, known from Aachen, was fighting near Hamich; Combat Command B of the 3d Armored Division, also an old opponent of the *116th Panzer Division,* fought near Hastenrath. Between these two units was the 47th Infantry Regiment of the 9th Infantry Division, which was attached to the 1st Infantry Division; it mission was to seize Gressenich. Thanks to the brave defense by the *12th Volks-Grenadier Division,* up to the morning of 17 November, only Gressenich, Werth, and Scherpenseel had been lost. The dominating high ridge from Hamich to the northwest remained in German hands.[13]

The attack by the 4th Infantry Division against the *LXXIV Corps' 275th Infantry Division* between Schevenhütte and Hürtgen also had only marginal success. Here again, vicious forest battles took place, as in previous battles in this area. The 8th Infantry Regiment was only able to penetrate the German positions at the boundary between the two corps at the extreme right wing of the *275th Infantry Division,* but it suffered high losses.[14] Since the *275th Infantry Division* lacked an infantry reserve, a second combat group was ordered up from the *116th Panzer Division.* For this, the Division allocated the remnants of both of its *Panzer-Grenadier* Regiments, under the command of *Oberstleutnant* Grollmann. The group was of approximately battalion strength. It consisted of the staff from *Panzer-Grenadier Regiment 156,* the staff from *2d Battalion, Panzer-Grenadier Regiment 156* with two rifle companies each from *Regiments 60* and *156,* as well as the *8th Company, Panzer-Grenadier Regiment 156* as a "heavy weapons group" under the staff of *2d Battalion, Panzer-Grenadier Regiment 60.*[15] Apparently, units from the *Panzerjäger* Battalion were ordered to follow.[16]

Group Grollmann, approaching via Gürzenich, was deployed during the night of 17/18 November west of the Schwarzenbroich cloister ruins. There, it sealed off the breach of the 4th Infantry Division's 8th Infantry Regiment.[17] During the period from 18 to 21 November, it repulsed numerous attacks in heavy fighting. On 18 November, contact with the adjacent unit on the right was lost. There, the 26th Infantry Regiment of the 1st Infantry Division fought its way up to Laufenburg Castle against *Grenadier Regiment 115* of the newly-inserted *47th Volks-Grenadier Division.*[18] On 19 November, contact was reestablished near the Franzosenkreuz. From there, the forward line ran almost exactly south to the hill northeast of the junction of the Roter and Weisser Wehbach.[19] South of it, in the *275th Infantry Division* sector, the most dangerous breach developed. It was aiming toward Grosshau.[20]

On 19 November, the *275th* was relieved by the newly-brought-up *344th Infantry* (formerly the *91st Air Landing*) *Division.* The changeover was completed on 21 November.[21] On the same day, *Group Grollmann* also left the battlefield and returned to the Division.[22] In these battles, *Hauptmann* Banaski, commander of the units allocated from *2d Battalion* of *Panzer-Grenadier Regiment 60,* especially distinguished himself. Even though his troops were just put together from the remnants of the Vossenack battles, he advanced at the front of a platoon and succeeded in taking "back five bunkers occupied by the enemy in the heaviest forest fighting."[23] The efforts of *Leutnant* Schalon from *7th Company, Panzer-Grenadier Regiment 156,* were also mentioned with praise. He received the German Cross in Gold.[24]

After the relief of the *275th,* the *Armored Artillery Regiment 146,* together with the Army anti-aircraft battalion, remained with the *344th Infantry Division* until it was relieved on the morning of 26 November by units from *Volks-Artillery Corps 405.* Only *5th Battery* was pulled out on the evening of 16 November, and attached to *Group Bayer.* On 18 November, six twin-engine bombers attacked and destroyed the firing position of the *6th Battery,* which was deployed in the southerm part of Gey. The rest was pulled out, and with it the staff of *2d Battalion.* The remaining *4th Battery* was subordinated to *3d Battalion.* On 23 November, the staffs of *2d* and *3d Battalions* exchanged their roles. The *3d Battery* of *1st Battalion* was pulled out and relinquished its guns to *2d Battery.* At the end, the regiment's firing positions were at the east bank of the Roer.[25]

During these days, *Group Bayer* probably had the most unpleasant task of all the combat groups from the *116th Panzer Division* of *LXXXI Corps.* As mentioned, it was subordinated to the *12th Volks-Grenadier Division,* which actually should have been relieved by the newly-arriving *47th Volks-Grenadier Division* during the night of 16/17 November, but this was delayed. Not until the night of 18/19 November did the *47th Volks-Grenadier Division* take over the left sector of the *12th* from Hastenrath up to the left corps boundary, northeast of Schevenhütte. There, it linked up with *Group Grollmann* fighting near the Franzosenkreuz within the framework of the *275th Infantry Division.* This put *Group Bayer* under the command of the *47th Volks-Grenadier Division.*[26] On the morning of 17 November, Bayer reported the following battle strengths to *LXXXI Corps*:

— Staff, *Panzer Regiment 16*: 5 officers, 8 NCOs, 43 enlisted men.

— *1st Battalion, Panzer Regiment 24*: 11 officers, 61 NCOs, 143 enlisted men, 17 *Panzer Vs,* 1 *Panzer V* command vehicle, 1 *Panzer IV* anti-aircraft tank, 3 four-barrelled anti-aircraft guns, and 2 engineer armored personnel carriers.

— *Armored Reconnaissance Battalion 116* (without recon units): 6 officers, 19 NCOs, 176 enlisted men, 13 machine guns, 4 medium mortars, 6 3.7cm anti-tank guns, 1 7.5cm anti-tank gun, 4 three-barrelled anti-aircraft guns.

— *5th Battery, Armored Artillery Regiment 146*: 3 Officers, 24 NCOs, 80 enlisted men, 3 light field howitzers with 300 rounds.

— *3d Company, Armored Engineer Battalion 675*: two Officers, 12 NCOs, 74 enlisted men, 17 light and 2 heavy machine guns, 2 medium mortars, 1 rocket launcher.[27]

Bayer further reported that the units from the *1st Battalion* of *Panzer-Grenadier Regiment 60* had not yet arrived. Bayer's command post was located in Jüngersdorf. At 0830 hours, he received an order from the *12th Volks-Grenadier Division* to report to the commander of *Grenadier Regiment 48*. At 1550 hours, the Division reported to corps that *Group Bayer* had been pulled forward to mop up an eventual breach near Hamich. At 1825 hours, the Division commander, *Generalmajor* Engel, informed corps headquarters that Bayer's unit was deployed with seven tanks near *Grenadier Regiment 48*, and with three tanks each, north and south of Heistern. *Armored Reconnaissance Battalion 116* and the *3d Company* of *Armored Engineer Battalion 675* were moved forward with the tanks. The advance by *Group Bayer* suffered from enemy fighter bomber action, even with an overcast sky on that day. The anti-aircraft weapons from the *Panzer* Regiment shot down two of the aircraft.[28]

The next day, 18 November, developed as a day of the heaviest fighting for *Group Bayer. Rittmeister* Weidemann's book includes the following:

On the morning of 18 November, *Oberleutnant* von Quadt and his tanks take up position west of the road on a dominating hill, north of Hamich, to engage enemy tanks in an assembly area north of Gressenich which had been identified from here. The Americans also recognize the significance of this hill. Quite soon, it is under massive and still-increasing artillery fire. Our tanks, "like being served on a platter," are getting hit over and over, even receive direct hits, catch fire, burn, are immobilized, and finally are forced to give up their positions, which shortly therafter are taken by the pursuing American infantry. One still-battleworthy tank returns from this operation![29]

Hill 232, northwest of Hamich, was the dominating hill that was lost. It was taken by the 2d Battalion, 16th Infantry Regiment on the afternoon of 18 November, while the regiment's 3d Battalion again attacked Hamich and entered the village.[30] To counteract this, *Leutnant* Turowski's Panther platoon, together with the infantry, were able to retake the town.[31]

The daily report of *12th Volks-Grenadier Division* from 18 November states that in the sector of *Grenadier Regiment 48*, the southern part of Hamich changed owners several times and that a counterattack with the deployment of *Combat Group Bayer* was under way.[32] According to American sources, this attack took place in darkness, between 2150 and 2330 hours. *Major* Stephan, commander of *Armored Reconnaissance Battalion 116*, reported after the war that he received orders from *Generalmajor* Engel to attack Hamich and to take it.[33] Because of the enemy's dominance of the air, Stephan suggested not mounting the attack until the onset of darkness. This was agreed upon. Stephan continues:

> Along with an attached tank company, the battalion occupied its position in a forest south of the railroad by Langerwehe. When darkness set in, riding on armored vehicles and tanks, the battalion raced toward the town of Hamich, about two kilometers away. This attack came as such a surprise to the enemy that he left everything behind and fled the town. The town was taken and, as agreed upon, handed over to the infantry battalion that was following.
>
> About an hour passed when devastating enemy artillery fire came down. It seemed as if the entire enemy artillery in area the Aachen had received orders for "concentrated fire on Hamich." The commander's vehicle was the first to receive a direct hit by a phosphorous shell, which killed both radiomen and the driver immediately, while the commander was unhurt. Two tanks and several armored vehicles also received direct hits and caught fire. After a barrage of about 20 minutes, enemy infantry attacked. There were so many casualties of both soldiers and vehicles that the battalion had to withdraw from the town. While on its way there, the infantry battalion that was to occupy the town was destroyed by enemy artillery fire. Again, due to enemy fire superiority, a victory was ruined, many wounded, high losses of lives and materiel were inflicted on the battalion.

On 18 November, 15 battalions of American artillery fired 5,350 shells on Hamich; this amounted to almost two-thirds of the normal daily expenditure of the whole German *LXXXI Corps*.[34]

The description of the battles of Hamich by Weidemann places the emphasis a little differently. According to that, *Rittmeister* Böke, with the platoon of *Oberleutnant* Abt, advanced to Turowski in Hamich. Böke's command tank was destroyed by a direct hit. The description continues:

> Despite several hours of barrage, our tanks who are jointly fighting with our brave *Grenadiers* [probably *Armored Reconnaissance Battalion 116—Author*] in Hamich, have succeeded in repelling the repeated attacks by the enemy and to hold on to the town. During the following day, when the massive artillery fire causes more complete losses, and the other tanks, due to their damages, can no longer be used in battle, the tanks, by order of combat group, are being pulled out out of Hamich.[35]

In the battles of Hamich on 18 November, *Rittmeister* Böke and *Wachtmeister* Lenz of *1st Battalion, Panzer Regiment 24,* distinguished themselves particularly. Twelve enemy tanks were destroyed and six of our own lost.[36]

According to *Supreme Command–West* on 19 November, the climax of the battle of Aachen was apparent. However, the breakthrough could be prevented.[37] On this day, the 1st Infantry Division pushed via Hamich toward Heistern, and in the forest east of it, got close to Laufenburg Castle.[38] A battalion supported by four tanks attacked Heistern. Only the remnants of *Combat Group Bayer,* a few tanks of *1st Battalion, Panzer Regiment 24,* and the *3d Company* of *Armored Engineer*

Battalion 675 fought against them. As per the report by the commander of the *47th Volks-Grenadier Division,* infantry was not available.[39] In the late morning, *Armored Reconnaissance Battalion 116* had been pulled out and ordered to march north to the *246th Volks-Grenadier Division.* It was there that corps expected the main effort of the enemy attack. The strength of the battalion still consisted of 100 men (40 men with armored personnel carriers and six self-propelled 7.5cm anti-tank guns).[40] Weidemann reported about the fighting between Hamich and Heistern:

> Hamich can no longer be held. The Americans are already at the southern edge of Heistern. His infantry, supported by tanks, achieved a penetration along the road up to three kilometers before Langerwehe. During the following days, bitter fighting rages at Heistern; already encircled by the Americans, the town is again freed by the engineers. Enemy tanks rolling forward along the hills further west are forced to turn around by our "security" tank; one "Sherman" was destroyed.[41]

On 19 November, Bayer had two battleworthy tanks available.[42] On this evening, *LXXXI Corps* formed a corps reserve west of Jülich, behind the *246th Volks-Grenadier Division.* It consisted of *Grenadier Regiment 48, Füsilier Battalion 12,* both from the *12th Volks-Grenadier Division,* and *Armored Reconnaissance Battalion 116.*[43]

At 1945 hours, corps was told it would receive one tank destroyer company from the *116th Panzer Division.* Headquarters *15th Army* ordered that it was only to be deployed jointly with infantry. On 20 November at 0300 hours, the commander of *Panzerjäger Battalion 228, Major* Bochnig, reported to corps headquarters. His twelve tank destroyers stood combat ready in Arnoldsweiler. They were moved forward as corps reserve into the vicinity of Langerwehe–Luchem. Deployment with the *12th* and *47th Volks-Grenadier Divisions* had to be prepared, and liaison with the command post of the *47th Division* had to be maintained.[44]

In the morning, deployment of the tank destroyers had already become necessary. The enemy, the *1st Infantry Division,* attacked with four regiments along the whole front between Laufenburg and Nothberg. The tank destroyers were pulled forward to the eastern edge of Langerwehe and released for deployment against the enemy, who was attacking on both sides of the Bovenberger Forest. At 1547 hours, *Generalmajor* Engel reported to corps that they should attack via Bovenberg, on both sides of the forest, and free the area. In the evening, it was said that a counterattack by the *12th Volks-Grenadier Division* with the *Panzerjäger Battalion* of the *116th Panzer Division* and all available forces was mounted against the enemy breach in the Bovenberger Forest. There is no report about the success of the attack, but with support from a combat command of the 3d Armored Division, the enemy was not able to gain posssession of Hücheln (500 meters northeast of Bovenberg) until 24 November. This points to at least a complete success in the defense of this area. However, on 20 November, Wenau and Laufenburg Castle fell. The battle of Heistern has already been portrayed: During the night of 20/21 November, the town was lost for good.[45] In *The Siegfried Line Campaign,* it is noted:

> As often happened, the Germans in a swift and futile counterattack had wasted the very troops who in a stationary defense might have prolonged the fight considerably.[46]

On 20 November, the situation that developed further north was substantially more critical than that in the Eschweiler–Wenau area. The enemy penetrated deeply between Gereonsweiler and Aldenhoven; Geilenkirchen was lost.[47]

On 21 November, *LXXXI Corps* again reported attacks along the whole corps front.[48] *Supreme Command–West* discerned the main effort near Eschweiler.[49] The 21 November order from *15th Army* permitted withdrawing the front back to the line Bourheim (due southwest of Jülich)–Pattern–Fronhoven–Dürwiss, and the evacuation of the Eschweiler salient. Simultaneously, *Combat Group Bayer* had to be pulled out as army reserve and placed on standby in Lucherberg (three kilometers northeast of Langerwehe). During 22 November, Bayer was not moved back to Lucherberg, but to Mariaweiler. In the evening, he reported his strength: six Panthers, one command tank, four light field howitzers and the remnants of *3d Company, Armored Engineer Battalion 675* with three NCOs and nineteen men.[50] On 21 November, Staff Paymaster Wolff-Boenisch wrote in his diary, "Except for a few enlisted men, our *3d Company,* deployed in the Hürtgen forest, has been captured along with its commander and officers."[51]

This must have happened during the battle of Heistern on 19 and 20 November.

On the morning of 22 November, *2d Battalion, Panzer Regiment 16* received orders to push its battleworthy tanks forward into the area northeast of Buir. The battalion commander was to relieve *Rittmeister* Böke during the night of 22/23 November. The order was canceled in the evening. Instead, the battalion received orders to relocate to the area northeast of München-Gladbach [Today, Mönchen-Gladbach—*Translator*]. The entire Division now was to be reconstituted; the units still deployed were to be pulled out and were to follow into this area.[52] On 22 November, the situation of *LXXXI Corps* in the Linnich–Jülich area improved because the newly arrived *340th Volks-Grenadier Division* relieved the very battered *246th Volks-Grenadier Division.* The *12th* and *47th Volks-Grenadier Divisions* essentially held their positions. The corps daily report mentioned a barrage of unprecedented force.[53] *Supreme Command–West* declared the main effort of the battles of this day to be the assault by the enemy toward the Roer, between Linnich and Jülich. This headquarters figured our losses since 16 November to be 12,000 men, and estimated enemy losses to be 20,000 men and 320 tanks.[54]

On 23 November at 0100 hours, *15th Army* informed *LXXXI Corps* that they had to reckon with giving up *Group Bayer* during the night to 24 November. It ordered that the tank destroyers of the *116th Panzer Division* be brought up to *Bayer* in Mariaweiler. The *12th Volks-Grenadier Division* was very distressed when it received the order to give up the tank destroyers, because they formed its right flank protection south of Pützlohn (about four kilometers northeast of Eschweiler) where they destroyed an enemy tank.[55] It is not clear if the tank destroyers ever got to Bayer in Mariaweiler. On 23 November, at 0935 hours, *15th Army* ordered them alerted and sent them to Geich (three kilometers east of Langerwehe). At 1005, the *12th Volks-Grenadier Division* reported that five of seven tank destroyers had become stuck near Merberich (one kilometer west of Langerwehe) and could not get restarted on their own. To haul them out, 18-ton tractors were requested.[56]

Now, a tug-of-war started for Bayer and the tank destroyers. The Commander-in-Chief of the *15th Army, General der Infanterie* von Zangen, encountered tank destroyers on his way to the rear, allegedly with the objective being München-Gladbach, and ordered them to stop. At 1059 hours, Corps ordered the *47th Volks-Grenadier Division* to keep *Group Bayer* at the disposal of Army Group in Mariaweiler; the corps is said to have requested release. Toward 1130 hours, Zangen appeared at *LXXXI Corps* and gave the order to find out if the commander of the tank destroyers had received orders to march to Mariaweiler. If not, a summary of evidence was to be submitted, and he could possibly face a court-martial.[57] Since during the night, it had been *15th Army* itself which ordered the tank destroyers to be brought up to Bayer—who was in Mariaweiler—a trial would have become superfluous.

At 1200 hours, Army headquarters gave the order to advance *Group Bayer* to Langerwehe. At 1625 hours, *Group Bayer* was released, subordinated to the *47th Volks-Grenadier Division* and deployed to seize Rösslershof (1,700 meters west-southwest of Langerwehe). Rösslershof was lost at noon. A deep breach threatened the boundary between the *12th* and the *47th Volks-Grenadier Divisions.* The order for Bayer was about like this, "*Combat Group* frees Rösslershof and defends on both sides of it against enemy advancing north."[58]

Weidemann offers the following description of the course of battle:

> On 23 November, at 1830 hours, *Rittmeister* Böke receives orders from commander of the *47th Volks-Grenadier Division* to recapture "Rössler Hof," which was taken by the enemy in the afternoon. He was to deploy the three remaining battleworthy Panthers and the still available command tank. Since there are enemy tanks near the farm houses, the *Grenadiers* stop 50 meters in front of them, due to lack of weapons with which to fight tanks at short range. Even as the battalion commander refers to the difficulties of such a night attack with tanks, the *General* adheres to his given order. At 1900 hours, our tanks attack; the *Grenadiers,* although informed of our plan, remain in their holes; at 1945 hours, our tanks stand there, in complete darkness, all by themselves in front of the farm, in whose courtyard, like in a cage, the enemy tanks "rumble."

For moments, flares cover the battle ground with their eerie flickering light. Our tanks cannot drive in, because the entrance is too narrow! Now, the enemy artillery fire, probably requested and controlled by the Americans in the inner courtyard, starts hitting directly in front of the farm and in the adjacent forest. For our tanks that were forced to stand still, but presumably also for the enemy tanks inside the farm complex, a witch's cauldron develops. Two commanders with their vehicles attempt to fire near the entrance; the effect of the fire from enemy tanks forces them to break off this firefight; the two other tanks are damaged by artillery hits. At 2015 hours, four no-longer-battleworthy tanks roll back to their starting positions, after attempts to burn down the farm by gunfire were not successful either. But earlier, the enemy tanks were "taken care of" with *Panzerfausts* by the dismounted *Leutnant* Wolter and his men.[59]

The order from *15th Army* on 23 November stated the following:

> The *116th Panzer Division* is being relocated as Army Group Reserve for replenishing in area Viersen–Erkelenz–Liedberg (towns inclusive)–Neuss–Krefeld (towns exclusive).
>
> Upon arrival, subordinated to *Group von Manteuffel* for personnel and logistical arrangements.
>
> Order for Bayer follows.[60]

For now, *Group Bayer*, including the tank destroyers, was to remain in Langerwehe as Army reserve. However, elements evidently remained deployed with *12th Volks-Grenadier Division*; *Oberleutnant* Borgert then noted in his diary that on 24 November an attack was mounted through a minefield near Lamersdorf.[61]

On 24 November, *Supreme Command–West* reported, "Major defensive battle at Aachen close to a decision."[62]

It was considered providing *LXXXI Corps* with eight Panthers from *1st Battalion, Panzer Regiment 16* that had meanwhile arrived from Grafenwöhr. Thank God, *Feldmarschall* Model did not release the tanks![63]

On the evening of this day, corps received orders to release the last twelve engineers from *3d Company, Armored Engineer Regiment 675* and to start marching them to the battalion.[64] The fight for Bayer's remaining units went on. On 25 November at 1745 hours, *15th Army* finally gave orders that by the evening of 26 November, all units were be released, with Böke and the engineers already released on 25 November.[65] On the morning of 26 November, *LXXXI Corps* reported that all units from the *116th Panzer Division* had been released.[66] This may not have been exactly true in the case of the tank destroyers, because Borgert maintained that he was still in the Lamersdorf–Frenz area on 25 and 26 November, and was not released before 27 November.[67] *Armored Artillery Regiment 146* and *Army Anti-Aircraft Battalion 281* reached the new Division area in the course of 26 November.[68]

The battles abated by the end of November/beginning of December. To that point, the American major offensive reached a line that ran from the area north of Geilenkirchen east toward the Roer near Linnich, then along the Roer to south of Jülich, from there south toward Langerwehe. It continued along the eastern edges of the forests south toward Gey, which was still in German hands. From there it continued toward Bergstein. Hürtgen, which was so heavily embattled during the fighting by the *116th Panzer Division* in the first half of November, fell on 28 November, and Kleinhau on the next day. Brandenberg and Bergstein followed in the beginning of December. Between 10 and 16 December, VII Corps advanced its front almost everywhere between Jülich and Bergstein to the Roer. However, all in all, the offensive was a failure. In one month, it gained only local terrain, but it missed its objective, the Rhine, by a great deal.

Further north, the British were able to bring the German Venlo bridgehead to a collapse. A planned attack east of the Maas, between the Maas and Geilenkirchen, did not take place because Montgomery deemed the ground to be too soggy. On 7 December, Eisenhower, Montgomery, and Bradley met in Maastricht and set a date for a new offensive toward the Rhine for mid-January 1945. The British were to push southeast from Nijmegen, the American armies (Ninth, First, and Third) across a broad front east toward the Rhine. Thereafter, the encirclement of the Ruhr region was planned with two armies each from north and south.

With the approach toward the Roer, the American side raised the fear that the Germans could flood the river valley by opening the reservoirs to make the crossing considerably more difficult. Therefore, the attempt was made to destroy the dams from the air.

That failed. After this, they were to be taken by attack. For this, on 13 December, V Corps attacked Kesternich (eight kilometers southwest of Schmidt) and also toward Dreiborn from the southwest. Until 15 December, only modest successes could be claimed. The offensive was stopped by 16 December.[69] For the time being, all plans of the western Allies were shelved. The German side took the initiative.

Chapter 9

The Ardennes Offensive

Part 1: Planning and Preparation

Since the American breakthrough at Avranches on 31 July 1944, Hitler had been looking for ways to turn the situation in the West to the better by counterattacks. However, the armored divisions needed for such a plan had been worn out earlier in static defense. Therefore, all attempts to seize the initiative failed; the first attempt was the German counterattack at Mortain on 7 August. The initial consideration of a decisive counterattack with new forces can be traced back to 19 August. On that day, when *7th Army* was encircled in the Falaise cauldron and prepared to break out, *Generaloberst* Jodl noted in his dairy, "19 August. *Führer* discusses situation West. . . . Prepare for offensive in November, when the enemy is unable to fly. Basic requirements, about 25 divisions must go to the West in one to two months."[1]

On 6 September, while the German Army in the West streamed back toward the border of the *Reich* without stopping:

> the *Führer* agreed with the judgment of the Chief of *WF* Staff (Armed Forces Operations Staff) whereby a decisive, major attack in the west would not be possible before 1 November and that it is now important to pull out as many units as possible for replenishment, and to get them battleworthy by then.[2]

After the morning meeting of 16 September, for the first time Hitler spoke to a larger group about his plans for the West. The personal diary of the former Chief of Staff of the *Luftwaffe*, *General der Flieger* Kreipe, provides the following information:

> Special conference in small circle. . . . Decision by the *Führer*, counterattack from the Ardennes, objective Antwerp. Forces to be balanced between positions and strength of defense. Present front is easy to defend. Our attack group: 30 new *Volks-Grenadier* divisions and new *Panzer* divisions, in addition *Panzer* divisions from the east.
>
> Rip open boundary between the English and the Americans, a new Dunkirk. Guderian objects, because of situation in the East. . . .
>
> Request by Hitler for 1,500 fighter planes by 1 November! . . . Offensive to be carried out during period of bad weather, the opponent then cannot fly either.[3]

On 18 September, Kreipe noted, "*OKH* (*Oberkommando des Heeres*, or the Army High Command) has most serious concern about plan for the Ardennes."

The negative attitude of *OKH* was more than understandable. The Eastern Front between East Prussia and the Carpathian Mountains, which had been entrusted to this headquarters, had been somewhat stabilized, but in the area of Hungary, the Soviets advanced farther and Army Group North in Kurland was threatened with encirclement. There were no reserves. New formations that were considered for occupying the fortifications in the East had to be placed at the disposal of the West. With their help, it was possible to basically defend the *Westwall.*

Hitler's plan to go over to the offensive in the West required the East to almost completely forfeit the supply of newly established or replenished units as well as personnel and materiel replacements.[4] *OKH* expected a new, major offensive in the East by the onset of winter. Therefore, it was important to mount the attack in the West, if at all, rather soon; strong forces could then be sent back to the East again in time for other contingencies. This was the only way *OKH* could come to terms with this plan.

Hitler's objective was the destruction of a considerable proportion of the Anglo-American formations. He believed that he could achieve success with about thirty attack divisions in the main effort against the approximately sixty enemy divisions that were spread out along the whole front from the *Scheldt* up to the Swiss border. Such an offensive would weaken the Western Allies for a long time. Hitler hoped to gain time, and to shake the belief of his enemies in total victory to the extent that they would relinquish their demand for unconditional surrender. At the same time, he promised himself an invigoration of the will to persevere in the German people and in his *Wehrmacht.*[5]

On 12 October, *Supreme Command–West* received the first order to "explain the preparation for the operation and at the same time to conceal it."[6] The emplacements of attack units were camouflaged as formations of reserves for the upcoming defensive battle; these remained *OKW* reserves, as did the arriving supply of materiel. While the replenishment of four *SS-Panzer* divisions and the *Panzer Lehr Division* was already finalized to a large extent in October, the tactical situations of the *2d, 9th,* and *116th Panzer Divisions,* as well as the *10th SS-Panzer Division*, only allowed replenishment close to the front in November.[7] However, this also did not take place, except in the case of the *2d Panzer Division*. The battles in the Aachen area forced the employment of these divisions in action.

On 1 November, Jodl sent the "basic thoughts" of Operation WACHT AM RHEIN ["Watch on the Rhine," the title of a 19th-century German patriotic song—*Editor*] to *Supreme Command–West.* He remarked that Hitler's basic ideas were not yet an order, but, "unchangeable is the risk of the major objective which, looked at theoretically, seems to be out of proportion with our available forces.

But in our present situation, we must not be afraid to stake everything on one card."[8]

That objective was outlined in the "basic thoughts" as follows, "The objective of the operation is the destruction of the enemy north of the line Antwerp–Brussels–Bastogne." The *6th Panzer Army* is to seize the Maas crossings undamaged on both sides of Lüttich and then, by building a defensive line oriented northward, push on to Antwerp. As the first objective, the Maas east of Namur was given to *5th Panzer Army,* which was later to protect the rear of *6th Panzer Army* along the line Antwerp–Brussels–Namur–Dinant. The *7th Army* was assigned to protect the flank of the entire operation toward the south and southwest. At the same time, *OKW* issued very strict directives for secrecy.[9] These rules proved valuable since the enemy did not recognize the significance of the deployment of the troop concentration. However, the rules limited the preparations of the attacking troops, making a penetration of the enemy's most forward positions more difficult.

On 3 November, Rundstedt commented on the "basic thoughts."[10] He expressed some concerns and proposed a second attack from the area north of Aachen "at once, in other words, simultaneously" with the main thrust. Ultimately, however, Rundstedt accepted the plan and wrote, "It is clear to me . . . that now we have to stake everything on one card. This is why I retract my concerns."

On 10 November, Hitler issued the "order for marshalling and preparation for the attack."[11] He maintained the "basic thoughts," but partially agreed with Rundstedt's suggestion to also attack at Aachen, but not "immediately." Hitler increased the armies involved by adding *15th Army* and gave it the following order:

> First, *15th Army* to take over the front between the Roer and Maas from *6th Panzer Army* and thereby secures the Maas crossing of *6th Panzer Army* at northern flank and rear. Its further task is to tie down the strong enemy forces in the area north of Roermond–Lüttich–east of Eupen with numerous individual attacks from north, east, and south, and at the very end to breakthrough and destroy them.

The first paragraph of the order now read as follows:

> Objective of the operation is to achieve a decisive turn of the campaign in the West, and thereby perhaps even for the entire war, by destroying the enemy forces north of the line Antwerp–Brussels–Luxembourg. I have decided to follow through with the execution of the operation by taking the greatest risk, even if the enemy attack on both sides of Metz and the upcoming thrust to the Ruhr area should lead to large losses of terrain and positions.

The assembly was to be concluded by 27 November. From the assembly, units were to arrive at their preparation areas "in no more than three nights." According to changes in the weather, units had to be able to halt movement on short notice, because when it came to the enemy's air superiority, other than the element of surprise, the weather was the most important prerequisite for the success of the operation. The "guidelines for the course of attack of Operation WACHT AM RHEIN followed on 18 November."[12] They contained detailed instructions about the selection of time of attack; the action of the artillery; the organization of the attack troops; the attainment of the breakthrough and the conduct of the subsequent advance "to and across the Maas"; and the cooperation with *Luftwaffe* and logistical support. Their ultimate results can be found in the still more detailed "directives for course of battle" from *5th Panzer Army*.[13] An excerpt is added as Appendix 16. This is indicative of all that was ordered and everything that was imposed on the divisions at the last minute.

Back to the preparation of the operation! On 16 November, Model reported his intent for the conduct of the offensive.[14] Beside surprise, he pronounced sustainment of the attack as a prerequisite for success, and therefore requested nine to ten more divisions. In the event that developments in Lorraine and around Aachen forced a premature deployment of attack units, Model suggested a surprise counterattack against the enemy, who was battle weary after the "unsuccessful breakthrough battle in the larger area of Aachen." Rundstedt forwarded Model's suggestion to *OKW* and requested that Model "now already be given fundamental freedom of action . . . even for the short-term start of the attack." This was the beginning of the dispute about a "little solution." The major American offensive at Aachen on 16 November provided Model with grounds to point out the extensive ongoing engagement of forces—including the *116th Panzer Division*—and he renewed his request for his little solution. As he said, he wanted to capture a fat sparrow first, and then the pigeon.[15]

Rundstedt accepted Model's proposal. It promised him that he could "with certainty destroy a group of strong enemy forces, "to create a "safe prerequisite" for the big solution and to achieve a strong "psychological effect."[16] *OKW* declined these proposals.[17] Meanwhile, not only did the American offensive near Aachen gnaw at the strength of *Supreme Command–West,* but the attacks in Lorraine and Alsace did, too. The front of *Army Group G* was close to collapse. Requests by *Supreme Command–West* for the release of forces fell on the almost deaf ears of *OKW*. However, on 11 November, the *Panzer Lehr Division* was released [to *Army Group G—Editor*] to push into the flank of the American attack through the Saverne Gap.[18] It had only minor success.

On 26 November, Jodl went to see *Supreme Command–West*. Again they wrestled with the question of whether the big solution could be carried out. Jodl wrote in his diary, "1. The big solution remains. 2. Missing units must be procured."[19]

Besides this, it was decided to postpone the commencement of the attack; 10 December was now being considered.

On 29 November, *Army Group B* presented its operation order under the name of *HERBSTNEBEL* ["Autumn Fog"—*Translator*].[20] This plan included a chronologically-staggered deployment of *15th Army,* with the *116th Panzer Division* still part of it, although only in the new draft of the order from 4 December was the *116th* assigned to *5th Panzer Army* for deployment with *LVIII Panzer Corps*.[21] After the beginning of the offensive, Hitler completely abandoned the plan for the attack by *15th Army*. Available mobile units were ordered to follow the *Panzer* armies.[22]

On 2 December, Hitler discussed the execution of the operation with Model and Westphal, as well as with both *Panzer* army commanders, *SS-Oberstgruppenführer* Dietrich and *General der Panzertruppe* von Manteuffel.[23] Model took this opportunity for a last attempt for the "little solution," but in vain. The time of attack was also discussed. Model suggested 0800 because the attack troops were not sufficiently trained for night attacks; Hitler, however, decided on 0530 hours. On 11 December, Hitler permitted the postponement of the day of attack to 15 December, and on 12 December, he allowed a further postponement to 16 December. This was due to the still-insufficient fuel supply.[24]

Hitler gave a speech for all troop leaders from the attack units. In two groups they were ordered to come to the *Führer*'s headquarters, the *"Adlerhorst"* ["Eagle's Nest"—*Translator*] near Bad Nauheim, where Hitler had been since 10 December. *Generalmajor* von Waldenburg was present on 11 December and was awarded the Knight's Cross by Hitler.[25] He had already been promoted to *Generalmajor* on 3 December and appointed Division Commander.[26] There is a written record of the *Führer*'s 12 December speech which affords a glimpse into Hitler's patterns of thought and argumentation.[27] The speech did not fail to impress the audience, in spite of many absurdities that are recognizable today.

The last attempt to change destiny in the West, therefore, could not start in November, but only on 16 December. Nevertheless, it was possible to bring the enemy attacks to a halt without having to use too much of our combat strength. It was to be expected that the ongoing enemy attacks would be terminated with the onset of our offensive. Even if the cargo of the first ships to use the port facilities in Antwerp could be unloaded on 28 November—improving the supply situation for the enemy—the prerequisites for the offensive in the West were still adhered to by "taking the greatest risk," in fact, staking "everything on one card." If the risk in the West could be calculated to an extent, in the East, the Soviet winter offensive between East Prussia and the Carpathians was looming. In Hungary, it had already started. Was there hope of moving units back into the east again in time? Were the advantages of interior lines still enough, with the transportation system so badly damaged and the lack of fuel? Hardly! One can well imagine the concerns of *OKH*. War on two fronts takes its toll—for centuries the problem of the defense of the *Reich*!

The *116th Panzer Division* provides an example of how the preparation for the great offensive progressed for the units that were not fortunate enough to enjoy an extended period of rest and replenishment. The previous chapter portrayed the scattered deployment of the troops of the Division in the defensive battle east of Aachen. On 23 November, when the Division received orders to replenish its units in the vicinity of Viersen–Erkelenz–Liedberg–Neuss (exclusive)–Krefeld (exclusive), the remnants of *Group Bayer* and the whole artillery were still in action. They did not return to the Division until 26 November.

Consideration was initially given to carrying out the replenishment in the vicinity of Düren, so that the transfer to the above-mentioned quiet area could be achieved.[28] The Division was not yet fully in the new area, the Division staff being in Gerkerath, Rheindahlen, and Hardt (southwest of München-Gladbach), when it received orders on 25 November to have a reaction force standing by.[29] At the same time, it was directed that the replenishment had to be completed by 28 November.

Model already went to see the Division on 25 November to be informed of the progress of the replenishment and to hasten it.[30] The composition of the reaction force is listed in the journal of *2d Battalion, Armored Artillery Regiment 146* as follows:

> Reaction force of the *116th Panzer Division* with reinforced *Panzer-Grenadier Regiment 60,* one tank company and *2d Battalion, Armored Artillery Regiment 146,* one company of *Armored Reconnaissance Battalion 116,* one company of *Armored Engineer Battalion 675.*
>
> Deployment of reaction force planned for areas of Venlo, Roermond, Heinsberg, Linnich-Jülich. . . .[31]

After an essentially stronger reaction force was ordered on 27 November, its composition was reduced to the above-mentioned units on 1 December. The *Panzer Regiment* had to provide a company with 15 *Panzer IVs* and the *Anti-Aircraft Platoon* from *2d Battalion. Oberleutnant* Erdmann assumed command of this reinforced company.[32] In the evening of the same day, a two-hour march alert was ordered; during the night, the group moved out under command of *Oberstleutnant* Zander.[33]

At midnight, Vogelsang wrote:

> One should celebrate the holidays as they come! Zander from *Panzer-Grenadier Regiment 60* became *Oberstleutnant*; Risse, his Adjutant, received the Knight's Cross. It is such a rare occasion when all commanders and adjutants can get together. In any case, the evening was very stimulating and went by quite nicely.
>
> Unfortunately, the joy was short-lived. An order popped up right in the middle for [*Panzer-Grenadier Regiment*] 60 to march with several tanks, engineers, and an artillery battalion as a reserve against American intentions to attack across the Roer.[34]

The reason for the deployment of the combat group was the Americans' entry into Linnich and the fear of further attacks at the Roer. The group was relocated into the area southeast of Erkelenz as Army Group reserve; it was only to be deployed when the opponent tried to cross the Roer. Its composition and location were as follows:

Panzer-Grenadier Regiment 60 staff and elements of *Panzer Regiment 16* at Kückhoven

1st Battalion, Panzer-Grenadier Regiment 60 at Ralshoven and Gevelsdorf

2d Battalion, Panzer-Grenadier Regiment 60 at Lövenich

2d Battalion, Armored Artillery Regiment 146 with *4th, 5th,* and *8th Batteries* at Bellinghoven, Tenholt, Granterarth

1st Company, Armored Engineer Battalion 675 at Holzweiler.[35]

Unit displacement during the night of 1/2 December proceeded without friction, however, this separation caused problems for replenishment. The commanders were already concerned with reconnoitering different possibilities for deployment for several days before the transfer. Even as the *15th Army*'s defensive battle continued with increasing intensity, the Division's combat group did not get into action. It remained in position until 7 December. *Oberst* von Waldenburg went to see the two corps engaged in the Ruhr sector, *XII SS-Corps* and *XLVII Panzer Corps* to get information about the planned deployment of Group Zander. From the *XII SS-Corps* he learned something about "new plans for deployment."[36] At this time, a deployment with *15th Army* was still planned for *116th Panzer Division.*

The replenishment in personnel and materiel progressed surprisingly quickly. On 22 November, Vogelsang still remarked:

> Since there can hardly be any talk of effective combat strength regarding our depleted units, today at least both of our *Panzer-Grenadier* regiments were released from action. *Armored Reconnaissance Battalion* was to follow. . . .
>
> In response to our urgent request, today we received 300 soldiers from the *Luftwaffe.* They are going to the *Field Replacement Battalion* for training, which in turn will provide 300 trained infantrymen to the units.[37]

On 25 November, Vogelsang wrote, "The announced 600 trained replacement *Grenadiers* have arrived and were assigned."

On 1 December, he noted, "Now, the regiments fortunately were replenished in this short time span, at least in terms of numbers." He adds:

> Meanwhile, word got around in the higher staffs that we train our replacements thoroughly for action before deployment in battle, which increases the battle value and decreases the losses caused by the typically inexperienced. With respect to this, we are supposed to soon receive 1,400 men all at once to replenish the units, as well as to build a reserve within the Division, which until now was not permitted by higher authorities to this extent.
>
> The *Field Replacement Battalion* is now capable at any time of organizing the training of up to 1,000 men as replacements of all kinds.

A few days earlier, Vogelsang visited the *Field Replacement Battalion* and reviewed the Division combat training course. He wrote about this on 19 November:

The live-fire exercise using all infantry weapons was splendidly laid out and was breathtakingly exciting for the spectator. I believe that the combat units receive really well-prepared replacements from here.

On 7 December, we find the following note in Vogelsang's diary:

> To extend the *Field Replacement Battalion* still further by increasing its enrollment ability and training capacity, we have reinforced it by adding more combat-experienced training personnel from the regiments. It now consists of five rifle companies, two heavy weapons companies (heavy machine gun, medium and heavy mortars, anti-tank guns, anti-aircraft guns), one infantry cannon company, one artillery and tank destroyer company, and one combat engineer platoon, besides the earlier special supply and cadre units. Special care was taken to equip the combat course conducted for the training of junior leaders. This is now already the cadre of two battalions!
>
> The *Field Replacement Battalion* once again sent 460 trained men to the units, and after many new arrivals of replacements, now has a head-count of 1,800 men, including a sufficient officer reserve.

On the next day, Vogelsang wrote:

> Crazy world! Last night at three o'clock, the duty officer of the *Field Replacement Battalion* came with the report that on one day 1,800 more replacements had arrived—with the best intentions, this is really beyond our capacity! In a flash, all the food was eaten, and there was not enough transportation available for the increase. Our duty officer had to drive to *Supreme Command–West* at once, to have 600 men transferred to another place—what have they planned that they treat us so well!

All these numbers should not misrepresent the fact that the Division lacked officers and NCOs in the infantry units. In the status report from 1 December, the Division reported about the training situation:

> After assigning the last replacements, the training status of *Panzer-Grenadier Regiments,* the *Armored Reconnaissance Battalion,* and the *Armored Engineer Battalion* is not yet adequate due to the lack of a longer training period.
>
> A period of 14 days would suffice to bring the assigned personnel replacements into a condition suitable for any deployment, in spite of a lack of sufficient and capable NCOs.
>
> Training courses for specialists in all areas are in process. The weak state of health of some of the replacements, mainly the *Grenadier Regiments,* impedes the training that was started with vigor.[38]

Progress regarding equipment was also made.[39] In exchange for the *1st Battalion, Panzer Regiment 24,* which was released for replenishment, our own *1st Battalion* under command of *Major* Tebbe arrived, however, it was not fully equipped with Panthers. It took over the few remaining Panthers from *1st Battalion, Panzer Regiment 24* and on 10 December, had 45 of them. Thirteen were in transit, but arrived too late for the beginning of the offensive. The *2d Battalion* did not look this good. On 24 November, it received 13 new *Panzer IVs* in addition to the eight it had. This was only enough for two weak companies; a third company was to receive assault guns, but these did not reach the Division before the attack on 16 December, either. The tank destroyers, artillery, and anti-aircraft units of the Division were almost fully equipped with their weapons.

On 1 December, the Division reported the following "special difficulties":

a) Lack of winter clothes for the *Grenadier* Regiments in the trenches.
b) Lack of command tanks in the *Panzer* Regiment
c) Lack of NCOs in the *Grenadier* Regiments, the Armored Artillery, and the *Armored Engineer Battalion*.
d) Only 50 percent of the equipment of heavy tonnage for the artillery. Here, help is urgently required.[40]

As "degree of mobility" the Division stated 75 percent. In numbers, this means, among other things, an absence of the following:

432 trucks
111 *"Maultier"* tracked transports
32 tractors of all sizes (1 to 18 tons)

In a status report from *Supreme Command–West* on 10 December about heavy weapons of the *Panzer* divisions in the beginning of December, the numbers of the *116th Panzer Division* look as follows:

	Authorized	On-Hand	Battleworthy	In Transit	Lack	Surplus
Panther	60	45	43	13	2	–
Panzer IV	30	26	26	–	4	–
Assault Guns	45	25	13	14	6	–
Hvy AT Guns	13	19	17	–	–	6
Lt.Fld.How.	19	20	–	–	–	1
Wespe	3	3	–	4	–	4
Hv.Fld.How.	8	8	–	–	–	–
Hummel	9	6	–	2	1	–
10cm Fld. Gun	4	4	–	–	–	–[41]

The "Authorized" quantities do not correspond with the table of organization. Evidently, there was a special "Authorized" quantity for the upcoming offensive, in accordance with the supply possibilities. For example, there were 172 tanks and assault guns authorized by the Table of Organization, as opposed to only 135 here. The "On-Hand" quantity was 96 because the vehicles in transit did not arrive in time.

To strengthen the connection between the population and *Wehrmacht,* and to make the men who worked at the fortifications understand the purpose of their work, the Division was ordered to organize social evenings for the soldiers and workers. These events took place on 3 and 4 December. *Generalmajor* von Waldenburg gave a speech each time.[42]

On 7 December, Vogelsang recorded:

> On one of the last evenings, we were invited with a delegation of officers and front soldiers to a community event *"Landser und Schanzer"* ["(Common) Soldiers and Diggers"—*Translator*], to document the solidarity of worker and front soldier. Besides us, the Commander-in-Chief of the *15th Army* and several generals and general staff officers from Army Group took part.
>
> We were all surprised by the excellent and confident attitude of these workers, who were bombed out in the Ruhr area, the farmers and city folk from the Rhine, who, far away from their families build fortifications, dig foxholes and trenches, from sun-up to sun-down, in rain and in filth.[43]

On 4 December, the Division received orders to relocate southward by railroad. The advance echelon departed on 5 December. These events were reported in the journal of *2d Battalion, Panzer Regiment 16* as follows:

> 4 December, 2300 hours. Still tonight, a transport notification must to be submitted, separated by combat company and other units. *Company Erdmann* marches and rides, respectively, with *Combat Group Zander.*
>
> 5 December, 1000 hours, order arrives that *Hauptmann* Brinkmann is to command the regimental advance echelon. How, where to, why, is still shrouded for now.
>
> 1330 hours, *Hauptmann* Brinkmann comes from regiment and brings the march order for the advance echelon. . . . There is a Divisional release point in Altenahr, and this is where *Hauptmann* Brinkmann is to also install one.
>
> 1400 hours, advance echelon departs for the new area.[44]

The Division command post was established in Altenahr. On 5 December, *Generalmajor* von Waldenburg drove there. He went to see the Division's new superior, the Commanding General of *LVIII Panzer Corps, General der Panzertruppe* Krüger, and *General der Panzertruppe* von Manteuffel, the Commander-in-Chief of *5th Panzer Army.*[45] The Division was subordinated to them as of 5 December. The *5th Panzer Army* was in Manderscheid, *LVIII Panzer Corps* in the Bergfeld hunting castle near Eisenschmidt (eight kilometers southwest of Manderscheid). The *5th Panzer Army* performed its duties under the code name *"Feldjäger-Kommando z.b.V."* ("Military Field Police" *zur besonderen Verwendung,* or "for special use"—*Translator*). Besides the *116th Panzer Division,* the now-approaching *560th Volks-Grenadier Division* was subordinated to corps headquarters, as was—temporarily—the *Führer Escort Brigade.* The subordination of the *11th Panzer Division* was planned, but did not go into effect, because this Division did not arrive.[46]

In the evening of 5 December, Waldenburg wrote in his pocket calendar, "God willing, all things planned will work out. This can get intense!—It may bring the decision."[47]

On 6 December, the transport began, and of the 53 trains that were planned, three departed.[48] Waldenburg noted, "Division transports start slowly. Railroad situation, due to much destruction by enemy air force very difficult!"[49]

On 7 December, *Generalmajor* von Waldenburg drove to the sector of the *26th Volks-Grenadier Division* for the initial reconnaissance. It concentrated mainly on the approach routes. Unfortunately, the impression gained of the attack area was only superficial. I was informed at corps headquarters by the Chief of Staff, *Oberst i.G.* Dingler.[50]

Vogelsang wrote:

> Activity is everywhere, like in a beehive. Army and *Waffen-SS* vehicles with the most varied division insignias are buzzing all over the place on the roads. Something out of the ordinary hangs in the air. What could it be? Nobody knows. (7 December 1944)[51]

At the end of this entry, Vogelsang noted that the Army Personnel Office wanted to transfer the commander of the *Artillery Regiment, Oberst der Reserve* Pean to command a *Volks-Artillery Corps,* which was a very great honor for Pean, but a very undesirable move for the Division at this point in time. The attempts to prevent the transfer failed. Pean left the Division on 15 December and became artillery commander with *LXVI Corps,* the adjacent unit to the right of *LVIII Panzer Corps.* His successor was *Major* ten Hompel, not unknown to the Division because he had served as commander of the *2d Battalion* of the *Artillery Regiment* in Russia.

There were several other changes in personnel during replenishment period. In the Division Staff, the *Ib* and the Division physician were changed. *Major i.G.* Issbrücker arrived to take over for the *Ib, Major i.G.* Wolf, and *Oberfeldarzt* Professor Doctor Bickert arrived and replaced *Oberfeldarzt* Dr. Baselt. *Hauptmann der Reserve* Geigenmüller assumed command of *Panzerjäger Battalion 228* from *Major* Bochnig, who was transferred to the *Oberfähnrichschule* (advanced officer candidate school) at Wischau. The *1st Battalion* of the *Artillery Regiment* was now led by *Hauptmann* Vinke. *Major* Sandkuhl was ordered to the homeland for *IIa* training. *Hauptmann* John became Vinke's successor as Regimental Adjutant.[52] The commander of *2d Battalion, Panzer Regiment 16, Hauptmann der Reserve* Count Brühl, became a *Major* and received a special document of recognition from the *Führer.* On 10 December, Count Brühl, suffering from diphtheria, had to be taken to the field hospital; he was replaced by *Hauptmann* Brinkmann.[53]

On 7 December, the Division command post was moved to Nohn (11 kilometers southwest of Adenau); the *Ib* command post was established in Nürburg. The area into which the Division now entered, the intervention assembly area, can no longer be precisely determined. It was quite large and included approximately the area bordered by the towns Stadtkyll (exclusive)–Antweiler–Döttingen (by the Nürburg Speedway)–Oberelz (eight kilometers southwest of Monreal)–Gerolstein (exclusive).[54]

On 8 December, *Generalmajor* von Waldenburg took part in a planning exercise at corps headquarters in Wittlich.[55] In the afternoon, 12 Lightnings attacked Nohn and set two vehicles afire. Vogelsang noted contently, "They became, however, more careful after the two new self-propelled armored anti-aircraft guns from the *Escort Company* opened fire with four barrels."[56]

Leutnant Schwörer from *2d Battalion, Armored Artillery Regiment 146* probably again found time this day for his diary. He wrote down the following:

> We are being transferred to the Eifel. Reason not yet known. I am driving ahead with the advance party and then probably can well discern the reason. The Eifel area is packed with troops. *SS-Reich, SS-Hohenstaufen, SS-Adolf Hitler, Panzer Lehr,* and our Division.
>
> In addition, there are special units of all sorts. Every little village is filled with them. It looks as though there is no room for even one more person. But it has to work. I have big fights with the stubborn, local offices. Each bed and every kitchen has to be emptied. . . .
>
> When the units arrive, everything will be different anyway, the masses will just come and go in, and nobody can take them out anymore. . . . There are also launching pads for V-1s in our lodging area and many more are under construction. No sooner does the weather clear, than the fighter bombers are here. Have they already noticed something?[57]

On 9 December, *Generalmajor* von Waldenburg took part in a conference at *5th Panzer Army* headquarters in Manderscheid with *Generalfeldmarschall* Model.[58] Sixteen trains carrying the *116th Panzer Division* arrived, with seven more in transit.[59] Waldenburg noted, "Trains arrive very slowly. In Eifel—snow, ice."[60]

Under the assumption that the operation would begin as planned on 14 December, the regimental commanders could be instructed on their tasks on 10 December. This happened at the *116th Panzer Division*. This is why the first moves into the intervention assembly areas already started during the night of 10/11 December. *Anti-Aircraft Battalion 281* and the heavy battalion (*3d Battalion*) of *Armored Artillery Regiment 146* were to advance to their area of emplacement.[61] This only succeeded in part, since some parts of these units had not yet reached the intervention assembly area in the Eifel. On the evening of 12 December, 51 of 53 trains of the *116th Panzer Division* had departed and 34 were unloaded, with 17 still on their way.[62] One-third of the Division was still missing. Vogelsang wrote in his diary:

> Day after day, bomber squadrons passed over us—but we did not actually expect that they would also attack our insignificant nest.
>
> Suddenly, a smaller group turned in our direction and unloaded 40 really large suitcases on our little village. We just had enough time to throw ourselves against the walls of the houses when we heard the whistling of the bombs. But it still went well! Ten 500 kg bombs ripped open the ground east of the house, while the rest plowed the land and street north of the village.
>
> Immediately, the home guard, police and all available infantrymen moved out to make the street passable again. A tedious job, with craters of 20-meters' diameter and five- to eight-meters' depth! Solid walls of mud, stones, and rubble from houses obstructed the road, but by this evening, traffic was moving again, at least on a single lane.
>
> . . . work, work!—but there is success: The Division is well replenished in personnel and materiel. Today we celebrate the award of the Knight's Cross to the Division Commander in his attractive, solid quarters in a forest villa next to the mill in the low ground west of the village.[63]

On 13 December, corps issued its "order for traffic regulation" with the date of 10 December.

In part I: In general, it says among other things:

1. Rigid traffic regulations are the deciding prerequisites for the planned course of every motorized movement.
2. Traffic jams and stagnation during the march, which occur due to difficult road conditions, must be nipped in the bud. . . .
3. During the time of the march, supply and individual traffic is to be carried out during daytime. . . . Traffic to the rear is desired during daytime to increase the deception.
4. Every motorized movement must be completed by daybreak. . . .
5. During the night, moving is done without lights. Only the lead vehicles in each unit drive with the lowest degree of light.
6. The moves are to be carried out without breaks or technical stops.
7. Strict march discipline is to be maintained; any passing is prohibited. . . .
8. For quick repair of bad roadways, all units have to carry fascines, knotted carpets, and straw.[64]

During the night of L-Day to M-Day [13/14 December: since "O-Day was the day on which the attack would begin—in this case, 16 December—the days leading up to it corresponded with the alphabetical letters preceding the letter "O"—*Editor*], *Panzer Regiment 16,* the bulk of *Panzerjäger Battalion 228,* and *Armored Artillery Regiment 146* were actually supposed to move forward.

However, apparently only the artillery moved up. The journal of *2d Battalion, Armored Artillery Regiment 146* records the following about 13 and 14 December:

> Battalion relocates during the night of 13/14 of December 1944, to a preparation area in the vicinity of the area of operations.
>
> March route: Waldsdorf–Rockeskyll–Gerolstein–Mürlenbach–Schönecken–Lünebach–Heilhausen.
>
> Preparation area south of Lünebach.
>
> Battalion gives up *5th Battery* to *3d Battalion* and receives *8th Battery*. However, *8th Battery* is still on the train, but is expected during the next days.
>
> During the whole day, brisk enemy aircraft activity. Ahr Valley railroad is continuously attacked by groups of fighter bombers.[65]

On 14 December, M-Day, the battalion commanders were allowed to receive their instructions. The journal of *2d Battalion, Panzer Regiment 16* includes the following:

> 0730 hours, the battalion commander drives to the front for a reconnaissance.
>
> 0900 hours, the regimental scout platoons drive out to reconnoiter march routes and preparation areas.[66]

On this day, *LVIII Panzer Corps*—if its journal is correct—issued the corps order for *"ADELHEID,"*[67] the code name for the offensive in the corps zone. The contents of the order must have been announced earlier, at least as far as the march and preparation, as well as the secrecy, were concerned. In some respects, the order was even changed; for example, the mission for the *Führer Escort Brigade (Brigade Remer)* was taken over by a second regiment of the *560th Volks-Grenadier Division*; it arrived just in time for the attack (Appendix 17).

On the afternoon of 14 December, Manteuffel and Krüger visited the *116th Panzer Division*. Waldenburg remarked, "Fuel and essential parts of the Division are still missing, but the plan is adhered to."[68]

Vogelsang wrote:

> Everything is rolling! We almost feel the way we did during the offensive in France in 1940, weeks that seem to have been an eternity ago! All preparations are completed, but everything is still very secretive. Many good and familiar divisions are starting their march. A certain anticipation has gripped even the most grizzled fighters. If we only had enough fuel—everything else is here![69]

The Division issued a report about the "fuel situation for planned operations" as of 1000 hours on 14 December to corps. In this report, among other things, the following was noted:

> With this amount of fuel, it is possible to move the units into the assigned preparation areas, where the vehicles, however, will remain immobile due to inadequate

quantities of fuel. . . . Therefore, it is urgently necessary to either postpone the set date . . . or to bring up fuel by army columns to the units in the preparation areas, at the latest in the evening of N-Day, in the amount of three fuel quotas.[70]

The letter, composed by the *Ib* and me, was signed by the Commander. On 15 December, in the original of the documents of *LVIII Panzer Corps*, it is noted, "According to phone conversation with *Oberstleutnant* Guderian, the Division does not expect arrival of fuel in assembly area in time."

Still, on the evening of 14 December, 250 cubic meters of Otto-fuel [Gasoline—*Translator*] and 50 cubic meters of diesel had been allotted.[71] But much time elapsed until the troops received them. Soon, the consequences will be apparent. On the evening of 14 December (M-Day) 48 trains were unloaded and four more were to arrive; one train was still waiting to be loaded.[72]

Both *Panzer-Grenadier* Regiments and the combat engineer battalion (minus one company in the advance echelon) were supposed to arrive at Assembly Area II southwest of Pronsfeld during the night of 14/15 December. The *Panzer* Regiment had to advance to Assembly Area I, east of Prüm.

Early on 15 December (N-Day), the status of the movements was as follows: In Assembly Area II, four to five kilometers behind the front, the following units arrived: *Panzer-Grenadier Regiment 156* and units of *Panzer-Grenadier Regiment 60* (a weak battalion and an armored engineer company).[73] Behind them, *Army Anti-Aircraft Battalion 281* was in position, as well as *Armored Artillery Regiment 146* (without *8th Battery* and without the two batteries of *Hummels*). In Assembly Area I [which was further back from the line of departure than Area II—*Editor*] were *Panzer Regiment 16* (without one company of *Panzer IVs* and without the company whose assault guns were still stuck somewhere on the railroad) and one armored engineer company. Remaining in the intervention assembly area were: the Division Staff; *Armored Signal Battalion 228; Armored Reconnaissance Battalion 116,* which was planned to be an advance battalion; most of *Panzer-Grenadier Regiment 60*; and all supply units that were not immediately needed for the operation. In the course of the day, *Panzer-Grenadier Regiment 60* was to be advanced to Assembly Area II.

The staff and one company of *Panzerjäger Battalion 228* were still marching toward Assembly Area I, near Kelberg; two tank destroyer companies and the *8th Battery* had only reached the vicinity of Koblenz, still on the railroad or perhaps unloading. The whereabouts of the *Hummel* batteries, which are the bulk of the *1st Battalion, Armored Artillery Regiment 146,* and of one *Panzer IV* and one armored engineer company, were unknown.

Nevertheless, *Supreme Command–West* stated in its journal that the march was almost completed, including fuelling. On the morning of 15 December, on the other hand, *Army Group B* requested a postponement of the attack. *Supreme Command–West* declined, because the danger of decamouflaging had become too great; also, there was concern for the situation of the *1st Army*, which could only be eliminated by preparing to attack quickly. [Third Army was attacking the right wing of *1st Army* in the Saar–Moselle Triangle, while the VI and XV Corps of Seventh Army were pressing the other end of the *1st Army* line in the Low Vosges and eastern end of the Saar Valley—*Editor*] The same was true for the threat to the right wing of the offensive near Monschau. There, the Americans pushed toward the Roer dams via Kesternich.

At 1530 hours, *Supreme Command–West* gave the order to commence the attack on 16 December.[74] In a letter to Model, Hitler gave the last directives. The opening sentences shifted the responsibility for success or failure to the lower levels, "I have made my decisions. The prerequisites for the success of the operation are all there. Size and extent of the success now depend solely on the leadership during the course of the operation."[75]

The letter closed, "If these principles for the course of the operation are followed, a great success is certain."

Manteuffel provided the final instructions:

1. We will march and fight, as appropriate, day and night. All armored vehicles also, as well as the tanks themselves, march at night. The creator of our weapons, *Generaloberst* Guderian, wants every tank commander to know, "The night is the tanker's friend."

2. Any *Grenadier, Panzer-Grenadier,* scout, or engineer who has a damaged vehicle continues to his objective by marching on foot! What we lose in the coming weeks on sweat, we will save in following months on blood!

3. Over-exposure to the enemy air forces must be dealt with! Remedy: Spread out vehicles according to width and depth, active air defense by everyone, camouflage, dugouts for vehicles, weapons and men. The ground war mission must be continued! There is no other way to reach our objective!

4. No tank officer, no tank crewman must disappoint, they all must be aware of the tradition that they carry within themselves "onward to the enemy and beyond!"[76]

All Commanders-in-Chief issued orders of the day. Rundstedt wrote:

Soldiers of the Western Front! Your great hour has come! Strong attack armies set out against the Anglo-Americans today. I do not have to tell you anything else. All of you can sense it: Everything is at stake!

Carry within yourself the holy commitment to give your all and make superhuman efforts for our Fatherland and our *Führer*!

> *Supreme Commander–West*
> von Rundstedt
> *Generalfeldmarschall*[77]

In the unit journals which still exist, the thoughts prior to the attack made an impression. The *2d Battalion* of the *Panzer* Regiment recorded on 15 December,

If what now supposedly seems to be suggested works out, then tomorrow morning it will open the opponent's eyes. He really does not seem to have any idea of what is going on here. Until now, camouflage and secrecy of the planned operation has been excellent.[78]

With this, we got a little ahead of the events and must once more return to the last phase of the march. It was concluded on 15 December and during the night leading to the day of attack. However, at the beginning of attack, the *8th Battery* and the 14 assault guns, which were announced in place of *Panzer IVs* for the *2d Battalion, Panzer Regiment 16* were still missing. It was very questionable whether the ghostly wandering units, still far away, would arrive on the morning of 15 December in time for the beginning of the attack. The only company of the *Panzerjäger* battalion that arrived in its entirety joined the advanced battalion of the Division.[79]

During the night of 15/16th December (O-Day was 16 December) the *Panzer-Grenadier* Regiments moved into their attack positions beyond the former main battle line; the artillery moved, if it had not happen already, into its firing positions and observation posts, the tanks, with the onset at 0120 hours, were advanced via Schönecken–Lünebach–Euscheid up to the forest west of the town. They arrived there, after some march delays, on 16 December at about 0700 hours.[80] The Division command post was established in a bunker of the *Westwall* near Oberüttfeld.[81] The newly-established advance battalion of the Division advanced during the night to the day of attack into the vicinity of Strickscheid–Lünebach–Matzerath. The organization as ordered, is shown in the corps order (see Appendix 17). The artillery assigned to it, the *2d Battalion, Armored Artillery Regiment 146,* in the beginning was in position to support the attack by the *Panzer-Grenadiers.* The armored rocket launchers and the anti-aircraft battery assigned to it naturally also took up position. After all, the number of battleworthy tanks, tank destroyers, and assault guns that went to battle was, in fact, quite modest.

The *2d Battalion* of the *Panzer* Regiment had 16 battleworthy *Panzer IVs*, out of 21 on hand. It looked slightly more favorable for the *1st Battalion,* which was equipped with Panthers. It had 41 Panthers, 29 of which were in place and battleworthy.[82] *Panzerjäger Battalion 228,* after complete arrival, had about 18 battleworthy tank destroyers and assault guns for the battle. How difficult the materiel situation still remained, in spite of the accomplished replenishment, is shown in the report of *2d Battalion, Armored Artillery Regiment 146* from 15 December, 1000 hours (Appendix 18).[83] This battalion was slated for incorporation in the Division's advance battalion, and therefore needed mobility more than anything.

The 15th of December was still used for some reconnaissance, as far as the strict orders for secrecy would allow. It was hardly possible to reconnoiter the area of attack. The information about the deployment of the enemy in the attack area of the Division was quite poor. The paragraph, "Enemy position and presumed development" of the "Directives for the course of battle" by the *5th Panzer Army* (Appendix 16) hardly offered any intelligence about the course of the attack by the Division, and neither did the *"Feindnachrichtenblatt,"* (enemy intelligence bulletin).[84] The introduction by the units that were holding the front did not give fully satisfactory insights, as we shall soon see. The Division's attack had to be started in uncertainty.

The enemy front line ran in the attack zone of the Division, three to six kilometers east of the Our. At the front were the towns Heckhuscheid, Grosskampenberg, and Berg, as well as Lützkampen; by the left neighbor was Sevenig. South of it, the Our formed the front line.

It could not be clearly explained how it looked in the attack zone of the Division along the Our, or which and what kind of crossings were indeed available. The corps staff assumed that the bridges between Burg Reuland and Ouren were in working order and effective, since here the enemy front ran east of the Our. For this reason, the attack by the corps was directed toward this sector.[85]

Who was the enemy that now was opposite the *116th Panzer Division*?[86] The 2d Battalion, 424th Infantry Regiment of the 106th Infantry Division, reinforced by units from the 820th Tank Destroyer Battalion, was defending in the sector from Heckhuscheid–Berg–forest edge northeast of Lützkampen. Between Lützkampen and the Our, west of Sevenig, the 1st and 3d Battalions of the 112th Infantry Regiment of the 28th Infantry Division, were emplaced in well-constructed positions. The *116th Panzer Division* was up against the 1st Battalion. The 2d Battalion of this regiment and Company C of the 630th Tank Destroyer Battalion, equipped with towed anti-tank guns, stood west of the Our as the backbone and reserve of the regiment. During the day, this battalion sent out men to secure the Our sector south of Ouren up to the right boundary of the 112th Infantry Regiment, east of Kalborn. The regimental command post was in Ouren.

The attack by *LVIII Panzer Corps* with the *116th Panzer Division* and the *560th Volks-Grenadier Division* came up against three battalions of the front line, in positions that had been carefully prepared for a long time, as well as against a battalion in reserve and a company of the 110th Infantry Regiment, linking up in Heinerscheid. In contrast, the whole *XLVII Panzer Corps* was confronted by an enemy with the strength of only one battalion in the forward line. Along a ten-kilometer front, a company base was established in each of the fortified villages, Marnach and Hosingen. Another battalion stood as division reserve west of Clerf. During the night, there were no enemy troops in this sector directly near the Our. American defense posts that were advanced there pulled back during the night, up to the hills west of the Our. While the 106th Infantry Division, which just arrived from the United States, did not take up its position until 11 and 12 December, the 28th Infantry Division had already been there since mid-November, to be replenished after the heavy losses in the battle of Schmidt, Vossenack, and Hürtgen. It made good use of time. The 112th Infantry Regiment especially made considerable progress under a new command. The *116th Panzer Division,* once again, met a well-known opponent. It made life very difficult for it.

Did the opposite side really not notice the German preparation at all? Some signs were recognized, but they were not taken seriously. The Americans were too concerned with plans for their own attacks and thought a modest number of troops would suffice in the Ardennes. The rush of retreat from Normandy to the *Westwall* led to the optimistic belief that the *Wehrmacht* was finished, or at least no longer capable of a major offensive. The replenishment of the *6th Panzer Army* and of some *Panzer* divisions was known, but it was not sufficiently clear where they were. It was assumed that the armored reserves were mainly positioned to counterattack an American offensive in the direction of Cologne, and to attack them from the rear. This assumption was supported by the German tactics of deception. Nobody expected that *Feldmarschall* von Rundstedt would send his reserves into the "game" prematurely. After all, there was consolation in the fact that the value of the replenished divisions could not be regarded as very high, since the *Panzer Lehr Division,* during its deployment in Lorraine, was not convincing.

As in the summer of 1943 in the East, Hitler did not believe in attacking from the rear. Besides, the winter offensive by the Soviets was now looming, which pressed him to attack as soon as possible. The attack in the West had already been delayed for almost a month. It was high time!

Part 2: The Attack

The attack by *Army Group B* began on the morning of 16 December with three armies, *6th Panzer Army* in the north, *5th Panzer Army* in the center, and *7th Army* in the south. The *6th Panzer Army* conducted the main effort. The *15th Army* did not join the attack. With its left wing, it was to support the offensive's right pivot northeast of Monschau. The corps order, as seen in Appendix 17, indicates the tasks of *5th Panzer Army,* and *LVIII Panzer Corps,* which was attacking from its center.[1] Within the scope of these tasks, the first objective for the *116th Panzer Division,* after breaking through the enemy's main battle line, was to capture the crossings of the Our near Stupbach and Welchenhausen, and to establish bridgeheads west of the Our. The important crossing at Weweler—in the course of the *Panzer* corps' march route, leading via Lützkampen to Burg Reuland—was to be opened from the rear.

To the left of the *116th Panzer Division,* the *560th Volks-Grenadier Division* attacked Ouren with one *Grenadier* regiment and the already-destroyed Our crossing, southeast of Kalborn, with another, since the enemy front there already ran west of the Our.[2] The main thrust of the right adjacent unit, the *62d Volks-Grenadier Division,* aimed toward Winterspelt on the road to St. Vith. Its attack on the village of Heckhuscheid, which was on the Division boundary, failed. The opponent also held his position here on 17 December.

The corps order and the "directives for the course of the battle" of the *5th Panzer Army* (see Appendix 16) were very detailed and did not leave the Division leadership much room for its own decisions.[3] Thus, the Division was ordered to:

> Attack with both *Panzer-Grenadier* Regiments, each with both of its battalions; the Division, therefore, with all four of its *Panzer-Grenadier* battalions in the forward line.

> — Have each of the four *Panzer-Grenadier* battalions send two to three assault platoons ahead, with a company behind them as the assault company (*"Sturmkompanie"*) under the personal command of the battalion commanders; the remainder of the battalion is to follow.

> — "Amply" reinforce the assault companies with minesweeper platoons, tank destroyer platoons, flamethrower groups, and forward observers with wireless sets.

> — Assign the best commanders and junior leaders to these assault companies; the rule of conduct for *Panzer-Grenadiers* is "Advance with silence and speed."

> — Move up tanks and tank destroyers only during the night before the attack. Consequence: tank support for *Panzer-Grenadiers* only possible in the course of the morning.

> — Attack by the *Panzer-Grenadiers* at 0500.

> — Commence artillery fire not before 0530.

> — Turn on searchlights 0535.

— Have an advance battalion stand by for the disposition of corps, consisting of the *Armored Reconnaissance Battalion*, a company of the *Panzerjäger* Battalion (the other two companies had not fully arrived anyway), an engineer company, a light artillery battalion, an armored rocket launcher battery, and a light anti-aircraft battery.

— Limit information to the attack troops in the forward line.

[A comparison of these minutely restrictive instructions with those given the 28th Infantry Division for its attack on Schmidt in early November (p. 236) is instructive—*Editor.*]

How could the Division command have any influence in this? What remained was the attack by the four *Panzer-Grenadier* Batallions to their assigned objectives, the Our crossings at Stupbach and Welchenhausen. To undertake anything reasonably, the Division would have needed more precise knowledge about the organization of the opposing enemy and the terrain, but this was inadequate, as already reported. Knowledge basically depended on the instructions to the commanders by the leadership of units that had been holding the line at the time of the attack. The most important men, the four commanders of the *Panzer-Grenadier* Batallions, were briefed on M-Day and, therefore, could not reach the forward line before the night of M/N-Day. During this day, they had to stay inside their positions, and during the following night, they had to mount the attack with their battalions which had in the meantime arrived at the front. This only left one minor possibility for the regimental commanders to coordinate, but next to none for the Division command. Everything was subordinate to maintaining secrecy and surprising the opponent.

The "directives" by *5th Panzer Army* included:

The status of training calls for an attack plan with the *simplest structure,* as well as attacks conducted in sectors with close-range or intermediate objectives . . . advance of strike troops and assault companies along clearly-recognizable terrain features.

However, the corps order demanded a thrust "in one push to the Our crossings." This was at least five to six kilometers. "Clearly recognizable features" in this cut-up terrain could only mean following a path. But these paths led through the enemy-occupied villages of Berg and Lützkampen. Therefore, attempts had to be made to get around the villages without following "clearly-recognizable terrain features," and to also avoid the roads later, wherever possible.

The attack by the four assault companies can no longer be clearly reconstructed. The *2d Battalion, Panzer-Grenadier Regiment 60* probably attacked between Heckhuscheid and Berg, while the *1st Battalion* probably attacked south of Berg with the objective of seizing Stupach. The two assault companies of *Panzer-Grenadier Regiment 156* most likely advanced on both sides of Lützkampen with the objective being Welchenhausen. In any case, the company of *1st Battalion,* commanded by *Hauptmann* Winter, pushed by Lützkampen to the north toward Diedrichsborn.[4]

The reports about the spearheads' advances were poor. Only two are entered in the journal of *LVIII Panzer Corps*.[5] At 0705 hours, *Generalmajor* von Waldenburg reported that the line from Heckhuscheid–Grosskampenberg had been crossed at 0620 hours by *2d Battalion, Panzer-Grenadier Regiment 60*. At 0820, the report came from the corps artillery commander that the customs house had been reached. I confirmed this and added that "units entered Berg."

Besides that, it remained unclear what the four companies had achieved. A most unpleasant situation developed. Not only did the four companies disappear, but so did the four battalion commanders. The remainder of the battalions, meaning the larger part of each, were now without leadership. To mount the attack as it was planned, the battalions first had to be newly organized. Direct support for the assault companies by the artillery had not been possible because the radio communication with the forward observers had been broken. To provide tank support to the *Panzer-Grenadiers* for the new attack, the Division ordered the deployment of the *2d Battalion* of *Panzer Regiment 16*.[6] It was ordered that one company each was to cooperate with the *Panzer-Grenadier* regiments. The *1st Battalion* remained directly under Division control, in the forest of Oberüttfeld. The journal of *2d Battalion, Panzer Regiment 16* reported about the deployment of *6th Company* with *Panzer-Grenadier Regiment 60*:

> In the morning, *Oberleutnant* Erdmann tries to attack Grosskampenberg from the southeast, but gets hung up at the tank obstacles (dragons' teeth), which were not reported by the Division that had been holding the line before the attack. After turning south and southwest via the western edge of Leidenborn toward Lützkampen, he then tries to strike west-southwestward from there. Thereby, due west of the area near Nöll, one tank was destroyed by an anti-tank gun and another one hit mines. Both vehicles are momentarily immobile and must be towed.

This is how Erdmann wound up with *Panzer-Grenadier Regiment 156,* but apparently, did not initially establish communication, and thereby also lacked success. The *5th Company, Panzer Regiment 16,* under *Leutnant* Schaller, was already with this regiment. Meanwhile, *Generalmajor* von Waldenburg rushed forward to mount the attack anew. He decided to conduct it with *Panzer-Grenadier Regiment 156,* reinforced by *2d Battalion, Panzer Regiment 16,* out of Lützkampen to the north. The extent to which *Panzer-Grenadier Regiment 60* participated in the attack from the east can no longer be established. *Panzer-Grenadier Regiment 156* attacked at 1630 hours.[7] Unfortunately, the staff of *2d Battalion, Panzer Regiment 16* did not arrive in front in time to assume control of both its companies. The journal of *2d Battalion, Panzer Regiment 16* includes the following about the attack:

> At 1630 hours, while *Hauptmann* Brinkmann was still en route to Lützkampen, all tanks attack after a rocket bombardment. Since the tanks had to exit the Lützkampen village on the road in a single file, protective fire from six tanks was set up right

and left. After a little more than 100 meters, the first tank, with *Leutnant* Einwächter, receives fire from up ahead. The tank burns at once and *Leutnant* Einwächter is killed, along with part of his crew. At this moment, the tanks draw heavy anti-tank gun fire from an anti-tank blocking position in the vicinity of Diedrichsborn–Bock. Six tanks are destroyed and burn within a few minutes. The road is blocked. Under covering fire from the security element that was established, the remaining tanks withdraw to their starting positions. Although three anti-tank guns are destroyed by our overwatching tanks, the attack must be terminated.[8]

According to American reports, one single 3-inch gun from the 820th Tank Destroyer Battalion, deployed at the right wing of the 106th Infantry Division north of Lützkampen, destroyed five German tanks at a distance of 1,800 meters, with only 18 rounds![9]

The results of the first day of the attack were sobering. In the late afternoon hours, the opponent mounted a counterattack and threw *Panzer-Grenadier Regiment 156* back to Lützkampen. Point 509 northwest of it, and Nöll, southwest of the village, were lost again.[10] In the evening, our forward line ran from the sunken road north of Berg, via Berg to the forest southwest of it, thence to the western edge and along the western edge of Lützkampen up to Hill 513, southeast of the village. The Division's daily report read as follows:

> Breach through enemy main battle line not successful. Whereabouts of three assault companies that broke through not known at this time. Continuation of attack in same direction as before does not look promising, mainly because support of these attacks by tanks would be very limited. By changing the direction taken until now, it is still possible to attack Ouren with combined forces by slanting toward the northwest near Berg and toward Diedrichsborn at dawn on 17 December, or to try to break through toward Welchenhausen during the night.[11]

These suggestions were developed after multiple considerations in discussion with the corps staff. They were also influenced by the results of the *560th Volks-Grenadier Division.* It had crossed the Our with its left regiment east of Kalborn and established a small bridgehead around the village; the road to it, however, was extensively blocked and sown with mines, and the bridge crossing the Our was destroyed. Yet there was hope to make the crossing passable in reasonable time with the help of the corps' engineers, and the advance battalion of the *116th Panzer Division* was told to march there.[12] But when it became obvious that the repairs would not be accomplished that quickly, corps orders from 1915 hours directed the advance battalion across the bridgehead established by the *2d Panzer Division* near Dasburg. It received orders to seize Heinerscheid, link up with the units of the *560th Volks-Grenadier Division* near Kalborn, and to defend the bridgehead there.[13]

The regiment of the *560th Volks-Grenadier Division* on the right had a fate similar to that of the *116th Panzer Division.* Its assault company on the right was bogged down north of Sevenig, while the one on the left succeeded in breaking through the enemy's forward line south of Sevenig. It pushed through to the Our, and seized the Our bridge south of Ouren undamaged. However, the bulk of the battalion came to a halt under defensive fire. The assault company was hit by an enemy counterattack with tanks. It suffered considerable losses, and by 1000 hours the bridge was lost again. Further attempts by the regiment to advance the attack failed.[14] Here too, the opponent mounted a counterattack in the evening.[15]

Corps headquarters ordered the *116th Panzer Division* to attack Ouren on 17 December, to seize the crossing there, and to establish a bridgehead on the west bank of the Our. On the afternoon of 16 December, among other things, Vogelsang wrote the following:

> The Division . . . conducted the attack, even if all units had not yet arrived in the assembly area, and were only insufficiently provided with fuel. . . . At 0500 hours, the offensive started on a wide front. During total darkness, selected assault troops sneaked up on the enemy's combat outposts and rolled over the occupiers. At 0530 hours, numerous searchlights lit up as the prelude for the sudden commencement of fire from all heavy weapons. . . . The western horizon was bathed in glittering, sparkling and quivering light.
>
> The most-forward enemy positions were quickly overrun. Toward noon, however, our attack became stuck in front of and within the enemy's main battle line.[16]

At 2100 hours, Vogelsang added:

> The four assault companies from [*Panzer-Grenadier Regiments*] 60 and 156, which broke through the American front line in an energetic thrust, are gone, and with them, by orders from Army Group, all four battalion commanders. The commander of *2d Battalion, Panzer-Grenadier Regiment 60,* the commanders of *1st Company, Panzer-Grenadier Regiment 60* and *1st Company, Panzer-Grenadier Regiment 156,* in the meantime, are back, wounded, and everything else is still missing. This is a shock! The commander of the *Division Escort Company* and the commander of the *Field Replacement Battalion* have to help out at once. Our attack this afternoon is completely scattered to the winds. Five of our tanks were destroyed.

Not until the following evening was Vogelsang able to make notes:

> The picture became clearer. *Hauptmann* Kroll (*1st Battalion, Panzer-Grenadier Regiment 60*) is back with the bulk of his assault company: He was bogged down all day in a minefield in front of enemy bunkers and could only free himself during the night. *Hauptmann* Gerke [*2d Battalion, Panzer-Grenadier Regiment 156—Author*] . . . broke clear through the enemy positions, and for the whole day and half the night, roamed around behind enemy lines. He came back with 250 prisoners and valuable information from reconnaissance. Still nothing accurate is known about *Hauptmann* Winter [Commander *1st Battalion, Panzer-Grenadier Regiment 156,* killed—*Author*] and the second company of *Panzer-Grenadier Regiment 60.* . . .

The *Army Group B* daily report summary for 16 December states the following:

> On 16 December, after strong, heavy fire preparation with all weapons, *Army Group B* mounted an attack toward the west, along the 100-kilometer-wide front of the Eifel. . . .
>
> The attack completely surprised the opponent, rolled over his forward defenses, and initially quickly gained ground everywhere. The attack's tempo was sometimes slowed by stubborn defense in the enemy's main strongpoints, which are generally three to five kilometers behind the forwardmost security positions. By evening, after a gain of three to ten kilometers of terrain, the opponent's main battle line, which was completely in low areas, could be reached, and the main battle area could be penetrated at several points. . . .
>
> After the completion of bridges across the rivers near the front, and after local regrouping, the attack is being continued along the entire front during the night.[17]

Besides one bridge at Dasburg, *XLVII Panzer Corps* had already completed a second one across the Our near Gemünd by noon. The *26th Volks-Grenadier Division* and the *Panzer Lehr Division* crossed there. The plan of the *116th Panzer Division* for 17 December was to deploy *Panzer Regiment 16* with *Panzer-Grenadier Regiment 156* and *2d Battalion, Panzer-Grenadier Regiment 60* as *Group Bayer* from Lützkampen toward Ouren, under the protection on the north flank by *Panzer-Grenadier Regiment 60* (minus *2d Battalion*). The nine still battleworthy *Panzer IVs* of *2d Battalion, Panzer Regiment 16* were attached to the *1st Battalion*. (See Appendix 19, the Division attack order.)[18]

The regiment of the *560th Volks-Grenadier Division* on the right was supposed to renew its attack on Sevenig. Its attack failed again. This caused a disadvantageous situation on *Group Bayer*'s flank. During the day, the regiment was subordinated to the *116th Panzer Division*.

Bayer started the attack at 0600 hours.[19] The Division's daily report states:

> *Group Bayer* succeeded in penetrating the heavily-fortified enemy main battle line west of Lützkampen. In a swift attack, it reached high ground east of the Our. Due to heavy anti-tank weapons and enemy tanks, however, it was temporarily halted. At 1800 hours, the group started to attack again.[20]

Vogelsang's notes complete the picture of these battles:

> It [*Group Bayer—Author*] was temporarily halted, confronted by heavy anti-tank weapons and enemy tanks, with the loss of three Panthers and because of very heavy flanking effect from the area of Sevenig. In very heavy fighting, and after bringing up more units of the Division, Ouren and the bridge could finally be taken without damage. This brought high, bloody, and materiel losses to the opponent.[21]

The bravely fighting opponent was, as already mentioned, the 112th Infantry Regiment of the 28th Infantry Division, known to the Division from the battles at Vossenack.[22] The battles of 16 December near Lützkampen tore the front of its

1st Battalion open but overall, it held its position east of the Our. Bayer's attack broke through the front of 1st Battalion and could eliminate the flanking situation from the direction of Harspelt and Sevenig. Near Harspelt, a platoon of tank destroyers from the 811th Tank Destroyer Battalion attached to the 9th Armored Division was destroyed just after it arrived. Bayer came to a halt before the 112th Infantry Regiment command post in Ouren. The regimental commander, Colonel Nelson, had emplaced all his anti-tank weapons around Ouren, to protect the crossings and his command post, which he defended with 50 men of his Headquarters Company.

The artillery took Bayer's tanks under direct fire. At noon, the 2d Battalion of the 112th Infantry Regiment mounted a counterattack and the German pressure subsided. In the afternoon, this battalion again counterattacked and reestablished the front of the 3d Battalion, 112th Infantry Regiment near Sevenig. In the evening, the entire regiment was withdrawn to the west bank of the Our. Contact with the division on the right was lost. After this, the 112th Infantry Regiment subordinated itself to the division on its left, the 106th Infantry Division; during the evening of 17 December, this division also retreated across the Our, because it had been penetrated further to the north.

The *XLVII Panzer Corps* thrust tore apart the 28th Infantry Division, as did the attack of the advance battalion of the *116th Panzer Division* on its north wing. During the night of 16/17 December, it crossed the Our near Dasburg, and at 0700, set out on the major road from Marnach to the north toward Heinerscheid. At Fischbach, it already encountered the enemy, captured the village, and took prisoners. Since the *560th Volks-Grenadier Division* reported that its left group had entered Heinerscheid, at 0930 hours, the advance battalion received orders to attack Binsfeld via Hüpperdingen [in the maps of that time: Hupperdingen]. At 1046 hours, however, *Major* Stephan reported back, "Heinerscheid not yet taken. Attack on Heinerscheid. 15 more prisoners."[23]

At 1440 hours, Stephan reported, "Heinerscheid taken. Three enemy tanks destroyed. Considerable losses of our own. Two company commanders are casualties. Replacement urgently required. 38 prisoners."

The daily report of the *116th Panzer Division* from 17 December included the following about the advance battalion:

> After crossing the Our near Dasburg, advance battalion of the Division mounted attack on Heinerscheid via Fischbach. Thereby, in the northwest part of Fischbach, strong enemy was thrown back by destroying seven tanks, taking 211 prisoners, and Heinerscheid was entered in a swift attack. Then, Heinerscheid was taken, despite heavy enemy resistance. In the afternoon hours, the battalion attacked Hupperdingen and captured it by evening.

The left group of the *560th Volks-Grenadier Division* joined the advance battalion of the *116th Panzer Division*. For 17 December, the Division reported 373 prisoners and 16 tanks destroyed, but our own losses were also extensive. Vogelsang noted:

> As far as can be seen, our losses are 300 men. The *Panzer Regiment* lost eight tanks with four officers and 30 men. . . .
>
> In the afternoon, we too got hit badly. The *Division Escort Company* was to be deployed and had just gotten ready in Lützkampen when a heavy mortar shell exploded in the middle of the circle of commanders. Twelve men, among them our outstanding Division physician, Professor Bickert, were killed immediately. The company commander, *Hauptmann* Schneider and our *Ic*-duty officer were seriously wounded.[24]

The latter, *Leutnant* Bischoff, succumbed to his injuries.

Referring to the weather, Vogelsang noted:

> Until now, the weather throughout was German-friendly—fog and drizzle. Today, it cleared up temporarily. Right away, numerous fighter bombers appeared. However, they had only limited effect because the unusually heavy anti-aircraft fire was obviously very unpleasant for them. Wherever they show up, they are sprayed by the countless bursts of the machine cannons.

During the whole night and the morning of 18 December, the struggle continued about the further deployment of the *116th Panzer Division*. At 17 December, at 2015 hours, *Oberst i.G.* Dingler, chief of staff of the *LVIII Panzer Corps*, gave me the following order:

> *116th Panzer Division* remains in the attack [on Ouren—*Author*]. If there is no report of a crossing passable for all vehicles by 2200 hours, terminate the attack and advance the Division across the Kalborn bridge. . . . First, make all preparations for a guaranteed, rapid departure.[25]

Yet the bridge near Kalborn was not quite ready. One hoped that it would be completed by the morning of 18 December. At 2215 hours, corps headquarters ordered, "Advance battalion to move forward relentlessly beyond Hupperdingen." At 2230 hours, orders followed to discontinue the attack on Ouren. At 2350, *Generalmajor* von Waldenburg reported to corps headquarters via radio from his location up front with *Group Bayer,* "Attack in full swing, can no longer be stopped." Five minutes later, the corps received the report, "Bridge near Ouren in our hands undamaged." At 0120 of 18 December, corps headquarters ordered the Division, "Cancellation of order for movement toward the east. Continue at Ouren, break through in the direction of Weiswampach."

Half an hour later, *Oberst* Dingler added, "Widen bridgehead by deployment of all forces, break through in the direction of Weiswampach, so that by tomorrow all motorized units have crossed."

By 0630 hours, he further urged, "Follow with all available and transferred units, and reinforce bridgehead so that eventual counterattacks can be destroyed."

The higher command now became restless. At 0915, the Chief of Staff of *5th Panzer Army* insisted, "that the corps must advance. If resistance is too strong at Ouren, then advance from the south via Dasburg, following advance battalion."

The advance battalion reported that it reached Binsfeld at 0730 hours, Massen and Ulflingen at 0945, Asselborn at 1050, and that the town was free of the enemy. *Major* Stephan urgently asked to receive a tank company, since he had only two battleworthy assault guns left.[26]

Now finally—after a suggestion by *5th Panzer Army*—the decision was made to have the entire *116th Panzer Division* follow the advance battalion via Dasburg. It was made easier by Bayer, who reported that the Ouren bridge was too weak for tanks and had to be reinforced. Of course, now everything was to move quite quickly, but the fuel situation had not yet experienced a basic improvement. In the afternoon, the corps commander issued a short order to both divisions:

116th

With personal action by the Division Commander and the Division staff, all available tanks, assault guns that can be procured by any means are to follow the advance battalion as an armored group. The *Supreme Commander–West* orders that no commander will be found in a house tonight.

The movement must be kept going!

Route for the Division: Further advance along road C. Resistance in larger villages to be bypassed.

Objective: West bank of the Ourthe bend at Noiseux.

560th

Basic remarks same as for the *116th*.

Mission: Advance westward, change to road B en route. . . .

Objective: Vicinity of Mont.

This meant that the *560th Volks-Grenadier Division* was now assigned the right side of the corps sector, and the *116th Panzer Division,* the left one. Road C ran close to the Ourthe, from Houffalize on its right bank and later on, on the left one. Road B ran north of C. The distance from Binsfeld to the objective at Noiseux was about 50 kilometers' straight line distance. It was 20 kilometers to the objective for the *560th Volks-Grenadier Division.*

Generalmajor von Waldenburg, with a small command party from the Division staff, went to the advance battalion, while I organized the release of the Division near the Our and its march via Dasburg.

The following march sequence was ordered:

1. In front, *Panzerjäger Battalion 228* (without the company that was already with the advance battalion.)
2. *Group Bayer (Panzer Regiment 16; 1st Battalion, Panzer-Grenadier Regiment 60; 1st Battalion, Armored Artillery Regiment 146; 3d Company, Armored*

> *Engineer Battalion 675*; the regimental staffs of *Armored Artillery Regiment*
> *146* and *Panzer-Grenadier Regiment 60,* the latter with its regimental units).
> 3. *3d Battalion, Armored Artillery Regiment 146.*
> 4. *Army Anti-Aircraft Battalion 281.*
> 5. *Division Escort Company.*
> 6. *Group Grollmann* (*Panzer-Grenadier Regiment 156*; *2d Battalion, Panzer-*
> *Grenadier Regiment 60*; *2d Company, Armored Engineer Battalion 675*).
> 7. One battalion of *Assault Anti-Aircraft Regiment 1.*[27]

In Daleiden, a Division release point was established under the command of
the *IIa, Major* Vogelsang. During the afternoon, the Division command post was
advanced to Hüpperdingen. By noon, the advance battalion passed through
Helzingen and by evening reached Tavigny in Belgian territory, where it assembled and refueled. The journal of *2d Battalion, Armored Artillery Regiment 146,*
which belonged to the advance battalion, recorded the following about the 18
December:

> 0500 hours, continue march without major enemy resistance via Rossmühle-
> Binsfeld.
>   1000 hours, Ulflingen is taken after a brief fight. Prisoners taken. Continue via
> Weiler, between Helzingen and Hoffelt, to Buret. . . . Spearhead rolls on to Tavigny.
> Again, prisoners are brought in and a huge munitions depot by the road is captured.
> Batteries follow toward Tavigny to close up for the planned continuation of the
> march in early morning.
>   Expended: 200 rounds.[28]

At 2030 hours, the advance battalion still reported:

> Stronger enemy resistance, enemy tanks at Houffalize. Stop for supplies in
> Vissoule. 209 prisoners. Captured and destroyed many trucks and armored vehicles.
> One Sherman destroyed.[29]

The leader of the advance battalion, *Major* Stephan, the Commander of
Armored Reconnaissance Battalion 116, received the Knight's Cross for his
valiant attack on 17 and 18 December.[30] Besides him, the commander of the *2d*
Company, Oberleutnant Andreis, especially distinguished himself. He, most of
all, had to be thanked for the quick capture of Heinerscheid. When he destroyed
an enemy tank with close combat weapons, his leg was so severely wounded that
he could only walk with assistance. Despite this, he continued to lead his company until the village was completely captured. Then, *Leutnant der Reserve* Auert
assumed command of the *2d Company.* He distinguished himself on the following day, during the assault on Buret, the first town on Belgian soil, and for this,
received the Knight's Cross.[31]

In the meantime, I arrived in Hüpperdingen and rendered the following report
to the corps at 2000 hours, "Most forward elements of Bayer arrived in
Ulflingen–Asselborn–Binsfeld area. Continue attack after arrival of fuel."[32]

At 2100 hours, I radioed to the advance battalion, "Day's target for Division on 19 December is Noiseux via Road C. How large radius of action for advance battalion, if necessary only elements?"

In the evening of 18 December, the unit to the left of *LVIII Panzer Corps,* with its three divisions, had reached the Luxembourg–Belgium border about everywhere. The unit to the right, *LXVI Corps,* was still clinging to the Our with its left wing, while the Division on the right, strengthened by the *Führer Escort Brigade,* fought for the stubbornly-defended St. Vith.[33] The *560th Volks-Grenadier Division* made quite an effort to keep pace with the *116th Panzer Division.*

The *Supreme Commander–West* insisted on accelerating the attack.[34] Naturally, this had a ripple effect downward. At 1945 hours on 18 December, the corps commander ordered the *116th Panzer Division* to clear the roads at once by accelerating the march, and at 2335, he sent a message to the division commanders:

> By highest order, under the personal leadership of the Division commanders, the line Mont–Houffalize–Noville must be crossed to the west by the morning of 19 December.
>
> Krüger[35]

General von Manteuffel also radioed the corps and division commanders:

> Spearheads too thin and narrow. When near enemy, attack him from broader formations with fire.
> Heavy weapons throughout much too far back. Armored groups to the front everywhere, not just *Panzer-Grenadiers* by themselves.
>
> v.M.

All these exhortations could not help much. Fuel was not nearly sufficient. There were not enough crossings over the Our. In view of these difficulties, the Division was quite proud of its accomplishments. After all, by 0230 hours on 19 December, it could report the arrival of *Group Bayer* and the entrance of *3d Battalion, Armored Artillery Regiment 146.*[36] At 0515 hours, it amended its reports to the effect that most of both mentioned groups had arrived, that *Army Anti-Aircraft Battalion 281* was in the Dasburg area, the *Division Escort Company* was near Daleiden, *Group Grollmann* and the *Anti-Aircraft Assault Regiment* were still approaching Daleiden. Further, it reported the march of a 15cm battery toward the advance battalion and said about the fuel situation, "No fuel. All units that have arrived have enough for 20 kilometers, the advance battalion for ten kilometers. Roads in the back jammed. Nothing coming in. Some tanks usable by siphoning."

In the evening of 18 December, in Daleiden, despite all the turmoil, Vogelsang still found time to write:

> The spell is finally broken! With a determined sprint west, our *Reconnaissance Battalion* has already arrived on Belgian soil by reaching Vissoule. . . .

The paper war has lost all priority! From 1400 to 1800 hours, I stood at the inter-section in Irrhausen and directed traffic—my most important task at that time! And it was necessary! . . .

Until 2130 hours, I stood at the intersection here. Now, everything is rolling smoothly in both directions, but above all, into the area of the breach. . . . The weather is again misty, damp, cold, and rainy. For our offensive, it could not be any better! However, mud and dirt on the ruined roads and in the torn-up terrain almost remind of Russian conditions! In most cases, the grey of the uniform only shows through in some spots. . . .

The hole in the enemy front now finally seems to be bored through. Merrily, the attack rolls west—hopefully for long![37]

The upbeat attitude was not shared by the Commander of *5th Panzer Army, General* von Manteuffel. At 0559 hours on 19 December the Division had report-ed that the advance battalion had not yet moved on due to enemy tanks blocking the way between Buret and Tavigny; the report also said that the advance battal-ion was under attack by them. It was probably due to this that *General* von Manteuffel criticized the leadership of *Generalmajor* von Waldenburg and threat-ened to relieve him.[38,39]

The corps commander obviously did not consider this critique justified. At 1100 hours, together with *Oberst i.G.* Dingler, he visited me at my command post in Hüpperdingen, where he was briefed and showed no ill feelings at all.[40] There was really no reason for it anyway, and Manteuffel's judgment of the Division's achievements was to change very soon. Meanwhile, it was reported that the advance battalion had beaten back the enemy attack and destroyed 18 tanks. Besides that, after his visit with the *116th Panzer Division, General* Krüger could report to Manteuffel that the Division's armored group in Tavigny had linked up with the advance battalion at 1030 hours.[41] The journal of *2d Battalion, Armored Artillery Regiment 146* provides details of the battles near Tavigny:

Advance battalion moved into Tavigny. At 0005 hours 14 Sherman tanks coming from west roll through Tavigny, without noticing that the town was already occu-pied by the enemy. At 0040 another seven enemy tanks (Shermans) roll along the same street. All 7 enemy tanks are put out of action by *Panzerfausts.* The 14 enemy tanks that passed through earlier are destroyed in the rear area. *Unteroffizier* Grünewald, *4th Battery,* destroys one Sherman with a *Panzerfaust.* At 0500 hours, continue march via Vissoule–Mabompré–Bertogne.[42]

The Commander of the *6th Battery, Oberleutnant* Steinmeier, distinguished himself in Tavigny through special fearlessness. With only a few soldiers, he forced an enemy convoy to stop, brought in 98 prisoners, and captured six armored reconnaissance vehicles and three anti-tank guns.[43]

The American tanks were part of Combat Command R of the 9th Armored Division, which was to defend forward of the line Houffalize–Bastogne. In part, they were scattered and rolled over by the assault of the *2d Panzer Division* on the St. Vith–Bastogne road.[44]

The advance battalion's reconnaissance reported Houffalize occupied by the enemy. For this reason, *Generalmajor* von Waldenburg decided not to approach the first Division objective, La Roche, along the road via Houffalize, but to swing around south via Bertogne.[45] On the morning of 19 December, however, Houffalize was in fact free of the enemy, whereas only the night before, long American convoys crossed through the town in both directions.[46] The Ourthe River bridges in the town were undamaged.

On the morning of 19 December, after the advance battalion mopped up the situation around Tavigny, in which units of the *560th Volks-Grenadier Division* took part, it attacked as ordered. At 1300 hours, it reached Compogne; at 1530 hours, Bertogne; and after a brief fight there and near Givroulle, at 1910 hours it reached Salle, two kilometers short of the major Marche–Bastogne road, one of the most important American lifelines. By the evening, *Group Bayer*, which was following, stood with its spearhead in front of Givroulle. *Generalmajor* von Waldenburg established his command post 500 meters east of Bertogne.[47] The *Ia* and his element moved from Hüpperdingen first to Buret, and by the evening further to Bertogne, where he arrived during the night of 19/20 December. The reconnaissance of the southwest Ourthe tributary resulted in blown-up bridges along the Bertogne–Ortho–La Roche road and near Wiompont. Therefore, the advance battalion again detoured to the southwest, to now find their salvation by the Ortheuville bridge, along the major road to Marche. It advanced up to the road in darkness, and interrupted the American traffic. Two tanks and 20 trucks were set on fire and 20 more were captured.[48] The journal of *2d Battalion* of the *Artillery Regiment*, which belonged to the advance battalion, reports the following on 19 December:

> Brief battle in Bertogne with a few American reconnaissance vehicles. Vehicles are destroyed. . . .
>
> Continuing march to Gives–Givroule, where a large fuel-and supply depot is captured. On to the Berhain-Wiompont farm. Bridge blown up in Wiopont and passage not possible. Advance battalion tries to gain another crossing by force. March via 329 [south of bridge Wiompont—*Author*] toward Castle Roumont.[49]

The continuation from 20 December reads as follows:

> Short break in Castle Roumont. Spearhead pushes on toward Herbaimont. In swift action and by surprise, it succeeds in capturing a convoy of the opponent's motorized vehicles.
>
> Continue march to Moriville, to attack Ortheuville. Spearhead is being stopped by emplaced anti-tank guns; one assault gun was destroyed.
>
> Batteries were brought up in forced marches and positioned in vicinity Roumont.

The advance battalion was not causing trouble only to the American supply road, but also unwittingly to *Group Bayer*. The journal of *2d Battalion, Panzer Regiment 16* reports the following:

> In the evening, our anti-aircraft platoon with elements of the scout platoon of the *1st Battalion, Panzer Regiment 16* follows the combat group past Bertogne. The anti-aircraft platoon misses a right turn taken by the combat group. At the intersection, 15 kilometers southwest of Bertogne, the anti-aircraft platoon turns right and hits upon a strong enemy convoy of about 60 trucks and cars with mounted infantry. A fierce skirmish with close combat developed. The opponent suffers high losses. The bulk of the enemy convoy, about 40 trucks and 500 men, were captured by our approaching *Grenadier* units. Our anti-aircraft platoon also has losses. An anti-aircraft gun prime mover is lost to a close combat weapon.[50]

The approaching *Panzer-Grenadiers* were the *1st Battalion* of *Panzer-Grenadier Regiment 60* under *Hauptmann* Kroll.[51]

While all this took place, I was driving by Houffalize in the evening of 19 December and found out that the town was free of the enemy.[52] If my memory does not fail, after I discussed it with corps headquarters, or by its order, I prepared *Group Zander* for an attack (*Panzer-Grenadier Regiment 60*—without its *1st Battalion* and the *3d Battalion, Armored Artillery Regiment 146*) via Houffalize, along the road in the valley toward La Roche. The decision was made easier by the good advance of the *560th Volks-Grenadier Division,* north of Houffalize. On the afternoon of 19 December, its left group took Mont (three kilometers northwest of Houffalize) and was to further advance via Wibrin–Nadrin toward Samrée.[53] The *116th Panzer Division,* which was drifting increasingly more to the left and had a long, open, left flank, caused corps headquarters much concern. At 2350 hours, it was radioed, "Do not distance yourself too far from the southern corps boundary."[54]

Ortheuville was about ten kilometers to the left. Boundaries are not supposed to be blinders, but the corps ran the danger of splintering. Besides, both of its flanks were open, the left one from Noville (eight kilometers southwest of Houffalize) and the right one almost still up to the Our. The left division of *LXVI Corps* fought further north, near Burg Reuland, while the remaining units tried to gnaw their way through north of St. Vith. In contrast, the right group of the *560th Volksgrenadier Division* fortunately closed up to Geileg and Lamerscher (ten to twelve kilometers northeast of Houffalize).[55]

After I ordered *Group Zander* to attack La Roche via Houffalize, I moved *Group Grollmann* (reinforced *Panzer-Grenadier Regiment 156*), which followed, and *Army Anti-Aircraft Battalion 281,* into the vicinity south of Houffalize. I then continued my trip to Bertogne. After arriving, the commander and I evaluated the situation. To get a clear picture, officers were sent out to reconnoiter the crossings over the Ourthe. There were no new results about the *Armored Reconnaissance*

Battalion. At that time, the following report about 19 December must have been sent to corps headquarters:

> In the early morning hours, during the attack to the west in vicinity Tavigny, the advance battalion was attacked in the rear by 26 enemy tanks.
>
> Attack rebuffed by destroying nine tanks and fought to free communication to the rear. Since Houffalize is heavily occupied by enemy, turning southward via Mabompré, Bertogne, Ortho, La Roche, is ordered.
>
> *Combat Group Bayer,* with orders to follow behind the advance battalion, repeatedly joins in the battles and breaks strong enemy resistance, mainly along the Houffalize-Bertogne road.
>
> Because of bridge demolition north of Bertogne, Commander orders new march route via Gives, Givroulle to Erneuville. Along this road, it was established that the Wiompont bridge is also destroyed. Reconstruction by our engineers is ordered. If this bridge cannot be rebuilt in shortest time, new crossing is to be found.
>
> Because the adjacent unit on the left is involved in heavy battles at Noville, the Division's deep advance has created an unsecured left flank. It forces the opening of the passage through Houffalize as soon as possible, to again unite the Division in the direction of La Roche.
>
> After it is determined in the evening that Houffalize is free of the enemy, and the impression exists that the enemy only has small forces on both sides of the Ourthe sector, the Division decides to order the approaching *Group Zander* to attack La Roche from Houffalize. *Group Grollmann* and *Army Anti-Aircraft Battalion 281* are ordered forward into the vicinity of Houffalize and receive orders to defend to the south.
>
> During the battle south of Houffalize, 400 prisoners were taken and a large number of tanks and motor vehicles were captured or destroyed.
>
> Intention of the Division is to combine the forces of *Group Zander,* which is heading toward La Roche from Houffalize, with the units that came out from the corps sector to the south, in the direction of La Roche.
>
> The Division attack on the morning of 19 December suffered considerable delays due to lack of fuel. The Division reached the vicinity of Heinerscheid generally with a supply of 0.4 units of fuel.[56]

On 20 December at 0810 hours, the Division reported that the bridge across the Ourthe south of Wibrin was destroyed, and that the repair of the bridge at Wiompont would require too much time.[57] The report ended with, "Division turns off via Houffalize Road C." Most likely, corps headquarters pushed for this action and finally ordered it. The journal of *LVIII Panzer Corps* contains nothing besides the above-quoted report by the Division. Still, at 0710 hours, when *General* Krüger reported to Manteuffel by telephone, there was no mention that the *116th Panzer Division* would turn off.[58] Only Vogelsang's diary mentions an order by corps headquarters:

With considerable delays due to shortage of fuel, most of the Division mounted the attack on the objective, Noiseux. The attack was behind the advance battalion, which was already far ahead, but, to avoid potentially great losses in a battle in Houffalize, the attacking elements turned off the intended march route southward toward Mabompré–Bertogne–Ortho–La Roche. They, along with the advance battalion, followed by *Group Bayer,* had to move forward further west via Gives-Givrolle due to the demolished bridge north of Bertogne. Against heavy enemy resistance, during this move, the advance battalion gained the partially-destroyed Wiompont bridge, and this morning, the intact Ortheuville bridge. Since the repair of the bridge at Wiompont would require too much time, since the report about the capture of the bridge at Ortheuville arrived too late, and since Houffalize was deemed free of the enemy, this morning, corps staff ordered the Division to do the following: Turn to the north bank of the Ourthe via Houffalize and press on from there, via the bridge at La Roche or any other crossing that would have to be captured to push toward the old objective, Noiseux.

By all these movements, the Americans are completely surprised and are in substantial turmoil. Long columns of prisoners march toward the east, many tanks were destroyed or captured. Our *Landsers* are loaded with cigarettes, chocolates, and canned food, and are smiling from ear to ear. The combat units were able to fill the gaps caused by missing vehicles in their convoys with captured ones. Along the roads are immense piles of artillery ammunition. Along the Helzingen via Trotten (Luxembourg) road up to here alone, I estimate the captured amount to be 25,000 rounds. How wonderful that this blessing will not fall on our heads!

Sometimes, complete American motorized convoys with all of their crew roll back past us. The faces of the prisoners are full of disbelief and amazement.[59]

To turn during the advance toward Ortheuville was not easy for *Generalmajor* von Waldenburg. In his presentation for the Americans in 1945, he wrote:

Reasons leading to this order or those that necessitated it were not known to the Division. Against my will and all my principles, I had to halt the Division, and still during the night of 19/20 December, give the corresponding orders to have the Division turn off from what was probably a very promising direction, which turned out to be a considerable loss of time for the continued march.[60]

As mentioned earlier, the situation portrayed in the journal of *LVIII Panzer Corps* does not coincide with this picture. A correction, which I proposed to the Commander while we were in captivity in 1947, was not completely accepted. It said:

The corps order to turn toward the north bank of the Ourthe was issued on the morning of 20 December, in Bertogne, after *Panzer-Grenadier Regiment 60* (Reinforced) was ordered to attack via Houffalize on the north bank toward La Roche, by request of corps headquarters. The crucial report from the *Armored Reconnaissance*

Battalion that it captured the Ourthe bridge at Ortheuville near the Bastogne–Marche road did not arrive in the hands of the Division until noon; in other words, too late to stop the corps order.[61]

In their study, the commanding general and the Chief of Staff of *LVIII Panzer Corps* also speak of a corps order, but are mistaken, at least, regarding the point of time, that is, "still during the night."[62]

But now, back to Bertogne on the morning of 20 December. At 0820 hours, *Major* Stephan reported to the Division, "Encountered enemy tanks near Ortheuville road bridge."[63] That message was monitored by corps headquarters, as were almost all communications between Division and the advance battalion. At about the same time, the following order from the Division went to Stephan by radio, "Division turns off via Houffalize on Road C, behind *Group Zander*. Advance battalion behind Bayer to Houffalize. Commander ahead to Division."

Bayer received a corresponding order. Still at 1010 hours, Stephan reported, "Ortheuville heavily occupied by enemy (tanks). Deployed assault platoon toward bridge. One of our assault guns destroyed."

Not until 1030 hours—two and a half hours after the decision to turn off—he radioed, "Took Ortheuville bridge intact." At about the same time, the report came from Zander that he had linked up with the *560th Volks-Grenadier Division* and reached Maboge (four kilometers southeast of La Roche). Shortly thereafter, he reported that La Roche was occupied by the enemy and 24 enemy tanks stood 1.5 kilometers west of town. During the confrontation with the enemy near La Roche, the regimental Adjutant, *Hauptmann* Risse, who drove in the front of his regiment, was seriously wounded. *Oberleutnant* Holtkamp, previously the Adjutant of the *2d Battalion* of the regiment, succeeded him. Bayer had already passed Bertogne in the direction of Houffalize at 1015 hours. The corps ordered the Division to advance along Road B, which is via Nadrin–Samrée toward Beffe. Therefore, Bayer was to attack Samrée. The Division staff followed in the direction of Houffalize, with *Generalmajor* von Waldenburg up front with Bayer. Corps headquarters assigned Road A to the *560th Volks-Grenadier Division*. This road ran furthest to the right in the corps sector, from north of Houffalize to Manhay.

It is hard to judge if the turn by the Division was a mistake. During the following night (20/21 December) the bridge at Ortheuville was again captured by the *Armored Reconnaissance Battalion* of the *2d Panzer Division*. However, due to lack of fuel, this division could not take advantage of the success.[64] The *116th Panzer Division* would not have fared much better. By the push northward, it was relieved of this problem; in Samrée, it captured a huge supply depot. The main advantage of an advance along the west bank of the Ourthe would have been that the confrontation with the units of the 3d Armored Division, that were now arriving east of the river, as well as another Ourthe crossing, could have been avoided. The 84th Infantry Division, that arrived one day later at Marche, might have been an opponent with less combat power. But in 1944, nobody knew anything about this.

Before we dedicate ourselves to the further advance of the *116th Panzer Division,* let us look at the opposing side, which was obscure to us at that time.[65] On 19 December, there were only weak American security elements in the *LVIII Panzer Corps* zone. The 51st Engineer Combat Battalion stood along the Ourthe between Durbuy and La Roche. The supply installations of the 7th Armored Division were arrayed around La Roche. Its commander established security elements at the destroyed Ourthe bridge, south of Ortho. After the destruction of some vehicles by an assault gun from the *116th*'s advance battalion, this unit retreated to the hills. Under the impression that his supply installations would be in danger west of the Ourthe, the commander relocated them to the east bank. There, in Sambrée, he already had a larger depot.

The American leadership could only gather weak forces for the protection of the Ourthe bridge at Ortheuville, along the most important supply road from Marche to Bastogne. The forces consisted of an engineer company and eight tank destroyers with long 76mm guns.

By 20 December, however, Eisenhower's actions regarding the events in the German breach area had an obvious effect. In the south, Patton assumed control and brought up new forces from his army's area of operations to mount a counterattack as soon as possible. In the north, Montgomery took over command of the Ninth and First Armies, and started to take generous measures to bring up forces from those armies that had not been attacked. They were to foil the German advance and ultimately also mount a counterattack. In the south, Bastogne developed into the center of resistance. One task force each of the 9th and 10th Armored Divisions, and the recently moved up 101st Airborne Division were fighting here.

In the north, the 82d Airborne Division had arrived at and west of Vielsalm. Next to it, on 20 December, units of the 3d Armored Division (Combat Command R and the reconnaissance battalion) moved to the west. The 3d Armored Division commander deployed three mixed reconnaissance groups out of Hotton. A reinforced battalion remained in the vicinity of Soy–Erezée as reserve. The right reconnaissance group advanced via Soy–La Roche toward Houffalize. Southeast of La Roche, it encountered the *2d Battalion* of *Panzer-Grenadier Regiment 60* and came to a halt. On 21 December, it retreated via La Roche to the north and was supposed to join another task force in Amonines. That failed. It was encircled near Marcouray. Lack of fuel made it immobile. It stayed there until 25 December, without being severely attacked by the Germans. During the following night, after destroying their tanks and vehicles, the men fought their way back to their own lines on foot. The middle group was to reconnoiter via Samrée toward Baraque de Fraiture. It ran into the attack by the *116th Panzer Division,* which will be reported about later. The third, the eastward group, also had Baraque de Fraiture as its objective and reached it without a fight. As of 21 December, a part of this group became entangled in the fighting there, while another part moved up for the battle at Dochamps (north of Samrée).

The 84th Infantry Division marched on west of the Ourthe. Its first regimental group arrived in Marche during the night of 20/21 December. The 2d Armored and 75th Infantry Divisions were to assemble further north. The British XXX Corps, which was brought up by Montgomery, stood by north and west of the Maas, while one tank brigade advanced to the Maas, between Namur and Givet.

Back to the *116th Panzer Division*! At noon on 20 December, at Zander's command post in Bérisménil, Waldenburg gave Bayer the order to attack Samrée.[66] *Group Bayer* consisted now, as before, of:

> *Panzer Regiment 16* (still with 15 Panthers and six *Panzer IVs* battleworthy)
> *1st Battalion, Panzer-Grenadier Regiment 60*
> *3d Company* of the Division's engineer battalion
> *1st Battalion* of the Division's artillery regiment

Bayer's attack was supported by more artillery, most likely from the *3d Battalion, Armored Artillery Regiment 146*, and armored rocket launchers. The *2d Battalion, Panzer-Grenadier Regiment 60* secured the advance to the west toward La Roche. The *560th Volks-Grenadier Division* joined in the attack with a regimental group to the right of the Nadrin–Samrée road.[67]

This attack started at about 1500 hours. Samrée was captured by 1600 hours. As of 1800 hours, the attack was continued at Dochamps toward the north. After a heavy battle in Dochamps, the spearhead reached the area south of Beffe at about midnight. Twelve enemy tanks were destroyed near Samrée.[68] The journal of the *2d Battalion, Panzer Regiment 16* recorded the following:

> In the meantime, *Combat Group Bayer* has advanced via Nadrin to Samrée. At Samrée, enemy tanks tried to stop the group. Four of our *Panzer IVs* bypass Samrée in the west and push into the enemy's flank. After this, the opponent retreats to the forest north of Samrée and north of Dochamps. Units of the combat group destroyed eight enemy tanks.
>
> At the intersection near Samrée, a fuel depot with about 100 cubic meters of fuel is captured, which is very helpful to the Division.
>
> The combat group pushes further ahead from Dochamps, past Beffe, and reaches the withdrawal route of the opponent, north of Melines.
>
> The successes of the past days create great enthusiasm among our soldiers, especially since many prisoners were brought in during the last days.[69]

The commander of *1st Battalion, Panzer Regiment 16, Major* Tebbe, who had just returned from the hospital at the outset of the attack, took command of his battalion at once, and distinguished himself through energetic leadership. He was awarded the *Ehrenblattspange (*German Army Honor Roll Clasp).[70]

As reported, the supply installation of the 7th Armored Division was in Samrée, until now only protected by several quadruple anti-aircraft guns and a light tank. Trusting in help from the approaching 3d Armored Division, work went on to the last moment and nothing was destroyed. The few Americans were quickly overrun, but most trucks, loaded with ammunition, succeeded in escaping. One hundred cubic meters of fuel and 15,000 food rations, however, were left behind intact; clothing was also captured.

Shortly after the capture of the town by *Combat Group Bayer*, six tanks and two halftracks from the 3d Armored Division appeared from the north. The tanks were destroyed, but after picking up the surviving tank crews, the halftracks escaped in the direction of La Roche. From there, a brave supply officer with two tanks and a tank destroyer tried to offer help. Everything was annihilated. Even the attempted advance by units from a reconnaissance troop of the 7th Armored Division from the east along the Baraque de Fraiture to Samrée road, ended without success. Now the Commander of the 3d Armored Division ordered the recapture of Samrée. Therefore, the reconnaissance troop was reinforced with two armored infantry companies, but was content to only block the road to Erezée, north of Dochamps, during the night. As a result, Bayer was able to advance along Road B, bypassing it toward Beffe without being noticed.[71]

The achievements of the *116th Panzer Division* on 19 and 20 December were something of which to be proud. The decision was made at about 0800 hours to turn around and head for La Roche via Houffalize. After preparatory fires by artillery and mortars, Samrée, 30 kilometers away, had by 1600 hours already been taken in a coordinated attack. Subsequently, the attack was continued into the dark for another twelve kilometers via Dochamps up to Beffe. Thirteen kilometers separated the spearhead from objective, Noiseux. During the night, the Division command post was established in Samrée.

The following morning, *General* von Manteuffel expressed his appreciation to *Generalmajor* von Waldenburg by radio:

> Appreciation and gratitude to your magnificent men, your commanders and to you. Your successes adhere to proud tradition.
>
> Signed, von Manteuffel[72]

The corps order from 20 December sounded confident indeed and stated in paragraph 1, not quite correctly, "During advance on both sides of Houffalize and across the line Durbuy-Noiseux, *LVIII Panzer Corps* took about 1,600 prisoners and destroyed or captured 50 tanks."[73]

Intent and tasks remained unchanged. The *6th Panzer Army*'s *2d SS-Panzer Division "Das Reich,"* which could not get going, was to be brought up to the right wing of the corps for the attack.[74] However, its arrival was delayed for days by lack of fuel, which made securing the long right flank the continued task of the *560th Volks-Grenadier Division.* One regimental group jointly fought with the *116th Panzer Division,* while the second one was lagging behind, east of Houffalize.[75] The adjacent unit on the left, *XXXVII Panzer Corps,* did not advance well. Although *Armored Reconnaissance Battalion 2* recaptured the bridge at

Ortheuville, most of its division [The *2d Panzer Division—Editor*] was still involved in heavy fighting north of Bastogne.[76] Most of the *Panzer Lehr Division* was also tied down there until 21 December.[77]

On 20 December, *Supreme Command–West* ordered *Army Group B* to deploy the *5th Panzer Army* toward Huy, Dinant, and, if necessary, Givet, because the *6th Panzer Army* could not advance.[78] This order pointed in a dangerous direction. Its execution had to result in longer unprotected flanks and in fragmenting the forces. Both of these happened in the next few days. After the war, Keitel and Jodl said it was already obvious on 18 and 19 December that the more distant objectives could not be reached, and that a battle in the Maas bend was imminent.[79] If the *Supreme Commander–West* shared this opinion at that time, his order is even more incomprehensible. On 20 December in the *Führer* Headquarters, the Chief of Staff oriented himself about the prospects of the offensive and concluded that it could not reach its objective.[80] On 21 December, the *Supreme Commander–West* continued to consider and ordered, "It is of *decisive importance* that the *right wing of the 6th Panzer Army* regain its freedom of movement quickly."[81]

The situation there, however, developed in the opposite direction. Therefore, success had to be sought at the free wing where it connected with the *5th Panzer Army*. This required march movements to the west for the units that were still available or had to be freed up. These again suffered from the restrictiveness of the area and from lack of fuel. At least the weather still cooperated.

Not until 22 December did the *Supreme Commander–West* take the development of the situation into account and, by moving the objectives back, he ordered, "It is important to advance north out of the vicinity of Marche and to the west of it with strong units, and to force the enemy away from the river on this side of the Maas, and to destroy it."[82]

Besides this, *Supreme Command–West* ordered *15th Army* to at "once attack along the whole front in the manner of strike troops." *Army Group G* was ordered to prepare for a diversionary attack in the direction of the Saverne Gap.[83] All these measures were correct, but came too late.

Early on the morning of 21 December, the *116th Panzer Division* again set out on its approach march toward Hotton. Bayer deployed reconnaissance out of Beffe toward the northeast, in the direction of Magoster, north to Wy and via Trinal toward Melines. It was established that the enemy was north of Wy. At 0725 hours, Bayer reported that Hotton was heavily occupied by the enemy. *Generalmajor von Waldenburg* went to Bayer and at 0940 hours, reported to corps headquarters that Bayer was involved in a heavy battle near the road to Hotton, and that Soy and Erezée were occupied by the enemy. At 1020 hours, therefore, he asked that the *560th Volks-Grenadier Division* advance toward Grandmenil–Erezée. An hour later, corps received the report that the bridge in Hotton was intact.[84]

The following report about the attack on Hotton can be found in the journal of the *2d Battalion, Panzer Regiment 16*:

In the morning . . . the combat group mounts an attack northward out of Beffe. Trinal is captured without incident. From the forest edge south of Melines, enemy traffic retreating from Soy to Hotton is recognized and attacked. Then, the combat group continues along the main road toward Hotton. *Oberfeldwebel* Pichler, along with another tank remain near a road crossing north of Melines and establish security toward Soy. The combat group still fights enemy traffic in the vicinity of Ny and then pushes on toward Hotton. The village, especially the bridge, is well secured by enemy tanks, anti-tank guns, and sharpshooters.

Due to loss of the lead *Panzer V* and the wounding of several commanders by headshots, the attack, which is only escorted by very weak infantry units, comes to a halt.

After heavy fighting with enemy tanks, by which the opponent suffers heavy losses, the battle units of the combat group move back to the eastern edge of Hotton and establish security there.

Supported by our combat engineer platoon, our units in Hotton are in their defensive positions and are under heavy fire during the whole day.[85]

Toward noon, the enemy made himself noticeable in an unpleasant way out of Soy. The journal of *2d Battalion, Panzer Regiment 16* reports, "Around 1500 hours, the opponent tries to attack with tanks from Soy in the direction of Hotton, but is beaten back with losses by *Oberfeldwebel* Pichler's security positions."

Sitting along the road west of Soy, the opponent held the only connection between the fighting units of *Group Bayer* near Hotton under constant direct fire from tank guns. Therefore, supply had to be limited to periods of darkness. With his command post in the forest east of Hotton, Bayer was compelled to deploy the bulk of *1st Battalion, Panzer-Grenadier Regiment 60,* east of Melines, for protection against the enemy near Soy.[86] During the day, the *2d Battalion* of *Panzer-Grenadier Regiment 60* arrived, and was deployed to protect Bayer's left flank near Werpin.

The reinforced *Armored Reconnaissance Battalion* that also arrived first received orders to attack northward via Dochamps. North and northwest of the town, it met stiffening resistance. After this, swinging around the east via Lamorménil, the battalion was deployed against Amonines. There, however, the forward units encountered strong defensive fire and suffered considerable losses. The attack came to a halt. Since the *560th Volks-Grenadier Division* took over the task of attacking northward via Dochamps, the battalion was released on the morning of 22 December and deployed toward Erezée by swinging around westward via Devantave and Amonines. In the evening, the battalion again joined the battle in front of Amonines.[87] *Panzer-Grenadier Regiment 156* was brought up and advanced to the vicinity of Beffe. Vogelsang wrote about the events of 21 December in the evening in Bérisménil:

> But now, *Group Bayer* was bogged down against very strong counterattacks in Hotton. Decimated American units tried to break out from the east, brought in

reserves, made an effort to open their escape route from the outside. Units of two American armored divisions were identified opposite the group.

In consideration of this difficult situation, it was urgently necessary to bring *Panzer-Grenadier Regiment 156* forward, but it was completely blocked in the narrow, rubble-strewn roads with intermingled convoys.

Again I was just in time to help the *Ia!* With a few officers from the Division staff and some rural policemen, we got to work. After an hour, we had aleardy occupied and cleared up all important intersections, removed unimportant vehicles and units, and put order into the remaining convoy, so that the regiment could attack.

We now marveled at the organizational foresight of the Americans, who left us 150–180,000 liters of fuel, neatly packed in canisters, at the road crossing north of Samrée. By using all available infantrymen, we could refuel the almost empty regiment while driving by and throwing the full canisters up to the vehicles without any loss of time.[88]

Perhaps a little too optimistically, the corps staff daily report from 21 December stated the following:

a) The continuation of the enemy's active defense in the Dochamps–Soy–Hotton area, to protect its forces that detour to the northwest, must be reckoned with.

b) Since yesterday, uninterrupted continuation of the attack by *LVIII Panzer Corps.* After throwing back the enemy along the advance routes, the following were reached: The road intersection four kilometers west-southwest of Regné, [Baraque de Fraiture—*Author*] by the *560th Volks-Grenadier Division* with its right combat group, and due south of the Forge a Laplez estate (three kilometers northwest of Dochamps) with the left combat group; the forest edge one kilometer southeast of Amonines by the *116th Panzer Division* with its Reconnaissance Battalion, and the southeastern edge of Hotton by the armored combat group. Since the early afternoon hours, heavy enemy counterattacks Hotton with tanks from the northeast, north, west, and southwest. Main effort from the northeast. Attacks repelled after heavy combat. Another enemy counterattack on Dochamps at noon, repulsed.[89]

The orders given during the night of 21/22 December by the staffs of *5th Panzer Army* and *LVIII Panzer Corps* were for advancing, but already disclosed the looming obstacles. The leadership of *5th Panzer Army* ordered the operation be conducted this way, "Bypass resistance, only cover the flanks, bulk remains in advance toward Maas, continue to confuse, split up, surround, reconnoiter in force, deceive."[90]

Misery is reflected in the missions. On the right, *LXVI Corps* was still fighting at St. Vith; the town was finally captured on the evening of 21 December. To the left, *XXXVII Panzer Corps* was hung up at Bastogne and was supposed to reconnoiter the Maas between Dinant and Givet. This does not even mention the bogged-down *6th Panzer Army*. In the middle of the *5th Panzer Army, LVIII*

Panzer Corps was to be reinforced by the arriving *2d SS-Panzer Division* near Durbuy. However, most of the division was still without fuel and was stuck behind the Our. The *560th Volks-Grenadier Division* and the *116th Panzer Division* were supposed to attack "still during the night," "to gain crossings . . . over the Ourthe;" the *116th* was to seize the one near Hotton. Given the way the situation was on the evening of 21 December, this was unthinkable.

The daily report about the situation of *Army Group B* by *Supreme Command–West* from 21 December was very optimistic; but after all, it ended with the following sentence:

> Since the beginning of the attack, the continuous action of the *116th Panzer Division* and the *2d Panzer Division,* under difficult terrain conditions and heavy enemy resistance, has caused combat effectiveness to drop heavily. Therefore, it is necessary to stick closely to the second echelon (*9th Panzer Division* and *15th Panzer-Grenadier Division*).[91]

On the evening of 22 December, Vogelsang wrote the following:

> A break in the attack! The Division charged 15 to 20 kilometers beyond the attack line and has its hands full defending the captured towns. The enemy's entire thrust concentrates on our spearhead in and around Hotton. In addition to his reserves already locally deployed, the opponent brings up units from his fronts at Aachen, from Holland, and the Saar, with great speed. . . .
>
> After all the forced marches in difficult terrain, and with the unavoidable casualties caused by heavy combat, our materiel situation is very tight. We had no more battleworthy tanks this morning. At noon, however, six new ones came rolling in, 17 more will follow, soon, ten more will come back from repair. It is high time!
>
> To compensate for the resulting personnel losses, replacement officers have already arrived. Replacements from the *Field Replacement Battalion* will be brought in as soon as possible.[92]

And now another glance at the opposing side.[93] In the morning of 21 December, parts of the staff of 3d Armored Division, messengers, engineers, supply, and rear echelon services of the division—about 200 men without heavy weapons—were in Hotton. Aside from this, there were one medium and one light tank, as well as a 57mm anti-tank gun. At the left bank of the Ourthe, the bridge was secured by a platoon from the 51st Engineer Combat Battalion, reinforced by one light anti-tank gun and two 40mm anti-aircraft guns. A second platoon from this battalion was stationed at a pedestrian footbridge near Hampteau, about two kilometers south of Hotton. Nobody was expecting an attack.

Toward 0700 hours, a few German *Panzer-Grenadiers* entered the eastern part of Hotton and took some prisoners. That must have been the reconnaissance deployed by Bayer out of Beffe, most likely a reinforced *Panzer-Grenadier* platoon from *Panzer-Grenadier Regiment 60.* At 0730 hours, eight grenades exploded in Hotton. This woke up the Americans and they prepared the defense of the town. Command was assumed by Major Fickessen from the 23d Engineer Battalion (Armored) of the 3d Armored Division.

At about 0900 hours, German tanks mounted the attack on Hotton, along the Soy–Hotton road, initially concealed by the forest that came close to the town. About seven tanks and several armored vehicles appeared in front of the town. According to residents, four tanks entered the town, but could not get to the bridge. They did destroy the two American tanks and other vehicles in town, but could not achieve anything against the anti-tank and anti-aircraft guns at the opposite bank. Quickly-laid mines and vehicles that were placed across the streets hindered the movements. One armored personnel carrier was destroyed by an American anti-tank gun, and one Panther sustained engine damage and had to be abandoned.

Meanwhile, the American occupation of the west bank was reinforced by units from the 84th Infantry Division, brought in from Marche. Exactly at the right moment, a platoon of tank destroyers equipped with heavy anti-tank guns from the 638th Tank Destroyer Battalion appeared, and destroyed the Panther that got closest to the bridge. After this, the two remaining Panthers withdrew from the town. Shortly thereafter, the occupation of Hotton received further reinforcement. A small task force from Combat Command R of the 3d Armored Division, consisting of seven tanks and twenty infantrymen, swinging around Ny, came to the town from Soy. Two platoons of infantry and, temporarily, one platoon of tanks from the 84th Infantry Division reinforced the defenders on the left bank of the Ourthe. With this, the Americans around Hotton were stronger than Bayer's units in front of Hotton. Luckily for Bayer, the cooperation of the Americans on the left and right of the Ourthe was limited exclusively to the fire support of the tank destroyers and heavy weapons from the 84th Infantry Division from the left bank. The leadership of the 84th Infantry Division strictly declined to send its units beyond the Division boundary to the right river bank. Yet, the platoon from the 638th Tank Destroyer Battalion still achieved decisive successes from the left bank of the Ourthe against the German tanks. Immediately after arriving on the morning of 21 December, it destroyed *Oberleutnant* Köhn's lead Panther, which came to within 80 meters of the bridge. Köhn lost an eye and three men from his crew were killed. The grievous loss of tanks on the afternoon of 21 and 22 December is also attributed to the deployment of that platoon of tank destroyers from different positions on the opposite bank. Obviously, its guns were not detected.

The surprise attack failed. Several days' fighting ensued. The forward-echeloned units of *Group Bayer* were under increasing danger of being cut off by the attacks of Combat Command R out of Soy. They started in the morning of 21 December, were repeated in the afternoon with the strength of a mixed battalion, and continued on the morning of 22 December. On 22 December, the journal of *2d Battalion, Panzer Regiment 16,* stated the following:

The morning begins quietly. Later, toward 0830 hours, the opponent tries to attack again out of Soy with tanks and infantry via the Melines mill, and across the major road in the direction of Hotton. *Oberfeldwebel* Pichler lets the tanks come as close as possible and from his covered position destroys the first Sherman. Upon on this, the others retreat to their starting positions. Two *Panzer Vs,* coming back from repair, succeed in establishing good firing positions in the forest south of Melines. The opponent is mainly caught along the forest path from Soy to Melines. Four more Shermans are destroyed from this position.[94]

On the evening of 22 December, another American attack hit the flank of *Group Bayer.* A parachute infantry battalion, reinforced by a tank destroyer company, arrived in the afternoon to reinforce Soy. It was immediately sent into battle to free the trail to Hotton. In the unfamiliar terrain, after darkness had set in, the attack toward Bayer's security positions near Melines failed. The *LVIII Panzer Corps* daily report about 22 December, summarized as follows:

a) Corps counts on further local counterattacks to delay our attack across the Ourthe.

b) Numerous counterattacks by the *116th Panzer Division* in the vicinity of Hotton, as well as several enemy attacks with tank support repelled. Heavy, bloody losses for the enemy. During the whole day, severe effects of fire from both sides on the Soy–Hotton and Trinal–Melines roads. Afternoon enemy attack from the vicinity of Amonines toward Magoster repulsed.[95]

The corps' intention remained the "attack across the west bank of the Ourthe." Nevertheless, now at least an advance battalion of the *2d SS-Panzer Division* appeared east of the Baraque de Fraiture intersection, which was still in enemy hands.[96]

The daily reports by *Army Group* and *Supreme Command–West* again sounded quite optimistic. About the *5th Panzer Army* they stated, "Advance battalion of *5th Panzer Army* and armored spearheads are in further attack everywhere toward the northwest, against enemy reserves that were quickly thrown into battle."[97]

Spearheads of the *XLVII Panzer Corps* reached the area south of Marche and closed up to St. Hubert on 22 December. However, *58th Panzer Corps* was bogged down. Bastogne was still the thorn in the side and continued to tie up strong elements of the *Panzer Lehr Division.* The *LVIII Panzer Corps* was tasked to "first gain the line Durbuy–Ciney," while the *XLVII Corps* was deployed toward the Dinant bridge.[98] Above all, a change in the weather became apparent. The *Supreme Commander–West* issued a warning.[99] Out of concern about the dangerously tight fuel situation, he again gave energetic orders to conserve.[100]

On 22 December, reconnaissance elements deployed by the *116th Panzer Division* toward La Roche established that the town was free of the enemy and that the bridge was hardly damaged. It was immediately secured and repaired. The Division and corps staffs now faced the decision of breaking off the battle at

Hotton, but first, a last attempt was to be made to seize it. For this, *2d Battalion* of *Panzer-Grenadier Regiment 156* was advanced during the day into the forest east of Hotton.[101] It received the support of all available tanks, while the *1st Battalion, Panzer-Grenadier Regiment 60,* with several tanks, kept its rear toward Soy open. *Hauptmann* Kroll, Commander of *1st Battalion, Panzer-Grenadier Regiment 60,* especially distinguished himself eduring these battles at Melines. He was seriously wounded and lost a leg.[102]

The night attack by *2d Battalion, Panzer-Grenadier Regiment 156* failed. The morning report of 23 December to corps headquarters stated the following:

> 2400 hours, *Combat Group Bayer*'s surprise attack on the Hotton bridge unsuccessful. 0215 hours, renewed attack repulsed. Attack terminated. Division is diverted across La Roche bridge toward the west bank of the Ourthe.
>
> 0400 hours, reinforced *Division Escort Company* in Beausaint. Armored reconnaissance ahead of *Escort Company.*
>
> 0530 hours, after leaving security positions along Hotton–Soy road, Division moves out.[103]

The reports in the morning by other divisions provided only little hope. The attack by the *560th Volks-Grenadier Division* from Dochamps on Amonines again could not break through. The *2d SS-Panzer Division* attacked Baraque de Fraiture.

On 23 December, the *116th Panzer Division* could turn its intention into action only with weak forces. Tanks and *Panzer-Grenadiers* could not be released during the day because of increasing enemy fire, repeated attacks out of Soy, and the enemy air forces, which got back into action after the change in the weather. Besides the *Division Escort Company,* only the reinforced *Armored Reconnaissance Battalion* could being marching. It followed the reconnaissance that was sent ahead, via Ronchamps–Halleux–Gênes into the vicinity of Grimbiémont, which it reached by noon. Reconnaissance showed that the bridge on the road to Marche, 3.5 kilometers west of Grimbiémont, was destroyed, and that the enemy occupied newly improved positions south of the Hotton–Marche road, ahead of the *Division Escort Company* near Hamoul and ahead of *Reconnaissance Battalion* at the southern borders of Marenne and Verdenne.

On the afternoon 23 December, in the forest south of Verdenne, *Armored Reconnaissance Battalion 116* prepared for the attack to the north. Its artillery, *2d Battalion, Armored Artillery Regiment 146,* moved into position east of Grimbiémont. Contact with the *2d Panzer Division* was established in Bande; on this day, its *Armored Reconnaissance Battalion 2* advanced up to five kilometers east of Dinant.[104] It reached its objective along side roads with hardly any enemy contact. The *Panzer Lehr Division* was fighting near Rochefort. The first units of the *9th Panzer Division* approached Bande. However, the *2d Panzer Division* lacked the fuel to bring up stronger forces to take advantage of the success of its reconnaissance battalion. It also felt threatened in its right flank near Marche.[105]

At noon on 23 December, headquarters, *LVIII Panzer Corps* sent two orders to the *560th Volks-Grenadier Division* and the *116th Panzer Division*. The *2d SS-Panzer Division* left the corps area and was subordinated to the *II SS-Panzer Corps*. The first order was as follows:

> During the night of 23/24 December, *LVIII Panzer Corps* attacks Ciney with the *116th Panzer Division* across line Hotton–Marche. Without awaiting the bulk of the Division, it is important to use available forces to interrupt the roads leading from northeast and north toward Marche early.
>
> During the night of 23/24 December, the *560th Volks-Grenadier Division* relieves the *116th Panzer Division* in its entire sector and holds the former main battle line of the *116th Panzer Division*. The right flank near Amonines is to be secured with sufficient forces.[106]

Given the experiences of recent days, the second order, which aimed at considerably more distant objectives, did not reflect much reality. Thereby, the *560th Volks-Grenadier Division* was not only to relieve the *116th Panzer Division,* but also to continue the attack to the northwest across the Ourthe, southwest of Durbuy; it was then to take over the protection of the corps' right flank between Maffe (ten kilometers west of Durbuy) and the Ourthe. The mission for the *116th Panzer Division* was very much directed at the leadership of the Division:

> *116th Panzer Division* with *Armored Reconnaissance Battalion* arrives at the vicinity of Ciney–Leignon via Marenne, Baillonville, Pessoux, and from there reconnoiters toward the line Namur–Dinant.
>
> The next following regimental combat group gains the Soy–Heure area via Marenne, Baillonville and covers the corps' right flank toward the north and northeast.
>
> Armored combat group and last infantry combat group via Hogne–Pessoux to area Ciney–Leignon.

This reads like a march order. However, when this order was issued, it was known that one had to reckon with a refreshed enemy along the line Hampteau–Marche. On 23 December, the paragraph about the enemy in the daily report by the *116th Panzer Division,* therefore, stated the following:

> Enemy defends tenaciously south of road Erezée, Hotton, Marche, and mounts numerous counterattacks. All breakthrough attempts by the enemy were repelled. Retrograde movements from east toward Erezée may indicate a retreat across the Ourthe; whether the opponent also has tendencies to pull back west of Hotton remains to be seen. It is important for the Division to achieve a quick breakthrough toward the north, between Hotton and Marche, to prevent reinforcement of the opponent in his position.[107]

The following was reported about the events involving the units of the Division which had not yet been relieved:

Enemy pressure increased in the vicinity of Hotton, Melines during the morning. Numerous enemy attacks with tank support out of the vicinity of Soy were repulsed. Continuous, heavy artillery fire on main battle area and roads in rear.

Our tanks provided covering fire to the *Volks-Grenadiers* attacking east of Dochamps.

During afternoon hours, continuous air raids on supply roads and towns of the rearward areas.

No *Luftwaffe*.

The surrounded enemy group [from the 3d Armored Division—*Editor*] was still near Marcouray. At 1600 hours, the Division requested their surrender through a parliamentarian, but the commander of the enemy group declined. The parliamentarian reported about 30 tanks and armored vehicles, trucks and cars. Shortly after the negotiations, 40 to 50 twin-engine aircraft appeared and tried to resupply the encircled unit from the air, but, according to American reports, were unsuccessful.[108] As already portrayed, this enemy group endured, without being seriously attacked from the German side, until, after destroying its equipment, it found its way back on foot to its own lines on 26 December.

On 23 December, at 1600 hours, Vogelsang wrote down the following:

> Enemy pressure at Hotton became too strong. It was no longer possible to capture the dominant enemy cornerstone at Soy and to advance beyond Hotton. Since it was important to prevent the enemy from further occupying the already battered points, this morning, however, corps headquarters ordered a halt to the attack on Hotton bridge, and released the Division for an attack via the La Roche bridge, which meanwhile was reported free of the enemy and occupied by our advance units in the direction of Marenne. . . .
>
> On top of everything, the favorable, foggy weather gave way to clear winter sun. Right away, across the entire western horizon, the countless streaks of white vapor trails moved across the sky, an impressive but scary show. The air is filled with uninterrupted humming. The number of bombers, fighter bombers, and fighters cannot be counted![109]

While on 23 December the eyes of the *116th Panzer Division* were already fixed past Marche to the north, most of the Division remained tied down in its old position. During the night of 24 December, the *560th Volks-Grenadier Division* relieved these units. The relief was not halted even though the enemy entered Hotton, but the Soy–Hotton road was now again entirely in the opponent's possession. This could be tolerated, since on the evening of 23 December, Manteuffel ordered, "the *560th Volks-Grenadier Division* to cease its attack toward the north. The *LVIII Panzer Corps* continues its attack westward toward Marche and Ciney with strongly combined forces even at night.[110]

The strong combination of forces could only apply to the *116th Panzer Division*. However, by orders of its superiors on 24 December, this unit went into action completely scattered, as could be seen by the corps order and as will be seen momentarily in a scary way.

According to the available German and American sources, the events of the ensuing days cannot be explained to the last detail. Despite this, I will attempt to present a summary, with the help of my memory.

Armored Reconnaissance Battalion 116 succeeded still during the night of 23/24 December to push into a gap in the enemy position west of Verdenne and to advance up to the Hotton–Marche road.[111] On 24 December, at 1200 hours and 1700 hours, it was even reported to corps headquarters—probably by mistake—that the Marche–Baillonville road had been reached.[112] In the morning, the Division command post was relocated first to Grimbiémont, and later to Lignières. *General* von Manteuffel showed up in Grimbiémont and ordered an attack on the move without waiting for the bulk of the Division.[113] At 1045 hours, via radio, the corps staff also urged an attack.[114] However, the Division advanced only slowly via Samrée–La Roche, since the enemy air forces again zoomed about undisturbed in the sky.[115,116]

The next unit to arrive during the morning was *Panzer-Grenadier Regiment 156,* minus its *2d Battalion,* which was the last one to be relieved at Hotton. At noon, under the command of *Hauptmann* Baumgarten-Crusius and reinforced by elements of *Panzerjäger Battalion 228,* the *1st Battalion* launched an attack toward Verdenne. The purpose of the attack was to reestablish contact with the forward elements of the *Armored Reconnaissance Battalion,* which had been cut off as a result of an enemy attack. Verdenne was taken, but the link-up could not be achieved. An American tank and infantry counterattack hit the units of the *Armored Reconnaissance Battalion* that were in the forest northwest of Verdenne in the flank and inflicted heavy losses. The *1st Battalion, Panzer-Grenadier Regiment 156* was probably hit by the same counterattack, suffered losses and again lost a part of the town.[117] Now the arrival of the armored group was anxiously awaited to get the attack moving and, if possible, to advance in depth toward the objectives indicated by Manteuffel. Bayer's combat group consisted of *Panzer Regiment 16* (13 *Panzer Vs* and two *Panzer IVs!*), the entire *Panzer-Grenadier Regiment 60,* the *3d Company* of *Armored Engineer Battalion 675,* and the *1st Battalion* of *Armored Artillery Regiment 146.*[118] Its arrival was delayed by difficulties when crossing the bridge at La Roche, so the attack could not be mounted before 1720 hours. The engineer company lost contact and did not take part in the attack. The artillery got into position, but the assignment of observers to the attacking battle troops seems to have not worked out. Only the commander of the *1st Battalion, Hauptmann* Vinke, accompanied the attack in his armored radio vehicle; however, he seems to have failed to establish functional fire control because Bayer reported "the breakdown of the artillery-armored radio vehicle."

Verdenne was captured after a hard battle in which the *2d Battalion, Panzer-Grenadier Regiment 60* fought dismounted, and the enemy was mopped up to the extent possible. The forest area north of the town was subsequently gained, and from there, reconnaissance elements were deployed across the Hotton–Bourdon–Marche road toward the Narve stream crossings. It reported strong enemy occupation and minefields everywhere. Therefore, a continuation of the attack during the night was not possible. Bayer reported to the Division that he would like to attack again on the morning of 25 December, and asked for the support of the Division's entire artillery. He also asked that the remaining combat troops join his attack. At 0515, Division ordered Bayer to, "Defend what has been gained, dig in. By all means, block Hotton–Marche."

During the night, the Americans recaptured Verdenne through a tank-supported counterattack and Bayer was surrounded in his hedgehog position. Contact remained interrupted with the forwardmost elements of *Reconnaissance Battalion* and with the *1st Battalion, Panzer-Grenadier Regiment 156*. On the morning of 25 December, only the *2d Battalion, Panzer-Grenadier Regiment 156*, which arrived in the meantime, was at the Division's disposal. Additionally, nine tanks under the command of *Hauptmann* Kuchenbuch arrived from the maintenance shops. The attempt finally to seize Verdenne was to be made with these forces, which were also to restore contact with the groups that were cut off near and north of the village.[119] The journal of *2d Battalion, Panzer Regiment 16* from 25 December contains the following description of this attack:

> The five *Panzer IVs*, which are to be led forward by *Leutnant* Grzonka, are being combined with four *Panzer Vs* under the command of *Hauptmann* Kuchenbuch; initially, their mission is, with only a few *Grenadiers* [the *2d Battalion, Panzer-Grenadier Regiment 156—Author*] to take Verdenne, to free *Battalion Baumgarten*, and then to push through to the *Combat Group. Platoon Grzonka* has to take over security of the right flank. . . .
>
> At 1130 hours, the tanks roll out of their positions and lay a barrage on Verdenne.
>
> In heavy artillery and anti-tank fire, four *Panzer Vs* are destroyed within a few minutes. *Platoon Grzonka* succeeds in entering the town first. Thereby, the lead vehicle is destroyed by an enemy tank. After assembling near the town exit toward Marenne, the remaining tanks again attack the center of town and reach the bend in the street, east of the church. There, the weak combat group is dug in. Two *Panzer-Grenadier* companies that are to be brought up have not arrived as of yet. [Probably written in the evening of 25 December—*Author*].[120]

Already in its preparation area, the *2d Battalion, Panzer-Grenadier Regiment 156* was caught in a heavy enemy artillery barrage, which prevented it from attacking in concert with the tanks. Its commander, *Hauptmann* Gerke, was seriously wounded, and died of his wounds shortly thereafter. At least, the attack led to freeing the remnants of this regiment's *1st Battalion*. Even some cut-off units from the Division *Armored Reconnaissance Battalion* managed to get back. *Group Bayer* was left on its own. At 0800 hours, it repelled the attack of an infantry company supported by tanks, and numerous assault and reconnaissance troops during the course of the day. It mopped up enemy infantry near its positions, and with fire blocked the Hotton-Marche road in the vicinity of the railroad station (Halte) and the little village of Bourdon.[121]

On the evening of 25 December, the situation of the *116th Panzer Division* was most unpleasant. Most of its combat units were destroyed or encircled by the enemy. A weak security line was established from the remnants of *Panzer-Grenadier Regiment 156* along the verge of the forest south of Verdenne. Luckily, the artillery was intact and in position. *Army Anti-Aircraft Battalion 281* was also here, and in the morning of 25 December, was in position in the vicinity of Roy–Lignières. The *Division Escort Company,* which since the morning of 23 December had secured the right flank of the Division in the Ourthe Valley toward Hampteau, was to be relieved on the evening of 25 December by the *Corps Escort Company,* and brought back to the Division.[122]

The *2d Panzer Division* fared even worse on 25 December. On the day before, it was arrayed in a long, spread-out line between Dinant and the area southwest of Marche. The 2d Armored Division threw itself upon its forward-echeloned units and destroyed the individual groups that were hindered in their mobility by lack of fuel. A British tank brigade took part in the fight against *Armored Reconnaissance Battalion 2* near Dinant.

Even the approaching *9th Panzer Division* and units from the *Panzer Lehr Division* that were called upon to help could no longer save much. However, the *9th* at least closed off the gap between the *2d* and *116th Panzer Divisions* and relieved their worries about their respective deep flanks.[123] On 26 December, the *Führer Escort Brigade* was to be inserted to the right of the *116th* to attack toward the line Hampteau–Menil with Noiseux as its objective.[124]

Despite all the setbacks, the corps order from the evening of 25 December, requested:

> *LVIII Panzer Corps* to protect the northern flank of *5th Panzer Army*, first by closing off the area northeast of Marche, then, following the attack of *6th Panzer Army,* with the right wing to start another attack toward the northwest along the whole front as soon as possible. . . .
>
> The *116th Panzer Division* joins the attack of *Brigade Remer,* advances via Baillonville toward Sinsin to protect the north flank. . . .
>
> Maximum damage to the opponent must be inflicted continuously ahead of the front by strike units, especially in vicinity north of Marche. . . .
>
> Common boundary to *XLVII Corps*: Houffalize (inclusive)–Marche (exclusive).[125]

The *5th Panzer Army* order from 25 December was a little more careful and only required *LVIII Panzer Corps* to protect the Army's northern flank.[126] The *XLVII Panzer Corps* was ordered to reestablish contact within the *2d Panzer Division*, to take Bastogne, and to advance toward Dinant by slanting to the south.

The *Supreme Commander–West* ordered the *6th Panzer Army* to stop the attack toward Elsenborn, and to strengthen the spearheads of the left wing.[127] This was an urgently needed measure to provide relief to the *5th Panzer Army,* which was ordered to mop up Bastogne. It was also ordered to advance to the Maas, and thereby achieve all the prerequisites for the continuation of the offensive. All these orders were obviously drafted before the extent of the losses of the first day of Christmas were first recognized. [In the European Christian tradition, 24 December is Holy Night and the 25th and 26th of December are the first and the second days of Christmas—*Translator.*] The daily report to *OKW* still sounded optimistic, even as the enemy conducted diversionary attacks against the *15th Army,* and the enemy air forces devastated the front and rear areas. Among other things, this report states the following:

> On 25 December, the attack by *Army Group B* was the target of strong enemy coun-terattacks from the north and west against the spearheads of the *5th Panzer Army.* The back-and-forth battles lasted the whole day. With the approach of the *9th Panzer Division* and the *Führer Escort Brigade*, as well as the advance of *II SS-Panzer Corps,* relief will be forthcoming here and will make it possible to continue the attack on the Ourthe and beyond.[128]

On the morning of 26 December, under the leadership of the commander of *Armored Reconnaissance Battalion 116, Major* Stephan, the *116th Panzer Division* gathered all its combat units to make a last attempt to free Bayer and to support the attack of the *Führer Escort Brigade.* The journal of the *2d Battalion, Panzer Regiment 16,* depicts its course as follows:

> In the morning, units from *Armored Reconnaissance Battalion 116* conducted an attack on Hill 326, due west of Verdenne. *Combat Group Kuchenbuch,* with the remaining units and mounted *Grenadiers,* pushes through the western part of Verdenne, which is occupied by the enemy, to support the attack by the reconnais-sance battalion. The reconnaissance battalion is able to take Hill 326, but then remains pinned down under the strongest enemy fire. Near the western edge of town, the tanks run into heavy artillery fire and the opponent succeeds in breaking up the reconnaissance battalion's attack by fire.
>
> Toward 0800, individual enemy tanks join the battle. Through hits and direct hits, the remaining tanks are immobilized. Hereby, our crews sustain heavy losses. *Leutnant* Grzonka is wounded, dismounts, and is killed by enemy machine-gun fire.
>
> Nevertheless, due to our tanks, the much superior opponent suffered consider-able losses.
>
> The dismounted crews, under *Hauptmann* Kuchenbuch, prepare to defend in the last houses, and by 1200 hours, beat back an enemy attack.
>
> During a new attack by the enemy with tanks and infantry, these units have to fight their way back to our lines.[129]

Four *Panzer IVs* were lost right here. On 26 December, at 0830 hours, the *Führer Escort Brigade* reached the Hampteau–Menil road, fought at Menil at

0930 hours, and at 1430 hours attacked Hampteau. At 1625 hours, Headquarters *LVIII Panzer Corps* received orders to relieve the brigade immediately and to set it in motion to *XLVII Panzer Corps*. Allegedly, the situation at Bastogne required this.[130]

On 26 December, at 0330 hours, *Group Bayer* already started to hold its breath. During the night, the opponent attacked the hedgehog five times. All these attacks were beaten back, but the ever-increasing fire from heavy weapons caused the combat group many losses of men, weapons, and vehicles. Despite this, the group supported the attack by *Armored Reconnaissance Battalion 116* against Hill 326 with an advance toward direction Verdenne. It even succeeded in taking the castle situated between it and the village; but this attack was then brought to a halt by fire from Verdenne and Hill 326, which in the meantime was again lost. In the afternoon, the fire on Bayer's hedgehog increased—three very heavy barrages—and with infantry and tanks, the enemy pushed closer and closer to our lines. Ammunition became scarce. The last two *Panzer IVs* were lost and *Oberfeldwebel* Pichler was seriously wounded. *Oberst* Bayer now asked for permission to break out.

The Division granted permission at 1625 hours.[131] The *116th Panzer Division* went over to the defense. At 1730 hours, *Group Bayer* broke away from the enemy, and at 1830 hours it started the breakout via Marenne, which was overrun. At that point, it was organized as follows:

Spearhead: seven *Panzer Vs* and four assault guns.
Command element.
Panzer-Grenadier Regiment 60 (dismounted, because armored vehicles were needed to transport about 130 wounded),
Rearguard: two *Panzer Vs* with infantry.

Since there was a heavy artillery curtain laid on the verge of the forest south of Marenne, the spearhead platoon commander decided to turn off to the left toward Menil. The lead tank was destroyed near Menil. After this, by order of *Major* Tebbe, the combat group turned right and continued cross-country through an enemy position and minefields to the forest. When the movement up front started to falter, the rear units of the combat group did not follow to Menil, but used the route originally planned from Marenne through the forest toward Sur Waha. There, they again met up with the spearhead. *Group Bayer* then marched from Sur Waha to Chéoux.[132] For his dedication as commander of the tanks at the spearhead during the breakout, *Leutnant* Weissflog received the Knight's Cross, while *Oberst* Bayer and *Oberfeldwebel* Pichler each received the Honor Roll Clasp; nominations for awards were also submitted for *Oberstleutnant* Zander and several other soldiers of the combat group.[133,134] On 26 December, at 2210 hours, the Division reported to corps headquarters, "Bayer breakthrough successful, heavy losses, no details available."[135]

The corps order for the changeover to the defensive had been issued shortly before.[136] In addition to its existing sector, the *116th Panzer Division* was assigned the sector of the *Führer Escort Brigade*. If the enemy had attacked, this would have been an insoluble task. The Division feared it. Fortunately, the enemy remained passive.

Who was this opponent?[137] The 84th Infantry Division was defending west of the Ourthe, up to and including Marche. By 23 December, it had arrived with all its units. Two of its battalions were echeloned far to the south and became entangled with the *2d Panzer* and *Panzer Lehr Divisions*. The 335th Infantry Regiment, (minus one battalion) was in position around Marche. The 334th Infantry Regiment was defending between Verdenne and Hampteau. The 333d Infantry Regiment (also minus one battalion) formed the division reserve. Thus, the *116th Panzer Division* encountered the 334th Infantry Regiment, with its 3d Battalion near Verdenne and its 2d Battalion in the Menil–Hampteau sector. During the first American counterattack on 24 December against the penetrations by *Armored Reconnaissance Battalion 116,* units from the 1st Battalion and a company from the 771st Tank Battalion were taking part next to the 3d Battalion's reserve company. The *1st Battalion, Panzer-Grenadier Regiment 156* also collided with them. Besides, during the night of 24/25 December, the 84th Infantry Division had most of the 3d Battalion, 333d Infantry Regiment, with a tank company, deployed for the recapture of Verdenne. First, this attack hit Bayer, but left his hedgehog alone and took the town. In turn, the town was attacked and in part recaptured by noon on 25 December by the *2d Battalion, Panzer-Grenadier Reigment 156*. Obviously, the 3d Battalion, 333d Infantry Regiment remained inserted in the front between Verdenne and Menil, because two of its companies fought near Menil on 26 December and during the night of 26/27 December. During the night of 25/26 December, the 1st Battalion, 333d Infantry Regiment finally attacked Bayer's position, but without success.

Besides the enemy air forces, which since 24 December again became overpowering, the artillery of 84th Infantry Division caused the biggest problems for the *116th Panzer Division*'s attack. The opponent's side had approximately 150 guns. "The deployment of guns was overwhelming."[138] In addition to the division's organic artillery, the 84th was supported by four battalions from VII Corps—including one with heavy 8-inch howitzers—and one battalion from 3d Armored Division. The infantry of the 84th Infantry Division also deserves recognition. It was rested, as opposed to the combat troops of the *116th Panzer Division*, and fought bravely.

The last Christmas of the war went down in a hail of fire for both sides. Only further to the rear was it possible to give it some thought. On 25 December [the day after Holy Night—*Translator*], in Gènes, Vogelsang wrote:

> Holy Night! . . . The infantrymen got a little fir tree from the snowy winter forest and decorated it with the silver strips thrown from allied airplanes. Our nice Belgian hosts donated a rabbit, the kitchen supplied a few bottles of wine and baked goods. Cigarettes and chocolate came from the Americans, involuntarily. Christmas songs were playing on the radio.[139]

On 26 December, Vogelsang summarized:

> The Division, which bounded forward at a swift pace and led the spearhead of the
> whole offensive for a long time, became the target of ever-increasing, fierce con-
> centric attacks from the ground and from the air. During its uninterrupted, heavy
> attack, pursuit, and breakthrough battles, it suffered losses that were so high that the
> *Panzer-Grenadier* regiments, the *Reconnaissance Battalion,* and the *Panzer* regi-
> ment, at this time, have to be considered as nearly destroyed. The Division is now
> forced to go over to the defensive along a thinly-secured line.

Vogelsang then shows numbers, from which the following details about prisoners (28 officers and 1,250 men), as well as destroyed or captured materiel, were
taken:

Materiel:

Type	Destroyed	Captured	Immobilized
Tanks	80	4	4
Other armored vehicles	8	1	–
Anti-tank guns	17	–	–
Aircraft	16	–	–
Mortars	36	–	–
Machine guns	174	–	–
Prime Movers	2	–	–
Trucks	192	35	–
Armored Vehicles	122	?	–

Vogelsang adds the following:

> These numbers only depict the quantities compiled by the Division. It is not possi-
> ble to establish the losses of materiel in the area held by the opponent, nor the cap-
> tured vehicles that were integrated, but not yet counted, by our individual troop
> units, but which could amount to a multiple of the above-mentioned numbers.

The Division's condition after the eleven days of the offensive is best
described in a 29 December report to corps headquarters. It says:

> The uninterrupted, continuous, heavy battles in which the Division has been
> involved since 16 December—especially the breakthrough battles of the first days
> and the offensive and defensive battles near Hotton and Verdenne—brought the
> Division heaviest losses of men and materiel. With the loss of a very many officers,
> including a large number of battalion commanders, adjutants, and company com-
> manders—regarding the *Panzer-Grenadiers,* most of the officers in these posi-
> tions—most of the junior leaders, and with the total loss of a considerable quantity
> of tanks and armored vehicles, mainly armored radio and other communication
> vehicles, or command vehicles, the Division lost much of its combat value, inner
> strength, quality, speed, and flexibility of leadership. The Division will be able to
> compensate for the numbers of these losses through its reserves, but not for those

of valuable officers and junior leaders, nor for the losses of tanks and armored vehicles. In these areas, immediate help from higher headquarters is essential. . . . Of special impact is the loss of 15 radio and 3 other armored communications vehicles. Here, quick relief is urgent, if the control of the Division is not to suffer.[140]

Table: 1 "Personnel Losses" speaks for itself:

	Killed	Wounded	Remaining w/units	Missing	Accidental Injuries	Sick	Total	
Officers	14	69	23	14	4	3	104	(23 present)
NCOs/EM	210	718	114	763*	25	87	1,803	(114 present)
							1,907	(137 present)

* Most of these were killed or wounded and captured (with four strike companies on the first day of the attack and during the breakthrough on 26 December via Marenne to our main battle line.

Tables 2 to 4 are included as Appendix 20.

The *1st Battalion, Panzer-Grenadier Regiment 156,* which took Verdenne on 24 December and was later overrun there by the opponent, was especially weakened. Vogelsang noted on 26 December, "*1st Battalion* must be rebuilt from scratch. It appears to be about the same for the rest of the units. To replace such losses, even the high number of replacements in the *Field Replacement Battalion* may hardly be enough."[141]

A total of seven tanks and four tank destroyers were still battleworthy.[142] On 30 December, 28 tanks and tank destroyers were reported.[143] The loss of officers was hard on the Division. On 16 December, all four *Panzer-Grenadier* battalion commanders became casualties. Furthermore, the bearer of the Oakleaves, *Hauptmann* Baumgarten-Crusius, and the wounded commander of the *1st Company, Armored Artillery Regiment 146, Hauptmann* Vinke, remained missing. The commanders of both *Panzer-Grenadier* Regiments were wounded, but remained present for duty. *Hauptmann* Ruppert, bearer of the Knight's Cross and Acting Adjutant of *Panzer-Grenadier Regiment 156,* was killed. *Major* Stephan had to go to the field hospital for some time, because an old neck wound opened up. *Oberfeldarzt* Dr. Maassen became the new Division physician.[144]

During 27 December and the following night, the Division regrouped for the defense. The front line, to be occupied only as a line of strongpoints, ran from Hamoul on the Ourthe via Waharday to the verges of the forests south of Marenne and Verdenne, from there through the forest, southwest to the mill, and to the destroyed bridge across the Hedrée stream (2.5 kilometers southeast of Marche). There it abutted the *9th Panzer Division,* which moved in next to the *116th.*[145] The *9th* stood in a bend, from there across the hills south of Waha–south of Marloie to Rochefort, where it abutted the *Panzer Lehr Division.*

The foreward-echeloned units of *2d Panzer Division* tried to fight their way back to this line.[146] In the sector of the *116th Panzer Division, Armored Reconnaissance Battalion 116* took over the right sector, with the *Corps Escort*

Company being temporarily attached, and as of the evening of 26 December, only the *3d Company* of *Armored Engineer Battalion 675* established security in the center. After a short rest period, *Panzer-Grenadier Regiment 60* was deployed there. First, *Armored Engineer Battalion 675* was on the left in the sector west of Grimbiémont, and later *Panzer-Grenadier Regiment 156* (without the weakened *1st Battalion,* which remained the Division reserve). After its relief, most of the combat engineers dedicated themselves to their basic task, namely building obstacles. All battleworthy units from both battalions of *Panzer Regiment 16* were combined in a mixed battalion under *Major* Tebbe; men and materiel from the regiment that were not needed at present were moved toward the rear. Eight battleworthy batteries were reported; the *1st Battalion* of the *Artillery Regiment* seems to have been divided between the two other battalions.[147] The reinforcing artillery and the rocket launchers were evidently already pulled out on 23 December because on this day, they ended their logistical dependence on *LVIII Panzer Corps.*[148] *Army Anti-Aircraft Battalion 281* prepared to participate as field artillery in the ground battle. The Division command post relocated to Halleux on 27 December.[149]

On 26 December, La Roche and Houffalize were attacked by enemy aircraft. In Houffalize, rearward units of the *Panzer Regiment* suffered losses, and the bridge was destroyed in La Roche.[150] On the afternoon of 28 December, a replacement bridge with a capacity of 16 tons was built from combat bridging material. Vogelsang noted the following on the evening of 26 December:

> This morning, fighter bombers and bombers turned La Roche, in the valley between the hills near the Ourthe, into a smoking pile of rubble. Our anti-aircraft guns were able to shoot down some of the attackers. . . . If only the weather would turn bad again![151]

The enemy artillery was also very busy. Toward midnight on 27 December, in Mierchamps, Vogelsang noted:

> Early this morning, we were smoked out of Gènes. First, fighter bombers appeared and took care of some of the few houses, including the occupants who did not flee in time, as well as the vehicles nearby. Then, artillery planes began to circle and presented us with well-controlled fire from heavy guns. Finally, it became too uncomfortable; nobody can conduct a paper war in a foxhole! Thus, during a break in the fire, we moved here. Explosions everywhere!

On 26 December, for the first time, the daily report by *Army Group B* did not sound optimistic.[152] Our attack came to a standstill and the opponent mounted a counterattack against our spearheads. The air raids on the traffic network in the rear made the supply situation worse. Parts of the convoys had to drive back to the Rhine. Despite this, *Feldmarschall* Model did not judge the situation pessimistically and adhered to his plans of attack.[153] After this, however, Model put his statement in perspective:

The Supreme Commander of *Army Group B* not only assumes that all of the reserves, including *OKW* reserves, in his area will be available for deployment to achieve these objectives, but also expects the addition of three to four *Panzer* divisions from other theaters of war, for the formation of an operational reserve.

As further prerequisites for the success of this operation, not only will sufficient supply, especially fuel, and sufficient manpower replacements be required, but also a weather situation that excludes unhindered actions of the enemy air forces.

The question must be asked whether this was the correct method for influencing Hitler: First, to present a prospect of the objective, and then to bring up requests. Hitler probably only took notice of the first half. In his heart, the *Supreme Commander–West* did not share Model's assessment of the situation. On the evening of 26 December, he reflected on the following:

A supplement to the evening report of *Army Group B* and a situation report by its Chief of Staff more clearly depict the reinforcement of the enemy resistance that meanwhile arrived in front of our spearheads. The *II SS-Panzer Corps* could no longer achieve any substantial advances; the most forward units of the *5th Panzer Army* had to fend off heavy enemy attacks. Thereby, the *2d Panzer Division* was split into two groups. Any transport of troops and supplies during the present weather is just about impossible, since our *Luftwaffe* does not have sufficient impact on the superiority of the enemy, in spite of strong deployment. In addition, the reinforcements of the enemy in the vicinity of Bastogne forced the withdrawal and deployment to the south of the *Führer Escort Brigade,* which was to support the *116th Panzer Division* in the attack toward the northwest. In any case, the impression remains that the battles of 26 December reached a certain climax and that if the weather stays as is, a supply and provision crisis can develop.[154]

With resignation, the *Supreme Commander–West* arrived at the following noble decision:

Based on a personal description of the situation in Army Group South by the Chief of the Army General Staff, who is staying at *Supreme Command–West*'s command post, the *Supreme Commander–West* cannot deny the necessity of making an infantry division available for the prevention of a complete Russian breakthrough in the vicinity of Budapest. Therefore, the *Supreme Commander–West* orders (and *OKW* later permits) the immediate transportation of the *711th Infantry Division* to Army Group South.[155]

The following day, at *Generaloberst* Guderian's urging, the *344th Infantry Division* was also released by *OKW* for transportation to the Hungarian border. This was quite an achievement, but with the major Soviet offensive looming along the whole front between the Baltic Sea and the Carpathian Mountains, this was only a drop in the bucket. The *OKW* journal quotes an assessment of the situation by the *Wehrmacht* Operations Staff on 26 December, "which was approved by the *Führer* and Chief of the Armed Forces Operations Staff and shared by the *Supreme Commander–West*."[156] At the end it says, "The planned advance across the Maas toward the northwest, therefore, still seems to be possible, but depends on the restoration of balance at the Sauer and the destruction of the forces deployed between the Ourthe and Maas, north of the line Marche–Dinant."

On 27 December, as the *116th Panzer Division* was trying to establish a thin defensive front, it was reported that the Americans broke throught the encirclement of Bastogne.[157] At 2200 hours, *Supreme Command–West* received a *Führer* order to clear up the situation near Bastogne by attacking the deep flanks of the enemy's spearhead. All attempts for this failed, although the attacks were always continued with new forces until 8 January, even including the *6th Panzer Army*. Bastogne developed into a battle of attrition.

On 28 December, Model offered a status report, in which he put forth prerequisites and conditions, respectively, and he had to know that most of them could not soon or could not at all be realized.[158] Among other things, Model opined that an attack with the objective of destroying the enemy south of the Maas would be promising and necessary. The old objective [Antwerp—*Author*] would have to wait "for now." On 31 December, Model's status report still left a certain hope alive, but it was much more subdued than that of 28 December.[159]

In the daily reports from 28 and 30 December, the *Supreme Commander–West* expressed the suspicion that the enemy might attack Houffalize from the north as well as from the south, to cut off the bend in the front line west of the Ourthe.[160] On 27 December, one English division was detected in the vicinity of Dinant; more could be counted on. On 29 December, *Supreme Command–West* ordered *Army Group B* to take Bastogne first, then further plans can be made.[161]

The Rhine bridge near Remagen, along the main supply line of the railroad, was heavily damaged by air raids.[162]

Meanwhile, *OKW* and *Supreme Command–West* prepared the attack by *Army Group G* against the Saverne Gap, to provide relief to the southern front of the spearhead in the Ardennes. On 28 December, Hitler spoke to the commanders deployed in that area.[163] Among other things, he said, offensive operations would be the only way to change the situation in the West. He admitted that the attack in the Ardennes unfortunately did not have the expected, stunning success, but consoled himself with the fact that the opponent had to give up his plans, whereby along the entire Western front, an "immense reduction in tension took place." *Army Group B* now had the task of tying down the enemy forces, while the forces south of it were going to be destroyed in individual attacks. Once all this is done, he implied that the old operation could be resumed. *Army Group H* was to simulate an attack. That was all it could do. Since the strength for the attack by *Army Group G* also remained modest, it is hard to understand that they still had hopes of achieving successes that would make an impact.

In the East, the Soviet offensive threatened to break loose any day. Even if it was still quiet on the main front between the Baltic Sea and the Carpathian

Mountains, in Hungary the Soviets had encircled Budapest and had advanced to the River Gran between the Carpathians and the Danube.

On 29 December, *Generaloberst* Guderian telephoned the *Wehrmacht* Operations Staff, requested to break off the Ardennes offensive, and demanded that "everything be thrown into the East," but his effort was unsuccessful.[164] Even a repeat visit by year's end was in vain. A presentation by Guderian on 9 January 1945, based on an enemy status report from 7 January by the Intelligence Office, *Foreign Armies–East,* which said that a major offensive by the Soviets should be expected within "four to five days," also failed. Hitler declared General Gehlen's account as "totally idiotic."[165]

The Russians attacked on 12 January.

Part 3: Defense and Retreat

The last days of December of the year 1944 and the beginning of the month of January 1945 were quiet for the *116th Panzer Division*. It found time to strengthen its severely battered units and to bring in replacements. Even the weather was agreeable. First fog, then rain and snow hindered the enemy's air forces. His artillery, however, was therefore more active, especially during the night. The enemy infantry, in general, behaved passively.

On the morning of 28 December, the Americans penetrated south of Verdenne in about company strength. A counterattack cleared up the situation.[1] On 29, 30, and 31 December, the enemy also tried to reconnoiter out of Verdenne and Marenne into the forest. It was repelled everywhere.[2] The opponent pushed reconnaissance patrols forward out of Menil up to the area north of Sur Waha. On 30 December, because of frequent artillery fire, the Division command post relocated to Petit Halleux. *Generalmajor* von Waldenburg noted, "Fantastic quarters, like in Russia."[3]

Major troop movements by the enemy were detected near Marche on 29 and 30 December. First, it seemed as if the opponent near Marche was being reinforced. On 29 December, civilians reported extensive convoys with numerous tanks coming into Marche from the northwest. This raised concerns about an attack from this area and compelled corps headquarters to order, "*116th Panzer Division* provides artillery fire with emphasis on the vicinity southeast and south of Marche; *Panzer* reserve stands by at left wing."[4]

On this day, the Division was in possession of twelve battleworthy tanks and five tank destroyers.[5] On 30 December, continuing enemy troop movements through Marche toward the northeast were observed. Two English soldiers were taken prisoner south of Rochefort, and on 1 January, a member of the British 53d (Welsh) Division was captured, southwest of Marche.[6,7]

On 29 December, *LVIII Panzer Corps* also took command of the *9th* and *2d Panzer Division*s, whose forward line, after the withdrawal from Rochefort, ran from the left wing of the *116th Panzer Division* south of Waha toward Jemelle on the Lomme, and then south along the stream toward Grupont, halfway between Rochefort and St. Hubert. On 31 December, the Grupont–Mirwart sector, where the *Panzer Lehr Division* was fighting earlier, was added to this. Southeast of it, *XLVII Panzer Corps* conducted the battle for Bastogne together with Headquarters, *XXXIX Panzer Corps*—which was brought in from the Eastern Front— at times as *Group von Lüttwitz*.[8]

The 30 December order by the leadership of *5th Panzer Army* reckoned with the enemy's intention of cutting off our forces west of the Ourthe. The task for *5th Panzer Army* was to defend its front and to take Bastogne. While *LVIII Panzer Corps* defended the salient in the front that jutted out to the west, the other two corps were to encircle Bastogne from east and west and seize it.[9]

However, the enemy attacked the right wing of the *XLVII Panzer Corps,* between St. Hubert and Bastogne on 30 December.[10] On the right of the *116th Panzer Division,* east of the Ourthe, the *560th Volks-Grenadier Division* was relieved by the *2d SS-Panzer Division.* As of 29 December, *II SS-Panzer Corps* assumed control there. Its attack northwest did not succeed in breaking through. The front line ran north of Beffe–south Amonines and further northeast toward Stavelot. The *6th Panzer Army* could not make any further progress and had to relinquish the *I SS-Panzer Corps* with three *Panzer* divisions to Bastogne.[11]

To provide at least temporary relief to the units of the army, on 1 January, with a last major attack, the German *Luftwaffe* attempted to hit the opponent's tactical air force on the ground. In the morning, 1,035 German fighters took off for operation *BODENPLATTE* ("GROUNDPLATE") against the airfields in Holland and Belgium. The report from the German Armed Forces stated that about 400 aircraft were destroyed on the ground, 100 damaged, and 79 shot down during aerial combat. The estimate of these numbers was too high. The opposite side counted 180 destroyed and 100 damaged. Our own losses were very high: 277 machines were lost, including their pilots, among them almost 60 experienced unit leaders. A large portion fell victim to the fire of our own, uninformed antiaircraft units. The operation was a failure. The *Luftwaffe* did not recover from this bloodletting.[12]

At the beginning of the new year, Hitler made a speech on the radio, in which he called upon the German people

> not to grow weak in the future, but to trust in the leadership of the movement and to fight this difficult battle with the utmost fanaticism for the future of our people.[13]

He admitted the setbacks but,

> a people, who at the front and in the homeland achieve such an immeasurable feat, suffer and bear such terrible acts, can never go under. To the contrary: from this cauldron of tests it will rise stronger and more powerful than ever before in its history.

The soldiers at the front entered the new year with uneasy hearts. *Generalmajor* von Waldenburg, who celebrated his 46th birthday on 30 December, and for which Model expressed best wishes and appreciation, wrote in his calendar on New Year's Eve:

> For our Fatherland, as well as for me, probably the most difficult year imaginable came to an end. . . . The last attack gave all of us a lift. Even if the major objectives have not been reached, we keep on hoping. We have to persevere or we will be ruined! . . . God be with us in the new year, and may it finally bring us the long desired peace after the victory![14]

On New Year's Day, he confided in his new calendar:

What will the new year bring us? After we win, God, finally give us peace!—But how can we win?

Staff Paymaster Wolff-Boenisch wrote in his diary:

> Our high hopes have vanished. The enemy is attacking with strong forces again, and we changed over to the defense. Our cities are destroyed. The Russians reached East Prussia, and our troops in Italy are involved in bloody defensive battles. It is difficult to still believe in a victory. But can we give up and leave our families to the mercy of the enemy?[15]

Leutnant Schwörer from *2d Battalion* of the *Division Artillery Regiment* had little hope and cleared his soul of anger by writing:

> Our attempts get bogged down everywhere. Our Division lacks tanks, and most of all, ammunition. Infantry once again destroyed. Enemy resistance strong. . . . Where did our big plans go? Have they all been disposed of already? Or can we not do it anymore?
>
> *Luftwaffe* is no longer to be seen. If the weather is nice, all connections to the rear are cut off during the day. . . . They already destroyed all the bridges. We cannot understand how one can mount such an attack, knowing that there is nothing anymore, except us, a couple of attack divisions.
>
> There is no more aerial reconnaissance. We run forward, and when that's not possible, then backwards. . . .
>
> We celebrate the new year in a very depressed mood. Soon it will all be over.[16]

On 30 December, Vogelsang ordered the *Field Replacement Battalion* to dispatch 700 trained NCOs and soldiers; on 31 December, the *General der Panzertruppe—West* in Bad Ems promised to quickly replenish the *Field Replacement Battalion.*[17]

On 1 January, the commander of *1st Battalion, Panzer Grenadier Regiment 60, Hauptmann* Nagel, who was wounded near Vossenack, returned to the Division. During the night of 1/2 January, when he wanted to be shown the layout of his battalion's position, the engineer officer who was guiding him stepped on a mine and was killed immediately. Nagel was seriously wounded. Later, his left leg was amputated.[18] *Hauptmann* von Watzdorf assumed command of the battalion.

The opposing side regrouped in preparation for the attack on the northern flank of the German spearhead. Both sides attacked on the southern flank, as mentioned earlier. The Third Army continued its offensive against the German *7th Army* and against the southern front of the *5th Panzer Army* near Bastogne. The British XXX Corps appeared opposite *LVIII Panzer Corps,* west of the Ourthe. In the *116th Panzer Division*s sector, between the Ourthe and Marche, the 53d (Welsh) Division relieved the 84th Infantry Division. The British 6th Airborne Division arrived as the adjacent unit to the south. The main effort of the attack by the First Army was east of the Ourthe, with the VII Corps, which had two tank and two infantry divisions subordinated to it. Its objective was Houffalize, where it was to meet with the units attacking from the south. The 2d Armored Division attacked between the Ourthe and the Lüttich–Bastogne road, supported and followed by the 84th Infantry Division and one regiment of the 75th Infantry Division.[19]

For the Americans, the attack was to commence on 3 January. The British were to join the following day. The relief of the 84th Infantry Division by the 53d (Welsh) Division began on 1 January and was completed on the morning of the next day. On 2 January, the daily report by *LVIII Panzer Corps* about the situation of *116th Panzer Division* stated that vehicles from Marche were on the move to the southeast and east, that the infantry was relieved and thereby strengthened, and that a new formation had arrived.[20] Thus, the relief was discovered. The 53d (Welsh) Division deployed two infantry brigades at the front—the 71st to the right, the 158th to the left—and kept one more, the 160th, as well as the 33d Armoured Brigade in reserve. Eight artillery battalions [the British Army then called them "artillery regiments"—*Author*] were additionally subordinated to the 53d.[21]

On 3 January, the Americans mounted an attack east of the Ourthe against the *6th Panzer Army*. They achieved breaches up to three kilometers in depth.[22] In the sector of the *2d SS-Panzer Division*—immediately to the right of the *116th Panzer Division*—the opponent penetrated into Beffe and Magoster, so that the right wing of the *116th* at the Ourthe was left hanging in the air.[23]

At 1400 hours, the *116th Panzer Division* was subordinated to *II SS-Panzer Corps*, while the *9th* and *2d Panzer Division*s were again attached to *XLVII Panzer Corps*. *LVIII Panzer Corps* was released and took over command and control functions near Bastogne. The Division's left boundary was now also the boundary between the *6th* and *5th Panzer Armies*.[24] The most unpleasant side effect of the change in subordination was the order to give up the *1st Battalion* of *Panzer-Grenadier Regiment 156*, which had been hastily replenished. This sole, weak Division reserve had to be sent to the *12th Volks-Grenadier Division*, from whence the Division later got it back with a battle strength of one officer and four men. In its closing report about the defensive battles from 3 to 15 January 1945, the *116th Panzer Division* lamented the situation:

> Since a change in this decision could not be reached, in spite of all remonstrances, the Division now had to look ahead to the upcoming defense battles with the greatest concern. This was due even more to the fact that the supply of fuel, ammunition, and food continues with the greatest difficulties, at no time enough for the advance and the later battles of withdrawal, and not even for an emergency. Concern also sprang from the fact that the battle, as could be already predicted, would at times have to be fought on both sides of the Ourthe, which, in the vicinity of the front line, could only be crossed at one small bridge near La Roche. This bridge was continuously suffering from the effects of low-flying enemy aircraft and twin-engine bomber units.[25]

Fortunately on this day, the *7th Company, Panzer Regiment 16* finally arrived up front in the Division sector. In the middle of December, it took over the aforementioned 14 assault guns in Neuwied, trained the crews in the unfamiliar equipment, and on the evening of 1 January, having set out from the Eifel during favorable weather, quickly reached the area of deployment.[26]

On 3 January, Hitler admitted:

that the continuation of the originally-planned operation no longer had prospects for success, since *Army Group B* drew more than half of all enemy forces toward itself.[27]

Army Group B received orders from *Supreme Command–West* to maintain the "area gained, by and large" and to "clear up the situation at Bastogne under all circumstances." "The long defensive flanks" should receive "special attention," and, besides that, "the defensive capability of the *Westwall* should always be improved."

On 4 January, Hitler ordered *Supreme Command–West*:

Conduct rapid attacks against the Anglo-American armies, one after the other, in sectors which the *Führer* kept to himself, to destroy them one at a time. In this way, retain the initiative under all circumstances.[28]

The attack by the *1st Army* in Lorraine that had begun on 1 January was to be continued and the *19th Army* was to establish a bridgehead across the Rhine north of Strasbourg.

On the morning of 4 January, the British also attacked, using the 53d (Welsh) Division, against the *116th Panzer Division* between Hotton and Marche. In the evening, Vogelsang wrote down the following:

Early this morning . . . at all important points . . . extremely violent battles started, during which *"Das Reich"* and we lost some ground. The *1st Battalion, Panzer-Grenadier Regiment 60* and the *Division Escort Company* as reserve, closed off dangerous breaches. In spite of heavily blowing snow, the fighting continued with relentless force and did not abate until dark.[29]

The Division's final report stated the following:

On the morning of 4 January, after a one-hour barrage, the enemy mounted the expected assault along the entire Division front.

At first, the majority of the enemy advances were repulsed, however, the opponent succeeded in achieving several breaches . . . that could only be sealed off by deploying the last reserves. Since, in view of our high losses, one could not think of gaining back the old main battle line, during the night of 4/5 January, the Division withdrew according to orders to the line Hamoul–Boican-Bach–Waharday–Hills north of Grimbiémont–La Rochette, which had more favorable terrain and did not run exclusively through impenetrable forest terrain.[30]

The *7th Company* of the *Panzer* Regiment under *Oberleutnant* Harder, which had just arrived, went into action near Waharday.[31]

The history of the 53d (Welsh) Division reports that the attack by the 158th Brigade started at 0800 hours.[32] Two battalions attacked; by 1015 hours, the left one had crossed the forest between Menil and Waharday, while the right one reached its objective by noon. Heavy snowfall throughout almost the whole day, as well as deep snow on the ground, hindered all movements. While the resistance by infantry was not very strong, heavy artillery fire, mines, and hidden demolitions claimed their victims.

Even if the reserve battalion of the brigade was deployed in the afternoon beyond the right one in the front, and even if the left front battalion started to attack once more, the attack on Waharday did not get off the ground again.

At 1030 hours, a battalion of the 160th Brigade attacked along the Ourthe. It came to a halt in front of an obstacle near Rendeux-Bas. Attempts to go around it failed. During the night, the 160th Brigade received orders for more attempts to capture the town, and to thereby open the important road along the river. The brigade on the right, the 70th, attacked at 1300 hours with two battalions forward, while a third one covered the division's right flank, southwest of Marche. After fierce fighting and in the face of difficult conditions, at 1730 hours, the two attacking battalions had taken their objectives. At 1530 hours, the battalion on the right had to stave off an energetic counterattack. The description of the battles from 4 January, closes with the following:

> The battles of the day gave the division an idea of what winter attack operations in the Ardennes entail. The troops had no special clothing, no boots or camouflage suits, no special means of transportation at their immediate disposal. In the forests—and the largest part of the land was forests—it was often difficult to overcome the snowy and wet ground after leaving the vehicle. Map reading was mostly a matter of guesswork.

The weather on 5 January was similar, but it allowed the employment of aircraft. No progress was made along the Ourthe road, even though one of the attacks was supported by special ground attack aircraft. The brigade in the center slowly pushed forward, to the left without enemy resistance, and to the right with difficulties in combat against some German armored personnel carriers. In the afternoon, at 1730 hours, a strong German infantry counterattack, supported by tanks, hit this battalion and inflicted such heavy losses that it had to be relieved, and therefore, the 53d (Welsh) Division postponed its attack planned for 6/7 January. According to a note from Waldenburg, the *116th Panzer Division* was subordinated, probably in the evening of 4 January, to the *XLVII Panzer Corps,* which by now controlled the entire forward-echeloned front bend, west of the Ourthe.[33] The journal of the *2d Battalion, Armored Artillery Regiment 146* describes 5 January as follows:

During the day, the opponent tries to break into the front of our sector with strong reconnaissance patrols.

In the Aux Bruyères sector [1.5 kilometers southwest of Waharday—*Author*] he succeeds in trickling through the forest edge with weak forces. A group deployed immediately with several tanks throws the opponent back toward his line of departure. . . .

Sector along the Ourthe toward the northwest, up to Hamoul, is secured by reconnaissance patrols from the *Armored Reconnaissance Battalion*. . . . During the whole day, the battalion combats enemy movements with very brief bursts of fire, since very little ammunition is still available, and new supplies were not to arrive until the next day. New ammunition had to be brought in from Luxembourg (near Clerf) with ammo convoy. *6th Battery* supports the defensive battle of *SS-Reich*.[34]

From its forward-facing salient, as it already had during the previous days, the *116th Panzer Division* assisted its hard-pressed neighbor. In the history of the 84th Infantry Division, the heavy enemy artillery-, mortar-, and machine-gun fire from the west bank of the Ourthe is mentioned several times, as it hindered the attack on 5 January, and forced the forward units to be withdrawn to Beffe.[35] On the evening of 5 January, Vogelsang noted the following:

Luckily, the weather continues to be misty, dreary, and mixed with flurries. . . .

It must be strongly counted on that the opponent will pursue his intentions to fight for the road connecting to Bastogne via La Roche and Houffalize, and to cut us off. . . . In front of our left sector, the British 53d Division now showed up, and the English are unpleasantly tough!

On 6 January, Vogelsang wrote:

But now, it is again getting uncomfortable in our village. Since yesterday evening, huge pieces come down in front and in back of our few houses at regular intervals. . . . It also became very uncomfortable near the *Ia* in Petit Halleux. . . . Even the situation as a whole is getting uglier. On the right, the Americans were able to achieve a large breach. During the night, Houffalize was tossed about by a bomber squadron.[36]

The journal from the *2d Battalion, Armored Artillery Regiment 146* reports about that day:

During the night, searchlights light up the enemy's rear area.

The night passes—like the previous one—with strong, combined, barrages. . . .

During the whole day, no infantry fighting. Only some reconnaissance patrols probing our own line.[37]

The *116th Panzer Division* again experienced a day of major combat on 7 January. Its closing report summarized the events from 6 and 7 January as follows:

On 6 January, the expected continuation of enemy attacks on a broad front still did not take place. . . . On 7 January, the enemy resumed his attacks against Waharday, and with tanks and mounted infantry from Haye à Banny [1.5 kilometers northeast of Grimbiémont—*Author*] toward the southeast. After very strong artillery preparation, he extended them until noon to the entire Division sector. In spite of bitter resistance, his penetration into the village of Grimbiémont could not be prevented. All the other breakthrough attempts, however—right down to the last man—were stemmed or sealed off in the area of the road Chéoux—the road intersection east-southeast of Grimbiémont. Thereby, the Division again had such heavy losses, mainly among the *Grenadiers,* that the infantry's strength would not be sufficient to occupy the new line. At the same time, by order of corps headquarters, it had to release armored units from the front during this most dangerous situation and give them up to the unit to the right. There it was to prevent the threatening breakthrough toward Samrée and avoid the necessity of having to recapture the position in the sector north of Samrée in the future, which the Division was to take over after relieving *2d SS-Panzer Division "Reich."*[38]

The following entry about 7 January can be found in the journal of the *2d Battalion, Armored Artillery Regiment 146*:

The battalion that received ammunition during the night resists the attack with heavy barrages. With well-aimed fire, it succeeds in repelling the attack forward of the reconnaissance zone of the battalion and beats back the enemy. At the left wing, in the sector of *Panzer-Grenadier Regiment 60,* the opponent succeeds in breaking through the woods and takes Grimbiémont in the evening hours. Infantry retreats.

The battalion resists the enemy attack in front of its sector and throws the opponent back.

In the sector of the adjacent unit to the right (*SS Reich*), where there are also very heavy tank supported attacks, the AVKO [*"Artillery Verbindungs Kommando"*— Artillery liaison unit—*Translator*] Artillery Liaison Commander fights these attacks with barrages by the entire regiment. . . .

In the evening hours, the Division withdrew to the line Dochamps–Marcourt–Hodister–Roy.[39]

On this day, the battalion fired 225 rounds, not exactly a lot for such a battle. In the new position, it depended on cooperation with *Panzer-Grenadier Regiment 156*. The latter took over the part of the Division sector on the left of the Ourthe all by itself. *Panzer-Grenadier Regiment 60* and *Armored Reconnaissance Battalion 116* were fighting on the right of the river. Units of the *2d SS-Panzer Division* and *Engineer Battalion 62,* for the time being, remained deployed east of the Ourthe, and were subordinated to the leaders of the *116th Panzer Division* who were in command there. It was ordered that the railroad loop, one kilometer northeast of Dochamps, would be the contact point for the unit on the right. The closing report by the Division stated the following:

With regard to the high casualties, as well as numerous illnesses which the continuous battles claimed among the completely exhausted troops, and with regard to the lack of any kinds of reserves, only an occupation in the form of strongpoints could be considered from the beginning. The situation became more aggravated by the fact that the sector, which was covered with the densest forests and which the Division had to newly take over, was at the main effort of the previous enemy attacks, as well as those still to be expected.[40]

The new Division sector was very wide and split down the middle by the Ourthe River. The Division's leadership was quite worried about how to survive the next day. On 8 January, it was again put under the command of *II SS-Panzer Corps.* The Division command post was relocated to Borzée (four kilometers east of La Roche).[41]

The history of the 53d (Welsh) Division reports that on 7 January, the 158th Brigade, which attacked first with one battalion in the center, "met considerable resistance," but nevertheless around noon took its objective, the hills southwest of Waharday.[42] Now, next to it on the right, another battalion attacked and in the early afternoon took Grimbiémont. The battalion suffered heavy losses. Each of the two companies in front had only 25 men left. For the defense of the captured village, fortunately for the weakened battalion, some tanks arrived that were able to overcome the difficult terrain. Also around noon, the 71st Brigade, deployed to the right, started its attack with two battalions against the Hedrée stream, west of Grimbiémont. They took 95 prisoners. Their own losses were relatively small, despite very heavy fire and some harsh skirmishes. Nothing is reported in the history about this brigade's gain of ground.

The left sector of the *116th Panzer Division,* between Grimbiémont and the boundary to the *9th Panzer Division,* was defended on 7 January by the *2d Battalion, Panzer-Grenadier Regiment 156.* The German Army Honor Roll Clasp had been requested for the officer who had been its commander since 26 December, *Oberleutnant* Krüger.[43] The British complain in their history about insufficient support by artillery.[44] They had to be satisfied with the fire from their mortars, which nevertheless, for example, fired 1,000 rounds in 30 minutes against the *2d Battalion, Panzer-Grenadier Regiment 156.*

In the course of 8 and 9 January, most of the 53d (Welsh) Division was relieved by the 51st (Highland) Division. An astonishing undertaking! This provided some relief for the *116th Panzer Division* in its distress, at least west of the Ourthe.

During the night of 7/8 January, Hitler gave permission to abandon the salient that jutted toward the west, and also allowed a withdrawal toward the line Dochamps–Longchamps (northwest of Bastogne).[45] Since the opponent's objective no longer seemed to be worthwhile after this, it was assumed that he would move the main effort of his attack further east, or pull out ten to twelve divisions and employ them against empty front lines. To confront this danger, strong forces were to be released from the front immediately and be prepared as a reaction force. For this, Hitler ordered the withdrawal of *I* and *II SS-Panzer Corps* with its four *Panzer* divisions. The German attack in Lower Alsace and Lorraine also failed, although heavy fighting continued in Alsace until the end of January. The *Führer* directive from 8 January already showed signs in the actions ordered on the evening of 7 January. Vogelsang wrote at 2200 hours in Nieder-Besslingen (already on Luxembourg soil) in his diary:

> Superior pressure by the enemy and the threatening danger of encirclement made the command decide to withdraw in small bounds toward the east. The order for it arrived today.
>
> With all units of the staff that were not immediately needed for the battle, and with consideration of the extremely tight situation for quartering the troops, as well as the murky development in this strange, serpentine front line, we moved back here in one continuous march.
>
> Supply from the rear becomes more and more difficult. All needs for the front must be brought by trucks from the vicinity of Cologne. And this, across the frozen Eifel, always observed by aircraft, and with its countless traffic problems.
>
> Mainly, there is the lack of fuel, which had an especially bad effect in this difficult, mountainous terrain. It is almost impossible to tow the damaged tanks. Yesterday, a duty officer had to bring fuel in canisters to La Roche, so that a tank could change position![46]

In the *116th Panzer Division* sector, 8 January passed relatively quietly west of the Ourthe, thanks to the relief operations being conducted by the British. In the Dochamps–Cielle sector, which had just been taken over, the enemy's attack activity concentrated toward Cielle (two kilometers northwest of La Roche). The town was lost in the afternoon. It was possible to seal off the attack east and west of Cielle, under the leadership of the commander of *Armored Reconnaissance Battalion 116*. Units from *SS-Panzer-Grenadier Regiment "Deutschland"* fought here jointly with the *Armored Reconnaissance Battalion 116*.[47] The *2d Battalion, Armored Artillery Regiment 146,* on the left bank of the Ourthe, joined with its fire, supporting the units in combat on the east bank. In front of their sector, meaning in front of *Panzer-Grenadier Regiment 156,* in the vicinity of Chéoux–Hodister, enemy movements associated with the ongoing British relief were engaged.[48] The battleworthy tanks were mostly deployed in the vicinity of Dochamps.[49] The engineers supported the *Panzer-Grenadiers* in diligent construction of barricades.[50] The terrain offered very good possibilities for this.

The main effort of the enemy's attack on 8 January was further east in the sector of *LXVI Corps*. On 9 January, the opponent continued to attack the *6th*, as well as the *5th Panzer Army*. He achieved several breaches, but was essentially repulsed.[51] More unpleasant for the *116th Panzer Division* was a deeper penetration of the unit on the right in the forest west of Chabrehez. The right flank remained open, "because the adjacent division to the right, due to its weakness, was no longer capable of establishing the ordered link-up. The Division had to search for it with its own reconnaissance patrols."[52]

In the *116th Panzer Division* sector, the Americans attacked near Dochamps toward Samrée, and near Cielle toward La Roche. They were brought to a halt by the pitiful remnants of the *Panzer-Grenadiers* of the *116th Panzer* and *2d SS-Panzer Division*s, with the support of the few tanks and tank destroyers, as well as by the combined fire from the artillery and anti-aircraft. The engineers also had their share of success in the defense with their obstacles—mines, tree barricades, rock blasting—as well as with action in the battle.[53] Snowstorms made life difficult on both sides.

On the evening of 9 January, the unit on the left, *XLVII Panzer Corps,* withdrew to the line La Roche–St. Hubert. With it, the left wing of the *116th Panzer Division* moved back to the road from La Roche toward the southwest. Advanced command posts remained echeloned forward for about three kilometers.[54] The force of the American attack against *6th Panzer Army* subsided on 10 January.[55] During the morning, however, the enemy succeeded in seizing Samrée in the sector of the *116th Panzer Division* and in the afternoon entered La Roche with reconnaissance patrols. By the evening, the Division was deployed in a thin security line in the forest, southeast and south of Samrée, as well as one kilometer east of La Roche, west of the Ourthe, along the road La Roche–Beausaint–Vecmont. The Division command post moved to Wibrin.[56]

In a letter home, *Leutnant* von Elterlein from *7th Company, Panzer Regiment 16*, wrote about the battles of 10 January:

> Near Samrée security position at forest lane opposite Hill 568 [2.5 kilometers southeast of Samrée—*Author*] where the enemy is dug in . . . distance 1,200 meters! During day, heavy "ari-magic," our artillery shoots very well at 568, *Nebelwerfer* firing almost non-stop! Samrée–Nadrin road is under heavy enemy barrage. . . . In the evening we advance from the forest to the edge of the road and take Hill 568 under fire. Perform security duties all night, forest is swarming with enemy reconnaissance troops. Icy cold.[57]

According to this, rocket launchers were again subordinated to the Division and strengthened its defensive power. The infantry forces of the Division, however, were finished. In the evening of 10 January, *Generalmajor* von Waldenburg wrote, "Troops completely finished and cannot go on."[58] On 11 January, he added, "The battle is too uneven." In the evening of 9 January, Vogelsang stated:

> Now as before, the situation is frightfully bad. The battalions' strengths again dropped down to 100 men or less. . . . The troops are exhausted, the casualties very high.[59]

On 10 January, he lamented:

The condition of the troops is shocking! The infantrymen are completely worn out. Besides the bloody losses, illnesses and increasing frostbite cause painful gaps. In spite of everything, the opponent has not yet achieved a decisive breakthrough.

And on 11 January:

To justify our request for replacements and the urgent references by the *Ia* about the state of the Division to Army Group, today we compiled the losses since Arnhem (end of Sept.) They are:

225 officers, 6,400 NCOs and men, of them

115 officers, 2,850 NCOs and men, in the winter battle of the Ardennes alone.

These numbers paint a shocking picture!

East of the Ourthe, 11 January went by relatively quietly. Apparently, the Americans had a day of rest. But west of the river, at the left wing of *116th Panzer Division*, the 51st (Highland) Division now became active. In the early morning hours, it attacked Beausaint and in the afternoon entered La Roche, which had already been vacated by the *116th*. Leaving the town, the British tried to advance south. A heavy skirmish developed and at 2000 hours, they succeeded in breaking through to Hives, and taking the village by surprise in the dark. The battles west of the Ourthe were described in the closing report of the *116th*:

In the meantime, in agreement with *II SS-Panzer Corps,* this sector suffered a further weakening by releasing one company of *Panzer-Grenadier Regiment 156* from the front, and moving it to the decisive east bank of the Ourthe as reserve. Thus, there were now only two weak *Panzer-Grenadier* companies along a front line of six kilometers, opposing an enemy several times superior, which was well-rested and mounted an attack with fresh forces. At dawn, after the enemy first overran the outposts north of Beausaint and captured the village, there were alternating battles of several hours' duration with high losses on both sides. In spite of the bravest opposition by *2d Battalion, Panzer-Grenadier Regiment 156,* the enemy succeeded in advancing to the southern edge of the forest, south of La Roche. There, in a combined attack, he pushed to, and several kilometers southward beyond, the strongpoint at the main road from La Roche to Ortho.[60]

On the night of 11/12 January, *XLVII Panzer Corps* withdrew as planned across the western tributary of the Ourthe.[61] Rear guards remained ahead of the river, the remnants of the *2d Battalion, Panzer-Grenadier Regiment 156* which were temporarily subordinated to *2d Panzer Division,* at their right wing.

The Division command post was relocated from Wibrin to Achouffe.[62] The whole area was covered with snow, about 20 centimeters deep. It was clear and cold. Since 10 January, the enemy air forces were again buzzing around in the sky.

Supreme Command–West reported about 12 January, "The enemy attacks in the Ardennes were weaker than on the previous day."[63]

The strongest attack of the day hit the corps to the right, the *LXVI Corps*. The enemy took Chabrehez from the *560th Volks-Grenadier Division,* which was the division to the right of the *116th.* On 11 January, the *2d SS-Panzer Division* was again inserted to the right of the *560th.* On 12 January, the *9th SS-Panzer Division* *"Hohenstaufen"* again had to move to the front, to the right wing of *LXVI Corps.* On 12 January, numerous advances by the enemy in the forests between the Samrée–Nadrin road and the Ourthe were "repulsed" by the *116th Panzer Division* in "bloody battles with high losses on both sides."[64] In the vicinity of Borcée, the Americans surprised a platoon of the *1st Company, Armored Engineer Battalion 675,* which was laying mines. Suddenly, armored vehicles appeared in the sparse forest and shot the platoon to pieces. Several soldiers were killed, the remainder were wounded and captured.[65] During the battles at Borcée, the commander of *2d Battalion, Panzer-Grenadier Regiment 60, Hauptmann* Banaski, distinguished himself. With six men of his staff, he opened the return route out of a little mountain village for his already cut-off battalion and defended his position until the withdrawal in the evening, in spite of a bullet through the thigh.[66]

During the night of 12/13 January, within the framework of a general withdrawal, the *116th Panzer Division* pulled back to a line which led from the road fork, five kilometers east-southeast of Samrée, via Bérisménil toward the Ourthe bend, two kilometers southwest of Bérisménil (the Ourthe being left boundary of the Division). The widening of the Division sector to the east up to the road Chabrehez–Wibrin called for the deployment of all available Division forces in the assigned line. This also precluded leaving rear-guards behind near the enemy. Numerous mines and tree barricades were to slow down the enemy's pursuit as much as possible.[67]

Panzer-Grenadier Regiment 156 (without its *1st Battalion,* which was still on stand-by) returned to the Division during the night and was deployed at once at its right wing, north of Wibrin. With it came the *2d Battalion* of the *Artillery Regiment,* which went into position east of Wibrin. During 12 January, thank God, nothing happened with *Panzer-Grenadier Regiment 156* west of the Ourthe.[68] The adjacent unit on the left, on the other side of the river, was now the *Panzer Lehr Division.*

On 13 January, Vogelsang wrote:

> Yesterday, I visited the *Ia* in Achouffe near Mont. The battle strengths have indeed dropped catastrophically—each regiment only 100–150 men. . . . Instead of taking back this man-consuming bend in the front, it has to be held on to further.[69]

On 12 January, the expected storm began on the Eastern Front. The Soviets attacked out of their Weichsel bridgehead near Baranow and achieved deep penetrations. On 13 January, the attack was extended to further parts of the front.[70] Soon, the entire front between the Baltic Sea and the Carpathian Mountains was engulfed in flames. The attacks also increased again in the Ardennes, on 13

January. The main efforts were east of Stavelot, northeast and east of La Roche—which means, toward the *116th Panzer Division* and the unit to its right, the *560th Volks-Grenadier Division*—as well as in the vicinity of Bastogne. *Supreme Command–West* reports about this:

> South of Bihain, the enemy achieved two deep penetrations that were able to be closed off along the line Baclain–Montleban. Attacking from the vicinity of Samrée, stronger infantry and tank forces succeeded in advancing up to 1.5 kilometers northwest of Wibrin and due north of Nadrin.[71]

In the journal of the *2d Battalion, Armored Artillery Regiment 146,* this reads as follows:

> During the morning hours in front of our sector, generally quiet. Enemy attacks unit to the right (*560th Volks-Grenadier Division*) and achieves breakthrough.
>
> At about 1400 hours, its armored spearhead stands before Sommerain and one hour later, in front of Fontenaille. Supply units flee from the vicinity.
>
> In the afternoon hours, attacks also in front of our sector. Infantry withdraws. . . .
>
> At 1545 hours, when opponent attacks Bérisménil with two tanks and infantry and takes the village, a change of position is ordered and a new main battle line established. . . .
>
> During the day, the battalion engages the enemy attack with heavy barrages.
>
> Short of ammunition. Our own ammo convoy set off to Germany, to bring in ammo from there. Own supply detachment cannot make it anymore.
>
> Still very low on fuel. To relocate to new main battle line, battalion was allocated 200 liters.
>
> Enemy artillery 3,000 to 4,000 rounds. During the entire day, very heavy attacks by fighter bombers on Wibring and all the forests.[72]

In the battles around Bérisménil, the commander of *7th Company, Panzer-Grenadier Regiment 156, Leutnant* Junge, especially distinguished himself. He was recommended by the Division for the Knight's Cross, but unfortunately without success.[73] In the evening of 13 January, the commander of *1st Battalion, Panzer-Grenadier Regiment 60* was captured in an unusual way. The history of the 84th Infantry Division reports about this episode:

> Later that night, a reconnaissance patrol was sent to investigate the enemy's tour position south of the hill but failed to return. At that, the battalion commander, Major Roland L. Kolb, decided to see for himself. Leading another patrol, he suddenly observed a German command car pull to the base of the hill and halt. Two men stepped out and began to walk up the hill. When the pair approached near enough, the patrol jumped out of hiding.
>
> One of the prisoners turned out to be Captain Hans Gottfried von Watzdorf, commander of the *1st Battalion, 60th Panzer Grenadier, 116th Panzer Division.*

Unaware that his lines had been penetrated to a depth of more than 1,000 yards, the German commander was out on a tour of inspection. In perfect English, he exclaimed, "I am astonished."[74]

During the night of 13/14 January, the *116th Panzer Division* withdrew to a line north of Wibrin and Nadrin. It was only secured by a few tanks and over-watched by the artillery. There were hardly any *Panzer-Grenadiers* left.[75] The Division command post was relocated to Taverneux.[76] Vogelsang wrote about 14 January in his diary:

> There is no liaison with the *Ia*. Therefore, I drove to the corps in Watermal. Artillery fire in every village, mainly in Holdingen, where the dead were laying between smoking shell and bomb craters.
>
> At corps, I finally learned more precise facts about the Division. The opponent had indeed broken through toward Sommerain and Brisy, blocked the supply road, and squeezed together our Division and units from the *560th Volks-Grenadier Division* and the *3d Panzer-Grenadier Division*, into the narrow area Wibrin–Mont–Fontenaille–Ourthe. The Division now has about a 100-man infantry battle strength! Despite everything, it has to defend the protruding nose in the front with these few men, a few tanks and assault guns. Luckily, the artillery is still halfway in order.
>
> With a newly arrived commander for the *1st Battalion* of the *Artillery Regiment*, I immediately drove away from the corps to contact the *Ia* in Taverneux. Via . . . Steinbach, we arrived south of the point of the breach at Cetturu and left our cars there, because Houffalize was impassable due to artillery fire and air-raids.
>
> Through a winter forest in deep snow, we plodded across lanes and narrow paths down to the Ourthe, waded through the half-frozen stream, and climbed the hill on the other side up toward Taverneux. Up there was a lot of action!
>
> Fire from all weapons roared and thundered in a wide semi-circle, so that it was hard to see where the front actually was. In a clear sky, fighter bombers circled and, like birds of prey, swooped down on targets in this half-cauldron, firing and glistening from all barrels.
>
> After a short conference regarding relevant questions with the Division Commander and *Ia*, we trudged back to the river, again waded through the icy water and toiled through deep snow drifts back up to Cetturu. . . . Everyone made use of the dark. The roads were occupied by a long column of vehicles in a single file. Total congestion; one could only advance little by little. Getting in and out, looking for detours, untangling knots, until we were finally completely wedged in, in front of Ober-Besslingen.[77]

January 14 brought the crisis to a climax. The main pressure was further to the right again, near Cherain and north of Sommerain.[78] Near the *116th Panzer Division,* the opponent also continued his attack, with Houffalize as the objective. The closing report of the Division says:

On 14 January, in spite of toughest defense, the enemy entered Nadrin with superior forces. The brave defenders fought for the town to the last man. After minor initial successes, our attempted counterattack failed. The reaction force promised by the *Panzer Lehr Division* could not be felt anywhere; they probably did not even exist.[79]

The following remarks can be found in the history of the *Panzer Lehr Division*:

After further withdrawal, the *Panzer Lehr Division* received orders on 13 January to move a combat group to the unit on the right north of the Ourthe, to secure its own flank. *Combat Group von Poschinger,* which was assigned to this, arrived during the night in Nadrin, but in the dark could not establish contact with the *116th Panzer Division.* At dawn of 14 January, the *Panzer-Grenadiers* north of the Ourthe were not only attacked along the front from the north, but also from the northeast, by superior enemy forces (1st Battalion, 334th Infantry Regiment), which took Nadrin and Filly by afternoon. Despite heavy losses, the *Panzer-Grenadiers* could still lay mines along the road, and at the last moment blew up the Ourthe bridge. With this, the retreat route was blocked for many. Only a few waded across the icy river. The few fords were blocked by wrecked vehicles, many *Panzer-Grenadiers* were captured.[80]

The closing report by the *116th Panzer Division* continues:

At noon on the same day, after heavy artillery fire with strong support by low-flying aircraft, the enemy attacked Wibrin with tanks. Even with its brave resistance, the weak occupation force could not prevent the enemy from entering the village, and finally, without contact to the right or left, had to retreat to the hills south of the village. At this point in time, the Division only had a battle strength of 50 men.[81]

Details about the battle of Wibrin are offered in the journal of *2d Battalion, Armored Artillery Regiment 146*:

In the morning hours, enemy attacks Wibrin. Enemy attack remains stalled by well-placed artillery fire from the entire battalion.

Toward the afternoon, when the enemy recommenced his attack after strong artillery preparation, Wibrin is lost. Dinez also falls into enemy hands.

Strong barrages fall on the firing position of *6th Battery,* which were probably detected by the *Artillery Observation Section.* Exit road is blocked. Two guns are blown up.

In the evening hours, a change of positions is ordered. The battalion command post moves to Cetturu. The batteries take up position near the village.

During the whole day, heavy barrage by enemy artillery in entire battle sector (approx. 1,500 to 2,000 rounds).[82]

The battalion was able to fire all but 180 rounds on this day. In a letter on 14 January, *Leutnant* von Elterlein recorded the experiences he had in assault gun number 706:

Toward morning . . . to the eastern edge of Wibrin, moved into position, well camouflaged, security in direction of road fork. . . . In the late morning hours, artillery fire increases! Suddenly, 1030 hours, quiet, and at 1100 hours, most heavy artillery- and mortar-barrage fire starts! In addition, anti-tank fire from the flank, 800 meters from the verge of the forest. Suddenly, six American tanks appear in front of us. The two *Panzer Vs* destroy four of them! Two Shermans with mounted infantry, breaking out of a gully, want to roll over me. *Unteroffizier* Reinecke, my gunner, shoots and destroys both in less than three minutes at close range. . . . All of a sudden, the 706 is all by itself, all hell breaks loose, seven artillery planes circle above my assault gun, I am in concentrated fire, receive orders from [*Hauptmann*] Kuchenbuch to withdraw to the southeast! Go into new position on Hill 428 [1km southeast of Wibrin—*Author*] and there find the *Panzer Vs* again. . . . Remain four more hours on 428, withdraw by 1700 hours to southeast of Achouffe–Mont main road and establish security near the Mont–Houffalize road intersection, oriented north. . . .

Withdrawal of our troops proceeds on track and without friction.[83]

The commander of *1st Company, Armored Engineer Battalion 675, Oberleutnant* Varnholt, wrote about 14 January in his diary, "Company command post in Mont. Obstacles, detonating craters in the road, demolition of slopes and bridges. After taking back all units, Achouffe bridge was blown up, after one enemy tank just pulled up to the enemy's side.[84]

Varnholt personally took care of the demolition of the important bridge in Achouffe at the last moment.[85] The closing report of the Division portrays the threatening event in the afternoon as follows:

Meanwhile, in the sector of the *560th Volks-Grenadier Division* along the road leading to Houffalize from the north, strong enemy units with tanks had broken through and advanced to the vicinity north of Mont. This created the danger that the Division units deployed west of this road were cut off. In this situation, on the evening of 14 January, the Division Commander decided to prepare a centralized command of the forces available for the defense of Houffalize, to prevent a breakthrough to the road. He also decided to subordinate units of the *560th Volks- Grenadier Division* which, however, only had minimal battle strength, the *Armored Reconnaissance Battalion* of the *Panzer Lehr Division*, which was without a mission in Mont with two medium companies, and *Combat Group von Eckartstein* of the *3d Panzer-Grenadier Division*. These units, together with the available forces of the *116th Panzer Division,* are to be *Group von Waldenburg,* and were to form a bridgehead around Houffalize, along the line Sommerrain–Fontenaille–Mont– Achouffe. Despite the urgent suggestion by the Division that its departure would make a catastrophe unavoidable, and despite the orders finally received from the Commanding General of *LXVI Corps,* which would have forced it to remain in its position, the *Armored Reconnaissance Battalion* moved out anyway during the night of 14/15 January.

There were no other forces available on the morning of 15 January to cover the hole this created. The Division could only set up a few damaged tanks on both sides of the road to Houffalize, and with the few still battleworthy tanks try to delay the advance of the enemy toward Houffalize for as long as possible.[86]

The Commanding General of *LXVI Corps, General der Artillerie* Lucht, had visited the Division's command post in Taverneux in the evening of 14 January, and approved of its measures. Waldenburg wrote in his notebook, "*General* Lucht is here, cannot change anything either! Infantry battle strength of Division equals zero, it cannot go on!"[87]

On 14 January, Hitler gave permission to withdraw from the bend in the front to a line from Cherain–east of Houffalize (which was to remain under fire by our artillery)–Bourcy–Longvilly. Finally! The following was added to the *OKW* journal, "And just in time, so that no further painful losses would occur at *Army Group B*."[88]

General Lucht noted the following about 14 and 15 January in his post-war writings [writing in the third person—*Editor*]:

14 January. Orders came from the army that I had to immediately take over the sector further to the west, on both sides of the road north of Houffalize, with the *560th Volks-Grenadier Division* and the *116th Panzer Division*. It was a cold, clear day, with extremely lively fighter bomber activity. Since there was no contact with these divisions, the commanding general himself drove ahead, to take over control of the battle right then and there. . . .

Due to congestion on the road in the vicinity south of Brisy, the trip to Taverneux, where both division staffs were, had to be done on foot. The commanding general arrived at the command posts in late evening. There, the situation was as follows:

Along the road from Houffalize to the north, *Combat Group Eckartstein* of the *3d Panzer-Grenadier Division* was deployed on both sides in area Dinez. West of it stood weak units of the *560th Volks-Grenadier Division*, and further southwest, the weak units of the *116th Panzer Division*. The *Armored Reconnaissance Battalion* of the *Panzer Lehr Division*, with six to eight tanks, which was available until now in Mont, was pulled out during the night of 14/15 January, causing a further weakening of the front. In my opinion, this protruding part of the battle front was nonsense, and could only have led to heavy losses.

15 January. Early in the morning and just in the nick of time, the Army order arrived to take the front back toward the southeast, and to leave security elements behind near Taverneux and east of Houffalize. This succeeded in the course of 15 January, without the enemy giving strong pursuit. Thus, this combat group escaped the encirclement.[89]

In the early morning of 15 January, the Division command post was relocated via Houffalize east to the Hof Rouvroy farm (4 kilometers northeast of Tavigny).[90] The closing report by the Division portrays 15 January as follows:

The enemy attack from north and northwest, however, soon leads to the collapse of the bridgehead, whereby the units from the *3d Panzer-Grenadier Division* and the *560th Volks-Grenadier Division* were pushed east; and the armored units of the Division toward Houffalize.

Meanwhile, the remnants of *Panzer-Grenadier Regiment 156* were deployed for the immediate protection of the town. These remnants were under the command of the regimental commander, and had a strength of 20 men with three assault guns. Later, they were to be moved forward from the vicinity of Nadrin via Houffalize to the north. However, they could not make it possible for the *Armored Reconnaissance Battalion*—which was once more charged with the security of Houffalize and was again brought back—to reach the security line north of the town. But with their brave persistence, they prevented the opponent from entering the town prematurely, and by blowing up the bridges in time, made it possible for all units of the Division and numerous columns of the nearby units to move out of Houffalize.[91]

The journal of *2d Battalion, Armored Artillery Regiment 146* says about 15 January:

> In the morning hours, again enemy attack. After a long battle, opponent succeeds in entering Taverneux and Houffalize.
> Battalion opposes the enemy attack with heavy barrages.
> In the evening hours, disengagement is ordered.
> New positions for battalion in the vicinity of Steinbach.[92]

On 16 January, the *116th Panzer Division* was, as far as could be established, deployed with other remnants of the Division in a sector northeast of Houffalize, which reached from Cherain to Houffalize (exclusive). On this day, the enemy only attacked near Cherain and Brisy and was repulsed. The tanks of the *116th* assembled in a preparation area 1.5 kilometers west of Liherain, under the command of *Hauptmann* Kuchenbuch.[93]

The history of the 2d Armored Division presents these battles as follows:

> On 15 January, Combat Command A reaches Achouffe, while Combat Command B captures Taverneux. Reconnaissance patrols that reconnoiter toward Houffalize shortly after dark return after midnight and report Houffalize to be free of the enemy. The next day, 16 January, at 0930 hours, a reconnaissance patrol . . . advances to the Ourthe and links up with a reconnaissance patrol from the 11th Armored Division that came from the south. Thereby, contact between the First and Third Armies is established. Meanwhile, Houffalize is captured by Combat Command B.[94]

The author of this presentation evaluates the German battle conduct in these words:

> Embittered. . . . The Germans defend their positions very tenaciously until 8 January, the day that Hitler permits the withdrawal at the front. The retreat,

beginning on 9 January, is conducted offensively; the advance of the Allies is delayed by numerous local counterattacks. In foxholes surrounded by minefields, some infantrymen with a few tanks or anti-tank guns defend vital points, hills, or intersections.

Many minor counterattacks, by a few tanks with infantry in company strength or less, are mounted against the allied positions. The Germans evolved as masters in this kind of ongoing battle and have learned to make use of the experiences from the Eastern Front.

The linkup of the two reconnaissance patrols from the First and Third Armies signified the end of the offensive against the German attack spearhead, but not one German unit was captured. The objective was placed too far west and the advance not forceful enough to achieve a major success. Nevertheless, the attacked German formations suffered heavily. *Generalmajor* von Waldenburg stated in the following in the closing report of the *116th Panzer Division*:

> The total casualties during the time from 3 to 15 January 1945 amount to 26 officers and 1,183 NCOs and men.
>
> This includes:
>
> | | | |
> |---|---|---|
> | Killed | 5 Officers | 91 NCOs and men |
> | Wounded | 16 | 339 |
> | Missing | 4 | 600 |
> | Accidents | 3 | 12 |
> | Sick | 2 | 180 |
>
> The high number of missing can be traced to the battles with high losses in the dense forest area, which often did not allow recovering the wounded and the sick. Very many of these were so completely exhausted that they could not move on their own any longer.[95] [The difference between the grand total and the sum of the individual numbers could be traced to the fact that the wounded and sick who remained with the troops were only deducted from the grand total—*Author.*]

On 17 January, Vogelsang wrote:

> Yesterday morning I drove again to the *Ia* . . . the *General* and *Ia* were on their way to Army Group [we were only with *5th Panzer Army,* which stood near Trotten—*Author*], to ask for the relief of the Division, since only about 200 *Panzer-Grenadiers* in the whole formation including the *Armored Reconnaissance Battalion* and *Division Escort Company* were still fit for battle.
>
> After their return, the following rules were ordered:
>
> *Panzer-Grenadier Regiment 156* remains deployed with the remnants of one engineer platoon, one and one-half artillery battalions, and one *Panzer* company, combined as one battalion.
>
> The remainder of the Division assembles in the vicinity of Ulflingen–Heiner-scheid and establishes a receiving position in the Clerf sector. To carry out this task, the available infantry cadre units are replenished with emergency companies of

soldiers, at this time without weapons, or from dispensable tank, artillery, and anti-aircraft soldiers, as well as men from supply and communication units.

Besides this, all staffs and rear guards were scrutinized to free soldiers who were fit for battle—like in Russia in 1944![96]

In Kalborn, still on Luxembourg soil, west of the Our, Vogelsang added, "In view of the situation here and the Russian breakthrough in the East, the mood is generally one of depression—probably the worst since Aachen!"

Staff Paymaster Wolff-Boenisch noted on the same day:

We want to look the truth straight in the eye. The offensive, for which we had so much hope, failed. All good intentions, all bravery, and all devotion did not help against the materiel supremacy. We are again going back to the place from whence we mounted the attack one month ago.[97]

The journal of *2d Battalion, Armored Artillery Regiment 146,* which remained deployed with *Combat Group Grollmann* with the *5th, 6th,* and *8th Batteries* and one platoon of *Anti-Aircraft Battalion 281,* stated the following about 17 January:

During the day, generally quiet. Enemy only attacks in the Cherain area, but is repelled. In the evening hours, it is announced that the combat group is placed near Trotten as reserve. March off after receiving of fuel. Battalion receives 500 liters for relocation.[98]

In the evening of 17 January, *Generalmajor* von Waldenburg wrote in his pocket calendar that everything ordered on 16 January would change. On 18 January, he entered:

Conference by Manteuffel with *Feldmarschall* Model. Division is pulled back with all units to again be deployed in the vicinity of Aachen, against threatening English penetration!—Should receive two march battalions—But not sufficient. For time being, no fuel![99]

Vogelsang wrote the following about 17 January:

During the night of 17 January, the surprising order arrived to immediately pull-out the Division for the likely relocation to the Aachen area. At the same time, an *NSFO* appeared, [*"National Sozialistische Führungs Offizier,"* or National Socialist Guidance Officer–*Editor*] commissioned by Army Group, who was to examine a supposedly defeatist mood and attitude. In an hour and a half meeting, Guderian explained the actual condition to him, based on excessive battle demands, impossibilities ordered by the highest command, the lack of supplies, and other causes, with such effectiveness that any objection, any attempt of an examination by him, simply vanished. Guderian bared his soul with the long-accumulated anger so severely that we feared the worst for him if the *NSFO* were to repeat it point blank to the higher-ups. It was, however, impudent to approach a unit that had been destroyed in spite of its exemplary devotion, in such a way![100]

The story that preceded the *NSFO's* visit was as follows: In Achouffe, a nice duty officer from Model visited the Division. Per Model's order, he was to find out about our problems. I mentioned them to him and added that confidence in the higher leadership has suffered. You cannot, for example, give the units Antwerp as their objective on 16 December, and by year's end declare in an *NSFO* order, signed by *General* Krebs, that the enemy claims we had far reaching objectives; this was wrong, the *Führer* alone knows about the objectives. Model reacted by sending his *NSFO*. The *Ic* of the Division, *Hauptmann der Reserve* Dr. Holtermann, who was also present during the discussion with the *NSFO,* reported in a letter to *General* Count von Schwerin:

> Guderian also found the courage to take a stand against the higher leadership and make them responsible for their part in the Division's awful devastation. There was talk of an open crisis of confidence in the leadership, and it was said that Army Group handled a *Panzer* Division like a three-year-old boy handles an electric train![101]

On 18 January, Vogelsang drove off to bring back new personnel. He visited the *Field Replacement Battalion* in Eitorf on the Sieg and *General of Panzer Troops West,* in Bad Ems. There, he was promised 1,000 men. The *Field Replacement Battalion* was able to prepare 100 trained junior leaders and 500 men. In addition, there was a convalescent march company of 200 men from *Reserve Regiment Rheine.*[102]

The reason for Model's decision to relocate the Division to the vicinity of Aachen was a British assault with more than three divisions at the east bank of the Maas, southeast of Maaseik, which gained ground toward the east and lasted until 27 January.

The objective of this British operation was to capture the Heinsberger *Dreieck* (triangle) and to advance of the British front to the lower Roer.[103]

On 19 January, the Division staff arrived in Nohn again, the point of departure for the offensive that had been begun with so much hope. For an operation of this kind, our forces had been no longer sufficient. As soon as the weather cleared, the enemy air forces were overwhelming. Supply was insufficient from the beginning. No offensive can succeed without fuel. Enemy resistance was also stronger than expected; the bravery of small units slowed down the speed of the march; just think of Hotton. Through this, the opposing command had time to bring in reserves. It did it quickly and energetically by exposing other fronts. And after all, in spite of all good intentions, the troops were no longer those from 1940.

Five years of war, since 1943 almost always on the defensive against superior opponents, were not without consequences for soldiers' ability to attack and endure. Nevertheless, astonishing feats were achieved in attack and defense. One must only take a ride along the road the Division took, from Lützkampen all the way to Ortheuville, Hotton or Verdenne! Even today, a tourist would be amazed by the difficult terrain. Yet roads and bridges have been much improved since

1944. And it was in winter with all the challenges of that season! Or drive just once along the former front between the Ourthe and the little bridge, four kilometers southeast of Marche, which the Division had to defend beginning on 27 December, and try to imagine the few *Panzer-Grenadiers* and tanks in the wide stretches of this mountainous land, when on 4 January 1945, the rested 53d (Welsh) Division mounted an attack against them with four brigades. One could also drive the distance from Dochamps via Cielle and La Roche up to the hills west of Gênes, which had to be defended on 8 January. In this last-ditch effort of the German Western Army, the German soldier once more was larger than life. But the final defeat was a huge disappointment, and the daily reports from the Eastern Front that sounded increasingly terrible, filled the soldiers with great concern. This was especially true for those whose homeland fell into the hands of the Soviets, and who were worried about their relatives.

Some notes from diaries may indicate these worries. On 22 January, *Generamajor* von Waldenburg, a Silesian, noted, "The Russians in Silesia, in the Warthe district and deep in East Prussia. Terrible, what will be?"[104]

And, on 25 January he wrote, "The battle of Breslau has begun. . . . Heavy frost, almost -20 degrees Celsius [-4 degrees Fahrenheit], the poor fleeing population. The tragedy is immeasurable. But we have to persevere or ?? But where?"

After visiting *Panzer Regiment 16*, on 27 January, Waldenburg wrote, "The same problems everywhere: Fuel! I was very depressed. Where does one get faith and hope? Both should be given to the people, but the unbelieving faces increase in number!"

Back to real life in the West, which demanded all strengths and left the busy people little time for reflection. In the daily report by *Army Group B* from 19 January, it stated, among other things:

> The defensive battle between the Maas and the Moselle continued at the main efforts in unrelenting force, through snowstorms and snow drifts. The road conditions in the Eifel Mountains are the main problems right now for our movements. At this moment, everything is at a standstill. The urgently-needed fuel convoys cannot continue due to the huge snow drifts. There are not enough snow plows, or they have no fuel. By noon, strong, low-flying enemy forces engaged in the ground battles.[105]

The same day, Hitler demanded:

> that the *Supreme Commander–West* assemble the *6th Panzer Army* and the *Führer-Grenadier* and *Führer Escort Brigade* in the shortest time, to be at the disposal of the *Führer* in the vicinity of Euskirchen–Prüm–Bitburg–Adenau.[106]

On 20 January, the order followed to ship out *I SS-Panzer Corps* to the east via Berlin.

On 22 January, a new *Führer* directive was issued which provided for further transfers to the East and also dealt with the future conduct of battle in the West.

Now, priority was given to the Eastern Front—too late! The effects of shifting the main effort would take weeks to be felt. Due to losses and damages in the offensives, and after all the relinquishment, the Western Front became so weak that it could barely stand up to the increasing supremacy of the Western Powers. After the loss of Upper Silesia, the significance of the Saar and the Ruhr for armament production heightened. Now, the fighting in the West was for its preservation. With difficulty, *Supreme Command–West* could at least accomplish the cessation of our attacks in Alsace, which continued to consume its strength. After all, there was not much room for directives. It was just important to group the weak forces in such a way that they would be placed somewhat correctly for the attacks that were expected from the Western powers. The *Supreme Commander–West* expected that, "the enemy will shortly resume the attack against Cologne. This, with participation of the British Second Army, means he will also attack the western front of *Army Group H.* For this, the enemy may deploy about 24 formations with about 2,500 tanks."[107]

Besides this, the *Supreme Commander–West* counted on an attack against the Moselle gateway, but a weaker one, and not before February. He pointed to the poor supply situation, which would delay a quick regrouping of the forces, and also delay the transportation of the units that had to be transferred to the East. *Supreme Command–West* reported that the autumn battles were only possible thanks to considerable employment of artillery. But now, there was a shortage of ammunition. He therefore voiced concerns about being able to beat back the upcoming attacks by the enemy. The pull-out of three *Luftwaffe* fighter groups had to increase the concerns about supply further.

On 20 January, *Generalmajor* von Waldenburg went to see *Army Group B,* and there received orders to get a combat group ready to march by 22 January. This unit was to be relocated to the vicinity of Erkelenz, ahead of the Division.[108] It was formed from *Panzer-Grenadier Regiment 156* (without the *2d Battalion*), the *2d Battalion* of the *Artillery Regiment,* and several other units, under the command of *Oberstleutnant* Grollmann. Indeed, Grollmann set out on his march on 22 January. The *2d Battalion, Armored Artillery Regiment 146* was still stuck at the Prüm without fuel. By 28 January, the combat group was finally assembled south of Rheydt. Since it was clear winter weather, marching could only be done at night. Even during the night, fighter bombers attacked the traffic on the roads with bombs and machine guns.[109]

Most of the Division slowly forced its way back to the area of the Eifel, where it had been before the beginning of the offensive. On 24 January, Waldenburg wrote in his notebook, "Continuous fuel problems. Cannot assemble Division."[110]

Vogelsang's notes from 25 January in Nohn were:

We are still stuck up here because of lack of fuel. From Luxembourg to here, most unit vehicles are scattered on many roads, wherever they ran out of fuel. It is indeed a tragedy!

Since the trip to the *Field Replacement Battalion,* we are also sitting dry. Necessary short trips are only possible by siphoning fuel from other vehicles.

But at least replacements are coming in. The units coming from the *Field Replacement Battalion* are 800 men strong, and are on their way in a foot-march toward Adenau. Baggage and provisions are brought along on horse-drawn carts (*Panzer* Division 1945!). In Adenau, they should be received by the individual units. A new march battalion for us, with a strength of 350 men, marches tonight from Mayen to Wirft [five kilometers west-southwest Adenau—*Author*], where I am going to divide it. Against our will, another 300 men were set to march to München-Gladbach, as replacements for *Panzer-Grenadier Regiment 156,* that had been ordered to go there as a combat group. A third march battalion and one more convalescent march company have been announced. Our trip to Bad Ems was not in vain!

After we also receive 30 officers, we should numerically again be fully battleworthy. The future will show how the battle strength and morale will be after the incorporation of so many new people! . . .

The fighter bomber activity prevented any driving during daytime. In the clear weather, between 1000 and 1700 hours, they are always out hunting in flocks of fiveto 25 aircraft, and, of course, find any vehicle in the wide-open, snowy landscape.

Three experienced officers from the *Panzer Regiment* were killed by bombs.[111]

[*Hauptmann* Kuchenbuch, two company officers, and his *Hauptfeldwebel* were at his company command post and fell victims to a bomb—*Author*][112]

On 25 January, Army Group announced the intended relocation of the Division. First, the cadre of the *2d Battalion* of *Panzer-Grenadier Regiment 156* was to follow *Group Grollmann,* and there be replenished with replacements.[113] On 27 January, still in Nohn, Vogelsang added to his entries from 25 January:

In the forest of Wirft, I dissolved the march battalion that arrived there. Replacements are steadily getting worse. Hardly 50 percent are fully capable as *Panzer-Grenadiers.* The rest are old, sick, or half-trained men plucked from industry and the *Replacement Army.* The number of junior leaders is much too small, their quality is moderate. After all the immense losses, from whence should we actually get usable replacements?[114]

At 1700 hours on 27 January, orders came from *Army Group B* that, beginning in the evening of this day, the Division should move additional combat units into the Wegberg–Schwanenberg–Venrath–Rheydt (exclusive)–Gerkerath– Rickerath area. On 28 January, the Division staff had to send strong advance parties on the march, and on 29 January, all the others. The staff moved to Gerkerath, (west of Rheydt). *Combat Group Grollmann* was to remain in its present area for the time being.[115] The journal of *2d Battalion, Armored Artillery Regiment 146* laments:

Battalion is with *Combat Group Grollmann* in the vicinity of Rheydt and is being replenished. With a march readiness requirement of two hours, the vehicles cannot be overhauled properly.[116]

The Division's orders for relocation were issued during the night of 27/28 January.[117] Only the combat units and the supply units that were absolutely necessary for the battle were to be deployed in the designated area. Everything else, especially the maintenance units, was to disperse toward the rear, mainly in the vicinity of München-Gladbach–Neuss. The main effort of the repair work, however, remained in the present area, in the Eifel, where all damaged vehicles either stood around or would arrive. *Oberst* Bayer was assigned as commander of all remaining units of the Division in the Eifel, with his command post in Nohn.

On 29 January, *Generalmajor* von Waldenburg drove to Gerkerath. On his way, he reported to headquarters, *15th Army* and visited *Combat Group Grollmann,* which on this day returned to the care of the Division.[118] The Division was subordinated to the *XLVII Panzer Corps,* where Waldenburg reported on the evening of 30 January.[119] The relocation of most of the Division got off to a slow start due to completely insufficient fuel allotments. The *1st Battery* of *Army Anti-Aircraft Battalion 281,* under the command of *Oberleutnant* Wilhelm, arrived on 30 January. The following day, the staff of *Panzer-Grenadier Regiment 60* arrived. Most of its units (without two armored personnel carrier companies and the *10th Company*), as well as *3d Battalion* of the *Artillery Regiment,* were on their way. The snow started to melt. The Division staff conducted a continuous fight for fuel allotment.[120] It had only modest success. Strong Division units—the *Panzer Regiment, Armored Reconnaissance Battalion,* the *Armored Engineer Battalion,* and large elements from the supply and maintenance units, remained pinned down in the Eifel, in some cases for weeks.

The battles in the lower Roer had subsided. The enemy achieved his objective, gaining the left bank of the Roer. The frontline in the Ardennes had essentially been thrown back to the starting position of December. In the northern Eifel, between Lützkampen—the first village taken by the *116th Panzer Division* on 16 December—and Monschau, an American attack was in progress. In the East, the Soviets continued their major offensive with increasing success, conquering almost all of East Prussia and separating it from the *Reich*. The entire length of the River Oder had been reached, up to northwest of Küstrin, and was crossed in Upper Silesia, as well as northwest of Breslau.[121] The units from the *6th Panzer Army* that were moved out were not transported toward Berlin, as requested by the Chief of Staff, *Generaloberst* Guderian, but were detoured on orders from Hitler toward Vienna, for deployment in Hungary.[122] On 25 January, the *Reich's* foreign minister was asked by Guderian to join him in suggesting a cease-fire to Hitler, at least toward one side. But Ribbentrop refused, and in spite of an agreed-upon confidence, informed Hitler. He went into a rage and declined rudely.[123] It is also questionable whether the West would have agreed to such a proposal, since it was demanding unconditional surrender. Thus, the battle went on.

Generalleutnant Gerhard Count von Schwerin
Commander, 116th Panzer Division
Until 14 September 1944
Knight's Cross with Oak Leaves and Swords
4 November 1943

Generalmajor Siegfried von Waldenburg
Commander, 116th Panzer Division
From 19 September 1944
Until capitulation 16 April 1945
Knight's Cross
6 December 1944

Oberstleutnant i.G.
Heinz Günther Guderian
Ia, 116th Panzer Division
Knight's Cross
5 October 1944

Major Fritz Vogelsang
Division Adjutant, 116th Panzer Division
Last Commander of Armored Artillery Regiment 146

Major i.G. Lothar Wolf
Ib, 116th Panzer Division
Until November 1944

Oberst Otto Fischer
Cmdr, Pz-Gren Reg 156
Until 12 August 1944
Knight's Cross
27 August 1943

Oberst Heinrich Voigtsberger
Cmdr, Pz-Gren Reg 60
Until September 1944
Knight's Cross with Oak
Leaves 9 December 1943

Oberst der Reserve
Dr. Ernst Pean
Cmdr, Artillery Reg 146
Until December 1944

Oberst Johannes Bayer
Cmdr, Pz Reg 16
From September 1944 to
March 1945

Oberstleutnant
Heinrich Grollmann
Cmdr, Pz-Gren Reg 156
From August 1944
to April 1945

Oberstleutnant Helmut Zander
Cmdr, Pz-Gren Reg 60
From September 1944 to
February 1945
Knight's Cross 5 April 1945

Major Gerhard Tebbe
Cmdr, 1st Bn, Pz Reg 16
Cmdr, Pz Reg 16 late
March 1945

Major Eberhard Stephan
Cmdr, Arm Recon Bn 116
August 1944 to February 1945
Cmdr, Pz-Gren Reg 60
March to April 1945
Knight's Cross 12 Jan 1945

Major Helmut Bochnig
Cmdr, Pzjgr Bn 228
Until November 1944
Knight's Cross 9 June 1944

Soldiers of the 116th Panzer Division and Its Subordinated (or Attached) Units Who Received the Knight's Cross While with the Division

Hauptmann
Eberhard Risse
Adjutant, Pz-Gren Reg 60
Conferred 26 November
1944

Major Kuno von Meyer
Cmdr, 1st Bn, Pz Reg 24
Attached to the 116th Pz Div
Until November 1944
Conferred 26 November 1944

Leutnant Johannes Lutz
Platoon Leader in the
Division Escort Company
Conferred 9 December
1944

Leutnant
Joachim Weissflog
Acting Cmdr, 2d Company,
Pz Reg 16
Conferred 5 March 1945

Hauptmann
Eduard Hübner
Cmdr, Assault Bn, 1st
Parachute Army
Conferred 17 March 1945

Leutnant der Reserve
Heinz Auert
Acting Cmdr, 2d Company,
Arm Recon Bn 116
Conferred 28 March 1945

Leutnant Herbert Käseberg
Acting Cmdr, 5th Comp,
Pz-Gren Reg 156
Conferred 14 April 1945

Feldwebel Fritz Muster
Platoon Leader,
Arm Recon Bn 116
Conferred 14 April 1945

Major Hans Jungwirth
Cmdr, Para Recon Bn 12
Conferred 9 May 1945

Soldiers of the 116th Panzer Division Who Were Awarded the Knight's Cross Prior to Their Assignment in the Division

Major i. G. Heinz-Jürgen
Issbrücker
Ib, 116th Pz Div
Conferred 12 September
1941 as *Oberleutnant*

Hauptmann
Hermann Ruppert
Pz-Gren Reg 156
Conferred 12 January
1942 as *Oberleutnant*

Hauptmann Werner
Baumgarten-Crusius
Acting Cmdr, 1st Bn, Pz-Gren
Reg 156; Knight's Cross with
Oak Leaves Conferred 27
February 1943 as *Oberleutnant*

Leutnant Josef Vernhold
Plt Ldr, Pz-Gren Reg 60
Conferred 22 February
1942 as *Unteroffizier*

Oberleutnant Hans Bunzel
Act Cmdr, 3d Comp, Pz Reg 16
Conferred 10 February 1943
as *Oberfeldwebel*

Soldiers of the 116th Panzer Division Who Were Awarded the Knight's Cross Prior to Their Assignment in the Division

Major der Reserve Friedrich
Count von Brühl
Cmdr, 2d Bn, Pz Reg 16
Conferred 3 November 1942
as *Hauptmann der Reserve*

Oberleutnant
Heinrich Schulze
Panzer Regiment 16
Conferred 14 August 1943
as *Stabsfeldwebel*

Feldwebel
Georg Thumbeck
2d Comp, Pz-Gren Reg 60
Conferred 12 November
1943 as *Obergefreiter*

Oberwachtmeister
Hermann Wehking
Arm Artil Reg 146
Conferred 15 January 1944

Unteroffizier Karl-Heinz
Drees; 3d Comp, Pzjgr Bn
228; Conferred 8 February
1944 as *Gefreiter*

Leutnant Willi Tanneberger
Act Cmdr, 3d Comp,
Pz-Gren Reg 156;
Conferred 10 February
1944 as *Oberfeldwebel*

Discussion about operations of the *Panzer* divisions in the event of an invasion, April 1944, in La Roche-Guyon. From left: *Generalleutnant* Dr. Speidel, Chief of Staff, Army Group B; *Generalfeldmarschall* Rommel, Commander, Army Group B; *Generaloberst* Guderian, Inspector General of Armored Troops; *General der Panzertruppe* Imperial Baron Geyr von Schweppenburg, General of *Panzer* Troops West; *Major i.G.* Baron von Woellwarth, from the staff of the Inspector General of Armored Troops.

Arrival of *Major i.G.* Guderian at the Division, 24 May 1944, in Bézu-St. Eloi. From left: *Oberst* Fischer, *Hauptmann der Reserve* Dr. Holtermann (partially obscured), *Major* Grollmann, *Oberst* Voigtsberger, *Oberstleutnant* von Trotha (partially obscured), *Major i.G.* Guderian, *Oberst der Reserve* Dr. Pean, *Generalleutnant* Count von Schwerin.

Generalfeldmarschall Rommel's visit to the 116th Panzer Division in Bézu-St. Eloi, early June 1944. *Major i.G.* Guderian reports.

Major i.G. Guderian with the commander of Armored Reconnaissance Battalion 116, *Hauptmann* Kurt Zehner in Hélicourt, south of Abbeville, June 1944.

Above: *Generalfeldmarschall*
Rommel at the 116th Panzer
Division, 12 June 1944, in
Perriers-sur-Andelle. From left:
Major Wolf, *Generalfeldmar-schall* Rommel, *Major i. G.* von
Ekesbarre, *Generalleutnant*
Count von Schwerin, *Major i.G.*
Guderian, *Major* Vogelsang.

Right: 12 June 1944,
Generalfeldmarschall Rommel
and *Generalleutnant* Count
von Schwerin in Perriers-sur-Andelle.

Left: *Oberst* von Waldenburg (seated) with *Oberst* Bayer, autumn 1944.

Below Left: *Oberstleutnant i.G.* Guderian in the bunker in Grosshau, November 1944.

Below Right: *Hauptmann der Reserve* Küpper, *01,* 116th Panzer Division, in the bunker in Grosshau.

Right: *Oberstleutnant i.G.* Guderian (left) and *Major* Vogelsang after being captured by the Americans in the Ruhr Cauldron, 16 April 1945, at the command post of the US 7th Armored Division at Menden.

Below: Memorial service for the fallen at the monument of the 116th Panzer Division near Vossenack in the Eifel.

Left: A knocked-out Panther adds to the debris of battle in Argentan. Behind it (center) is the destroyed St. Germain cathedral.

Below: A British Sherman VC throws up a spray of mud, and American soldiers watch from a 2½-ton truck as a GI examines a destroyed Panther, probably of the 116th Panzer Division, in the Falaise Cauldron.

Above: Allied soldiers examine a knocked-out *Sonderkraftfahrzeug* (*Sdkfz.*) 234/3 of Armored Reconnaissance Battalion 116 in the Falaise Cauldron.

Below: Generalleutnant Count von Schwerin leads the 116th Panzer Division back to Aachen after being reinstated in command.

Left: American infantry advance with the support of Sherman tanks in Aachen.

Below left: *Generalfeld-marschall* Walther Model (left) confers with then-*Oberst* von Waldenburg outside the 116th Panzer Division command post in Würselen, 25 Oct 1944. Note the Greyhound Division symbol and arrow indicating the way to the CP behind Model.

Below right: *General der Panzertruppe* Hasso von Manteuffel, Commander, 5th Panzer Army (left), confers with then-*Oberst* von Waldenburg, autumn 1944.

Above: Officers of the 116th Panzer Division
prepare to attack British forces near Arnhem,
1 October 1944, around 1600 hours. At left is
a forward observer for a *Waffen-SS* rocket
launcher unit; marking the map and smoking a
cigarette is *Oberstleutnant* Grollmann, Commander, Panzer-Grenadier Regiment 156;
Hauptmann Voigt, Adjutant, Regiment 156, is at
right, and *Oberleutnant* Holthoff, duty officer,
looks on from the back.

Right: *Hauptmann der Reserve* Walter Küpper,
the Division 01 (1st Assistant Adjutant) (right),
with an escort officer from Army headquarters,
autumn 1944.

Above: A 116th Panzer Division *Landser* bails water out of his fighting position, autumn 1944. A *Panzerfaust* 60 anti-tank rocket launcher lies ready on his right.

Below: The fighting in the muddy, densely-forested maze of the Hürtgen was bitter and vicious. Some German and American soldiers' remains, like these, were not found and interred until 1949.

Above: View from the commander's cupola of a 116th Panzer Division Panther. The target appears to be a Sherman tank.

Below: *General der Panzertruppe* von Manteuffel, confers with officers of Panzer Regiment 16. On the right is *Oberleutnant* Penzler, to his right is *Oberleutnant* Gittermann. Manteuffel's escort officer is in the back.

Above: Knocked-out 116th Panzer Division Panther near the chapel in Houffalize.

Below: Medics evacuate a wounded Greyhound Division soldier on a litter as a heavily-camouflaged late-model *Sdkfz.* 251 Armored Personnel Carrier of Panzer Regiment 16 moves up in the Ardennes. Note swastika aerial recognition aid on top-rear of the armored vehicle.

Above: German Red Cross nurse and American medic provide first aid for a wounded 116th Panzer Division soldier.

Below: Hunting Panther tank destroyer of Panzer Regiment 16 in the Ruhr Cauldron, April 1945.

A half-tracked *Schützenpanzer* (armored personnel carrier) of the 116th Panzer Division and crew passes a knocked-out American M10 tank destroyer in the Ardennes, December 1944.

Inscription on Left Tablet:
May this memorial, where soldiers of the Greyhound Division (16th Rhenish–Westphalian Infantry Division; 16th Motorized Infantry Division; 16th Panzer-Grenadier Division; and 116th Panzer Division, consecutively) fought and died in 1944, remind the world of peace.

Inscription on Right Tablet:
Memorial of the Windhund Division.
Enter with reverence for the sacrificial deaths of the soldiers from all nations who died in the Hürtgen Forest.

CHAPTER 10

Defensive Combat
Between Rhine and Maas

On 31 December, when the German Ardennes offensive was brought to a halt, Eisenhower informed Montgomery in a letter about his intentions for the future course of operations. He considered reaching the Rhine a prerequisite for the further advance into the interior of the *Reich*. Montgomery was to lead the thrust to the Rhine in the north with his army group, to which Ninth Army was subordinated, and later, advance north of the Ruhr area. Bradley's army group, with First and Third Armies, was to reach the Rhine south of the Ruhr region, and later push on via Frankfurt to Kassel.[1] Montgomery ordered the First Canadian Army to attack between the Rhine and the Maas southward from the area southeast of Nijmegen, and to overrun the German Maas position (Operation VERITABLE). Then, by crossing the Lower Roer between Düren and Roermond, the Ninth Army was to attack Neuss and Krefeld, and break open the German Maas position from the south (Operation GRENADE). The First Army had to cover the right flank of Ninth Army. The days planned for the commencement of the operations were 8 February for the attack by the British and 10 February for the Americans.

The following prerequisites had been established for the execution of these intentions:

1. The Americans had to move north; their Ninth Army had to relieve the British at the Lower Roer and the First Army was to relieve the Ninth south of the Aachen–Cologne *Autobahn*.
2. The Ninth Army was to be sufficiently supplied and reinforced with five divisions, mainly from the First Army.
3. The Roer dams must be taken to prevent the Germans from opening their sluices and allowing the Roer to swell; such an action could cut the lines of communication of Ninth Army units that had advanced beyond the river.

On 6 February, the Ninth Army took over the sector up to Roermond from the British. The Roer dams were captured between 5 and 9 February, but earlier, the Germans had opened their sluices to the extent that the Roer was high for about two weeks, which turned the Roer Valley into a water-and-mud wasteland. This delayed Operation GRENADE until 23 February. Provisions for the attacking British and American field armies were no problem.

Supplies moved quickly via Antwerp. German bombardment with V-2 rockets had no serious impact on this. Even though Eisenhower ordered the 12th Army Group to cease further attacks, Patton's 3d Army punctured the front at the Eifel during the whole month of February, seized Prüm and Bitburg, and shackled the German forces, as well as the attention of the German High Command. By this, Patton prevented a relocation of the German main effort toward the north.

The British prepared their attack with great thoroughness.[2] The British XXX Corps took control of the attack forces between the Maas and Rhine. For the initial phase, five forward-deployed infantry divisions were at its disposal, along with three tank brigades and most of the special armored units of the 79th Armoured Division. One infantry and one armored division were in reserve. The fire from 1,050 guns was to prepare the attack and keep it going on a front that was 15 kilometers wide, thus achieving a density of 70 tubes per kilometer. Strong air support was also planned. Before the commencement of the attack, air raids were to be directed toward bridges and railroad installations in the hinterland. Thanks to careful camouflage and radio discipline, these enormous preparations for the attack remained almost completely hidden from the German side. Even if there were some signs for the upcoming attack against the German position between the Rhine and Maas southeast of Nijmegen, *Army Group H* and *Supreme Command–West* judged the situation differently. They expected the main thrust to be across the Maas, on both sides of Venlo, and reckoned with only on a diversionary or supporting attack in the *Reichswald*. Most of the commanders at the *Reichswald* front were of a different opinion.[3]

Our own forces between the Rhine and Maas were weak. Here, only the insignificantly reinforced *84th Infantry Division* was deployed, and at the last moment a parachute infantry regiment was inserted at its left wing, due north of the Maas. The Division, together with the *180th Infantry Division* along the adjoining Maas front, was under command of *LXXXVI Corps*. The adjacent unit on the left—along the Maas up to Roermond—was the *II Parachute Corps*. Both corps were under the command of *1st Parachute Army*, commanded by *General der Fallschirmtruppe* Schlemm. The only worthwhile reserve along the whole front from the Rhine up to Roermond was the *7th Parachute Division*, which in part was being transported to the area east of Venlo. In the beginning of February, the army also received a minor reinforcement of artillery and tank destroyers, including *Heavy Tank Destroyer Battalion 655*.[4] The *XLVII Panzer Corps*, with the *15th Panzer-Grenadier* and *116th Panzer Divisions*, constituted the *Supreme Command-West* reserve. This corps' units were arrayed along the boundary between *Army Groups H* and *B*, specifically, along the boundary between the *1st Parachute* and *15th Armies*, in the vicinity of Sevelen-Krefeld–München-Gladbach.[5]

The previous chapter has already showed how cumbersome it was to assemble the *116th Panzer Division*. It was not much different for the *15th Panzer-Grenadier Division*. During a conference on 1 February with *Feldmarschall*

Model at *15th Army* headquarters, the Commander of the *116th Panzer Division* learned that the Division was to be pulled further north into the *Army Group H* area of operations, in the vicinity of Aldekerk–Straelen–Geldern. The first step was to relocate the *1st Battalion, Panzer-Grenadier Regiment 156* in the new sector, and to dispatch an advance party to *II Parachute Corps.*[6] On 2 February, the Dülken–Viersen area was assigned to the Division. The Division remained *Supreme Command–West* reserve, was subordinated regarding unit formation to *XLVII Panzer Corps,* and regarding logistics, to the *II Parachute Corps.*[7]

On this day, the *1st Battalion, Panzer-Grenadier Regiment 156* reached the vicinity of Boisheim (five kilometers northwest of Dülken). In the evening, more units of the Division marched off. During the course of 3/4 February, *Panzer-Grenadier Regiment 156* reached the vicinity of Boisheim, *2d Battalion, Armored Artillery Regiment 146* the vicinity of Oedt (eight kilometers north of Viersen), and all the Division's battleworthy tanks, combined in *Panzer Company Brinkmann,* arrived at the forest south of Hardt (seven kilometers west of München-Gladbach).[8] On 4 February, the commander of *1st Parachute Army, General* Schlemm, and the Commanding General of *XLVII Panzer Corps, General der Panzertruppe* Baron von Lüttwitz, visited the Division. The following was noted in the Division's journal:

> Army Headquarters expects attack at the *Reichswald,* because the Canadians are very active there. Behind the front of the English, are new forces, namely the 51st and 53d Infantry Divisions, three divisions from England and three tank brigades. *Supreme Command–West* expects an attack on Erkelenz and near Venlo. Army Headquarters however, believes in an attack first near Roermond, proceeding via Erkelenz, at the same time as attack on the *Reichswald.*
>
> Results from reconnaissance corroborate this opinion. The Maas itself is a hindrance until high water recedes. As of 9 February, the Maas can be crossed north of Venlo, because the English opened the locks.[9]

Yet, after 9 February, the Maas continued to run high, because now the opening of the Roer dam took its effect. On 8 February, the German command began opening Rhine dikes, to flood land forward of the front. This was successfully continued until the beginning of March.[10]

The *116th Panzer Division* had to prepare for two directions of deployment, namely Case Heinsberg, at the right wing of *15th Army,* and Case Kaldenkirchen, south of Venlo, at the left wing of the *1st Parachute Army.* For the latter case, the battleworthy artillery of the Division (the *2d Battalion, Armored Artillery Regiment 146* with *4th, 6th,* and *8th Batteries*) still had to go into position during the night of 4/5 February in the vicinity of Bracht in such a way that it controlled the Maas crossings between Kessel and Baarlo. It depended on cooperation with the *190th Infantry Division* and *Group Wadehn (8th Parachute Division).*[11] The corresponding Division order was issued on the evening of 4 February. It said that after the weather improved, a major enemy assault could be expected and that the

Division was to stand by in the vicinity of Dülken–Viersen. The enemy attack was expected from the direction of Venlo-Roermond, or north of Heinsberg, with the intention of pushing forward toward Cologne–Düsseldorf. At the same time, it was to roll up the front of the Maas from the south.[12] On 1 February, the Division already ordered that every unit establish a base on the eastern bank of the Rhine, "in which immobile materiel, motor vehicles that are not needed for combat, and supplies should be deposited."[13]

On 5 February, the Division staff moved to Venn (four kilometers northwest of München-Gladbach). On the evening of this day, *Panzer-Grenadier Regiment 60* reported that it arrived with all units in the vicinity of München-Gladbach; those which had been hung up in the Eifel were finally able to link up. Elements of *Panzerjäger Battalion 228* (five *Jagdpanzer IVs*) [The *Jagdpanzer IV* was a well-armored turretless tank destroyer based on the *Panzer IV* chassis, mounting a 75mm main gun—*Editor*] also arrived in Pongs, near Rheydt. To strengthen the very minimal artillery firepower of the Division, the heavy anti-tank guns were ordered to fire with the artillery during the next action.[14]

Vogelsang wrote the following in Venn, on the evening of 5 February:

> A number of officers and a few hundred enlisted replacements have also arrived. The *Panzer-Grenadier Regiments* are numerically replenished. Yet, there is little left of the old stock. Even awards have again arrived! The Knight's Cross for *Major* Stephan, . . . the German Cross in Silver for our specially distinguished *Major* (Ing.) Hartung. . . .
>
> We are again in the target area of the heavy bomber packs. In these few days alone, four heavy air raids hit the towns in our nearby surroundings. Our night fighters really prove themselves exemplary, but in their limited number they are not in a position to decisively affect these masses, in spite of their sacrificial efforts. . . .
>
> It is raining torrents. Hopefully it stays that way! This way, the American takes his time with his offensive. Every day is a gain with regard to the battle strength of the Division; in view of the necessity for recuperation of the infantry, it is a gift![15]

During the night of 5/6 February, the *2d Battalion, Armored Artillery Regiment 146* took up position in the vicinity of Bracht as ordered. It established observation posts along the Maas, between Belfeld and Reuver. It remained there until the evening of 10 February. All was quiet at the front, except on 8 February, at 0800 hours, when the opponent was firing near and north of Venlo to divert from his attack at the *Reichswald*.[16] On 6 February, the Division was placed under *XLVII Panzer Corps* in every respect. The only anti-aircraft battery of the Division that had arrived, the *1st Battery, Army Anti-Aircraft Battalion 281* with three heavy and three light guns, received orders to go into position in the vicinity of Busch, south of Dülken.[17]

On 7 February, the corps commander ordered the Division Commander to deliver a short speech to every battalion to raise the morale of the troops. For 10 February, he announced a planning exercise for the corps.[18] The Division's new

Ib, Major i.G. von Carlowitz, led an ongoing fight for fuel, on the one hand, to be able to carry out the relocation to the newly assigned area, and on the other hand, to move up the units still stuck in the Eifel. On 7 February, he reported to me that the units still encamped in the Eifel could not be supplied, that the scattered, damaged vehicles could not be recovered, and that with the advance of the enemy in the vicinity of Schleiden, the situation there was intensifying. Ten trucks had already been lost due to artillery fire. Not even the few *Jagdpanzer IVs* could be moved up from Pongs to *Panzer Company Brinkmann,* because of lack of fuel; the distance was only about six kilometers.[19]

The journal of *OKW* reports about this day:

> On 7 February, during a meeting of the Supreme Commanders . . . situation and preparations for the upcoming defensive battle were discussed. Special consideration was given to the lack of fuel and the consequences of the impossibility of quickly relocating reserves, the decreased combat strength of *Army Group B,* the fatigue and over-exertion of the troops, as well as their emotional state ("generally, the soldier has had it up to his eyeballs"). Independently of this, every officer, NCO, and soldier must be clearly aware that in view of the situation in the homeland and in the East, he must persevere to the last.[20]

During the night of 7/8 February, the *116th Panzer Division* issued a new order for the preparation of an emergency deployment to close off enemy breaches or to mop them up by counterattack. It mentioned five different situations to be reconnoitered. The troops were also ordered to disperse, and it was also ordered that all unnecessary vehicles were to be displaced to near- and far-collection areas in the rear, because when the enemy started the offensive, the heaviest air activity could be counted on. Every battalion was to have an emergency company standing by for action against airborne landings. To improve training, a company training exercise was conducted by each *Panzer-Grenadier Regiment.* On the evening of 8 February, *General* Lüttwitz reported that the enemy attacked in the *Reichswald* during the morning hours and achieved a breach. However, the Division received 40 cubic meters of fuel to move more units up from the Eifel. It ordered that the armored units were to be given priority for departure.[21]

The next day, 9 February, passed without any particularly significant events. According to *Supreme Command–West*'s weekly report of 10 February, the Division consisted of three strong and two medium-strength battalions, as well as one average-strength battalion; one anti-tank gun; three artillery batteries; 44 tanks, assault guns, and tank destroyers.[22] Unfortunately, two of those battalions and several tanks were still in the Eifel. On this 10 February, at 1000 hours, the announced planning exercise began at the headquarters of *XLVII Panzer Corps.* At 1700 hours, corps headquarters ordered the Division to prepare to march toward Kleve. For the transportation of *Panzer-Grenadier Regiment 156,* it provided 30 tons of truck cargo space. Thank God, it also allotted 80 cubic meters of fuel, and an additional 25 for the units in the Eifel. The Division was to reach the vicinity of Marienbaum–Sonsbeck–Xanten during the night of 10/11 February. The Division designated Pauelshof as the release point (four kilometers south-west of Xanten).[23]

The march into the new area became difficult. There was still a lack of fuel, and in part also of cargo space. At 2200 hours, *Panzer Company Brinkmann* was the first unit to march; at 0300 hours the Division staff started to move, and established a temporary command post in the Köppenhof farm (five kilometers south-west of Xanten).[24] By 0900 hours, the Division Commander received the following order for the Division from the Commanding General, *XLVII Panzer Corps,* at the *LXXXVI Corps* command post:

— Preparation in area south of Hau during night 11/12 February.
— Attack on 12 February at dawn via the forward line of the *84th Infantry Division* to recapture the high ground west and southwest of Kleve.
— Attack by *15th Panzer-Grenadier Division* to the left of the *116th* through the northern part of the *Reichswald.*
— Carry out reconnaissance immediately. As soon as possible, begin trickling *Panzer-Grenadiers* into the preparation area by foot march from the western edge of the Xanten state forest.[25]

Reconnaissance of the preparation area and the area of attack, as far as it was possible, as well as the link-up with the unit currently holding the position, disclosed that in the meantime, the opponent had advanced further than was first reported. The situation southeast of Kleve and in the northeastern part of the *Reichswald* was not clear. Therefore, the Division ordered the forward edge of the preparation area to be the Kleve–Goch railroad line.[26] For the aforementioned reasons, the Division's flow into the area west of Xanten proceeded reluctantly. At first, only one battalion each from the two *Panzer-Grenadier* Regiments was available. Fortunately, bad weather—strong rain and blowing snow—allowed daytime marching.[27]

In Venn, at noon on 11 February, Vogelsang wrote:

Lack of fuel is frightening, the vehicle situation is bad, armored equipment is insufficient.

Shortly before setting out, besides smaller transports of officers and enlisted men, another march battalion arrived, which we were still able to hastily divide. Another 300 men from the non-combat units of the Division were mustered and passed on to the *Field Replacement Battalion,* whose training was now in full force again with 1,200 men.

The intensity of the air war has increased again. Bombers and fighter bombers drone day and night. Rheydt, Gladbach, Viersen, Dülken suffered heavy raids.[28]

What had happened at the *Reichswald* since 8 February?[29] In the late morning hours of 8 February, British XXX Corps attacked with four reinforced infantry divisions between the Maas and the Rhine. At 0500 hours, more than 1,000 guns and countless weapons of various kinds opened their destructive fire on the *84th Infantry Division*. It was the strongest barrage of annihilation the British fired during the whole war. It was interrupted at 0730 hours for ten minutes to coax the Germans out of their shelters, but at 1000 hours, it intensified to an inferno, and at 1030 hours it was advanced. With the support of ground attack aircraft, the British and the Canadians now attacked and penetrated the main battle line almost everywhere. In the evening, the 3d Canadian Infantry Division joined the attack in the flooded lowland north of the road Nijmegen–Kranenburg–Kleve with amphibious vehicles. The first objective of the offensive was the line Gennep–Asperden–Kleve, the next one the line Weeze–Uedem–Kalkar–Emmerich. The breakthrough toward Geldern–Xanten was to follow. It was hoped to reach this objective in a few days, and it was assumed that the ground would be frozen. However, this did not happen. On the contrary: the rain caused the ground to be bottomless. Flooding filled the lowlands and was increased by the high waters from the Maas, as well as by the demolition of Rhine dams by the Germans. On 8 February, the water in the Rhine lowlands northwest of Kleve rose by about one half meter.

The *84th Infantry Division* was in a difficult position and suffered considerable losses.[30] The only armored support it had was *Heavy Tank Destroyer Battalion 655*; all three infantry regiments and the parachute infantry regiment at the left wing were deployed on the front. In the evening of 8 February, the one in the middle, *Grenadier Regiment 1051,* took quite a beating, and the front line fell back to a weakened area of the *Westwall*. On 9 February, all three of the Division's regiments began to falter, and the enemy advanced to a line five kilometers northwest of Kleve–Westrim Kleve–Westrim Materborn–Gelden-Berg–two kilometers northeast of Gennep. The British reached their first attack objective.

Army Group H was constantly very concerned about its left wing at the Maas, and only released the *7th Parachute Division* after some hemming and hawing.[31] It was inserted with most of the Division to the left, next to the *84th Infantry Division*. Besides this, *Parachute Infantry Regiment 16* of the *6th Parachute Division*, brought in from the Lek, was deployed at the northern verge of the *Reichswald*.[32] It offered tenacious resistance southwest of Kleve and near Materborn against the reserve of the British XXX Corps, the 43d (Wessex) Division, which was brought in for the penetration of Goch. However, this Division, reinforced by the 8th Armoured Brigade, was sent into battle too early: freedom of mobility had not yet been gained. On 10 February, terrible traffic jams developed on the few passable roads; the German side gained time.[33] But, on 11 February, Kleve and Materborn fell, and Hau followed (four kilometers southeast of Kleve) on the morning of 12 February. The British also advanced in the *Reichswald* further toward the east, and Gennep fell into their hands.[34]

By now, there was not much left of the infantry of the *84th Infantry Division*. Only *Grenadier Regiment 1052* on the right was still somewhat intact; *Grenadier Regiment 1051,* in the center, and *Grenadier Regiment 1062,* on the left were more or less destroyed. *Parachute Infantry Regiment 16,* which fought bravely within the framework of the Division, had also suffered much.[35] Since the reports about the strength of the attacking enemy on 9 and 10 February clearly showed that the British deployed the bulk of their large formations at the *Reichswald, Supreme Command–West* and *Army Group H* decided on 10 February to release *XLVII Panzer Corps.* Army Group also moved up the *346th Infantry Division's Grenadier Regiment 858* from the Netherlands.[36]

At 0900 hours on 11 February, *XLVII Panzer Corps* assumed control in the *84th Infantry Division* sector, with the left boundary extending from Goch (exclusive) to the southern edge of the *Reichswald.* The instructions were to attack the high ground left of Kleve no later than 12 February at 0600 hours. Corps suggested abandoning the plan for an attack and deploying the two approaching divisions—they were only division combat groups—for defending the line Bedburg–Asperden. The suggestion did not find any consent.[37]

This was the situation when, on 11 February, the *116th Panzer Division* was about to advance into its preparation area for the attack.

The commanders in the vicinity of Ueden reported the results of their reconnaissance at 1745 hours. The Division then verbally forwarded the attack order.

The written version was issued on 12 February, at 0030 hours, and included the following:

> Enemy pushed back front line of *LXXXVI Corps* with strong force superiority, took Kleve, and achieved a deep penetration in the *Reichswald.* Continuation of the attack with strengthened deployment of tanks to gain exit from the *Reichswald* must be expected. Task for *XLVII Panzer Corps* with *116th Panzer Division* is, after assembly in the area south of Hau, to attack the opponent at 0630 hours, and to capture the high ground west and southwest of Kleve. *Heavy Tank Destroyer Battalion 655* is subordinated to *Hauptmann* Brinkmann. The attack is to be conducted beyond the forward units of the *84th Infantry Division.* In view of the minimal state of training of the *Panzer-Grenadiers,* the attack has to be conducted rigidly, sector by sector.[38]

In his post-war report, *Generalmajor* von Waldenburg wrote:

> The Division reported, dutifully, that its combat group was not suitable for a counterattack with the insufficiently-trained, newly-arrived *Panzer-Grenadiers* and only a few tanks against a concentrated attack by the opponent who, above all, had extremely strong and superior artillery with unlimited ammunition. The Division suggested deploying them for the defense in a partially-finished position south of Kleve. The *XLVII Panzer Corps* was of the same opinion and agreed with the suggestion, but nevertheless, a higher command ordered the counterattack.[39]

Besides *Heavy Tank Destroyer Battalion 655,* two more artillery battalions were subordinated to the *116th Panzer Division, Heavy Artillery Battalion 1152,* and the *1st Battalion, Artillery Regiment 184.* The *116th* only brought its

2d Battalion and some guns from the *3d Battalion,* which were subordinated to the *2d.* It had eight to ten tanks, as well as some tank destroyers, including about six heavy tank destroyers, which were attached. The *2d Battalion, Panzer-Grenadier Regiment 156* did not arrive in time, so only three *Panzer-Grenadier Battalions* were available. *Panzer-Grenadier Regiment 60* was to attack to the right, and *Panzer-Grenadier Regiment 156* to the left, out of the southern part of the Kleve state forest. The only anti-aircraft battery of the Division arrived on the morning of 12 February. Everything else was still pinned down in the Eifel.[40] The Division command post was advanced to Louisendorf on the evening of 11 February.[41]

Corps postponed the attack because the *15th Panzer-Grenadier Division* did not arrive in its preparation area in time, and because the enemy took Hau. The instructions for the *116th Panzer Division* were therefore formulated less stringently: Attack out of the Bedburg area toward the northwest with the objective of recapturing Hau and advance to the line Freudenberg (six kilometers northwest of Hau)–Palandswald, which meant up to the narrow area between the little Wetering river and the northern edge of the *Reichswald* south of Kleve. The attack was to commence at 0930 hours.[42] Therefore, after combined fire by the entire artillery and the heavy weapons from *Panzer-Grenadier Regiment 60,* the *1st Battalion, Panzer-Grenadier Regiment 60,* reinforced by *Panzer Group Brinkmann,* attacked Hau, while *1st Battalion, Panzer-Grenadier Regiment 156,* with the heavy tank destroyers, advanced along the major road from Goch–Kleve to the north, toward the northeast corner of the *Reichswald.*

At first, the attack on Hau progressed well. The road bend south of Hau was reached, but then the attack came to a halt under fire from the northern part of the town and out of the right flank from the vicinity of Bedburg. Even after reforming, a subsequent attack failed; for this, the *1st Battalion, Panzer-Grenadier Regiment 60* attacked once more at 1445 hours, but had to abort the attempt under heavy artillery fire. The effect from the right flank was felt more and more. Here, the enemy achieved a deep breakthrough along the Kleve–Kalkar road at what was now the left wing of *84th Infantry Division.*

Initially, the attack by the reinforced *1st Battalion, Panzer-Grenadier Regiment 156* encountered only minor resistance. However, an enemy attack with tanks and reconnaissance vehicles along the Kleve–Goch road pushed straight into its front; it was repelled, and all six reconnaissance vehicles and one tank were destroyed. The attack was conducted by the reconnaissance regiment [a battalion-sized unit—*Editor*] of the 43d (Wessex) Division. After this, the *1st Battalion* reached the northeastern corner of the *Reichswald* near Horstmannshof and by noon, pushed into it about one kilometer deep. There, the battalion repulsed an attack by a British infantry battalion, which was conducted after an massive artillery preparation from the vicinity of Resepütt, along the verge of the forest.[43] The attack by the *15th Panzer-Grenadier Division* into the *Reichswald* achieved no noteworthy success.[44]

During the course of the day, the British attack against Bedburg and along the Kleve–Kalkar road was especially unpleasant. In the late morning, the enemy seized Bedburg and advanced up to Hasselt. The *116th Panzer Division* placed the *2d Battalion* of *Panzer-Grenadier Regiment 60* behind the *1st Battalion,* northeast of the pine woods, in such a manner that it could be deployed to protect the right flank to the north but, if necessary, also along the boundary with *Panzer-Grenadier Regiment 156.* For the latter task, the Division Commander permitted the deployment of one company of this battalion at 1445 hours. Shortly thereafter, *General* von Lüttwitz ordered the release of three heavy tank destroyers to the *84th Infantry Division* for deployment against the enemy near Hasselt.

This situation forced the cessation of the attack. At 1715 hours, *Generalmajor* von Waldenburg ordered the changeover to defense. I informed the commanders of the necessary measures. At 1845 hours, the Division Commander ordered *Panzer-Grenadier Regiment 60* to at once pull up the *2d Battalion* to the vicinity south of Bedburg and to block the roads out of town to the east and southeast. The *84th Infantry Division* was subordinated to the *116th Panzer Division.* The written Division order was sent out at 0100 hours on 13 February.[45] The British captured it. Its translation to English is (excerpt):

2. *116th Panzer Division* with subordinated *84th Infantry Division* . . . stops the attack south of Kleve and changes to defense in line Erfgen [five kilometers east of Kleve—*Author*]–Hasselt–Esels–Berg [two kilometers southeast of Bedburg—*Author*]–northwestern corner of pine woods–western edge of pine woods [*Tannenbusch*].

3. On the right: *84th Infantry Division*
   Center: *Panzer-Grenadier Regiment 60*
   On the left: *Panzer-Grenadier Regiment 156*

4. Conduct of battle:

a) *84th Infantry Division* with attached *Grenadier Regiment 858* (approaching) defends line Erfgen–Stammenhof, Hasselt railroad station–Hasselt–Rosendahl. *Grenadier Regiment 858* and units formed from stragglers are to be deployed to establish a rear support line Kapitelshof [3.5 kilometers southeast of Erfgen—*Author*]–Rubenkath–eastern edge of Rosendahl Park. . . .

   Commander, *84th Infantry Division* is personally responsible to the commanding general for collecting all stragglers, to form units of them, and to bring them forward for deployment to hold the remaining sector of the Division. Main effort of defense on both sides of road Kleve–Kalkar. The tanks must be deployed there, and a strong local reserve must be established.

b) *Panzer-Grenadier Regiment 60* has only the *2d Battalion* at its disposal. The armored battalion remains at the disposal of the Division in the forest southeast of Kal. Kotten [one kilometer northeast of Esels-Berg—*Author*] to conduct limited objective attack on the morning of 13 February via Rosendahl toward Hasselt. . . .

c) *Panzer-Grenadier Regiment 156* defends in sector, relieves *1st Battalion* with the *2d* and as soon as possible withdraws all units of *Panzer-Grenadier Regiment 60* in its sector. . . . [T]he *15th Panzer-Grenadier Division* has orders to establish a reaction force behind its right wing.

6. Tanks and assault guns:

Commander, *Panzerjäger Battalion 228,* to whom heavy *Tank Destroyer Battalion 655* and the active company of *Panzer Regiment 16* are attached, coordinates the deployment of tanks and assault guns in both division sectors. One group is to be added to each for support.

a) The *84th Infantry Division* along road Kleve–Kalkar.

b) *Panzer-Grenadier Regiment 60* along the roads leading out of Bedburg toward the east and southeast.

c) *Panzer-Grenadier Regiment 156* north of the pine woods.[46]

Hauptmann Brinkmann was seriously wounded and died on 13 February. Therefore, the commander of *Panzerjäger Battalion 228, Hauptmann der Reserve* Geigenmüller assumed command of all tanks and tank destroyers.

The Division journal reports the following about the night of 12/13 February:

At 0500 hours, after reforming during the night with the newly-arrived units from *Grenadier Regiment 858,* the *84th Infantry Division,* which was subordinated to the Division, occupied the line Kapitelshof–Brünskath–Ruwenkath, 500 meters southeast of Rosendahl. The *116th Panzer Division* could not move into the assigned line until 0800 hours. The reorganization of the Division was delayed by extremely heavy enemy artillery fire and by the enemy attack at the eastern edge of the *Reichswald* at dusk.[47]

The attack by *1st Battalion, Panzer-Grenadier Regiment 60* toward Hasselt, initially requested by headquarters, *1st Parachute Army,* was cancelled after a long-distance call between *General* von Lüttwitz and *Generalmajor* von Waldenburg. The corps commander ordered, "Press forward to the line Trägerskath–Rosendahl–Fahnenkamp."

To this, the journal adds, "The *84th* reached the line without a fight, however, it encountered minor enemy resistance in the Rosendahl–Esels–Berg sector."

Commencing at 1030 hours, the enemy artillery fire increased to a barrage, and the terrain was screened with smoke. An attack on the Kalkar–Kleve road pushed the just-advanced units of *84th Infantry Division* back to their line of departure. The advanced assault groups of the *2d Battalion, Panzer-Grenadier Regiment 60* had a similar fate. Besides this, a gap had developed between *Panzer-Grenadier* Regiments 60 and 156. A company from *1st Battalion, Panzer-Grenadier Regiment 60,* which was kept in reserve, was released to close it. The journal further reports about the course of events on 13 February:

At 1500 hours, the enemy began to attack on both sides of the Bedburg–Uedem road with strong infantry (regimental strength), supported by tanks. Again, preceding the attack was an extraordinarily heavy artillery preparation with phosphorous and smoke. The enemy succeeded with heavy, simultaneous action by fighter bombers, and after eliminating all assault guns and tank destroyers in this sector, broke in and advanced toward Esels-Berg, Trippenberg, Castel, and the road intersection southwest of it.

The immediately-mounted counterattack by the units still available from *1st Battalion, Panzer-Grenadier Regiment 60,* along with the remaining battleworthy assault guns and the deployment of *Panzer-Grenadier Regiment 156*'s reserve company closed off the opponent and destroyed three enemy tanks.

With the enemy capturing the Eselsberg and the road junction 500 meters northeast of the northeastern corner of the pine woods, the Division's situation became critical. Disposed in the pine woods, *Panzer-Grenadier Regiment 156* was threatened in its flank and contact with the unit to its right was jeopardized. Therefore, at the Division command post, which had been in Heidkamp since 1400 hours, the corps commander ordered at 1800 hours that the breach would be mopped up the next morning. To increase its reduced infantry strength, the *Training School* troops of the *1st Parachute Army* was to be added to the Division. It had the strength of a battalion and brought with it a battery of light field howitzers. However, it was not to be deployed in an attack. Its commander was *Hauptmann* von Hütz. Nevertheless, this gave the Division a reserve behind the most threatened sector along the road to Uedem. The *84th Infantry Division* was again subordinated to corps headquarters. During the night of 13/14 February, its sector was to be widened toward the south and up to the Bedburg–Kalkar road, to free up the units from *Panzer-Grenadier Regiment 60* that were fighting there. Fortunately, the *84th Infantry Division*'s situation had stabilized, mainly due to the flooding which affected both sides of the Kleve–Kalkar road. The main effort of the enemy thrust was now in the open area southeast of Bedburg, opposite the *116th Panzer Division.*

Vogelsang wrote the following on the evening of 13 February:

In past actions, one counted the duration of barrages by hours. Here, it would be easier to just note the hours during the day when there is no barrage.

During the whole night, nuisance fire in a strength thus far never experienced rolled across all roads, towns, road junctions along the front and deep into the rear. After a pause during the late morning hours, it started again toward noon. . . .

The gaps in the artillery fire are closed by countless fighter bombers and light bomber units, which go after every town and every movement between the front line and the Rhine. Earlier, Sonsbeck was the target in our vicinity. The explosions were so violent that one could literally see a reflecting wave of compressed air extending around the point of impact. . . .

If one experiences this and then reads the report by the *OKW*, one really does not know how all this will turn out! One must not write or speak about this. But the thoughts cannot be suppressed, even if one would almost like to do that. If one only knew what the continuous rumors about new decisive weapons were all about: otherwise, one can hardly see any sense to all this![48]

On 14 February at 0700 hours, attacking on a broad front after a barrage from all of the Division's artillery, the strike troops from both regiments gained some ground. The Eselsberg, however, remained in enemy hands, and the previously captured road intersection northeast of the pine woods was lost after an immediate enemy counterattack. Thereby, three enemy tanks were destroyed by one assault gun.[49] The journal of the *2d Battalion, Armored Artillery Regiment 146,* reports, "Attack advances well at first, but when weather clears and multitudes of fighter bombers control the entire battle field, the attack halts."[50]

The enemy attacked several more times in the course of the day. At 1200 hours, a battalion supported by six tanks attacking from Castel was repelled. At around the same time, the same fate befell a renewed attack along the Bedburg–Uedem road. At 1300 hours, another one with the support of five tanks from the direction of Eselsberg was also beaten back. Attacks conducted at 1100 hours against the northwestern corner and the northern edge of the pine woods near *Panzer-Grenadier Regiment 156* were without success. At 1400 hours, *Regiment 156* repelled a renewed attack at the northwestern corner of the forest. All these enemy attacks were supported by very heavy artillery and by fighter bombers. These and twin-engine ground attack aircraft dominated the air and joined the battles with bombs and machine guns, bombing villages, groups of houses, and the artillery's firing positions.[51] The Ic of *Supreme Command–West* estimated 2,500 fighter bombers and 540 twin-engine aircraft over the battle area.[52] The journal of *2d Battalion, Armored Artillery Regiment 146,* however, praised the well-organized air defense, which effectively hindered the attacks by the low-flying planes.[53]

Vogelsang wrote down in the evening:

The Division again has had a hard day. The English were beaten back everywhere by defense and counterattack. . . . In this tough fight, we again had losses including three officers and 60 men. With respect to the artillery fire, some World War [meaning World War I—*Editor*] veterans state that there was never a barrage like this during their days.[54]

For his exemplary action during the fight at the northwestern corner of the pine woods, the acting commander of *5th Company, Panzer-Grenadier Regiment 156, Leutnant* Käseberg, received the Knight's Cross.[55]

For 15 February, the Division expected the continuation of the British breakthrough attempts with the main effort in the direction of Uedem.[56] The deployment of the *1st Parachute Army Training School* troops in the sector of *Panzer-Grenadier Regiment 60* permitted the formation of a weak mobile reserve. The *1st Battalion, Panzer-Grenadier Regiment 60* moved into a rear defense position on both sides of the Bedburg–Uedem road, near Blacknik (1.5 kilometers west of

Louisendorf) and kept its armored vehicles ready, so that it could be moved quickly, and if needed, by order of corps headquarters, also to the adjacent divisions.

It was announced to the Division that by 15 February, it would be joined by *Parachute Reconnaissance Battalion 12.* The night of 15 February again brought a continuous, very heavy harrassing fire by the enemy artillery. The *2d Battalion, Armored Artillery Regiment 146* estimated 10,000 rounds in the Division sector.[57] In the meantime, the opponent probed the front with strong assault troops, in part supported by tanks. Two small breaches near *Panzer-Grenadier Regiment 60* were immediately mopped up.[58]

On 15 February, after two hours of the heaviest barrage on the front and far into the rear, the enemy attacked along the entire Division front.[59] An attack conducted by tanks and infantry in battalion strength on the Bedburg–Kalkar road, along the boundary with *Panzer-Grenadier Regiment 60* to the unit on the right, gained a breach 400 meters deep at about 1000 hours, before it could be closed off. One enemy tank was destroyed. At the same time, another attack, also in battalion strength, against the northwestern corner of the pine woods was turned back. One-half hour later, the attack by two battalions at the northern edge of the pine woods suffered the same fate. The repetition of both attacks a short time later was finished off in the same way by *Panzer-Grenadier Regiment 156.* Along the Castel–Louisendorf road, a battalion supported by three tanks attacked at 1130 hours near *Panzer-Grenadier Regiment 60*, but failed, losing one tank. At the same time, tanks with mounted infantry attacked a little further west and captured a group of farm houses in the regiment's main battle line. At 1200 hours at the northeastern corner of the pine woods, a new attack in battalion strength, accompanied by tanks, was repelled by *Panzer-Grenadier Regiment 156.*

No sooner was this over than an enemy battalion attacked the northern front of the pine woods twice, in vain. In the afternoon, the attacks against *Panzer-Grenadier Regiment 156* continued, at 1400 hours against the northeast corner, at 1550 hours against the entire northern front, repeated twice, and at 1630 hours against the northwestern corner of the forest. With the help of the outstanding support provided by the Division's artillery, *Panzer-Grenadier Regiment 156* repulsed all attacks. For his excellent fire control, in spite of heavy enemy fire, *Oberwachtmeister* Frey, the forward observer from *5th Battery,* was mentioned in the Division's honor roll.[60]

At 1600 hours, the enemy attacked the *1st Parachute Army Training School* troops with one battalion and tanks along the road Bedburg–Uedem. The battles there continued during the night. Bröckel and Berkhöfel were lost. With a counterattack by the engineer company from the *1st Parachute Army Training School* under the personal command of *Hauptmann* von Hütz, the enemy that had penetrated was thrown back in the morning hours of 16 February. Four enemy tanks were destroyed by close combat weapons.[61]

On the afternoon of 15 February, the Supreme Commander of the *1st Parachute Army, General* Schlemm, visited the Division in its newly-established command post in a farm house 1.5 kilometers northwest of Delsenhof, and expressed his appreciation.[62] For his personal dedication during the mop-up of the breaches in his front line, *Oberstleutnant* Zander, commander of *Panzer-Grenadier Regiment 60,* was recommended for the Knight's Cross, which was awarded to him shortly before the war's end.[63] *Oberstleutnant* Grollmann and his *Panzer-Grenadier Regiment 156* also received special recognition. During the battles for the northeastern part of the pine woods, the commander of the *1st Battalion, Panzer-Grenadier Regiment 156, Hauptmann* Schneider, showed special tactical skills and great bravery on this day, as well as during the following morning.[64]

After the war, Waldenburg wrote:

All in all, on 15 February, the Division repelled 20 enemy attacks, ten alone by the superbly fighting *Panzer-Grenadier Regiment 156,* deployed in the pine woods under the leadership of its commander (*Oberstleutnant* Grollmann).

The major defensive success of this day can be attributed mainly to the fact that the strong, superior opponent only conducted local, separate, partial attacks, and thereby allowed the Division leadership to always throw the mobile reserves at the threatened points and to combine the fire of all heavy weapons to the endangered areas one at the time.[65]

In the evening of 15 February, the Division had no more reserves. The *1st Battalion, Panzer-Grenadier Regiment* was at the front again. The losses were high.

On 16 February, the opponent repeated his breakthrough attempts with reinforcements.[66] They ultimately led to a deep breach in the direction of Goch and threw the *XLVII Panzer Corps* into a crisis. During the night, at 0400 hours, an enemy attack hit the right wing of the *116th Panzer Division* at and west of the Bedburg–Kalkar road. It was intercepted by *Panzer-Grenadier Regiment 60* north of Louisendorf. Starting at 0930 hours, after preparatory fires, the enemy attacked along the entire front of the Division in various strengths, from company up to regiment. A minimum of 50 tanks supported the attack. While an attack in progress against the northwestern corner of the pine woods was repelled and one tank destroyed, the superior enemy forces achieved success on both sides of the Bedburg–Uedem road against the *1st Parachute Army Training School* troops, who fought with exemplary bravery in spite of high losses. The Bröckel and Berghöfel farms were lost again.

At about 1100 hours, the enemy's spearhead was at the road crossing, two kilometers southwest of Louisendorf. The Division was in danger of being torn apart in the center. *Panzer-Grenadier Regiment 156* and units from the *15th Panzer-Grenadier Division* were threatened with encirclement.

The Division intended to restore the situation by attacking with *Panzer-Grenadier Regiment 156* from the west and *Panzer-Grenadier Regiment 60* from the east. Corps headquarters subordinated the *2d Battalion* of *Panzer-Grenadier Regiment 115* of the *15th Panzer-Grenadier Division,* which was southeast of the pine woods, to the *116th Panzer Division* to clear up the situation. It was to attack Berghöfel from the south. At 1130 hours, *Oberstleutnant* Grollmann received orders to take his *Panzer-Grenadier Regiment 156* back to the southeastern part of the pine woods, to leave security elements at the edges of the forest, and to prepare it for an attack east against the enemy that had broken through. The Division did not receive permission for the complete evacuation of the pine woods. At 1145 hours, the order went out to *Oberstleutnant* Zander to attack from Louisendorf to the west, toward Berghöfel, by combining the assault guns that were still battleworthy and the infantrymen who were still available. They were ordered to attack at 1500 hours.

The attack did not occur. Instead, the enemy attacked in the afternoon toward Louisendorf, as well as from the breach near Berghöfel in the south toward Goch. After a renewed barrage, Louisendorf was attacked by infantry with about 20 tanks, and was lost. Under fire from all weapons, the enemy was brought to a halt and the breach was closed off by *Parachute Reconnaissance Battalion 12,* which, under the command of *Major* Jungwirth, had arrived just in time. The *3d Company* of *Panzer-Grenadier Regiment 60,* under the command of *Oberleutnant* Gebauer, bravely withstood all attacks at the hill north-northeast of Louisendorf and ultimately even those coming out of the village.[67]

The events southwest of Louisendorf became quite critical.[68] Here, the enemy attacked again in the afternoon, overran *2d Battalion, Panzer-Grenadier Regiment 115,* which by now had been deployed to seal of the breach, and then pushed further south toward Goch. *Panzer-Grenadier Regiment 156* was cut off, but it succeeded in escaping to the south during the night. In the late afternoon, two more attacks along the boundary with the unit on the right were turned back, in combined action with that unit. In the course of the day, 14 enemy tanks were destroyed.

During the night of 16/17 February, the Division moved into a new position along the trail which runs about one kilometer northwest parallel to the Kalkar–Goch road, with the right wing in the vicinity of Gross-Heselerfeld (three kilometers southwest of Kalkar), and the left wing at the Bedburg–Uedem road, and as of noon on 17 February, near Gross-Ackershof.[69] By order of corps headquarters, by 0500 hours on 17 February, a reinforced assault unit of *Parachute Reconnaissance Battalion 12* was to join the *15th Panzer-Grenadier Division* at Halvenboom (one kilometer south-southeast of Gross-Ackershof) to establish a defensive line forward of Goch.[70] The opponent captured Hassum and Afferden, west and southwest of Goch.[71]

To the right of the *116th Panzer Division,* the staff of the *6th Parachute Division* assumed control in the former sector of the *84th Infantry Division* with the paratroopers that were already deployed there (remnants of *Parachute Infantry Regiment 16* of the *6th Parachute Division,* from *2d Battalion, Parachute Infantry Regiment 19* and *2d Battalion, Parachute Infantry Regiment 21* of the *7th Parachute Division*) and with *Grenadier Regiment 858. Parachute Infantry Regiments 17* and *18* of the *6th Parachute Division* arrived later. The artillery of the *84th Infantry Division* remained deployed.[72]

Who fought against the *116th Panzer Division?* For an answer, a look at the opposite side is again needed.[73] When the *XLVII Panzer Corps* started to attack on 12 February, the British offensive had just gotten under way. The 15th (Scottish) Division, with tanks from the 6th Guards Armoured Brigade, seized Hasselt at the Kleve–Kalkar road. The 43d (Wessex) Division, reinforced by the 8th Armoured Brigade, had attacked Goch from the area south of Kleve and took Bedburg and Hau. It encountered the attack by the *116th Panzer Division,* south of these towns. Both sides came to a halt. Aside from this, the 53d (Welsh) Division, with the attached 34th Armoured Brigade, almost reached the eastern edge of the *Reichswald* on 12 February, when it encountered *Panzer-Grenadier Regiment 156* in the northeastern part of the forest; further south, it met the attack by the *15th Panzer-Grenadier Division.* South of the *Reichswald,* the 51st (Highland) Division reached the Kleve–Gennep road. At the other British wing, in the flooded area south of the Rhine, the 3d Canadian Infantry Division took Griethausen and Kellen.

On 13 February, all British attacks were beaten back; only south of Bedburg, could the 43d (Wessex) Division achieve the reported breach at the Eselsberg. British successes were also minor on 15 February. The Canadians advanced to the ferry landing opposite Emmerich. Due to flooding, the Scots abandoned any further attacks along the Kleve–Kalkar road, and moved their attack further south, to the Bedburg–Kalkar road. In the afternoon, when they attacked along the boundary between the *84th Infantry* and the *116th Panzer Divisions,* they achieved no noteworthy success. In the southern part of the British attack front, only two local breaches were recorded.

On 15 February, the massive attacks along the entire front line hardly produced any gain. However, the continuous fire and prodding in the main efforts toward Kalkar and Goch started to promise certain successes. In part, they were realized on 16 February. The 214th Infantry Brigade of the 43d (Wessex) Division, along with tank support, succeeded in the afternoon of 16 February to break through the *116th Panzer Division,* east of the pine woods. Then, the 214th Infantry Brigade overran the *2d Battalion, Panzer-Grenadier Regiment 115.* During the night, it pushed on to the Goch–Kalkar road, northeast of Goch. West and southwest of Goch, the British also had more breathing room. Instead of the 15th (Scottish) Division, the 3d Canadian Infantry Division meanwhile reached the objective, Kalkar. In the afternoon of 16 February, its 7th Canadian Infantry Brigade, supported by one regiment of the 6th Guards Armoured Brigade, entered the battle. It took Louisendorf and the "T" in the road, 1.5 kilometers to the northeast. With the appearance of this brigade, a new act of the offensive began. The Canadian II Corps took over the left attack sector, attacking along the Kleve–Uedem axis, while the British XXX Corps was to attack Kevelaer to the right, via Goch–Weeze. The 43d, 53d, 51st, 52d, and 15th Divisions were subordinated to the latter, while the 2d and 3d Canadian Infantry Divisions were at the disposal of the Canadian II Corps, as was its reserve, the 4th Canadian Armoured Division. First, only the 3d Canadian Infantry Division entered the battle and took the place of the Scottish. The 7th Canadian Infantry Brigade continued its attack on 17 February, but without noticeable success. The 130th Infantry Brigade of the 43d (Wessex) Division occupied the pine woods, which were vacated by *Panzer-Grenadier Regiment 156.* The 53d (Welsh) and the 51st (Highland) Divisions took advantage of the success of the 43d and hooked up in the direction of Goch. Their 214th Infantry Brigade widened its nocturnally-effected breach toward Goch, as well toward Uedem. This endangered the left flank of the *116th Panzer Division.*

As reported, during the night of 16/17 February, the *116th Panzer Division* occupied a thin security line between Gross-Heselerfeld and the Bedburg–Uedem road with *Panzer-Grenadier Regiment 60,* the *1st Parachute Army Training School* troops, and *Parachute Reconnaissance Battalion 12.* Here, with much concern, they awaited the continuation of the enemy attacks. Thank God, *Panzer-Grenadier Regiment 156* returned to the Division during the night and apparently took over the left of the Division sector with the attached *Parachute Reconnaissance Battalion.* Due to the situation in the sector of the unit to the left, at 1000 hours on 17 February, corps headquarters ordered, "Strengthen the left wing and hold the Am Lindchen road junction."[74]

The Division's left wing was deployed at this intersection without support on its left. The nearest of our troops was in Halvenboom; it was the assault element of *Parachute Reconnaissance Battalion 12.* At 1420 hours, corps headquarters informed the Division that the enemy was advancing toward Goch and passing south of Halvenboom toward Hollen. *Generalmajor* von Waldenburg therefore ordered the few battleworthy tanks to Klein-Ackershof. From there, they could quickly assist in the direction of Am Lindchen, as well as Hollen, and if necessary, help out on the Division's right wing. Furthermore, reconnaissance was deployed on the left flank. Fortunately, on 17 February it was relatively calm in front of the Division's forward line. Vogelsang's diary entry for 17 February states:

> Both regiments are again badly bruised. Total casualties so far are 800 to 850 men. In some cases, the company strengths are again down to 15 men. The men fought superbly in all the battles, otherwise we would certainly no longer be sitting west of the Rhine! . . .
>
> Today, the resolution of the allied Tripartite Conference was made known. Our indignation, caused by the demands stipulated in it, could create a further intensification of the battles.[75]

Corps headquarters was advised by the Division of the poor infantry combat strength. It subordinated *Parachute Infantry Regiment 7* to it for the defense of Uedem.[76] On 17 February, at 1100 hours, the Division command post was relocated to the "Nachtigall" ["Nightingale"—*Translator*] forester's station. The night of 17/18 February and the day itself were again rather quiet.

On the left wing, two reconnaissance probes were repelled in the morning. In joint action with the unit to the immediate right, units of *Panzer-Grenadier Regiment 60* took back Gross-Heselerfeld against weak resistance. At noon, with combined fires, the Division artillery effectively engaged an accumulation of 20 enemy tanks northeast of Louisendorf. At 1350 and 1630 hours, tank-supported enemy battalion-strength attacks near Gross-Heselerfeld were destroyed with fire from all weapons, and the farm southwest of it was captured in a counterstrike.

In contrast, 19 February was a hot day. After a quiet night, the enemy fired a 90-minute barrage on the right of the Division sector in the early morning without a subsequent attack. At 1100 hours, strong preparations by enemy infantry were detected around Louisendorf and resisted with the combined fire of our artillery. At noon, the enemy began another barrage for about 90 minutes. Then, following its firestorm, the enemy attacked across a broad front on both sides of the road from Louisendorf to the southeast, supported by more than 30 tanks. The deployment of tanks with flamethrowers had an especially uncomfortable effect. Despite bitter resistance and heavy defensive fire by our troops, the opponent succeeded in breaking through the Division's thin lines and in advancing across the Kalkar–Goch road, up to the next row of farms. First, most of the farms were lost. However, with a counterstrike by local reserves, mainly the *1st Parachute Army Training School* troops, the opponent was thrown back and the Mooshof, Taubenhof, and Brunshof farms were retaken. A counterattack with tanks, set for 1700 hours, also led to recapturing the Am Lindchen road junction.

At 1400 hours, the right wing of the Division repelled an attack on Gross-Heselerfeld and destroyed two enemy tanks. During the night of 19/20 February, *Panzer-Grenadier Regiment 60* finally succeeded in recapturing the "T" intersection via Schwanenhof, 500 meters northwest of it, on the Kalkar–Goch road. From there, it was able to advance another 500 meters southwest along the road toward the dairy farm.

On 19 February, a total of 32 enemy tanks and one armored personnel carrier were reported as destroyed, and 60 prisoners taken. The enemy pushed our main battle line back by about 500 meters. It also suffered heavy, bloody losses, mostly from the combined fire of heavy weapons. On this day, the *2d Battalion* of *Armored Artillery Regiment 146* expended 2,205 rounds.

Also on 19 February, under the command of *Major* Jungwirth, *Parachute Reconnaissance Battalion 12,* which defended the left portion of the Division sector between Louisendorf and Gross-Ackershof, especially distinguished itself. The Division recommended *Major* Jungwirth for the Knight's Cross, which was still awarded to him on 9 May.[77,78]

Toward midnight, Vogelsang noted the following about 19 February, "Barrages again and again! With 35 to 40 tanks, the Canadians break through the positions along the entire width of our front. The attack was brought to a standstill after hours of bitter fighting by destroying 25 enemy tanks, with minimal loss of terrain."[79]

More terrain had been flooded near the adjacent sector to the right, north of Kalkar. All attacks by the Canadians along and mainly south of the Kleve–Kalkar road, and along the boundary, were able to be repelled in joint action with the *116th Panzer Division*. Fresh units from the *6th Parachute Division* arrived and relieved fatigued units.[80] The situation in the sector of the unit on the left, however, was less pleasant.[81] There, the battle of Goch was raging. Besides this, the enemy poked further into the gap between the left wing of the *116th Panzer Division* near Gross-Ackershof and the Goch–Uedem railroad line. There was no physical contact with the unit to the left. At noon on 19 February, *Parachute Infantry Regiment 7* was, after all, moved from Uedem to the sector of the adjacent unit to the left for deployment south of the railroad. Therefore, the *84th Infantry Division* was to be moved up into the gap. From the remnants of its three regiments, it formed two.

Since 9 February, a vigorous exchange of opinions took place between *OKW* and *Supreme Command–West*, in which *Supreme Command–West* portrayed its worrisome situation candidly, and asked for help.[82] In view of the overall situation, *OKW* was unable to help and deliberated how to conduct command in the West and what kind of help could still be found. On 16 February, *Supreme Command–West* received Hitler's "directives in case the Anglo-Americans might succeed, in spite of the determined resistance by the troops, to achieve a breakthrough out of the *Reichswald* or across the Roer toward the Rhine." According to the journal of *OKW*, they determined the following:

> In such a case, the decisive task of *Supreme Command–West* would be the defense of the Rhine, between Arnhem and Bonn (including the prepared bridgeheads on the west bank). . . . To establish the defense of the Rhine, the construction of a system of positions along the east bank between Emmerich and Karlsruhe was ordered. . . .

In spite of the impending American attacks across the Roer, the *Supreme Commander–West* made the difficult decision to release one of his few reserves, the *Panzer Lehr Division*, for a one-time deployment with the *1st Parachute Army*. A combat group of the division arrived on 18 February in the Hochwald, west of Xanten. It consisted of *Panzer-Grenadier Lehr Regiment 901*, one artillery battalion, 22 battleworthy tanks, and ten to twelve tank destroyers. The second *Panzer-Grenadier Regiment* remained in reserve.[83]

The combat group was alerted at 1000 hours on 19 February. At 1350 hours, at the climax of the *116th Panzer Division*'s crisis, the corps commander announced that this combat group was being deployed to restore the main battle line.[84]

At 1630 hours, he appeared at the command post of the *116th Panzer Division* and gave the *116th* and the combat group of the *Panzer Lehr Division* orders for a counterattack for the night of 20 February. The attack's objective, the reestablishment of the old main battle line, was to be achieved in concert with the unit on the right, the *6th Parachute Division*. For this, the combat group of the *Panzer Lehr Division* was to attack at the right wing of the *116th*. Their leaders reconnoitered in preparation for the attack during the day. Occupation of the preparation positions was delayed, however, so that initially, the *116th*'s counterattacks were conducted in isolation, with the results described. The combat group of the *Panzer Lehr Division,* reinforced by the *116th Panzer Division Escort Company* with support from its artillery, attacked at 2000 hours on 19 February, joined on the right by units from the *6th Parachute Division,* and on the left by units from *Panzer-Grenadier Regiment 60*. The combat group advanced via Schwanenhof up to the Kalkar–Goch road, but then came to a halt in a heavy barrage from artillery of all calibers. A renewed attempt on the morning of 20 February, after initial successes, had to be stopped due to heavy losses.

At 0900 hours, the enemy mounted an attack with infantry and ten tanks against the left wing of the *116th Panzer Division* and threw back its weak defenses to the Brunshof, but two tanks were immobilized. The enemy's attack continued after a barrage of more than two hours' duration, but was destroyed in the combined fire from all weapons, forward of the Brunshof.

At this time, at the command post of the *116th Panzer Division, General* Schlemm expressed his appreciation of the *116th Panzer Division* for its devotion and "for prudent leadership, planning, and mop-up of the enemy breaches using stand-by reserves on 19 February."[85]

The journal of *116th Panzer Division* continues, "The corps commander [*General* von Lüttwitz—*Author*] is convinced that during the night of 19/20 February, the Division opposite the *Panzer Lehr Division* had to carry the main burden during the mop-up of the breaches."

Meanwhile, the enemy penetrated the lines of the unit on the left, now the *84th Infantry Division,* on a wide front, between the Bedburg–Uedem road and the Niers River.[86] Halvenboom and Bucholt were lost. Further left, Goch fell into enemy hands. The left wing of the *116th Panzer Division* hung in the air; Gross-Ackershof therefore, had to be given up. At 1250 hours on 20 February, *Panzer-Grenadier Regiment 156* received orders to protect the left flank. However, coming from Halvenboom and turning northeast, the enemy was able to encircle the weakly occupied strongpoint at the Am Lindchen road junction. During the night 20/21 February, the occupying element fought its way back.

Regrouping was planned for this night. The right side of the Division sector was to be turned over to the *6th Parachute Division. Panzer-Grenadier Regiment 60* and the *1st Parachute Army Training School* troops were to be released for replenishment, but without their heavy weapons. The release of the *Panzer Lehr Division*'s combat group was also to be prepared. All *116th Panzer Division* elements still deployed were now led by the commander of *Panzer-Grenadier Regiment 156*. The combat group of the *Panzer Lehr Division* was subordinated to the *116th*. In view of the situation of the unit to the left, the forward line had to be taken back to the line from the "T" intersection, southeast of the Schwanenhof–Mooshof–Felemannshof (one kilometer southeast of Halven-boom), while leaving behind advanced outposts.

Obviously, the heavy battles of the last two days had also exhausted the enemy, because the *116th Panzer Division* front was relatively calm. The enemy limited his activity to lively reconnaissance during the late morning hours and the usual artillery harassing fire. However, there was very strong fighter bomber activity again. Uedem was bombed in the afternoon. Our artillery observed and engaged enemy concentrations and movements in the rear area.

Finally, *Armored Reconnaissance Battalion 116*, *Armored Engineer Battalion 675*, and more units from *Panzer Regiment 16* came from the Eifel and joined the Division. After a discussion with the corps staff, the *Armored Reconnaissance Battalion* was deployed in a blocking position behind the left part of the Division sector. The other *Panzer-Grenadier* regiment from the *Panzer Lehr Division*, which was behind the *116th Panzer Division* as corps reserve, was temporarily also subordinated to the *116th*. The engineers that had just arrived were deployed to finish off a reception area, the so-called Schlieffen Position, situated at the western edge of the Hochwald. The unit to the right of the *116th*, the *6th Parachute Division,* withdrew from its salient near Moyland to the line Hönnepel–Kalkar, and thereby gained the use of forces to release units of the *116th*. These were probably the subordinated combat group of the *Panzer Lehr Division,* which was deployed at the front. On 22 February, the enemy took Moyland without a fight.[87]

On the evening of 21 February, Vogelsang wrote in his diary:

> No attacks took place at the front, but the artillery attrition fire rolls without inter-ruption. The fog gave way to clear pre-spring weather with increased air activity. In the late morning, a bulls-eye hit by a bomb blew up one of the steeples of the Xanten cathedral in front of our eyes. *Section Ib* from our staff lost several dead and wounded by hits on one of the neighboring farms.
>
> In the afternoon, for the first time in a long time, German planes showed up, some of the new "*Blitz* bombers" [*Arado 234* light jet bombers—*Editor*], that left everything else far behind with their tremendous speed. Is there indeed maybe some truth to the rumors of new weapons?[88]

Leutnant Schwörer from the *2d Battalion, Armored Artillery Regiment 146* looked at things with more skepticism:

> The people should be trained more than they have been to this point, this is what they tell you now. . . . A brand new *NSFO* order. How do the higher-ups still imag-ine the war to be. Do they really believe that something can still be done through

NSFO? The soldiers do not want talk, but action. We want more ammunition and more tanks. Our *Luftwaffe* was seen two days ago. Eight or ten *Blitz* bombers dropped bombs. Otherwise, there were only enemy fighter bombers in the sky. . . .

None of us believe in victory anymore. We do not even talk about it anymore. We all feel indifferent, we have our orders and we have to follow them.

We have no defectors, because they cannot even get to the main battle line at the front. If they were up front, we would not have most of the men anymore. Every so often, some of the infantry take off, sometimes whole groups.

The big ghost, the attack by the *Ami,* is still always at our back. I do not believe that we can finish both. The new front will be at the Rhine.[89]

Schwörer exaggerated regarding the defectors. There were, however, always some, sometimes even small groups, who would surrender without a fight, which is no wonder with the continuous replacements coming to the *Panzer-Grenadiers.* However, Schwörer did an injustice to the majority of the soldiers, especially to his artillerymen. They were members of intact units that did not bleed to death every couple of weeks and did not need to receive replacements who were less and less capable.

Now, let us again take a look at the opponent.[90] The relatively minor success of the 3d Canadian Infantry Division's 7th Canadian Infantry Brigade in the battles of 16 and 17 February delayed the plans of the Canadian II Corps. On 18 February, the 4th Canadian Infantry Brigade of the Canadian 2d Infantry Division received orders to attack on the afternoon of 19 February toward the southeast from the vicinity of Louisendorf, to push through to the Kalkar–Goch road, and to capture about three kilometers of the road, between the Bedburg–Uedem road and the area north of Schwanenhof. The attack was to be conducted by two battalions in front, each supported by a tank company. Twenty-one artillery battalions and two heavy batteries provided fire support.

After heavy artillery preparation, following the firestorm, the Royal Hamilton Light Infantry attacked in front to the left, the Essex Scottish Regiment on the right. Suffering heavy losses, they reached their objectives at about 1345 hours Then, both battalions were exposed to continuous counterattacks; their situations became critical, and they lost part of the conquered terrain. These were the reported counterattacks by *XLVII Panzer Corps* on the evening of 19 February and during the night of 19/20 February. On the morning of 20 February, the 4th Brigade reserve, the Royal Regiment of Canada, attacked twice to provide relief to the distressed Essex Scottish Regiment, but could not fully regain the objective. In these two days, the 4th Canadian Infantry Brigade lost about 400 men. The boundary between the Canadian II Corps and the British XXX Corps matched the left boundary of the *116th Panzer Division.* The forces causing trouble on the left flank of the *116th* belonged to 43d (Wessex) Division.

Now, the main effort of the British offensive was to be moved to the Canadian II Corps. The task for the XXX Corps was to cover the Canadians' right flank.

The Canadians chose the Uedem–Xanten railroad embankment as the axis of attack for the main effort. Along this embankment, the 4th Canadian Armoured Division was to break through the Hochwald toward Xanten, once both infantry divisions had fulfilled the prerequisite of capturing the Todtenhügel–Uedem hill mass. Besides this, the British 11th Armoured Division, deployed on the right of Canadian II Corps, received orders to take the hills northeast of Kervenheim by attacking south of Uedem, pushing toward Sonsbeck. A "gigantic artillery program" was planned for this operation, code-named BLOCKBUSTER, in which 30 artillery battalions were to take part in the firestorm during the first phase, with corresponding forces supporting the armored divisions during the breakthrough phase. The main effort of the whole operation hit the *116th Panzer Division.* While 26 February was intended to be the attack date for the Canadian II Corps and the bulk of the British XXX Corps, units from the British corps remained busy with local attack operations from the vicinity of Goch toward Weeze.

Due to the timing of these enemy plans, the *116th Panzer Division* gained a five-day respite. All its fighting units had now arrived from the Eifel. Reserves were incorporated and the number of battleworthy tanks increased. *Major* Tebbe assumed command of the tanks. On 22 February, however, the opponent caused the Division some excitement.

The journal of the *2d Battalion, Armored Artillery Regiment 146* reports:

> At about 1100 hours, the opponent commenced heavy artillery fire in entire sector and at 1200 hours, changes to infantry attack.
>
> Direction of thrust is Verkält. During the entire local attack operation by the opponent, which lasts into the evening, continuous heaviest harrasssing fire throughout the entire sector. Our units move out of Verkält, leaving the rubble of the farm houses to the opponent.
>
> Battalion supports the defensive battle of the *Panzer-Grenadiers* with heavy barrages in this area. Opponent suffers heavy, bloody losses.[91]

The Division staff, however, already saw things more clearly. The Division journal entry for 22 February included the following:

> After reconnaissance probes in the morning hours, in spite of strong, sometimes drumfire shelling, the enemy did not mount the expected attack today. In the early afternoon, it moved up toward our outposts near Verkält. Our reconnaissance patrols report preparation positions ahead of the right and left wings of the Division sector, which indicate intentions for an attack on the coming day. During the entire day, heavy, sometimes drumfire shelling on Hollen, the vicinity south of it, access roads, and rear area, also lively fighter bomber activity.[92]

At noon of 22 February, the Division command post relocated into a group of finished bunkers, one kilometer southeast of the Nachtigall forester's station. The next day passed quietly for the *116th Panzer Division,* but in the sector of the unit to the right, the enemy was able to advance into the forest south of the Goch–Uedem railroad, on toward the Weeze–Uedem road. The *Panzer Lehr Division* was deployed to oppose it. On the evening of 23 February, Vogelsang recorded, "*Ia* now moved into a bunker in the Xanten Hochwald, a generously laid-out and true fox's den, finished with all amenities—tiled walls, electric light, easy chairs and desks. Who was the local king taking up residency here!"[93]

On 24 February, it was also quiet on the Division front, but busy vehicle traffic to and from Louisendorf was detected, a total of about 200 to 250 trucks.[94] Our artillery and heavy infantry weapons engaged this traffic successfully. Large explosions, jets of flames, and fires were observed. The *116th Panzer Division* received orders to deploy the *1st Parachute Army Training School* troops in Uedem. *Hauptmann* von Hütz was appointed battle commandant of Uedem. Besides this, during the night of 24/25 February, the Division took over a sector from the *84th Infantry Division* using units of *Panzer-Grenadier Regiment 156*. Hereby, it was solely responsible for the entire area in which the Canadian II Corps, with two infantry and two armored divisions intended to attack.

The organization of the Division's units that were deployed at the front can no longer be precisely determined. In any case, in the Division sector, *Panzer-Grenadier Regiment 156* was on the left; behind it in Uedem were the *1st Parachute Army Training School* troops. *Parachute Reconnaissance Battalion 12* probably fought in the middle, and it is possible that the *Division's Escort Company* was to the right of it. It can no longer be verified whether units from *Panzer-Grenadier Regiment 60* were deployed there, and whether the staff of *Panzer-Grenadier Regiment 60* controlled the sector to the right. Finally, the location of *Armored Reconnaissance Battalion 116* remains an open issue. Most of the tanks and tank destroyers, together with *Panzer-Grenadiers* mounted in armored vehicles, stood by for mobile deployment behind the center of the Division, in the vicinity of Keppeln–Michelshof (1.2 kilometers northeast of Keppeln). The engineers continued building obstacles in the Schlieffen Position at the western edge of the Hochwald. It was again quiet on 25 February, except for very lively low-flying enemy aircraft activity. Uedem was bombed again in the morning. Twenty-four twin-engine bombers reduced the town to rubble and ashes. On the evening of 24 February, Vogelsang wrote:

> Near Wesel, we succeeded in locating a march battalion from our replacement regiment, which was actually not assigned to us, but we did not ask a lot of questions, we just picked it up with trucks. Well camouflaged in a forest, we divided it. About half of the men were combat ready, 50 to 80 men were so ill or wounded that they could not be used as infantry at all. The remaining ones were only good for rear echelon services or at its best, for manning heavy weapons. The available NCOs could not be utilized, while 30 officers and NCO candidates were exemplary.[95]

At midnight on 25 February, he wrote down the following:

In the sector of *15th Panzer-Grenadier Division,* heavy artillery drumfire rolling for hours.

The Americans mounted a major offensive east of Aachen.

A few minutes ago, our whole yard vibrated—a few especially heavy shells must have come down somewhere! Air landing alert was issued.

On 23 February, the Americans mounted their offensive that had been delayed because of the Roer's high water level, across a broad front between Roermond and Düren.[96] Eleven infantry and four armored divisions stood opposite six weak German infantry divisions. The only German reserve was the *9th Panzer Division.* The first units from the *11th Panzer Division,* which was en route aboard trains, had just arrived. The German *15th Army* opposed the 2,000 guns and 1,394 tanks of the Americans with only weak artillery, a modest supply of ammunition, and a few tanks and assault guns. In spite of the difficulties caused by the still wet Roer lowlands, on the first day of attack, 16 American infantry battalions settled in at the east bank. On 26 February, the day of the Canadian BLOCKBUSTER offensive, a wide bridgehead, about ten kilometers deep, had been established between Erkelenz and the road Düren–Cologne. German resistance decreased noticeably. The Americans advanced their armored divisions for the thrust toward the Rhine, between Duisburg and Düsseldorf.

On 25 February, the *Supreme Commander–West* sent *OKW* a status report, which did not fully convey the seriousness of the situation:

> Between the Rhine and the Maas no acute danger of penetration. Near the *15th Army,* however, the enemy crossed the Roer and gained up to seven kilometers of terrain; the main thrust to Cologne is still to come. *Supreme Command–West*'s main concern is the development of the situation on both sides of the Moselle.[97]

In view of the development at Erkelenz, on 26 February, the *Supreme Commander–West* requested permission to withdraw the southern wing of *Army Group H* and the right wing corps of *15th Army.* Hitler refused. Nevertheless, on 27 February, he answered the status report of *Supreme Command–West* from 25 February quite appropriately. He saw the opponent's main effort at the Roer front, where the enemy wanted to break through to the Rhine. Despite this, he again rejected the withdrawal of the southern wing of *Army Group H.* In the evening of this day, "with a heavy heart," he finally approved it. The *Supreme Commander–West* wanted to try to deploy forces that became free, together with the *Panzer Lehr Division,* to establish a line between the Maas, south of Venlo, and Rheindalen (west of München-Gladbach). During the night of 24/25 February, the *Panzer Lehr Division* was released, southwest of Uedem, and set to march south.[98]

On 27 February, the *Supreme Commander–West* issued a new status report to Hitler, in which he considered it his essential task to "maintain the entire Western Front intact and cohesively."[99] Therefore, he asked for a "certain freedom of action." On 28 February, Hitler expressed his confidence to Rundstedt and now urged "a speedy withdrawal of the left wing of *Army Group H*."

Back to the *116th Panzer Division* on 26 February 1945.[100] At 0340 hours, the enemy started a very heavy barrage, lasting several hours, on the positions of the Division and the units on both sides. While it was still dark, heavy infantry and armored forces mounted the attack. At the left wing of the *6th Parachute Division,* a group, supported by about 20 tanks, achieved a deep breach into Neu-Louisendorf. It threatened the right flank of the *116th*. The Division deployed a part of its mobile reserves, consisting of several tanks and some *Panzer-Grenadiers* under the command of *Oberleutnant* Harder, against the flank of the breach from the south via Todtenhügel. Harder encountered the enemy that had already turned south, pushed through to the road, crossing 1.5 kilometers northeast of Todtenhügel, and halted the attack there by destroying five enemy tanks. The *2d Battalion, Panzer-Grenadier Regiment 60,* which was kept in reserve, was alerted at 0700 hours and as a precaution was moved forward to the vicinity of the road triangle near Delsenhof. The only major road ran east from here through the lowlands toward the Hochwald.

Before daybreak, an enemy attack hit the left wing of the *116th Panzer Division*. The enemy pushed toward the southeast from the vicinity of Brunshof–Halvenboom–Lintzenhof. Felemannshof was lost in the late morning, after a bitter fight. Under cover of artificial fog, supported by numerous flamethrower-equipped tanks, the enemy entered the northwestern part of Keppeln and reached the area 1.5 kilometers southwest of Keppeln, two kilometers northwest of Uedem. Our counterstrike threw the enemy back out of Keppeln.

While Harder was able to temporarily stabilize the situation at Neu-Louisendorf, the opponent attacked the Division's right wing at the road junction northeast of Heibauershof. He was turned back and lost one tank. The Division's journal further reports the following:

> At about 1000 hours, with eight tanks, the enemy again pushed . . . toward Michelshof. There, in bitter tank battles, another five enemy tanks were destroyed, while the remaining three broke through toward the southeast and pushed forward to the vicinity north of Persel. Therefore, *Panzer Group Harder,* which had been sent to the sector of the Division on the right, had to be taken back to secure our right flank.

Despite the success at Michelshof, the front was torn open. The Division's battle report portrays the course of battle as follows:

> At 1400 hours, the enemy mounted an attack with tanks and infantry on a broad front from north, northeast, east, and west, on Kepplen. The town changed owners several times in hard and bitter street fighting, but finally succumbed to the concentrated thrust of the enemy's superiority. In the late afternoon hours, Persel was also taken by the enemy. Enemy tanks were north of Kirsel, but the village itself

was still held by our troops. On this one day, the Division's weapons destroyed 57 tanks, 37 alone by *Panzer Battalion Tebbe,* which stood firm in its area of operations in a heroic battle up to the last round. It did not retreat to the new blocking position front until dusk, as ordered.

All communication wires were disturbed by the morning barrage. A battalion observation post was established by the *2d Battalion, Armored Artillery Regiment 146* on the dominating hill southwest of the Paulsberg, from whence the entire battlefield could be overlooked. The battalion estimated the enemy artillery fire of 26 February to be 10,000 to 15,000 rounds. The reinforced *2d Battalion, Armored Artillery Regiment 146* fired a total of 625 rounds. Thank God it was raining, so no planes appeared.[101]

In the afternoon, the *1st Battalion, Parachute Infantry Regiment 7* was added to the Division. It moved into a receiving position on the Paulsberg–Hill 54.2– Katzenberg.[102]

In the evening, the Division journal noted, "A large part of the Division's forces deployed in the main battle line had fought to the end, and except for minor forces, must be considered destroyed. This includes *Parachute Reconnaissance Battalion 12, Panzer-Grenadier Regiment 156,* and the *Division Escort Company*."[103]

With emphasis, the Division Commander pointed out the Division's weakness to corps headquarters:

> Commander indicates weak combat strength of the Division. Because of heavy battles, presently only a few tanks ready. The newly-assigned replacements are still poorly trained and not combat experienced. Besides that, there are no reserves. Commander expresses his concerns for conduct of battle on the following day.[104]

Tank Destroyer Battalion 741 (38t) was subordinated to the Division.[105] It brought two companies into battle, each with four to five "*Hetzers.*" ["*Hetzers,*" or "Harriers," were fast, nimble, turretless tank destroyers built on the chassis of obsolete Czech Model 1938 tanks, taken by the Germans upon the occupation in 1938. They mounted a 75mm main gun—*Editor*] The commander of *Panzer-Grenadier Regiment 60, Oberstleutnant* Zander, was wounded on 26 February. *Major* Stephan assumed command of the regiment. At midnight, Vogelsang noted:

> Since this morning at 0315 hours, the Tommies have been firing barrages all day. The roar was simply unreal! According to estimates, they fired 80,000 to 100,000 shells.
>
> While they advanced the fire, they mounted a major attack with more than 100 tanks along the boundary between us and the *Parachute Division,* which was on our right. Hour-long bitter battles developed, in which our most forward units, mainly *Panzer-Grenadier Regiment 156* and *Parachute Reconnaissance Battalion 12,* were more or less destroyed. With the help from units of *Panzer-Grenadier Regiment 60*

and the *Armored Reconnaissance Battalion* that were pulled out quickly from another place, we succeeded in stemming the enemy breakthrough attempt after pulling back the front by three kilometers. By this evening, about 40 enemy tanks were destroyed by units and weapons of the Division.

The latest surprise by the Tommies is tanks with flamethrowers that have a range of 100 meters, the effect of which is very unpleasant. By these and the strong artillery fire, entire villages and farms have simply been obliterated. The infantry-men again had to accomplish the impossible against such superiority of men and materiel—not to forget the achievement of the tactical leadership. Again and again, this leadership was able to achieve defensive successes with our insufficient means, compensating for the lack of numbers with agility and talent.[106]

Sadly, this is the last entry in Vogelsang's diary that was preserved.

By nightfall, the Division attempted to establish a weak front along the heights between Delsenhof and Uedem. In the Schlieffen Position south of Schmachdarm and on both sides of the Nachtigall forester's station, *Armored Engineer Battalion 675* was building defenses, and at the same time formed a rear defensive line. At 2300 hours, the Division command post was relocated to Seelenhof, four kilometers west-southwest of Xanten.[107] The enemy did not let up during the night of 26/27 February. In the sector of the unit on the right, Kalkar was lost by encirclement from the south. The *6th Parachute Division* took its forward line back to the Schlieffen Position and held it during the ensuing days.[108]

Near the *116th Panzer Division*, the enemy attacked the high Delsenhof–Uedem ridge and pushed beyond, to the western edge of the Uedemer swamp. His attempt to capture Uedem from the east, however, was prevented by our tanks under *Major* Tebbe. Thirteen enemy tanks were left immobilized, eleven of them having been destroyed by the *Hetzers* from *Tank Destroyer Battalion 741*.[109] Uedem fell on the morning of 27 February. The Division's battle report states the following:

In the early morning hours, after strongest artillery preparation that often increased to a barrage, and after heavy street and house fighting, the enemy succeeded in entering Uedem and advancing to the southern edge of the town. During the fighting, the enemy lost numerous tanks, eight of which were destroyed with close combat weapons by the exemplary and decisively fighting *Group von Hütz*. Three more tanks were captured undamaged.[110]

The Division nominated *Hauptmann* von Hütz for the Oakleaves to the Knight's Cross, but unfortunately it was no longer awarded.[111] [The end of the war prevented it—*Author.*] The Division's defenses, meanwhile, were taken back to the Schlieffen Position at the western edge of the Hochwald. The enemy conducted numerous tank-supported reconnaissance probes against it during the morning hours. They were essentially turned back and six enemy tanks were destroyed, but two minor breaches were achieved, one at the Nachtigall forester's station, the other one northeast of Uedemer swamp. They could only be sealed off, but not eliminated. About further events of the day, the Division journal includes the following:

> Toward 1215 hours, the enemy pushed forward from Uedem to the southeast with infantry and 15 to 20 tanks. Despite the destruction of 11 more enemy tanks, he succeeded with a breach in the direction of Gochfortz-Berg. . . .
>
> In the late afternoon hours, after a renewed barrage, the enemy was able to enter the Hochwald via Nachtigall. An immediately-started counter strike was not successful.[112]

Now, *Armored Engineer Battalion 675* fought on the Division's right wing. Its company on the right, the *1st,* under *Oberleutnant* Varnholt, held its position connecting to the *6th Parachute Division,* most likely until the afternoon of 28 February. The left of it, south of the Nachtigall forester's station, the enemy entered the Hochwald.[113] The Division journal on 27 February concludes with the following:

> Larger enemy successes could only be prevented today by the fact that the Division, which was without any reserves, was able to quickly incorporate replacements and seize a larger number of stragglers from all units through appropriate measures and deployed them in the defensive lines.[114]

Toward noon of 27 February, corps headquarters announced that it would bring in and subordinate *Parachute Infantry Regiment 24* to the Division. Its commander was *Oberstleutnant* Hübner. The regiment, however, arrived with only two battalions, the *2d Battalion, Parachute Infantry Regiment 24* and the *Assault Battalion,* under *Hauptmann* Hübner. The latter was not immediately released by corps headquarters. After its arrival, the *2d Battalion, Parachute Infantry Regiment 24* was deployed in the especially threatened Hochwald gap, probably south of the railroad. The regiment fought with great bravery during the following days. For his dedication within the framework of the *116th Panzer Division,* *Hauptmann* Hübner received the Knight's Cross.[115] The *1st Battalion, Parachute Infantry Regiment 7* apparently returned to its regiment.

Corps headquarters did not inform the Division until 27 February of the great success that the American offensive had in its rear area. It reached the vicinity of Viersen–Dülken. The Division then ordered that all materiel not needed for the battle be moved out of the threatened area on the left bank of the Rhine and transported across the river.[116]

The worst was feared for 28 February. Danger in two places gave reason for concern. The breach into the Hochwald, south of the Nachtigall forester's station, and the thrust along the boundary with the unit to the left with the enemy at Gochfortz-Berg. The enemy attack already started during the night, at 0230 hours, searching for the decisive breakthrough to Xanten.

Infantry and tanks advanced behind a rolling firestorm after a heavy barrage and attacked south of the Nachtigall forester's station, directly toward the gap in the Hochwald on both sides of the Uedem–Xanten railroad. After subduing the Schlieffen Position, the enemy took the dominating Hill 73, due north of the railroad, and pushed further east to the Hufscher-Berg (one kilometer east of Hill 73). The few tanks in place here were destroyed by artillery fire. By deploying of a few tanks that were held in reserve, it was possible to halt the enemy. Counterattacking with *Assault Battalion Hübner,* which was subordinated to the Division at 1000 hours, it was possible for the tanks to throw the enemy back to a line east of the Villa *Reichswald*–Nabershof. An attempt during the afternoon to regain the old main battle line failed. The enemy defense was already too strong: a front line of anti-tank guns had been established; enemy tanks flanked the area from the northern forest edge; and the enemy employed massive artillery fire.[117]

On 28 February, our artillery helped as much as it could. The reinforced *2d Battalion, Armored Artillery Regiment 146* fired almost 1,000 rounds.[118] The enemy air forces were in the sky again. The unit on the right of the *116th Panzer Division*, the *6th Parachute Division*, repelled all attacks.[119] To the relief of the Division, the opponent opposite the unit on the left remained quite idle.[120] As far as can be established, *Parachute Infantry Regiment 24* was now alone in the forward line of the Division sector, supported by the Division's tanks and tank destroyers, as well as by *Tank Destroyer Battalion 741. Battalion Hübner* was deployed on the right, *2d Battalion, Parachute Infantry Regiment 24* on the left, with the boundary being approximately along the railroad. *Group Stephan* was formed from the remnants of the infantry units of the *116th Panzer Division.* It was deployed further back as the reaction force. After suffering heavy artillery fire at the Seelenhof at 1830 hours, in which *Oberleutnant* Franz, keeper of the journal, was wounded, the Division command post moved to the Schrammshof (3.5 kilometers south of Xanten) during the night of 28 February/1 March.[121] For his dedication on 26 and 28 February, the corps staff recommended the Division Commander, *Generalmajor* von Waldenburg, for the Oakleaves to the Knight's cross. *General* Schlemm forwarded the request with a recommendation for approval.[122] The Oakleaves were no longer being awarded. Time ran out.

The battle report of the Division says the following about the next day:

> On 1 March, the enemy remained quiet, except for brisk air activity with numerous bomb attacks on the main battle line and rear area, and a weak assault from Kunderenhof with infantry and tanks [at western edge of the Hochwald, south of railroad—*Author*] toward the east, which was repelled with combined fire from all heavy weapons.[123]

By contrast, 2 March was turbulent. The battle report states the following:

> During the night of 1/2 March, heavy artillery fire with intense barrages that lasted into the late morning hours fell on the main battle line and rear area. The enemy

attacked in the early morning with infantry and strong armored forces north of Xanten–Uedem railroad, on a wide front toward the east and from the north toward Nabershof. The attacks were turned back by the bravely and skillfully fighting Parachute Infantry Regiment 24, and a mixed combat group composed of all units of the Division [Group Stephan—*Author*], with high, bloody losses to the enemy. Enemy tanks that broke in via Hufscher-Berg–Pauelshof were thrown back to their starting position by immediate counterattacks resulting in the destruction of 14 tanks, six of them by close combat weapons. Thereby, 66 prisoners from the 4th Canadian Armoured Division were brought in.

The telephone log of the Division indicates a more differentiated picture.[124] *Reaction Force Stephan*, which first was held back, received orders at 1030 hours to take up position at the Division's left wing on both sides of the Wesselshof, because the situation in the forest was evidently not quite clear. At 1140 hours, the *Ia* of the division on the left—by now the *180th Infantry Division*—also reported that the enemy entered the southwestern edge of the forest in Neuenbauershof, and that the situation in the forest itself was not clear. *Major* Stephan then received orders to weaken the right wing near Wesselshof to echelon his forces to the left rear in the forest to the south. Moreover, *Battalion Jungwirth,* in the rear, was moved up into the deep left flank toward Blauhaus (two kilometers north of Sonsbeck). According to the records, this battalion was formed by order of the *1st Parachute Army* headquarters, by combining *Parachute Reconnaissance Battalion 12* and the *1st Parachute Army Training School* troops.

During the recapture of the Hufscherberg, several *Sturmtigers* from *Assault Mortar Battery (RW 61) 1002* supplied much help.[125] ["Storm Tigers" were heavily armored self-propelled 380mm rocket launchers, built on Tiger (*Panzer VI,* Type E) chassis. Only 18 were produced.—*Editor*] At 1415 hours, *Oberstleutnant* Hübner reported, "1002 fired four rounds in area of Villa. Villa completely destroyed. Ammunition pile blown up."[126]

In the afternoon, a crisis developed at the boundary between *Parachute Infantry Regiment 24* and *Group Stephan.* Steinhügel and Wesselshof were lost, and tanks entered the Nabershof. In the evening, Waldenburg confided the following in his calendar:

> Very optimistic speech by Goebbels, hopefully he is right!—Population here wishes for quick advance by the enemy; one can understand that, but the influence on our soldiers is very damaging—we still have to fight (?) . . . Despite the brave fighting by the remainder of my Division, the enemy, with its outrageous superiority, cannot be stopped. . . .[127]

March 3 again brought a few crises. The "battle report" relates the following:

> On the next morning, the enemy attempted to advance with infantry and 15 tanks through a gap in the front of the sector of the unit on the right. From there, he attempted to attack and overrun the Division's right wing. but was closed off by

units of *Parachute Infantry Regiment 24* along the line Waldmannshof–Pauelshof. The attempt was thereby thwarted. Further enemy attacks along the Uedem–Xanten railroad line and against the right wing of *Group Stephan* were repulsed. Later, because of the enemy's breach in the left adjacent sector, the Division's left wing had to be turned and withdrawn to the eastern edge of the Hochwald-Xanten state forest, along the line Rosental–Pauhof–Hasenacker–Lindenhecke. In the afternoon, after a short but violent barrage, enemy infantry and tanks pushed into a mixed combat group of the Division at several places. The group consisted of insufficiently trained replacements, who had only been in the unit for a few days. These replacements that were not strong enough and could not withstand the pressure from the enemy. The enemy advanced east from land tract 122 beyond the verge of the forest where, however, it came to a halt under the combined fire of all heavy weapons. During these battles, the enemy again lost ten tanks and two armored personnel carriers. During the night of 3/4 March, the units of the Division which were still deployed were withdrawn from the front and moved northwest. The Division itself was relocated as an army reserve in the vicinity of Alpen, to be deployed against the Americans who were advancing from the south from the vicinity of Moers.[128]

According to *Major* Stephan's report at 1600 hours, the penetration through land tract 122, north of Pauhof, was the result of an entire platoon of about 25 men surrendering to the enemy, which was the first time something of this kind had happened to the *116th Panzer Division*.[129] In the evening, however, a more or less continuous line existed from Waldmannshof via Pauelshof–Lindenhecke up to Blauhaus, where the unit on the left linked up while retreating to Sonsbeck. On the evening of 3 March, the unit on the right was also pushed out of the Hochwald. The non-organic units fighting within the framework of the *116th Panzer Division* remained deployed except for the *1st Parachute Army Training School* troops and *Parachute Reconnaissance Battalion 12*. The staff of the *180th Infantry Division* assumed control of the former sector of the *116th Panzer Division*. The new Division command post was established in Wallach.[130]

Once again, it is necessary to look at the opposite side and the situation at large.[131] In the early morning of 26 February, the two Canadian infantry divisions initiated the major BLOCKBUSTER offensive against *XLVII Panzer Corps* between Kalkar and the Kleve–Uedem road. They were supported by the 2d Canadian Armoured Brigade. To the left, two brigades from the 2d Canadian Infantry Division encountered the *6th Parachute Division*. To relieve the latter situation, the *116th* deployed *Group Harder* against the right flank of the 2d Canadian Infantry Division. Very soon, Harder also entered the battle with the left wing of the 3d Canadian Infantry Division, which attacked at 0440 hours. These were units from the 8th Canadian Infantry Brigade. Most of its units did not attack until 0845 hours, on both sides of the Kleve–Uedem road, with Keppeln and Hollen its objectives. By evening, it had reached its objective.

The attack by the 4th Canadian Armoured Division started at midmorning, about 1000 hours. It attacked between the two infantry divisions with five mixed combat groups, supported by minesweeper and flamethrower-tanks from the British 79th Armoured Division. The objective of the attack was the Paulsberg–Katzenberg mountain range, northeast of Uedem. The two forward groups did not firmly capture Todtenhügel until 1600 hours. The attack was continued after regrouping. During the evening, the Canadians seized the mountain range.

At 2100 hours, the 9th Canadian Infantry Brigade of the 3d Canadian Infantry Division, passing by the 8th Canadian Infantry Brigade, initiated the attack on Uedem. In spite of heavy resistance by the *1st Parachute Army Training School* troops, the town was seized on the morning of 27 February. Thereby, the way south was open for the attack by the British 11th Armoured Division toward Gochfortz-Berg. They did not energetically use 27 February for a breakthrough, but mostly spent the time reorganizing.

The Canadian 2d Infantry Division relieved units from the Canadian 4th Armoured Division that had remained in the vicinity of Todtenhügel. After two hours of artillery preparation, this division was to attack the Schlieffen Position with its 10th Infantry Brigade on the morning of 27 February, still during hours of darkness, with the objective being Hill 73 near Villa *Reichswald*. The attack was delayed by German fire and broke down after dawn. Another attack along the railroad line by units of its 4th Armoured Brigade failed in the evening.

During the night of 27/28 February, at 0200 hours, the 10th Canadian Infantry Brigade started attacking the gap in the Hochwald again. It did take Hill 73, but due to the strong defense by *Parachute Infantry Regiment 24* and Tebbe's tankers, it came to a halt under fire. The attack by a fresh regiment beyond the stalled troops failed during its approach due to German artillery fire. Even support by the 4th Canadian Armoured Brigade could not get the attack restarted. The diary of the 29th Reconnaissance Regiment (The South Alberta Regiment) describes the German fire as "the most concentrated this regiment has ever been exposed to." Montgomery wrote, "The extent of the enemy fire was the strongest that British troops have so far encountered during the campaign."

On 1 March, the exhausted troops from the 4th Canadian Armoured Division were relieved by the 2d Canadian Infantry Division. On 2 March, the battle along the entire front of the Canadian II Corps started to rage again. Five divisions commenced the attack, with the 4th Canadian Armoured Division again in the forest gap. It was to push through the Hochwald and to establish a bridgehead across the Hohe Ley stream, flowing about one kilometer east of the forest. The division suffered high losses and had to be relieved by the Canadian 5th Infantry Brigade during the night of 2/3 March. South of the forest gap, the 8th Canadian Infantry Brigade from the 3d Canadian Infantry Division fought laboriously from 2 to 4 March through the south part of the forest Tüschenwald. Further south, the British 11th Armoured Division, strengthened by the 7th Canadian Infantry Brigade, advanced on Sonsbeck. To the right of it, British XXX Corps, now with three divisions, reached Kapellen, Berendonk (five kilometers northwest Geldern), and Well on the Maas. The English and Americans met at Berendonk.

The Ninth Army reached the Rhine between Neuss and Uerdingen and was at Moers and near Sevelen.[132] The *1st Parachute Army* and a few units from *Army Group B* that had had to detour to the north were pushed back toward a bridgehead near Wesel. Its right wing leaned against the Rhine north of Xanten. From there, a somewhat secure front ran south, up to Sonsbeck. Further southeast, since 1 March, along the western edge of the wooded Bönninghardt mountain range, via Lintfort toward Moers and Homberg, a loose security line was being established from the remnants of the drained returning divisions, under command of *II Parachute Corps* and *LXIII Corps*.[133]

On 2 March, the army received permission to move their rearward units across the Rhine under the premise that no combat-capable man and no weapon must go across the Rhine.[134] It was high time, for there was only one bridge near Homberg; both bridges near Wesel were damaged and, for the time being, not passable for vehicles.

During the night of 3/4 March, the *116th Panzer Division* moved everything it could do without toward Homberg. The move back was a success.[135] On 3 March, *General* Schlemm requested the evacuation of the west bank.[136] *Army Group H* shared this view. Hitler refused. He wanted to keep a wide bridgehead opposite Duisburg to continue the transportation of coal for the navy along the Rhine between Duisburg and Wesel, via the canals that flowed into the Rhine near these cities.[137] The combat report from the *116th Panzer Division* describes the events of these days:

> While our troops were still deployed with the front line toward the northwest against the English and Canadians, American tank spearheads already pushed north via Moers–Lintfort. In clear cognizance of the dangerous situation developing in the rear of the entire *Parachute Army,* on 2 March, on its own initiative, the Division had already sent out armored reconnaissance patrols to the south that were to observe the enemy's movements and if possible, to delay him until a defensive front could be established. On 3 March 1945, at 1000 hours, a reconnaissance patrol reported that the enemy had crossed the Sevelen–Issum road and had already advanced with several tanks north of Sevelen. Based on this report, a reaction force was immediately withdrawn from the northwest front, mounted on three tanks of *Combat Group Tebbe* and sent to secure the Issum–Alpen road against the enemy advancing from the direction of Sevelen.[138]

The rest of the *1st Parachute Army Training School* troops, about 70 men, marched along with Tebbe's tanks.[139] Due to the reconnaissance reports, the Division, being the only available motorized unit, proposed that it be withdrawn from the front and thrown against the new enemy. As reported, the deployment of reconnaissance patrols and of the combat group was approved and at noon on 3

March, the order was issued to release the Division from the front. The combat report continues:

> The departure of a reaction force was delayed by the strongest enemy air activity—sometimes there were more than 100 fighter bombers simultaneously above the Division's sector. However, before it reached its destination, a reconnaissance patrol, consisting of two eight-wheeled reconnaissance vehicles, came into contact with the enemy north of Lintfort, as he was attacking Hill 57. In concert with a company of *Parachute Infantry Regiment 21,* the attack was turned back and 22 prisoners from the 35th Infantry Division were brought in.
>
> Thereafter, the reaction force occupied security positions south and southwest of Rheinberg to repel enemy attacks from Moers and Kamp toward Rheinberg.[140]

Hill 57 is the Dachsberg on the Aldekerk–Rheinberg road, nine kilometers southwest of Rheinberg. After the war, *Generalmajor* von Waldenburg wrote about 4 March in his report for the Americans:

> The relief of the Division during the night went well. Assembly in the vicinity of Alpen lasted until late morning. While still assembling, the Division received orders to establish security positions oriented toward the south along the general line Saalhoff–Rheinberg. The Division was relieved of responsibility for the Issum–Alpen road. Thus, the combat units of the Division, coming from a major battle of several weeks' duration, at once attacked again, without ever having a little time to rest, or putting their units in order.
>
> The Division was formed by two combat groups, each equivalent to about one weak battalion in strength. To begin with, the number of battleworthy tanks did not even reach ten.[141]

The *116th Panzer Division* was subordinated to *LXIII Army Corps,* which was in charge at the left wing of the bridgehead.

The combat report states this about 5 March:

> On 5 March, the enemy attacked Rheinberg with strong tank forces from the 8th Armored Division from the direction of Kamp and shortly thereafter, with infantry and tanks, from the direction of Moers. The attack was turned back by destroying several tanks. Other enemy tank forces advanced on Orsoy. . . . An attack mounted from there on Driessen and Budberg was repelled by our security forces [here, remnants of the *Panzer Lehr Division—Author*] and at the same time an assault coming from Kamp, north toward Rossenray, was brought to a halt north of the village. In the early afternoon, the enemy broke through our security positions with 20 to 30 tanks west of Winterswick and entered Rheinberg. In a counterattack, the town was recaptured and thereby, again, several enemy tanks were destroyed.
>
> By combining all units of the Division that were still battleworthy, it was finally possible to establish a new line of blocking positions along the southern edge of Rheinberg. The enemy mounted another attack against this line in the late

afternoon, which was repelled with the destruction of seven more enemy tanks. On this day, in heavy fighting near and in Rheinberg, a total of 30 enemy tanks and two reconnaissance vehicles were destroyed by tanks, artillery, anti-tank guns [and anti-aircraft guns—*Author*], and close combat weapons. In the evening, the Division retreated to a new security line, which ran along the Heidecker Ley–Dickskath–Lois-Berg– . . . to the S.M. [saw mill—*Author*], northwest of Rheinberg. The Rheinberg bridges were blown up.[142]

This sounds relatively simple. The Division telephone log and the journal of the *2d Battalion, Armored Artillery Regiment 146*, however, show quite dramatic situations.[143] The two deployed *Panzer-Grenadier Battalions* of the Division, the *2d Battalion, Panzer-Grenadier Regiment 60* under *Hauptmann* Bröker, and the *1st Battalion, Panzer-Grenadier Regiment 156* under *Hauptmann* Schneider, put together with difficulty and replenished with replacements, were at the end of their strength and did not withstand the enemy onslaught. Only a few brave men and the heavy weapons of the Division saved the situation. The swift deployment of the few tanks and tank destroyers and the well-guided fire from the artillery made the difference. The last protection north of Rheinberg came from two immobile, damaged tanks and an anti-aircraft battery. A recommendation for the German Cross in Gold was submitted for *Oberleutnant* Varnholt, commander of the *1st Company, Armored Engineer Battalion 675*.[144] *Feldwebel* Muster, born in Vienna, commander of an eight-wheeled reconnaissance troop of *Armored Reconnaissance Battalion 116*, was still awarded the Knight's Cross by the end of April 1945.[145]

As indicated by the combat report, 6 March was also an active day:

After preparation in Rühlshof, the enemy already attacked the next morning with 20 tanks and mounted infantry against the new security line, rolled over it in the first assault, and pushed through to the Millingen railroad station. There, after heavy fighting and the destruction of five enemy tanks, the attack was brought to a halt, and toward noon, a new security line was established south of the *Siedlung II. Bauernschaft* ["Farmer's settlement"—*Editor*]–southwestern edge of Millingen–eastern part of Vitten-Berg–western and southern edge of Lois-Berg. Enemy tank attacks. . . . on Vitten-Berg, as well as on Vittenhof were turned back. . . . The newly brought in *2d Battalion, Parachute Infantry Regiment 18*, was deployed for the support of the right side of the Division sector, south and southwest of Millingen.[146]

The journal of the *2d Battalion, Armored Artillery Regiment 146* adds to this report:

During the night, heavy harassing fire by the enemy on all ferry landings. Both bridges are passable as of midnight.

Situation in bridgehead: No one bearing arms may cross the Rhine, no vehicle can pass without the Division Commander's signature, the staffs also remain in the bridgeheads. All firing positions are being prepared for close-in defense. . . .

Rheinberg is taken by the enemy during the night. New main battle line is being established north of Rheinberg and is held. . . .

Enemy attacks Millingen railroad station with seven tanks and infantry. . . .

The whole day, while there was a low cloud ceiling, continuous air raids on the bridge positions. Despite all the attacks, the bridge remains intact and the flow of the non-essential motor vehicles proceeds without major disturbances.

Heavy losses by the infantry requires deployment of all non-essential men. By regimental orders, the battalion, therefore, must form a rifle platoon consisting of one officer, one NCO and 40 men. Batteries take men out of their positions, so that only three men are left at the guns. . . . Rifle platoon is subordinated to *Battalion Jungwirth* and together with other rifle platoons, occupies the artillery defensive position at the southern borders of Borth and Wallach.

Further subordinated to the battalion are: one battery of horsedrawn light field howitzers and one battery of horsedrawn heavy field howitzers (both from Artillery Regiment 26).[147]

The attack across Heidecker Ley hit *Armored Reconnaissance Battalion 116.* Tanks and artillery saved the situation. The Division's *Panzer-Grenadiers,* under command of the staff of *Panzer-Grenadier Regiment 156,* were deployed in the sector north and northwest of Rheinberg. The remnants of the *Panzer Lehr Division* were on the left wing, between the Old Rhine and the Rhine, the last two tanks at the boundary in the vicinity of Am Anker.[148] The British had success in the center sector of the bridgehead. They took the decisive hills around Bönning-hardt from which they were able to overlook the entire lowlands in the Rhine bend near Wesel.[149] On 6 March, the Division came under command of *II Parachute Corps.* The other two corps were finally allowed to leave the bridgehead.[150]

The Division expected the main effort of the enemy attack on the next day, 7 March, again in the vicinity of Millingen. The movements by the enemy and the favorable terrain for tanks pointed to it.[151] However, the combat report states the following:

> On the morning of 7 March, the enemy advanced with strong infantry and and tank forces from Rheinberg toward Ossenberg and pushed our security elements back toward the line brickyard–southern edge "Am Anker." More enemy advances against this sector were turned back by destroying five enemy tanks.[152]

The journal of the *2d Battalion, Armored Artillery Regiment 146* continues:

> During the night, the opponent lays heavy harrasing fire in the vicinity of both Rhine bridges. Bomber units carpet-bomb Wesel and the area of the bridge. Bridges are hit. Traffic rolls on. . . .
>
> The whole day continuous attacks by the enemy. . . .
>
> The battalion's fire missions alternately fall into the various offensive main efforts of the enemy. . . .

The bridgehead is full of heavy weapons. There are no longer new firing positions. Behind every house, behind every bush, is a gun or a mortar. Ammunition is scarce, but every so often, some more arrives.

Toward 1700 hours, opponent takes Solvay works, south of Ossenberg. Thereby, he can observe the ferry near Haus Momm. Ferry service has to be stopped there. Ferries go to the ferry landing near Büderich.[153]

In the evening of 7 March, the Corps Commander, *General der Fallschirmtruppe* Meindl, permitted the heavy batteries to cross to the other Rhine bank.[154] On the late morning of 8 March, units from the artillery, together with the damaged guns that were repaired, stood at the east bank in the vicinity of Spellen, ready to fire. During the night, the Division command post moved from Wallach into the Sandsenhof (1.6 kilometers north of Wallach).[155]

March 8 was again a day of heavy fighting:

At 0700 hours the next morning, after heaviest artillery preparation, the enemy again attacked the entire front of the Division with far superior infantry and tank forces. Favored by the natural morning fog and artificial smoke screens from the enemy artillery, blinding all observation posts and obstructing the view for our tanks . . . after heavy combat he succeeded in entering the town via the railroad embankment and Millingen railroad station, and at the same time . . . capturing the Solvay works and the northern part of Ossenberg. After many losses of infantry and heavy weapons, the attack was brought to a halt at about noon, in the depth of the main battle line. A new defense line was established along the Grünthal–Rheinberg road.[156]

The journal of the *2d Battalion, Armored Artillery Regiment 146* supplements this with the following:

Barrage starting along the entire bridgehead front at 0400 hours. Fire also in the rear. . . . All wire connections are disturbed and two guns are destroyed at *5th Battery.* . . .

0800 hours, enemy mounts attack. Division command post . . . prepares for close-in defense. Positions of *5th Battery* are included. . . .

Toward noon, enemy attacks are decreasing. Continuing strongest artillery fire in entire bridgehead.[157]

Combat Group von Poschinger from the *Panzer Lehr Division,* subordinated to the *116th Panzer Division,* still had about 12 men who were securing the left wing near the road junction northwest of Ossenberg.[158] On this day, the British mounted a new assault on Xanten, Veen, and Alpen. Here, the front also had to be withdrawn everywhere.[159] In a telephone conversation that evening, *Generalmajor* von Waldenburg informed the corps commander of the following:

1. Troops are demoralized. They have only one thought: "How do we get back across the Rhine?"

2. Officers and troops do not know each other, since everything has been thrown into disorder. No inner structure.

3. Most of the leadership have become casualties, troops are being led by officers who are strangers to them.

4. Concentrating the artillery in the narrowest space can no longer be justified. Due to direct hits in battery emplacements, heavy losses of personnel and materiel occur continuously. Artillery can fulfill the same tasks from the other side. Proposal: Relocate artillery to east of the Rhine.

5. Division has no more reserves of any kind.

6. The accumulation of staffs who do not have real leadership tasks can no longer be justified.

7. The final battle for the bridgehead signifies a full burn-out of the last cadres, so that a quick rebuilding of the Division is no longer guaranteed.[160]

General Meindl responded:

1. The smaller the area, the less freedom of mobility one has; therefore, the present line must be held under all circumstances.

2. Division must prevent the opponent from breaking in along the Rheinberg–Grünthal road: Endangers left flank of the *7th Parachute Division.*

3. Artillery shells expended on 8 March: Enemy, 180,000; Friendly, 5,000.

Hardly a comforting conversation! As *General* Meindl stated after the war, on this day, he again requested the evacuation of the bridgehead.[161] *General* Schlemm did the same on the previous day. On 8 March, an officer from *OKW* showed up and became convinced by the situation, so that by 9 March the evacuation was finally permitted.[162] *General* Meindl also remarked in his notes that besides the *6th* and *7th Parachute Divisions,* the *116th Panzer Division* also fought especially well.[163]

March 9 went by relatively quietly.

The order for the evacuation of the Wesel bridgehead finally arrived at 2120 hours. The following is noted in the telephone log:

> The *Ia* summons the adjutants and issues his orders. Division relocates to area east of Haldern [16 kilometers northwest of Wessel—*Author*]. Release point is Hamminkeln. Dismounted units reach the other bank via rubber rafts near Pottdeckel [2.5 kilometers south of Büderich—*Author*]. . . . All non-essential vehicles are being moved across the Wesel bridge as quickly as possible.[164]

The log further reports the following:

> 0500, start of retreat. 0300 hours, the emergency units of *Combat Group Jungwirth* already cross over near Pottdeckel. Toward 0615 hours, with the last units of the main body, the *Ia* also crosses the Rhine. Rear units follow around 0700 hours. At 0730 hours the last man is out of the bridgehead. Opponent did not discover our move. . . .

With the release from the bridgehead, the Division is again subordinated to *XLVII Panzer Corps* . . . together with the *15th Panzer-Grenadier Division.*
New command post Loikum (four kilometers north of Hamminkeln).
A good night's rest. Organize the units.[165]

The relief of the writer can be sensed. The release from the bridgehead was successful everywhere. Afterward, the bridges were blown up. At the end, the combat report from the *116th Panzer Division* summarizes as follows:

The severe battles for the Lower Rhine, accompanied by heavy losses, hereby came to a close. The Division again had to enter them under unfavorable conditions at a time when, after the difficult winter battle in the Ardennes, it was torn apart over an area of 250 kilometers, due to lack of fuel. Therefore, the new battle could not be taken up in an integral Division formation. . . . Besides this, after the battles of the Ardennes, the *Panzer-Grenadier* Regiments only had about one week's time to refit their fully-depleted units with replacements and to weld them together anew.

Despite these unusual difficulties and high casualties, all units of the Division reached . . . new, shining battle successes in combat against a massive enemy superiority. During sacrificial battles, they succeeded in preventing . . . any breach by the enemy and kept . . . the enemy from penetrating toward Wesel into the rear of the *Parachute Army.* . . .

In this sector, besides heavy, bloody losses that amounted to a multiple of our own casualties, the enemy lost 225 prisoners, 203 tanks, numerous armored vehicles, armored reconnaissance vehicles, Bren carriers, guns and anti-tank guns, as well as five aircraft. In contrast, after deduction of 22 officers, 85 NCOs and men who, in spite of their wounds remained with the troops, our own losses were 68 officers and 2,465 NCOs and men.[166]

The achievements of the *116th Panzer Division* during the four weeks of this battle still create astonishment today. The reader will feel the same way. Appreciation of the role played by the parachute troops must not be forgotten. They fought within the framework of the Division and at times replaced its depleted *Panzer-Grenadier* units almost entirely. The *1st Parachute Army Training School* troops and *Parachute Reconnaissance Battalion 12,* as well as *Parachute Infantry Regiment 24* during the Hochwald phase and the *2d Battalion, Parachute Infantry Regiment 18* in the bridgehead are all included . . . but even the bravest infantry could not have withstood the onslaught, if the Division's few tanks and tank destroyers had not intervened at the threatened places over and over. Together with the swiftly guided and combined fire of the artillery at the points of danger, these brought the opponent to a halt. He had an overwhelming superiority available in all areas and could relieve his attack units with fresh ones after very little time, but he neglected to attack all at once across a wide front. Thereby, he repeatedly made it possible for the swift command of the defender to concentrate his small reserves, his few tanks, and his fires on the major points of danger.

The British flamethrower tanks proved to be the enemy's most dangerous weapon in the battle against our infantry. The range of the flames was greater than that of the *Panzerfaust* and the stream of fire entered dugouts and houses.

The battles in the Wesel bridgehead saw only Americans as opponents of the *116th Panzer Division*: The 35th Infantry Division with the attached Combat Command B of the 8th Armored Division and the 784th Tank Battalion.[167] The reinforced 35th Infantry Division formed the left wing of XVI Corps of the Ninth Army. The attack on Rheinberg on 5 March was led by Combat Command B of the 8th Armored Division. It was still inexperienced in combat and was expecting "insignificant resistance." Its objective were the bridges near Wesel. It lost 39 of its 54 tanks, plus 92 dead, 31 missing and 220 wounded.

On 6 March, the 35th Infantry Division employed two task forces; on the right, Task Force Murray (the 137th Infantry Regiment and the remnants of Combat Command B, 8th Armored Division); on the left: Task Force Byrne (320th Infantry Regiment with the 784th Tank Battalion).

On 6 March, Task Force Murray occupied Rheinberg without a fight. On 7 and 8 March, it led the thrust toward Ossenberg. Task Force Byrne attacked Millingen from 6 to 8 March. In *The Last Offensive*, the author, Charles B. MacDonald states:

> Both task forces soon discovered that the hard fighting for Rheinberg on 5 March had been a harbinger of what was to come. Although a British Division on the left of Task Force Byrne provided help, the two task forces could do no more through the next three days than inch forward.
>
> Then as suddenly as the determined resistance had formed, it disintegrated.[168]

This was on the morning of 10 March, after the evacuation of the bridgehead. The Canadian history work, *The Victory Campaign,* sums up in the following way:

> So ended more than a month of uninterrupted, bitter fighting. . . . Day after day, a cloudy sky robbed the army of its air support. Too often, their tanks were immobilized by flood waters and mud. The enemy had an unusually high concentration of firepower. . . . The German resistance was enormous, in numbers as well as in quality.[169]

Now, according to the numbers, the defender was not exactly strong. Brought up as a basis for comparison, the number of ten German divisions that were deployed seems higher than what was there in reality. The example of the *116th Panzer Division* is clear proof. The reports of the individual days prove that the enemy's air activity was not severely hindered by the weather.

In the meantime, the situation in the West, as well as in the East became increasingly more dangerous. The Americans reached the Rhine between Rheinberg and Koblenz. Between Koblenz and Trier, they stood at the north bank of the Moselle, ready for an attack toward the south. From Lower Alsace, from Lorraine and Luxembourg, an attack toward the Saar district and the Palatinate could be counted on. But the worst part was that on 7 March the bridge at Remagen fell undamaged into American hands, and a large bridgehead was established at once. Hitler relieved *Generalfeldmarschall* von Rundstedt and appointed *Generalfeldmarschall* Kesselring as *Supreme Commander-West*.[170] The traffic and transportation system of the *Reich* was paralyzed, the fuel situation was catastrophic. In the interim, the most important industrial areas now were near the front or in enemy hands. The war was lost. Only a miracle could have turned things around. However, there was no Russian Czarina who died just at the right time, and no Czar who admired his opponent and therefore made peace. [As there had been in the Seven Years' War—*Editor*] In the beginning of February, in Yalta, the opponents again decided to destroy the German *Reich*. The German people and the German soldier had their backs against the wall and in spite of everything, continued to do what they considered their duty.

CHAPTER 11

The Ruhr Cauldron

The remnants of the *116th Panzer Division* that came out of the Wesel bridgehead joined the units that were moved over to the east bank of the Rhine earlier, in the area north and northwest of the town. They first had a good night's rest. On 11 March at 1330 hours, the Chief of Staff of *XLVII Panzer Corps, Oberstleutnant i.G.* Count Bernstorff, announced the relocation of the Division to Holland, into the vicinity north of Emmerich.[1] There, it was to be prepared for deployment against an anticipated English attack across the Rhine near Emmerich. It was believed that the attack would be combined with an airborne landing and continued toward the north.

Fifteen cubic meters of fuel were allotted for the relocation, which was only enough for weak units. In the afternoon of 12 March, the first formation to roll into the new Division area was *Armored Reconnaissance Battalion 116*, reinforced by the *3d Company, Armored Engineer Battalion 675* and six tanks.[2] This area was bordered approximately by the towns of Doetinchem–Hengelo–Ruurlo–Lichtenvoorde–Terborg. The Division staff moved to Halle. On his way there, *Generalmajor* von Waldenburg announced his departure to the commanding general of *II Parachute Corps, General der Fallschirmtruppe* Meindl, and received "gratitude and much appreciation" for the Division's achievements.[3] Depending on allotments of more fuel, the remaining units followed in the coming days. With great effort, the Division succeeded in saving its bogged-down units, partly in the Eifel and in the vicinity of München-Gladbach, and moved them across the Rhine in due time. Now, the tight fuel situation delayed their move into the Dutch area.

Jointly with the *15th Panzer-Grenadier Division*, the Division was subordinated to *XLVII Panzer Corps* as *Army Group H* reserve. It received the following orders:

1. Preparation for deployment against an enemy attack
   a) in the vicinity of Arnhem;
   b) across the Pannerdenschen canal southeast of Arnhem;
   c) near Emmerich;
   d) near Rees;
   e) near Wesel.
2. Warding off an enemy airborne landing in the area in which the Division is stationed.

3. Preparation for an attack against an enemy airborne landing in the vicinity of Duisburg–Emmerich–Winterswijk–Dorsten.[4]

From this, the following tasks emerged:

1. Reconnaissance and, through the promulgation of orders, definition of the different options for deployment.
2. Train commanders for these deployments.
3. Bring up all units still in other areas.
4. Establish a rear echelon organization, especially for motor vehicle repair, which would be able to provide services to all possible Division areas of operations. The Division moved it into the vicinity of Dorsten-Hamm.
5. Move up, incorporate, and train personnel replacements.
6. Repair motor vehicles and weapons. Move up new equipment as long as it is still made available.

This program was time sensitive since the initiation of the enemy offensive had to be reckoned with starting any day. All in all, it was accomplished. However, the training and the bonding of the units in the pallid formations could not be achieved so quickly. This was true for the two *Panzer-Grenadier Regiments,* both armored personnel carrier companies of the *Armored Reconnaissance Battalion,* and the *Armored Engineer Battalion.* Another discrepancy that would later have a decisive effect was the insufficient allotment of fuel. On 24 March, it just sufficed for a march of about 70 kilometers. For a deployment toward Arnhem or across the Lippe River, the Division would at best reach the battle area, only to then immobilized.

The replenishment of personnel succeeded as far as numbers were concerned. On 11 March, two convalescent and two march companies, as well as Combat Group Kobelinski were already announced.[5] The latter supposedly had a strength of 1,200 men and was put together from the Division's replacement units in *Wehrkreis VI.* On 15 March, they released 561 men to the Division. The remainder were cadre personnel from the training units, and their incorporation was not allowed. It can no longer be established if the request by the Division for the release of these very necessary personnel was ultimately fulfilled. Among the replacement personnel were numerous soldiers from the *Luftwaffe,* good people, but not trained as infantrymen.[6] Overall, the quality of the replacements left much to be desired. The Division *Field Replacement Battalion* delivered the men, who in the meantime were poorly retrained, to the combat units, and in turn received those arriving replacements who urgently needed further training. Among them were also some who until now were indispensable to industry, as well as people who were combed out from offices of the Replacement Army.[7] The supply of weapons, equipment and vehicles was within modest limits. The Division received only a few tanks from new production and furthermore had to depend on repairing its own.

In this situation, the Division was supposed to be restructured for the "Basic Organization of *Panzer* Division 1945."[8] The order for this came from the General Inspector of *Panzer* Troops and was delivered by *Oberst i.G.* Freyer. The written order by the *OKH* was not issued until 25 March. It is included as Appendix 21. The new organization was a child of deficiency. It only provided for a mixed armored regiment with one tank battalion and one *Panzer-Grenadier* battalion. The two *Panzer-Grenadier* Regiments—each with two strong battalions, each with one infantry gun and one engineer company—could no longer be fully motorized. The numbers for presumed assets of tanks and armored vehicles were radically lowered, to about one-third of the old stock. The Division was authorized 20 Panthers and 20 *Panzer IVs,* 20 tank destroyers, and eight armored, self-propelled anti-aircraft guns. The *Armored Reconnaissance Battalion* was denied almost all armored personnel carriers and its heavy company. *Panzer-Grenadier Escort Platoons* were to be incorporated with the tank destroyer companies and the *Panzerjäger* battalion. The rest of the Division's units remained essentially unchanged. In regard to supply troops, apparently three horsedrawn columns of 30 tons each were to take the place of the same number of motorized columns of 120 tons each, and one medical company was to be omitted.

The restructuring was only partially carried out "in the framework of the available personnel and materiel," as the order stated. For example, it can no longer be determined whether the mixed *Panzer* regiment was established. The tanks from both *Panzer* battalions were combined into one, although it remains unclear if the battalion of armored personnel carriers supposedly belonging to it was established and incorporated. Only a note addresses this, "*Oberst* Bayer takes over armored combat group with all tank and reconnaissance vehicle units."[9]

Thus, a new *1st Battalion, Panzer-Grenadier Regiment 60* (Motorized) would have to be established, as well as new motorized companies within the reconnaissance battalion. But obviously, neither happened. Even the escort platoons in the tank destroyer companies were probably hardly established. The *2d Battalion, Armored Artillery Regiment 146* was not restructured from three batteries with four guns each to two batteries with six guns each.[10] However, the three motorized *Panzer-Grenadier* battalions seem to have been reconstructed according to the new organization. A chart of *2d Battalion, Panzer-Grenadier Regiment 156* shows how such a battalion may have looked as of 17 March. The chart is added as Appendix 22.[11] The combination of all transport vehicles from the *Panzer-Grenadier* companies into one combat column as provided for in the *OKH* order apparently remained undone. The consequence of the consolidation of both battalions from the *Panzer* regiment was that 61 NCOs and men were dispatched to Herdringen near Neheim-Hüsten for retraining with the *Field Replacement Battalion.*[12]

The losses of commanders during the previous battles made it necessary to newly fill several positions. *Major* Stephan ultimately assumed command of *Panzer-Grenadier Regiment 60,* and *Major* Tebbe temporarily that of *Armored*

Reconnaissance Battalion 116. His substitute at *1st Battalion, Panzer Regiment 16* was *Hauptmann* Adam.[13,14] On 26 March, after the outbreak of the battles, *Oberst* Bayer was appointed commander of Army tank destroyer groups at *Supreme Command–West.*[15] *Major* Tebbe then took over command of the *Panzer* regiment, *Hauptmann* Kühne assumed command of *Major* Tebbe's *1st (Panzer-) Battalion,* and *Hauptmann* Fischer that of the *Armored Reconnaissance Battalion.* The battalions of the *Panzer-Grenadier Regiments* were led by *Hauptmann* von Ketteler (*1st Battalion, Panzer-Grenadier Regiment 60*), *Hauptmann* Bröker (*2d Battalion, Panzer-Grenadier Regiment 60*), *Hauptmann* Froemel (*1st Battalion, Panzer-Grenadier Regiment 156*), and *Hauptmann* Zanzinger (*2d Battalion, Panzer-Grenadier Regiment 156*).[16]

Reconnaissance and tactical exercises were eagerly carried out to prepare the deployment. On 17 March, corps headquarters arranged a tactical exercise regarding deployment against an enemy airborne landing. On 23 March, the *116th Panzer Division* executed "Case Emmerich."[17] The weather helped to revitalize. A glorious spring allowed the people to take a deep breath again. Shortly after the war, *Major* Vogelsang contemplated the following:

> These two weeks of rest were for the entire Division . . . a longed-for and deserved recuperation, a relaxation which provided a final opportunity to meet each other within circles of comrades of the entire Division and within the individual units, to chat and to free oneself from the immense physical and mental pressures of the events of the previous months.
>
> The Division staff was situated in a village with windmills and surrounding farms. The Dutch people, who were well disposed toward us, treated us like sons of their own country and spoiled us wherever they could. It was simply wonderful, after all the dirt, the turbulence, and the haste, to find some outward peace in these well-tended, undamaged houses.
>
> But on the inside? Anxiety gnawed about the future, the burden of a situation from which a way out could hardly be seen. The question always emerged: Why? What for?[18]

The enemy air activity increased. *Generalmajor* von Waldenburg noted in his calendar on 21 March, "Very, very strong enemy air activity, one formation after another flies into the *Reich*, barely any defense! Otherwise quiet."[19]

The command post of the *1st Parachute Army* was also attacked on this day and *General* Schlemm was wounded. *General der Infanterie* Straube from *LXXXVI Corps* took his place, until *General der Infanterie* Blumentritt assumed command of the Army on 28 March.[20]

The following were deployed in the *Army Group H* area for the defense of the Rhine: The *25th Army* from the coast up to Emmerich (inclusive), and the *1st Parachute Army* from Emmerich up to about ten kilometers north of Düsseldorf, where *Army Group B*'s area of operations began.[21] Subordinated to *1st Parachute Army* were: *II Parachute Corps,* deployed between Emmerich and northeast of

Xanten; *LXXXVI Corps* in link-up from there to Walsum; and *LXIII Corps* up to the Army Group boundary. *XLVII Panzer Corps* formed the army group reserve. Besides this, Army Group had the *190th Infantry Division* at its disposal, which was refitted in Holland.

The positions along the Rhine were weak. Almost all divisions of the *1st Parachute Army* deployed at the river had suffered in the battles west of the river and had been insufficiently replenished. The anti-aircraft artillery of the entire area came as a pleasant reinforcement. It served primarily for the protection of the industrial area and the traffic routes against the enemy air forces. Furthermore, its task was to defend against the expected airborne landing. Ultimately, it could provide useful service in ground combat, even if in most cases it was hardly mobile. Units from the *466th Replacement Division* arrived in the vicinity northeast of Wesel. Later, they were partially deployed within the framework of *XLVII Panzer Corps,* as long as they were not involved in the attack by the Anglo-Americans across the Rhine and the air landing related to it.[22]

While the German side prepared as much as was still possible for the daily expected onslaughts, the enemy's march for deployment was in high gear. During the previous month, the German Army in the West lost about one third of its strength, that is, 293,000 men captured and approximately 60,000 dead and wounded.[23] On 9 March, Montgomery gave his final order for the assault across the Rhine, Operation PLUNDER, to the three armies under his command. These were the Ninth Army to the right (11 divisions), the British Second Army in the center (11 divisions and six separate maneuver brigades), and the First Canadian Army to the left (eight divisions).[24] The allied airborne operation, VARSITY, was tied in with PLUNDER. The 17th Airborne Division and the British 6th Airborne Division, under the command of *XVIII Airborne Corps,* were designated for this. The day of attack was to be 24 March.

Plans for this day had been made for weeks, along with preparations for the technical control of the river crossing and the establishment of a supply line. Montgomery's 21st Army Group consisted of almost 1.3 million men; about 60,000 engineers were assigned for the crossing; 5,500 artillery pieces of various kinds were on hand; about 260,000 tons of supplies and engineer equipment were brought up. Considerable efforts were made to camouflage and for deception. Thus, a veil of smoke along the Rhine front prevented the Germans from obtaining a view of the allies' rear areas for more than ten days before the attack. The population was evacuated and put into camps. Since mid-February, the allied air forces conducted air raids over the Ruhr area and hoped to cut off the traffic coming from the interior of Germany, mostly targeting important railroad bridges. Commencing 11 March, the air raids increased and reached their climax during the last three days before the attack when 11,000 sorties were flown. Airfields, anti-aircraft gun positions, troop quarters, railroad stations, and traffic hubs were the preferred targets. Once again, an area that had already been heavily bombarded for years was hit by this violent storm with devastating force.

Montgomery did not consider the Rhine crossing a leisurely stroll, but a difficult undertaking that had to be prepared perfectly and to the last detail. Therefore, he declined plans for surprise attacks, urgently made by the commander of the Ninth Army, Lieutenant General Simpson. His field army was to cross the Rhine up-river from Wesel, while the British Second Army crossed between Wesel and Rees. The most important objective was Wesel, being a traffic junction. Therefore, the airborne landing was planned for north and northwest of the city. After establishing a sufficiently large bridgehead and having units from the Canadian First Army widen it toward the north, Montgomery wanted to push into the interior of the *Reich*, with the Canadians protecting his left flank.

Meanwhile, the situation further south dramatically came to a head for the German side.[25] The American bridgehead at Remagen was widened in the north up to the Sieg River, and in the south up to Neuwied; the Cologne–Frankfurt *Autobahn* was crossed on a wide front. German counterattacks produced no success. After much damage, the solid Rhine bridge caved in. However, eight army engineer bridges were set up, and the First Army in the bridgehead was ready to attack with seven divisions. Between Ludwigshafen and Koblenz, the Americans were positioned all along the Rhine. In the meantime, the Seventh Army attacked in lower Alsace and broke into the *Westwall*. The German *7th* and *1st Armies* consisted of nothing but wreckage. During the night of 22/23 March, Patton's Third Army established a bridgehead across the Rhine near Oppenheim and quickly extended it.

On 9 March, *Generalfeldmarschall* Kesselring reported to Hitler, to assume the Supreme Command in the West. Hitler made an effort to encourage Kesselring and declared that the Eastern Front would hold up and new U-boats and airplanes were on the way.[26]

On 23 March, all commanders of the *116th Panzer Division* were assembled for a tactical exercise.[27] *Generalmajor* von Waldenberg executed "Case Emmerich." The corps commander, Baron von Lüttwitz, took part. At 1700 hours, fierce enemy artillery fire started along the Rhine front and increased to barrage strength. At the same time, heavy bombardments were observed in the area north of Rees. Since all wires in this area were damaged, the Division sent out two reconnaissance patrols.[28]

After the tactical exercise, all the participants had supper and stayed together for a while.

In 1947, I wrote the following in my work for the Americans:

It was the last time that this circle was together. The officers were fully aware of the seriousness of the situation. Their loyalty oaths and their soldierly honor demanded this last difficult journey, especially since the enemy requested unconditional surrender. Many still hoped for a diplomatic solution with the Western powers. Thus, all responsible soldiers fulfilled their difficult duty for a last time, and the Division started its last passage of arms and sacrifice.[29]

At midnight, the Chief of Staff *XLVII Panzer Corps* informed me, "In battalion strength, the enemy succeeded in gaining a foothold on both sides of Rees on this river bank. The Division is being alerted, order to deploy still expected during the night."[30]

At 0100 hours, Count Bernstorff added, "*15th Panzer-Grenadier Division* is being deployed against enemy at Rees. Division remains . . . under alert."

Besides that, the *116th Panzer Division* received orders to relocate the reinforced *Armored Reconnaissance Battalion* still during the night into the area east of Bocholt. There, it was to stand by for use against an enemy airborne landing, or a crossing near Wesel, or, if necessary, also to provide support near Rees. The area west-northwest of Wesel was to be reconnoitered. At 0345 hours, the reconnaissance battalion reported its departure. It had been reinforced by *3d Company, Armored Engineer Battalion 675*; *2d Battery, Armored Artillery Regiment 146*; and by tank destroyers. *Major* Tebbe was in command.

In the morning hours, additional reports arrived about the enemy attack on both sides of Rees. According to these reports, the enemy established a bridgehead of at least two kilometers' depth on both sides of the town. There was vigorous air activity, including fighter bombers and twin-engine machines. Even the Division command post was attacked.[31] At 1100 hours, the message arrived: "Enemy advancing rapidly south of the Lippe."

A half-hour later, corps headquarters informed the Division of the following, "Airborne landing three kilometers north of Wesel. [Unreadable] area Dingden. *XLVII Corps*. . . is being subordinated to *1st Parachute Army*."

The *116th Panzer Division* received orders to have the *Armored Reconnaissance Battalion* at once determine the extent of the airborne landing. Shortly thereafter, corps headquarters reported that the enemy landed 3,000 men between Bocholt and Hamminkeln, and that 400 four-engine aircraft were detected north of Wesel, bearing east toward the Schwarze Heide forest (two kilometers northeast of Wesel). Soon after that, another 200 aircraft were sighted. At 1200 hours, corps headquarters issued the order to deploy the reinforced *Armored Reconnaissance Battalion* to attack the "enemy advancing from Dingden in the direction of Bocholt." It was retracted, however, "because other units tied down the opponent there."

At 1510 hours, the Division received orders to prepare to march at 1945 hours along two march routes, to reach the areas on both sides of Dorsten. Reconnaissance elements were to be sent ahead to and across the Lippe River. It was said that the enemy had also conducted airborne landings south of the Lippe, in the vicinity of Kirchhellen. The Division was to establish bridgeheads on the south bank of the Lippe during the night, and attack the enemy in the vicinity of Kirchhellen early on 25 March. During the afternoon, Count Bernstorff added to his order, "It is important to throw the strongest units across the bridges toward the south."

At 1800 hours, he reminded, "Keeping the bridges open and obtaining clear results from the reconnaissance of the Kirchhellen area decisive for success of the Division."

He announced that *Rocket Launcher Brigade 16* would be subordinated to the Division and moved into the area west of Raesfeld. It can no longer be established what condition it was in when it arrived at the Division. The Division Commander was ordered to the command post of the *1st Parachute Army,* south of Borken, to be informed about the situation and to receive the final order for the Division's deployment.[32]

At 1945 hours, the Division began its march. The Division staff also moved, first to a release point on the Raesfeld–Dorsten road, where it was to meet with *Generalmajor* von Waldenburg and where the commanders were told to go to receive orders.[33] The Division marched on two roads, the right column via Doetinchem–Aalten–Bocholt–Raesfeld at Schermbeck, the left one via Lichtenvoorde–Winterswijk–Borken toward Dorsten.[34] As far as can be determined, *Panzer-Grenadier Regiment 156* with the *2d Battalion, Armored Artillery Regiment 146* and the *1st Company* of *Engineer Battalion 675* marched on the right, while *Panzer-Grenadier Regiment 60* with *3d Battalion, Armored Artillery Regiment 146,* and probably the tanks, marched on the left.[35] In general, the march proceeded smoothly. The larger villages recently destroyed by bombs created delays and had to be partly circumvented.

The reinforced *Armored Reconnaissance Battalion* had established security positions at the Lippe and reconnoitered to the south. Thereby, it became obvious that no enemy airborne landings had taken place south of the Lippe.[36] Coming from *1st Parachute Army* headquarters at 0200 hours on 25 March, the Division Commander arrived at the Division release point northwest of Dorsten and brought the orders for the Division.[37] It was subordinated to *LXXXVI Corps* and was to throw the enemy that came across the Rhine south of the Lippe in the sector of *180th Infantry Division* back to the river. In the telephone log, the following is recorded:

> 0200 hours, return of *General* from Army Chief of Staff. Conference with *Ia* about intended course of attack: to the right *156th,* to the left *1st Battalion, Panzer-Grenadier Regiment 60* with *Armored Reconnaissance Battalion* and tank destroyers. [Unreadable] subordinated.

It is not clear who led on the left, in the Division's southern zone. It is possible that the commander of *Panzer-Grenadier Regiment 60, Major* Stephan, took charge there. But most likely, *Major* Tebbe, the leader of the reinforced *Armored Reconnaissance Battalion,* had command first. *Oberstleutnant* Grollmann set up the regimental command post for *Panzer-Grenadier Regiment 156* west of Schermbeck. The spearhead of the regiment's first march group from his *2d Battalion* arrived there at about 0200 hours.[38] The *2d Battalion, Armored Artillery*

Regiment 146, which was incorporated in this march group, was left behind due to lack of fuel. The *3d Battalion* of the *Artillery Regiment* encountered the same problem. It only got as far as the forest north of Dorsten.[39] In the log it says, "*General* reports to the army that artillery and tanks cannot reach assigned area of deployment due to lack of fuel. Until now, allocation has not taken place and should not be counted on until daybreak because of long distances."[40]

At 0300 hours, the commanders who were ordered to the release point received their orders. One hour later, a duty officer delivered the corps order; it specified that the Division should not attack until all of the artillery had taken up position.[41] Thereafter, the Division's units received orders not to attack, but to advance as far as possible and to change over to the defensive if they encountered the enemy. On the right, *2d Battalion, Panzer-Grenadier Regiment 156,* under the command of *Hauptmann* Zanzinger, had reached the western edge of Hünxe, when *Oberstleutnant* Grollmann personally delivered the order to cease the attack.[42] The *2d Battalion, Panzer-Grenadier Regiment 156* took up position on both sides of Hünxe, its right wing at the Lippe side-canal. During the day, the *1st Battalion* took up positions on the left of the *2d Battalion.* Stragglers from the *180th Infantry Division* came back and were stopped. The left group of the Division, the *1st Battalion, Panzer-Grenadier Regiment 60* with tank destroyers, advanced along the Kirchhellen-Dinslaken road. Its forwardmost units reached the forest east of the *Autobahn,* northeast of Lohberg. At 0600 hours, the Division command post was established in Besten (six kilometers west-southeast of Dorsten).[43]

Communications with the staff of the *180th Infantry Division* gave the impression, "that the *180th Infantry Division* is insufficiently informed about its own units, due to complete absence of communications."[44]

At 1415 hours, *LXXXVI Corps* received the report that according to information from the *180th Infantry Division,* the enemy attacked through Hiesfeld toward the east, and advanced up to "Hinter den Kempen." In so doing, they advanced about 1,000 meters past the *Autobahn* embankment. Furthermore, the Division reported that its artillery had used up its ammunition and was engaging attacking tanks with direct fire. I forewarned the corps staff, therefore, "that with further development of the situation, by evening most of the *116th Panzer Division* would be tied down in battle." [Americans would say that most of the Division would be "decisively engaged"—*Editor.*]

At 1600 hours, the corps Chief of Staff determined the following, "Since the units of the *180th Infantry Division* no longer have the strength to defend the extended front, the *116th Panzer Division* becomes the front unit. Remnants of the *180th* retreat where they cannot hold any longer. . . . Units of the *180th* remain deployed and must be picked up during retreat."

The Chief of Staff pointed out the necessity of maintaining liaison with the right wing of the adjacent unit on the left. The insertion of the *2d Battalion, Panzer-Grenadier Regiment 60* was discussed. It is not clear if it was deployed on the Division's left wing or in its center, in the forest forward of Hövelsberg. As will be shown later, the latter is closer. This is how the *116th Panzer Division* experienced the attack by the British and Americans across the Rhine. Before its further battles are described, a look at the enemy's side and the situation at large is presented.[45]

During the night of 23/24 March, 21st Army Group commenced its attack. It was preceded—beginning at 1700 hours on 23 March—by a preparatory barrage from 3,560 tubes, lasting several hours. It reached its climax at 2100 hours. After this, a British Division began crossing the Rhine near Rees. This was followed by a second crossing downriver from Wesel, while the already-destroyed city was heavily bombarded once more. At 0200 hours on 24 March, another British Division crossed northeast of Xanten. Simultaneously, the XVI Corps with the 30th Infantry Division started its crossing southwest of Wesel. One hour later, the 79th Infantry Division followed north of Orsoy. The crossings were successful everywhere. Resistance at the river bank was weak. There was hard combat only in Rees and Wesel. In the late morning hours of 24 March, two airborne divisions landed in the area north of Wesel. Approximately 1,500 airplanes and 1,300 gliders set down 17,000 men, 800 vehicles and guns, as well as 600 tons of ammunition. In the afternoon, the air-landed troops linked up with those who had crossed the river. The airborne operation resulted in considerable losses of men and planes, because it headed directly into heavy anti-aircraft fire. On the evening of 24 March, the British, together with the airborne forces, had established a bridgehead 25 kilometers wide, with varying depths. Near Hamminkeln it reached a depth of about twelve kilometers, further north only of two to five kilometers. The *84th Infantry Division,* deployed down river from Wesel, was hit by the airborne landing and destroyed, as were the troops in Wesel. The *7th* and *8th Parachute Divisions* north of it defended themselves with everything that was available.

Army Group H subordinated the *XLVII Panzer Corps* to the *1st Parachute Army,* which at midnight ordered the deployment of the *15th Panzer-Grenadier Division* against the enemy that had crossed near Rees. Evidently, only one reinforced *Panzer-Grenadier* regiment was deployed via Bienen toward the enemy who had landed west of Rees. It was without success.[46] The entire *15th Panzer-Grenadier Division,* however, was thereby pulled into the defensive battle near the *II Parachute Corps* sector, while the *116th Panzer Division*—as reported— was told to march across the Lippe against the Americans. With this, the only operational reserve was dispersed. The *XLVII Panzer Corps* received orders on 24 March to assume control in the former sector of the *180th Infantry Division,* south of the Lippe, as of the evening of 25 March. Subordinated to it from this time on were the *180th Infantry Division,* the *116th Panzer Division,* and the *190th Infantry Division,* which was in transit from Holland.[47]

In this sector, after an artillery preparation from 2,070 guns and the expenditure of 65,000 shells, *XVI Corps* succeeded in crossing on a wide front with

almost no losses.[48] On the evening of 24 March, the better part of five infantry
regiments was on the right bank of the Rhine. Dinslaken was captured and a
bridgehead was formed between Walsum and the Lippe. Its forward line generally ran along National Highway 8. The *180th Infantry Division* suffered heavy
losses. About 4,500 German soldiers were captured by the Americans. By 1600
hours, they completed the first bridge and transferred artillery and tanks.

While the 79th Infantry Division deployed on the right and turned southeast
toward the Emscher Canal, still on 25 March, the commander of the 30th Infantry
Division strove for the breakthrough to the east toward Kirchhellen and Dorsten.
A regiment from the 35th Infantry Division was inserted between the two divisions. On that day, one tank destroyer and two tank battalions had already moved
into the 30th Infantry Division's bridgehead. The 30th's Division Artillery occupied positions on the right bank of the Rhine. Two regiments formed mobile task
forces: on the left, the one from the augmented 117th Infantry Regiment with
Dorsten as its objective; on the right, the one from the augmented 120th Infantry
Regiment, with the mission of seizing Kirchhellen. Establishing the task forces
and preparing them for the attacks took time, so the attacks could not be mounted until late in the afternoon of 25 March. The left group hit *Panzer-Grenadier
Regiment 156,* the right one *1st Battalion, Panzer-Grenadier Regiment 60.* The
attack against still-defending units from the *180th Infantry Division* near Hiesfeld
may have been led by the 79th Infantry Division. The American war history
works describe the battles of 120th Infantry Regiment as follows:

> Almost from the outset, the tankers and infantrymen had to fight for every little
> gain. The Germans suffered—they lost four halftracks armed with multiple-barrel
> 20mm anti-aircraft guns, two 75mm guns, three 105mm pieces, and several motor
> vehicles, including an ammunition truck that caught fire and set a patch of the for-
> est ablaze—but they imposed the delay they wanted. Night was falling when inter-
> rogation of prisoners revealed the story: the task force was no longer fighting
> *Volkssturm* nor even disconsolate survivors of the *180th Division;* the prisoners
> were from the *60th Panzer-Grenadier Regiment, 116th Panzer Division.*[49]

The leftmost American task force from the augmented 117th Infantry Regiment, confronted *Panzer-Grenadier Regiment 156,* took Hünxe in the evening,
and had experiences similar to those of the group on the right. On 25 March, the
79th Infantry Division also met strong resistance: southeast of Dinslaken, a regiment of the *2d Parachute Division* was deployed against it. The American history continues:

> The 30th Infantry Division on the third day, 26 March, made some impressive gains,
> despite continuing problems with narrow, muddy forest trails and despite an enemy
> bearing no resemblance to the one who first had opposed the Rhine crossing. One
> battalion of the 119th Infantry reached Gahlen . . . but they became so involved in
> a fight that a second battalion had to come to its aid. The 117th Infantry reached

open ground just over three and a half miles from Dorsten but had trouble holding the position because of fire from tanks in a nearby town and woodlot and from 128mm anti-aircraft guns emplaced in concrete near an airfield.

The 120th Infantry had the roughest going of all at first, but in the end, crowned the day with a strikingly successful maneuver. Continuing through the woods toward Kirchhellen, the regiment's 2d Battalion first had to disperse a counterattack by a company of the *116th Panzer Division*'s *Grenadiers* supported by five tanks. From that point it was a slow, yard-by-yard advance until just before nightfall when the men reached the edge of the woods to look down on the airfield from which anti-aircraft guns were harassing the neighboring 117th Infantry.[50]

During the night a fresh battalion was deployed, and captured the airfield without major losses. The American report continues:

These were impressive gains, but they were not breakout. By nightfall of 26 March, the enemy's *116th Panzer Division* had clearly thwarted immediate breakout and, though incapable of decisive counterattack, was strong enough to hold an attacker to limited gains.[51]

Since most of the *116th Panzer Division* could now gradually be expected, the commander of the 30th Infantry Division would have liked to take smaller steps, to "afford his tired infantry battalions a chance to rest."[52] But the Ninth Army urged him on. To give the 30th Infantry Division more room, the 8th Armored Division was deployed beyond it. But even this measure did not solve the problem.

Although the fatigued infantrymen of the 30th Division had fought through the night of the 26th and the day of the 27th to open a route for the armor, they failed to do more than dent the positions of the enemy's *116th Panzer Division*. Dense forest and poor roads, when combined with determined resistance from German tanks and anti-aircraft guns, prevented the armor from gaining more than three miles. When the fighting died down with the coming of night on 28 March, the Germans still held Dorsten. Prospects of a breakout faded.[53]

A radio message by war correspondent John MacCormac from 27 March that indicates how much the resistance of the *116th Panzer Division* impressed the Americans appeared in *The New York Times* the following day:

Last resistance by the Nazis against the 30th Infantry Division. . . .

The story of the Ninth Army bridgehead became the chronicle yesterday of the desperate attempt by Field Marshal Albert Kesselring to prevent this breakthrough by throwing the famous *116th Panzer Division,* the best *Panzer* unit of the German army, toward it. . . . With support by tanks, since yesterday it led counter attacks in classical German defensive tactics against the spearhead of the bridgehead. . . . Its presence in the sector of the 30th could be interpreted as respect, however it destroyed the prospects for a quick use of the Ninth Army bridgehead for a

breakthrough. . . . Since then, the *116th* fought outstandingly, the way one is used
to it. . . . It did not give up anything without fight. . . .[54]

On the next day, MacCormac reported the following:

Also today, on the fifth day of the bridgehead offensive by the Ninth Army, the
feared German *116th Panzer Division* continued to carry out its task with unrelenting tenacity. Now today, the tired 30th, which fought without let-up since the
crossing of the Rhine, opened its ranks to allow armored forces to pass that were to
advance against the German *Panzers*. . . . The *116th Panzer Division* did justice to
its reputation in this sector of the bridgehead, but it had to pay dearly for its
determination. . . . But all in all, the *116th* fights now as before, exceedingly
effectively. . . .

On 28 March, Combat Command A of the 8th Armored Division attacked
toward Dorsten and Polsum, with the CCR south of it, toward Kirchhellen. It
"was pinned down by the stubborn resistance it encountered on the east bank of
the Rhine."[55] North of the Lippe, however, a larger success paved the way for the
enemy. On the afternoon of 28 March, tanks from the British 6th Armoured
Brigade, mounted with American paratroopers, pushed far to the east and reached
Haltern, in the deep flank of the German defenders near Dorsten.[56] The British
stood approximately on a line from Borken to ahead of Emmerich. The 79th and
35th Infantry Divisions advanced slowly along the right wing of the Ninth Army.
Thereby, Hamborn, Sterkrade, and Königshardt were taken.

Meanwhile, the First Army reached Marburg and Giessen and the Third Army
arrived at Hanau.[57] On 28 March, Montgomery issued a new order for operations
across the north German low country, toward the Elbe. On the same day,
Eisenhower delivered a directive which foresaw that after encircling the Ruhr
area, the Ninth Army was to come under the command of Bradley; he was to
advance with three field armies as the main effort of the offensive toward the east.
Thereby, Montgomery's responsibility was only the protection of the northern
flank, while 6th Army Group protected the southern flank. Thus, Eisenhower
abandoned his original objective, Berlin. He informed Stalin about this; protests
by the British were to no avail. A change in the future division of the German
Reich into occupation zones would probably not have been possible with the capture of Berlin, since this was already politically predetermined.[58]

Let us return to the *116th Panzer Division*. We left it at 1600 hours on 25
March, when it became obvious that the remnants of the *180th Infantry Division*
were to fall back on the *116th,* which would then have to take over its entire front.
In the evening, *Panzer-Grenadier Regiment 156* fought for Hünxe and to the
south of it. *Hauptmann* Zanzinger wrote the following in his diary:

Toward 1800 hours, violent artillery and tank fire on Hünxe. *Oberleutnant* Schutow
[Acting Commander, *6th Company, Regiment 156—Author*] reports heavy enemy
attack. Simultaneously heavy combat noise south near *1st Battalion.* Fleeing

soldiers of the *1st Battalion* report: Battalion commander, *Hauptmann* Froemel, seriously wounded—missing. Americans with tanks break through the *1st*.[59]

The Americans also continued to attack near *2d Battalion*. Hünxe was lost. By 1800 hours, *Panzer-Grenadier Regiment 156* had already reported to the Division that the enemy was advancing out of Hünxe toward the east with tanks.[60] The *1st Battalion, Panzer-Grenadier Regiment 60,* with attached tank destroyers, encountered the enemy in the forest northeast of Lohberg. In heavy combat on both sides of the road from Kirchhellen to Dinslaken, the battalion delayed the American advance considerably, but suffered painful losses. Its commander, *Hauptmann* von Ketteler, was captured.[61] At 1900 hours, the Division received the following report:

> Near *2d Battalion, Panzer-Grenadier Regiment 60*, breach with tanks toward Hövelsberg and toward Schwarze Heide [1.5 kilometers southeast of Hövelsberg— *Author*]. Blockade by Stephan [meaning *Panzer-Grenadier Regiment 60—Author*] north of Schwarze Heide being established. Tanks in Kirchhellen being alerted, to go into position toward Hövelsberg.[62]

It is questionable if "*2d Battalion, Panzer-Grenadier Regiment 60*" is correct. It could also haven been the *1st Battalion.*

On the evening of 25 March, orders were issued by the Commanding General of *XLVII Panzer Corps, General* Baron von Lüttwitz, at the *116th Panzer Division* command post in Besten. At 1800 hours, he assumed command in the sector between the Lippe and the Emscher Canal. To the south, *LXIII Corps*, with *Division Hamburg* and the *2d Parachute Division,* linked up. The former unit consisted only of the division staff with its communications section, and also commanded some elements of the *2d Parachute Division.* The commander of the *180th Infantry Division, Generalmajor* Klosterkemper, was present when the order was briefed.[63]

Lüttwitz ordered the *180th Infantry Division* to be released from its former sector and to take over a narrow sector at the right wing. On 26 March, the *116th Panzer Division* initially had the task of defending across the entire corps sector. For the time being, *Panzer-Grenadier Regiment 156* had to remain deployed along the Hünxe–Dorsten road, until the remnants from the *180th Infantry Division* assembled and reorganized behind it. Lüttwitz announced that the newly arriving *190th Infantry Division,* coming from the Netherlands, would take over the southern sector during the course of the day. Its commander was *Generalleutnant* Hammer.

Most of the division's units that remained behind due to lack of fuel, mainly most of the artillery and the tanks, arrived at the battlefield little by little during the night of 25/26 March. By morning, *Panzer-Grenadier Regiment 156* moved into a new position between Hünxe and Gahlen. *Panzer-Grenadier Regiment 60,* in the center, was deployed on both sides of the road from Dinslaken to

Kirchhellen, approximately in a line east of Hövelsberg–Grafschaft–Sträterei. A weak combat group formed from units of the *Armored Reconnaissance Battalion* with some tanks was deployed in the left sector, forward of the *Autobahn* bend.[64]

As of 1000 hours, the enemy attacked along the entire front between the Lippe and Sträterei. Reports about the action reached the Division between 1030 and 1100 hours. At the right, near *Panzer-Grenadier Regiment 156,* the enemy attacked with tanks across the Hinsenberg and along the Lippe side-canal and against the brickyard, 2.5 kilometers west of Gahlen, and penetrated the Gartroper thicket. At noon, the enemy appeared with 20 tanks at the road triangle south of Heisterkamp. At 1345 hours, the Division ordered—most likely the *Panzer Regiment*—to bring this attack to a halt by deploying all available tanks. There were two points of heavy attack in the *Panzer-Grenadier Regiment 60* sector. One was north of the road to Kirchhellen, coming out of the forest near Hövelsberg toward Schwarze Heide, the other along the southern road from Oberlohberg toward the east, across Sträterei. The Schlägerhardt forester's station (3.5 kilometers northeast of Oberlohberg) was lost. Sometime later, the enemy advanced east again for about 2.5 kilometers in the dense forest area. During the night, it attacked again at Schwarze Heide.[65] This could have been the night attack on the airfield, four kilometers northwest of Kirchhellen, that was described earlier by the American side.

During the night of 26/27 March, the *Panzer-Grenadier Regiments* moved into a line that ran from the western edge of Gahlen via Besten toward the south, somewhat west of the north-south trail (which today is a finished road), through the Kirchheller Heide (two kilometers west of Federal Highway 223). South of the Dinslagen–Kirchhellen road, units from *Panzer-Grenadier Regiment 60* were still in the forest up to 1.5 kilometers west of the trail. The *Division Escort Company* was inserted near Besten. The *190th Infantry Division* relieved the combat group of *Armored Reconnaissance Battalion 116* that was fighting on the Division's left wing. Initially, the boundary between the two divisions probably ran about 1.5 to two kilometers south of Kirchhellen. There, the staff of the *190th* assumed control at 2000 hours on 26 March. The *116th's* Division command post was relocated to the area east of Kirchhellen.[66]

The next day, 27 March, turned out to be a critical one for the Division.[67] During the night, the impression had already arisen that the enemy had trickled into a gap between the *Escort Company* and *1st Battalion, Panzer-Grenadier Regiment 60,* and reached the road south of Besten. In the morning, the Americans attacked along the entire front, between Besten and the Division's left boundary. At 0840 hours, *Oberstleutnant* Grollmann reported four enemy tanks at the western exit of Besten. Shortly thereafter, a report arrived from *Panzer-Grenadier Regiment 60* about an enemy attack with tanks along both trails out of the southern part of the Kirchheller Heide toward the east, to the southern part of Holthausen. At 0905 hours, *Panzer Regiment 16* received orders to push north on a wide front with all tanks deployed in the vicinity of *Panzer-Grenadier Regiment*

60, to remove the threat south of Besten. But now, *Regiment 60* itself was attacked on a wide front, south of the Dinslaken–Kirchhellen road and could not spare the tanks. Therefore, our attack apparently did not take place. *Generalmajor* von Waldenburg drove to the *Panzer Regiment* to get an overview of the situation. Corps headquarters was informed of the danger of a breach. The *180th Infantry Division* took over the right sector directly south of the Lippe, after it fortunately had released the *2d Battalion, Panzer-Grenadier Regiment 156* in Gahlen in the meantime, so that the Division would again have a reserve on hand.

An enemy attack against the Schäfer road triangle (2.5 kilometers southeast of Besten) was reported at 1140 hours. Twelve of our tanks established a security line against this to prevent the Division from being torn apart. A short time later, Grollmann reported that the *180th Infantry Division* was attacked near Gahlen and was retreating to the Baumbach (stream), 2.5 kilometers southeast of Gahlen. Grollmann received the order for his *2d Battalion* and the *Division Escort Company* to establish a security line, which was to run from the Baumbach across the gravel pit (two kilometers east of Besten) toward Im Loh. At least he could still report the destruction of three enemy tanks near Besten. At noon, Corps staff issued an order that was preserved in the telephone log:

1. Opponent's spearheads broke through center and left wing *116th Panzer Division* on broad front, gained southern edge of Besten–forest south of Horstkamp–forest south of Frankenkamp. More opponent in west of Holthausen, weak enemy achieved exit out of Kirchheller Heide near Stemmer and Grafenmühle.
2. *XLVII Panzer Corps* prevents enemy breakthrough toward Dorsten–Kirchhellen and maintains liaison with *LXXX Corps* as before. For this, new main battle line in approximately following line is being established: . . .
3. Missions:
   a) *180th Infantry Division* . . .
   b) *116th Panzer Division* must establish a new defensive front by deploying *Ersatz und Ausbildungs Battalion 464* (*Replacement and Training Battalion 464*) Nothelle–Im Loh–Holthausen–farm 1.5 kilometers northwest of the Jandewerth Inn. It is important to organize our troops and by all means prevent an enemy breakthrough toward Kirchhellen.
   c) *190th Infantry Division* . . .
4. It is important to combine all tubes to prevent the enemy from breaking through toward Dorsten–Kirchhellen until the new defensive front has been established.

This order offers quite a good picture of the critical situation. The fighting diminished somewhat during the afternoon, however, a dangerous situation developed on the right wing of the adjacent unit on the left. *Panzer Regiment 16* reported at 1545 hours that the Otte farm, along the road three kilometers south of Kirchhellen, was occupied by the enemy. One kilometer further south, the enemy advanced across the road toward the railroad line. *Panzer-Grenadier Regiment 60* reported enemy pressure at the left wing. The Janknecht farm and Hill 72.0 fell into enemy hands. The combat strength of *Panzer-Grenadier Regiment 60* and of the *1st Battalion, Panzer-Grenadier Regiment 156* had dropped significantly. *Regiment 60* reported 60 men for the *1st Battalion* and 40 for the *2d*. The *2d Battalion, Panzer-Grenadier Regiment 156*—released by the *180th Infantry Division* near Gahlen—was pulled behind the Division's right wing to the railroad line near Haus Repel. On this day, a Hitler Youth company was subordinated to *2d Battalion, Panzer-Grenadier Regiment 156*. *Hauptmann* Zanzinger confided in his diary, "About seventy boys, still children, with big helmets, overcoats too long, old rifles, commanded by a war-wounded *Feldwebel*. I moved the company back as reserve and sent them quietly to their hometowns; they came from this area."[68]

During the night of 27/28 March, the Division was withdrawn to the line Im Loh–Kirchhellen–railroad southeast of Kirchhellen. The Division command post moved into the area east of Feldhausen.[69]

The intensity of the battles on 28 March surpassed that of the day before; because now the 8th Armored Division appeared on the scene in full strength. By 0800 hours, the first reports of the enemy attack west and south of Kirchhellen had already arrived.[70] Preparation areas were detected near the Jandewerth Inn, south of Kirchhellen, already in the sector of the unit to the Division's left. The Division engaged all detected targets with combined fire by its artillery and the rocket launchers from *Regiment 83*. At 0830 hours, I still could report to the Corps Chief of Staff that "for the time being, everything is still in order." At 0910 hours, the *Artillery Regiment* reported that the enemy was making smoke south of Kirchhellen and soon thereafter, it broke in near Holbeck (1.5 kilometers south of Kirchhellen). At about the same time, *Major* Stephan reported that the enemy entered the western part of Kirchhellen. In spite of a brave defense, the town was lost around noon. South of it, *Feldwebel* Podlech from the *2d Company* of the *Panzerjäger Battalion* destroyed two enemy tanks, his twenty-eighth and twenty-ninth. *Panzer-Grenadier Regiment 60* and the tanks and tank destroyers that were supporting it retreated to the railroad line east of town.

Panzer-Grenadier Regiment 156 was also attacked. Initially, it destroyed four enemy tanks, but then the enemy pushed ahead via Nothelle and Rexfort up to the Dorsten–Kirchhellen road. Schenke, Rotthof, and Im Loh were lost. Still in late morning, the enemy advanced further via Im Loh, southeast toward Riesener (one kilometer northeast of Kirchhellen). It thereby threatened *Panzer-Grenadier Regiment 60*, also in the right flank. Therefore, the regiment reported at 1225 hours that it occupied a rear defensive line. It may have run along the Dorsten–Kirchhellen railroad line on both sides of Haus Repel, because at 1345 hours *Oberstleutnant* Grollmann reported that his *2d Battalion* was at the railroad and that the *1st Battalion* and the *Division Escort Company* were retreating. The regiment was under heavy enemy artillery fire. But the Division's artillery, the attached rocket launchers, and sometimes the anti-aircraft artillery were firing as much as they could. Ammunition, for a change, was not scarce. On 28 March, the *2d Battalion, Armored Artillery Regiment 146* alone fired 2,128 rounds.[71] Some Storm Tigers also took part in the fire duel. A battery of these weapons, under the command of *Hauptmann* von Gottberg, was subordinated to the Division on the morning of 28 March.[72] It joined *Panzer Regiment 16* and played a large part in stalling the enemy attack near Kirchhellen. To avoid civilian losses, the Division ordered the battery not to fire on villages.[73] Enemy troop concentrations around the road junction northwest of Kirchhellen were a rewarding target. *Hauptmann* Adam, who led the *1st Battalion* of the *Panzer Regiment,* reported the following after the war:

> Four Storm Tigers were subordinated . . . to me. . . . Since, due to the rocket propulsion, the projectiles left a long, meteor-like smoke trail behind them and thereby gave away the firing position, the position had to be changed after every round.
>
> The first deployment was in the Dorsten-Kirchhellen area. After the evacuation of Kirchhellen, we took up position in the forest north of Feldhausen. . . . We had a good view of the fork in the road north of Kirchhellen and observed that strong American combat units were assembled there and had come to a standstill. With all four Storm Tigers, a salvo . . . was fired. The effect . . . was hard to comprehend in those days. Vehicles flew through the air, and tanks flipped over like cardboard boxes. Of course, we had to immediately leave our position, but it took hours for the enemy to recover.[74]

The engineers also contributed to strengthening the defense by building obstacles. They laid hasty minefields and demolished bridges across the little streams. In the Ninth Army chronology of events for the period 27–30 March, the resistance ahead of the 30th Infantry Division, that is, against the 8th Armored Division, was described as heavy or resolute.[75] On 30 March, it was mentioned, that "many mines" were encountered.

In the sector of the adjacent unit on the left, on 28 March, the enemy was four kilometers west of Gladbeck, as well as at the railroad. In the sector of the corps on the right, he took the part of Dorsten situated north of the Lippe River.[76]

In the early afternoon, the enemy advanced beyond the railroad at several points. Near *Panzer-Grenadier Regiment 156,* he took Haus Repel and Enberg; near *Panzer-Grenadier Regiment 60,* he seized Haus Brabeck. At 1450 hours, I informed the *XLVII Panzer Corps* Chief of Staff about this attack along the entire front and requested permission to withdraw. Permission was denied at 1530 hours. The Division "believes, therefore, a breakthrough to be unavoidable," the log recorded. One half hour later, *Regiment 156* reported that it was forming a new line forward of the Dorsten–Gladbeck railroad, between Hülsmann and Schulte zur Wieschen. At 1630 hours, the frightening report came from *Panzer-Grenadier Regiment 60* that the enemy was attacking on a broad front with tanks and infantry, and had entered the Zweckel mine. In the sector of the unit adjacent to the left, the opponent reached the western edge of Gladbeck.

Now, the corps commander did decide to withdraw to the Hasseler Mühlenbach (western edge of Hassel to the eastern edge of Dorsten). At 1800 hours, he gave me the order for this. The log reports the following:

> 1900 hours, *Ia* issues order for assembling and organizing the Division for further combat operations. To the right, *Panzer-Grenadier Regiment 156,* then *Panzer-Grenadier Regiment 60* with the *Armored Reconnaissance Battalion* on the left wing.
>
> *Panzer Group Tebbe* at left wing, because main effort there.

The danger of an enemy penetration between the *116th Panzer Division* and the unit to its left was thereby avoided. The unit to the right, the *180th Infantry Division,* left advanced combat outposts in Dorsten, while the unit to the left, the *190th Infantry Division,* did so in Gladbeck. On 28 March, the log closes with the following entry:

> The withdrawal of the units takes place during the night. New command post in Kotten as of 1900 hours. [2.8 kilometers east of Polsum—*Author*]

On 28 March, the critical development of the situation north of the Lippe and the news of the enemy's advance toward Marburg caused the *116th Panzer Division* to deploy reconnaissance patrols from the *Armored Reconnaissance Battalion* against the enemy's two pincers. It was important to have advanced awareness of the dangers that threatened the deeply echeloned Division supply installations.[77] One could no longer rely on the knowledge and information of the higher command authorities. On the afternoon of 28 March, *Oberleutnant* Nommensen's reconnaissance patrol reported that Lippramsdorf and Wulfen were occupied by the enemy, that the bridge across the Lippe near Haltern had been demolished, and that none of our units were in the village anymore, except for fleeing columns.

On this day, the Supreme Commander of *Army Group H, Generaloberst* Blaskowitz, suggested to *Supreme Command–West* and *OKW* the withdrawal of the defense to the Weser and the northeastern part of the Netherlands. He experienced a harsh rejection.[78]

During the night of 28/29 March, emergency units were brought up to the Division and incorporated into the *Panzer-Grenadier Regiments.* Thus, an emergency company of 100 men came to join the *2d Battalion* of *Panzer-Grenadier Regiment 156.*[79]

From 1100 hours on 29 March, the first reports from the new main battle line arrived at the Division, including, among others, "25 enemy tanks advancing east from Bur-Scholven."[80]

The enemy did not attack again until the afternoon, namely near *Panzer-Grenadier Regiment 60,* in the vicinity of Vicarie (one kilometer northwest of Buer-Hassel) and at the railroad branch line near Buer-Hassel. It was beaten back. In the later afternoon, the enemy attacked *Panzer-Grenadier Regiment 156* and broke into Heiken and Polsum. The enemy had pushed into Polsum with 18 tanks. A counterattack supported by twenty tanks was mounted and threw the enemy out again during hours of darkness. The old main battle line at the stream was repossessed. *Hauptmann* Zanzinger recorded the events of *Regiment 156* in his diary:

> Late morning, new position at Mühlenbach. Enemy about six to eight kilometers away—therefore still quiet. In the afternoon, increasing pressure from Dorsten toward Marl and Polsum. Whoever has Polsum has Marl and the position at the Mühlenbach. There stands *1st Battalion, Panzer-Grenadier Regiment 156,* reinforced by *Division Escort Company.* The *6th Company* maintains contact and is under heaviest pressure. The *1st Battalion* retreats to Polsum. Our blocking position is holding. Enemy stops; advances instead on the northern road coming from Dorsten. The *8th Company* is cut off. Under covering fire from the mortars of *10th Company* and the *2d Battalion, Armored Artillery Regiment 146,* as well as a diversionary attack by *12th Company* under *Oberleutnant* Höltje, it was possible to free the *8th.* It also became quiet for the *6th.* The enemy is not budging.
>
> Order from regiment: "Immediate counterattack—regain old position."
>
> Without a sound the company makes its way forward. Mühlenbach and Polsum are again occupied, in Polsum two tanks are destroyed in close combat.[81]

With the successful counterattack near Polsum, 29 March ended with a minor success, which had not happened in a long time. During the day, the Division command post relocated to Haus Niering (four kilometers north-northwest of Recklinghausen). Nommensen reported from Buldern that the enemy tank spearhead was holding up east of Dülmen. He suspected that most of the tanks had turned east toward Lüdinghausen. The Division decided to send heavy mobile units of its supply troops and the *Field Replacement Battalion* marching toward Paderborn.[82]

On March 29, *Supreme Command–West* denied the request of *Army Group H* to give up both its southern corps, the *LXIII* and the *XLVII* to *Army Group B*. The *Supreme Commander–West* criticized that *XLVII Panzer Corps* had not attacked north to reestablish contact with the rest of the army group; this was an adventurous evaluation of the situation in recognition of what was just described.[83] After the war, *General* Baron von Lüttwitz wrote that in view of the development of the situation at large, he considered it an urgent task to maintain contact with *Army Group H* to prevent encirclement. He continued as follows:

> Therefore, on the evening of 29 March, the corps requested the *1st Parachute Army* to:
>
> 1. Quickly withdraw the corps behind the Dortmund-Ems Canal between Datteln and Herne.
> 2. Pull out *116th Panzer Division* to maintain mobile contact with *1st Parachute Army.*[84]

The request was denied and the corps was ordered to hold the present line. On 29 March, *Army Group B* was denied its request to break out toward the east.[85] Hitler issued the order to halt. Army Group judged the situation in such a way that if it was encircled in the Ruhr area, it could hold out until about mid-April. To keep the connection open, in this case it also considered an attack to the east as practical. *Army Group* hoped for an attack from Kassel toward the west to break through the encirclement. Its *5th Panzer Army* stood at the Rhine and along the Sieg up to Siegen, hardly bothered by the enemy. The *15th Army,* connecting to the left, was splintered; its units established a security line from Siegen to Brilon, via Winterberg. Two of its corps—almost without troops—detoured toward Fulda and Kassel. During the night of 29/30 March, the *LIII Corps* commander, *Generalleutnant* Bayerlein, received orders from Model to attack from the vicinity of Schmallenberg to the east and northeast, and to establish contact with the units attacking from the east.[86] The attack was to start on the evening of 30 March or early on the next day, a very optimistic plan in view of the great difficulty of moving up the forces.

For the *116th Panzer Division,* 30 March was again a day of heavy defensive battles.[87] They started in the morning with *Panzer-Grenadier Regiment 60,* which at 0830 hours reported house-to-house fighting in Buer-Hassel South. A short time later, an attack southwest of Polsum was in progress. At 0900 hours, *Oberstleutnant* Grollmann reported enemy in the western part of Polsum. Soon thereafter, news came from the artillery that the enemy near Polsum was making smoke and trickling through north of it. Near Polsum, the artillery detected an enemy attack by 20 tanks and 30 men. The enemy also mounted an attack on the left wing of the *180th Infantry Division.* Through defense and counterattack the enemy was brought to a standstill near Buer-Hassel and Polsum. Several enemy tanks were destroyed. However, by noon, he attacked again, reached the left wing at the eastern edge of Buer-Hassel, and attacked *Panzer-Grenadier Regiment 156* so vigorously that Grollmann considered detouring to a new line near Marl.

In the late afternoon, it was apparent that the battles slacked off. At 2000 hours, a withdrawal was ordered to a line west of Hüls–Kleverbeck–Schulte–western edge of Elpe–600 meters west of Disteln. The *190th Infantry Division* linked up to it in the south. Its front ran south from west of Herten, through the Emscher Bruch, up to the Rhine-Herne canal. The withdrawal proceeded as planned. The reconnaissance patrols north of the Lippe reported enemy before Buldern, and ongoing combat there. The same held true in front of Senden, from Lüdinghausen toward the east and south, as well as west of Selm, deep in the corps' right flank.[88] The other pincer approached Paderborn and Brilon.

Without knowledge of the deliberations of its superiors, on the evening of the 30th, the Division suggested to corps headquarters that it be released from the front facing the west and relocated in the vicinity of Beckum–Lippstadt–Wiedenbrück. Perhaps there the Division could still have prevented the enemy spearheads from uniting and avoided the threatening encirclement. In an emergency, the only still-fully-mobile unit in the northern part of the area of encirclement would have at least had a way out toward the east. Corps headquarters declined rather harshly.

Enlightened by experience in Normandy and in the Wesel bridgehead, the Division moved out its ballast during the night of 30/31 March. After the war, I wrote the following in my report for the US Army:

> To at least save from encirclement the elements that were not immediately necessary for combat, and to not have to drag them as dead weight during a breakout, the Division decided to move them out during the night of 30/31 March to the vicinity of Melle (northwest of Bielefeld). Thus, during this night, all parts of the Division not needed for the movement of combat troops and for its most necessary supply and repair, were leaving. Later, they were transferred by orders transmitted by radio further to the vicinity east of Hameln, and from there into the Harz Mountains. There they formed a combat group to be at the disposal of the local authorities for battle. After relinquishing its tanks to the *Panzer Regiment,* the Division's *Panzerjäger* battalion was also set to march. It was to receive new armored vehicles near Warendorf (east of Münster). It also escaped the encirclement and was later united with the Division combat group in the Harz. To keep a base for the Division for a breakout toward east, the *Field Replacement Battalion* received orders to reach Beckum and to hold it for a breakout by the Division. At this time, the battalion was on a foot march toward Paderborn.[89]

Major Dunker, who was ordered to the Division for preliminary General Staff training, was assigned as commander of the *Field Replacement Battalion.* He was a proven infantry officer. The battalion soon got into a difficult situation which will be described later.

An enjoyable event occurred on 30 March. The Division received 14 new "Hunting Panther" tank destroyers, receiving them in the forest near Siepen (five kilometers northeast of Recklinghausen).[90] The *Panzer Regiment* was able to man them and somehow deal with them because it already had Panthers and assault guns, therefore, Panther drivers, commanders, and gunners. On 30 March, soldiers from the *116th Panzer Division* were fighting apart from it near Buldern and obviously confused the opponent's intelligence personnel.[91] They belonged to *Panzer-Grenadier Replacement and Training Battalion 60* from Rheine. It fought with other units against the British 6th Guards Armoured Brigade. Nommensen's armored reconnaissance patrol observed the event and reported at 1000 hours, "*Panzer* spearhead at southwest exit of Buldern. Enemy attacks with tanks and infantry. Eight tanks destroyed."[92]

The battalion was not able to offer protracted resistance.

On the morning of 31 March, the *116th Panzer Division* stood along the assigned line Hüls–Disteln; it was not challenged as much as it had been during recent days.[93] Toward noon, preparation areas were detected forward of *Panzer-Grenadier Regiment 60,* at the left wing east of Langenbochum, as well as in the Arenberg Forest. At 1315 hours, *Regiment 60* reported an enemy attack against its entire front. It led to a breach with infantry and tanks near Scherlebeck–Elpe, but achieved no major success; six enemy tanks were destroyed. The day was less fortunate for the units to the Division's right and left. At 1530 hours, the Corps Chief of Staff informed me of this. The telephone log read as follows:

> Enemy at the *180th Infantry Division* in the Auguste Victoria Mine. Our four reaction tanks must set out. . . . Enemy at adjacent unit in Hüls. Entered left in Herten. We strengthen our left wing.

At 1800 hours, an order arrived from corps headquarters for the withdrawal to a new line at the western outskirts of Recklinghausen. *Panzer-Grenadier Regiment 60,* with *Armored Reconnaissance Battalion 116* attached, remained at the front. With its new Hunting Panthers, *Panzer Regiment 16* apparently took over a sector along the boundary with the *180th Infantry Division. Panzer-Grenadier Regiment 156* was pulled out as reserve into the vicinity of Bockum (nine kilometers northeast of Recklinghausen).[94] The engineers received orders to erect obstacles and carry out demolitions in front of Recklinghausen. As far as can be deciphered from the telephone log, *Army Anti-Aircraft Battalion 281* was relocated to the Dortmund-Ems Canal, with the heavy batteries already beyond it. Fortunately, on 31 March, a large ammunition depot was discovered, from which the Division's stock could again be replenished.[95]

After the war, the quartermaster of *XLVII Panzer Corps* reported about its supply status from 30 March to 4 April. It was during the time when contact with *1st Parachute Army* was broken and the corps was not yet subordinated to *Army Group B*:

> Therefore, the corps made itself logistically self-sufficient. First, for this purpose, special inventory teams were formed, whose task was to determine all supply goods at hand in the corps area.
>
> Afterwards, the following measures were taken.
>
> Ammunition: Take-over of the Bork Army Ammunition depot [six kilometers northwest of Lünen—*Author*] and take-over of all ammunition trains, that is, railroad cars found at railroad stations or on the open track.
>
> Fuel: Take-over stock of Hydrier Works, mostly by free filling permits for the troops, creating fuel-reserve convoys.
>
> Food, clothes, and gear: Takeover stock of Army Garrison Administration.
>
> Supplies: Incorporation of presently unused columns in the corps area.
>
> With this, the following logistical situation was created:
>
> —Ammunition secured for about eight days with frugal use.
>
> —Some types of ammunition were completely missing.
>
> —Fuel: Sufficient for four weeks.
>
> —Food: Sufficient without reductions for three weeks.[96]

On 31 March, *Major* Vogelsang, the former Division Adjutant, assumed command of the *Armored Artillery Regiment* from *Major* ten Hompel, who was transferred; *Major* Sandkuhl was appointed *IIa.*[97]

In my report for the US Army shortly after the war, I noted the following:

> The Division's reconnaissance reported the advance of the enemy in the areas east of Lippstadt and Rheda-Wiedenbrück, as well as its advance toward Beckum. During the night of 31 March/1 April, the last units assigned to pull out of the encirclement area to the east got on their way. They reported strong enemy columns on the *Autobahn* from Wiedenbrück to the east.[98]

The Division command post moved to Hagem on 1 April at 0500 hours. It was Easter Sunday! When I arrived at the new command post, I received an Easter egg from my men with two closing pincers painted on it in red, and in the open gap, a blue arrow pointing east with a question mark. Count Bernstorff asked me at 0730 hours if and when the Division would be released to march off toward the east.[99] I answered that it naturally would have been better to release the Division during the night, but it would probably also be possible in the late morning. The Americans then would most likely not seriously attack the newly occupied line, and the misty weather was favorable. Bernstorff announced that the *116th Panzer Division* would be pulled out and would still move to the east during the day. For the time being, one regiment of the Division was to remain deployed in the bridgehead ahead of the Rhine-Herne and Dortmund-Ems Canal. The corps leadership's change of mind resulted from an order by *1st Parachute Army*. This radioed, "Attack immediately with all available forces from the Werne–Hamm area to the north toward Münster. Detour behind Dortmund-Ems Canal is permitted."[100]

Unfortunately it was too late, as will soon be seen.

At 0830 hours, Count Bernstorff arrived at the Division command post with the first general staff officers from the *180th* and *190th Infantry Divisions*. He arranged the *116th*'s relief, as well as the takeover of the Division's entire sector by the two adjacent units. This would occur by withdrawing the front to a line east of Recklinghausen, and later to the canal between Datteln and Herne.[101] The *116th Panzer Division* was to march at 1230 hours, leaving rear guards behind in the former sector, and was to reach the area south of Beckum and attack from there north toward Münster. Leaving a regiment at the bridgehead as originally planned was waived, even though that morning, the enemy had penetrated the *190th Infantry Division*'s sector in Hochlar and, by noon, had entered Recklinghausen from the south (that is, from Hochlar). This forced *Panzer-Grenadier Regiment 60* to withdraw to the railroad east of Recklinghausen. After the Division's units received their marching orders, the Division command post was displaced to Nateln (ten kilometers northwest of Soest). All leaders were told in advance to go there, so that radio silence could be maintained during the march. The fog lifted at noon. A bright sun shone from the sky. It was a wonderful Easter

Sunday. Astonishingly, no enemy fliers showed up in the sky. Therefore, the march went by without interference from the air. My post-war report states:

> After the Division was already marching along the *Autobahn* and the Unna–Werl–Soest road, the picture of the situation underwent a significant change. The Division's reconnaissance reported: Enemy east of Lippstadt and near Beckum. Enemy north of the Lippe, opposite Hamm, Werne, Lünen, one of our bridgeheads still at the north bank near Hamm. *Field Replacement Battalion* reported: Beckum lost, fighting for Lippstadt. The corps reported: All bridges across the Lippe between Lippstadt and Hamm destroyed.
>
> After this, the order for the Division was changed to the extent that it was not to go to the area south of Beckum, but was rather to reach the area east of Soest, to be able to mount an attack to the east from there.[102]

The commanders received their corresponding orders in Nateln. The turn by the Division went without friction. The aforementioned report continues as follows:

> In the evening and during the night, the troop units reached the assigned areas: *Armored Reconnaissance Battalion*–southeast of Soest; *Combat Group Panzer-Grenadier Regiment 60* and *Panzer Regiment 16*–west of Erwitte; *Combat Group Panzer-Grenadier Regiment 156*–northeast Soest, reconnaissance and security elements were advanced, liaison established with *Field Replacement Battalion*. It was in combat east of Erwitte and south of Lippstadt. It was subordinated to *Panzer-Grenadier Regiment 60*. By evening, the Division command post was in Bad Sassendorf.
>
> Communications with the *Field Replacement Battalion* provided the following picture about its situation and enemy activities from 31 March and 1 April. According to this, the enemy had now closed the cauldron near Lippstadt, however, the enemy forces east of Erwitte seemed to be weak. The Division's reconnaissance within and outside of the cauldron reported: Near Paderborn our forces are still in combat, near Winterberg are units from the *Panzer Lehr Division,* with their front toward the east, near Belecke weak security measures by the *Reichs Labor Service,* with front toward east.
>
> The Division intended to break through to the Weser south of Paderborn during the night of 2/3 April. Therefore it was ordered: Secure preparation position in line Belecke–Erwitte–south of Lippstadt–Lippe up to Uentrop *Autobahn* bridge and reconnoiter toward southeast at Winterberg, Brilon, Rüthen. *Field Replacement Battalion* was incorporated into *Panzer-Grenadier Regiment 60*. The bulk of the Division was to assemble and conduct preparations behind the security line in the course of 2 April.

On 1 April, a conversation I had with *Oberstleutnant* Grollmann is listed in the log: "The *1st Battalion, Panzer-Grenadier Regiment 156* becomes *Volkssturm (Home Guard) Battalion.*"[103]

Apparently an entire *Volkssturm* battalion was merged with the remnants of *1st Battalion, Panzer-Grenadier Regiment 156*. *Leutnant* von Elterlein from the *Panzer Regiment* noted:

> Easter Sunday, 1 April 1945: . . . At 1300 hours, orders came for entire *Combat Group Hauptmann* Adam to retreat to Recklinghausen, on to Horneburg–Brambauer, refuel there.
>
> 2300 hours, continue march on *Autobahn*, then via Unna–Werl–Soest to Schmerlecke.
>
> Easter Monday, 2 April 1945: Toward 0900 hours in Schmerlecke.
>
> Occupied quarters in village with security oriented south. Quiet! Afternoon, technical service and maintenance of vehicles' weapons.[104]

Before *Group Adam, 2d Battalion, Panzer-Grenadier Regiment 156* had already rested in Brambauer. The battalion commander, *Hauptmann* Zanzinger, recorded, "At noon we march into Brambauer. Enthusiastic reception by the civilians. . . . Our men are being served coffee and cake. The people obviously give everything they have."[105]

Combat Group Zanzinger—2d Battalion, Panzer-Grenadier Regiment 156 with *2d Battalion, Armored Artillery Regiment 146*—had orders to advance along the *Autobahn* and to keep the crossing over the Lippe and the Lippe side-canal near Uentrop open for the Division or, if occupied by the enemy, to capture it. Zanzinger further reports:

> March continues 1600 hours. *8th Company* under Junge drives in front. I drive ahead to reconnoiter. Near Rynern, bridge guards make us stop, "From third bridge on [evidently it was meant to be Lippe bridge—*Author*] in view of enemy, fire on bridge." Then the Regimental Adjutant, *Hauptmann* Voigt, comes also, "Stop—everything changes!" . . . Junge with *8th Company* is made to turn toward Dinker on the Ahse. The Division blocks toward the east near Lippstadt. . . .
>
> Pitiful columns of concentration camp inmates and prisoners of war move along the roads. They are supposed to be relocated to the east, but it is too late, thus, they walk around in confusion in the front area.

On the evening of 1 April, *Generalmajor* von Waldenburg sums up:

> We are being relocated from the Recklinghausen area to the area around Lippstadt, but too late! Our proposal was accepted too late, the cauldron is closed. The spearheads of the opponent move forward with giant steps.[106]

As mentioned, on 30 March, *Major* Dunker received the mission of assuming command of the *Field Replacement Battalion*. He was to use it to prevent the merger of the two enemy spearheads around Lippstadt–Beckum–Hamm, and thereby maintain the possibility for the Division to break out.[107] He was to form two battalions from the combined *Field Replacement Battalion* (Commander, *Hauptmann* Inboden) and the Division combat school (Commander, *Hauptmann*

Schörken). However, this did not succeed. Dunker could only move the staff of the *Field Replacement Battalion* and two to three companies up to Beckum. The remaining units were already marching further to the east, but by 1 April, Dunker caught up with most of them and deployed them south of the Lippe.

At 1000 hours on 31 March, Dunker and his staff reached Beckum and established a command post in the recruiting office. He established liaison with the local officials who were glad to cede responsibility. He then went toward Ahlen to reconnoiter. Three kilometers east of it, he met the commander of a reserve officers candidate course, which had already been in combat west of Ahlen and had lost about half of its 1,400 young men. Dunker subordinated these troops to himself and ordered them to disengage from the opponent. Leaving strong combat outposts along the *Reichs Autobahn* west and northwest of Beckum, he ordered the troops to reach the town, to organize the units there, and receive new orders. Furthermore, Dunker ran into the commander of the 600-man strong *SS-Battalion 600.* He also put this under his command and ordered it to Beckum. Ultimately, he could still incorporate five assault guns and four Tigers into his fighting force. They were supposed to be moved up to the *Panzer Lehr Division,* and even though they had been resupplied with ammunition, they had no more fuel.

With all these units, a defensive position was established adjacent to the outskirts of Beckum; the tanks were deployed, two each at the main exit roads, since they were just about immobile. One tank served as the mobile reserve. Reconnaissance patrols were sent out toward Ahlen and Neubeckum. Toward 1600 hours, Dunker received binding orders from the district battle commandant of Soest, whose domain also included Beckum, to defend the town to the last man and to render an hourly status report. Since this order did not conflict with the Division order, Dunker was not concerned. In the afternoon, the enemy mounted his first assault against Beckum; it was repelled with two enemy tanks destroyed.

In the early evening, the first two companies of the *Field Replacement Battalion* arrived, and Dunker first granted them some rest. He ordered the responsible gentlemen of the town to come see him at 2200 hours, appointed a new mayor to replace the ailing one, and ordered the utilities to be shut down. He instructed the newly-appointed mayor to evacuate the civilians from the city and, after a harsh exchange of words with the district battle commandant from Soest, he managed to exempt the Lippe bridge near Herzfeld from the demolition that had been ordered for all of the Lippe bridges at midnight.

At 2245 hours, Dunker received a phone call from enemy-occupied Ahlen, where about 3,000 wounded were in the field hospital area. *Oberfeldarzt* Dr. Rosenbaum was on the phone, and after telling Dunker of his impression of the great strength of the Americans, he urged him not to defend Beckum, since it otherwise would be turned into rubble and ashes by 2330 hours. Dunker asked for time to think. After he received positive information about Dr. Rosenbaum, he carefully thought through the situation. In a second conversation with him at 2315 hours, Dunker tried to gain time and proposed a cease-fire until 0100 hours, to be able to enter negotiations with the American commander about declaring Beckum an open city. Dunker asked Dr. Rosenbaum to come see him as a parliamentary.

He then ordered the commanders of his units to report to him and asked them if any of them felt duty bound by the *Führer* order of 25 November 1944 and were willing defend Beckum and thereby assume command. After every single one refused, Dunker issued his orders for the evacuation of the city before 0130 hours on 1 April, for the retreat across the Lippe Bridge at Herzfeld, and for establishing a defense on the southern Lippe bank, between Lippstadt and Lippborg. He sent the staff officers of the *Field Replacement Battalion* out to stop the remaining companies of the battalion in their approach toward Beckum and to bring them the orders for deployment south of the Lippe. At 2340 hours, Dr. Rosenbaum telephoned again and reported that the order to fire had been cancelled. Now, an American translator got involved in the conversation, from whom Dunker requested that American troops not enter Beckum before 0600 hours. In further negotiations with the translator, behind whom an American colonel was standing who did not want to give his name, the Americans insisted on having their troops enter Beckum by 0200 hours. At 0050 hours, the talks came to an end.

Shortly thereafter, the Soest district battle commandant telephoned Dunker and objected to the absence of the hourly reports. A violent argument developed. Despite all reproaches, Dunker stuck to his decision and finally ended the conversation by declaring that he had no more time and would report in Soest and be available after leading his troops back. As he was leaving Beckum toward 0200 hours, the Americans already approached the city and announced their entrance with loudspeakers. At 0300 hours they moved in. Beckum was spared from the war. The city owes this to *Major* Dunker.

Now, Dunker wanted to drive to his staff in Oestinghausen, south of the Lippe, passing by the marching troops. But, when he came close to the bridge of Herzfeld, it blew up. Therefore, he had to divert his entire unit toward Lippstadt and it was largely possible to preserve them on the south bank of the river. One company, however, was destroyed by the enemy in Lippstadt.

Dunker drove via Oestinghausen to Soest and reported to the district battle commandant at 0900 hours on 1 April. After he sustained a severe bawling out, threats of a court-martial and a firing squad, his situation suddenly improved by the report that the enemy was advancing from the east toward Soest. Dunker and his troops were the only forces that could prevent a further advance. He received the order to take up position along the Rüthen–Erwitte–Lippstadt railroad line, and to hold there. This succeeded. At close range, Dunker experienced the linkup of the two American pincer armies south of Lippstadt in the afternoon. He passed this information on by radio to the *116th Panzer Division,* which departed from Recklinghausen to the east at just about this time. In its answer, the Division confirmed Dunker's new orders and informed him that he was again under the command of the *116th Panzer Division*. The first units from the Division arrived in the evening, reinforced Dunker's front, and took it over in the course of 2 April.

On this day, three different orders from corps headquarters were recorded in the duty officer's telephone log. The time of the first one was not recorded, but the log reflects the following, "New instructions: Division area Hamm for assault toward north, direction Münster. . . . The *Autobahn* bridge is to be seized in a surprise attack."[108]

At this point, the enemy had already reached Münster. The second order recorded was, "At 1700 hours, new order: Elimination of bridgehead near Hamm and also, further closing off in the area east of Soest."

Then, a third order that came in at 2320 hours noted, "Most of Division assemble south of Hamm for assault toward north or other directions. Secondary mission is to establish security east of Soest. If enemy in counterstrike tries to cross, demolish bridge."

In my report of 2 April, I described the events as follows:

At noon of this day, the Division was prohibited from attacking toward the east, and was ordered to leave a combat group near Erwitte, and then to attack north across the Lippe to push into flank and rear of the enemy that was advancing south of Münster toward the east.

The Division was of the opinion that:

1. For this, its forces were much too weak.
2. There was no longer any bridge available to cross the Lippe, or one that could be restored with our own means; therefore, the only remaining possibility to attack was toward the east.

In spite of this, the corps insisted on the order. The Division was told that the enemy forces advancing east were still weak, and that a breach through its rearward units in combined action with the assurance of an attack from area Münster would be quite possible. Thus, the Division was ordered to capture and repair the *Autobahn* bridge Uentrop and from there to attack toward north. When the Division, therefore, sent out an assault platoon from the *Engineer Battalion* and it established that the bridge could not be repaired with the Division's means, the Division was ordered to attack toward north out of bridgehead Hamm.

It turned out that this order could not be accomplished either since, in the meantime, the enemy pushed in the bridgehead, took possession of the undamaged Hamm railroad bridge, and, on its part, established a bridgehead there across the Lippe. In the evening, the Division was ordered to remove the enemy Hamm bridgehead and to destroy the bridge. Then, the Division ordered the reinforced *Panzer-Grenadier Regiment 60* to take over the front between Belecke and the Lippe, and *Panzer-Grenadier Regiment 156* (minus one battalion) to control the Lippe up to the Uentrop bridge. For the battle in Hamm, a combat group was formed from the *Engineer Battalion,* the *Armored Reconnaissance Battalion,* and one battalion of

Panzer-Grenadier Regiment 156, as well as most of the Division's artillery. This combat group was relocated to Hamm-South during the night of 2/3 April.

With this, the last possibility of breaking out of the cauldron was wasted. Two weeks of heavy defensive battles in the cauldron began.[109]

Now, again, we take a glance at the enemy and at the development of the situation at large since 29 March. The American war history states the following:

> Renewing the attack on 29 March, the 8th Armored Division found the enemy's *116th Panzer Division* which, as part of *General* Lüttwitz's *XLVII Panzer Corps,* had thwarted a breakout from the Rhine bridgehead, still making a fight of it. By nightfall, the American armor claimed Dorsten, but it had been a plodding fight against an enemy helped by marshy ground, woods, and deadly nests of big anti-aircraft guns in concrete emplacements. Given the wooded nature of the terrain east of Dorsten, there was no evidence but that the same kind of slow, dogged advance might be in the offing for days.[110]

As we saw, this assessment proved to be correct. The American offensive north of the Lippe and in the breach area south of the Sieg, however, unfolded quite differently. The 2d Armored Division pushed forward north of the Lippe. It took Ahlen on 31 March and stood at the *Autobahn* near Wiedenbrück. It chased *Major* Dunker out of Beckum, pushed up to the Teutoburg Forest on 1 April, and together with units from the 3d Armored Division, which arrived from south at the spearhead of First Army, the 2d closed the cauldron near Lippstadt. North of the 2d, the 5th Armored Division passed by Münster and reached Telgte.

The situation in Hesse and Franconia became more dangerous still. The First and Third Armies streamed into central Germany on a wide front. Paderborn fell on 1 April. The enemy stood before Kassel and Fulda, and was near Eisenach by 2 April. The southern 6th Army Group fought at Würzburg and advanced toward Heilbronn and Bruchsal. On the next day, the enemy already stood near Osnabrück, Herford, Vlotho on the Weser, Mühlhausen, Gotha and Meiningen. The enemy reached the Weser on 4 April near and north of Minden, as well as near Rinteln and Hameln. In the east, the Soviets took Wiener-Neustadt. The battles of Danzig and Königsberg were coming to an end. The front by the Oder was still quiet.

On 4 April, the aforementioned Eisenhower directive went into effect, which moved the main effort of the offensive to the interior of the *Reich,* to the center in the zone of the 12th Army Group (Bradley). For his center field army, First Army, Bradley set Leipzig as the objective, for the Third Army on the right, it was Chemnitz. The Ninth Army on the left was to reach the Elbe between Dessau and Wittenberge and to "be ready to continue the attack on Berlin or toward northwest." This plan by Bradley kept the Ninth Army's vain hope alive, to still be able to seize Berlin before the Russians arrived. But not all units from the First and Ninth Armies could start advancing toward the east. Two corps from each, with fifteeen divisions combined, remained back for the encirclement of *Army Group B.* Aside from this, the three divisions of the Fifteenth Army were kept at the Rhine front, between Sieg and the Ruhr estuaries. Thus, *Army Group B* tied down a total of eighteen American divisions. The boundary between the First and Ninth Armies was established along the Ruhr.

In the beginning, opposite the *116th Panzer Division* at the eastern front of the cauldron, were units from the 1st Infantry Division north of the Möhne, as well as units from the 2d and 3d Armored Divisions near Lippstadt. Elements of the 15th Cavalry Group were deployed along the Lippe between Lippstadt and Hamm. On 2 April, units from the 83d Infantry Division appeared near Lippstadt and Hamm. On 4 April, under command of the 19th Corps, the 8th Armored Division, known from Rheinberg and Kirchhellen, fought between the Möhne and the Lippe, and the 95th Infantry Division fought near and east of Hamm. South of the Ruhr, in the First Army area of operations, the III Corps assumed control. Subordinated to it were the 7th Armored and the 99th Infantry Divisions. The 9th Infantry Division, which first fought at the right wing of the corps, was later replaced by the 5th. The attack from the south against *Army Group B* was led by General Ridgway's XVIII Airborne Corps.

On 31 March, shortly before its encirclement, *Army Group B* rendered a status report to *Supreme Commander–West,* and requested the establishment of a strong front behind the Army Group, out of which "attacks were to be mounted with sufficient forces to cut off the penetrating enemy and to establish the link-up with Army Group."[111] Otherwise, Model requested to be granted freedom of action in the form of a directive for a longer period of time.

To establish a front east of *Army Group B, Headquarters 11th Army* was brought in.[112] As far as troops were concerned, almost the only units available were those battered elements of *LXVI* and *LXVII Corps* of the otherwise encircled army, and *Heimat Truppen Teile* ("Home Units") of the substitute *VI* and *IX Corps* areas [These are garrison and administrative units assigned to *Wehrkreise VI* and *IX,* or *Corps Areas VI* (Westphalia) and *IX* (Hesse), which answered to the *Commander, Replacement Army—Editor*]. A strong assault toward the west was not to be considered with these troops. The only attempt, by *SS-Brigade Westfalen* south of Paderborn, failed after minor initial successes. The *11th Army* sector stretched from Hameln up to the middle of Thuringia. As of 2 April, *11th Army* appears in the daily reports within the framework of *Army Group B,* even though it could no longer be controlled by it anymore, but received its orders directly from *Supreme Command–West.*

On the evening of 4 April, *11th Army* Headquarters received orders to attack south into the left flank of Patton's Army, which had pushed into Thuringia near Mühlhausen and Gotha. It was attempted with weak forces and failed. An attack to free *Army Group B* was now totally impossible. As consolation, the *12th Army,* known also as *"Army Wenck,"* was established. This did not show up in the "daily reports" until 12 April, when it was near the Elbe and ultimately made an about face toward the east to free Berlin.

After declining a breakout, *Army Group B* postured itself to defend its area. Its attack toward the east near Winterberg failed on 1 April. On 3 April, the opposing attack came to a halt near Willebadessen (22 kilometers southeast of Paderborn). That was 60 kilometers northeast of Winterberg! There could also be no help expected from the Kassel area. This city fell on 4 April, after four days of fighting.

On this day, "*Group Lüttwitz*" (*XLVII Panzer Corps* and *LXIII Corps*) subordinated to *Army Group B,* appears in the "daily report" for the first time. Earlier, the reports about the events of *XLVII Panzer Corps* are still found under *Army Group H* with the *1st Parachute Army.* On 31 March, *OKW* ordered *Army Group H* to reestablish contact within the *1st Parachute Army* by attacking to the south and from the south toward Münster. *Generaloberst* Student appeared at Army Group to command the counterattack. On 1 and 2 April at the *1st Parachute Army,* he convinced himself of the impossibility of carrying out this *OKW* order.[113] Here is where to find the source for the orders for the *116th Panzer Division* by *XLVII Panzer Corps.*

On the evening of 2 April, the *116th Panzer Division* prepared to carry out the order that was forced on it to attack Hamm. *Hauptmann* Zanzinger wrote about this day:

> New command post at the Hense farm. There, the regimental commander assigns to me the Hovestadt–Benninghausen sector and the *Volkssturm* units there.
>
> The commander of *Battalion Benninghausen* declares to make it on his own in his sector. He needs no help. "A US officer, being a parliamentary, was just turned back! We defend our homeland!"
>
> Afternoon US artillery fire. The *Volkssturm* commander calls up in despair, "I have only 15 men left, the others went home." The abandoned weapons are lying in the empty foxholes.
>
> I deploy the *6th Company* as motorized fire fighters in this section. Eikelborn is in the security sector. This village serves as a "hospital town" and cannot be approached from any side closer than one kilometer. We, as well as the Amis precisely hold to these rules.[114]

Leutnant Schwörer from *2d Battalion, Armored Artillery Regiment 146* also reports about parliamentarians. One of them announced a major attack and carpet bombing if there were no negotiations. In Benninghausen at 1320 hours, the deadline for the surrender was set for 1430 hours. The rejection had no consequences. On 2 April, the opposing side was still too weak for this. Schwörer further noted:

> A loudspeaker is set up on the other side of the Lippe. Following this, the veterinary soldiers . . . surrender to the enemy. [These were medical personnel from a

horse cavalry unit—*Editor.*] In front of all eyes, 75 men out of 100 run away. To us, this is understandable. We no longer blame these people.

At Benninghausen, [most] of a *Hauptmann's* men went over to the other side. He . . . still has a total of 6 men.[115]

In the latter case, it may have been the same troop unit that Zanzinger mentioned.

Unfortunately, the telephone log of the Division relates little about 3 April.[116] Accordingly, *Armored Reconnaissance Battalion 116* and *Armored Engineer Battalion 675* were already set to march toward Hamm on the evening of 2 April, while *Panzer-Grenadier Regiment 156* (but obviously only its *2d Battalion*), the *2d Battalion, Armored Artillery Regiment 146,* and 25 tanks followed on the morning of 3 April. *Panzer-Grenadier Regiment 60,* with the *Division Escort Company* and ten tanks, remained east of Soest, supported by an artillery battalion. Per *Hauptmann* Tzschentke's description, *Regiment 60* had deployed its *2d Battalion* in front of Anröchte, and the *Field Replacement Battalion* was near Erwitte. The command post of *Hauptmann* Inboden, who in the morning of 3 April again took over command of the battalion from *Major* Dunker, was in Stirpe. The *1st Battalion, Panzer-Grenadier Regiment 156* linked up to the left with its command post in the Brockhof farm, the commander now being *Hauptmann* Gerling. On 3 April, this battalion was relieved by the *Division Escort Company* under the command of *Hauptmann* Rudolph.[117] The *1st Battalion, Panzer-Grenadier Regiment 156* probably assumed the security mission at the Lippe, instead of the *2d Battalion* that was pulled out. Exactly where the *1st Battalion, Panzer-Grenadier Regiment 60* was deployed cannot be established. Tzschenke also reported that he gave one *Volkssturm Company* each to *2d Battalion, Panzer-Grenadier Regiment 60* and *1st Battalion, Panzer-Grenadier Regiment 156*; the latter consisted of miners from Marl and was deployed in Overhagen, southwest of Lippstadt. On 3 April, the log closes, "Attack planned for removal of bridgehead and establishing our own."[118]

Command for the attack was assigned to *Major* Dunker.[119] *Hauptmann* Zanzinger's diary offers information about the preparation for the attack.[120] His battalion was in Westtünnen as the Division reserve. Very soon, Zanzinger was ordered to the advanced command post of the Division in the Argonne Barracks in Hamm. *Generalmajor* von Waldenburg was also there, while the Division command post moved to Osterbönen. The battle commandant of Hamm was subordinated to the Division.[121] Reconnaissance showed that the Americans widened their bridgehead and already occupied the preparation areas we had intended to use for the attack. Therefore, the attack could not be carried out as planned. A request by the Division to completely abstain from it was denied. The attack's objective was now limited to the removal of the American bridgehead and the destruction of the 11-track railroad bridge.

Therefore, the order for the Division, which was preserved by Zanzinger, said:

Order for the attack on Hamm railroad station.

1. Enemy. In battalion strength, enemy has occupied the railroad station, post office, Hotel Schloss, and the northern part of the Union-Works south of the Lippe.

2. The *116th Panzer Division* attacks enemy with *Armored Reconnaissance Battalion 116* and *2d Battalion, Panzer-Grenadier Regiment 156* using strike troops conducting a pincer movement, destroys enemy, and occupies terrain until relief by other units.

3. Execution in detail:

   a) *Armored Engineer Strike Force.*
   One tank with three trucks in tow drives from the east on the road along the river bank to below the bridge. Under the bridge, it unhooks the trucks and ignites the charge (trucks to be loaded with seven tons of explosives), then drives west under the bridge and strives to push through to *2d Battalion, Panzer-Grenadier Regiment 156.* Behind the trucks rolls a second tank, which, in case the ignition fails, fires at the charge.

   b) *Armored Reconnaissance Battalion 116* and *2d Battalion, Panzer-Grenadier Regiment 156,* after detonation succeeds, attack the enemy with strike platoons on the bank from east and west, close off near the crater with one group from each toward the north, and clear out the positions of the enemy toward the south.

   c) The two clearing platoons follow immediately behind the assault platoons and mop up remaining enemy resistance, take over the positions stormed by the strike platoons, and secure the captured positions toward the east and west, respectively.

   d) The reserve platoons follow the clearing troops, to immediately replenish losses of personnel and materiel, respectively, and to relieve the remaining elements of the strike platoons.

   e) Artillery support: Total available artillery (approximately 10 battalions) fires box barrage during operation to the area north of the detonated bridge. . . .

8. Commence attack: 0630 hours.[122]

The explosion failed. The tank towing the trucks hit a mine shortly before it reached the bridge.[123] The engineer riding on it, *Leutnant* Fütterer, remained missing. The trucks were fired at by the accompanying tank and exploded, but without effect on the bridge.[124] The *Armored Reconnaissance Battalion* mounted the attack and achieved some success. The *2d Battalion, Panzer-Grenadier Regiment 156* did not hear the detonation and, therefore, did not attack.

Soon after the failure in Hamm became known, alarming news arrived from the east and northeast fronts of the Division. On 3 April, vigorous movements and brisk reconnaissance activity by the enemy were already reported by *Panzer-Grenadier Regiment 60*. Strong enemy movements north of the Lippe did not promise much good. During the night of 3/4 April, the enemy crossed the Lippe northeast of Hamm, south of Dolberg.[125] On 4 April at 1000 hours, the first reports of enemy attacks arrived at the Division: From Eikeloh with tanks west toward Erwitte, and from Lippstadt southwest, upstream along the Gieseler creek near Overhagen.[126] An assault across the Lippe near Herzfeld was turned back. Besides this, an attack was reported across the Lippe from Lippborg toward the Ahse, between Hachenei and Dinker. Enemy reconnaissance patrols were already in Berwicke (two kilometers south of the Ahse). Ultimately, the enemy crossed the Lippe side-canal near Uentrop in battalion strength.

After this, corps headquarters permitted cessation of the attack in Hamm. In the interest of the city and the population, this was indeed urgently needed. The entire front from Belecke on the Möhne up to Hamm, including the area for which the Soest battle commandant was responsible, were subordinated to the Division (a sector of more than 60 kilometers). Like the battle commandant of Hamm, the one in Soest had only weak forces unused to battle, without heavy weapons and without sufficient leadership at his disposal.[127] Along with the tanks at Hamm, the *1st Battalion, Panzer-Grenadier Regiment 156* was deployed against the enemy attacking south and southwest from Lippborg. The remaining forces of the *116th Panzer Division* in Hamm were also withdrawn from the front at noon. The *2d Battalion, Panzer-Grenadier Regiment 156* was relocated to Mawicke (eight kilometers west of Soest) as reserve, and the *1st Company* of the *Engineer Battalion* was deployed to secure the *Autobahn* bridge across the Ahse, west of Dinker.[128,129] The staff of *Panzer-Grenadier Regiment 156* took over control of the sector north of Soest up to the *Autobahn*.[130] The *2d Battalion* of *Armored Artillery Regiment 146,* which depended on joint action with the regiment, took up positions in the area northwest of Werl.[131]

In the evening, the enemy stood at the Ahse, in some places already south of the stream. The Division's eastern front had to be withdrawn. The enemy advanced up to Schmerlecke–Millinghausen–Eickelborn.[132] The second to last entry in the duty officer's log recorded the destruction of 22 enemy tanks on 4 April, including 15 by *Panzer Regiment 16* and 7 by *Panzer-Grenadier Regiment 60.*[133] In the evening, the commander of Combat Command R of the 8th Armored Division, Colonel Wallace, fell into the hands of the *116th Panzer Division* near Horn.[134] Our own losses affected the Division painfully. Among others, three of four *Panzer IVs* from the *8th Company* of *Panzer Regiment 16* were lost south of Norddorf.[135]

Supreme Command–West's daily report of 4 April about *Group Lüttwitz* stated the following:

> The enemy pushed out of Geseke with heavy infantry and tank forces along the road to the west, took Erwitte, and was brought to a standstill during his further advance toward Soest by our counterattack along the line Waltringhausen–Schmerlecke–Merklinghausen (ten kilometers southeast, east and northeast of Soest) and lost ten tanks. A second enemy spearhead pushed forward via Nateln (24 kilometers west of Erwitte), up to Dinker. Along the *Autobahn*, the opponent attempted to push via

Uentrop (nine kilometers east of Hamm) toward Dortmund. The enemy advanced south via Waltrop (14 kilometers east of Recklinghausen) and was brought to a halt north of Brambauer. However, he succeeded in pushing forward via Ickern south of the *Autobahn* toward the east, north of Mengede, and to advance to the northern outskirts of Castrop-Rauxel.[136]

On 5 April, the enemy continued his attack along the entire front between the Möhne and Hamm. At the east front, the main effort was on both sides of the Soest–Erwitte road. There, Waldhausen, Altenmellrich, Altengeseke, Sehringhausen and Schallern were lost. Northwest of Soest, the opponent pushed ahead to the Soest–Hamm railroad and crossed it in some places. In Hamm, he also gained terrain. Our front line was taken back to the eastern part of the Möhnesee–Bad Sassendorf–Soest Nord, then along the Soest–Hamm railroad.[137]

On 5 April, the engineers of *1st Company, Armored Engineer Battalion 675* erected barricades in the vicinity of Flerke–Scheidingen. The engineers' task for 6 April was to secure the bridge across the Möhnesee near Delecke.[138] The Division reserve, *2d Battalion, Panzer-Grenadier Regiment 156,* located northwest of Soest, had remained untouched until this point. Its commander, *Hauptmann* Zanzinger, wrote, "On both sides of Schwefe [five kilometers northwest of Soest—*Author*], we established a blocking position—to the south *Panzer-Grenadier Regiment 60,* to the north, *1st Battalion, Panzer-Grenadier Regiment 156.*[139]

The Division command post was relocated to Hünningen (seven kilometers southeast of Werl).[140]

The *116th Panzer Division* got into a very critical situation on 6 April. It was again attacked along the entire front. The last entry in the telephone log, unfortunately without mentioning the time, reads, "Enemy in Borgeln. Enemy allegedly in the direction of Rhynern."[141] Hamm was lost, as well as East and West Tünnen. At first, only weak thrusts took place between the *Autobahn* and Soest-North. Aside from Borgeln, the enemy took Hattrop. In the evening, Soest was attacked from the north and during the night it was seized. South of Soest, near *Panzer-Grenadier Regiment 60,* the enemy made a deep breach with tanks and pushed through to southwest of the city.[142] Parts of the Division were encircled. *Major* Schmeermann, commander of *3d Battalion, Armored Artillery Regiment 146,* with his command post in Wippringsen (seven kilometers south of Soest), recorded in his diary, "Crazy day, afternoon changing position (Haarweg). 2200 hours breakout from small cauldron near Soest."[143]

Leutnant Schwörer from *2d Battalion, Armored Artillery Regiment 146,* took the following notes:

More attacks at noon. *Panzer-Grenadier Regiment 60* is overrun. . . . *60* is completely torn apart. Enemy in front of Gerlingen [five kilometers southeast of Werl—*Author*]. . . . 2100 hours, firing positions change into area east of Werl to fire at tanks.[144]

Hauptmann Zanzinger recorded the following about the events at *2d Battalion, Panzer-Grenadier Regiment 156* on 6 April:

> Advances by the *Amis* against our front [on both sides of Schwefe—*Author*], then separation from *Panzer-Grenadier Regiment 60* and *1st Battalion.* We are between pincers, retreat to the sinew.[145]

Finally, *Leutnant* von Elterlein from *Panzer Regiment 16* wrote the following:

> 1500 hours, departure . . . to Sieveringen to the regimental command post. From there by car for reconnaissance to Niederense (*Ami* is said to have broken through near Möhne-Dam, emergency report!). Surprised by 40 Shermans, back to Sieveringen. There too, enemy with tanks in front of town. Machine-gun bursts and tank shells already hit the walls of our house. In wild flight, the entire regimental command post jumps out the windows into the vehicles . . . and off we go! . . . I escape the *Amis* by the skin of my teeth.[146]

Soest and Hamm were lost. About 4,500 imprisoned French officers and 600 men were in a camp in Soest. The Americans found them in good condition.[147] On 7 April, with much trouble, the torn-open front of the Division was successfully stabilized approximately along the following line: Niederense on Möhne–Westönnen–Niederbergstrasse–west of Rhynern–west of Hamm. In this approximately 30-kilometer-long front, the miserable infantry remnants assembled, with *Panzer-Grenadier Regiment 60* on the right; *Panzer-Grenadier Regiment 156* in the center, east and northeast of Werl; and at the left wing, the thrown-together units of the battle commandant of Hamm. Any energetic grip would cause the house of cards to collapse.

On the late morning of 7 April, the Division command post moved from Hünningen to Hohenheide near Fröndenberg.[148] On the afternoon of 6 April, after the arrival of the emergency report, it prepared to defend with everything available.[149] Shortly before, *Generalfeldmarschall* Model visited the command post in Hünningen. The situation was presented to him with all candor. He listened to it, but then spoke of the importance of defending Ruhr cauldron, of his plans for relief from the east by the new *12th Army,* and about mobilizing men and materiel in the cauldron. I added to it in 1947:

> After learning the situation at large, nobody from the Division believed in the possibility of a rescue force, and after the experiences with the *Volkssturm* and the elements that had been formed by "combing out," nobody believed the promises of personnel and materiel replacements.
>
> It was clear to us that we had to be self-reliant and persevere until the end with honor.[150]

As mentioned earlier, the opponent of the *116th Panzer Division* at the front in the east was the 8th Armored Division, and at the northern front, between Soest and Hamm, the 95th Infantry Division.[151] Both divisions were reinforced by tank destroyers and artillery, and the 95th also had an attached tank battalion. The decisive breakthrough by the 8th Armored Division passed south of Soest and followed this route: Brüllingsen–Ellingsen–Echtrop; along the hillside path of the Haarstrangs up to the vicinity of Bittingen; finally turning north via Sieveringen up to Ostönnen. It was conducted by Task Force van Houten of the 8th Armored's Combat Command B. According to the history of this division, it thereby took 500 prisoners, captured three tanks, four personnel carriers, four anti-tank guns, and other materiel. If all US units would have operated in this manner, the German resistance would have faltered quickly. On 5 March, van Houten had led the totally unsuccessful attack on Rheinberg, but since then had obviously gathered experience and applied what he learned.

The 194th Glider Infantry Regiment, which was attached to the 8th Armored Division, was deployed south of the Möhne. It took Kallenhardt and Warstein. On the German side, only weak forces from *Sperrverband* (*"Blocking Group"*) *Wirtz* fought there. *Generalleutnant* Wirtz was commander of engineers of *Army Group B* and he and his staff were assigned by Model to command the units that were thrown together on both sides of the Ruhr.[152] The leadership of the *116th Panzer Division* knew next to nothing about the existence of Wirtz. On 7 April, Task Force Twaddle was formed by the Commanding General of XIX Corps, to be commanded by Major General Twaddle of the 95th Infantry Division. It consisted of the elements of the corps that fought against *Army Group B,* including the reinforced 95th Infantry Division, the reinforced 8th Armored Division, the 194th Glider Infantry Regiment, and the 15th Cavalry Group. The remaining units of the corps had already crossed the Weser and pushed toward Hildesheim. This is where the corps staff needed to focus their attention. Therefore, on 8 April, Task Force Twaddle was subordinated to XVI Corps, which now commanded the entire northern front between the Rhine and the Ruhr near Meschede. The forces of the First Army that encircled the cauldron from south and east also mounted an attack on 5/6 of April against the cauldron, and achieved successes. Siegen, Schmallenberg and Winterberg were lost; the Americans stood before Meschede. In the western part of the northern front, XVI Corps crossed the Rhine-Herne Canal, north of Gelsenkirchen, and approached Dortmund from northwest.

On 7 April, the temporary security line of the *116th Panzer Division* was first only attacked in the sector held by *Panzer-Grenadier Regiment 156. Leutnant* Schwörer from *2d Battalion, Armored Artillery Regiment 146,* which supported *Regiment 156,* noted the following about mid-morning:

> From 0800 hours on, things go haywire. They already sit in Flerke, Niederbergstrasse, and Scheidingen. Some of our units still in Flerke. The *6th Company* encircled in Oberbergstrasse. Enemy with tanks from north toward Westönnen.
>
> *2d Battalion* [*Panzer-Grenadier Regiment 156*] retreats. [*2d*] *Battalion* [*Armored Artillery Regiment 146*] must change position.[153]

The commander of the *2d Battalion* had a somewhat different picture:

> At the crack of dawn, US tanks break through the position of *1st Battalion, Panzer-Grenadier Regiment 156* and encircle the *6th*, which is in position in Niederbergstrasse. The *8th Company* with 30 men and the *12th Company* with 15 men block off behind the *6th Company*; the *9th* and *10th Companies* are also still battleworthy. Toward noon, a company messenger from the *6th* arrived, "Tanks run down our houses, set them on fire. Schutow."
>
> This is the last message from the *6th*.[154]

It remains to be seen who was wrong. In any case, the 3d Battalion from the 377th Infantry Regiment took Nieder- and Oberbergstrasse and pushed through up to the vicinity northeast of Werl.[155]

Hauptmann Zanzinger further noted the following:

> A tragic incident happens in Westönnen. *Oberleutnant* Junge reports, "The civilians pit the soldiers against the officers, and nab messenger." The people are actually urging the soldiers to stop the senseless war and to disarm the officers. Besides this, supply vehicles are plundered near Westönnen. A patrol under *Leutnant* Fricke re-establishes calm.
>
> The mood varies. Soldiers who are at home in the area quickly visit their families and return to the troops, some in civilian clothes, since they have to beat their way through the US front line. My driver, Anton Bauer simply says, "In the good days, I was *116th*; now down and out, I will stick with it."
>
> On 27 March, *Oberleutnant* Noltensmeyer, commander of the *7th Company*, became a prisoner, battled his way through and returns to the battalion completely exhausted. He remains with the supply company and established a new *7th* from stragglers. A new *6th* is also being formed; by the evening, a *Leutnant* reports that it has 40 men.[156]

In this manner, the infantry units are always being replenished, but easy come, easy go.

In the afternoon of 7 April, the 8th Armored Division mounted an attack toward the west, out of Ostönnen and Ampen. Combat Command B took Westönnen and Gerlingen despite strong resistance, but at dusk remained its newly-gained line.[157] In addition to the two arches already destroyed, the engineers of the Division stationed at the bridge across the Möhnesee south of the Lecke blew up a third one just as the enemy was on it.[158]

Now the town of Werl became the front line and was called a "stronghold." A battle commandant had to be appointed and *General* von Lüttwitz assigned *Major* Dunker to the job.[159] Lüttwitz had initiated a court-martial against him because he surrendered Beckum without a fight against orders, as it was reported by Soest battle commandant. Lüttwitz counted on Dunker becoming a prisoner in Werle and, thereby, the trial would take care of itself.

Dunker assumed his duties on 7 April. Besides the units that were in Werl, including the *Volkssturm Battalion Werl,* the *2d Battalion, Regiment 156* was subordinated to him. Before the Americans entered, the *Volkssturm* threw its weapons into the water basins of the fire brigade and dispersed. Zanzinger wrote:

> New order: *"2d Battalion, Panzer-Grenadier Regiment 156* is ordered to occupy *Stronghold Werl.* Report 2400 hours in command post to battle commandant of Werl, *Major* Dunker." With *Leutnant* Holzinger I drive into town. Darkness, heavy damage in the streets, artillery fire on the town. I report to Dunker and present my request, to release us from Werl, since it makes no sense to stay in town. He faces a dilemma but decides, "Immediately relocate battalion to western outskirts of Werl. I take full responsibility."
>
> Werl was quickly traversed and a new position taken up in the vicinity of Budberg. We thereby got into a village already occupied by the *Amis,* which caused losses, especially to the *8th.*[160]

On the morning of 8 April, the *116th Panzer Division* stood approximately along the line Neheim–Höingen–Bremen–Werl–Budberg–Westhilbeck–Pelkum. From there, the front of *Group Lüttwitz* stretched to the northern edge of Dortmund and further across the northern edge of Gelsenkirchen up to the Rhine-Herne Canal, to Duisburg on the Rhine.[161] There was only insufficient news about the developments on the Division's right flank and its rear.

Early on 8 April, the enemy attacked the Division's right wing, as well as the sector between Werl and the Lippe. At the eastern front of the Division, Höingen and Bremen were lost.[162] The opponent here was Combat Command R of the 8th Armored Division. North of it, Combat Command B was turned back. The history of the 8th Armored Division states the following:

> Attempting to carry out the original attack plan on Werl, Task Force Roseborough jumped off at 0700. Meeting heavy resistance at Blumenthal, the advance bogged down. At 1030, Colonel Kimball ordered Colonel Roseborough to break contact, return to West Onnen, and pass through Task Force van Houten, which would remain to form a base of fire. Since the infantry elements of Task Force Roseborough were heavily engaged, a lengthy delay was involved in breaking contact.[163]

In the afternoon of that day, after artillery preparation, the enemy, Combat Command B with Task Force van Houten, mounted the attack on Werl and captured it by evening. Prior to this, the Americans telephoned from Westönnen and requested the surrender of the town. When *Major* Dunker refused, Werl was covered with artillery fire from 1500 to 1700 hours. With the last shots, the first tanks rolled into town. Upon renewed request to surrender the town, the mayor and police chief surrendered. Earlier, *Major* Dunker left the command post and went to the nearby forest. From there, with 30 men, he beat his way back through the enemy to our lines during the night.[164]

On 8 April, west of Werl the situation again came to a head for *Panzer-Grenadier Regiment 156*. The diaries of *Hauptmann* Zanzinger and *Leutnant* Schwörer show it clearly. Schwörer noted:

> Enemy attack on Budberg. It is also lost right away. We fire at it. It should be closed off . . . enemy advances further. Tanks are always there; without these, the enemy would not advance either.
>
> *Hauptmann* Gerling, *1st Battalion, Panzer-Grenadier Regiment 156,* wounded, taken prisoner. Firing on Budberg. Thereby, one enemy tank was damaged. We can see it being towed away.
>
> Battalion has to provide two platoons of riflemen. They are now supposed to hold everything in check.[165]

Zanzinger wrote, "The *1st Battalion, Panzer-Grenadier Regiment 156* again suffers heavy losses, the commander is taken prisoner, the remnants are subordinated to *2d Battalion, Panzer-Grenadier Regiment 156.* At the eastern edge of Büderich, new position."[166]

Zanzinger's command post was in Holtum. By evening, the battalion was withdrawn toward Hemmerde, the command post established in Stockum. Between Budberg and the Lippe, the enemy attack was conducted by the 95th Infantry Division. On the left, between Sönnern and Rhynern, was the 379th Infantry Regiment; on the latter's left wing, the 1st Battalion fought against *Panzer-Grenadier Regiment 156* at Hilbeck and Budberg. In Budberg, the Americans committed an atrocity. There, they took several prisoners. One of them, the then-17-year-old Friedrich Schmidthausen, reported the following after the war:

> In the early morning hours of 8 April, during an American surprise attack, we were taken prisoner. Besides me, there were seven members of the *116th Panzer Division,* including the already-severely-wounded *Hauptmann* Gerling. A few minutes after we were captured, additional American soldiers brought another six prisoners from a street not far from the Borg house. Shortly after the arrival of this group, we had to stand against a wall, facing it. At almost the same moment, shots were fired out of some windows of the Borg house. Shots by the Americans and the screams of women and children now intermingled in the ensuing chaos. I could not observe exactly what was happening, since we were hindered by the American MPs. After the skirmish was over, we were taken into the house and kept under heavy guard. In the meantime, the American soldiers killed in the early morning battle were placed under our window. We were then forced to look at the dead. After an infantry lieutenant from our group had been interrogated, we were informed at 1030 hours that we would be shot toward 1830 hours in the evening.
>
> In the course of the afternoon, the seven youngest of us were picked out to be shot ahead of the others. However, this plan was dropped after the insistance of the infantry lieutenant and our protests. Toward 1800 hours, the Americans took us to their command post. We carried the seriously-wounded *Hauptmann* Gerling on an

unhinged door. At the command post, a few American officers questioned us again about the events. The correct response to the questions was in part impossible, because we did not understand them. During the march through Budberg, the commanding officer gave orders to line us up and to fire.

From the 14 of us, three were wounded, but stayed alive. These were an elderly *Volkssturm* man, an officer cadet, and me. I would also like to mention that the Americans used explosive ammunition for the executions. Two comrades who fled into a nearby barn were recaptured the following day. I cannot give any information about their whereabouts. At dusk on the same day, the fallen comrades were taken away by truck. I myself was hit seven times and with the kind help of a Russian and a German girl, I got to a field hospital in the afternoon of 10 April.[167]

The history of the 95th Infantry Division does not mention this incident. For the fighting in the West, this was an unusual incident.

On 8 April, the *116th Panzer Division* withdrew its right wing behind the Ruhr and gave up Waltringen. On the morning of 9 April, the front stretched from west of Waltringen toward Hemmerde. The Hamm battle commandant's troops were attacked on 8 April again and retreated to a line that ran approximately from Lenningsen via Bönen toward Nordbögge.[168] On 8 April, between the Möhne and the Ruhr, Hirschberg fell into enemy hands. The 377th Infantry Regiment of the 95th Infantry Division, which was released near Soest, was deployed here to the right of the 194th Glider Infantry Regiment. From both regiments and with additions from other service branches, Task Force Faith was established under the acting commander of the 95th, Brigadier General Faith.[169]

The events in this area remained more or less hidden from the leadership of the *116th Panzer Division.* Not until after the capture of Neheim on 11 April did it come into direct enemy contact.

The example of *2d Battalion* of *Panzer-Grenadier Regiment 156* shows how the ever-dwindling infantry forces of the Division were replenished. On 8 April, the commander of that battalion recorded the following:

> . . . *Anti-Aircraft Battalion Jäger* is being attached. The battalion commander, *Oberstleutnant* Jäger, harbors concerns that he should be subordinated to a *Hauptmann.* But the arrangement is as follows: He remains with the staff, takes care of the logistical part, establishes the new command post, and always keeps the morale up with stories he has in stock. The employment of his men is more difficult. It was a heavy homefront anti-aircraft battalion that was taken out of action, and instead of the 8.8cm, was only equipped with rifles, machine guns (Danish ones nobody could operate), and *Panzerfausts* (which nobody could handle). It was to go into an infantry battle. The officers—elegant, with ties and high boots—are being issued clothes by me through the supply company and the soldiers are divided into our companies. The battle value of this unit was about equal to that of the *Hitler Youth Company* which was subordinated on 27 March near Besten.[170]

On 9 April, *Generalmajor* von Waldenburg wrote down, "Very dense fog! Attack along entire front! Relocate command post behind the Ruhr!"[171]

On 9 April, near *Panzer-Grenadier Regiment 60,* the enemy penetrated into the forest northwest of Waltringen. *Major* Schmeermann, who supported the regiment with his *3d Battalion,* recorded, "Enemy attacks destroyed with artillery fire. In the evening, quiet."[172]

It was also calm on the right wing, between Neheim and Echthausen. In contrast, *Regiment 156* was again hard hit by the enemy attack. *Leutnant* Schwörer wrote about 9 April in his diary, "During the whole day, the enemy attacks everywhere and throws the units. . . . We fire heavily into all villages."[173]

Hauptmann Zanzinger noted the following:

0430 hours, tank attack by the *Ami* against Hemmerde.

Defense all around Stockum. On the roads leading to the rear, I position officers to collect stragglers and bring them to the unit. It is now important to continue the turn to the south across the Ruhr. In the afternoon, new position near Siddinghausen, staff in Ostbüren.[174]

In the evening, Wiehagen at the northwestern edge of Wickede, was attacked. Here, the *1st Company* of the *Engineer Battalion* occupied positions. *Oberleutnant* Varnholt's diary says, "Company secures Wiehagen near Werl. Road Werl–Wickede. Toward 2100 hours a tank attack occurred that was a complete surprise. Hereby, an undetermined number of engineers were killed or taken prisoner."[175]

As a consequence, the front was taken further back north of the Ruhr. *Hauptmann* Zanzinger remarked:

At 0100 hours, pull back west of Wickede, east of Bausenhagen, staff in Tummelplatz.[176] [500 meters southwest of Stentrop—*Author*]

In the evening, the Division staff relocated from Hohenheide into the Barge and Werringsen farmhouses, south of the Ruhr. *Generalleutnant* Bayerlein, commanding general of *LIII Corps,* visited the Division while it was still in Hohenheide. He and his staff were released from the eastern front near Schmallenberg. On 10 April, he was to assume command in the former sector of *XLVII Panzer Corps,* which means, of the *116th Panzer Division,* the staff of *190th Infantry Division* with *Combat Groups Unna* and *Hamm,* as well as of a security regiment and of the *180th Infantry Division* near Dortmund. As of 10 April, *General* von Lüttwitz and his corps staff, as a higher headquarters, commanded both corps of the northern front, the *LIII* and *LXIII Corps,* and not only their three divisions with *LXIII Corps.* The sector of the *190th Infantry Division,* to the left of the *116th,* which was still able to be held on 9 April, stretched from south of Lünern to Weddinghofen, northwest of Kamen.[177] Since *Generalmajor* von Waldenburg was with *Panzer-Grenadier Regiment 60* on the afternoon of 9 April, I presented the situation to *General* Bayerlein, who "approved of the Division's opinion that the only remaining course was to persevere until an honorable end and to avoid any somehow unnecessary sacrifice of men and valuables."[178]

General von Lüttwitz reported about a conversation with Bayerlein from 8 April:

> In a very serious discussion, the hopeless situation is addressed and an agreement is reached on all points. It is established that, as before, no unnecessary losses should result from senseless resistance. Special reference was made to avoid the destruction of the Ruhr bridges, since this would make the water supply for the industrial areas impossible.[179]

During the prior days, Lüttwitz had already come to an agreement with an industry representative that no factory would be seriously destroyed, only some individual ones were to be paralyzed. A hospital situated in the vicinity of Wimbern in the new Ruhr front was evacuated using the Division's ambulances during the night of 9/10 April; the area around the hospital was kept free of troops.

On the morning of 10 April 10, enemy tanks fired on the Division command post from the hills north of the Ruhr near Wiehagen.[180] The 8th Armored Division and the 95th Infantry Division again mounted an attack along the entire front between the Ruhr and the Lippe.[181] Combat Command R attacked with its southern group due north of the Ruhr and pushed forward up to Stentrop. A northern group took Bausenhagen and pushed into Frömern by evening. Combat Command B was to continue the attack on Unna. Lünern was taken with help from units of the 95th Infantry Division. Other units took Ostbüren and Kessebüren. On 10 April, the 95th Infantry Division reached the following line: Mühlhausen (3.5 kilometers northeast of Unna)–Kamen–Horstmar–southern part of Lünen. Task Force Faith occupied the remaining area between the Möhne and the Ruhr, and now stood between Arnsberg and Neheim at the northeast bank of the Ruhr. On 10 April, it was quiet between Neheim and Wickede.

Again, the whole burden rested on *Panzer-Grenadier Regiment 156,* north of the Ruhr. *Leutnant* Schwörer wrote about it:

> Early in the morning, enemy attacks along entire front.
>
> Bausenhagen is taken by opponent, and a strong tank assault rolls over the entire main battle line, west of Wickede. Also near Ostbüren, the opponent's armored forces succeed in overrunning our main battle line. Large parts of all the infantry are captured, or better, let themselves be captured. Many desert.
>
> Grollmann moves into a new main battle line with fewer people each time. Strength of the battalions not more than 30 men.
>
> During the whole day in very bright weather, continuous fighter bomber attacks over the entire sector. Commanding General Bayerlein at command post. Division receives new orders to prevent opponent's breakthrough south of Unna. Grollmann continues command in this sector.

Ten *Jagdtigers* are deployed south of Unna to prevent the breakthrough. [The *Jagdpanzer VI Jagdtiger,* or "Hunting Tiger" was the tank destroyer variant of the King Tiger, or Tiger II heavy tank. It mounted a 128mm main gun in its turretless superstructure, and was the most heavily-armored—and heaviest—armored vehicle of WWII—*Editor.*][182]

Hauptmann Zanzinger's notes supplement this:

> In the morning, sounds of combat, especially near the *8th Company.* I drive to Junge by motorcycle. Breakfast on the table—bread, coffee half-consumed—this must have happened quickly.
>
> Rifle shots hit . . . .
>
> Back to the command post. There, tank rounds burst in.
>
> Relocate further toward Hohenheide. Even there, already enemy fire.
>
> Back to Fröndenberg, on to Ardey. There, the Regimental Commander, "give you six tanks, at once counterstrike on Fröndenberg." Whatever for? The commander says, "Quickly, so I can report it as carried out!" Company commanders for conference, "We attack Fröndenberg." The answer of the commanders is, "Idiocy, my men cannot do it anymore!" Then I report, "Against strong enemy resistance, battalion could not advance and holds Ardey." Answer by the regiments, "We have tried it; if it didn't work, there is nothing one can do."[183]

In my 1947 report, I wrote about the end of the battles of 10 April:

> During the night, the Division retreated to the south bank of the Ruhr up to Fröndenberg. Only one combat group (*Panzer-Grenadier Regiment 156*) remained north of the river on a line Fröndenberg–west of Frömern.
>
> Since the main effort of the enemy's attack was expected there, *Heavy Tank Destroyer Battalion 512* (consisting of four Hunting Tigers) depended on cooperation of the combat group and was deployed in the area west of Frömern. The Ruhr bridges were not destroyed, only barricaded, to ensure the continued supply of gas and water for the population. The replacement and emergency formations that had been deployed by the territorial authorities for the defense of the Ruhr were subordinated to the Division for incorporation. This was the last addition of replacements for the *Panzer-Grenadiers*, but their battle value was extremely low.[184]

In the afternoon, the Division command post moved to Lürbke (two kilometers northeast of Lendringsen). On this day, the troops under the command of the *190th Infantry Division* were able to hold Unna. Dortmund was still in the hands of the *180th Infantry Division,* however, the enemy pushed through west of the town up to Witten. *LXIII Corps* was, except for two narrow bridgeheads, also thrown back to the Ruhr. Bochum and Essen were occupied by the enemy. A dangerous development emerged at the southern front of the cauldron. Here, the enemy took Olpe and attacked further toward the north. The situation in the east also became threatening. The enemy units which advanced in the Ruhr valley via Meschede pushed toward Sundern and Arnsberg.[185] The development of this

situation had implications for the logistical support of the *116th Panzer Division.*
Its installations echeloned toward the rear suffered from a diminishing quantity of
suitable facilities. Ammunition became scarce. In my post-war report about the
battle of 11 April, I wrote the following:

> In the morning, the expected attack at Frömern began. With support from the
> Hunting Tigers, the breakthrough was able to be prevented. However, the Hunting
> Tigers were recognized and attacked without surcease by fighter bombers, until
> three were out of action by noon. In the sector of the unit to the left, Unna was lost,
> and the enemy broke through to the southwest up to Holzwickede. In the Division's
> sector, the enemy pushed into Fröndenberg north of the Ruhr. Thereby, the Divi-
> sion's combat group was in danger of being cut off north of the Ruhr. It was there-
> fore subordinated to the *190th Infantry Division,* which controlled the area north of
> the river and was to be pulled out to follow the Division to the south bank. This did
> not happen until the night of 12/13 April.[186]

Hauptmann Zanzinger wrote the following about 11 April:

> New position near Dellwig. . . . I take in reinforcements: Sharpshooter School Army
> *Wehrkreis VI,* Münster, 20 men; *SS*-NCO School Unna, 40 men; four Hunting
> Tigers.
>
> It is quiet again. Once more, I drive to Höltje (*12th Company*) and Junge (*8th
> Company*). Slowly, the *Ami* again starts to press—the tanks with open hatches, in-
> between jeeps with recoilless anti-tank guns, are forced to turn back by the fire from
> the sharpshooters. One US jeep loses its way and is destroyed 50 meters in front of
> the battalion command post. Earlier, this would have been a good catch. The US
> lieutenant is communications officer of a US brigade; map material up to Berlin,
> roster of code names, radio code, placements of units, and so on—but now only
> paper trash.
>
> Now, heavy artillery fire and tank attack. The Tigers destroy some Shermans, but
> soon the reconnaissance aircraft discover the Tigers and finish them off with rock-
> et bombs.[187]

The above-mentioned Hunting Tigers belonged to the *1st Company* of *Heavy
Tank Destroyer Battalion 512.* Its commander was *Hauptmann* Schärf, the *1st
Company* was commanded by *Oberleutnant* Ernst. The *2d Company* of the battalion fought to the left in front of the *1st,* obviously already in the sector of the
190th Infantry Division. Together with the Hunting Tigers, almost all available
tanks of *Panzer Regiment 16* were deployed with *Panzer-Grenadier Regiment 156*
on 11 April. Very few supported *Panzer-Grenadier Regiment 60. 1st (Panzer)
Battalion* of *Panzer Regiment 16* was now led by *Hauptmann* Kühne, while its
tanks with *Regiment 156* were under the command of *Leutnant* Rose. According
to his statement, he had three *Panzer IVs,* one Panther, and one Hunting Panther.
On the morning of 11 April, about 15 to 17 tanks went into position on the hill
one kilometer north of Strickherdicke, east of the Bismarck tower and *Reichs*

Route 233 (R233). From there they had a wide-open view to the north toward Kessebüren and Unna.[188]

On the morning of 11 April, after artillery preparation, the 8th Armored Division attacked Unna via Kessebüren, and swung by south of it from the southeast and south. This attack was led by Combat Command A under the covering fires of Combat Command B, which remained in position east of Unna. Combat Command R attacked north of the Ruhr, took Fröndenberg and Hohenheide as well as Frömern, and from there pushed ahead toward the Unna–Langschede road (R233), the latter probably not before afternoon. During its attack, enveloping the south of Unna, the left group of Combat Command A was hit in its left flank by German "rapid fire" from the hill and requested artillery fire on that area. For their part, the artillery fliers requested an air raid on the enemy tanks detected in that area, which was carried out very quickly. The US Army Air Forces reported 11 German tanks destroyed. The German reports mention an attack by the Americans against the hill, some also of one or two repeat attacks. They list considerable success, up to 15 enemy tanks destroyed.

The American history does not mention any losses, even though it can be assumed that in this ideal situation of an ambush from the flank, there must have been some. In any case, the deployed German tanks suffered considerable losses due to fighter bombers and during the battles, so that evidently only one Hunting Tiger from *Company Ernst* remained battleworthy and one Hunting Panther from *Panzer Regiment 16* remained mobile, but with a damaged gun. *Leutnant* Rose carried his wounded away on this armored vehicle.

In the evening of 11 April, units from Combat Command A still pushed through from Unna to Holzwickede. The 95th Infantry Division reached a line from Holzwickede to the northern edge of Dortmund. The *LIII Corps* still held one bridgehead north of the Ruhr, between Lüttgenmühle (*2d Battalion, Panzer-Grenadier Regiment 156*) and south of Witten. Further west, *Group von Lüttwitz* essentially detoured to behind the Ruhr.[189] The daily reports of *Army Group B* show the desperate situation. On 11 April, one includes the following:

> For ten days, units of Army Group are encircled without sufficient supply and without sufficient *Luftwaffe* support, in heavy defensive battle against superior enemy forces. The opponent is mounting an operational breakthrough out of the area on both sides of Olpe toward the northwest to achieve the fragmentation of Army Group with the assault that is expected from the vicinity of Bochum. With a concentric advance of strong tank spearheads, the enemy also attempts to break the structure of the front from all sides.[190]

The enemy already stood before Lüdenscheid and near Attendorn. The day after, on 12 April, Army Group reported the following:

> The enemy still strengthened the force of its concentric attacks against the fortress. Along the entire front, even outside of the main efforts, in spite of our stubborn

resistance in north, south, and east of the fortress, the enemy pressed part of our troops back considerably. Army Group's means for preventing the enemy from achieving his goal of fracturing the fortress into several smaller cauldrons are, as of today, completely exhausted. Weapons and ammunition are totally insufficient (about 60 to 70 percent without weapons).

In the Army Group's rear, the enemy was already before Bremen and near Celle. Near Tangermünde and on both sides of Magdeburg, it reached the Elbe, and on 12 April, even crossed it south of the city. There, *12th Army* assumed control on the German side, because *11th Army* was also encircled by the enemy who was advancing on both sides of the Harz Mountains. The enemy stood in front of Halle near Zeitz and Jena, in front of Bamberg and Rothenburg ob der Tauber. Eisenhower's planned objective, the Elbe–Mulde line, was almost reached. In the east, the resistance in Königsberg faded. On 12 April, Roosevelt died. There were no hopes attached to this. The miracle of 1762 did not repeat itself. [The death of the Russian Czarina Elizabeth in January 1762 precipitated the Treaty of St. Petersburg, by which the new czar, Peter III, removed the Russians from the Seven Years' War. This turned the tide of the war in favor of Frederick the Great of Prussia—*Editor.*]

This date, 12 April, brought exciting events to the *116th Panzer Division*. In my post-war report, I wrote the following:

> Since the situation in the unit on the right (*Group Wirtz* of *15th Army*) was very unclear, the Division sent reconnaissance elements there, mainly in the area southeast and east of the Sorpe Dam and on Arnsberg. The Division's right wing was extended up to Herdringen. Thus, the Division's front ran along the Ruhr from Neheim up to Langschede. *Combat Group 156* was still north of the river with the *190th Infantry Division.*
>
> To fully clear up the situation regarding the unit to the right, in the late morning, the Division Commander drove to *Group Wirtz,* whose command post was not to be found, and he had to search for it. . . . The group only had minimal forces, without battle value and without artillery at its disposal. It was pushed back by a superior opponent and at this moment was fighting in the vicinity of Westenfeld, seven kilometers east of the Sorpe Dam. It was also engaged in combat near Arnsberg. The Division's reconnaissance that was deployed in its area reported at the same time that the opponent rolled over the weak forces near Westenfeld and was swiftly advancing toward Seidfeld and Sundern, and that Arnsberg was captured by the enemy.
>
> On its own, the Division at once deployed weak, scraped-together blocking units (some tanks, anti-tank guns, and *Panzer-Grenadiers*) toward Amecke and Langscheid–Hachen, to prevent an enemy penetration on both sides of the dam into the right flank and rear of the Division. The troops deployed toward Amecke encountered a superior enemy and were thrown back toward Balve. The enemy continued to push toward Neuenrade and, in the evening, took Balve. The group

deployed toward Langscheid–Hachen was blocking the roads west of both villages. The enemy advancing through Arnsberg met the Division's security elements near Herdringen. In an attempt to cross between Hüsten and Neheim, the enemy was able to reach the west bank of the Ruhr.

In the evening, the Division stood in a large bend from the vicinity of Balve via Hövel–Herdringen–Ruhr up to Langschede. It no longer had any reserves. The Balve–Herdringen sector was only secured by blocking groups at the roads. The Division's right flank was completely unprotected. The Division's main aid station near Neuenrade was lost.

In spite of this situation, by order of Army Group, a change in command status was to take place. The staff of the *190th Infantry Division* was to take over the sector of the *116th Panzer Division* south of the Ruhr, the staff of the *116th Panzer Division,* the sector of the *190th Infantry Division* north of the Ruhr. It was reasoned that the *Panzer Division* staff would be better qualified for the command and control of the tanks in what was assumed to be the point of main effort north of the river. The Division strongly resisted this plan, since most of its troops were on the south bank. The communications equipment was in full action and could not be released, and the development of the situation on the right wing of the Division would in no way any longer allow a change in leadership. None of the objections were acknowledged. The communications equipment of both divisions was to be exchanged and if not possible, the Division was to operate with the equipment from the other Division. The *Ia* from the *190th Infantry Division* had already appeared at the *116th Panzer Division* command post for the takeover. Ultimately, the catastrophic development of the situation by *Group Wirtz* made this plan fail. As the Division only now [1947—*Author*] could see from the report by *Generalleutnant* Bayerlein, the reason for this order was *Feldmarschall* Model's intentions for breaking out of the cauldron to the north with the mobile forces under command of the *116th Panzer Division,* a plan that would have had prospects for success twelve days previously, but now was completely hopeless.[191]

In the afternoon, the enemy rolled over the staff of *Group Wirtz* in Stemel and captured it.[192] The staff of *LXXXI Corps,* which was its higher headquarters, allowed the enemy to march it off and capitulated on 13 April without regard for units on its left or right.[193] On 12 April, the remnants of the *Panzer Lehr Division* were near Werdohl and Neuenrade. They lost Neuenrade the following day and were ultimately pushed back to Altena.[194] In the evening of 12 April, a ten-kilometer gap opened between the right wing of the *116th Panzer Division* near Balve and Neuenrade, directly inviting the opponent to break through.

The diaries of *Hauptmann* Zanzinger and *Leutnant* Schwörer portray the events at *Panzer-Grenadier Regiment 156,* which on 12 April was further subordinated to the *190th Infantry Division.* Schwörer says the following about 12 April:

Enemy took Keller. Attack on Opherdicke and Hengsen. It is reported at 1145 hours that the last of our Hunting Tigers was damaged. . . .

2000 hours, enemy attacks with 500 men and seven tanks from 168 toward Kemmele [most likely, Krümmde, two kilometers south southwest of Hengsen—*Author*]. No combat noise to be heard. Evidently, nobody is there to bother its march. . . .

Grollmann himself drives off for reconnaissance. He finds complete calm, but not one man from his *2d Battalion*.[195]

Zanzinger's diary, of course, sees things from a different angle:

Battalion command post Krümmde, *12th Company* established security toward the north and *8th Company* along the river toward the east. West of the *12th*, US infantry advances, Opherdicke is occupied by the enemy. The *12th* is forced back, the *8th* retreats along the bank toward the west. Battalion command post is under direct fire. An assault gun drives up. Behind me, the Shermans—let's get out of here. Höltje [*Commander, 12th Company—Author*] also arrives, "Go, just go! They are after us!" . . . Phone call from the Regiment, "More orders?" *Hauptmann* Voigt answers, "Do what whatever you want to do, we have to run, too."[196]

After this, Zanzinger and his battalion changed positions to the south bank of the Ruhr with the command post in Hennen. His people were totally exhausted. In the middle of the night, a duty officer from *Regiment Zanzinger* delivered the order that the Division—the *190th*—wanted to have the old positions at the north bank occupied again, since the enemy seemed to be weak. The officer added that the regimental commander was displeased with the change of position to the south bank and spoke of consequences for the battalion commander. That led to a fit of anger from Zanzinger, who remained where he was. At 0230 hours, a messenger from the regiment brought the order from the *190th Infantry Division* to evacuate the north bank and establish security positions on the south bank. Zanzinger had the regiment informed that his battalion would clear the north bank and occupy positions on the south bank. In the morning of 13 April, *Oberstleutnant* Grollmann came and relieved Zanzinger of his command. *Oberleutnant* Junge assumed command of the battalion. Zanzinger was placed at the disposal of the supply company; he was captured along with it on the evening of 15 April in Iserlohn. He writes, "I know that during this event I broke every rule one calls the virtue of soldiers and refused orders. But I found, and find even now, that it was justified due to the situation at large."

He could hardly be disagreed with. The extraordinary situation of the collapsing resistance, the evidence of deterioration and the increasingly obvious senselessness raised doubts for the most steadfast old soldier. The morale of a good unit withstands the most difficult crisis, but if the bow is too taut, sooner or later it will snap.

On 12 April, the 8th Armored and the 95th Infantry Divisions were still fighting on the north bank of the Ruhr.[197] Units of the 8th seized the Dellwig–Opherdicke–Hengsen area and might have thrown Zanzinger out of Krümmde, while the 1st Battalion of the 379th Infantry Regiment of the 95th Infantry Division was the opponent of *2d Battalion, Panzer-Grenadier Regiment 156* during a night battle for the Ruhr crossing near Geisecke. The following day, the 8th Armored Division was released and sent off toward Wolfenbüttel, while on 13 and 14 April, the 95th Infantry Division closed in on the Ruhr everywhere. Task Force Twaddle was dissolved. The main opponents of the *116th Panzer Division* were now the 5th Infantry Division and the 7th Armored Division from First Army's III Corps. The 5th conducted its attack across the Ruhr and the valley of the Röhr, between Hüsten and the Sorpe Dam in the southern sector, supported by the 7th Armored Division. Bypassing the dam to the south of it, most of this Division pushed via Balve to the northwest and toward Neuenrade. The 99th Infantry Division followed it, echeloned to the left rear. Fortunately, the enemy forces north of the Ruhr remained quiet and did not carry out an assault across the river.

My report about 13 April says:

> During the night, the Division strengthened the southeastern front as much as possible and subordinated all units that were deployed there to the Commander of *Panzer Regiment 16*. This group secured the Division's flank in a line from southwest of Beckum–Hövel–Ainkhausen. *Panzer-Grenadier Regiment 60* controlled the Herdringen–Wimbern sector, and connecting to Langschede were *Armored Reconnaissance Battalion 116* and *Panzer-Grenadier Regiment 156*. The right flank of the Division in the forest northwest of Balve remained unprotected. It was only poorly guarded by weak reconnaissance from units of the supply troops. There was great danger of the Division being split by an enemy attack from the south toward Iserlohn. The Division constantly reckoned with it, but was not in a position to do anything about it.
>
> As expected, in the morning, the enemy mounted an attack along the entire front between Beckum and Neheim. In severe combat, a breakthrough near Beckum and Hövel was prevented. However, Herdringen was lost and the opponent entered the forest northwest of the village, where he established a link-up with the forces that had already crossed the Ruhr between Hüsten and Neheim. In the afternoon, a deep breach occurred via Wettmarsen–Ainkhausen and toward Holzen. A completely surprising tank assault through the forest from Balve toward Deilinghofen in the late afternoon was decisive. Since the reconnaissance patrols from the supply troops deployed there had not returned, the opponent advanced through the forest unnoticed and, in the evening, appeared in Deilinghofen at the airfield. Hemer was under artillery fire. The withdrawal behind the Hönne sector, west of Volkringhausen–Menden–Fröndenberg, which was ordered for the night, was threatened. By deploying some hurriedly-gathered tanks, the Division was able to stop the opponent's

advance near Hemer and Deilinghofen, and succeeded in establishing a line of strongpoints from Sundwig via Hemer-East–a group of houses north of Deilinghofen–Lendringsen–Hönnetal. During the night, the Division command post was relocated to Hemer-North.[198]

In 1947, I wrote this about 14 April:

The Division's losses, mainly of tanks, were so large, and the lack of artillery ammunition so considerable that there could no longer be talk of regulated battle conduct.

In the late morning, the security line was extended from Sundwig south up to Ihmert.

The enemy mounted an attack from Deilinghofen to the north and near Lendringsen to the west. It threw the security forces back to the Hemer–Menden road.

The Division command post was relocated to Gerlingsen during the morning.

Since there were several thousand wounded and a large prison camp in Hemer, by noon, the Division held negotiations with the opposing 7th Armored Division, which led to the agreement that Hemer would be neutral.

The opponent continued to attack during the afternoon south and north of Hemer, as well as out of Menden. He achieved several breaches, so that the withdrawal of the security line during the night to the line Dahlsen–Westig–Landhausen–Sümmern–southwest of Langschede was ordered. The Division command post was moved to Refflingsen-South.

In the cauldron, people and vehicles were shoved together in frightening masses, but there was a lack of weapons, munitions, and operational possibilities. By order of Army Group, the older age groups were to be discharged. They wandered about in the cauldron and broke the spirit of the younger ones, who were still supposed to fight.

Hagen fell, still on the evening of 14 April, so that the Division's tank maintenance facility in Letmathe was lost and had to be blown up. The Division now had no more battleworthy tanks.

In view of this situation, on the evening of 14 April, the Division ordered the commanders to stop fighting at a given keyword to prevent further senseless bloodshed. In this case, whether to capitulate or attempt a breakout toward the east was left open. It explained that the Division staff would capitulate together with most of the troops, since there was no chance of pushing through the enemy-occupied area to the Elbe or still further toward the east.[199]

Major Dunker, who was in command of a battalion of anti-aircraft soldiers who were deployed as infantry, was captured near Apricke during this day's battles.[200] In his addition to my post-war report, *Generalmajor* von Waldenburg noted the following:

The first negotiations on 14 April with officers from the 7th Armored Division— which led to agreeing that Hemer would be neutral ground—were carried out in a friendly and helpful manner. With this, a great danger was removed for thousands of prisoners and wounded and for the overcrowded town itself. I had to decline a request by the American officers to cease resistance in general. Some of the Division's individual, laboriously-established security positions still stood loosely touching and connecting with the adjacent units; the last shell was not yet fired; a few tanks were still fighting into the evening of this day against an indeed powerful superiority; and the orders necessary for the cessation of the battle were not yet given. The corollary preparatory directives went out to the commanders during the following night.[201]

The negotiations with the Americans were initiated by *Generalleutnant* Bayerlein.[202] He had sent a captured American officer over to them. Consequently, the American officers appeared at the command post of the *116th Panzer Division.*

On 14 April, the Ruhr cauldron was split into two parts by the American penetration from the south via Lüdenscheid toward Hagen; the *116th Panzer Division*, the entire *LIII Corps,* and more units of the *15th Army* were in the smaller cauldron in the east. *Group Lüttwitz* had been subordinated to *15th Army,* but there was no longer any effective command. Army headquarters, like the staff of *Group Lüttwitz,* was captured on 15 April.[203] In 1947, I wrote the following about 15 April:

> The movements during the night of 14/15 April led to the fact that some of the *Panzer-Grenadiers* of *Regiment 60* were missing, causing a hole in the front near Landhausen, which could no longer be closed. Without finding any resistance, the enemy pushed through this gap into the forest south of Landhausen. Furthermore, it pushed through south of Westig, so that the security positions there had to be taken back to the eastern edge of Iserlohn. Iserlohn itself was to be defended by the Iserlohn battle commandant. However, his units were so weak that the Division had to leave behind its units that were deployed there. In the Division's left sector, Sümmern was lost to a superior enemy with tanks. In the evening, there were no combat-capable troops left. There were no longer any battleworthy tanks, the *Panzer-Grenadiers* were almost entirely overrun, and the artillery was out of ammunition. For the night, the Division tried to establish a security line, approximately along the Iserlohn–Kalthof railroad, but it no longer succeeded. The Division command post was moved back into the forest near the Reingser stream.[204]

Now almost the entire III Corps attacked the Division, with the 5th Infantry Division south of the Ruhr, the 7th Armored Division in the center near Hemer, and most of the 99th Infantry Division in the southern sector near Westig and south of Iserlohn.[205] On 15 April, the remnants of the *Panzer Lehr Division* capitulated in Altena.[206] On this day, weak units of the *3d Panzer-Grenadier Division* retreated into to the area west of Iserlohn.[207] My report for the Americans states the following:

During the night of 15/16 April, after consultation with the Division Commander, the corps ordered . . . the capitulation.

During the night, the entire area of the Division was still under heavy artillery fire, which was halted at daybreak, based on the agreement between the corps and the 7th Armored Division. Also at daybreak, on behalf of the Division, a parliamentary was sent to the tanks of the 7th Armored Division, which had closed in to within 500 meters of the Division command post.[208]

Generalmajor von Waldenburg added:

On 15 April, the Division's resistance became lame, all artillery ammunition was used up to the last round, the last tank was immobilized in combat, the left-over remnants were crowded together in the narrowest area. In the afternoon of this day, in view of the situation, I reported to *General* Bayerlein at my command post that it was no longer possible—and rather senseless—to continue resistance, and that the disabled remainder of the Division would cease combat operations. During the night of 15/16 April, after consultation with all of the Division's commanders at the corps command post, corps ordered the capitulation. On the morning of 16 April, per instructions from the corps, I led the first negotiations with the Chief of Staff of the 7th Armored Division, after first sending a duty officer from my staff to ask for a cessation of the fire that could not longer be returned. I then brought the Chief of Staff of the 7th Armored Division to *General* Bayerlein's command post, where the latter led further negotiations. I promptly turned over several captured American officers to the Americans, including a colonel. They had asked not to be put into a prison camp, but to be allowed to stay with the *116th Panzer Division*. At the same time, the remnants of my Division laid down their arms. The remaining guns, heavy weapons, and so on, were blown up. To the commander of *Panzer-Grenadier Regiment 156,* as the next senior officer of the Division, I gave the final orders for the concentration, supply, and conduct of all troops subordinated to me. I was brought to the American Army by the 7th Armored Division, situated opposite from us at Bad Wildungen. There, the *Ic* [that is, the G-2—*Editor*] of the Army told me the following, and with this judgment by our former opponents, I conclude my reports about the *116th Panzer Division*. He said that the *116th Panzer Division,* known to them for a long time and very respected, has always fought heroically, tenaciously, but fair and with honor, until the last moment.[209]

The captured American officers who were with the Division included the aforementioned Colonel Wallace from the 8th Armored Division; Major Ludeman from the 2d Armored Division, who was captured between Halen and Beckum on 31 March by *Group Dunker*; and Lieutenant MacGraw, along with two crews from the 8th Armored Division.[210] As a parliamentary, *Leutnant* Weyand was sent to the Americans. He reported the following to me:

Toward the evening of 15 April 1945, I was ordered to the Division command post, which was located in a forest gorge. In your presence, I received orders from

General Waldenburg to establish communications with the forward American troops and to ask for a cease-fire. Thereby, the three American officers who stayed within or near the Division command post were mentioned.

Together with an NCO as translator . . . we drove off in a VW. Despite a white flag . . . we were initially shot at by the *Ami,* but then we were able to establish communications with the Americans and asked for a cease-fire.

After long radio conversations between the Americans and their higher headquarters, the cease-fire was promised. I was sent back with instructions to pick up the Americans right after daybreak and hand them over.

At dawn, I picked up the American officers and took them to the Division command post.[211]

In his final report, *Generalleutnant* Bayerlein said that enemy fire was halted at 0300 hours on 16 April, and at 0700 hours the Chief of Staff of the 7th Armored Division arrived at the corps command post.[212] He brought directives about the collection areas for the troops and the surrender of weapons. After those orders were sent on to the units, all generals, the first general staff officers of the divisions, and the commander of *Armored Artillery Regiment 146, Major* Vogelsang, were led to the 7th Armored Division's command post near Menden. They were allowed to drive there in their own vehicles and to keep their pistols. Then, however, these were taken from them and the men were brought, like all the rest, into the collection camp in the meadows near Brilon; only Bayerlein and Waldenburg drove on to the First Army command post. An example from the *Panzer Regiment* shows how the capitulation played out with the troop units of the Division. *Leutnant* von Elterlein noted the following:

16 April 1945: At 1000 hours, departure of regiment's remnants to a collection point near Iserlohn for surrender. We drive up to a hill surrounded by woods under the observation of an artillery liaison plane. In the forest clearing, all comrades dressed in black fall in for the last roll call by *Major* Tebbe. Tebbe thanks them for genuine German front comradeship during difficult times. A stirring moment is the parting of the officer corps from the NCOs and soldiers. All eyes glisten with tears! After a speech by our commander, the destruction of all weapons and equipment, ammunition, binoculars, optical instruments, and so on, follows. Around 1600 hours, an American captain arrives by jeep. Surrender to the 99th Infantry Division, very appropriate treatment; no interrogations take place. Entire regiment remains together under command of its officers. . . .

17 April 1945 at 0600 hours with our vehicles . . . almost up to Menden. There, we suddenly have to surrender our vehicles. At the Menden airfield, thousands of German infantrymen wait to be transported by truck. From Menden . . . we are transported by semi-trucks to Brilon to the large prisoner collection camp. Guarded by Negroes, no more front troops, treatment gets worse! Almost all baggage is taken away from the soldiers. 70 men on one truck! The camp is on extensive cattle

pastures, guarded at the corners by tanks and recon vehicles. The entire *116th Panzer Division* together and still others . . . a very sad picture for us, but nobody has lost his sense of humor. . . .[213]

Others had a more difficult fate. *Leutnant* Schwörer wrote the following about 17 April:

60 men per vehicle, this is much, even very much. Not even room for our baggage, and all we have is blankets. They are just being ripped away from the men. . . . If some infantrymen do not want to give up their blankets or haversacks, they are hit with sticks. . . . In Brilon, thousands of soldiers. All on a large meadow. There are hardly any provisions. Hardly any water. . . . Mess kits and canteens are already being missed. Only blankets are still around, but not everybody has one. Now we already miss those things bitterly.[214]

The following days near Brilon are described by Schwörer:

Camp life is hardly bearable. 36,000 soldiers are here. Hardly any provisions. Last two days nothing but rain and nothing to eat, and then in an open meadow with only one blanket. . . . After hours of standing in line, water was received. A farmer from Brilon was provided, who brought water in a manure barrel for 36,000 men. Dysentery has already affected some men. . . . There were enough doctors from every unit, but nothing is here. Medicine is completely missing . . . there are no toilets. We could not have made any, because we had no spades. . . .

On 21 and 22 April, most members of the Division were transported to Remagen. At first, it was no better there than in Brilon. On 25 April, the officers were taken out and moved by railroad to Attichy, near Soissons.[215] *Obergefreiter* Mattischewski wrote about Remagen:

From the frying pan into the fire. . . . Once more, thoroughly filched. . . . The *Amis* especially loved our watches, rings (including wedding bands) and most of all, our medals.[216]

This is how captivity started for the soldiers of the Division. It's duration varied and showed different faces, but hardly anyone was happy. Nobody felt liberated.

We must, however, take a look back to the Ruhr cauldron.[217] After the smaller eastern cauldron capitulated on 16 April, organized resistance also died down in the western part on the next day. On the evening of 16 April, *Feldmarschall* Model rejected a request to surrender. He hid in the vicinity of Düsseldorf and on 21 April put an end to his life. He is now buried in the military cemetery of Vossenack in the Eifel, a few meters from the *116th Panzer Division* memorial. On 19 April, the *Wehrmacht* report announced:

The battle between Ruhr and Rhine has ended. During weeks of heaviest fighting, troops of all branches of the *Wehrmacht,* under the supreme command of *General-feldmarschall* Model, tied down the superior forces of two American armies and offered resistance in exemplary performance of duty to the last breath. The opponent thereby suffered heavy losses of men and materiel.

On 16 April, when the *116th Panzer Division* capitulated, the armies of the western powers stood before Bremen and Lüneburg, at the Elbe between Wittenberg and Dessau, in front of Leipzig and Chemnitz, near Plauen and by Bayreuth, in front of Nuremberg and Stuttgart. The Harz Mountains were encircled. The Soviets mounted their attack across the Oder and the Neisse toward Berlin. Vienna fell on 13 April. The Russians stood before Brünn and near St. Pölten. In Italy, the British and Americans mounted the offensive into the Po Valley.[218]

With this situation at large, did the battle for "Fortress Ruhr" make any sense at all? Why did the German soldiers continue to fight? Why did the leaders responsible not capitulate?

The Chief of Staff of *Army Group B, Generalmajor* Wagener, the first advisor to Model, referred to this while in captivity. Dated 2 April 1945, he portrays the considerations of Army Group Command after the encirclement:

> After the tanks of the Third and First American Armies met in the area west of Paderborn, the *encirclement of Army Group B is completed.* The Army Group had the clear, unequivocal order to hold its positions, and to link up with the *Group of Forces-Kassel* by attacking in the direction of the Edertal Dam.
>
> The hope was that a new German front would form and hold for some time on both sides of Kassel, at the Weser and the Fulda, and that units of the Army Group would be able to reach it. This hope had, however, already collapsed due to the successes of the Third Army at the Kinzig and the Fulda. All relief attempts prepared by the *11th* and *12th Armies* from the outside would probably be overtaken by the development of the situation. The condition of our strength to achieve a link-up through an attack out of the cauldron made that possibility now seem already hopeless. It would be completely illusory to try and beat a way through to a German front that dissapears in ever-increasing distance toward the east.
>
> *Army Group B* nevertheless still made an effort to carry out the orders it received, but was clearly aware that it would have to rely on itself and probably make its own decisions if it did not want to be idly destroyed in a "Cannae" of the largest scale.
>
> Therefore, in contrast to the present order, the *thought of breaking out* with the entire army group remained fully alive and was repeatedly debated. . . .
>
> During these days, the question of *capitulation* has, therefore, also been discussed between the Supreme Commander and Chief of Army Group. It is a bitter and, most likely, the hardest decision for any soldier, because it requires him not to

act as a soldier anymore, and to violate what he had to demand countless times during the war from his subordinates. It was not only about giving up the oath, discipline, duty, and honor, but also about the betrayal of sacrifices by the fallen and the comrades who were still fighting on all fronts. Even the capitulation of 300,000 men under their *Feldmarschall* would, at this time, not have had any effect that would decide and end the war. As long as there were still possibilities to continue the battle, as long as connections to the highest command existed, the decision for capitulation had to be put aside. Supreme Commander and Chief were, however, in agreement that the decision for it must at no time be passed to the middle or lower command, but that *Army Group* had to take responsibility for it at the proper time.

At this time, the possibilities for Army Group to continue the battle were still there. It had been promised relief from the outside. By tying down large enemy forces that the opponent lacked for its push toward central Germany, Army Group still fulfilled a certain purpose in the overall picture, while the protection ordered for the Ruhr area certainly remained imaginary. After all, it was encircled along with Army Group and lost for Germany.[219]

On 5 April, a breakout request by Army Group was rejected. On 8 April, Wagener proposed to the Field Marshal obtaining permission for capitulation. Model declined. On 13 April, the situation came to such a head that the collapse was imminent. The news from outside the cauldron also depicted a picture of hoplessness. *Generalmajor* Wagener wrote of it:

By considering all possibilities, Army Group arrives at a solution which hardly has any precedents in the history of modern war, if one does not credit the behavior of the Russians with this invention after many of this war's cauldron battles in the East.

Army Group will dissolve, but by order and as far as possible, in an orderly fashion. The date fixed for this was the morning of 17 April, the day on which provisions and ammunition would be used up, and therefore the day on which the last possibilities for a continuation of the battle were gone.

Thus, Army Group issues the order to cease resistance on 17 April. All younger and older age groups are at once to be discharged from the armed forces to go home. On the morning of the same day, officers, career soldiers, and the middle age group are to be divided into three groups, based on voluntary reporting: a. Non-fighting units and those without weapons or ammunition, by order of their corresponding commander, will allow themselves be overrun by the enemy and surrender; b. Groups of volunteers in uniform, civilian clothes, without weapons, who, under command of the most senior officer, try to beat their way through to their homeland; c. Groups of volunteers, who, under command of an officer, armed and in uniform, break out to one of our fronts outside of the cauldron. An order or even a request to become Werewolves [A German guerrilla, designated to continue the war after Allied or Soviet occupation—*Editor*] was not issued. Specifically requested, in any case, was leadership by an officer. . . .

With this solution, Army Group believed to have saved the troops from the disgrace that comes with unconditional surrender. The term "unconditional" even questions the rules of the Geneva convention! By order, furthermore, the individual was relieved of responsibility to act on his own; and with the principle of volunteering during the establishment of the groups, the peculiarity of every individual and of the units was taken care of. Ultimately, further bloodshed and senseless self-sacrifice was prevented. Perhaps with this solution, some would even avoid becoming prisoners of war and reach their place of work at home faster than by unconditional surrender to the enemy.

As we saw, the intentions of Army Group Command remained theory. The events of 14 and 15 April destroyed all plans. In an article from 1957, Wagener judged more critically:

> Nothing could give any meaning to the senselessness of further resistance after the collapse of the Rhine defense! It was as senseless to retreat to behind the Weser as it was to defend the Ruhr cauldron, or to capitulate in it. Here, the complete breakdown between the political leadership and the Army was evident. Therefore, toward the end, the troops were not really fighting anymore, but in a justified case of self-help, only conducted *faux* combat. . . .
>
> In the overall situation, the loss of *Army Group B* did not change anything, but it, indeed, tore a hole in the Western Front, because 300,000 men were missing in the fight in Germany's interior. However, *Army Group B* tied down 20 enemy divisions to the end, against which it would probably have succumbed earlier in continuous battle within the retreating remainder of the front.[220]

The question of why Army Group did not capitulate when the situation looked so hopeless, Wagener answered as follows:

> A capitulation requires the readiness of the opposite side to negotiate, which, after the announcement of the unconditional capitulation, was no longer proffered.

The above-quoted sentences by *General* Wagener about the bitter significance of a capitulation were true for the soldiers of the *116th Panzer Division*. The demand for "unconditional" capitulation sharpened the situation. Today, we may see some things in a different way. In any case, the Division conducted the battle in a way that somehow spared soldiers, civilians, and buildings of all kinds from unnecessary victimization. The soldiers of the Division fought with loyalty to their oath, even if fate could no longer be changed. Special respect is due from the survivors to all who sacrificed their lives. The report I wrote for the Americans during imprisonment closed this way:

> Thus the battle ended for the *116th Panzer Division* with an honorable capitulation, after the destruction of all its tanks, after the expenditure of all its artillery ammunition, after the extermination of its *Panzer-Grenadiers,* and in view of the impos-

sibility of a breakout, in closed formation or in small groups, due to the development of the situation at large.

The Division kept its shield of honor clean at all times and in every respect. Its achievement and conduct was also recognized by the enemy.

The personnel strength of the capitulating units was about 3,000 men. The units that were moved out of the Ruhr cauldron continued to fight under the leadership of others in the Harz and at the Saale, until they, too, were captured by the Americans.[221]

CHAPTER 12

The End in the Harz Mountains

As described in the previous chapter, shortly before the closure of the Ruhr cauldron, the *116th Panzer Division* moved out all units that were not required for the movement of combat units and its most necessary supplies. They left the Division during the nights of 30/31 March and 31 March/1 April, under the leadership of the commander of the Division's supply troops, *Major der Reserve* Degenhard. Their first objective was to reach the vicinity of Melle, northwest of Bielefeld, on the other side of the Teutoburg Forest.[1] The movement just about succeeded, because not only did the cauldron near Lippstadt close up on 1 April, but American spearheads also advanced east along the *Autobahn* to the Teutoburg Forest and crossed the Münster–Rheda road, east of Warendorf.[2]

The receipt of new tank destroyers by *Panzerjäger Battalion 228,* which was sent to Warendorf for that purpose, also still succeeded, but other units had already picked up some of them. However, ten Hetzers were received. Between 1 and 2 April, they were in combat with swiftly advancing American spearheads near Sassenberg, Versmold, and at the southwest edge of the Teutoburg Forest.[3] Coming from Holland, the Division convalescent field hospital also arrived in the vicinity of Melle, and followed Degenhard.[4] Reconnaissance patrols of *Armored Reconnaissance Battalion 116* which had escaped from the cauldron also met up with them.[5] Units from the *Field Replacement Battalion* that were able to get out of the encirclement near Lippstadt marched on foot from there to the Harz.[6]

After it became obvious that the enemy advanced toward the Weser near Hameln and Minden, and after a radio consultation with the Division command, *Major* Degenhard moved across the Weser into the area east of Hameln.[7] Tank destroyers from the Division took part in the defense of the Weser near Minden.[8] When the defense did not hold, Degenhard ordered his units to further detour into to the western Harz; they arrived there around 5 or 6 April. In Clausthal-Zellerfeld, Degenhard reported to an operations staff. He called him "General Harz Area." The general, whose name could not be clarified, requested the establishment of a combat group in a strength of five companies with 100 men each.[9] Its leadership was assumed by *Major der Reserve* Count Brühl, who was released by the field hospital.[10] He had commanded the *2d Battalion, Panzer Regiment 16* until his illness in December 1944. The way *Combat Group Brühl* looked in detail can no longer be ascertained. According to statements by some members of the combat group, it had only a few tanks; about four tank destroyers under the command of *Hauptmann der Reserve* Geigenmüller; a few *Panzer-Grenadiers,* some mounted on armored personnel carriers; and an engineer platoon, in part also on armored personnel carriers, under *Leutnant der Reserve* Golly.[11] A reconnaissance platoon was also established, which was commanded by *Leutnant der Reserve* Beckmann. On 6 April, the combat group was drawn up for the first time. As a whole, the combat group certainly did not reach the requested strength. On one hand, the supply columns could not provide enough fighters; on the other hand, the tendency to put one's life or that of entrusted subordinates on the line, was—in this obviously hopeless situation—small, and became smaller from day to day.

On the day the Combat Group was drawn up, Hamm and Soest in the Ruhr cauldron were lost. The American field armies that were pushing further toward the east reached the line Weser–Werra on a broad front. The Weser was crossed between Minden and Hameln. The continuation of the American attack toward Hannover and Hildesheim became clear. In the south of the Harz, the enemy entered Thuringia and stood before Erfurt.[12]

Headquarters, *11th Army* was brought in from the East to command the German formations in the Paderborn–Kassel–Eisenach sector. As mentioned in the previous chapter, its task was to link up with the enclosed *Army Group B* and reestablish a closed front in the West. Both failed. *The LXVI and LXVII Corps,* with some of the remnants that had escaped the encirclement of the Ruhr cauldron, as well as the *Wehrkreis IX* replacement and training troops from Kassel, were subordinated to *11th Army.* On 4 April, the *Wehrkreis VI* headquarters from Münster, which retreated from the Teutoburg Forest to the Weser between Hameln and Höxter, was also subordinated. Thereby, the sector of the *11th Army* expanded to the north. The forces of *Wehrkreis VI* did not suffice to cover its area.[13] On 7 April, the command relationships in the West were newly organized by *OKW. Army Group H* departed from the area of *Supreme Command–West.* A *Supreme Commander-Northwest* was appointed. Between its left wing and the right wing of the *11th Army,* the enemy pushed into the weakly-covered area north of the Harz. It was only a matter of days before *11th Army* would have to march out of there. The same danger loomed in the south of the mountains after an insufficient push against the left flank of the Americans advancing on Erfurt failed.[14]

On 8 April, *General der Artillerie* Lucht assumed command of the *11th Army.* By a directive from *OKW, Supreme Command–West* ordered him to hold the Harz as a "fortress" for the assembly of the *12th Army,* which was to be newly established. As a right boundary for the *11th Army,* the line Oschersleben–Salzgitter–Holzminden was ordered; the line Weimar–Erfurt as the left one.[15] Their corps retreated to the Leine; the enemy already pushed beyond their right wing toward Salzgitter, and seized Gandersheim and Seesen. At the Army's left wing, contact with *Army Group G* was lost, whose right wing fell back to the northern edge of the Thuringian forest. This development accelerated on 10 and 11 April. North of the Harz, the enemy reached the Elbe near Magdeburg and also pushed further east via Halberstadt. The western and southwestern edges of the Harz were reached by the enemy. He took Osterode, and on 11 April, surprisingly entered the mountain range near Lautenthal and Bad Grund. At the southern edge of the Harz, the enemy stood before Bad Lauterberg and in Nordhausen. Enemy forces streamed east through Thuringia toward Naumburg and Jena without being bothered.[16]

At the Elbe, mostly east of the river, the new *12th Army* was established under *General der Panzertruppe* Wenck. Hitler wanted it to come out of the Harz and relieve *Army Group B* in the Ruhr cauldron. This was a utopian scheme like the earlier one regarding the *11th Army*. For some time, the *12th Army* had trouble holding at the Elbe and lower Saale, and then at the lower Mulde.[17] That it was able to do this at least for a while was owed mainly to Eisenhower's order to stop, which was mentioned in the previous chapter.

For the largest part, the Harz was situated in the First Army's zone of attack. Only the northwestern part, approximately north of the line Clausthal-Zellerfeld–Brocken–Quedlinburg–Dessau, was assigned to the Ninth Army. It passed by the Harz, leaving it to its right. Only units of the 83d Infantry Division and later of the 8th Armored Division were fighting here. All of the remaining Harz Mountains were in the area of the First Army's VII Corps. Its 1st Infantry Division—known from Aachen—pushed from the west and southwest into the Harz, while its 3d Armored Division with the 104th Infantry Division pressed forward, south of it. The 9th Infantry Division ultimately took the eastern Harz, advancing via Nordhausen and Sangerhausen into the mountain range.[18] In a surprise attack on 11 April, the 26th Infantry Regiment of the 1st Infantry Division overran Bad Grund. North of it, on the same day, the reinforced 330th Infantry Regiment of the 83d Infantry Division entered the upper Harz via Lautenthal and took Hahnenklee, Bockswiese, and Wildemann.[19]

Headquarters, *Wehrkreis VI,* leading the German side at the right wing of *11th Army* on 10 April, made an effort to establish a security line at the western edge of the Harz. That failed. The staff of *Group Goerbig* leading here was obviously completely surprised by the development of the situation, and was captured in Bad Grund on 11 April.[20] A *"Battle Commandant Harz"* was deployed behind the staff, probably by the headquarters of *11th Army.* On the morning of 11 April, he issued the order enclosed in Appendix 23.[21] According to this, he was put in charge of defending the northwestern part of the Harz. His sector reached from Stapelburg (east of Bad Harzburg) almost up to Osterode, with a front more than 50 kilometers wide. His forces were modest. Even the favorable defensive terrain did not change this.

The following units were subordinated to *Battle Commandant Harz* and deployed as indicated:

— To the right, *Battle Commandant Goslar,* from Stapelburg to Hahnenklee (exclusive). Goslar itself was not defended by *Oberst* Poppe, the battle commandant, but on 10 April was occupied without a fight by the Americans as a hospital town.

— In the center, *Combat Group Zahn* from Hahnenklee to Lautenthal.

— To the left, *Combat Group von Fallois* ahead of Wildemann and Bad Grund.

Furthermore, there still was *Battle Group Count Brühl,* "pulled out for other uses." It was supposed to "leave security elements as verbally ordered in former sector." Wherever that was is not clear.[22]

Battle Group von Fallois was mainly put together from the units of the *9th Panzer Division* that had escaped from the Ruhr cauldron.[23] On 11 April, it lost Bad Grund, while the breach via Lautenthal to Hahnenklee and Bockswiese played out in the center with *Group Zahn.* According to various statements, *Battle Commandant Harz* was the elderly *Oberstleutnant* Lindner. His identity could not be clarified. The order is signed by *Major i.G.* Uhl, who earlier and afterwards belonged to *Wehrkreis IX.*[24]

On the afternoon of 11 April, after Hahnenklee and Bockswiese had been occupied out of Lautenthal without a fight because they were full of wounded, the Harz battle commandant wanted to regain Bockswiese in the evening.[25,26] Therefore, despite the objections of the local commanders of *Combat Group Brühl,* above all the tank leaders *Oberleutnants* Weissflog and Schmidt, he mounted an attack against Bockswiese during darkness. He hoped to overrun the enemy in a surprise assault, using the two available Panthers and six armored personnel carriers with mounted crews from the *Panzer-Grenadiers* and engineers. The enemy and difficulties in the terrain during the night were underestimated. The attack failed. The Panther in front—Commander *Oberleutnant* Schmidt—was destroyed; likewise, three armored personnel carriers. Chaos developed. The attempt to continue the attack dismounted also failed. Schmidt and his gunner were wounded and brought to safety.

Amazingly, one enemy tank, whose crew had left it with the motor still running, was able to be taken over by *Leutnant* Beckmann and brought back from the battlefield by *Oberleutnant* Weissflog, the commander of the second Panther. This combat action can be reconstructed up to this point. During the night, the combat group went back along the road toward Zellerfeld. The engineers laid three tree barricades; *Leutnant* Beckmann was assigned to defend the most forward one. For this, he was allotted a group of soldiers and six Hitler Youths with *Panzerfausts.* When the enemy attacked at 0900 hours on 12 April, six of his soldiers ran away, while the Hitler Youths bravely persevered. After firing all *Panzerfausts,* Beckmann cleared the position and retreated to the rearward obstacles. Two soldiers and two Hitler Youths were killed.[27]

Meanwhile, the 26th Infantry Regiment of the 1st Infantry Division pushed through from Bad Grund toward Clausthal-Zellerfeld, and cut off the units of the combat group that were fighting at the tree barricades. On 13 April, some of the encircled, including Beckmann, were able to beat their way through to our lines, which were now east of Clausthal.[28] On the evening of 12 April, the village of Clausthal-Zellerfeld was cleared and in the morning of 13 April, it was occupied by the enemy.[29]

Another attempt to stem the enemy was made between Clausthal and Altenau. On the evening of 12 April, the remnants of *Combat Group Brühl* took up positions east of Clausthal-Zellerfeld, *Hauptmann* Geigenmüller among them with two tank destroyers on the road to Altenau. *Oberleutnant* Weissflog took part with his Panther, as did *Panzer IV 818* from the *8th Company, Panzer Regiment 16* and an assault gun from the *7th Company, Panzer Regiment 16*. *Leutnant* Golly and his engineers took up position in an ammunition factory there. On 13 April, Golly was marched out by the Americans, again by the 26th Infantry Regiment, and was captured. The remaining units retreated to Altenau. The village fell on 13 April.[30] During a counterstrike in Altenau, combined with units from *Combat Group Fallois, Feldwebel* Arnold, the commander of *Panzer IV 818*, was killed.[31]

From here on, there was no longer a cohesive deployment of the combat group. Most soldiers hid in the woods, mainly in the vicinity of Braunlage–Elend, and were discovered little by little and taken prisoner. A few succeeded in escaping.

On Sunday, 15 April, the last day of combat for the *116th Panzer Division* in the Ruhr cauldron, the defenders of the western front of the Harz were pushed back toward the Brocken–Achtermannshöhe mountain range west of Braunlage. The enemy entered the mountain range from the south on a broad front and stood before Benneckenstein, Stiege, and Harzgerode.[32]

On this 15 April, *Major* Degenhard issued the following order:

Commander of Division Supply Unit 60   O.U., 15 April 1945
    1915 hours
    Engineer battalion scout reports road open to the east. Relocate units, marching at once via Ballenstedt–Aschersleben toward east and march east of Elbe to Lauenburg. There, report at release point Clausewitz for regrouping.
    Command: Company commanders personally. Scout ahead as far as engineer battalion, which is already rolling!
    Degenhard
    Battalion Commander[33]

Obviously, the remnants of the *116th Panzer Division* were to contribute to the regrouping of *Panzer Division "Clausewitz,"* which together with *Division "Schlageter,"* under the command of the *XXXIX Panzer Corps,* was to attack south out of the Ülzen area, west of the Elbe, to reestablish contact with the *11th Army* in the Harz. Originally, *OKW* intended to combine this assault with an attack by the *12th Army* west across the Elbe. The attack by *12th Army* was not realized because all its troops were involved in combat at the Elbe and Mulde. The attack by the *XXXIX Panzer Corps*—actually only the incomplete *Division "Clausewitz"*—began on 15 April with incomplete formations.[34] They attacked one after the other. It can no longer be established which unit of the *116th Panzer Division* found its way to *Division "Clausewitz."* Degenhard himself remained in the Harz and was captured there.

It is certain that the maintenance detachment of *Armored Artillery Regiment 146*, under the command of *Oberleutnant* Kempe, reached the Lauenburg area and joined *Division "Clausewitz."* It was its only maintenance unit.[35] On 17 April, Kempe received the order to cross the Elbe and to reach the Göhrde Forest. From there, he and his troops marching during the night ultimately reached Königslutter at the Elm forest via Fallersleben. Everything from *Division "Clausewitz"* that came this far moved into the Elm. Kempe dated this as 22 April. In fact, it probably was already so on 20 April. Weak groups of *Division "Clausewitz"* thereby caused some trouble in the rear of the enemy. The one in the front came to an end on 18 April near Gardelegen. The main group, under the Division Commander, *Generalleutnant* Unrein, was caught in a trap near the Elm and was overrun by the enemy on the evening of 20 April.[36] Also on 20 April, remnants of the *116th Panzer Division* were taken prisoner in the vicinity of Blankenburg at the northern edge of the Harz. The same fate befell *Hauptmann* Geigenmüller in Wienrode, with what was left of *Panzerjäger Battalion 228*.[37] Near Timmenrode, facing the 8th Armored Division, horse-drawn baggage units, probably mostly from the convalescent hospital, capitulated. They had 177 horses and 144 vehicles. They caused such a sensation that the Commander of the 9th Army, General Lieutenant Simpson honored them with a visit on 21 April.[38]

The last battles in the Harz took place on 21 April in the vicinity of Blankenburg.[39] The *12th Army* could never give any thought to mounting an attack toward the west. On 15 April, it reported to *OKW* that it saw its mission as the defense of the Elbe-Mulde front.[40]

On 16 April, the Soviets mounted a major assault across the Neisse and the Oder. On 24 April, they stood before Dresden and Berlin.[41] During the night of 22/23 April, *General der Panzertruppe* Wenck, Commander of *12th Army,* received orders from *Generalfeldmarschall* Keitel in person, to double back and attack Berlin.[42] On 24 April, the Army made an about-face and turned east, leaving security guards opposite the Americans.[43] Its attack reached the area south of Potsdam and made it possible for units that were surrounded by the Russians, mainly the *9th Army* under *General der Infanterie* Busse, to break out to the west, and for many refugees to escape the Russians. But Berlin could not be relieved. Hitler learned about this on 30 April; approximately 14 hours later, he took his life.[44] On 18 March, he had declared to Speer:

> If the war is lost, the people will also be lost. This fate in unavoidable. It is not necessary to give consideration to the basics that the people will need for their most primitive further existence. To the contrary, it would be better to even destroy these things. The people have proved to be the weaker ones and the future belongs exclusively to the stronger people from the East. What is left after the battle are only the inferior ones anyway, because the good ones have fallen![45]

On 22 April, Eisenhower told the Soviets that he would stop along the Elbe–Mulde line. On 30 April, he informed them of the following line: Wismar–Schwerin–Dömitz–Elbe–Mulde–Karlsbad–Pilsen–Budweis–Enns. Berlin, Vienna, and Prague were left to the Soviets. On 30 April, Churchill attempted to at least save Prague, without success.[46] Ultimately, all of Mecklenburg, the province of Saxony-Anhalt, the rest of Saxony, and Thuringia were surrendered to the Soviets; only a part of Berlin was taken from them.

The Empire of all Germans was destroyed, the dream that finally became realty for all patriots was shattered. The Germans were chased out of flourishing areas. Most of the cities laid in rubble. The arrogance of a criminal leadership pushed the people into disaster and even burdened it with a stain of guilt. The German people had fought bravely and in good faith, passed unspeakably hard tests, and made horrible sacrifices, but it was not "lost" as Hitler prophesied. New life grew out of the rubble, and now the core of its area is again united in liberty, and therefore, the partition of Europe is removed and the danger of a still more terrible war probably banned. Now it is up to all of us to bring our whole *Vaterland* into full bloom. We have honored the legacy of our dead to keep the peace and to reestablish German unity in liberty, as far as it is in our power. We remember their sacrifices in mourning, but now at least with a better conscience.

Organization Diagram, Panzer Division 44

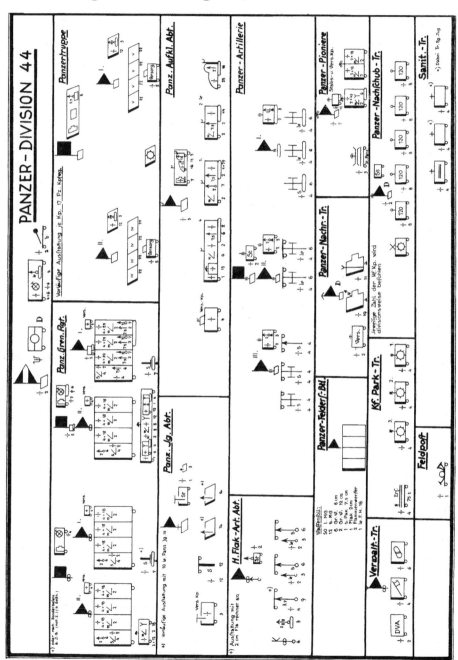

APPENDIX 2

Roster of Officers and Duty Positions of the 116th Panzer Division (to the extent they can be determined today) and the Division's Knight's Cross Recipients

Appendix 2a (as of June/July 1944)

Staff, 116th Panzer Division

Commander	Generalleutnant	Gerhard, Count von Schwerin
Ia (1st General Staff Off/Opns Off)	Major i.G.	Heinz Günther Guderian
0 1 (1st Asst. Adjutant/ Asst. Opns Off)	Leutnant d.R.	Dietrich Bisping
0 4 (4th Asst. Adjutant/ Asst. Opns Off)	Leutnant d.R.	Karl-Heinz Büscher
Ic (Intelligence Officer)	Hauptmann d.R.	Dr. Arthur Holtermann
0 3 (3rd Asst. Adjutant/ Asst. Intel Off)	Leutnant d.R.	Karl-Peter Bischoff
IIa (Adjutant, for Officers)	Major	Fritz Vogelsang
IIb (Adjutant, for Enlisted Men)	Hauptmann d.R.	Fritz Stukenberg
Ib (2d General Staff Off/Supply Off)	Major	Lothar Wolf
0 2 (2d Asst. Adj/ Asst. Supply Off)	Oberleutnant d.R.	Alexander Erdland
Division Physician	Oberstabsarzt (Major)	Dr. Gerhard Baselt, M.D.
Adjutant	Stabsarzt d.R. (Hauptmann)	Dr. Werner Mehring, M.D.
Div. Kfz. Offz. (Div. Engineer)	Major	Karl Hartung
W.u.G. (Weapons and Equipment Off)	Hauptmann	Willibald Butz
Div. Intendant (Admin Off)	Oberstabsintendant (Major)	Dr. Eberhard Falck
Div. Richter (Judge Advocate)	Kriegsgerichtsrat d.R. (Hauptmann)	Hans-Georg Manteufel

Protestant Chaplain	Pfarrer	Dietrich Baedeker
Roman Catholic Chaplain	Pfaffer	Josef Strickstrock
Headquarters Commandant	Oberleutnant d.R.	Kurt Volckerts

Panzer Regiment 16

| Commander | Major | Hans-Georg Lueder |
| Adjutant | Hauptmann | Klaus Kühne |

1st Battalion (Panther) (in Grafenwöhr)

Commander	Major	Gerhard Tebbe
Adjutant	Oberleutnant	Horst Gittermann
1st Company	Hauptmann	Franz Kuchenbuch
2d Company	Hauptmann	Hans Kratzsch
3d Company	Hauptmann	Karl-Hermann Flath
4th Company	Oberleutnant d.R.	Walter Penzler

2d Battalion (Panzer IV)

Commander	Hauptmann d.R.	Friedrich, Count von Brühl
Adjutant	Oberleutnant d.R.	Horst Templin
5th Company	Oberleutnant	Werner Adam
6th Company	Oberleutnant d.R.	Willi Erdmann
7th Company	Oberleutnant d.R.	Ernst Harder
8th Company	Hauptmann	Werner Brinkmann

1st Battalion, Panzer Regiment 24 (Panther) (attached)

Commander	Major	Kuno von Meyer
Adjutant	Leutnant d.R.	Albrecht Stein von Kamienski
1st Company	Rittmeister	Christoph von Helldorff
2d Company	Oberleutnant	Heinrich, Baron von Schlotheim
3d Company	Rittmeister d.R.	Arnold von Günther
4th Company	Oberleutnant	Gert-Axel Weidemann

Panzer-Grenadier Regiment 60

Commander	Oberst	Heinrich Voigtsberger
Adjutant	Hauptmann	Eberhard Risse
9th (Infantry Gun) Company	Oberleutnant d.R.	Martin Röttger
10th (Combat Engineer) Company	Leutnant d.R.	Joachim Degner

1st Battalion (Armored Personnel Carriers)

Commander	Major	Helmut Zander
Adjutant	Leutnant d.R.	Wolfgang Möller
1st Company	Oberleutnant	Gerd Gorges
2d Company	Oberleutnant d.R.	Emil Reunert
3d Company	Oberleutnant d.R.	Harald von Löbbecke
4th Company	Hauptmann	Helmut Nagel

2d Battalion (Motorized)

Commander	Major	Wilhelm Carstensen
Adjutant	Oberleutnant d.R.	Helmut Holtkamp
5th Company	Oberleutnant	Werner Neuhaus
6th Company	Oberleutnant	Karl Flörchinger
7th Company	Oberleutnant	Ernst-Werner Weiss
8th Company	Oberleutnant d.R.	Theo Kuhlmann

Panzer-Grenadier Regiment 156

Commander	Oberst	Otto Fischer
Adjutant	Oberleutnant	Gerhard Voigt
9th (Infantry Gun) Company	Oberleutnant d.R.	Wilhelm Lehmkämper
10th (Combat Engineer) Company	Oberleutnant d.R.	Karl-Heinz Swenson

1st Battalion (Motorized)

Commander	Major	Herbert Flecke
Adjutant	Leutnant	Günter Hoppe
1st Company	Oberleutnant d.R.	Kurt Heiberger
2d Company	Oberleutnant	Phidias Triantaphyllides
3d Company	Oberleutnant	Dietrich Doneit
4th Company	Oberleutnant	Hermann Ruppert

2d Battalion (Motorized)

Commander	Hauptmann	Alois Nitsch
Adjutant	Oberleutnant	Gerhard Model
5th Company	Oberleutnant	Hans Nürnberg
6th Company	Oberleutnant	Hans Eric Best
7th Company	Oberleutnant	Fritz Strackerjahn
8th Company	Oberleutnant d.R.	Karl Kaden

Armored Reconnaissance Battalion 116

Commander	Hauptmann	Kurt Zehner
Adjutant	Leutnant d.R.	Richard Nommensen
1st Company	Rittmeister	Jürgen Schliep
2d Company	Oberleutnant d.r.	Jakob Gärtner
3d Company	Oberleutnant	Kurt Michler
4th Company	Oberleutnant	Otto Hellhammer

Panzerjäger Battalion 228

Commander	Major	Helmut Bochnig
Adjutant	Leutnant d.R.	Wenzel Borgert
1st Company	Oberleutnant	Hubert Hartlieb
2d Company	Oberleutnant d.R.	Ludwig Resch
3d Company	Hauptmann d.R.	Wilhelm Wohlgemuth

Armored Artillery Regiment 146

Commander	Oberst d.R.	Dr. Ernst Pean
Adjutant	Hauptmann	Werner Vinke

1st Battalion (Self-Propelled)

Commander	Major	Wilhelm Sandkuhl
Adjutant	Oberleutnant	Franz Säcker
1st Battery	Oberleutnant d.R.	Heinz Brockhaus
2d Battery	Oberleutnant d.R.	Detmar Meiners
3d Battery	Hauptmann	Theodor Ammermann

2d Battalion

Commander	Hauptmann d.R.	Gerhard Müller
Adjutant	Oberleutnant d.R.	Friedhelm Herring
4th Battery	Oberleutnant	Gerhard Willerding
5th Battery	Hauptmann	Wilfried Segebarth
6th Battery	Oberleutnant d.R.	Egon Steinmeier

3d Battalion

Commander	Hauptmann	Heinz Schmeerman
Adjutant	Leutnant	Erwin Poth
7th Battery	Oberleutnant	Karl-Ernst Tielker
8th Battery	Hauptmann	Hans-Werner Kusenberg
9th Battery	Hauptmann d.R.	Alfred Henrich

Army Anti-Aircraft Battalion 281 (Motorized)

Commander	Hauptmann d.R.	Alfred Beug
Adjutant	Leutnant d.R.	Paul Massman
1st Battery	Oberleutnant d.R.	Hans Wilhelm
2d Battery	Hauptmann	Gerhard Lutz
3d Battery	Oberleutnant	Wolfgang Horney

Armored Engineer Battalion 675

Commander	Hauptmann	Klaus Hossenfelder
Adjutant	Leutnant	Horst Baecker
1st Company	Oberleutnant	Kurt Oberfeuer
2d Company	Oberleutnant	Gerd Kuschel
3d Company	Oberleutnant	Heinrich Diekmann

Armored Signal Battalion 228

Commander	Hauptmann	Richard Kleckel
Adjutant	Oberleutnant	Günther Prophet
1st Company	Hauptmann	Alexander Stachowitsch
2d Company	Hauptmann d.R.	Karl Agne

Armored Field Replacement Battalion 146

Commander	Major	Heinrich Grollmann
Adjutant	Oberleutnant d.R.	August-Wilhelm Inboden
Division Combat School	Hauptmann	Hans Winter

Armored Supply Troop 66

Commander	Hauptmann d.R.	Ernst Degenhard
Adjutant	Oberleutnant d.R.	Hermann Buschmann

Appendix 2b (as of about 16 December 1944)

<u>Staff, 116th Panzer Division</u>

Commander	Generalmajor	Siegfried von Waldenburg
Ia (1st General Staff Off/Opns Off)	Oberstleutnant i.G.	Heinz Günther Guderian
0 1 (1st Asst. Adjutant/ Asst. Opns Off)	Hauptmann d.R.	Walter Küpper
0 4 (4th Asst. Adjutant/ Asst. Opns Off)	Oberleutnant d.R.	Otto Franz
Ic (Intelligence Officer)	Hauptmann d.R.	Dr. Arthur Holtermann
0 3 (3rd Asst. Adjutant/ Asst. Intel Off)	Oberleutnant d.R.	Karl-Peter Bischoff
IIa (Adjutant, for Officers)	Major	Fritz Vogelsang
IIb (Adjutant, for Enlisted Men)	Hauptmann d.R.	Fritz Stukenberg
Ib (2d General Staff Off/ Supply Off)	Major i.G.	Heinz-Jürgen Issbrücker
0 2 (2d Asst. Adj/ Asst. Supply Off)	Oberleutnant d.R.	Alexander Erdland
Division Physician	Oberfeldarzt (Oberstleutnant)	Professor. Dr. Wilhelm Bickert
Div. Kfz. Offz. (Div. Engineer)	Major	Karl Hartung
W.u.G. (Weapons and Equipment Off)	Hauptmann	Willibald Butz
Div. Intendant (Admin Off)	Oberstabsintendant (Major)	Dr. Eberhard Falck
Div. Richter (Judge Advocate)	Kriegsgerichtsrat d.R. (Hauptmann)	Hans-Georg Manteufel
Headquarters Commandant	Hauptmann d.R.	Günter Tscheuschler
Div. Escort Company	Hauptmann	Wilhelm Schneider

<u>Panzer Regiment 16</u>

Commander	Oberst	Johannes Bayer
Adjutant	Oberleutnant	Horst Gittermann

<u>1st Battalion (Panther)</u>

Commander	Hauptmann	Karl-Hermann Flath
Adjutant	Oberleutnant d.R.	Hermann Gekle
1st Company	Hauptmann	Franz Kuchenbuch

2d Company	Oberleutnant d.R.	Kurt Köhn
3d Company	Leutnant	Hans Bunzel
4th Company	Oberleutnant d.R.	Walter Penzler

2d Battalion (Panzer IV)

Commander	Hauptmann	Werner Brinkmann
Adjutant	Oberleutnant d.R.	Horst Templin
5th Company	Leutnant d.R.	Horst Schaller
6th Company	Oberleutnant d.R.	Willi Erdmann
7th Company	Oberleutnant d.R.	Ernst Harder
8th Company	Oberleutnant	Wilhelm Mielke

Panzer-Grenadier Regiment 60

Commander	Oberstleutnant	Helmut Zander
Adjutant	Hauptmann	Eberhard Risse
9th (Infantry Gun) Company	Oberleutnant d.R.	Martin Röttger
10th (Combat Engineer) Company	Oberleutnant d.R.	Gottfried Lichtenfeld

1st Battalion (Armored Personnel Carriers)

Commander	Hauptmann	Bernhard Kroll
Adjutant	Oberleutnant	Karl Jochum
1st Company	Leutnant d.R.	Walter Bohnert
2d Company	Oberleutnant d.R.	Emil Reunert
3d Company	Oberleutnant	Franz von Schrom
4th Company	Oberleutnant d.R.	Josef Schelz

2d Battalion (Motorized)

Commander	Major	Wilhelm Carstensen
Adjutant	Oberleutnant d.R.	Helmut Holtkamp
5th Company	Leutnant	Alfred Krümmling
6th Company	Hauptmann	Ernst Banaski
7th Company	Leutnant	Wilhelm Schalon
8th Company	Hauptmann	Paul Schneider

Panzer-Grenadier Regiment 156

Commander	Oberstleutnant	Heinrich Grollmann
Adjutant	Hauptmann	Hermann Ruppert
9th (Infantry Gun) Company	Oberleutnant d.R.	Wilhelm Lehmkämper
10th (Combat Engineer) Company	Oberleutnant d.R.	Horst Stoltenberg

1st Battalion (Motorized)

Commander	Hauptmann	Hans Winter
Adjutant	Leutnant d.R.	Egbert Möcklinghoff
1st Company		
2d Company		
3d Company		
4th Company	Oberleutnant d.R.	Kurt Heiberger

2d Battalion (Motorized)

Commander	Hauptmann	Heinrich Gerke
Adjutant	Oberleutnant	Gerhard Model
5th Company	Oberleutnant d.R.	Jürgen Löffler
6th Company	Leutnant	Rudolf Krefeld
7th Company	Leutnant d.R.	Oskar Junge
8th Company	Leutnant	Rudolf Seeger

Armored Reconnaissance Battalion 116

Commander	Major	Eberhard Stephan
Adjutant	Oberleutnant d.R.	Richard Nommensen
1st Company	Rittmeister	Jürgen Schliep
2d Company	Oberleutnant d.R.	Karl Andreis
3d Company	Oberleutnant	Johann Sesterhenn
4th Company	Oberleutnant	Otto Hellhammer

Panzerjäger Battalion 228

Commander	Hauptmann d.R.	Helmut Geigenmüller
Adjutant	Leutnant d.R.	Walter Kaspers
1st Company	Oberleutnant	Hubert Hartlieb
2d Company	Leutnant d.R.	Wenzel Borgert
3d Company	Oberleutnant d.R.	Eilhard Dierks

Armored Artillery Regiment 146

Commander	Major	August-Wilhelm ten Hompel
Adjutant	Hauptmann	Erhard John

1st Battalion (Self-Propelled)

Commander	Hauptmann	Werner Vinke
Adjutant	Leutnant	Karl Wessel
1st Battery	Leutnant d.R.	Wolfgang Pich
2d Battery	Oberleutnant d.R.	Wilfrid Kisker
3d Battery	Hauptmann	Theodor Ammermann

2d Battalion

Commander	Hauptmann d.R.	Gerhard Müller
Adjutant	Leutnant d.R.	Walter Hasenpatt-Prigge
4th Battery	Hauptmann	Gerhard Willerding
5th Battery	Hauptmann d.R.	Hans Heim
6th Battery	Oberleutnant d.R.	Egon Steinmeier

3d Battalion

Commander	Hauptmann	Hans-Werner Kusenberg
Adjutant	Oberleutnant	Erwin Poth
7th Battery	Oberleutnant	Karl-Ernst Tielker
8th Battery	Leutnant d.R.	Josef Blome
9th Battery	Oberleutnant	Wolfgang Heestermann-Königsbeck

Army Anti-Aircraft Battalion 281 (Motorized)

Commander	Hauptmann d.R.	Alfred Beug
Adjutant	Leutnant d.R.	Paul Massman
1st Battery	Oberleutnant d.R.	Hans Wilhelm
2d Battery	Hauptmann	Gerhard Lutz
3d Battery	Oberleutnant	Wolfgang Horney

Armored Engineer Battalion 675

Commander	Hauptmann	Klaus Hossenfelder
Adjutant	Leutnant d.R.	Richard Alpers
1st Company	Leutnant	Otto Varnholt
2d Company	Oberleutnant d.R.	Karl-Heinz Hölling
3d Company	Leutnant	Günter Panneck

Armored Signal Battalion 228

Commander	Hauptmann	Helmut Bartels
Adjutant	Oberleutnant	Günther Prophet
1st Company	Oberleutnant	Siegfried Matern
2d Company	Oberleutnant d.R.	Helmut Böttcher

Armored Field Replacement Battalion 146

Commander	Hauptmann	Werner Baumgarten-Crusius
Adjutant	Oberleutnant d.R.	August-Wilhelm Inboden
Division Combat School	Hauptmann	Otto Schörken

Armored Supply Troop 66

Commander	Hauptmann d.R.	Ernst Degenhard
Adjutant	Oberleutnant d.R.	Hermann Buschmann

Appendix 2c (as of about 15 March 1945)

Staff, 116th Panzer Division

Commander	Generalmajor	Siegfried von Waldenburg
Ia (1st General Staff Off/Opns Off)	Oberstleutnant i.G.	Heinz Günther Guderian
0 1 (1st Asst. Adjutant/ Asst. Opns Off)	Hauptmann d.R.	Walter Küpper
0 4 (4th Asst. Adjutant/ Asst. Opns Off)	Oberleutnant d.R.	Otto Franz
Ic (Intelligence Officer)	Hauptmann d.R.	Dr. Arthur Holtermann
0 3 (3rd Asst. Adjutant/ Asst. Intel Off)	No longer staffed. Oberleutnant Bischoff killed in action	
IIa (Adjutant, for Officers)	Major	Fritz Vogelsang
IIb (Adjutant, for Enlisted Men)	Hauptmann d.R.	Fritz Stukenberg
Ib (2d General Staff Off/ Supply Off)	Major i.G.	Hans-Christoph von Carlowitz
0 2 (2d Asst. Adj/ Asst. Supply Off)	Oberleutnant d.R.	Alexander Erdland
Division Physician	Oberstabsarzt (Oberstleutnant)	Dr. Helmut Maasen
Div. Kfz. Offz. (Div. Engineer)	Major	Karl Hartung
W.u.G. (Weapons and Equipment Off)	Hauptmann	Willibald Butz
Div. Intendant (Admin Off)	Oberstabsintendant (Major)	Dr. Eberhard Falck
Div. Richter (Judge Advocate)	Kriegsgerichtsrat d.R. (Hauptmann)	Hans-Georg Manteufel
Headquarters Commandant	Hauptmann d.R.	Günter Tscheuschler
Div. Escort Company	Hauptmann	Johann Rudolph

Panzer Regiment 16

Commander, until 26 March	Oberst	Johannes Bayer
Commander, after 26 March	Major	Gerhard Tebbe
Adjutant, until 26 March	Hauptmann	Klaus Kühne
Adjutant, after 26 March	Oberleutnant	Horst Gittermann

1st Battalion (Panther)

Commander, until 26 March	Hauptmann	Werner Adam
Commander, after 26 March	Hauptmann	Klaus Kühne
Adjutant	Leutnant d.R.	Hermann Gekle
1st Company	Oberleutnant	Richard Wich
2d Company	Oberleutnant d.R.	Johannes Wolters
3d Company	Oberleutnant	Horst Glitterman
4th Company		

2d Battalion (Panzer IV)*

Commander	Major d.R.	Friedrich, Count von Brühl
Adjutant	Leutnant d.R.	Paul Aufleger
5th Company	Oberleutnant	Joachim Weissflog
6th Company	Leutnant	Horst Rink
7th Company	Oberleutnant d.R.	Ernst Harder
8th Company	Oberleutnant d.R.	Horst Templin

Panzer-Grenadier Regiment 60

Commander	Major	Eberhard Stephan
Adjutant	Oberleutnant d.R.	Helmut Holtkamp
10th (Infantry Gun) Company**	Hauptmann d.R.	Martin Röttger
11th (Combat Engineer) Company**		

1st Battalion (Armored Personnel Carriers)

Commander	Hauptmann	Joseph von Ketteler
Adjutant		
1st Company		
2d Company		
3d Company		
4th Company	Oberleutnant d.R.	Josef Schelz

**Both battalions were eventually consolidated into one, with two companies from each former battalion.
**The former 8th Company was divided into two new companies (8th Company—direct fire and 9th Company—indirect fire); after this, the former 9th and 10th Companies became the 10th and 11th Companies, respectively.

2d Battalion (Motorized)

Commander	Hauptmann d.R.	Ernst Bröker
Adjutant	Leutnant	Wolfgang Vogel
5th Company	Leutnant	Alfred Krümmling
6th Company	Leutnant	Rudolf Krefeld
7th Company	Leutnant	Wilhelm Schalon
8th Company**	Oberleutnant d.R.	Otto Wilms
9th Company**	Oberleutnant d.R.	Hans-Joachim Tzschentke

Panzer-Grenadier Regiment 156

Commander	Oberstleutnant	Heinrich Grollmann
Adjutant	Hauptmann	Gerhard Voigt
11th (Infantry Gun) Company***	Hauptmann d.R.	Wilhelm Lehmkämper
12th (Combat Engineer) Company***	Oberleutnant	Wilhelm Höltje

1st Battalion (Motorized)

Commander	Hauptmann	Walter Froemel
Adjutant	Oberleutnant	Wilhelm Bellmann (?)
1st Company		
2d Company		
3d Company	Leutnant	Willi Tanneberger
4th Company***		
5th Company***		

2d Battalion (Motorized)

Commander	Hauptmann	Erich Zanzinger
Adjutant	Oberleutnant d.R.	Horst Stoltenberg
6th Company	Oberleutnant	(?) Schutow
7th Company	Oberleutnant d.R.	Karl Noltensmeyer
8th Company	Oberleutnant d.R.	Oskar Junge
9th Company***	Leutnant	Bruno Tröster
10th Company***	Leutnant	Claus (?) Fricke

***The former 4th and 8th Companies were divided into two new companies (direct fire and indirect fire); after this, all companies above 5th Company were renumbered.

Armored Reconnaissance Battalion 116

Commander, until 26 March	Major	Gerhard Tebbe
Commander, after 26 March	Hauptmann	Walter Fischer
Adjutant	Oberleutnant d.R.	Theodor Adam
1st Company		
2d Company	Oberleutnant d.R.	Karl Andreis
3d Company	Oberleutnant	Johann Sesterhenn
4th Company	Oberleutnant	Kurt Michler

Panzerjäger Battalion 228

Commander	Hauptmann d.R.	Helmut Geigenmüller
Adjutant	Leutnant d.R.	Werner Vöhl
1st Company	Oberleutnant	Erwin Neusch
2d Company	Oberleutnant d.R.	Wenzel Borgert
3d Company	Oberleutnant d.R.	Eilhard Dierks

Armored Artillery Regiment 146

Commander	Major	August-Wilhelm ten Hompel
Adjutant	Hauptmann	Erhard John

1st Battalion (Self-Propelled)

Commander	Hauptmann	Heinz Lüsse
Adjutant	Oberleutnant	Karl Wessel
1st Battery	Leutnant d.R.	Wolfgang Pich
2d Battery	Hauptmann d.R.	Wilfrid Kisker
3d Battery	Hauptmann	Theodor Ammermann

2d Battalion

Commander	Major d.R.	Gerhard Müller
Adjutant	Leutnant d.R.	Walter Hasenpatt-Prigge
4th Battery	Hauptmann	Gerhard Willerding
5th Battery	Hauptmann d.R.	Hans Heim
6th Battery	Hauptmann d.R.	Egon Steinmeier

3d Battalion

Commander	Major	Heinz Schmeermann
Adjutant	Oberleutnant	Erwin Poth
7th Battery	Hauptmann	Karl-Ernst Tielker
8th Battery	Hauptmann	Hans Krass
9th Battery	Oberleutnant	Wolfgang Heestermann-Königsbeck

Army Anti-Aircraft Battalion 281 (Motorized)

Commander	Hauptmann d.R.	Alfred Beug
Adjutant	Leutnant d.R.	Reinhold Peetz
1st Battery	Oberleutnant d.R.	Hans Wilhelm
2d Battery	Hauptmann	Gerhard Lutz
3d Battery	Oberleutnant	Wolfgang Horney

Armored Engineer Battalion 675

Commander	Hauptmann	Klaus Hossenfelder
Adjutant	Leutnant d.R.	Reinhard Golly
1st Company	Oberleutnant	Otto Varnholt
2d Company	Leutnant	Josef Willoh
3d Company	Oberleutnant d.R.	Karl-Heinz Hölling

Armored Signal Battalion 228

Commander	Hauptmann	Erwin Jeglinski
Adjutant	Oberleutnant	Günther Prophet
1st Company	Hauptmann	Siegfried Matern
2d Company	Hauptmann d.R.	Helmut Böttcher

Armored Field Replacement Battalion 146

Commander	Hauptmann d.R.	August-Wilhelm Inboden
Division Combat School	Hauptmann	Otto Schörken

Armored Supply Troop 66

Commander	Major d.R.	Ernst Degenhard
Adjutant	Oberleutnant d.R.	Hermann Buschmann

Appendix 2d

Soldiers Who Received the Knight's Cross While
Assigned to the 116th Panzer Division

9 June 1944	Major Helmut Bochnig, Commander, Panzerjäger Battalion 228
5 Oct 1944	Major i.G. Heinz Günther Guderian, Ia, 116th Panzer Division
26 Nov 1944	Major Kuno von Meyer, Commander, 1st Battalion, Panzer Regiment 24
26 Nov 1944	Hauptmann Eberhard Risse, Adjutant, Panzer-Grenadier Regiment 60
9 Dec 1944	Oberst Siegfried von Waldenburg, Acting Commander, 116th Panzer Division
9 Dec 1944	Leutnant Johannes Lutz, Platoon Leader, Division Escort Company, 116th Panzer Division
12 Jan 1945	Major Eberhard Stephan, Commander, Armored Reconnaissance Battalion 116
5 Mar 1945	Leutnant Hans-Joachim Weissflog, Acting Commander, 2d Company, Panzer Regiment 16
17 Mar 1945	Hauptmann Eduard-Georg Hübner, Commander, Assault Battalion, 1st Parachute Army
29 Mar 1945	Leutnant Heinz Auert, Acting Commander, 2d Company, Armored Reconnaissance Battalion 116
5 Apr 1945	Oberstleutnant Helmut Zander, Commander, Panzer-Grenadier Regiment 60
14 Apr 1945	Leutnant Herbert Käseberg, Acting Commander, 5th Company, Panzer-Grenadier Regiment 156
14 Apr 1945	Feldwebel Fritz Muster, Platoon Leader, Armored Reconnaissance Battalion 116
9 May 1945	Major Hans Jungwirth, Commander, Parachute Reconnaissance Battalion 12

Appendix 2e

Recipients of the Knight's Cross Who Served in the 116th Panzer Division After the Medal was Awarded

Generalleutnant Gerhard, Count von Schwerin, Commander, 116th Panzer Division. Swords, 4 Nov 1943 as Commander, 16th Panzer-Grenadier Division

Hauptmann Werner Baumgarten-Crusius, Acting Commander, 1st Battalion, Panzer-Grenadier Regiment 156. Oakleaves, 27 Feb 1943, as Oberleutnant, Acting Commander, 1st Battalion, Grenadier Regiment 156 (Motorized)

Oberst Heinrich Voigtsberger, Commander, Panzer-Grenadier Regiment 60. Oakleaves, 9 Dec 1943, as Commander, Grenadier Regiment 60 (Mot.)

Major i.G. Heinz-Jürgen Issbrücker, Ib, 116th Panzer Division. Knight's Cross Awarded 12 Sep 1941, as Commander, 3d Company, Armored Reconnaissance Battalion 7

Hauptmann Hermann Ruppert, Acting Adjutant, Panzer-Grenadier Regiment 156. Knight's Cross Awarded 12 Jan 1942, as Leutnant, Inf Reg 15 (Mot.)

Leutnant der Reserve Josef Vernhold, 8th Company, Panzer-Grenadier Regiment 60. Knight's Cross Awarded 22 Feb 1942, as Unteroffizier, 8th Company, Infantry Regiment 60 (Mot.)

Major der Reserve Friedrich, Cont von Brühl, Commander, 2d Battalion, Panzer Regiment 16. Knight's Cross awarded 3 Nov 1942 as Hauptmann der Reserve, Commander, 8th Company, Panzer Regiment 2.

Oberleutnant Hans Bunzel, Acting Commander, 3d Company, Panzer Regiment 16. Knight's Cross awarded 10 Feb 1943 as Oberfeldwebel, Platoon Leader, 3d Company, Panzer Battalion 116.

Oberleutnant Heinrich Schulze, Acting Commander, Support Company, 1st Battalion, Panzer Regiment 16. Knight's Cross awarded 14 Aug 1943, as Stabsfeldwebel, Platoon Leader, 2d Company, Panzer Battalion 116.

Oberst Otto Fischer, Commander, Panzer-Grenadier Regiment 156. Knight's Cross awarded 27 Aug 1943, as Oberstleutnant, Commander, Grenadier Regiment 156 (Mot.).

Feldwebel Georg Thumbeck, 2d Company Panzer-Grenadier Regiment 60. Knight's Cross awarded 12 Nov 1943 as Obergefreiter, 10th Company, Grenadier Regiment 60 (Mot.).

Oberwachtmeister Hermann Wehking, Armored Artillery Regiment 146. Knight's Cross awarded 15 Jan 1944 as Oberwachtmeister, Forward Observer, 1st Battery, Artillery Regiment 146 (Mot.).

Unteroffizier Karl-Heinz Drees, 3rd Company, Panzerjäger Battalion 228. Knight's Cross awarded 8 Feb 1944 as Gefreiter, Gunner, 14th Company (Panzer-Jäger), Grenadier Regiment 552.

Leutnant Willi Tanneberger, Act. Commander, 3d Company, Panzer-Grenadier Regiment 156. Knight's Cross awarded 10 Feb 1944 as Oberfeldwebel, Company Headquarters Section Leader, 3d Company, Grenadier Regiment 156 (Mot.)

Appendix 3

Appeal by the Führer to the Soldiers in the West

Soldiers of the Western Front! The enemy has mounted the attack on Europe that we have long expected. All of us are familiar with his intentions. You are called upon to foil them and thereby secure the national safety, the existence, and the future of our people. The military and materiel prerequisites for this conflict were created during the victorious western offensive of May and June 1940. Since then, in years of work, enormous fortifications have been built along the coasts of Europe. Here, you will now defend our continent. Here, you will destroy the attack by our enemies against the people and the Reich.

Soldiers! In this historic hour, I appeal to your courage, to your proven bravery, and to the steadfastness of your hearts. Your task is to deny the enemy entrance to Europe under all circumstances. In this confrontation, you will connect the power of your weapons with the strength of your souls. The repulse of this assault is a matter of life for our people and a historic task, whose fateful dimension obligates each of you to the utmost. Here is no escape and no maneuver; what matters here is to stand, to hold, or to die. Every leader, every commander of a base, an island, or a fortress, or of a ship, is responsible to me with his honor, never to capitulate and to continue the battle to the last fighter and to the last grenade and round. In these days, the German people and the whole world are looking at you.

I know that each of you, my brave soldiers, is deeply filled with the will to fight in the coming days and ultimately to secure a fortunate future for our people. Wherever the enemy attacks, he must be destroyed. he will not succeed in gaining a foothold on the coast defended by us. Victory will, therefore, be ours. You are called upon to fight for it and thereby to fulfill the legacy of our fallen comrades.

signed, Adolf Hitler[*]

---

[*] From KTB HQ, 15th Army Ic, RH 20-15/208

Appendix 4

116. Pz.-Division   Division Command Post, 12 June 1944
Section Ia   2000 hours

Division Order
Orders for combat:
1.) Army Group B expects immediate upcoming major attack against the front Dunkirk–mouth of the Somme.
2.) Division prevents breach of coastal front on both sides of Le Tréport from the rear by airborne troops and remains prepared to mount counterattack against penetrated enemy near and north of Ault. Intervention also possible in the direction of Dieppe.
3.) Onset of enemy attack and coordinated airborne landings further inland of Ault and Le Tréport are already possible in the coming night.
It is important that the troops march quickly during the night and reach their designated areas before daylight. Subsequently, they must dig in with the greatest speed and take up position so that open areas primarily used for airborne landings will be controlled by fires. Therefore, do not go into the forests and villages, but rather build positions with regard to the terrain. Dominating points in our hands serve as strongpoints. Motor vehicle echelons to be camouflaged and dug-in in the woods.
4.) Rapid establishment of communications important!
5.) In particular, the following are tasked:
Combat Group Panzer-Grenadier Regiment 60 to secure the high plateau southeast of Ault, north of the Bresle sector.
Combat Group Panzer-Grenadier Regiment 156 to secure the high plateau south of Eu, between the Bresle and Yeres sector, as well as the high plateau northeast of Bailly.
Panzer Group in area west of Gamaches stands by for intervention in both combat groups' areas and reconnoiters accordingly.
Pz.A.R.146 reconnoiters artillery deployment in cooperation with 348th I.D. (command post in Friville).
6.) All combat groups take up position against enemy airborne landings and stand by in highest alert status until further order.

F.d.R.   draft form signed
signed, Bisping   Count von Schwerin
Leutnant and 01

Appendix 5

TRANSCRIPT
Secret!

Headquarters, LXVII Corps   Corps Command Post, 13 June 1944
Ia No. 6000/44 (1547) g.II.Ang.

Order for Deployment of 116th Pz.Div.
(Map, 1:200,000)

1.) 116th Pz.Div. (Army Reserve) moves into positions vicinity of Incheville (excl.)–St. Martin le Gaillard (excl.)–Envermeu–Londinieres–Senarpont–Feuquieres (excl.), and will be subordinated to Headquarters, LXVII Corps. Land front incl. the towns to the 348th Infantry Division. . . .

2.) Mission
    a.) Destruction of opponent's airborne landings in area of operations.
    b.) Counterattack immediately to destroy seaborne opponent in St. Valery–Ault (incl.) swamp or near both sides Le Tréport, respectively.
    c.) Counterattack to destroy opponent seaborne opponent between Yeres and Dieppe.

3.) For this, the Division conducts its main effort north of the Bresle
    with
    1 combat group north of the Bresle,
    1 combat group south of the Yeres,
    further units between the Bresle and the Yeres.
    As support for the defense in the area of operations, the second position . . . is to be occupied by combat-ready units.
    The artillery is to be organized in such a way that it can intervene with strong units in the coastal battle in the area on both sides of Ault.

4.) Deployment in Area of Operations
    Dispersed, weapons including artillery, ready to fire at all times with all-around effect in the terrain, dispersed toward the eastern boundary of the area of operations, securing the most important Bresle and Yeres bridges (see Paragraph 7).

5.) In the area Cahon–Chepy–Moyenneville (one reinforced Grenadier Regiment is already deployed there), one parachute infantry regiment will be deployed with the following missions:
    a.) Defend its area of operations against the airborne enemy,
    b.) Counterattack against seaborne opponent landing south of the mouth of the Somme. ·

Anticipate attachment of this unit to 116th Pz.Division.

Another parachute infantry regiment will be deployed to keep the Somme bridges open on both sides of Abbeville.

6.) Communications are to be established and maintained

    a.) Mainly with the 348th Infantry Division—exact orientation about the action of this division and cooperation in the reconnaissance of 116th Pz.Div.

    b.) With the combat group deployed in the vicinity of Cahon–Chepy–Moyenneville

    c.) Combat Group Abbeville

    d.) 245th Infantry Division

Command posts are announced verbally.

7.) To be reconnoitered

    a.) Deployment north of the Bresle in the vicinity of St. Valery–Ault (incl.), Both sides of Ault

       Vicinity of Le Tréport.

    b.) Deployment on both sides of the Bresle toward Le Tréport.

    c.) Deployment south of the Bresle toward Le Tréport

       Swamp and vicinity of Ault (crossing point swamp with steep shore) are considered a threatened region in corps area south of the Somme.

    d.) Deployment between Yeres and Dieppe.

    e.) Special attention to be given to the reconnaissance of the crossings of the Bresle and the Yeres, to move up the respective combat groups.

. . .

9.) Corps command post announced verbally.

Corps area in Stage II alert.

                         The Commanding General

                         I.V.

                         signed, Sponheimer

                         General der Infanterie

Appendix 6

116th Panzer Division   Command Post, 23 July 1944
Section Ia   1000 hours

To
Panzer-Grenadier Regiment 60

Today, reinforced Panzer-Grenadier Regiment 60 arrives via St. Pierre in the area east of St. Silvain, and with the armored personnel carrier battalion on its left goes into position in the hills south and southwest of Poussy in such a manner that it can repel an eventual breakthrough by the opponent.

Right boundary with 156:	Trail from Cinq Autels–Hill 47 (southwest of Chicheboville). (Responsibility for trail to 60).
Left wing:	Northern part of forest three km southeast of St. Aignan (incl.)

Armored personnel carrier battalion is to stand by so that it can mount a counterattack toward the north and northwest, together with the Panzer Regiment, which after arrival will be employed with one battalion on a wide front southwest of Poussy with the Panther battalion in the area west of St. Silvain.

Elements of Armored Reconnaissance Battalion 116 deployed in the regiment's sector are to be relieved. They assemble later to be at the Division's disposal near Vieux-Fumé. Commander travel ahead to Division commander at the command post of Armored Reconnaissance Battalion 116 in Rue Vilaine.

Distributor:
for the correctness   signed, Count von Schwerin
of the draft:
signed, Guderian
Major i.G.

Appendix 7

116th Panzer Division   Command Post, 9 August 1944
Commander

To the
Commanders

Gentlemen, you may know that on the part of the Commanding General of XLVII Panzer Corps, General der Panzertruppe von Funck, most serious reproaches were raised against the command and battle conduct of the Division from the beginning of its subordination under the mentioned corps. These have been answered by me with increasing severity, unfortunately without any success. These differences apparently led to the request for my relief for cause on the part of the corps commander; by command of Feldmarschall von Kluge, it was ordered this morning.

To begin with, I ask you, gentlemen, to meet Oberst i.G. Reinhard, who was assigned to command the Division, with confidence. He has nothing to do with the whole situation; he himself was just recently relieved of his position as Chief of Staff of XLVII Panzer Corps, because of differences with General von Funck. Besides this, he is a good friend of mine and will certainly do everything to help the Division in this difficult situation.

I will personally first ask for clarification by the Army Supreme Commander, Oberstgruppenführer Hausser, of the reasons that led to my relief, and what reproaches were raised against me. My further actions will depend on the result of this step.

Gentlemen, I expect you to hold your troops and the Division together tightly, in view of the situation at large, which is also known to you. I furthermore expect you and the troops to continue without exception to do your duty with all devotion, so that your shield of honor remains clean and without stain, and that the troops can live with their own consciences.

> signed, v.S.
> Generalleutnant and Commander
> 116th Panzer Division

Appendix 8

TRANSCRIPT

Fellow Countrymen and fellow Countrywomen!

If the enemy approaches the German positions in the West, he should meet our fanatical resistance! His intentions to destroy the Reich and to exterminate our people must be foiled.

He must not be allowed to achieve now that which he could not achieve five years ago, when his highly-equipped armies stood in front of our fortifications. Our children's eyes, which want to see a future, remind us to resist with all means to the last breath. The voices of the many hundreds of thousands who remained on the battlefields for the honor and freedom of our Fatherland, or those who lost their lives to enemy terror bombing, are calling us. The spirits of the heroes of liberty of our glorious history shake us, so that we do not weaken or become cowards during the decisive part of the fight for our existence!

The ruins of our cities and the millions of our fellow countrymen's homes that were destroyed by terror bombing are a silent accusation against anyone who does not give everything for the victory, without which there will be no rebuilding.

Fellow Countrymen and fellow Countrywomen!

We must expect the western forward areas of our fortifications and also the towns within the fortifications to soon become a battle area. Therefore, the Führer ordered the evacuation of the towns and villages in the upcoming battle area for the safety of German life and war-important valuables!

The evacuation proceeds according to plan and without haste. The safeguarding of valuables that are important for the war is handled by the appropriate authorities; the orderly evacuation of men, women, and children has been taken over by the Party.

The Ortsgruppenleiter [Nazi Party village group leaders—*Editor*] issue the necessary instructions according to the directives from the Kreisleiters. The evacuation proceeds to previously-designated areas of the Reich, where all preparations for shelter have been arranged. The relocated people will receive the same assistance as those who were bombed out.

Males between the ages of 16 and 60 who are capable of work will for now not be evacuated, but will be deployed at fortifications under construction, as long as they do not belong to the work force who, because of relocation of its factories, move out with them to another part of the Reich.

The fellow countrymen working on the fortifications will be brought back as soon as their work is completed or the situation at the front requires the fortifications to be released to the fighting Wehrmacht.

Fellow Countrymen and fellow Countrywomen!

In the difficult years of war behind us, you had to make extraordinary sacrifices without ever forgetting your duty. It is important that the evacuation now necessary takes place with discipline and mutual helpfulness!

Whoever disturbs measures of the evacuation, or tries to refuse to join the withdrawal, not only puts himself in deadly danger, but has to be considered a traitor against the public community and dealt with accordingly.

And now more than ever:

Long live our Führer, our Reich, and our People!

Grohé

Gauleiter and Reichs Defense Commissioner

APPENDIX 9

Citizens of Aachen!

The most difficult days in the history of our old, venerable city are ahead of us.

The committee empowered by the Wehrmacht and the city administration will install a temporary administration for the remaining citizens. Provisions can only be assured if everyone does his part.

Remain calm and orderly!

Looting will be punished by the Wehrmacht according to martial law with death by firing squad.

All members of the administration report at the Neues Kurhaus ("New Spa").

Intentions are to establish a self-defense.

Willing and suitable personnel will report this afternoon at 1700 hours in front of the Monheimsallee Spa Park.

If an occupation of the city by enemy forces should occur, no unauthorized actions must occur.

Do not forget that you are Germans. Maintain your dignity as Germans. But avoid anything that could give the enemy cause for coercive measures.

Follow the directives of the undersigned that will be announced in the bunkers or by posters.

Aachen, 14 September 1944

M. Kremer   Dr. Kuetgens   Dr. Drouven   Packbier

Organization Diagram, 116th Panzer Division, 15 September 1944

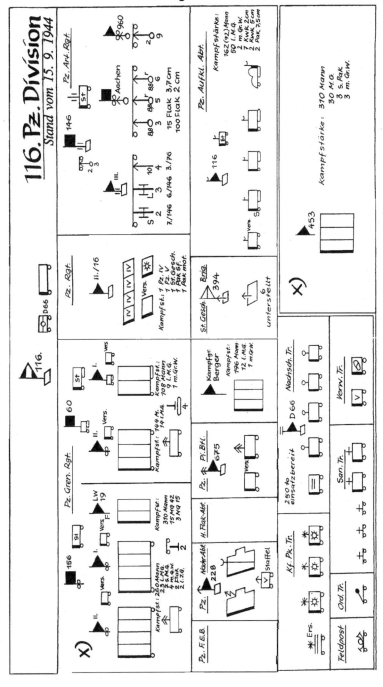

Organization Diagram, 116th Panzer Division, 24 September 1944

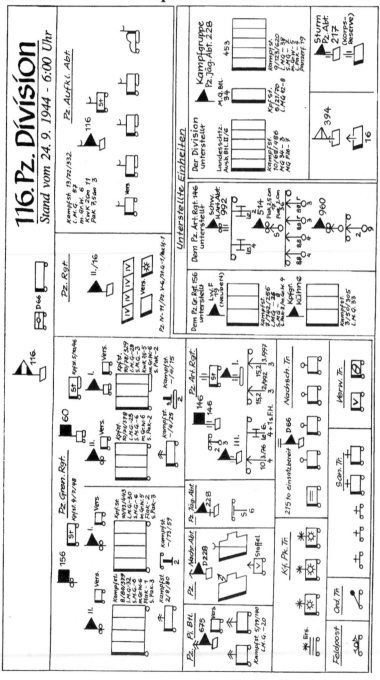

Appendix 12

TRANSCRIPT

116. Panzer Division   Division Command Post, 25 September 1944
Section Ia

Order for the Installation of a Battle Commandant for the City of Aachen
(With accompanying instructions for combat)

1.) Major Zander, commander of Panzer Grenadier Regiment 60, will be appointed Battle Commandant of the city of Aachen.
2.) As per Führer order, the city of Aachen is to be defended as a stronghold ("ein fester Platz") to the last round.
3.) In case of encirclement of the city of Aachen, Major Zander is responsible for command of all encircled troops and formations in the city of Aachen.
4.) As the area of operations for the Commandant of the city of Aachen, the Aachen bridgehead southwest of the main Westwall position is specified in the sector of the 116th Pz.Div.
5.) The battle commandant immediately makes all preparations needed for a longer defense of the city of Aachen (laying of minefields, road barricades, bridge demolitions), and now secures the uniformity of battle conduct and improvements. All units and formations in the city of Aachen that do not belong to combat units are to be employed for these projects to the largest extent possible.
   Nothing is changed for the independent course of battle for reinforced Pz.Gren.Rgts. 60 and 156, or for their subordinations to the 116th Pz.Div.
6.) Combat-ready reserves are to be formed now in anticipation, preparation areas are to be determined and made safe against bombs and fragments.
7.) Supply of ammunition and provisions must be arranged according to the directives already issued by the Ib in direct coordination with the Battle Commandant.
8.) Division Signal Officer, in direct coordination with the Battle Commandant, secures a telephone connection to the Division and between the Battle Commandant and the individual sector commandants, who are to be appointed by the Battle Commandant.
9.) All baggage and other equipment not necessary for defense of the city of Aachen are to be moved out now to holding areas.
10.) Battle Commandant Aachen reports conclusion of preparations by 30 Sept. and submits a plan in duplicate for the defense of the city.

Distributor   v. Waldenburg
Draft

Appendix 13

Headquarters, LXXXI Corps   26 September 1944
Ia

Nr. 153/44 g.Kdos.   18 copies
                                   13th copy

Secret Command Matter

Order for the Release of the 116th Pz.Div.

1.) Enemy has not shown any greater intentions to attack during recent days, apparently due to the high losses he has suffered. Brisk strike troop and artillery activity leads to the conclusion that further attacks must be reckoned with at any time.

2.) LXXXI Corps, with the newly subordinated 246th Volks-Grenadier Division, continues holding the present main battle line, and after regrouping and moving up more forces, is to bring the Westwall position at the left wing back into our possession.

3.) 246th Volks-Gren.Div. is to be inserted into the Aachen sector, and first of all, relieves the infantry units of the 116th Panzer Division. Subordinated for this will be:
Parachute Infantry Battalion,
Luftwaffe Fortress Battalion XIX,
Machine Gun Battalion 34,
Militia Training Battalion II/6
with Infantry Training Battalion 453 attached
A special order will be issued for incorporation of these formations.
It is important for the division to accelerate the transportation of the division and the relief of the 116th Panzer Division by using all available means.
The relief is to be carried out beginning on the night 26/27 only in darkness, or if weather permitting, during the day in close coordination with both divisions.
The relief must be completed by daybreak on 28 September.
Assume command in sector 0600 hours on 28 September.

4.) 116th P.D. remains in command during the conduct of the relief until 0600 hours on 28 September.

The Division ensures that the strength of defense will not be weakened during that time.

Therefore, at first, the following are to be left in the sector:

a) All tanks and anti-tank guns

b) All artillery

Special order to be issued about release of these units.

With assumption of command by 246th Infantry Division, these units first will be subordinated to the 246th Infantry Division.

Special order will be issued referring to transfer of six heavy anti-tank guns (7.5 cm) of the former Fortress Anti-Tank Battalion 302.

116th Panzer Division assembles with released units north and northeast of Jülich.

5.) Artillery Commander 117 ensures that after release of artillery from the 9th Panzer Division and the 116th Panzer Division, heavy fire concentrations are available at any time by combining as many batteries as possible in the area south and southwest of Schevenhütte, Stolberg, Eilendorf, as well as in front of the 49th Infantry Division.

6.) Corps Signal Officer establishes telephone and radio connections.

7.) To be reported:

a) by 116th Panzer Division: continued state of release movements,

b) by 246th Infantry Division: continued state of transport movements,

c) by 246th Infantry Division: assumption of command.

8.) Corps command post as before.

signed, Köchling

General der Infanterie

Distributor:

As per draft.

APPENDIX 14

116th Panzer Division   Division Command Post, 26 September 1944
Section Ia

Order for the Relief of Panzer-Grenadier Regiment 156 by Grenadier Regiment
404 of the 246th Volks-Grenadier Division

1.) 116th Pz. Div. will be pulled out of the Aachen bridgehead for other uses.
2.) For this, during the night of 26/27 September 1944, Gren. Rgt. 404 relieves
    Pz.Gren. Rgt. 156 with 1st and 2d Battalions and regimental units from pre-
    sent deployment; after completion of relief, assumes command in former sec-
    tor of Pz.Gren.Rgt. 156.
3.) For this will be subordinated:
    Parachute Infantry Battalion
    Luftwaffe Fortress Battalion 19
    4 heavy anti-tank guns of Panzerjäger Battalion 228
4.) Assault Gun Brigade 394 as of 26 September 1944 is brought in with all units
    and subordinated to the 12th Infantry Division.
5.) During the relief, it is important that by using all available means of trans-
    portation, Gren. Rgt. 404 be brought forward at nightfall and Pz. Gren. Rgt.
    156 be moved back.
    Assembly in Steinstrass–Stetternich–Hambach forest area to continue march
    north on the evening of 27 September 1944.
6.) After Gren.Rgt.404 takes over the sector, Rgt. will be subordinated to 116th
    Pz.Div.
7.) Arm.Art.Regt.146 prepares to withdraw 6th Battery/146 and the 3d
    Battery/76 in such manner that in the course of 27 September, if the situation
    in the air permits, during day or in the evening, the batteries can be pulled out
    and moved ahead into the assembly area of Pz.Gren. Rgt. 156.
8.) Telephone connections of Pz.Gren.Rgt.156 are to be transferred to 246th
    Volks-Gren.Div.
9.) Gren.Rgt.404 and Pz.Gren.Rgt.156 report successful changeover and relief,
    respectively.
10.) Rear guards [Nachkommando] with sufficient strength are to be left in the
    former positions for 24 hours in coordination between Pz.G.R.156 and
    G.R.404.
    They are to be led to the regiment in closed formation by an officer.

signed, von Waldenburg

Distributor:
In draft

Appendix 15

TRANSCRIPT

Order of the day
Soldiers of the Army Group!

The battle in the West has reached its climax, we are defending German homeland in wide sectors.

Now is the time to protect the holy ground of the Fatherland, tenaciously and doggedly. We go against the enemy onslaught with the greatest strain on the material forces of the German people, with our fighting will, our faith, and our deliberately heightened fanaticism.

The order of the hour is: None of us, while alive, gives up one foot of German soil!

Every bunker, every block of houses in a German town, every German village, has to be made a fortress, on which the enemy will break into pieces. This is expeced by our Führer, our people, and our fallen comrades.

The enemy shall know that there is no way into the heart of the Reich, except over our dead bodies.

There are no rear echelons, everyone are combat troops. Wherever the enemy shows up, a battle must be mounted with all forces.

We do not listen to cowardly doubters and constant know-it-alls who stand aside in fear, without faith and without will.

There is no indolence and comfortable calm if German life is at stake.

More than ever, it is now important to prove faith, confidence, and perseverance.

Each must aim to surpass the other one in courage and conduct. Veteran fighters should set a special example for the younger ones or those comrades who are new to battle! Egotism, forgetfulness of duty, slackness, or even cowardliness must not have any room in our hearts.

He who gives in without a fight, is a traitor to the people!

We know that the enemy tidal wave now presents the utmost threat to our living space (*Lebensraum*).

Our enemies know that German technical developments will decisively back our fight with new war materiel. Therefore, the opponent's intentions are to overrun us before that. Those intentions must come to nothing, due to our determined will and our readiness to fight. In these decisive battles, this is our historic task.

We will confirm this readiness to fight with the resolution: No enemy soldier shall be better than we soldiers of our Führer Adolf Hitler!

Soldiers, our homeland, our women and children are at stake!
Our Führer and all of them trust us soldiers!
We want to be worthy of this trust.

Long live our Germany and our beloved Führer!

Model
Generalfeldmarschall

APPENDIX 16

TRANSCRIPT

Annex 3 to Military Police Command z.b.V/Ia
Nr.0100/44 g.Cmd.-Chief

40 copies
6th copy

DIRECTIVES FOR BATTLE CONDUCT
(Distributed to Divisions)

I. In general

1.) In the West, we attack to completely destroy the opponent's strong forces, and thereby influence the decision of the war.

   The objective is the encirclement of the 21st English Army Group and the Ninth and First American Armies by a quick assault on Antwerp, and to destroy them in cooperation with our forces attacking south from Holland.

   The prerequisite for the success of this operation is to surprise the enemy, which requires secrecy, speed, and mobility—everything must be subordinated to these.

   For the attack, sufficiently-strong infantry and Panzer forces will be prepared with concentrated artillery, mortar, and air support. Reserve divisions will follow in depth; a considerable number of strong replacements are prepared. The day of attack if possible, will be during bad weather. Start of attack at the same hour on the entire front under the protection of darkness.

   Selected units and commanders, as well as the superiority of the German soldier, offer security for complete success. Every soldier from the 5th Panzer Army must be permeated with the thought that the fate of our people and Fatherland is being placed in his hands at this hour. There is only one watchword:

   > "Forward, without looking right or left, across the Meuse towards Antwerp."

   This watchword is to be announced to every soldier (after start of attack)!

2.) Adjacent Units

   a) 6th SS-Panzer Army has the task to advance across the Meuse on both sides of Lüttich and to gain the Albert Canal from Maastricht to Antwerp.

   b) 7th Army is responsible for the protection of the operation's flanks toward the south and southwest. For this, it is to gain and hold a defensive front in the line Gedinne–Libramont–Medernach.

II. Enemy situation and likely developments

1.) Suspected enemy situation on day of attack see enemy intelligence summary.
2.) If surprise is successfully maintained, only relatively-weak enemy resistance is to be expected in the sector of the Army (weak artillery, no tank units). Most of all, no strong reserves in depth have been detected. However, even weak defensive forces of the enemy are, from experience, structured in several security lines in depth. Surprise is not guaranteed with certainty. Therefore, all preparations for the attack must be geared toward an opponent better prepared for defense.

. . .

4.) In the Army sector, the enemy main battle line in general is far back from our own (up to 2.5 km). While strong security forces have been advanced in the northern sector and in the center, the ones in the southern sector are situated mostly west of the Our, but are established accordingly densely.

. . .

III. Course of attack and time sequence

. . .

Thereby it must be assured that most of the armored units survive the breakthrough battles in such a way that they retain the combat capabilities for their original task, operation in open terrain, and that the armored units of the second echelon still mount their attack during daylight on the first day of the offensive.

According to this, the infantry divisions are to be deployed on a wide front in the forward line and not to be kept back. As many assault guns and self-propelled artillery pieces as possible are to be provided to them.

2.) To eliminate the enemy airforce and to heighten surprise, the attack will be mounted during darkness.

For this, the attack divisions must establish, equip and train assault companies [Sturm-Kompanien] and strike platoons [Stosstrupps] under the most suitable, that is, best, leaders (commanders). They are to be sufficiently reinforced with mine detector platoons, tank destroyer platoons (with smoke materials to make tactical smoke), flamethrower groups, and artillery forward observers. Their task is to attack, capture, or cut off forward security positions and individual enemy strongpoints. The attack of several assault platoons, one after another in overlapping formation, can be practical.

The attack objective is to break through the forward enemy security lines, opening a road and gaining bridgeheads across the Our and Clerf. After reaching the objective, changeover to the defensive at once.

The state of training calls for an attack plan with the simplest structure, as well as conduct of battle in sectors with close-range objectives or with intermediate objectives.

The status of training calls for an attack plan with the simplest structure, as well as attacks conducted in sectors with close-range or intermediate objectives. The best attack formation is a wedge with strong, deeply-echeloned spearheads, with the advance of strike troops and assault companies along <u>clearly recognizable terrain features.</u> (Designate navigation groups or platoons!)

During the night it is not the amount of men, but cunning, deception, and the pluck of courageous men ("tough guys") with many weapons that <u>decide the battle.</u> Silence, absence of light, no clattering gear. Surprise is the best trump! Deployment of <u>searchlights</u> in the attack area produces approximately the brightness of a half moon. <u>Setting houses and haystacks on fire</u> in the rear or on the flank of the enemy is another useful aid.

Most of the troops are ready to either quickly follow the assault companies or to mount an attack after artillery preparation during daylight. . . .

3.) After a successful breakthrough to the west bank of the Our and Clerf, leaders and troops have to be permeated by only one thought:

"Forward to the Meuse and across!"

For this, the following is needed:

a) Leaders and command posts far up front, where they have the best view of the terrain, and can at <u>any time</u> apply their <u>personal influence</u> to command, march, fight, and supply their troops.

b) Early departure of the mobile divisions with advance battalions and most of their forces, even through the narrowest gaps behind the attack troops. Relentless advance toward the west, also at <u>night</u>!

c) Units of artillery, mainly assault gun batteries, close behind the attack spearheads.

d) Continuous reconnaissance of enemy, since reconnaissance is the best security, and reconnoiter terrain, mainly crossings of waterways.

e) Strictest regulation of traffic and traffic discipline.

4.) During the advance to the Meuse, it is important that LXVI Corps and LVIII Panzer Corps move forward on a broad front by using all trails, that they circumvent enemy resistance, avoid larger villages, and that XLVII Panzer Corps advances deeply echeloned without allowing itself to be pulled toward the south. It is important to seize any Meuse bridge and keep it open by all means. To attack one particular Meuse bridge is wrong. Reconnaissance on a broad front in advance is specially important. Moving strike and command troops up ahead for capturing Meuse bridges by *coup de main* can be expedient; engineer reconnaissance platoons are to be incorporated to examine the bridges for charges and remove them. The more quickly the Meuse is reached, the greater the possibility of capturing undamaged bridges. The corps boundaries are not limits for attack spearheads, they are only binding for the supply and most of the units.

. . .

IV. Battle Conduct for Artillery and Rocket Launchers

1.) General tasks
   Due to a precisely worked-out firing plan, the artillery must be capable of
   either carrying out preparatory fires according to this plan or, per direction of
   forward observers, to provide fires in advance of the attacking infantry.
   Commence fire as of 0530 hours.
   . . .

V. Battle Conduct for Engineers

1.) Employment of engineers
   Units do not wait for engineers when difficulties arise! Use your own assets!
2.) Deployment of engineers with the attack divisions
   Within the strike groups of the attack divisions, in addition to the infantry
   strike platoons for main efforts, combat engineer strike platoons (of not less
   than platoon strength) are to be established. Flamethrower groups (at least
   two to three flamethrower squads) are to be incorporated. There will be no
   subdivision of engineer groups into individual squads for subordination to
   other units!
   Sufficient engineer forces are to be deployed for clearing paths through
   minefields.
   Divisions employ engineer officer reconnaissance patrols in the assault
   groups to carry out engineer reconnaissance, mainly for trail and bridge evaluation. Results are to be reported promptly to the army through corps.
   Small rubber boats, planks, and bridges are to be prepared by the divisions
   for the combat operations of the strike groups, and are to be serviced or
   installed by those forces that are not taking part in the further combat of the
   assault groups.
   . . .
4.) Requirements for the crossing
   Speed is decisive, and it must be considered that the installation of prepared
   auxiliary bridges of short span does not take more time than the installation
   of mechanical bridges. If possible, save bridging equipment, look to impro-
   vise, save bridging equipment for the Meuse!
   . . .

VI. Unit Organization

1.) Since deployment and use, thereby also unit battle strength, depend on unit
   organization as well as on the regulation and movement of supplies of all
   kinds, the entire organization must not be left to just anyone. It is the task of
   every unit commander, within the limits of the duties of supervision and

responsibility assigned to him. <u>Commanders</u> must become involved <u>in every detail,</u> since the largest part of our young officers and a high number of officials are inexperienced and inept in this; even the senior NCOs can no longer master their tasks.

2.) In the organization of <u>combat units,</u> we must rid ourselves of all habits and customs by voluntarily renouncing comfort for a short time. One must break with the conventional; new solutions have to be found for special purposes (speed, mobility, overcoming difficult terrain in bad weather), and indeed only take along that which is necessary for combat, and march! No trucks for officer baggage, officer mess equipment, and so on! Materiel not immediately needed to be moved forward in partial shipments. Adjust everything to the given task! No compromises! Clear decisions!

3.) The mobile divisions must already prepare their combat units for the thrust to the Meuse. Apportioning of heavy weapons, engineer forces, and anti-tank weapons will always be necessary.

Communications, apportioning of anti-aircraft guns and of supply units for the combat groups are to be organized and discussed during tactical games. Lack of supply is often of decisive significance!

4.) <u>An advance battalion</u> must be structured so that it contains nothing but tactical vehicles in good condition, manned by the best drivers. They are to be given anti-tank weapons, engineers, anti-aircraft guns, and artillery! Plan for deployment of blocking tasks, therefore amply apportion anti-tank guns. The light Pz.Jäg.38 [Hetzer] is too slow and has unnecessary technical problems. The Eifel terrain requires <u>strong apportionment of riflemen.</u> Fuel, ammunition, and provisions (hay-boxes) to be given special consideration! Combat engineer units are to be given mines, explosives, cable reels, and tools for building auxiliary bridges; if needed, equipment for auxiliary bridges. Engage leaders acquainted with the local area!

Advance battalions must provide room for freight (provision packages), since the roads are narrow and needed for forward movement!

Each Volks-Grenadier, Panzer-Grenadier, and Panzer division must have a bicycle battalion. [Remained theory—*Author*].

. . .

5.) <u>Special detachments are to be formed for blocking tasks</u>

. . .

6.) <u>Combat strength</u>

Companies not more than 80 men (without heavy weapons). There will eventually be surpluses from field replacement battalions, as well as from weapon reserves, so replacements will also bring weapons. Assign a maximum two officers per company or battery (except reconnaissance, Panzer, tank destroyer, and communications battalions).

7.) Transport of <u>baggage</u> needs most careful consideration. Every commander must fight with every vehicle he takes. . . .

8.) <u>Means of communication</u>

Telephone connections are mostly not working, therefore, use radio and other means.

Maintain duty officers as messengers in Volkswagens, half-tracked motorcycles, horses, and bicycles; in emergencies, travel on foot. Avoid main roads! No radio messages with more than 100 letters. Establish lines of communication. Be careful with messages by UKW (ultra short wave) sets! Use deception/codes during telephone conversations.

. . .

11.) <u>Provisions</u>

Clear messages, no intermediate messages! In case of wrong messages, army will proceed with punishment. Commanders and Ibs are responsible for the messages of their officials. <u>Supply in the wrong areas can be the cause of difficulties with provision.</u>

. . .

12.) <u>Personnel and materiel reserve</u> (Also see Nr.6) 20 percent of available armored vehicles are allotted to the materiel reserve; deployment only by order of the Army.

Thereby, those armored vehicles in short-term repair are also to be included. Details about establishing commander reserves will be ordered by IIa.

Appendix 17

TRANSCRIPT

Headquarters, LVIII Pz.Corps   Corps command post, 10 December 1944
Section Ia Nr. 341/44 g.commandos

10 copies
10th copy

Order for Operation "Adelheid"

1.) Enemy situation: see enemy intelligence summary.
2.) 5th Panzer Army breaks through enemy during hours of darkness in the Ormont–Rodershausen sector, passes across the Our sector, and without consideration of the situation, strikes left and right via the Ardennes and Meuse up to Antwerp. It is important to break through the enemy front at numerous points by surprise, to open the roads and Our River crossings from the rear, and to attack with the mobile forces on the first day of attack during daylight, through even the narrowest gaps, with a wide objective and following with the infantry on a broad front, without consideration for the enemy remaining. Cover the flanks by anti-tank gun units and fire. LXVI Corps to the right, LVIII Pz.Corps in the center, XLVII Pz.Corps to the left.
3.) **LVIII Pz.Corps** with main effort at the inner wings of the attack divisions, infantry in front, on O-day 0500 hours breaks through the enemy positions and in a quick thrust gains bridgeheads across the Our.
First target of attack: Dürler–Heinerscheid road! After opening of a road, the corps sets out early with mobile forces for an assault on the Andenne–Namur Meuse sector and captures the Meuse crossings by *coup de main.*
Hereby corps boundaries are not blinders!
After overcoming the Meuse, the corps pushes non-stop through to Antwerp with at least two attack spearheads, blocks toward the north and west there, and links up with 6th SS-Panzer Army and XLVII Pz.Corps.
4.) To break through the enemy main battle line, the following prepare themselves:
to the right: 116th Pz.Div.
to the left: Gren.Rgt. 1130 and elements of Brigade Remer. [This was later changed. Actually, the 560th Volks-Grenadier Division with two regiments—*Author.*]
Commencement of attack:
Infantry to fall in on O-day 0500 hours.
No soldier is allowed to cross the main battle line to the west before this time.
Artillery may open fire by 0530 hours.
Illuminate search lights 0535 hours.

5.) <u>Boundaries:</u>
LXVI Corps on the right.
. . . Pronsfeld (LXVI) . . .–Heckhuscheid (LXVI)–Alster (northwest of Burg
Reuland) (LXVI) . . . Fraiture (LXVI)–Clerheid (LXVI)–Septon (LXVI). . .
XLVII Pz.Corps on the left:
. . . Dahnen–Fischbach–Boxborn . . .Warempage–Beausaint . . .–Sinsin . . .
<u>Separation line:</u> . . . Stalbach-North, Herzfeld-Nord, Our loop due southwest
of Oberhausen, Leithum-North, road intersection three km west-southwest of
Beiler (to 116th), Limerlé-North, Sommerain-North, Wibrin-North, Samrée-
southwest, Soy-southwest, . . .

6.) <u>Tasks for the attack divisions:</u>

    a)   116th Pz.Div. deploys for attack in forward line with two regiments of
two battalions each.

          At start of attack, the division breaks through enemy main battle line
bypassing stronger nests of resistance, pushes through in one move
towards the Our crossings near Stupbach and Welchenhausen, and captures them firmly by forming bridgeheads on the hills west of the Our.
The crossing, 1.5km north of Stupbach, is to be opened from the rear.

          <u>Advance Btl. 116 Pz.Div.</u> (organization: Armored Recon Battalion, one
assault gun company, one combat engineer company, one light artillery
batallion, one armored rocket launcher battery, one light anti-aircraft gun
battery) is to be assembled and prepared in the area, see map. By corps
order, it will be deployed for the assault on the Meuse.

          <u>Division command post:</u> from O-day, 0400 hours, vicinity Oberüttfeld.

    b)   <u>Gren.Rgt. 1130</u> prepares for attack with both battalions in forward line
on both sides of Eschfeld–Sevenig road. After breaching enemy main
battle line, the regiment seizes the Our crossings near Ouren and protects
them by establishing bridgeheads along the hills west of the Our.

          <u>Command post:</u> vicinity of Roscheid

7.) <u>Conduct of battle:</u>
Both attack groups must attack with all battalions in front. For this, two to
three strike groups precede each battalion.
<u>Organization of battalions:</u> Assault company <u>ahead,</u> remainder of battalion
following.
<u>Leadership:</u> Battalion commanders with assault company.
Assign best company commanders and junior leaders to assault companies.
Attack without artillery preparation. Release of artillery fires by request from
forward observers or by order of the division or brigade, respectively, not
before 0530 hours.
Release of any kind of fire—heavy and light infantry weapons—not before
encountering enemy resistance.
<u>Rule of conduct:</u> Quiet and quickly forward!
It is of decisive importance for the Meuse crossing that existing bridges be
captured undamaged. Therefore, <u>engineer officer reconnaissance units</u> (not

less than reinforced platoon strength) are to be assigned to the front of the advance battalions, to examine the bridges for explosives. If existing bridges cannot be used, crossings with all available means (rubber dinghies, boats, whatever is available) is to be carried out at once.
Look for bridges newly built by the enemy.
. . .

12.) Marshalling and Activities in Preparation Areas
    I.   The operation can only succeed if everything is being done to conceal marshalling and and preparation. For this, all commanders must personally check the execution of the measures ordered and ensure they are supervised by apt, energetic officers. Careful camouflage is especially important in assembly and preparation areas and in firing positions. Camouflage officers are to be appointed, who supervise the measures specified.
    II.   Preparation areas, see map.
    III. Schedule for march movement, see. . .
         March routes, see . . .
    IV. Details:
         1.) Advance detachments are only to be sent into the main battle line in the number necessary, for example, the commander of one assault company. Advance detachments remain in their positions on N-Day. No black uniforms! Officers camouflage themselves! Other than under these circumstances, no members of attacking units may come into the main battle line.
         . . .
         4.) Noise deception
         While artillery, anti-aircraft, and searchlights are taking up positions, covering the noise by the deployment of night fighters is planned during the nights of K-L, L-M, M-N. This will be conducted three to four hours per night. Noise deception is to be supervised by listening posts directly behind the main battle line.

13.) Rules for Secrecy
    a)   Regimental commanders may be briefed on K-day, at the same time the corps order will be issued to the division. Until then, all written communications within the corps remain prohibited. Battalion commanders cannot be briefed before M-day. Soldiers may not be briefed before N-day. Reconnaissance may only be conducted when absolutely necessary, and may only be deployed in camouflaged form with the mission of reconnoitering for counterattacks, reliefs-in-place, or similar operations.
    b)   Rule of conduct must be:
        No member of any newly-arrived division may appear in the main battle line, no vehicle may drive within ten kilometers of the main battle line.
        . . .

APPENDIX 18

2d Bn, Armored Artillery Regiment 146   Battalion Cmnd Post, 15 Dec 1944
Section Ia   Time: 1000

To
Armored Artillery Regiment 146

The battalion reports:
1.) Battalion in readiness with 4th Battery, 6th Battery, and staff in forest area near the 3d Battalion command post.
2.) 1,350 rounds of light field howitzer ammunition stored in the vicinity of firing positions.
3.) Battery and battalion wire communications nets in place.
4.) Bunker command post occupied by officers as of 1200 hours.
5.) Rear command post still with 3d Battalion CP until this evening.
6.) Status of deployment of battalion:
Besides the vehicles already set aside in the old assembly area at Bongard, the following battalion vehicles are out of action:
   a) Armored personnel carrier for artillery A.V. commando by damage to gear box. Wheeled personnel vehicles for duty officer and A.V. commando are employed, so that entire staff must be moved in three of them, (including the physician)
   b) Two armored prime movers from 4th Battery, so that only three guns may be moved, namely one with a prime mover and two with mules. One of these mules must be transferred to the 1st Battalion. After carrying out the transfer, the battery can only move two guns.
   c) Two kitchen vehicles from 6th and Staff batteries have been replaced using vehicles from the battalion ammunition vehicles. The amount of ammunition which may be hauled is decreased by two trucks.
   d) Two anti-aircraft gun prime movers, so that only one anti-aircraft gun can be moved, while two more battleworthy guns are immobile.
   e) Regimental communications vehicle has defective clutch; may be rendered immobile at any time.
   f) Staff Battery's telephone installation vehicle broke its suspension during the night while laying cable. Telephone section must be made mobile by using one more of the battalion's ammunition trucks.

F.d.R.   In draft, signed, Müller
Ha   Hauptmann and Battalion Commander
Leutnant and Adjutant

APPENDIX 19

116th Panzer Division   Division Command Post, 16 Dec 1944
Section Ia

1.) In spite of beginning with a swift penetration of enemy security positions, the first attack stopped in front of the main battle line. After regrouping during the night, commencing 0600 hours on 17 Dec, the division again mounts an attack and breaks through the enemy main battle line on both sides of the Lützkampen–Ouren trail by slanting toward the northwest and combining all forces, then pushes through to the Our and captures the crossing at Ouren.

2.) For this, Group Bayer (Pz.Rgt.16, Pz.Gren.Rgt.156, 2d Bn./Pz.Gren.Rgt.60, 3d Co./Arm.Engr.Bn. 675) attacks out of the Lützkampen area.
Course of battle according to verbal directive.
One regimental group from the 560th Volks-Gren.Div. attacks simultaneously from the vicinity of Roscheid toward Sevenig, to tie down the enemy.

3.) Group Zander (Pz.Gren.Rgt. 60, minus 2d Battalion; Corps Escort Company, which was brought into Group Zander; and a tank destroyer company) secures the northern flank of the Division between Berg and Hill 509.0 (inclusive). Reconnaissance to advance toward the north and northwest.

4.) Group Schneider (Division Escort Company; 1st Company, Armored Engineer Battalion 675; and one assault gun company)
Division reserve "Im Spielmannsholz." Reconnoiter for approach march to the north and northwest, via Leidenborn, Lützkampen.

5.) Artillery:
The attack by Group Bayer is to be supported by all available artillery (incl. corps artl. and rocket launchers). Heavy combined fire! Enemy strongpoints around Nöll and in the vicinity of the road intersection west of it are to be destroyed. Flanking positions from the edge of the forest north of Hill 539.2 and out of Harspelt are to be eliminated. Part of the artillery must be prepared to defend against an enemy advance toward the screen protecting Group Zander.
After receiving fuel, 2d Battalion, Arm. Art. Regt.146 (minus 6th Battery) is to follow Advance Battalion-Stephan via Dasburg.

6.) Illumination of area by searchlights as per direction from Oberst Bayer.

7.) Division Command Post: Unchanged.

Distributor: Signed in draft
F.d.R.   von Waldenburg
signed Guderian
Oberstleutnant i.G.

APPENDIX 20

<u>Annex 2 to 116th Pz.Div. Ia #1101/44 as of 29 December 1944</u>
<u>Battle strengths</u>

		Offrs.	NCOs	Men
Pz.Gren.Rgt.60				
1st Battalion	Mounted	8	36	192
(Of which number are purely infantry)		(3)	(18)	(102)
Additionally, unarmed		-	11	55
2d Battalion		4	19	167
(Of which number are purely infantry)		(2)	(8)	(90)
Regimental Units		7	28	129
Total		19	94	543
Pz.Gren.Rgt.156				
1st Battalion		3	19	96
(Of which number are purely infantry)		(2)	(4)	(31)
2d Battalion		5	31	175
(Of which number are purely infantry)		(1)	(6)	(35)
Regimental units		6	31	162
Total		14	81	433
Armored Reconnaissance Battalion 116	(mounted)			
Staff, Recon Co. & Heavy Co.		8	44	196
Recon Companies		2	14	99
Total		10	58	295
Armored Engineer Battalion 675 (mounted)		5	28	260

<u>Annex 3 to 116th Pz.Div. Ia #1101/44 as of 29 December 1944</u>

<u>Total losses of Motor Vehicles</u>
(From Approximately 16 to 27 December)
Panzer IV	11
Panzer V	30
Panzerjäger & assault guns	6
Hummeln & Wespen	2
Medium Armored Personnel Carriers	54

(of them, 15 w/ radios;
3 w/ telephones;
1 w/ 75mm gun;
6 w/ triple gun mounts)

Light Armored Personnel Carriers	10
Motorcycles	64
Wheeled Personnel Vehicles	55
Wheeled Cargo Vehicles	57
Kfz. 31	4
Maultiere (Half-tracked trucks)	5
Prime movers	5

<u>Battleworthy tanks, assault guns and artillery tubes</u>
Panzer IV	-
Panzer V	7
Sturmgeschütz III	1
Panzerjäger IV	3
Light Field Howitzers	13
Heavy Field Howitzers	5
10cm Field Guns	3
Hummeln	3
Wespen	-

<u>Annex 4 to 116th Pz.Div. Ia #1101/44 as of 29 December 1944</u>
<u>Losses of Weapons</u>
Machine Pistols	163
Flare pistols	38
Rifle lg.gear	97
Light machine guns	158
Heavy machine guns	22
MG 151/15s	6
Heavy Anti-Tank Guns (7.5cm Pak 40)	5
8cm Mortars 34	15
Heavy Rocket Launchers	2

Appendix 21

TRANSCRIPT

General Inspector of Panzertroops	Headquarters 25 March 1945
OKH/GenStdH/Organization Section	Tel: Olga 31 45

I/1600/45 g.Kdos.

600 copies
367th copy

Secret Command Matter

<u>Re:</u> Basic Structure of Panzer Division 45
- 4 Appendices -

1.) For all <u>Panzer and Panzer-Grenadier divisions of the field army, the basic structuring of Panzer Division 45</u> goes into effect with immediate action. Appendix 1 addresses organization.
Appendix 2 is a tentative summary of personnel and material strength.
2.) Within the framework of available personnel and material, Panzer and Panzer-Grenadier divisions are to be reorganized in accordance with the structure of Panzer Division 45. Armored formations whose personnel and materiel strengths do not allow the attainment of this structure are to be structured temporarily as <u>combat groups.</u> Units that will be released, will be ordered individually.
For the <u>232d Pz.Div.</u> (field training div.) the former special organization is in effect.
3.) <u>Validation lists, establishments, and final summaries of personnel and material strength</u> will be forwarded by General Inspector of Panzer Troops.
4) Supreme Command–West and army groups report successful reorganization by subordinated Panzer and Panzer-Grenadier divisions to OKH/Army Gen. Staff/Organization Section <u>NLT 5 January 1945</u>.

> J.A.
> signed, Guderian
> Generaloberst and Chief of Gen. StdH

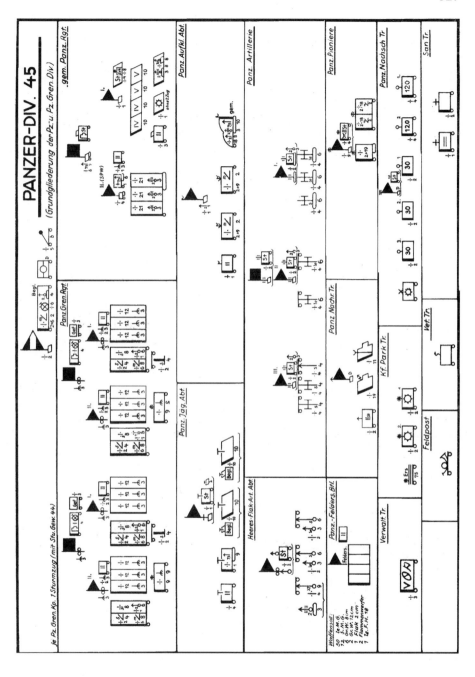

Bezeichnung	Gesamt-Kopfstärke	Lkw	restl. Kfz	Panzer (einschl. Flak u. Berge-Pz.)	SPW	Rad-späh Wagen	Jagd-panzer (einschl. Berge-Pz.)	Vergleich		
									Panz.Div. 45	Panz.Div. 44
Div.Kdo.Panz.Div. 45 m.Begl.Kp., Div.Kart.St u.Feldg.Tr:	420	27	41	-	-	-	-	Kopfstärke	11422	13213
Gem.Panz.Rgt.								Lkw-Soll	1080	1198 gek. Nol-Soll
Stab Panz.Rgt.mit Stbs.Kp.	106	12	13	2	2	-	-	restl.Kfz-Soll	1091	1190
I. (Panz.Abt.)	767	85	81	52	-	-	-	Panzer-Soll (einschl.Flak u.Berge-Pz.)	54	165
II. (SPW Batl.)	488	32	27	-	47	-	-	SPW-Soll	90	288
Summe gem.Panz.Rgt.:	1361	129	121	54	49	-	-	Radspähwagen-Soll	16	16
2 Panz.Gren.Rgter.								Jagdpanzer-Soll (einschl. Berge-Panzer)	22	22
2 Panz.Gren.Rgts.Stbe.m.Stbs.Kp.	252	26	66	-	-	-	-			
2 Gefechts-Kol. x)	196	86	16	-	-	-	-			
4 Panz.Gren.Btls.Stbe.	192	16	48	-	-	-	-			
4 Versorg.Kp.	308	72	36	-	-	-	-			
12 Panz.Gren.Kp.	1404		36	-	-	-	-			
4 M.G.Kp.	484	16	72	-	-	-	-			
4 schw.Kp.	508	44	48	-	-	-	-			
2 Panz.Gren.Pi.Kp.	288	28	30	-	-	-	-	Verteilung der SPW innerhalb der Panz.Div. 45		
2 s.J.G.Kp.	204	22	32	-	-	-	-	Einheit	251/1 251/3 251/16 251/21 251/22	Gesamt
Summe 2 Panz.Gren.Rgter.:	3836	310	384	-	-	-	-	Div.Kdo.u.Nachr.Abt.	5	5
								Artillerie	4	4
Panz.Aufkl.Abt.	648	35	130	-	9	16	-	Panz.Rgt. (gem.Rgts.Stb.)	2	2
Panz.Jäg.Abt.	522	38	52	-	10	-	22	Panz.Jäg.Abt.	1 9	10
Panz.Art.Rgt	1367	116	156	-	4	-	-	Panz.Aufkl.Abt.	3 3 3	9
Heer.Flak-Art.Abt.	440	48	19	-	-	-	-		15 3 12	30
Panz.Pionier Btl.	716	70	54	-	13	-	-	Panz.Gren.Btl.(gp)		
Panz.Nachr.Abt.	378	46	47	-	5	-	-	Stab	4	4
Panz.Felders.Btl.	173	2	7	-	-	-	-	Kan.Zg.	1 6	7
Gesamt-Summe der fechtenden Truppe Panz.Div. 45	9861	821	1011	54	90	16	22	1. Kp.	8 1 3	12
Gesamt-Summe der fechtenden Truppe Panz.Div. 44	11528	919	1042	165	288	16	22	2. Kp.	8 1 3	12
bei Panz.Div. 45 eingespart:	1667	98	31	111	198	-	-	3. Kp.	8 1 3	12
									24 8 9 6	47
Versorg.Truppen								Panz.Pi.Kp.	6 1 6	13
Panz.Nachsch.Tr.	702	116	44	-	-	-	-	Gesamt:	30 24 6 12 18	90
Krafft.Park Tr.	277	47	8	-	-	-	-			
San.Tr.	334	64	16	-	-	-	-			
Vet.Tr.	24	1	2	-	-	-	-			
Verwalt.Tr.	206	28	9	-	-	-	-			
Feldpostamt (mot)	18	3	1	-	-	-	-			
Gesamt-Summe der Versorg.Tr. Panz.Div. 45	1561	259	80	-	-	-	-			
Gesamt-Summe d.Versorg.Tr. Panz.Div. 44	1685	279	148	-	-	-	-			
bei Panz.Div. 45 eingespart:	124	20	68	-	-	-	-			

x) Gef.Kol. dient zur Verlastung der Pz.Gren.u deren Versorgung

Appendix 22

Organization of 2d Battalion, Panzer-Grenadier Regiment 156 under the New Structure, 17 March 1945

Battalion Staff:	Commander	Hauptmann Zanzinger
	Adjutant	Oberleutnant Stoltenberg
	Surgeon	Stabsarzt Dr. Bergmann
	Motor Officer	Oberleutnant (K) Dorsch
	Paymaster	Oberleutnant (TSD) Koppen
	Duty Officers	Leutnant Muntzig
		Leutnant Trede
		Leutnant Holzinger

Support Company:	Commander	Oberleutnant Gerner
6th Company (Rifle)	Commander	Oberleutnant Schutow
	Lieutenant	Leutnant Thomas
7th Company (Rifle)	Commander	Oberleutnant Noltensmeyer
	Lieutenant	Leutnant Krause
8th Company (Rifle)	Commander	Oberleutnant Junge
	Lieutenant	Leutnant Petersen
9th Company (MG)	Commander	Leutnant Tröster
10th Company (Mortar)	Commander	Leutnant Fricke

Armament; Organization

Rifle Company: Company HQ Section
      1 x Assault Squad   MG 34s and MP 44s
      2 x Rifle Platoons

Direct Fire   2 x Heavy MG platoons, each with three heavy MGs
Company   1 x Light Anti-Aircraft platoon w/ six 20mm guns

Indirect Fire 2 x Medium Mortar platoons, each with four 8cm mortars
Company   1 x Heavy Mortar platoon, with four 12cm mortars

Combat Vehicles:

Battalion Staff:
- 1 x motor vehicle 15
- 1 x Jeep
- 1 x Volkswagen
- 1 x Motorcycle w/ sidecar
- 3 x Motorcycles w/o sidecar

Signal Platoon
- 1 x Armored Personnel Carrier w/radio
- 3 x Personnel Vehicles w/radios
- 1 x Truck w/radio
- 2 x large, 4 x small Telephone Construction Vehicle
- 1 x Radio - Apparatus Vehicle (with Signal Officer)

Medical Platoon
- 1 x Doctor's personnel vehicle
- 1 x Motorcycle with sidecar
- 1 x High-speed Ambulance
- 2 x Ambulances, 1 x Armored Ambulance
- 1 x Medical Apparatus Truck (Dispensary equipment with 18 beds and two Red Cross nurses)

Support Company
- approx. 3 x Personnel Vehicles
- 40 Trucks (Field kitchens, Ammunition, Equipment, Weapons)

Each Rifle Company
- 1 x Personnel Vehicle (Jeep)
- 2 x Motorcycles w/o sidecars
- 4 x Trucks for personnel (3 ton)
- 1 x Truck for weapons, equipment, and baggage

Direct Fire Company
- 1 x Personnel Vehicle
- 2 x Motorcycles w/o sidecars
- 1 x Telephone Vehicle
- 2 x Personnel Vehicles w/ machine guns (for platoon leaders)
- 4 x Trucks w/ machine guns
- 2 x Ammunition trucks
- 6 x Self-Propelled 20mm guns

Indirect Fire Company
- 1 x Personnel Vehicle
- 2 x Motorcycles w/o sidecars
- 2 x Radio Vehicles
- 1 x Tracked Motorcycle
- 2 x Mortar Personnel Vehicles (platoon leaders)
- 4 x Trucks (for mortars)
- 2 x Trucks (for ammunition)
- 4 x Mules (prime movers for heavy mortars)

Combat Vehicle Summary:

22 x Personnel Vehicles

80 x trucks

2 x Armored Personnel Carriers

4 x Maultiere

6 x Self-propelled Anti-Aircraft guns

TOTAL: 114

2 x Motorcycles w/ sidecars

1 x Tracked Motorcycle

13 x Motorcycles without
sidecars

16

Appendix 23

11 April 1945

Battle Commandant "Harz"

Battle order # 1

1.) Enemy took Goslar. Münchehof [south of Seesen—*Author*] was lost again. Situation in 3rd Pz.Gren.Div. sector unclear. Continuation of enemy attacks on Bad Harzburg, Vienenburg and Lautenthal must be counted on.

2.) Battle commandant Goslar defends main battle line by extending right wing up to south of Ilsenburg.

3.) Assignment of sectors

To the right: Battle commandant Goslar (Volksturm Battalion Wittisch attached)

In center: Combat Group Zahn

To the left: Combat Group Fallois

Combat Group Count Brühl will be released for other use, leaves weak security positions in former sector as verbally ordered.

4.) Boundaries

To the right: Torfhaus–Stapelburg–East

To the left: Badenhausen-South–Eisdorf-North.

Between the right and center: Hahnenklee-East–Langelsheim-East–Upen-East.

Between center and left: Lautenthal–Seesen road for Combat Group Zahn

5.) Combat orders

a) All forces in sector will be subordinated to Battle Commandant Goslar. It is important for the course of battle that the roads leading from the north into the Harz are blocked off and the road blocks are manned. Volks-Sturm Btl. Wittich has orders from Battle Commandant Harz to erect barricades at the northern edge of the Harz, at the roads Bad Harzburg–Torfhaus and Oker to the south; also to reconnoiter if roads from Ilsenburg toward the southwest and from Stapelburg toward the southwest are blocked. If barricades are not prepared and secured by other units, Volks-Sturm Btl. has orders to take over erecting barricades on these roads.

b) For the course of battle, it is important to retain Lautenthal; therefore, all available forces are to be moved up.

c) A further advance by the enemy from the area of Münchehof toward the east is to be prevented; the Lautenthal–Wildemann road is to be blocked off effectively by engineer or other forces.

6.) Once again it is explicitly pointed out that all forces in the sectors are to be seized without consideration and brought up to the battle.

7.) <u>Reconnaissance</u> is to be advanced up to the line Ilsenburg–Stapelburg–Vienenburg–Immenrode–Jerstedt–Nauen–Gross-Rhüden–Westerhof. Main effort north of the Harz.

It must be established where the enemy brings up forces, where the enemy batteries are.

Signed, Uhl

NOTES

CHAPTER I

1. Memminger, Fritz. *Die Kriegsgeschichte der Windhund-Division* (Bochum-Langendreer: n.p., 1962) S. D 4
2. Vogelsang, Fritz, Binder with original orders and reports; further: Vogelsang, collection of orders.
3. Letter Count Schwerin to Oberstlt. Engel, 7 Sep 1993, copy in author's possession
4. Holtermann, Dr. Arthur, Documents of orders, reports, and personal letters by and to Count Schwerin [Holtermann docs.]
5. BA–MA (*Bundesarchiv-Militärarchiv*) RH 10/24, p 32
6. *Kriegstagebuch* (Operations Journal) of the OKW [*Wehrmachtsführungsstab* (armed forces operations staff)] *1940–1945,* vol. IV, 1. (Frankfurt am Main, 1961, licensed edition, Herrsching 1982), p 272, 275, 109, 116. The 10th Pz-Gren.Div. unfortunately could not be pulled out. Therefore, the 11th Pz.Div. was transferred to the West.
7. BA–MA RH 10/20, p 250 and 25, resp. RH 19 IV/30, p 29 and 30. As per OKH order 18 Mar 1944, it was established that the 179th Reserve Pz.Div. should be attached to the 16th Pz-Gren.Div. BA–MA RH 10/20, p 238, resp. RH 19 IV/30, p107–108
8. Vogelsang, collection of orders
9. Vogelsang, collection of orders
10. Holtermann docs, copy of draft of letter
11. BA–MA Rh 10/20, p 181–189, resp. Rh 19/IV/36, p 19-24
12. BA–MA RH 10/112, p 51
13. ftnt. 11 and Sandkuhl, Wilhelm, pocket calendar 1944
14. BA–MA RH 10/20, p 170–175
15. BA–MA RH 2/1308, 15 Aug 1944, (app. 1)
16. See ftnt. 14 and BA–MA RH 10/20. p 146
17. Order OKH/general StA/Org. Sect. # I/ 16816/44 g.K., 2 May 1944, depicted in app. 18
18. BA–MA RH 10/23 p 180 Org. Sect. # I/ 4909/44 geh., 20 May 1944
19. BA–MA RH 10/23 p 178
20. BA–MA RH 19/ IV/37, app. 352, p 283
21. BA–MA RH 24-67/4, 24 June 1944
22. Vogelsang, Fritz, diary. Not specifically mentioned in the future if quoted in text.
23. Vogelsang, collection of orders
24. BA–MA RH 19 IV/33 and 37, 21–30 Apr 1944, and 19 IV/34 and 38, 1–2 May 1944
25. BA–MA RH 10 IV/42 K, 22 Apr 1944
26. BA–MA Rh 10/163, p 1–3
27. Deutsche Volksliste III consists of men of Polish descent from the German Eastern territories—West Prussia, Warthegau, Upper Silesia—who wanted to acquire German citizenship. According to the order OKH-AHA, 28 Mar 1944, signed by Count Stauffenberg from app. 14, 8 percent of the units had to consist of soldiers from Volksliste III.
28. BA–MA RH 10/112, p 49–50
29. BA–MA RH 10/163 p 10
30. BA–MA RH 10/109 p 107
31. BA–MA-RH 10/89 p 31
32. BA–MA RH 19 IV/33, 29 Apr 1944 and 19 IV/37, app. 352
33. BA–MA RH 19 IX/83, 25 May 1944
34. BA–MA RH 19 IV/37, app. 203
35. BA–MA RH 19 IV/38, app. 390
36. BA–MA RH 10 IV/39, app. 719
37. BA–MA RH 19 IV/34, 3 May 1944 and 19 IV/38 app. 406
38. See ftnt. 29
39. BA–MA N 117/22, 5 May 1944
40. Guderian, Heinz. *Erinnerungen eines Soldaten* (Heidelberg: n.p., 1951) p 298
41. BA–MA RH 10/163, p 12
42. BA–MA RH 10/23, p 181, 12 Apr 1944
43. BA–MA RH 19 IV/38, app. 575 and 576, 15 May resp. 16 May 1944
44. BA–MA RH 19 IV/38, app. 567, 15 May 1944 and RH 19 IX/83, 15 May and 19 May 1944
45. Vogelsang, collection of orders
46. Vogelsang, collection of orders
47. KTB (*Kriegstagebuch,* or unit journal) #7 of 3d Bn./Arm.Art.Rgt. 146, 1 Apr 1943– 30 June 1944 photo copy p 90
48. KTB of 2d Bn./Arm.Art.Rgt. 146, 22 Aug 1943–10 Mar 1945, draft
49. See app. 47 and 48
50. BA–MA RH 10/163, p 11–13
51. KTB Army Group B, 4 June 1944, Irving collection, *Institut für Zeitgeschichte,* Munich

52. BA–MA RH 10/163, p 11–13, 14–16, also Beug, Alfred, Cdr. Army Anti-Aircraft Battalion 281, to the author

CHAPTER 2

1. Janske-Drost, Eberhard. *Am Rande des Grossen Geschehens: Skizzen aus dem Westen, Juli–Dezember 1944*, unpublished.
2. 7th Company, Pz-Gren.Rgt. 60, Newsletter #2, 15 May 1944.
3. Program of church services, 28 May 1944.
4. Eisenhower, Dwight D. *Invasion, General Eisenhowers eigene Kriegsbericht* (Hamburg, 1949), 35; Young, Peter, *Der Grosse Atlas zum II. Weltkrieg* (Munich, 1976), 493f.
5. OKW KTB, vol. IV, 2, 1530ff.
6. Ibid., 1, 277ff.
7. Ibid., 2, 1258, 1466.
8. Ibid., 1, 276, 277.
9. BA–MA From order of battle schematics for 15 May 1944 and 15 June 1944 in Ose, Dieter, *Entschiedung im Westen 1944* (Stuttgart: n.p., 1982), 95ff; Rückbrodt, Peter, *"Die Invasion in der Normandie, Operative Lehren and Probleme"* in *Europäische Wehrkunde* 2, 1977
10. OKW KTB, vol. IV, 1, 302; BA–MA 19 IV/33, 15 April 1944 and 19 IV/37, appendices 288, 352.
11. Eisenhower, 30.
12. BA–MA RH ZW/199 Situation West, 6 June 1944.
13. Eisenhower, 42, 43.
14. OKW KTB, vol. IV, 1, 458; BA–MA RH 19 IV/48, app. 348; BA–MA RH 19 IX/8/60, 61.
15. BA–MA RM 7/60, 15 May 1944; BA–MA RH 19 IV/40, app. 857.
16. OKW KTB, vol. IV, 2, 1530ff., directive 51; Hubatsch, Walther, *Hitlers Weisungen für die Kriegsführung 1939–1945* (Frankfurt: n.p., 1962), 338, Weisung 51a, 27 Dec 1943; Weekly evaluation of situation, Sup Cmd–West in BA–MA RH 19 IV/34 and 35 resp. 38, 39, 40; Pemsel, Max Joseph, USAREUR Series MS. B-763, 116ff.; Evaluation on 1 January 1944 by HQ, 15th Army BA–MA RH 20-15/64
17. BA–MA RM 7/260, 4 Nov 1943.
18. OKW KTB, vol. IV, 1, p117, 270, 300, 302; BA–MA RH 19 IV/29, app. 752;

BA–MA RH 19 IV/34 and 38, appendices 374, 386, 387, 444, 461; BA–MA RH 19 IV/41, app. 471; Ruge, Friedrich, *Rommel und die Invasion* (Stuttgart: n.p., 1959), 267–268.
19. BA–MA H 19 IX/4, 3 July 1944, 116ff.; Ruge, loc. cit., map across from 49, 155 and 172–175; Ruge, Friedrich, in *Europäische Wehrkunde* 10, 1979 and 4, 1980
20. OKW KTB, vol. IV, 1, 302, 303; BA–MA RH 19 IV/34, 4 May 1944; and BA–MA RH 19 IV/41, 49–50.
21. BA–MA RH 19 IV/33, 10 Apr 1944.
22. BA–MA RH 10 IX/83, 48, 50.
23. OKW KTB, vol. IV, 1, 277, 304; BA–MA RH 20-15/64, 1 January 1944; Salmuth, Hans von, USAREUR Series MS. B-746, 7–12.
24. Jodl, Alfred, letter to Rommel 4 May 1944, cited in Ruge, 270.
25. Speidel, Dr. Hans, *Invasion 1944* (Tübingen: n.p., 1949), 71.
26. Speidel, 126.
27. BA–MA RH 19 IV/38, app. 479
28. Irving, David, *Rommel: A Biography* (Hamburg: n.p., 1978), 474.
29. BA–MA N 117/22 from Rommel's daily report for 5 May 1944, from Irving collection.
30. BA–MA RH 19 IX/1, 14 May 1944; Ruge, 157.
31. See note 28, but date of 13 May is probably wrong, since events from 14 May were included.
32. Unit Journal, 3d Battalion, Armored Artillery Regiment 146, 6 May 1944.
33. Poth, Heinz, handwritten notes of the leading officers in the unit journal of 3d Battalion, Armored Artillery Regiment 146, 8 May 1944.
34. Schwerin, Gerhard, Count von, *Erinnerungen des ehem. Kommandeurs der 116. Panzer-Division*, Dec. 1977 (draft).
35. Ruge, 144
36. Eisenhower, 13ff., 56ff.; Montgomery, Bernard, L. *Von der Normandie zur Ostee* (Deutsche Ausgabe: Hamburg, n.d.) 19ff, 36, 45; Wilmot, Chester, *Der Kampf um Europa* (Frankfurt: n.p., 1954) 175ff.; Assmann, Kurt. *Deutsche Schicksalsjahre*

(Wiesbaden 1950, 413ff.; Ryan, Cornelius. *Der längste Tag* (Gütersloh: n.p., 1960, 42ff.; Bothing, Douglas. *The Second Front* (Alexandria, VA, 1978), p44ff.

37. Eisenhower, 128.

38. Eisenhower, 274.

39. Baldwin, Hanson W., *"Die Landung in der Normandie-der Anfang vom Ende"*. *Grosse Schlachten des 2. Weltkrieges* (*Great Battles of the Second World War*). (Düsseldorf: n.p., 1960), 244.

CHAPTER 3

1. BA–MA RH 19 IV/38, KTB Sup Cmd–West, 8 May 1944 app. 479

2. BA–MA RM 7/89, KTB Mar.Gruppe West, 2 May 1944

3. Assmann, loc. cit., p419 ff

4. Brown, Anthony Cave, *Die unsichtbare Front: Entschieden Geheimdienste den 2 Weltkrieg?* (Munich: n.p., 1976), p447 ff.

5. BA–MA RM 7/60, p272, KTB SKL, 15 May 1944; BA–MA RH 19 IV/40, p81 KTB Sup Cmd–West, 4 June 1944 app. 857

6. BA–MA RM 7/61, KTB SKL, 4 June 1944

7. BA–MA RN 11/22, 3 June 1944, apparently dictated later; on 6 or 7 June?

8. Irving, loc. cit., p491; Ruge, loc. cit., p116; BA–MA RH 19 IV/35 and 40, KTB Sup Cmd–West, 1 June 1944 app. 810; Meyer-Detring, Wilhelm, Letter to the author, 30 Jan 1978; Ryan, loc. cit., p66

9. BA–MA RH 19 IV/40, app. 887, 5 June 1944

10. Situation Briefing 2/6 from OKW/WFST/Op M, Kapitän z. See Assmann to the OKM/1 SKL Ia, 2 June 1944 Irving collection, Institute for Zeitgeschichte, Munich

11. Reile, Oscar, *"Knackten die Engländer den geheimen Wehrmachtsfunk und täuschten sie die Abwehr die Invasion,"* in *Wehrwissenschaftliche Rundschau,* 19 Apr 1978

12. BA–MA RH 19 IV/47, KTB Sup Cmd–West, 9 June 1944 app. 65; Meyer-Detring, loc. cit.

13. BA–MA RH IV/43 and 133, app. 126

14. BA–MA RH 20-15/64 and 15/89, 5 June 1944, KTB HQ, 15th Army Ia and Ic

15. Staubwasser, Anton, Ic Army Grp B, letter to the author, 11 Nov 1978; Speidel, loc.

cit., p 98. But Speidel is mistaken. HQ, 15th Army did not inform the neighboring armies, only the Army Group.

16. Assmann, loc. cit., p 424

17. BA–MA N 117/22

18. BA–MA RH 20–7/129, KTB HQ, 7th Army, 6 June 1944; BA–MA RH 20–15/64, KTB HQ, 15th Army, 6 June 1944

19. Different sources of opposing sides, mainly Willmot, p264 ff

20. See ftnt. 18

21. KTB Army Grp B, 6 June 1944, Irving collection, I.f.Z., Munich; BA–MA RH 20-7/129

22. BA–MA RH 19 IV/43 and 47, app. 3 and 4; KTB Army Grp B, loc. cit.

23. KTB Army Grp B, loc. cit.

24. KTB Army Grp B, loc. cit.

25. KTB Army Grp B, loc. cit.

26. See ftnt. 19

27. Kortenhaus, Werner, unpublished draft of Operations of the 21st Panzer Division in the Battle of the Invasion; Gottberg, Wilhelm von, letter to the author, 18 May 1978

28. BA–MA RH 19 IV/43 and 47 app. 11; KTB Army Grp B, loc. cit.

29. BA–MA RH 19 IV/47, app. 10

30. KTB Army Grp B, loc. cit.

31. BA–MA RH 19 IV/43 and 47, app. 15–16

32. Ritgen, Helmut, *The History of the Panzer Lehr Division in the West 1944–1945* (Stuttgart: n.p., 1979), p103 ff

33. BA–MA RH 20–7/129 and /137

34. BA–MA RH 20–7/129

35. BA–MA RH 19 IV/43 and 47, app. 26 and 28; BA–MA RH 19 IV/134 D(1), 7 and 8 June 1944; KTB Army Grp B, loc. cit.

36. BA–MA RH 20–15/64

37. BA–MA RH 19 IV/43 and 47, app. 26, 45

38. BA–MA RH 20–7/129

39. BA–MA RH 19 IV/43 and 47, app. 97

40. KTB OKW, vol. IV, 1, p314

41. KTB Army Grp B, 12 June 1944 loc. cit.

42. BA–MA RH 19 IV/43 and 47, app. 159

43. BA–MA RH 19 XI/1

44. BA–MA RH 19 IV/47, app. 189

45. BA–MA RH 19 IV/47, app. 190

46. BA–MA RH 19 IV/43, p66

47. BA–MA RH 19 IX/84, p22, 23, 26

48. BA–MA RH 19 IV/43 BA–MA RH 19 IV/84; BA–MA RH 20–7/129 and /137

49. Eisnehower, loc. cit., p129–135
50. BA–MA RH 19 IV/43; BA–MA RH 19 IX/84; BA–MA RH 20–7/137
51. KTB OKW vol. IV, 1, p317–321; BA–MA RH 19 IV/48, app. 306, 340, 348, 355, 356, 375
52. KTB OKW vol. IV, 1, p319
53. BA–MA RH 19 IV/48, app. 348
54. KTB OKW vol. IV, 1, p320
55. BA–MA RH 19 IX/1, p86–89; BA–MA RH 19 IV/48, app. 396
56. KTB OKW vol 4, 2, p 1594–1595
57. BA–MA RH 19 IX/4, 96–100
58. BA–MA RH 19 IV 1944 and 49, app. 409
59. BA–MA RH 19 IX/7, 13
60. BA–MA RH 19 IV 1944; BA–MA RH 19 IX/84
61. BA–MA RH 19 IX/4, 116–125
62. BA–MA RH 19 IV/49, app. 504
63. BA–MA RH 19 IV 1944
64. BA–MA RH 19 IX/85; BA–MA RH 19 IV 1944
65. KTB OKW vol. IV, 1, p458; BA–MA RH 19 IV 1944 and 49, app. 529
66. BA–MA RH 19 IX/85
67. BA–MA RH 19 IV 1944; BA–MA RH 19 IX/85
68. BA–MA RH 19 IV 1944 and 49, 615, 617
69. BA–MA RH 19 IX/8, 105 and 106
70. Speidel, loc. cit. p138
71. BA–MA RH 19 IX/8, 103 and 104
72. BA–MA RH 19 IV 1944
73. Eberbach, Heinrich, letters to the author, 30 Jan and 28 Feb 1979
74. BA–MA RH 19 IX/86; BA–MA RH 19 IV 1944
75. Piekalkiewicz, Janocz, *Invasion Frankreich 1944* (Munich: n.p., 1979), p181; Wilmot, loc. cit., p376ff, map before 353
76. BA–MA RH 19 IX/86; BA–MA RH 19 IV 1944
77. Piekalkiewicz, loc. cit., 181
78. BA–MA RH 19 IX/86; BA MA-RH 19 IV 1944 and 50, app. 725
79. BA–MA RH 19 IV/50, app. 729
80. BA–MA RH 10 IX/86

CHAPTER 4

1. Wolff-Boenisch, Richard, diary
2. Vogelsang, Fritz, diary
3. KTB 2d Bn./Arm.Art.Reg. 146, 6 June 1944
4. BA–MA RH 24-81/89, KTB LXXXI, Corps
5. BA–MA RH 24-81/89, KTB LXXXI, Corps
6. KTB 1, II and 3d Bn./Arm.Art.Reg. 146, 6 June 1944
7. BA–MA RH 20–15/208, KTB HQ 15th Army Ic (app. 3)
8. BA–MA RH 20–15/64, KTB HQ, 15th Army; KTB Army Grp B, 6 June 1944 1020 hours, Irving collection.
9. KTB 2d Bn./Arm.Art.Reg. 146, 6 June 1944
10. BA–MA RH 19 IV/43 and 47, app. 19 KTB Sup Cmd–West
11. KTB 2d Bn./Arm.Art.Reg. 146, 7 June 1944
12. KTB Army Grp B, loc. cit.
13. BA–MA RH 24–81/93, KTB LXXXI Corps
14. Strackerjahn, Fritz, Brockmeyer, Konrad and Bargstädt, Klaus Richard, to the author
15. KTB 2d Bn./Arm.Art.Reg. 146, 8 June 1944
16. BA–MA RH 20–15/64, KTB HQ, 15th Army; BA–MA RH 24–81/91 and 89, KTB LXXXI Corps
17. Ba-MA RH 19 IV/43 and 47, app. 85, KTB Sup Cmd–West
18. KTB 1/Arm.Art.Reg. 146, 9 June 1944; Wolff-Boenisch, loc. cit.
19. KTB Army Grp B, loc. cit.
20 KTB 2d Bn./Arm.Art.Reg. 146, 9 June 1944
21. BA–MA RH 24–81/91, KTB LXXXI Corps
22. Holtermann, Dr. Arthur, pocket calendar
23. BA–MA RH 24–81/91, KTB LXXXI Corps
24. Wolff-Boenisch, loc. cit.
25. BA–MA RH 19 IV/47, KTB Sup Cmd–West; KTB Army Grp B, loc. cit.
26. BA–MA RH 24–81/89, KTB LXXXI Corps
27. Holtermann, see ftnt. 22
28. Wendt, Kurt, report to the author
29. BA–MA RH 19 IV/43 and 47, app. 87, KTB Sup Cmd–West
30. BA–MA RH 19 IV/47, app. 122, KTB Sup Cmd–West
31. KTB Army Grp B, loc. cit.; BA–MA RH 20–15/64, KTB HQ, 15th Army

32. See ftnt, 31
33. BA–MA RH 24–81/91, KTB LXXXI Corps
34. BA–MA RH 20–15/64, KTB HQ, 15th Army
35. KTB Army Grp B, loc. cit.
36. Order 116 Pz.Div., Sect. Ia, 12 June 1944 2000 hours, from docs. Arm.Art.Reg. 146
37. Carell, Paul. *They Are Coming, Berlin.* (Vienna: n.p., 1960), p162 ff
38. BA–MA RH 24–67/4, KTB LXVII Corps
39. BA–MA RH 24–67/5, KTB LXVII Corps; BA–MA RH 24–67/6 K, KTB LXVII Corps
40. BA–MA RH 24–67/4, KTB LXVII Corps; BA–MA RH 20–15/64, KTB HQ, 15th Army
41. BA–MA RH 19 IV/47, KTB Sup Cmd–West
42. KTB OKW vol. IV, 1, p315
43. KTB OKW vol. IV, 1, p314; KTB Army Grp B, loc. cit.; BA–MA RH 19 IV/43, 47
44. BA–MA RH 24–81/91, KTB LXXXI Corps
45. KTB 3d Bn./PzArt.Reg. 146, 14 June 1944
46. KTB II and 3d Bn./Arm.Art.Reg. 146; Order 116 Pz.Div., Sect. Ia, 15 June 1944, from document Arm.Art.Reg.146
47. KTB 2d Bn./Arm.Art.Reg. 146
48. KTB Army Grp B, loc. cit.; Senger and Etterlin, Dr. F. M. von Jr.; *Div 24. Panzer-Division, vormals 1. Kavallerie-Division, 1939–1945* (Neckargemünd, 1962), p299
49. BA–MA RH 24–67/5, KTB LVII Corps
50. BA–MA RH 24–67/4, KTB LVII Corps; BA–MA RH 20–15/64, KTB HQ, 15th Army
51. BA–MA RH 20–15/64, KTB HQ, 15th Army
52. BA–MA RH 24–67/4, KTB LVII Corps
53. BA–MA RH 24–67/1, KTB LVII Corps
54. BA–MA RH 19 IV/43 and 47, KTB Sup Cmd–West; BA–MA RH 19 IX/84, KTB Army Grp B
55. BA–MA RH 19 IV/47, app. 130, KTB Sup Cmd–West
56. BA–MA N 117/22; BA–MA RH 20–15/64, KTB HQ, 15th Army; BA–MA RH 24–67/5, KTB LVII Corps
57. BA–MA RH 24–67/5, KTB LVII Corps
58. BA–MA RH 20–15/64, KTB HQ, 15th Army; BA–MA RH 24–67/4, KTB LXVII Corps; Area of operations and unit disposi-tions basically corresponded to the map as per 1 July 1944, also see ftnt. 64
59. BA–MA RH 24–81/90, KTB LXXXI Corps
60. KTB II and 3d Bn./Arm.Art.Reg. 146
61. BA–MA RH 20–15/64, KTB HQ, 15th Army
62. See ftnt. 61
63. BA–MA N 117/22; BA–MA RH 19 IX/84, KTB Army Grp B; BA–MA RH 20–15/64, KTB HQ, 15th Army; BA–MA RH 24–67/4, KTB LVII Corps
64. BA–MA RH 24–67/6, K, KTB LVII Corps, map 4
65. Holtermann, see ftnt. 22
66. BA–MA RH 19 IV/43, KTB Sup Cmd–West
67. BA–MA RH 24–67/4, KTB LVII Corps
68. KTB 2d Bn./Arm.Art.Reg. 146, 1 July 1944
69. BA–MA RH 2 W/203
70. Delmer, Sefton. *Die Geisterarmee oder Die Invasion, die nicht stattfand* (Munich–Vienna–Zürich: n.p., 1972,) p251 position report 1320 of btl. foreign armies West, 8 Jul 1944
71. Delmer, loc. cit., p254 position report 1339, btl. foreign armies West, 27 Jul 1944
72. BA–MA RH 19 IX/4, KTB Army Grp B
73. Borgert, Wenzel, pocket calendar
74. BA–MA RH 19 IV 1944 and 49, KTB Sup Cmd–West; BA–MA RH 19 IX/85, KTB Army Grp B
75. Schwerin, Gerhard Count von, letter to the Ia, Army Grp B, Oberstleutnant i.G. von Tempelhoff, 4 July 1944.
76. KTB 2d Bn./Arm.Art.Rgt.146, 27 June 1944
77. BA–MA RH 19 IV 1944 and 50 app. 728, KTB Sup Cmd–West
78. BA–MA RH 19 IV 1944 and 50; Order 116 Pz.Div.Sect. Ia, 23 July 1944 from docs. Arm.Art.Reg.146; KTB 2d Bn./Pz.Art.Reg.146
79. BA–MA RH 19 IV 1944 KTB Sup Cmd–West
80. Bargstädt, loc. cit., Grollmann, Heinrich and Inboden, August Wilhelm, reports to the author.
81. KTB 2d Bn./Arm.Art.Reg.146, 23 July 1944

82. Order 116th Pz.Div., 23 July 1944, same as in ftnt. 78

83. BA–MA RH 19 IV 1944 KTB Sup Cmd–West; KTB 2d Bn./Arm.Art.Reg. 146

84. BA–MA RH 19 IX/86, KTB Army Grp B, 20 July 1944

85. Schwerin, Gerhard Count von, letter to Major Tebbe, Kdo. 1st Bn.//Pz.Reg.16, 26 July 1944

86. Lademann, Gerhard, n.d.; Trauden, Fritz, letter 19 Jan 1974

87. Schwerin, Gerhard Count von, Reasons for the delayed deployment of the 116th Pz.Div. in the Normandy invasion, summer 1944, recollections by the Cdr., 116th Pz.Div., Selbstverlag, FM-12/1977

88. Irving, loc. cit., p518

89. Speidel, loc. cit., p71

90. Schwerin, Gerhard Count von, sworn statement, 16 May 1978

91. OIS Speidel, Dr. Hans, letter to the author, 4 Oct 1978

92. BA–MA RH 19 IV/47, app. 45, KTB Sup Cmd–West

93. Strauss, Dr. F. J., *Friedens- und Kriegseriebnisse einer Generation (*Schweinfurt, 1961), p167

94. Both quotations from BA–MA RH 19 IV 1944, KTB Sup Com–West, 19 and 24 July 1944

95. BA–MA RH 19 IX/86, KTB Army Grp B

96. BA–MA RH 19 IV 1944 and 51 app. 883, KTB Sup Cmd–West

97. See ftnt. 90

98. Wolff-Boenisch, loc. cit.

99. Strackerjahn, Fritz, letter to the author, 4 Oct 1981

CHAPTER 5

1. Strauss, loc. cit., p167

2. Wilmot, loc. cit.,p403 ff and map next to p400. Blumenson, Martin, *Breakout and Pursuit,* from the US Army in WWII series, (Washington, DC, 1961,) p197 ff and map VI

3. Ritgen, loc. cit., p167

4. Wilmot, loc. cit., p410 f

5. BA–MA RH 19 IV 1944 and 51, KTB Sup Cmd–West, 27 July 1944; BA–MA RH 19 IX/86, KTB Army Grp B, 26 July 1944

6. See ftnt. 5, 27 July 1944

7. BA–MA RH IX/86, KTB Army Grp B, 28 July 1944

8. See ftnt. 7

9. See ftnt. 7

10. See ftnt. 7

11. See ftnt. 7

12. BA–MA RH 19 IV 1944, KTB Sup Cmd–West, 28 Jul 1944; KTB 2d Bn./Pz.Art. Rgt. 146, 28 Jul 1944; Schmeermann, Heinz, diary; Schwerin, Gerhard, Count von, MS Ethint-17, *The 116th Panzer Division During the Battle of the Normandy*

13. BA–MA RH 19 IV 1944, KTB Sup Cmd–West, 28 July 1944; BA–MA RH 19 IX/86, KTB Army Grp B, 28 July 1944

14. Schwerin, Ethint-17, and letter, 8 Sep 1944 to *Generalleutnant* Dr. Speidel from Holtermann docs., see ftnt. 4, chapter 1; The description of events at the 116th Pz. Div. until 7 Aug 1944 is based on those two drafts by Schwerin to a large extent. Other sources used will be noted accordingly.

15. Ritgen, loc. cit., p173

16. Blumenson, loc. cit., p299 ff

17. BA–MA RH 19 IX/86, KTB HG.r.B., 29 July 1944; BA–MA RH 19 IV 1944, KTB Sup Cmd–West, 29 July 1944

18. Blumenson, loc. cit., p301

19. KTB 2d Bn./Arm.Art.Rgt. 146, 29 July 1944

20. Memo for KTB 116th Pz. Div., 29 July 1944 2120 hours from Holtermann docs., see ftnt. chapter 1, 4. In the memo the date of 30 July 1944 is noted erroniously

21. See ftnt. 20

22. BA–MA RH 19 IX/86, KTB Army Grp B, 29 July 1944

23. Sandkuhl, loc. cit., 30 July 1944

24. Nitsch, Alois, diary and reports to the author; BA–MA RH 27–116th/127, p129 ff, IIa document of 116th Panzer Division recommendation for award for Oberleutnant. Best

25. Senger, loc. cit., p300 ff; Weidemann, Gert-Axel, *Unser Regiment - Reiter-Regiment 2 - Panzer - Regiment 24,* (Gross-Umstadt, 1982), p.217 ff

26. KTB 2d Bn./Arm.Art.Rgt. 146

27. Nitsch, loc. cit.; Triantaphyllides, Phidias, diary

28. Blumenson, loc. cit., p301 ff

29. BA–MA RH 19 IX/86 KTB Army Grp B, 30 July 1944

30. Senger, loc. cit., p301

31. BA–MA RH 19 IV 1944 and 51, KTB Sup Cmd–West, 30 and 31 July 1944; BA–MA RH 19 IX/86, KTB Army Grp B, 30 July 1944

32. BA–MA RH 20–7/145 telephone conversations 7th Army, 31 July 1944 1045 hours

33. BA–MA RH 19 IV 1944, KTB Sup Cmd–West, 31 July 1944

34. BA–MA RH 19 IX/86, KTB Army Grp B, 30 July 1944; BA–MA RH 20–7/145 telephone conversations 7th Army, 31 July 1944; BA–MA RH 19 IV 1944, KTB Sup Cmd–West, 31 July 1944

35. BA–MA RH 19 IX/86, KTB Army Grp B, 7/31 1944

36. KTB 2d Bn./Arm.Art.Rgt. 146

37. Senger, loc. cit., p301

38. Nitsch, loc. cit.; Triantaphyllides, loc. cit.

39. Senger, loc. cit., p301

40. BA–MA RH 19 IV 1944, KTB Sup Cmd–West, 31 July 1944; BA–MA RH 19 IX/86, KTB Army Grp B, 31 July 1944

41. Wilmot, loc. cit., p416

42. BA–MA RH 19 IX/86, KTB Army Grp B, 31 July and 1 Aug 1944; BA–MA RH 19 IV 1944 and 51 KTB Sup Cmd–West, 31 July and 1 Aug 1944

43. Sandkuhl, loc. cit.,

44. BA–MA RH 19 IV 1945, KTB Sup Cmd–West, 1 Aug 1944; BA–MA RH 19 IX/87, KTB Army Grp B, 1 Aug 1944

45. Order 116th Pz.Div., Sect. Ia, 31 July 1944 from document Arm.Art.Rgt. 146

46. BA–MA RH 19 IX/87, KTB Army Grp B, 8/1 1944; KTB 2d Bn./Arm.Art.Rgt. 146

47. BA–MA RH 19 IV 1945 and 52, KTB Sup Cmd–West, 1 Aug 1944

48. BA–MA RH 19 IV 1945, KTB Sup Cmd–West, 1 Aug 1944

49. Nitsch, loc. cit.

50. KTB 2d Bn./Arm.Art.Rgt. 146; Triantaphyllides, loc. cit. ; Nitsch, loc. cit.

51. BA–MA RH 19 IV 1945 and 52, KTB Sup Cmd–West, 2 Aug 1944; Weidemann, loc. cit., p221 and 222

52. Weidemann, loc. cit., p222

53. Blumenson, loc. cit., p446 ff

54. 116th Pz.Div., commander, 2 Aug 1944 from Holtermann docs, see ftnt. ch. 1, 4

55. BA–MA RH 19 IV 1945 and 52, KTB Sup Cmd–West, 2 Aug 1944; BA–MA RH 19 IX/87, KTB Army Grp B, 2 Aug 1944

56. See ftnt. 55

57. BA–MA RH 19 IV 1945 and 52 Anl. 1050, KTB Sup Cmd–West, 2 and 3 Aug 1944

58. Headquarters 12 Army Group, letter of instructions number two, 3 Aug 1944; copy in possession of author.

59. KTB 2d Bn./Arm.Art.Rgt. 146; Nitsch, loc. cit.

60. BA–MA RH 19 IV/52, KTB Sup Cmd–West, 3 Aug 1944; BA–MA RH 19 IX/87, KTB Army Grp B, 3 Aug 1944

61. KTB 2d Bn./Arm.Art.Rgt. 146; Nitsch, loc. cit.

62. BA–MA RH 19 IV 1945 and 52, KTB Sup Cmd–West, 4 Aug 1944; BA–MA RH 19 IX/87, KTB Army Grp B, 4 Aug 1944; BA–MA RH 20–7/147, KTB 7th Army, 4 Aug 1944

63. See ftnt. 62, 5 Aug 1944

64. BA–MA RH 19 IX/87, KTB Army Grp B, 6 Aug 1944; BA–MA RH 19 IV 1945, KTB Sup Cmd–West, 6 Aug 1944; KTB OKW, vol. IV, 1, p336 ff

65. BA–MA RH 19 IX/87, KTB Army Grp B, 6 Aug 1944; BA–MA RH 20–7/147, KTB 7th Army, 6 Aug 1944; KTB 2d Bn./Arm.Art.Rgt. 146

66. BA–MA RH 19 IV 1945, KTB Sup Cmd–West, 6 Aug 1944; BA–MA RH 19 IX/87, KTB Army Grp B, 6 Aug 1944

67. Strackerjahn, Fritz, letter to the author, 4 Oct 1981

68. BA–MA RH 20–7/145, KTB 7th Army, 6 Aug 1944

69. BA–MA RH 19 IX/87. KTB Army Grp B, 7 Aug 1944; Senger, loc. cit., p302 ff; Weidemann, loc. cit., p224 ff

70. Senger, loc. cit., p303; Weidemann, loc. cit., p227 and 230; BA–MA RH 27-116th/127 p58/59, IIa-document of 116th Pz.Div

71. BA–MA RH 20–7/145, telephone conversations Army HQ, 6 and 7 Aug 1944

72. BA–MA RH 20–7/147, KTB 7th Army, 7 Aug 1944; Nitsch, loc. cit. ; Strackerjahn, loc. cit.

73. Memories of the author and note for KTB 116th Pz.Div, 6 Aug 1944 from document; Holtermann, see ftnt. chapter 1, 4. Obviously, there were two conversations mixed up, one from 6 Aug at 2135 hours, the other from 7 Aug late afternoon.

74. Letter 116th Pz.Div Cdr., 9 Aug 1944 from document Holtermann see ftnt. chapter 1. 4

75. BA–MA RH 19 IX/87, KTB Army Grp B, 7 Aug 1944

76. As of 6 Aug 1944, *"Panzergruppe West"* was called 5th Panzer Army.

77. Blumenson, loc. cit., p465 ff

78. KTB 2/Arm.Art.Rgt. 146, 6 Aug 1944

79. BA–MA RH 19 IV/52, Anl. 1176, KTB Sup Cmd–West, 7 Aug 1944

80. BA–MA RH 20–7/147, KTB 7th Army, 7 Aug 1944

81. BA–MA RH 19 IV/52, Anl. 1205, KTB Sup Cmd–West, 8 Aug 1944, adendum to morning report; BA–MA RH 19 IX/87, KTB Army Grp B, 8 Aug 1944

82. BA–MA RH 19 IX/87, KTB Army Grp B, 8 Aug 1944

83. BA–MA RH 20–7/145, telephone conversations 7th Army, 8 Aug 1944

84. BA–MA RH 19 IX/87, KTB Army Grp B, 9 Aug 1944

85. BA–MA RH 20–7/145, telephone conversations 7th Army, 9 Aug 1944

86. BA–MA RH 19 IX/87 kTB Army Grp B, 9 Aug 1944

87. 12 Army group, letter of instructions number four, 8 Aug 1944, copy in possession of author.

88. BA–MA RH 19 IX/87, KTB Army Grp B, 10 Aug 1944

89. BA–MA RH 20–7/147, KTB 7th Army, 8 Aug 1944

90. BA–MA RH 58/9, KTB LVIII Panzer Corps, 9 Aug 1944; BA–MA RH 27-116th/127, p92, recommendation for Rittmeister Schliep, IIa doc 116th Pz.Div.

91. BA–MA RH 19 IX/87, KTB Army Grp B, 10 Aug 1944

92. BA–MA RH 19 IV/53, Anl. 1458, KTB Sup Cmd–West, 16 Aug 1944

93. BA–MA RH 19 IV 1945, p80–82 and 53, Anl. 1270 and 1271, KTB Sup Cmd–West, 10 Aug 1944; BA–MA RH 19 IX/87, KTB Army Grp B, 10 Aug 1944

94. BA–MA RH 19 IX/87, KTB Army Grp B, 11 Aug 1944, 1510, 1535, and 1620 hours

95. BA–MA RH 19 IX/87, KTB Army Grp B, 10 Aug 1944; BA–MA RH 20–7/145, telephone conversations 7th Army, 10 Aug 1944 1800 hours

96. BA–MA RH 20–7/147, KTB 7th Army, 10 Aug 1944

97. See ftnt. 96

98. BA–MA RH 20–7/147, KTB 7th Army, 11 Aug 1944

99. Müller, Gerhard Paul, MS B-162; The description up to 24 Aug 1944 is mostly based on this work.

100. BA–MA RH 19 IX/87, KTB Army Grp B, 12 Aug 1944

101. BA–MA RH 19 IV/53, Anl. 1296 and 1314 KTB Sup Cmd–West, 11 Aug 1944; BA–MA RH 19 IX/87, KTB Army Grp B, 11 Aug 1944

102. BA–MA RH 24-81/100, KTB LXXXI Corps, 11 Aug 1944

103. Nitsch, loc. cit.

104. KTB 2d Bn./Arm.Art.Rgt. 146, 12 Aug 1944 ;Sandkuhl, loc. cit.

105. Blumenson, loc. cit., p502 ff

106. KTB II Arm.Art.Rgt. 146; Sandkuhl, loc. cit.

107. Blumenson, loc. cit., p502 ff

108. Hafemeister, Hans-Hermann, reports to the authors 1981 and 1982

109. Leiding, Alfred, personal notes and letters to the author, December 1982

110. Hafemeister and Leiding, loc. cit.

111. Nitsch, loc. cit.

112. Nürnberg, Hans (5/156), Best, Eric (6/156) and Strackerjahn, Fritz (7/156), reports to the author.

113. Nitsch and Strackerjahn, loc. cit.

114. Leiding, loc. cit.

115. Baedeker, Dietrich, *Das Volk das im Finstern wandelt,* Hannover 1987, p79 ff; 116th. KTB 2d Bn./Arm.Art.Rgt. 146; Senger, loc. cit., p303/304

116. KTB 2d Bn./Arm.Art.Rgt. 146; Senger, loc. cit., p304; Weidemann, loc. cit., p232

117. KTB 2d Bn./Arm.Art.Rgt. 146; Senger, loc. cit., p304; Weidemann, loc. cit., p232

118. Schüler, Helmut, reports to the author

119. BA–MA RH 24-81/97 and 100, KTB LXXXI Corps, 12 Aug 1944

120. BA–MA RH 19 IV 1945 and 53, Anl.1347,1357,1373 KTB Sup Cmd–West,

13 and 14 Aug 1944; Eberbach, Heinreich, MS A-922; BA–MA RH 20–7/147, KTB 7th Army, Eberbach's radio messages to Army Grp B

121. BA–MA RH 24-81/97 and 100, KTB LXXXI Corps, 13 Aug 1944

122. Blumenson, loc. cit., p504 ff

123. BA–MA RH 19 IV 1945 and 53, Anl. 1369, KTB Sup Cmd–West, 14 Aug 1944; BA–MA RH 19 IX/87, KTB Army Grp B, 12 and 13 Aug 1944; BA–MA RH 21-5/52, KTB HQ, 5th Pz Army, 12 and 14 Aug 1944

124. BA–MA RH 19 IV 1945 and 53, Anl. 1383, KTB Sup Cmd–West, 14 and 15 Aug 1944; BA–MA RH 19 IX/87, KTB Army Grp B, 14 Aug 1944

125. BA–MA RH 19 IV 1945 and 53, Anl. 1418, KTB Sup Cmd–West, 14 and 15 Aug 1944; BA–MA RH 19 IX/87, KTB Army Grp B, 15 Aug 1944; BA–MA RH 21-5/52, KTB HQ, 5th Pz Army, 15 Aug 1944

126. KTB II Arm.Art.Rgt. 146

127. BA–MA RH 24-81/97 and 100, KTB LXXXI Corps, 13 and 14 Aug 1944

128. KTB 2d Bn./Arm.Art.Rgt. 146

129. 116th Pz.Div.Sect. Ib, 14 Aug 1944 from document Holtermann see ftnt. chapter 1, 4

130. BA–MA RH 20–7/147, KTB 7th Army, 16 Aug 1944; BA–MA RH 21-5/53 p49, KTB HQ, 5th Pz Army, 16 Aug 1944; BA–MA RH 19 IX/87, KTB Army Grp B, 16 Aug 1944

131. Document Holtermann, see above ftnt. 129, Schwerin's letter, 16 Aug 1944

132. Harzer, Walter, MS P/162

133. Stückler, Albert, MS P/159

134. Blumenson, loc. cit., p530

135. BA–MA RH 27-116th/127, p55/56 and 85, recommendations for awards Brühl, Friedrich Count von and Pichler, Josef in IIa-document 116th Pz.Div.; BA–MA RH 19 IV/53, Anl. 1490, KTB Sup Cmd–West, 17 Aug 1944

136. V Corps, G3-Sitrep, 17 Aug 1944 1800 hours copy in possession of author

137. Weidemann, loc,cit., p232 f

138. BA–MA RH 21-5/52, KTB HQ, 5th Pz Army, 17 Aug 1944 1800 hours

139. BA–MA RH 19 IV 1945, KTB Sup Cmd–West, 17 Aug 1944 2000 hours

140. Blumenson, loc. cit., p533 ff; Order V Corps, 17 Aug 1944, 1800 hours copy in possession of author

141. BA–MA RH 19 IV 1945 and 53, Anl. 1498, 1512, KTB Sup Cmd–West, 18 Aug 1944; Harzer, loc. cit.

142. BA–MA RH 21-5/52, KTB HQ, 5th Pz Army, 18 Aug 1944

143. BA–MA RH 19 IV/53, Anl. 1522, KTB Sup Cmd–West, 19 Aug 1944

144. BA–MA RH 19 IV/53, Anl. 1513, KTB Sup Cmd–West, 18 Aug 1944

145. BA–MA RH 19 IV/53, Anl. 1521, KTB Sup Cmd–West, 19 Aug 1944

146. BA–MA RH 19 IV/53, Anl. 1482 and 1499 KTB Sup Cmd–West, 17 resp. 18 Aug 1944; KTB OKW, vol. IV, 1 p352 and 459

147. BA–MA RH 19 IV/53, Anl. 1530, KTB Sup Cmd–West, 19 Aug 1944

148. Twelfth Army Group, adenda to Letter of Instructions Number Five, 19 Aug 1944

149. BA–MA RH 19 IV 1945 and 53, Anl. 1533b, KTB Sup Cmd–West, 19 Aug 1944

150. BA–MA RH 27-116th/127, p55/56, proposal Brühl, Friedrich Count von

151. Blumenson, loc. cit., p540 ff

152. Order 116th Pz.Div.Art. Ib, 21 Aug 1944 from document Arm.Art.Rgt. 146

153. Harder, Ernst, report to the author, 4 Oct 1978; BA–MA RH 24-81/97 and 100, KTB LXXXI Corps, 17 and 18 Aug 1944; Meyer, Hubert, MS P-164 and report to the author

154. BA–MA RH 19 IV 1945 and 54, Anl. 1586, KTB Sup Cmd–West, 21 Aug 1944; BA–MA RH 19 IX/88, KTB Army Grp B, 21 Aug 1944; BA–MA RH 21-5/52, KTB HQ, 5th Pz Army, 21 Aug 1944

155. Bargstädt, Dr. Hans Richard, report to the author

156. BA–MA RH 21-5/53, Anl. 38 KTB HQ, 5th Pz Army, 21 Aug 1944

157. BA–MA RH 21-5/23, Anl. 37 KTB HQ, 5th Pz Army, 21 Aug 1944

158. BA–MA RH 24-8/97, KTB LXXXI Corps, 21 and 22 Aug 1944

159. See ftnt. 158

160. Order, Cdr 116th Pz.Div., 22 Aug 1944 from document Arm.Art.Rgt. 146

CHAPTER 6

1. BA–MA RH 19 IV 1945 and 54, Anl.1618 and 1620, KTB Sup Cmd–West, 22 Aug 1944; BA–MA RH 19 IX/88, p.77-78, KTB Army Grp B, 22 Aug 1944; BA–MA RH 21-5/52, KTB 5th Panzer Army, 22 Aug 1944; BA–MA RH 24-81/97, KTB LXXXI Corps, 22 Aug 1944
2. BA–MA RH 24-81/97 and 100, KTB LXXXI Corps, 22 Aug 1944
3. KTB 2d Bn./Arm.Art.Rgt. 146; Metzscher, Erich, notes; Schwörer, Ernst, diary
4. BA–MA RH 27-116/127, IIa-Akten 116th Pz.Div. proposal Hptm. Gerke
5. BA–MA RH 24-81/100, KTB LXXXI Corps, 23 Aug 1944
6. See ftnt. 3; BA–MA RH 19 IV/54, Anl. 1645 and 1647, KTB Sup Cmd–West, 23 Aug 1944; BA–MA RH 24-81/97, KTB LXXXI Corps, 23 Aug 1944
7. BA–MA RH 24-81/97, KTB LXXXI Corps, 23 and 24 Aug 1944; BA–MA RH 21-5/52 and 53, KTB 5th Panzer Army, 23 and 24 Aug 1944; Müller, Gerhard Paul, MS B-162
8. Voigtsberger, Heinrich, MS B-058
9. BA–MA RH 21-5/52 and 53 KTB 5th Pz Army, 23 and 24 Aug 1944; BA–MA RH 24-81/97 and 100, KTB LXXXI Corps, 23 and 24 Aug 1944
10. BA–MA RH 19 IX/88, KTB Army Grp B, 22 and 23 Aug 1944; BA–MA RH 21-5/52, KTB 5th Panzer Army, 22 and 23 Aug 1944; BA–MA RH 24-81/97 and 100, KTB LXXXI Corps, 23 and 24 Aug 1944
11. BA–MA RH 19 IX/88, KTB Army Grp B, 23 Aug 1944
12. BA–MA RH 19 IV/54, Anl. 1636, KTB Sup Cmd–West, 23 Aug 1944
13. BA–MA RH 19 IX/88, KTB Army Grp B, 23 Aug 1944
14. BA–MA RH 19 IV/54, Anl. 1645 and 1647, KTB Sup Cmd–West, 23 Aug 1944; BA–MA RH 19 IX/86, KTB Army Grp B, 23 Aug 1944; BA–MA RH 21-5/52, KTB 5th Panzer Army, 23 Aug 1944
15. Blumenson, loc. cit., p559 ff
16. KTB 2d Bn./Arm.Art.Rgt. 146; BA–MA RH 19 IV/54 Anl. 1684 and 1687, KTB Sup Cmd–West, 8/24 1944; BA–MA RH 19 IX/88, KTB Army Grp B, 24 Aug 1944;

17. BA–MA RH 21-5/52 and 53, KTB 5th Panzer Army, 24 Aug 1944
18. BA–MA RH 19 IX/88, KTB Army Grp B, 24 Aug 1944; BA–MA RH 21-5/52, KTB 5th Panzer Army, 24 Aug 1944
19. BA–MA RH 19 IV/54, Anl. 1687, KTB Sup Cmd–West, 24 Aug 1944
20. BA–MA RH 19 IV/54, Anl. 1687, KTB Sup Cmd–West, 24 Aug 1944; Blumenson, loc. cit., p610 ff
21. Twelfth Army Group, letter of instructions number six, 25 Aug 1944; Blumenson, loc. cit., p657 ff
22. BA–MA RH 19 IV/54, Anl. 1707, KTB Sup Cmd–West, 25 Aug 1944; BA–MA RH 21–5/53, p72, KTB 5th Panzer Army, 25 Aug 1944
23. BA–MA RH 24-81/99, KTB LXXXI Corps, 25 Aug 1944
24. BA–MA RH 19 IX/4, Army Grp B, 25 Aug 1944
25. Schwerin, Gerhard Count von, MS Ethint-18; Borgert, Wenzel, "Sonderausweis" of Combat Group Schwerin, 27 Aug 1944, copy with author.
26. Wendt, Kurt, report to the author
27. BA–MA RH 19 IV/54, Anl. 1705, 1712, 1713, KTB Sup Cmd–West, 25 Aug 1944; BA–MA RH 24-81/97 and 98, KTB LXXXI Corps, 25 Aug 1944
28. KTB 2d Bn./Arm.Art.Rgt. 146; Schwörer, diary
29. BA–MA RH 19 IV/54, Anl. 1713 KTB Sup Cmd–West, 25 Aug 1944; BA–MA RH 24-81/98, KTB LXXXI Corps, 25 Aug 1944
30. See ftnt. 27; Map from KTB 2d Bn./Arm.Art.Rgt. 146
31. Schwerin, MS Ethint-18; Varnholt, Otto, notes
32. BA–MA RH 24-81/97, KTB LXXXI Corps, 26 Aug 1944
33. See ftnt. 27
34. BA–MA RH 19 IV/54, Anl. 1748 and 1752, KTB Sup Cmd–West, 27 Aug 1944
35. BA–MA RH 24-81/97, KTB LXXXI Corps, 27 and 28 Aug 1944
36. Individual pieces from the following sources have been combined. It is not always possible to name them separately. a) Schwerin, MS Ethint-18; b) Voigtsberger, MS B-058; c) Wolf, Lothar, Map

entries and marginal notes on maps of the Ia 116th Pz.Div; d) Holtermann, pocket calendar 1944; e) Schmeermann, Heinz, Notes

36. Order 116th Pz.Div., Sect. Ia, 29 Aug 1944 from document Arm.Art.Rgt. 146
37. Stephan, Eberhard, Post War Report
38. Senger, loc. cit., p305
39. Bergstädt, Hans-Richard, Notes
40. Blumenson, loc. cit., p 671 ff
41. BA–MA RH 19 IV/54, Anl. 1808, KTB Sup Cmd–West, 31 Aug 1944; BA–MA RH 21-5/52, KTB 5th Panzer Army, 31 Aug 1944
42. BA–MA RH 19 IX/4, p427/428, KTB Army Grp B, 29 Aug 1944
43. BA–MA RH 19 IX/88, KTB Army Grp B, 28 Aug 1944
44. BA–MA RH 19 IV/54, Anl.1785 and 1789, KTB Sup Cmd–West, 29 Aug 1944
45. See ftnt. 42; BA–MA RH 21-5/52 and 53, KTB 5th Panzer Army, 29 Aug 1944
46. Bittrich, Wilhelm, MS B-749 and P-155
47. BA–MA RH 21-5/53, Anl.59, KTB 5th Panzer Army, 28 Aug 1944
48. Schwerin, MS Ethint-18; Count Schwerin did not give any dates in his report for the following days. The author tried to match Schwerin's statements with the KTB, Sup Cmd–West, Army Grp B and 5th Panzer Army. It was not possible in every case.
49. Order 116th Pz.Div.Sect. Ia, 29 Aug 1944 from document Arm.Art.Rgt. 146
50. Schwerin, MS Ehint 18
51. BA–MA RH 19 IX/88, KTB Army Grp B, 29 Aug 1944
52. See ftnt. 50
53. See ftnt. 51
54. BA–MA RH 19 IV/54, Anl.1799, KTB Sup Cmd–West, 29 Aug 1944
55. See ftnt. 54
56. BA–MA RH 19 IV/54, Anl.1811, KTB Sup Cmd–West, 30 Aug 1944
57. See ftnt. 56; BA–MA RH 19 IX/88, KTB Army Grp B, 30 Aug 1944
58. BA–MA RH 19 IV/54, Anl.1797, KTB Sup Cmd–West, 29 Aug 1944
59. BA–MA RH 19 IV/54, Anl.1812, KTB Sup Cmd–West, 30 Aug 1944
60. BA–MA RH 19 IX/88, KTB Army Grp B, 30 Aug 1944

61. See ftnt. 56
62. See ftnt. 60
63. See ftnt. 50
64. Order Arm.Art.Rgt. 146, Sect. Ia, 30 Aug 1944 1900 hours, doc. Arm.Art.Rgt. 146
65. Voigtsberger, MS B-058
66. Order 116th Pz.Div.Sect. Ia, 29 Aug 1944; Order 116th Pz.Div., div.-Kf. Offz. and Cdr. of Kf.Pk. troops, 30 Aug 1944, 1620 hours, from document Arm.Art.Rgt. 146
67. See ftnt. 50
68. Schwerin, MS Ethint-18; Voigtsberger, MS B-058; Wolf, Map entries; Schmeermann, Notes
69. Schmidt, Hans, MS B-371
70. BA–MA RH 19 IV/54, Anl.1838, KTB Sup Cmd–West, 31 Aug 1944
71. BA–MA RH 19 IX/88, KTB Army Grp B, 31 Aug 1944; BA–MA RH 21-5/52, KTB 5th Panzer Army, 31 Aug 1944
72. See ftnt. 70
73. Wolf, Original report and map entries
74. Schwerin, MS Ethint-18
75. KTB 2d Bn./Arm.Art.Rgt. 146
76. Blumenson, loc. cit., p679 ff and 684
77. BA–MA RH 19 IV/55, Anl. 1850, KTB Sup Cmd–West, 1 Sep 1944; BA–MA RH 19 IX/89, KTB Army Grp B, 1 Sep 1944; BA–MA RH 21-5/52, KTB 5th Panzer Army, 1 Sep 1944; Frank, Paul, MS B-729
78. As example of this is order 5th Panzer Army #3240 geh., 1 Sep 1944, BA–MA RHfdcr; 21-5/53, Anl.72
79. Bittrich, MS B-749
80. Schmidt, MS B-371
81. BA–MA RH 19 IV/54, Anl. 1838, KTB Sup Cmd–West, 31 Aug 1944
82. Schwerin, MS Ethint-18
83. BA–MA RH 27-116/127, p205, report Adjutant Pz.Gren.Rgt.156 about the action of regimental commander, 27 Oct 1944
84. Schwerin, Ethint-18
85. BA–MA RH 24-58/10, KTB LVIII Pz.Corps, 1 Sep 1944; Bittrich, MS B-749; Straube, Erich, MS B-824; Frank, MS B-729
86. BA–MA RH 19 IX/89, KTB Army Grp B, 2 Sep 1944
87. Schwerin, Ethint-18; Information for the US divisions from report of operations of 9th US Infantry Division

88. Schmeermann, Notes
89. BA–MA RH 24-116/127, p117, recommendation for award Schmeermann
90. See ftnt. 88
91. Holtermann, pocket calendar
92. Schwerin, Ethint-18; Schwerin says: II SS-Pz.Corps to Beaumont. This is an error. It was the I SS-Pz.Corps It remains unclear if the message came from 2d or 12th SS-Pz.Div. In all probability it was the 12th.
93. Wolf, Map entries
94. Keppler, Georg, MS B-623; Trierenberg, Wolf, MS B-169
95. Schwerin, MS Ethint-18; Wolf, Map entries; Schmeermann, Notes
96. Senger, loc. cit., p305
97. See ftnt. 95
98. Report of operations of 9th US-ID
99. Holtermann, pocket calendar 1944
100. Mayer, Hubert, *Kriegsgeschichte der 12. SS-Panzer-Division "Hitlerjugend."* (Osnabrück: n.p., 1982), p368; Stückler, Albert, MS P-032e
101. BA–MA RH 21-5/53, Anl. 75, KTB 5th Panzer Army, 3 Sep 1944
102. Schwerin, MS Ethint-18
103. Bargstädt, report to the author
104. BA–MA RH 21-5/53, KTB 5th Pz. Army, 3 Sep 1944
105. Schwerin, Ethint-18
106. Wolf, original order Ia 116th Pz.Div., 3 Sep 1944
107. Ibid., 4 Sep 1944
108. Schmeermann, Notes
109. Schwerin, MS Ethint-18; Voigtsberger, MS B-058; Trierenberg, MS B-164
110. Schwerin, MS Ethint-18
111. Straube, MS B-824
112. BA–MA RH 24-81/99, KTB LXXXI Corps, 4 Sep 1944
113. Trierenberg, MS B-164
114. Schwerin, MS Ethint-18
115. Bargstädt, Notes
116. BA–MA RH 19 IV/55, Anl. 1921, KTB Sup Cmd–West, 4 Sep 1944
117. See ftnt. 116
118. BA–MA RH 21-5/33, Anl. 79 and 81, KTB 5th Panzer Army, 4 Sep 1944
119. KTB 2d Bn./Arm.Art.Rgt. 146
120. BA–MA RH 21-5/53, KTB 5th Panzer Army, 3 Sep 1944
121. BA–MA RH 19 IX/89, KTB Army Grp B, 5 Sep 1944
122. Schwerin, MS Ethint-18
123. BA–MA RH 19 IV/55, Anl. 1885, KTB Sup Cmd–West, 3 Sep 1944; BA–MA RH 21-5/53, Anl. 80, KTB 5th Pz Army, 4 Sep 1944
124. BA–MA RH 19 IV/55, Anl. 1948, 2005, 2016, 2041; BA–MA RH 19 IV/56, Anl. 2110, 2136, 2143, 2151, 2159, 2166, 2180, 2208, 2262, 2263, 2278, 2288, 2292, 2301, 2309; BA–MA RH 19 IV/57, Anl. 2316, 2319, 2332, 2337, 2342, 2343, 2355, 2380, 2399, 2401, 2404, 2411, 2416, 2435, 2456, 2471, 2478, 2498; BA–MA RH 19 IV/78, KTB Sup Cmd–West, 5 Sep–begin. Oct. 1944
125. Tebbe, Gerhard, reports to the author
126. BA–MA RH 21-5/53, KTB PZ. HQ, 5th Army, 3 Sep 1944
127. BA–MA RH 19 IX/89, KTB Army Grp B, 4 Sep 1944
128. BA–MA RH 19 IX/89, KTB Army Grp B, 2 and 3 Sep 1944
129. BA–MA RH 19 IV/55, Anl. 1952, 2057, KTB Sup Cmd–West, 5 and 9 Sep 1944
130. Blumenson, loc. cit., p692 ff
131. BA–MA RH 19 IV/55, Anl. 1941 and 1956, KTB Sup Cmd–West, 5 Sep 1944; BA–MA RH 19 IX/89, KTB Army Grp B, 5 Sep 1944
132. Bargstädt, original report submitted to the author
133. Bargstädt, notes; Schmeermann, notes
134. Wolf, map entries
135. BA–MA RH 19 Iv/55, Anl. 1973, KTB Sup Cmd–West, 6 Sep 1944
136. Wolf, Map entries
137. Schmeermann, Notes
138. Bargstsädt, Notes; Löbbecke, Harald von, Report to the author
139. BA–MA RH 19 IV/55, Anl. 1975, 1977, 2003, KTB Sup Cmd–West, 6 Sep 1944; BA–MA RH 19 IX/89, KTB Army Grp B, 6 Sep 1944
140. Trierenberg, MS B-164
141. See ftnt. 139; Wolf, map entries
142. BA–MA RH 19 IV/55, Anl. 1973, KTB Sup Cmd–West, 6 Sep 1944
143. BA–MA RH 19 IV/55, Anl. 1977, KTB Sup Cmd–West, 6 Sep 1944

144. BA–MA RH 19 IV/55, Anl. 2003, KTB Sup Cmd–West, 7 Sep 1944
145. BA–MA RH 19 IX/89, KTB Army Grp B, 6 Sep 1944
146. BA–MA RH 19 IV/55, Anl. 2010, KTB Sup Cmd–West, 7 Sep 1944; Wolf, map entries
147. BA–MA RH 19 IX/89, KTB Army Grp B, 6 Sep 1944
148. Brandenberger, MS B-730; Trierenberg, MS B-164
149. Meant to be: Schwerin, MS Ethint-18
150. Schwerin, MS Ethint-18
151. Blumenson, loc. cit., p 694
152. BA–MA RH 19 IX/89, KTB Army Grp B, 7 Sep 1944
153. BA–MA RH 19 IV/55, Anl. 2019, KTB Sup Cmd–West, 7 Sep 1944
154. BA–MA RH 24-81/97, 100 and 101, KTB LXXXI Corps, 7 Sep 1944
155. See ftnt. 154; BA–MA RH 19 IV/55, ANl. 2022, KTB Sup Cmd–West, 7 Sep 1944
156. BA–MA RH 24-81/100, KTB LXXXI Corps, 7 Sep 1944; Wolf, map entries
157. BA–MA RH 24-81/101, KTB LXXXI Corps, 8 Sep 1944
158. BA–MA RH 19 IV/55, Anl. 2022, KTB Sup Cmd–West, 7 Sep 1944
159. BA–MA RH 24-81/103, KTB LXXXI Corps, 8 Sep 1944
160. BA–MA RH 24-81/101, KTB LXXXI Corps, 8 Sep 1944
161. BA–MA RH 19 IX/89, KTB Army Grp B, 8 Sep 1944
162. BA–MA RH 24-81/103, KTB LXXXI Corps, 8 Sep 1944
163. BA–MA RH 24-81/97, KTB LXXXI Corps, 8 Sep 1944
164. BA–MA RH 24-81/101 and 102, KTB LXXXI Corps, 8 Sep 1944
165. See ftnt. 164
166. BA–MA RH 24-81/97, KTB LXXXI Corps, 8 Sep 1944
167. BA–MA RH 24-81/103, KTB LXXXI Corps, 8 Sep 1944
168. Stephan, post-war report
169. BA–MA RH 24-81/97 and 103, KTB LXXXI Corps, 9 Sep 1944; Schmeermann, notes
170. BA–MA RH 19 IV/55, Anl. 2063 and 2066, KTB Sup Cmd–West, 9 Sep 1944
171. BA–MA RH 19 IV/55, Anl. 2035, KTB Sup Cmd–West, 8 Sep 1944
172. KTB OKW vol. IV/1 p 371; BA–MA RH 19 IV/55, Anl. 2053, KTB Sup Cmd–West, 8 Sep 1944
173. BA–MA RH 19 IV/55, Anl. 2013, KTB Sup Cmd–West, 9/7 1944
174. BA–MA RH 24-81/97, KTB LXXXI Corps, 9 Sep 1944
175. BA–MA RH 24-81/103, KTB LXXXI Corps, 9 Sep 1944
176. BA–MA RH 24-81/97 and 103, KTB LXXXI Corps, 9 Sep 1944
177. See ftnt. 176
178. See ftnt. 174
179. See ftnt. 174
180. BA–MA RH 24-81/103, KTB LXXXI Corps, 9 Sep 1944
181. BA–MA RH 24-81/98, KTB LXXXI Corps, 9 Sep 1944
182. See ftnt. 174
183. See ftnt. 174
184. BA–MA RH 19 IV/55, Anl. 2061, 2063, 2066 and 2084; KTB Sup Cmd–West, 9 and 10 Sep 1944
185. BA–MA RH 19 IX/89, KTB Army Grp B, 10 Sep 1944
186. See ftnt. 174
187. BA–MA RH 24-81/100, KTB LXXXI Corps, 8 Sep 1944
188. See ftnt. 174
189. Zander, Helmuth, note about battles at Aachen
190. BA–MA RH 24-81/98, KTB LXXXI Corps, 10 Sep 1944
191. BA–MA RH 24-81/98 and 103, KTB LXXXI Corps, 10 Sep 1944
192. BA–MA RH 24-81/103, KTB LXXXI Corps, 10 Sep 1944
193. See ftnt. 190
194. Ibid.
195. Ibid.
196. Ibid.
197. Ibid.
198. BA–MA RH 24-81/100, KTB LXXXI Corps, 10 Sep 1944
199. BA–MA RH 19 IV/56, Anl. 2088, KTB Sup Cmd–West, 10 Sep 1944; BA–MA RH 19 IX/89, KTB Army Grp B, 10 Sep 1944
200. BA–MA RH 19 IX/89, KTB Army Grp B, 10 Sep 1944

201. Piekalkiewicz, loc. cit., p 288 ff. Excerpts from KTB of 9 Pz.Div.; BA–MA RH 24-81/103, KTB LXXXI Corps, 11 Sep 1944; Müller, Gerhard Paul, MS B-345

202. BA–MA RH 24-81/98, KTB LXXX Corps, 11 Sep 1944

203. BA–MA RH 24-81/103, KTB LXXX Corps, 11 Sep 1944

204. BA–MA RH 24-81/97, 98 and 103, KTB LXXXI Corps, 11 Sep 1944; Piekalkiewicz, loc. cit., p 288 ff

205. BA–MA RH 24-81/97, 98 and 103, KTB LXXXI Corps, 11 Sep 1944

206. *Danger, Forward, The Story of the First Division in WW II* by several authors, (Atlanta: n.p., 1948), p 257

207. BA–MA RH 24-81/98, KTB LXXXI Corps, 11 Sep 1944

208. BA–MA RH 24-81/101, KTB LXXXI Corps, 11 Sep 1944

209. BA–MA RH 19 IV/56, Anl. 2088 A, KTB Sup Cmd–West, 12 Sep 1944; BA–MA RH 19 IX/89, KTB Army Grp B, 11 Sep 1944

210. BA–MA RH 24-81/97 and 100, KTB LXXXI Corps, 10–11 Sep 1944

211. BA–MA RH 24-81/97 and 103, KTB LXXXI Corps, 12 Sep 1944

212. See ftnt. 211; BA–MA RH 19 IV/56, Anl. 2123 and 2126, KTB Sup Cmd–West, 12 Sep 1944; BA– MA RH 19 X/89, KTB Army Grp B, 12 Sep 1944

213. Piekalkiewicz, p 298, there exerpts from KTB 3d US Armored Div.

214. BA–MA RH 24-81/100, KTB LXXXI Corps, 12 Sep 1944

215. BA–MA RH 24-81/97, KTB LXXXI Corps, 12 Sep 1944

216. See ftnt. 214

217. BA–MA RH 19 IV/56, Anl. 2134, KTB Sup Cmd–West, 13 Sep 1944; BA–MA RH 24-81/97, KTB LXXXI Corps, 13 Sep 1944; *Danger, Forward,* loc. cit., p 257

218. KTB OKW vol. IV/1, p 371 ff

219. Norman, Albert. *Die Invasion in der Normandy, aus Entscheidungsschlachten des Zweiten Weltkriegs* (Frankfurt: n.p., 1960), p 431; Wilmot, loc. cit., p 513 ff; Tippelskirch, Kurt von. *History of WW II* (Bonn: n.p., 1950), p 446 ff; Blumenson, Martin, *Liberation,* Alexandria, VA 1978, p 175

220. BA–MA RH 19 IV/55 and 56, Anl. 2078 and 2101; KTB Sup Cmd–West, 9/10 resp. 10 Nov 1944

221. BA–MA RH 19 IV/55, Anl. 2078, KTB Sup Cmd–West, 10 Sep 1944

CHAPTER 7

1. MacDonald, Charles, B. *The Siegfried Line Campaign,* from the series *United States Army in WW II* (Washington, DC, 1963), p. 37–115 [hereafter, referred to as MacDonald I]

2. KTB 9th Pz.Div., 13 Sep 1944, reprinted in *Mitteilungsblatt der Kameradschaft, #*30, June 1964

3. Schwerin, Gerhard Count von, report by commander of the 116th Pz.Div. to the Commanding General of LXXXI Corps, 15 Sep 1944, reprinted in *Zeitschrift des Aachener Geschichts-vereins,* vol. 73, 1961, Aachen 1962, p.82, author Poll, Bernard of part 'Das Schicksal Aachens im Herbst 1944, authentische Berichte II.'

4. Osterroht, Helmuth von, in the same essay, p. 54

5. Schmeermann, Heinz, diary

6. See as ftnt. 4, p. 54–56; BA–MA RH 24-81/97 and 101, KTB LXXXI Corps 13 Sep 1944; BA–MA RH 19 IX/89, KTB Army Grp B 13 Sep 1944

7. BA–MA RH 24-81/97 and 101, KTB LXXXI Corps 14 Sep 1944; BA–MA RH 19 IV/56, KTB Sup Cmd–West, 9/14 and 15 1944; BA–MA RH 19 IX/89, KTB Army Grp B 14 Sep 1944; Report Arm.Art.Rgt. 146, 22 Sep 1944 from document Arm.Art.Rgt. 146

8. BA–MA RH 24-81/97, KTB LXXXI Corps, 13 Sep 1944

9. BA–MA RH 24-81/98 and 101, KTB LXXXI Corps, 13 Sep 1944; Zander, Helmut, post-war report of battle area Aachen in September 1944

10. Schmeermann, Heinz, diary

11. Schwerin, Gerhard Count von, MS Ethint-18

12. Brandenberger, Erich, MS B-730

13. BA–MA RH 24-81/101, KTB LXXXI Corps, 13 Sep 1944

14. BA–MA RH 24-81/97 and 101, KTB LXXXI Corps, 13 Sep 1944

15. See ftnt. 8

16. Jodl, Alfred, MS A-927

17. Heiber, Helmut, Hitlers Lagebespre-chungen, Stuttgart 1962, p.620f and 614

18. Jung, Hermann, Hermann, *Die Ardennen Offencive, 1944–1945,* (Göttingen, 1972), p.89ff

19. Holsteiner Nachrichten, 17 Sep 1944

20. BA–MA RH 24-81/98, KTB LXXXI Corps, 13 Sep 1944

21. BA–MA RH 24-81/97, KTB LXXXI Corps, 13 Sep 1944

22. BA–MA RH 24-81/101, KTB LXXXI Corps, 13 Sep 1944

23. Zander, loc. cit.; Stephan, Eberhard, post-war reports

24. Schäfer, Hans, diary

25. BA–MA RH 24-81/97 and 101, KTB LXXXI Corps, 13 Sep 1944; Schwerin, see ftnt. 3

26. Thorné, Josef, diary, reprinted in "Heimat-blätter des Kreises Aachens," 2 Jan 1978

27. BA–MA RH 24-81/97 and 98, KTB LXXXI Corps, 13 Sep 1944; KTB 9 Panzer Division, 13 Sep 1944 see ftnt. 2

28. BA–MA RH 19 IV/56, Anl. 2150, KTB Sup Cmd–West, 13 Sep 1944; BA–MA RH 19 X/89, KTB Army Grp B, 13 Sep 1944; BA–MA RH 24-81/97, KTB LXXXI Corps, 13 Sep 1944

29. BA–MA RH 19 IV/56, Anl. 2150, KTB Sup Cmd–West, 13 Sep 1944

30. BA–MA RH 24-81/97 and 98, KTB LXXXI Corps, 14 Sep 1944

31. BA–MA RH 24-81/98, KTB LXXXI Corps, 14 Sep 1944

32. BA–MA RH 24-81/97, KTB LXXXI Corps, 14 Sep 1944

33. Schack, Friedrich-August, report KG LXXXI Corps to Sup Cmd 7 Army, 15 Sep 1944 reprinted see ftnt. 3, p. 86–87; BA–MA RH 24-81/97, KTB LXXXI Corps, 15 Sep 1944 0100 hours Osterroht, see ftnt. 4 p. 57/58

34. BA–MA RH 19 IV/56, Anl. 2157, KTB Sup Cmd–West, 14 Sep 1944; BA–MA RH 19 IX/89, KTB Army Grp B, 14 Sep 1944; BA–MA RH 24-81/97, KTB LXXXI Corps, 14 Sep 1944; KTB 9 Pz div., 14 Sep 1944; see ftnt. 2; BA–MA RH 24-81/98, KTB LXXXI Corps, 14 Sep 1944

35. KTB LXXXI Corps 14 Sep 1944

36. Schack, see ftnt. 33; BA–MA RH 24-81/97, KTB LXXXI Corps, 14 Sep 1944

37. BA–MA RH 24-81/108 K, map from KTB LXXXI Corps 14 Sep 1944

38. BA–MA RH 24-81/97, KTB LXXXI Corps, 14 and 15 Sep 1944; KTB 9th Pz.Div. see ftnt. 2

39. BA–MA RH 19 IX/89, KTB Army Grp B, 14 Sep 1944

40. See ftnt. 39

41. BA–MA RH 19 IV/89, Anl. 2162, KTB Sup Cmd–West, 14 Sep 1944

42. BA–MA RH 24-81/97, KTB LXXXI Corps 14 Sep 1944

43. BA–MA RH 24-81/103, KTB LXXXI Corps 14 Sep 1944

44. Zander, loc. cit.; Nagel, Helmut, reports to the author

45. Kühne, Klaus, brief of later history of Panzer Regiment 16, unpublished

46. Holtermann, Dr. Arthur, "Der Krieg im Dunkel," published as special issue by Gerhard, Count von Schwerin 1944 in the German family archive, vol. 76, Neustadt (Aisch) 1981 and in part by Memminger, Fritz, Aachen in Sept 1944, Bochum 1963

47. Schwerin, MS Ethint-18

48. Grollmann, Heinrich, oral reports to the author

49. Zimmermann, Paul, "Die Eroberung der Stadt Aachen," reprinted by Poll, corre-sponding with ftnt. 3, p.145

50. BA–MA RH 19 IV/56, Anl. 2088A, KTB Sup Cmd–West, 11 Sep 1944

51. Osterroht, see ftnt. 4, p. 53

52. Reprinted like ftnt. 3, p. 151

53. Zimmermann, see ftnt. 49, p. 146

54. Osterroht, see ftnt. 4, p. 57

55. Schack, see ftnt. 33, p. 84/85

56. Schwerin, original sketch in Holtermann docs., Dr. Arthur, reprinted see ftnt. 3, p. 92

57. Schwerin, in reports, 13 and 15 Sep 1944, to Chief of Staff, resp. Cmdr. genl. of LXXXI Corps, original sketch in Holtermann docs., reprinted see ftnt. 3 and 56, p. 81–83; Schwerin, MS Ethint-18

58. Photocopy of original in Holtermann docs. and with Memminger, Fritz, same as remarks 46, p. 41, reprinted as in ftnt. 3, p.70, original in city archive Aachen

59. This quote and the following ones from BA–MA RH 19 IX/89 KTB Army Grp B, 13 Sep 1944

60. Original of letter in Holtermann docs.

61. Schwerin, report to the Chief of Staff LXXXI Corps, 13 Sep 1944, see ftnt. 57

62. Original of document in cith archive Aachen, reprinted as in ftnt. 3, p.67 and with Memminger, p.42

63. Schwerin, MS Ethint-18

64. See ftnt. 63

65. BA–MA RH 24-81/97, KTB LXXXI Corps, 14 Sep 1944

66. BA–MA RH 24-81/101, KTB LXXXI Corps, 14 Sep 1944

67. Kuetgens, Dr. Felix, report about the time of my activity as representative of Oberbürgermeister of the city of Aachen, 11 to 15 September 1944, issued 15 Nov 1944, reprinted in Poll, Bernhard, 'Das Schicksal Aachens im Herbst 1944,' Aachen 1955, p.240ff Including the appeal to the citizens of Aachen on p.248/249

68. Kuetgens, Dr. Felix, statutory declaration, reprinted by Memminger, Fritz, Aachen, September 1944, Bochum 1963, p. 60/61, including the appeal to the citizens of Aachen, p. 63. This document, unfortunately, contains several grave mistakes.

69. BA–MA RH 19 IX/89, KTB Army Grp B 14 Sep 1944

70. Schack, report, 15 Sep 1944, see ftnt. 33

71. See ftnt. 69

72. BA–MA RH 24-81/97, KTB LXXXI Corps, 14 Sep 1944

73. BA–MA RH 19 IX/89, KTB Army Grp B, 15 Sep 1944

74. BA–MA RH 24-81/103, KTB LXXXI Corps, 15 Sep 1944

75. See ftnt. 4, p.58

76. Schwerin, report to Cmdg Gen. LXXXI Corps, 15 Sep 1944 Original in Holtermann docs., reprinted see ftnt. 3, p.82/83 and with Memminger, p.71, see ftnt. 68

77. Schwerin, see ftnt. 56

78. Schack, see ftnt. 55

79. Schack, see ftnt. 33

80. Schwerin to Himmler, original sketch in Holtermann docs.

81. Memminger, see ftnt. 68, p. 77/78

82. BA–MA RH 19 IX/90, KTB Army Grp B, 16 Sep 1944

83. BA–MA RH 19 IX/5, KTB Army Grp B, 15 Sep 1944; BA–MA RH 19 IV/56, Anl. 2222, KTB Sup Cmd–West, 6/19 1944. reprinted by Memminger, see ftnt. 68, p. 81

84. Schwerin, MS Ethint-18

85. BA–MA RH 19 IX/89, KTB Army Grp B, 15 Sep 1944

86. See ftnt. 85

87. Schwerin, MS Ethint-18

88. See ftnt. 87

89. Order 116th Pz.Div., division commander, 16 Sep 1944, 1132 hours, from document Arm.Art.Rgt. 146

90. BA–MA RH 24-81/97, KTB LXXXI Corps, 16 Sep 1944

91. BA–MA RH 19 IX/89, KTB Army Grp B 16 Sep 1944

92. Holtermann, Dr. Arthur, letter to Generalleutnant Count von Schwerin, 15 Sep 1944; Draft in document Holtermann, reprinted see ftnt. 3, 87/78; Holtermann, pocket calendar

93. Holtermann, Dr. Arthur, "Der Krieg im Dunkel," reprinted see ftnt. 46, contains wrong dates

94. Vogelsang, Fritz, diary

95. BA–MA RH 19 IX/90, KTB Army Grp B, 16 resp. 17 Sep 1944

96. BA–MA RH 19 IX/90, KTB Army Grp B, 17 Sep 1944

97. BA–MA RH 24-81/97, KTB LXXXI Corps, 17 Sep 1944

98. Kleer, Walter, post-war report, reprinted by Memminger, see ftnt. 68, p.94, also contains wrong dates

99. BA–MA RH 24-81/97, KTB LXXXI Corps, 17 Sep 1944

100. Zimmermann, see ftnt. 49, p.146, 147

101. BA–MA RH 19 IX/90, KTB Army Grp B, 20 Sep 1944

102. Risse, Eberhard, post-war report, reprinted by Memminger, p.89/90 see ftnt. 68

103. Vogelsang, diary

104. Risse, see ftnt. 102, p.98

105. Vogelsang, diary

106. Schwerin in a note, 7 Nov 1962 in Holtermann docs.

107. BA–MA RH 19 IX/90, KTB Army Grp B, 18 Sep 1944

108. Schwerin, orally to Memminger on 4/27/1963, printed by Memminger p.98, see ftnt. 68

109. BA–MA RH 19 IV/150, KTB Sup Cmd–West; Work report by legal advisor for the time of 1 July–31 Dec 1944

110. Holtermann, 'Der Krieg im Dunkel', see ftnt. 46

111. Holtermann, letter to Major i.G. Wolf, 24 Sep 1944, from Holtermann docs. reprinted see ftnt. 3, p. 90–92

112. Holtermann, pocket calendar; and see ftnt. 111

113. Holtermann, pocket calendar

114. Original letter in Holtermann docs.

115. Schwerin, letter, 11 Nov 1944 to Holtermann in Holtermann docs.

116. Holtermann, letter, 15 Nov 1944 in Holtermann docs.

117. Holtermann, letter to Count von Schwerin, 28 Nov 1944, in Holtermann docs.

118. See ftnt. 116

119. See ftnt. 117

120. Holtermann, letter to Count von Schwerin, 7 Dec 1944, in Holtermann docs.

121. Copy of document OKH HPA to Generalfeldmarschall Kesselring, 9 Dec 1944 in Holtermann docs., reprinted see ftnt. 3, p.96/97 and by Memminger, p.106 see ftnt. 68

122. Schwerin, letter, 4 Dec 1944 to Holtermann, original in Holtermann docs.

123. Schwerin, parting order, 5 Dec 1944, original order in Holtermann docs., 14 Dec 1944 to the troops

124. Voigtsberger, Heinrich, report, reprinted by Memminger, p.96, see ftnt. 68

125. Voigtsberger, Heinrich, parting order, 19 Sep 1949; Reprinted by Memminger, p.96–97 see ftnt 68

126. Schwerin, MS Ethint-18

127. See letters in chapter 1

128. "Der Windhund" #1/81

129. BA–MA RH 24-81/97 and 98, KTB LXXXI Corps, 14–15 Sep, 1944

130. BA–MA RH 24-81/97 and 98, KTB LXXXI Corps, 15 Sep 1944

131. Schmeermann, diary

132. KTB 2d Bn./Arm.Art.Rgt. 146

133. Order Arm.Art.Rgt. 146, Sect. Ia/Ib, 24 Sep 1944, from document Pz.Art. Rgt.146

134. BA–MA RH 24-81/97 and 98; KTB LXXXI Corps, 15 Sep 1944; KTB 9 Panzer Division, 15 Sep 1944, see ftnt. 2

135. BA–MA RH 24-81/98, KTB LXXXI Corps, 15 Sep 1944, daily report of Corps

136. See ftnt. 135, daily report 116th Pz.Div. 15 Sep 1944

137. See ftnt. 1, p.77

138. BA–MA RH 24-81/105, KTB LXXXI Corps, 15 Sep 1944

139. BA–MA RH 24-81/128, KTB LXXXI Corps, 16 Sep 1944

140. BA–MA RH 24-81/97 and 98, KTB LXXXI Corps, 15 Sep 1944

141. BA–MA RH 19 IX/90, KTB Army Grp B 15 Sep 1944

142. BA–MA RH 19 IV/56, Anl. 2202, 2208, 2209, KTB Sup Cmd–West, 16 Sep 1944; BA–MA RH 24-81/97 and 98, KTB LXXXI Corps, 16 Sep 1944; KTB 9th Pz.Div. 16 Sep 1944, see ftnt. 2

143. BA–MA RH 24-81/97, KTB LXXXI Corps, 16 Sep 1944

144. See ftnt. 143

145. See ftnt. 142

146. BA–MA RH 24-81/97 and 98, KTB LXXXI Corps, 16 Sep 1944

147. Triantaphyllides, Phidias, diary 16 Sep 1944

148. BA–MA RH 19 IX/90, KTB Army Grp B 16 Sep 1944

149. KTB 9th Pz.Div., 16 Sep 1944, see ftnt 2

150. BA–MA RH 19 IV/56, Anl. 2210, KTB Sup Cmd–West, 16 Sep 1944

151. BA–MA RH 24-81/99, KTB LXXXI Corps, 16 Sep 1944

152. BA–MA RH 24-81/100, KTB LXXXI Corps, 16 Sep 1944

153. BA–MA RH 19 IX/90, KTB Army Grp B 17 Sep 1944 BA–MA RH 1IV/56, Anl. 2245, KTB Sup Cmd–West, 17 Sep 1944

154. Wilmot, loc. cit., p.519

155. All entries from BA–MA RH 24-81/97, 98,109K, KTB LXXXI Corps, 17 Sep 1944

156. Vogelsang, diary, 20 Sep 1944

157. BA–MA RH 24-81/97 and 98, KTB LXXXI Corps, 17 Sep 1944; KTB 9th Pz.Div., 17 Sep 1944, see ftnt. 2

158. BA–MA RH 24-81/98, KTB LXXXI Corps, 17 Sep 1944

159. All entries from BA–MA RH 24-81/97 and 98, KTB LXXXI Corps, 18 Sep 1944

160. BA–MA RH 19 IX/90, KTB Army Grp B, 18 Sep 1944

161. See ftnt. 160

162. BA–MA RH 19 IV/56, Anl. 2292, KTB Sup Cmd–West, 18 Sep 1944

163. BA–MA RH 24-81/97 and 98, KTB LXXXI Corps, 19–20 Sep 1944; BA–MA RH 19 IV/56, Anl. 2309, KTB OBWest, 20 Sep 1944

164. BA–MA RH 19 IX/90, KTB Army Grp B 19 Sep 1944

165. BA–MA RH 24-81/97, 98, 100, and 108K, KTB LXXXI Corps, 19 Sep 1944

166. Waldenburg, pocket calendar

167. Waldenburg, Siegfried von, division order, 21 Sep 1944, from doc. Pz.Art. Rgt. 146

168. BA–MA RH 19 IV/56, Anl. 2309, KTB Sup Cmd–West, 20 Sep 1944

169. BA–MA RH 24-81/97, 98 and 109K, KTB LXXXI Corps, 20 Sep 1944; KTB 9th Pz.Div., 20 Sep 1944, reprinted in *Mitteilungsblatt der Kameradschaft,* Issue 31, Sept 1964

170. BA–MA RH 24-81/100, KTB LXXXI Corps, 22 Sep 1944

171. Vogelsang, diary, 20 Sep 1944

172. BA–MA RH 24-81/98, KTB LXXXI Corps, 21 Sep 1944

173. BA–MA RH 19 IX/90, KTB Army Grp B 21 Sep 1944

174. BA–MA RH 24-81/98, KTB LXXXI Corps, 21 Sep 1944

175. KTB 9th Pz.Div. reprinted as in ftnt. 169

176. Waldenburg, pocket calendar

177. BA–MA RH 24-81/97, 98, and 109K, KTB LXXXI Corps, 22 Sep 1944

178. BA–MA RH 19 IV/57, Anl. 2319, KTB Sup Cmd–West, 21 Sep 1944

179. BM-MA-RH 19 IV/57, Anl. 2343 and 2404, KTB Sup Cmd–West, 22 resp. 25 Sep 1944

180. BA–MA RH 19 IV/57, Anl. 2343, KTB Sup Cmd–West, 22 Sep 1944

181. BA–MA RH 24-81/97 and 98, KTB LXXXI Corps, 22 Sep 1944; KTB 9th Pz.Div., 22 Sep 1944, see ftnt. 169; Waldenburg, pocket calendar

182. BA–MA RH 24-81/97 and 98, KTB LXXXI Corps, 23 Sep 1944

183. BA–MA RH 19 IX/90, KTB Army Grp B, 23 Sep 1944

184. KTB 9th Pz. div., 23 Sep 1944, reprinted in *Mitteilungsblatt der Kameradschaft,* Issue 32, Dec 1964

185. BA–MA RH 24-81/98 and 109K, KTB LXXXI Corps, 23 resp. 24 Sep 1944; Order 116th Pz.Div.Sect. Ia, 27 Sep 1944, from document Arm.Art.Rgt. 146

186. BA–MA RH 19 IX/90, KTB Army Grp B, 23 Sep 1944

187. BA–MA RH 19 IV/57, Anl. 2366, KTB Sup Cmd–West, 23 Sep 1944

188. BA–MA RH 19 IV/57, Anl. 2380 and 2381, KTB Sup Cmd–West, 24 Sep 1944; BA–MA RH 19 IX/90, KTB Army Grp B, 24 Sep 1944

189. BA–MA RH 19 IX/90, KTB Army Grp B, 24 Sep 1944

190. BA–MA RH 19 IV/57, Anl. 2385, KTB Sup Cmd–West, 24 Sep 1944

191. BA–MA RH 19 IX/90, KTB Army Grp B, 24 Sep 1944

192. BA–MA RH 19 IX/5 and 90, KTB Army Grp B, 9/25 and 26 1944; BA–MA RH IV/57 Anl. 2400, KTB Sup Cmd–West, 25 Sep 1944

193. BA–MA RH 19 IV/57, Anl. 2416, KTB Sup Cmd–West, 26 Sep 1944

194. BA–MA RH 19 IX/5, KTB Army Grp B, 27 Sep 1944

195. BA–MA RH 19 IX/90, KTB Army Grp B, 27 Sep 1944

196. Bittrich, Wilhelm, MS P-155

197. KTB OKW, vol. IV/1, p.400

198. BA–MA RH 24-81/97, KTB LXXXI Corps, 24 Sep 1944

199. BA–MA RH 24-81/97, 105 and 111, KTB LXXXI Corps, 24 Sep 1944; BA–MA RH 19 IX/5, p.766, KTB Army Grp B, 25 Sep 1944

200. Waldenburg, pocket calendar 24 Sep 1944

201. Vogelsang, diary, 24 Sep 1944

202. Waldenburg, pocket calendar

203. BA–MA RH 24-81/97, KTB LXXXI Corps, 25 Sep 1944

204. Order 116th Pz.Div. Sect. Ia, 25 Sep 1944, from document Arm.Art.Rgt. 146

205. BA–MA RH 24-81/97, KTB LXXXI Corps, 25 Sep 1944

206. KTB 2d Bn./Arm.Art.Rgt. 146; Schwörer, Ernst, diary
207. BA–MA RH 24-81/97, KTB LXXXI Corps, 26 Sep 1944
208. Waldenburg, pocket calendar, 26 Sep 1944
209. BA–MA RH 24-81/97 and 100, KTB LXXXI Corps, 26 Sep 1944
210. Order 116th Pz.Div. Sect. Ia, 26 Sep 1944, from doc. Arm.Art.Rgt. 146
211. BA–MA RH 24-81/97, KTB LXXXI Corps, 26 Sep 1944
212. See ftnt. 209
213. BA–MA RH 24-81/97, KTB LXXXI Corps, 27 Sep 1944
214. See ftnt. 213
215. BA–MA RH 24-81/97, KTB LXXX Corps, 27 and 28 Sep 1944
216. BA–MA RH 24-81/97, KTB LXXX Corps, 28–30 Sep 1944; Order 116th Panzer Division, Sect. Ia, 28 Sep 1944, from doc. Arm.Art.Rgt. 146; Zander, Helmut; Grollmann, Heinrich; Stephan, Eberhard, reports to the author; Schmeermann, Heinz, diary; BA–MA RH 19 IX/90 and 5, KTB Army Grp B, 27 and 30 Sep 1944 and 1 Oct 1944; BA–MA RH 19 IV/57, Anl. 2435, 2453, 2471, 2473, 2477, and 2499, KTB Sup Cmd–West, 27–30 Sep 1944
217. KTB 9th Pz.Div., 23 and 25 Sep 1944, see ftnt. 184; Jollasse, Erwin, "*Einsätze der 9. Panzerdivision,*" reprinted in *Mitteilungsblatt der Kameradschaft,* issue 25, 1963
218. Waldenburg, Siegfried von, MS P-171; Waldenburg, pocket calendar and notes without date

CHAPTER 8, PART 1

1. Waldenburg, MS P-171, and pocket calendar and personal notes; Jollasse, Erwin, MS P-161 and "Deployments of the 9th Pz.Div."; Bittrich, Wilhelm, MS P-155; Harzer, Walter, MS P-162; Harmel, Heinz, MS P-163; Schmeermann, Heinz, diary; Bargstädt, Hans-Richard, diary; Utsch, Günther, notes
2. KTB 2d Bn./Pz.Rgt. 16, 1 October–31 December 1944
3. Varnholt, Otto, notes; Wolff-Boenisch, Richard, diary
4. BA–MA RH 19 IV/77, Anl. 27, KTB Sup Cmd–West, 2 Oct 1944
5. Jollasse, see ftnt. 1
6. Waldenburg, see ftnt. 1; KTB 2d Bn./Pz.Rgt. 16
7. Vogelsang, Fritz, diary
8. Wolff-Boenisch, Richard, diary
9. BA–MA RH 19 IX/90, KTB Army Grp B, 29 Sep 1944
10. BA–MA RH 19 IV/77, Anl. 10, KTB Sup Cmd–West, 1 Oct 1944
11. BA–MA RH 19 IX/5, KTB Army Grp B, 30 Sep 1944
12. Bittrich, Jollasse, Harzer, Harmel, ftnt. 1
13. Bittrich, see ftnt. 1
14. Bittrich, see ftnt. 1; Map Ib, 116th Pz.Div. in the possession of Major i.G. Wolf, Lothar
15. Jollasse and Harzer, see ftnt. 1; Order 116th Pz.Div.Sect. Ia, 1 Oct 1944; Map Ib 116th Pz.Div. see ftnt. 14
16. Beckmann, Gustav, diary
17. Stephan, Eberhard, addition to MS P-171
18. Waldenburg, MS P-171; Grollmann, Heinrich, addition to MS P-171
19. Waldenburg, MS P-171
20. BA–MA RH 19 IV/77, Anl. 3 and 10, KTB Sup Cmd–West, 1 Oct 1941; BA–MA RH 19 IX/13, KTB Army Grp B, 1 Oct 1944; Jollasse, see ftnt. 1
21. Order 116th Pz.Div. Sect. Ia, 1 Oct 1944
22. Jollasse, see ftnt. 1
23. BA–MA RH 19 IV/77, Anl.10 KTB Sup Cmd–West, 1 Oct 1944
24. BA–MA RH 19 IX/13, KTB Army Grp B, 2 Oct 1944
25. Jollasse, see ftnt. 1
26. Grollmann, Heinrich, addition to MS P-171
27. Junge, Oskar, letter to the author, 28 Dec 1984
28. BA–MA RH 27-116/127, IIa docs. 116th Pz.Div., award recommendation Heiberger, Kurt
29. BA–MA RH 19 IX/13, KTB Army Grp B, 2 Oct 1944
30. Jollasse, see ftnt. 1
31. BA–MA RH 19 IV/77, Anl. 25, KTB Sup Cmd–West, 2 Oct 1944
32. BA–MA RH 19 IX/13, KTB Army Grp B, 2 Oct 1944
33. See ftnt. 32
34. BA–MA RH 19 IV/77, Anl. 3, KTB Sup Cmd–West, 1 Oct 1944

35. BA–MA RH 19 IV/77, Anl. 23, KTB Sup Cmd–West, 2 Oct 1944
36. BA–MA RH 19 IX/10, KTB Army Grp B, 2 Oct 1944
37. Jollasse, see ftnt. 1; KTB 2d Bn./Pz.Rgt. 16, 8 Oct 1944
38. Vogelsang, loc. cit.
39. Beckmann, Gustav, diary
40. Senger, p.306; KTB 2d Bn./Pz.Rgt. 16
41. Jollasse, see ftnt. 1
42. BA–MA RH 19 IV/77, Anl. 33, 40, 44, 45, KYB Sup Cmd–West, 3 Oct 1944
43. Triantaphyllides, Phidias, diary
44. Vogelsang, loc. cit.
45. BA–MA RH 19 IV/77, Anl. 49, KTB Sup Cmd–West, 4 Oct 1944; Jollasse, see ftnt. 1
46. Waldenburg, pocket calendar
47. KTB II.Pz.Rgt. 16
48. Waldenburg, MS P-171; KTB 2d Bn./Pz.Rgt. 16
49. KTB 2d Bn./Pz.Rgt. 16
50. Senger, loc. cit., p.306
51. Weidemann, p. 244
52. Zander, Helmut, addition to MS P-171
53. KTB 2d Bn./Pz.Rgt. 16
54. Schäfer, Hans, diary
55. Tzschentke, Joachim, letter to the author, 1 Nov 1988
56. BA–MA RH 19 IV/77, Anl. 53, 54, 60 and 61, KTB Supreme Command–West, 4 Oct 1944
57. BA–MA RH 19 IX/10 and 13, KTB Army Grp B, 4 Oct 1944; BA–MA RH 19 IV/77, Anl. 54, 60, 61, KTB Sup Cmd–West, 4 Oct 1944; Jollasse and Bittrich, see ftnt. 1
58. KTB 2d Bn./Pz.Rgt. 16
59. Harmel, see ftnt. 1
60. Vogelsang, loc. cit.
61. BA–MA RH 19 IV/77, Anl. 70, KTB Sup Cmd–West, 5 Oct 1944
62. Zander, see ftnt. 52
63. Waldenburg, pocket clanedar
64. BA–MA RH 19 IV/77, Anl. 70, KTB Sup Cmd–West, 5 Oct 1944
65. Triantaphyllides, see ftnt. 43
66. BA–MA RH 27-116/127, IIa Doc. 116th Pz.Div., suggestion Grollmann, Heinrich, 16 Nov 1944
67. Triantaphylides, see ftnt. 43
68. KTB 2d Bn./Pz.Rgt. 16; BA–MA RH 19 IV/77, Anl. 78, KTB Sup Cmd–West, morning report, 6 Oct 1944
69. BA–MA RH 19 IV/77, Anl. 65a, 69, 70, KTB Sup Cmd–West, 5 Oct 1944
70. Bittrich, see ftnt. 1
71. BA–MA RH 19 IV/77, Anl. 79, KTB Sup Cmd–West, 6 Oct 1944 1200 hours
72. BA–MA RH 19 IV/77, Anl. 80, KTB Sup Cmd–West, 6 Oct 1944
73. BA–MA RH 19 IV/77, Anl. 84, KTB Sup Cmd–West, 6 Oct 1944; Bittrich, see ftnt. 1; Jollasse, see ftnt. 1
74. KTB 2d Bn./Pz.Rgt.16
75. BA–MA RH 19 IV/77, Anl.84, KTB Sup Cmd–West, 6 Oct 1944
76. Jollasse, see ftnt. 1
77. KTB 2d Bn./Pz.Rgt. 16
78. BA–MA RH 19 IV/77, Anl. 84, KTB Sup Cmd–West, 6 Oct 1944
79. Stephan, see ftnt, 17
80. Order, 116th Pz.Div. Section Ia, 8 Oct 1944
81. BA–MA RH 19 IV/77, Anl. 80, 83, 84, KTB Sup Cmd–West, 6 Oct 1944
82. BA–MA RH 19 IV/77, Anl. 91, KTB Sup Cmd–West, 7 Oct 1944
83. BA–MA RH 19 IX/6, KTB Army Grp B from 7 Oct 1944
84. BA–MA RH 19 IV/77, Anl. 95, KTB Sup Cmd–West, 7 Oct 1944
85. KTB 2d Bn./Pz.Rgt. 16; Jollasse, see ftnt. 1; Zander, see ftnt. 52
86. KTB 2d Bn./Pz.Rgt. 16
87. Jollasse, see ftnt. 1
88. Waldenburg, pocket calendar
89. Bittrich, Jollasse, Harmel, see ftnt. 1
90. BA–MA RH 19 IV/77, Anl. 99, KTB Sup Cmd–West, 8 Oct 1944
91. BA–MA RH 19 IX/6, KTB Army Grp B, 8 Oct 1944
92. BA–MA RH 19 IV/77, Anl. 96, KTB Sup Cmd–West, 8 Oct 1944
93. KTB 2d Bn./Pz.Rgt.16; Sandkuhl, Wilhelm, pocket calendar
94. Vogelsang, loc. cit.
95. BA–MA RH 19 IX/6, KTB Army Grp B, 7 Oct 1944
96. Strickhausen, Heinz, letter to the author, 31 Oct 1981
97. Vogelsang, loc. cit.
98. BA–MA RH 19 IV/77, Anl. 112, KTB Sup Com–West, 9 Oct 1944
99. KTB 2d Bn./Pz. Rgt. 16
100. Jollasse, see ftnt. 1

101. KTB 2d Bn./Pz.Rgt.16
102. BA–MA RH 19 IX/6, KTB Army Grp B, 9 Oct 1944
103. KTB 2d Bn./Pz.Rgt.16, 7–11 Oct 1944
104. Waldenburg, pocket calendar
105. Waldenburg, MS P-171
106. BA–MA RH 19 IX/10, KTB Army Grp B, 10 Oct 1944
107. KTB 2d Bn./Pz.Rgt.16
108. Löffler, Jürgen, letter to the author, 18 Dec 1979
109. BA–MA RH 19 IV/77, Anl. 114 and 134; KTB Sup Cmd–West, 8 and 9 Oct 1944; KTB OKW vol. IV, 1 p.406ff
110. BA–MA RH 19 IX/6, KTB Army Grp B, 13 Oct 1944; BA–MA RH 19 IV/74, KTB Sup Cmd–West, 13 Oct 1944; Jollasse, see ftnt. 1
111. BA–MA RH 19 IX/6, KTB Army Grp B, 3 Oct 1944

CHAPTER 8 PART 2

1. Mac Donald, Charles B., *The Siegfried Line Campaign* from the series *United States Army in WW II* (Washington, DC, 1963), p251–269
2. BA–MA RH 19 IV/74, KTB Sup Cmd–West, 2 and 3 Oct 1944; BA–MA RH 19 IV/77, Anl. 45, KTB Sup Cmd–West, 3 Oct 1944; BA–MA RH, 19 IX/6, KTB Army Grp B, 3 Oct 1944; BA–MA RH 24-81/97, KTB LXXXI Corps, 2–3 Oct 1944
3. BA–MA RH 19 IX/6, KTB Army Grp B, 3 Oct 1944
4. BA–MA RH 19 IV/74 and 77, Anl. 68, KTB Sup Cmd–West, 4 and 5 Oct 1944
5. BA–MA RH 19 IX/6, KTB Army Grp B, 5 Oct 1944
6. MacDonald I, loc. cit., p270-280
7. BA–MA RH 19 IV/77, Anl. 91 and 96, KTB Sup Cmd–West, 7 Oct 1944
8. MacDonald I, loc. cit., p285ff
9. MacDonald I, loc. cit., p295
10. BA–MA RH 24-81/97, 98 and 101, KTB LXXXI Corps, 8 and 9 Oct 1944; BA–MA RH 19 IV/77, Anl. 106 and 123, KTB Sup Cmd–West, 8 and 9 Oct 1944
11. MacDonald I, loc. cit., p297
12. BA–MA RH 19 IV/77, Anl. 123, KTB Sup Cmd–West, 9 Oct 1944; BA–MA RH 24-81/97, 98 and 101, KTB LXXXI Corps, 9 Oct 1944

13. BA–MA RH 19 IV/74 and 77, Anl. 143, KTB Sup Cmd–West, 10 Oct 1944; BA–MA RH 24-81/97, 98 and 101, KTB LXXXI Corps, 10–11 Oct 1944
14. BA–MA RH 24-81/97 and 98, KTB LXXXI Corps, 10 Oct 1944
15. BA–MA RH 19 IV/77, Anl. 134, KTB Sup Cmd–West, 10 Oct 1944
16. BA–MA RH 19 IX/6, KTB Army Grp B, 10 Oct 1944, 1045 hours
17. BA–MA RH19 IV/74, KTB Sup Cmd–West, 10 Oct 1944
18. BA–MA RH 19 IX/10, KTB Army Grp B, 10 Oct 1944
19. BA–MA RH 24-81/97, KTB LXXXI Corps, 10 Oct 1944
20. BA–MA RH 24-81/97, 98, p332 and 100, KTB LXXXI Corps, 10 Oct 1944
21. BA–MA RH 24-81/99, p254, 256, 253, KTB LXXXI Corps
22. BA–MA RH 24-81/97, KTB LXXXI Corps, 10 Oct 1944
23. BA–MA RH 24-81/100, KTB LXXXI Corps, 11 Oct 1944
24. BA–MA RH 24-81/97, KTB LXXXI Corps, 11 Oct 1944
25. BA–MA RH 19 IV/74 and 78, Anl. 156, KTB Sup Cmd–West, 11 Oct 1944; BA–MA RH 19 IX/10, KTB Army Grp B, 10 Oct 1944
26. Zander, Helmut, reports to the author; BA–MA RH 19 IV/79, Anl.402, KTB Sup Cmd–West, 26 Oct 1944, Report Combat Group Rink
27. Albert, Heinz, diary
28. BA–MA RH 24-81/100, KTB LXXXI Corps, 11 Oct 1944
29. See ftnt. 28
30. BA–MA RH 19 IX/10, KTB Army Grp B, 11 Oct 1944
31. BA–MA RH 24-81/97, KTB LXXXI Corps, 11 Oct 1944
32. KTB 2d Bn./Pz.Rgt. 16
33. Vogelsang, Fritz, diary
34. BA–MA RH 24-81/100, KTB LXXXI Corps, 11 Oct 1944
35. BA–MA RH 24-81/97, KTB LXXXI Corps, 11 Oct 1944
36. BA–MA RH 19 IV/74 and 78, Anl. 149, KTB Sup Cmd–West, 11 Oct 1944
37. BA–MA RH 19 IV/78, Anl. 150, KTB Sup Cmd–West, 11 Oct 1944

38. BA–MA RH 24-81/97 and 100, KTB LXXXI Corps, 11–12 Oct 1944

39. BA–MA RH 24-81/100, KTB LXXXI Corps, 11 Oct 1944

40. Waldenburg, Siegfried von, MS P-171; Keppler, Georg, MS B-623, most dates off by one day

41. BA–MA RH 24-81/100, KTB LXXXI Corps, 11 Oct 1944

42. BA–MA RH 19 IX/13, KTB Army Grp B, 12 Oct 1944; BA–MA RH 19 IV/78, Anl. 172, KTB Sup Cmd–West, 12 Oct 1944

43. BA–MA RH 19 IV/78, Anl. 174, KTB Sup Cmd–West, 12 Oct 1944

44. KTB 2d Bn./Pz.Rgt.16

45. BA–MA RH 19 IX/10, KTB Army Grp B, 12 Oct 1944; BA–MA RH 19 IV/78, Anl. 175, KTB Sup Cmd–West, 12 Oct 1944

46. MacDonald, loc. cit., p299ff

47. Wilck, Gerhard, "*Die 246. Volksgrenadier-Division in der Zeit vom September to November 1944,*" in the journal of the Historical Society of Aachen, vol.73,1961 p113ff; BA–MA RH 24-81/111, KTB LXXXI Corps, report, the battle of Aachen

48. BA–MA RH 19 IV/78, Anl. 172, KTB Sup Cmd–West, 12 Oct 1944; BA–MA RH 19 IX/13, KTB Army Grp B, 12 Oct 1944

49. BA–MA RH 24-81/97, KTB LXXXI Corps, 13 Oct 1944

50. BA–MA RH 19 IV/79, Anl.402, KTB Sup Cmd–West, 26 Oct 1944, Report of Combat Group Rink

51. Wolff-Boenisch, Richard, diary

52. BA–MA RH 19/IX /10, KTB Army Grp B, 13 Oct 1944

53. BA–MA RH 24-81/99, KTB LXXXI Corps, 14 Oct 1944

54. See ftnt. 53

55. BA–MA RH 19 IV/78,Anl.201, 207, 211 and 216, KTB Sup Cmd–West, 14–15 Oct 1944; BA–MA RH 19 IX/10 and 13, KTB Army Grp B, 14–15 Oct 1944

56. Beckmann, Gustav, diary

57. See ftnt. 55; BA–MA RH 24-81/97, KTB LXXXI Corps, 14–15 Oct 1944

58. Mac Donald, loc. cit., p313 and 318

59. BA–MA RH 19 IV/74 and 78, Anl. 225 and 229, KTB Sup Cmd–West, 15 Oct 1944; BA–MA RH 19 IX/10 and 13, KTB Army Grp B, 15 Oct 1944; Beckmann, Gustav, diary

60. BA–MA RH 27-116/127 and 128, IIa-doc. 116th Pz.Div., award recommendations Heiberger, Kurt and Orb, Helfried

61. BA–MA RH 24-81/97, KTB LXXXI Corps, 15 Oct 1944; KTB Sup Cmd–West, and Army Grp B as in ftnt. 59

62. BA–MA RH 19 IX/10, KTB Army Grp B, 15 Oct 1944

63. BA–MA RH 19 IV/78, Anl. 226, KTB Sup Cmd–West, 15 Oct 1944; KTB OKW, vol. IV 1, p405

64. BA–MA RH 24-81/97 and 99, KTB LXXXI Corps, 10 Oct 1944

65. Keppler, Georg, MS B-623

66. MacDonald, loc. cit., p303–306

67. BA–MA RH 19 IX/13, KTB Army Grp B, 16 Oct 1944

68. BA–MA RH 19 IV/78, Anl. 251 and 252, KTB Sup Cmd–West, 16 Oct 1944; BA–MA RH 19 IX/13, KTB Army Grp B, 16 Oct 1944; BA–MA RH 24-81/97 and 98, KTB LXXXI Corps, 16 Oct 1944

69. Beckmann, Gustav, diary, 15 Oct 1944, this date may be wrong

70. Vogelsang, Fritz, diary

71. See ftnt. 68

72. KTB 2d Bn./Pz.Rgt.16

73. Löffler, Jürgen, notes

74. See ftnt. 68

75. BA–MA RH 19 IV/78, Anl. 252, KTB Sup Cmd–West, 16 Oct 1944

76. Waldenburg, pocket calendar

77. BA–MA RH 19 IV/78, Anl. 262, 264, 269, 270, KTB Sup Cmd–West, 17 Oct 1944; BA–MA RH 24-81/97 and 98, KTB LXXXI Corps, 17 Oct 1944

78. MacDonald, loc. cit., p313

79. BA–MA RH 24-81/97 and 93, KTB LXXXI Corps, 17–18 Oct 1944

80. BA–MA RH 19 IV/78, Anl. 270, KTB Sup Cmd–West, 17 Oct 1944

81. BA–MA RH 24-81/97, KTB LXXXI Corps, 17 Oct 1944

82. BA–MA RH 19 IV/74 and 78, Anl. 278, 280, 282, 285, KTB Sup Cmd–West, 18 Oct 1944; BA–MA RH 24-81/97 and 98, KTB LXXXI Corps, 18 Oct 1944

83. BA–MA RH 19 IV/78, Anl. 286, KTB Sup Cmd–West, 19 Oct 1944; Beckmann, Gustav, diary

84. BA–MA RH 19 IV/78, Anl. 287, 299 and 300, KTB Sup Cmd–West, 19 Oct 1944

85. BA–MA RH 24-81/97, 98 and 127, KTB LXXXI Corps, 19 resp. 22 Oct 1944
86. Alsleben, Rolf, diary
87. Radio orders Ia 116th Pz.Div., 18 Oct 1944, 2045 hours, doc. Arm.Art.Rgt. 146
88. Vogelsang, Fritz, diary
89. BA–MA RH 19 IV/78, Anl. 299 and 300, KTB Sup Cmd–West, 19 Oct 1944
90. Sandkuhl, Wilhelm, diary
91. Löffler, Jürgen, notes
92. BA–MA RH 24-81/98, KTB LXXXI Corps, 18 Oct 1944
93. BA–MA RH 24-81/99, KTB LXXXI Corps, 18 Oct 1944
94. BA–MA RH 19 IV/78, Anl. 284, KTB Sup Cmd–West, 18 Oct 1944; BA–MA RH 24-81/97, KTB LXXXI Corps, 18 Oct 1944
95. BA–MA RH 24-81/98, KTB LXXXI Corps, 19 Oct 1944
96. BA–MA RH 24-81/97 and 98, KTB LXXXI Corps, 19–20 Oct 1944
97. KTB OKW, vol. IV, 1, p405
98. BA–MA RH 19 IV/78, Anl. 320, KTB Sup Cmd–West, 20 Oct 1944
99. BA–MA RH 24-81/97 and 127, KTB LXXXI Corps, 20 resp 23 Oct 1944
100. BA–MA RH 24-81/97 and 100, KTB LXXXI Corps, 20 Oct 1944, 2400 hours
101. BA–MA RH 24-81/97 and 98, KTB LXXXI Corps, 21 Oct 1944
102. BA–MA RH 24-81/97 and 98, KTB LXXXI Corps, 20–21 Oct 1944
103. BA–MA RH 24-81/97 and 98, KTB LXXXI Corps, 21 Oct 1944
104. BA–MA RH 19 IV/79, Anl. 339, 341, 342, KTB Sup Cmd–West, 21 Oct 1944 and Anl. 346, 22 Oct 1944; BA–MA RH 24-81/98 and 101, KTB LXXXI Corps, 21 resp. 22 Oct 1944; BA–MA RH 27-116/127, IIa-doc. 116th Pz.Div., recommendation Hauptmann von Linde-Suden, Jörg-Achim and points for recommendation German Cross in Gold for Oberst Siegfried von Waldenburg
105. KTB 2d Bn./Pz.Rgt.16
106. Waldenburg, Siegfried von, pocket calendar
107. BA–MA RH 19 IV/74, KTB Sup Cmd–West, 21 Oct 1944
108. BA–MA RH 19 IV/78, Anl. 298, KTB Sup Cmd–West, 19 Oct 1944
109. BA–MA RH 24-81/114, 120 and 125, KTB LXXXI Corps, 22 Oct 1944; BA–MA RH 19 IV/79, Anl. 355, KTB Sup Cmd–West, 22 Oct 1944
110. BA–MA RH 24-81/114 and 125, KTB LXXXI Corps, 23 Oct 1944
111. BA–MA RH 24-81/127, KTB LXXXI Corps, 23 Oct 1944; BA–MA RH 19 IV/79, Anl. 397, KTB Sup Cmd–West, 25 Oct 1944
112. BA–MA RH 24-81/128, KTB LXXXI Corps, 21 Oct 1944
113. BA–MA RH 24-81/120, KTB LXXXI Corps, 22 Oct 1944
114. BA–MA RH 24-81/144, KTB LXXXI Corps, 22 Oct 1944
115. Vogelsang, Fritz, diary
116. BA–MA RH 24-81/125, KTB LXXXI Corps, 23 Oct 1944
117. Waldenburg, Siegfried von, MS P-171 and pocket calendar
118. BA–MA RH 24-81/120, KTB LXXXI Corps, 24 Oct 1944
119. KTB 2d Bn./Pz.Rgt.16
120. Waldenburg, Siegfried von, pocket calendar; BA–MA RH 24-81/114 and 120, KTB LXXXI Corps, 24–26 Oct 1944
121. Waldenburg, Siegfried von, MS P-171
122. BA–MA RH 24-81/114 and 120, KTB LXXXI Corps, 26–28 Oct 1944
123. BA–MA RH 24-81/120, KTB LXXXI Corps, 26 Oct 1944
124. KTB 2d Bn./Arm.Art.Rgt. 146
125. Wolff-Boenisch, Richard, diary
126. Kleckel, Richard, and Agne, Karl, reports to the author
127. Vogelsang, Fritz, diary
128. OKW report, 28 Oct 1944, copy from Waldenburg docs

CHAPTER 8, PART 3

1. Waldenburg, Siegfried von, pocket calendar
2. BA–MA RH 19 IV/74 and 79, Anl. 449, KTB Sup Cmd–West, 28 Oct 1944
3. BA–MA RH 24-81/121, KTB LXXXI Corps, 28 Oct 1944
4. Hermann, Dr. Carl Hans, "*Bis zum bitteren Ende, Zum Kampf und Untergang der 9th Panzer-Division vor 25 Jahren,*" in *Mitteilungsblatt der Kameradschaft,* series

52, Dec 1969; Jollasse, Erwin, "Einsätze der 9. Panzerdivision," in *Mitteilungsblatt der Kameradschaft,* series 27–29, 1963–1964

5. BA–MA RH 19 IV/74 and 75, 79 and 80, Anl. 458, 468, 475, 489, 542, KTB Sup Cmd–West, 28 Oct–2 Nov 1944

6. BA–MA RH 19 IV/74 and 79, Anl. 490; KTB Sup Cmd–West, 30 Oct 1944 KTB OKW vol. IV, 1, p408

7. BA–MA RH 24-81/121, KTB LXXXI Corps, 28 Oct 1944

8. KTB 2d Bn./Pz.Rgt. 16; KTB 2d Bn./Arm.Art.Rgt. 146; Waldenburg, pocket calendar; Sandkuhl, Wihelm, pocket calendar; Bargstädt, Hans-Richard, diary; Zander, Helmut, post-war report; Löffler, Jürgen, post-war report

9. Waldenburg, pocket calendar

10. KTB 2d Bn./Arm.Art.Rgt. 146

11. KTB 2d Bn./Pz.Rgt. 16

12. KTB 2d Bn./Arm.Art.Rgt. 146

13. Vogelsang, Fritz, diary

14. KTB 2d Bn./Arm.Art.Rgt. 146; Zander, loc. cit.; Varnholt, Otto, notes

15. a) MacDonald I, p341ff. b) MacDonald, Charles B., *Battle Objective Schmidt: The History of the 112th Inf. Regt. of the 28th US-Inf. Division in the Battle for Schmidt, Germany—from Three Battles, Arnaville, Altuzzo and Schmidt,* (Washington, 1952), chapter I and II; translation (weak) in MGFA at Freiburg [hereafter, referred to as MacDonald II]; c) MacDonald, Charles B. *The Battle of the Huertgen Forest* (Philadelphia and New York, 1963), in the series *Great Battles of History,* chapter 10 [hereafter, referred to as MacDonald III]; d) Thompson, R.W., *The Battle for the Rhineland.* German edition (Klagenfurt, n.d.), p58ff.

16. Schmidt, Hans, MS B-810; Hohenstein, Adolf and Trees, Wolfgang. *Hölle im Hürtgenwald* (Aachen: n.p., 1981), p109ff; Scheele, Alexander, *Hürtgenwald 1944, Ausarbeitung an der Raketenschule des Heeres* (n.p.: n.d.); Brückner, Paul, "Die Schlacht im Hürtgenwald," *Truppenpraxis,* 3, 1970 and notes in the diary.

17. Gerdsdorff, Rudolf, Freiherr von, MS A-892

18. BA–MA RH 24-81/114, 121 and 123, KTB LXXXI Corps, 2 and 3 Nov 1944; KTB 2d Bn./Arm.Art.Rgt. 146; Brückner, diary; Hohenstein-Trees, loc. cit., p131

19. MacDonald I, p353

20. BA–MA RH 24-81/114 and123, KTB LXXXI Corps, 3 Nov 1944

21. BA–MA RH 24-81/121, KTB LXXXI Corps, 3 Nov 1944

22. Order 116th Pz.Div., Sect. Ia, 3 Nov 1944, from document Arm.Art.Rgt. 146; BA–MA RH 24-81/114, KTB LXXXI Corps, 3 Nov 1944

23. BA–MA RH 19 IV/75 and 80, Anl. 573 and 578, KTB Supreme Command–West, 3 Nov 1944

24. BA–MA RH 19 IV/75 and 80, Anl. 577, KTB Sup Cmd–West, 3 Nov 1944; BA–MA RH 26-89/3, Divisionsspiegel der 89. I.D., 9 Nov 1944; Haslob, Gevert, Ausarbeitung, Gegenangriff der 89. Inf. Div. on 4 Nov 1944 on Schmidt, 2 Mar 1983

25. Brückner, diary; BA–MA RH 19 IV/80, Anl.577, KTB Sup Com–West, 3 Nov 1944

26. BA–MA RH 19 IV/80, Anl.581, KTB Sup Cmd–West, 3 Nov 1944

27. BA–MA RH 24-81/114, KTB LXXXI Corps, 4 Nov 1944

28. Waldenburg, pocket calendar

29. BA–MA RH 19 IV/80, Anl.595, KTB Sup Cmd–West, 4 Nov 1944; Vogelsang, diary; Schmidt, MS B-810

30. Bargstädt, diary; Grollmann, Heinrich; Lehmkämper, Wilhelm; Noltensmeyer, Karl; Löffler, Jürgen; Varnholt, Otto, notes

31. KTB 2d Bn./Arm.Art.Rgt. 146

32. BA–MA RH 19 IV/80, Anl.595, KTB Sup Cmd–West, 4 Nov 1944

33. See ftnt. 30

34. Varnholt, Otto, report to the author

35. Schmidt, MS B-810; Borgert, Wenzel, notes in diary

36. BA–MA RH 19 IV/80 Anl.593, KTB Sup Cmd–West, 4 Nov 1944

37. Löffler and Noltensmeyer, see ftnt. 30

38. Nagel, Helmut, Information for the author; Dreiling, Hermann, diary and information for the author; Otten, Manfred, in Hohenstein-Trees, p139, see ftnt. 16; Palm,

Baptist, Hürtgenwald, Das Verdun des 2. Weltkriegs, Privatdruck, 1984, p59

39. BA–MA RH 19 IV/80, Anl.594, KTB Sup Cmd–West, 4 Nov 1944

40. MacDonald II, p67

41. BA–MA RH 24-81/114, KTB LXXXI Corps, 3–4 Nov 1944; BA–MA RH 10/247, Report of Heavy Tank Destroyer Battalion 682; Control cards of Org.Sect. of General Army Staff in BA–MA; Hohenstein-Trees, loc. cit., p131 (in part with mistakes); Bruns, Walter, MS B-032a; Several individuals questioned, MS C-089; Weidemann, p248ff.

42. BA–MA RH 19 IV/75 and 80, Anl.593, 594, 595, KTB West, 4 Nov 1944; BA–MA RH 26-89/3, Divisionsspiegel 89. I.D., 9 Nov 1944; Bruns, Walter, MS P-032a; Several individuals questioned, MS C-089

43. MacDonald II, p59ff.

44. KTB 2d Bn./Pz.Rgt.16; Adam, Werner, report to the author

45. BA–MA RH 26-89/3, Divisionsspiegel 89.I.D., 9 Nov 1944

46. Honor roll of 116th Pz.Div., 28 Nov 1944

47. MacDonald II, p70ff.

48. MacDonald II, p74

49. MacDonald II, p83

50. MacDonald II, p82

51. BA–MA RH 19 IV/80, Anl.602, 603, 607, 608, KTB Supreme Command–West, 5 Nov 1944

52. BA–MA RH 27-116/127, p217ff., IIa, docs 116th Pz.Div.

53. BA–MA RH IV/80, Anl.603, KTB Sup Cmd–West, 5 Nov 1944

54. BA–MA RH 26-89/3, Divisionsspiegel 89. I.D., 9 Nov 1944; BA–MA RH 19 IV/80, Anl.603, 607, 608, KTB Sup Cmd–West, 5 Nov 1944; KTB 2d Bn./Pz.Rgt.16

55. MacDonald II, p88ff.

56. KTB 2d Bn./Arm.Art.Rgt. 146

57. BA–MA RH 19 IV/80, Anl.603, 607, 608, KTB Sup Cmd–West, 5 Nov 1944

58. Bargstädt, diary

59. Varnholt, notes

60. Borgert, diary

61. Löffler and Noltensmeyer, notes

62. Nagel, report to the author; Dreiling, diary

63. Palm, loc. cit., p64ff.

64. Vogelsang, diary

65. Weidemann, loc. cit., p248

66. Palm, loc. cit., p65

67. Sandkuhl, pocket calendar

68. MacDonald II, p107

69. MacDonald II, p116

70. MacDonald II, p110

71. MacDonald II, p116

72. BA–MA RH 19 IV/80, Anl.618, KTB Sup Cmd–West, 6 Nov 1944

73. BA–MA RH 19 IV/80, Anl.621, KTB Sup Cmd–West, 6 Nov 1944

74. Heiber, p702

75. See ftnt. 73

76. KTB 2d Bn./Arm.Art.Rgt. 146

77. Sandkuhl, pocket calendar

78. Vogelsang, diary

79. BA–MA RH 19 IV/80, Anl.631, KTB Sup Cmd–West, 6 Nov 1944

80. MacDonald II, p138

81. Varnholt, report to the author; Grollmann, Heinrich, addition to MS C-089; BA–MA RH 19 IV/80, Anl.595, KTB Sup Cmd–West, 4 Nov 1944

82. Löffler, Noltenmeyer and Junge, Oskar, reports to the author

83. BA–MA RH 27-116/128, p137ff., IIa, docs. 116th Pz.Div. Proposition Lauer, Erich

84. Otten, Manfred, in Hohenstein-Trees, p140 and reports to the author

85. Nagel, reports to the author

86. KTB 2d Bn./Arm.Art.Rgt. 146; Löffler, report to the author

87. MacDonald II, p103 and 109

88. MacDonald II, p112 and 130

89. BA–MA RH 27-116/127, p173ff., IIa, docs. 116th Pz.Div.

90. a) MacDonald I, p364ff.; b) MacDonald II, p116ff., 132ff.; c) MacDonald III, p106ff.

91. MacDonald II, p118ff. and 136ff.

92. MacDonald II, p139ff.

93. MacDonald II, p142

94. MacDoanld II, p151

95. BA–MA RH 19 IV/80, Anl.638 and 639 KTB Sup Cmd–West, 7 Nov 1944

96. Stephan, Eberhard, post-war report

97. BA–MA RH 27-116/128, p98, IIa, docs. 116th Pz.Div. proposal Orb, Elfried

98. MacDonald II, p153 and MacD. I, p367

99. BA–MA RH 19 IV/80, Anl.621, 630, 631, KTB Sup Cmd–West, 6 Nov 1944

100. KTB 2d Bn./Pz.Rgt.16
101. BA–MA RH 26-89/3, Divisionsspiegel 89thI.D., 9 Nov 1944; Haslob, see ftnt. 24
102. Weidemann, loc. cit., p249ff.
103. KTB 2d Bn./Pz.Rgt.16
104. MacDonald II, p178ff.
105. BA–MA RH 26-89/3, see ftnt. 101
106. BA–MA RH 27-116/127, p45 IIa-doc.116th Pz.Div.
107. See ftnt. 105
108. KTB 2d Bn./Pz.Rgt.16
109. Weidemann, loc. cit., p253
110. MacDonald II, p161ff.
111. MacDonald II, p187ff.
112. MacDonald II, p194
113. MacDonald II, p204ff.
114. MacDonald II, p172ff., 181 and 185; MacDonald I, p366
115. BA–MA RH 27-116/128, p44 and 137, IIa-doc.116th Pz.Div., proposals Geyser, Eugen and Lauer, Erich; Dreiling and Varnholt, diaries; Grollmann, Zander, Nagel, Lehmkämper, Löffler, Palm, post-war reports
116. Borgert, diary
117. BA–MA RH 19 IV/80, Anl.630, KTB Sup Cmd–West, 6 Nov 1944
118. Brückner, diary
119. Löffler, postwar report
120. Dreiling, diary
121. BA–MA RH 27-116/128, p44, IIa-doc.116th Pz.Div.
122. BA–MA RH 27-116/128, p137ff., IIa-doc.116th Pz.Div.
123. KTB 2d Bn./Arm.Art.Rgt. 146
124. BA–MA RH 19 IV/80, Anl.639, KTB Sup Cmd–West, 7 Apr 1944
125. BA–MA RH 19 IV/80, Anl.646, KTB Sup Cmd–West, 7 Apr 1944
126. Order 116th Pz.Div., Sect. Ia, 7 Nov 1944 from doc. from Pz.Art. Rgt.146
127. Order 116 Pz.Div., Sect. Ia, 8 Nov 1944 from doc. from Arm.Art.Rgt. 146
128. KTB 2d Bn./Arm.Art.Rgt. 146
129. BA–MA RH 19 IV/80, Anl.724, KTB Sup Cmd–West, 10 Nov 1944
130. Vogelsang, diary
131. MacDonald II, p212
132. BA–MA RH 19 IV/80, Anl.630, KTB Sup Cmd–West, 6 Nov 1944

133. KTB OKW, vol.IV, 1, p414; BA–MA RH 19 IV/80, Anl.669 and 685, KTB Sup Cmd–West, 10 Nov 1944
134. BA–MA RH 19 IV/80, Anl.722 and 723, KTB Sup Cmd–West, 10 Nov 1944
135. Waldenburg, pocket calendar
136. MacDonald I, p372ff.; MacDonald II, p210ff.
137. See ftnt. 127
138. KTB 2d Bn./Arm.Art.Rgt. 146; Brückner, diary; Varnholt, diary; Order 116th Pz.Div., Sect. Ia, 10 Nov 1944 from doc.Arm.Art.Rgt. 146
139. MacDonald I, p372; BA–MA RH 19 IV/80, Anl.719, 722, 724, KTB Sup Cmd–West, 10 Nov 1944; KTB 2d Bn./Arm.Art.Rgt. 146
140. MacDonald I, p373
141. KTB 2d Bn./Arm.Art.Rgt. 146
142. BA–MA RH 19 IV/80, Anl.722, 724, 81, Anl.735, 738, KTB Sup Cmd–West, 10 resp. 11 Nov 1944
143. Order 116th Pz.Div., Sect. Ia, 10 Nov 1944 from doc. Arm.Art.Rgt. 146
144. Brückner, diary
145. BA–MA RH 19 IV/81, Anl.735, 738, 745a, KTB Sup Cmd–West, 11 Nov 1944
146. 116th Pz.Div., Sect. Ia, 10 Nov 1944, notice in document about deployment conference on 10 Nov 1944, 2300 hours from doc.Arm.Art.Rgt. 146
147. BM-MA RH 19 IV/81, Anl.745a, KTB Sup Cmd–West, 11 Nov 1944
148. See ftnt. 146
149. BA–MA RH 19 IV/81, Anl.745a, KTB Sup Cmd–West, 11 Nov 1944
150. Waldenburg, pocket calendar
151. MacDonald I, p137ff.; KTB 2d Bn./Pz.Art. Rgt.146
152. BA–MA RH 27-116/127, p36ff., IIa-doc.116th Pz.Div., proposal Linde-Suden, Jörg-Achim von
153. KTB 2d Bn./Arm.Art.Rgt. 146
154. BA–MA RH 19 IV/81, Anl.757, 760, 804, KTB Sup Cmd–West, 12 and 14 Nov 1944
155. KTB 2d Bn./Arm.Art.Rgt. 146
156. Waldenburg, pocket calendar
157. Vogelsang, diary
158. Schwörer, Ernst, diary
159. BA–MA RH 19 IV/81, Anl.782, 785, KTB Sup Cmd–West, 13 Nov 1944

160. Order 116th Pz.Div., Sect. Ia, 13 Nov 1944 from doc. Arm.Art.Rgt. 146
161. KTB 2d Bn./Arm.Art.Rgt. 146
162. Brückner, diary
163. MacDonald I, p429
164. Waldenburg, pocket calendar
165. BA–MA RH 19 IV/81, Anl.810, 814, 829, KTB Sup Cmd–West, 15 Nov 1944; Order 116th Pz.Div., Sect. Ia, 14 Nov 1944 from doc. Arm.Art.Rgt. 146; KTB 2d Bn./Pz.Art. Rgt. 146; BA–MA RH 27-116/128, IIa-doc. 116th Pz.Div., proposal Kroll, Bernhard
166. MacDonald I, p373
167. BA–MA RH 19 IV/81, Anl.829, KTB Sup Cmd–West, 15 Nov 1944
168. Hohenstein-Trees, loc. cit., p204 note 212; Palm, loc. cit., in the title
169. Vogelsang, diary

CHAPTER 8, PART 4
1. Vogelsang, Fritz, diary
2. MacDonald I, p397ff.; MacDonald III, chapter 12 and 13
3. BA–MA RH 19 IV/75 and 81, Anl.803, KTB Sup Cmd–West, 14 Nov 1944
4. KTB OKW, vol. IV, I, 1, p 414ff. and 429/430
5. BA–MA RH 19 IV/75 and 81, Anl.842 and 845, KTB Supreme Command–West, 16 Nov 1944
6. BA–MA RH 19 IV/75 and 81, Anl.847 KTB Sup Cmd–West, 16 Nov 1944
7. BA–MA RH 19 IV/75 and 81, Anl.871 KTB Sup Cmd–West, 17 Nov 1944
8. Jollass, March 1964
9. Order 116th Pz.Div., Sect. Ia, 15 Nov 1944, from doc. Pz.Art. Rgt.146
10. BA–MA RH 19 IV/81, Anl.831, KTB Sup Cmd–West, 15 Nov 1944
11. BA–MA RH 24-81/114, 121 and 123, KTB LXXXI Corps, 16 Nov 1944; BA–MA RH 19 IV/81, Anl.853, KTB Sup Cmd–West, 16 Nov 1944
12. Order 116th Pz.Div., Sect. Ia Addendum to this order, 16 Nov 1944, from doc. Arm.Art.Rgt. 146; Weidemann, Gert-Axel, p253ff.
13. MacDonald I, p397ff.; MacDonald III, chap.13; *Danger, Forward,* chap.7
14. MacDonald III, chap.14

15. BA–MA RH 24-81/114, KTB LXXXI Corps, 17 Nov 1944; Order 116th Pz.Div., Sect. Ia, 17 Nov 1944, from doc. Arm.Art.Rgt. 146; Schmidt, Hans MS B-810
16. Borgert, Wenzel, diary
17. BA–MA RH 19 IV/81, Anl.860, 880, 885, 895, KTB Supreme Command–West, 17 Nov 1944
18. MacDonald III, chap. 13 and 16
19. BA–MA RH 19 IV/81, Anl.917, KTB Sup Cmd–West, 19 Nov 1944; BA–MA RH 24-81/114 and 120, KTB LXXXI Corps, 19 Nov 1944
20. BA–MA RH 19 IV/82, Anl.991, KTB Sup Cmd–West, 22 Nov 1944
21. Schmidt, Hans, MS B-810
22. BA–MA RH 19 IV/82, Anl.991, KTB Sup Cmd–West, 22 Nov 1944; Waldenburg, pocket calendar
23. BA–MA RH 27-116/128, p8, IIa-doc. 116th Pz.Div.
24. BA–MA RH 27-116/126 and 127, p266, IIa-doc. 116th Pz.Div.
25. KTB 2d Bn./Arm.Art.Rgt. 146; Sandkuhl, pocket calendar
26. BA–MA RH 24-81/114 and 123, KTB LXXXI Corps, 16–19 Nov 1944; Engel, Gerhard, MS B-764; Bork, Max, MS B-602
27. BA–MA RH 24-81/125, KTB LXXXI Corps, 17 Nov 1944
28. BA–MA RH 24-81/114, KTB LXXXI Corps, 17 Nov 1944; KTB 2d Bn./Pz.Rgt.16
29. Weidemann, loc. cit., p254
30. MacDonald I, p417ff.; *Danger, Forward,* p303ff.
31. Weidemann, loc. cit., p254
32. BA–MA RH 24-81/120, KTB LXXXI Corps, 18 Nov 1944
33. Stephan, Eberhard, post-war report
34. MacDonald I, p418
35. Weidemann, loc. cit., p255
36. BA–MA RH 27-116/127, p45 and 258, IIa-doc.116th Pz.Div.
37. BA–MA RH 19 IV/81, Anl.917, KTB Sup Cmd–West, 19 Nov 1944
38. MacDonald III, chap.13
39. BA–MA RH 24-81/114, KTB LXXXI Corps, 19 Nov 1944

40. BA–MA RH 24-81/114, KTB LXXXI Corps, 19 Nov 1944
41. Weidemann, loc. cit., p255
42. BA–MA RH 24-81/123, KTB LXXXI Corps, 19 Nov 1944
43. BA–MA RH 24-81/114, KTB LXXXI Corps, 19 Nov 1944
44. BA–MA RH 24-81/114, KTB LXXXI Corps, 19 Nov 1944
45. BA–MA RH 24-81/114 and 120, KTB LXXXI Corps, 20 Nov 1944
46. MacDonald I, p478
47. BA–MA RH 19 IV/81, Anl.949 KTB Sup Cmd–West, 20 Nov 1944
48. BA–MA RH 24-81/114, KTB LXXXI Corps, 21 Nov 1944
49. BA–MA RH 19 IV/82, Anl.970, KTB Sup Cmd–West, 21 Nov 1944
50. BA–MA RH 24-81/114, 121 and 123, KTB LXXXI Corps, 21 Nov 1944
51. Wolff-Boenisch, Richard, diary
52. KTB 2d Bn./Pz.Rgt.16
53. BA–MA RH 24-81/120, KTB LXXXI Corps, 22 Nov 1944
54. BA–MA RH 19 IV/82, Anl.944, KTB Sup Cmd–West, 22 Nov 1944
55. BA–MA RH 24-81/114 and 127, KTB LXXXI Corps, 23 Nov 1944
56. BA–MA RH 24-81/114, KTB LXXXI Corps, 23 Nov 1944
57. BA–MA RH 24-81/114, KTB LXXXI Corps, 23 Nov 1944
58. BA–MA RH 24-81/114, 118 and 123, KTB LXXXI Corps, 23 Nov 1944
59. Weidemann, loc. cit., p255ff.
60. BA–MA RH 24-81/121, KTB LXXXI Corps, 23 Nov 1944
61. Borgert, diary
62. BA–MA RH 19 IV/82, Anl.1046, KTB Sup Cmd–West, 24 Nov 1944
63. BA–MA RH 24-81/114, KTB LXXXI Corps, 24 Nov 1944
64. BA–MA RH 24-81/114, KTB LXXXI Corps, 24 Nov 1944
65. BA–MA RH 24-81/121, KTB LXXXI Corps, 25 Nov 1944
66. BA–MA RH 24-81/114, KTB LXXXI Corps, 26 Nov 1944
67. Borgert, diary
68. KTB 2d Bn./Arm.Art.Rgt. 146
69. KTB OKW, vol. IV, 1, p426ff.; BA–MA RH 19 IV/75 and 76, 82 and 83, KTB Sup Cmd–West, 11/26 to 15 Dec 1944; MacDonald I, p581ff.; MacDonald III, chap. 16/19

CHAPTER 9, PART 1

1. Warlimont, Walter, *Im Hauptquartier der Deutschen Wehrmacht, 1939–1945,* (Frankfurt, 1962), p487
2. KTB OKW, vol. IV, 1, p367
3. Kreipe, Werner, diary; Jung, Anl.1
4. KTB OKW, vol. IV, 1, p435
5. Jung, loc. cit., p102ff; Guderian, *Memories,* p343ff; KTB OKW, vol. IV, 1, p430ff
6. KTB OKW, vol. IV, 1, p434 and 407
7. KTB OKW, vol. IV, 1, p434; BA–MA RH 19 IV/74 and 78, Anl.255, KTB Sup Cmd–West, 16 Oct 1944
8. KTB OKW, vol. IV, 1, p435; BA–MA RH 19 IV/247, p30, KTB Sup Cmd–West, 1 Nov 1944; Jung, loc. cit., Anl.15
9. KTB OKW, vol. IV, 1, p437 and 438; BA–MA RH 19 IV/247, KTB Sup Cmd–West, 5 Nov 1944; Jung, loc. cit., Anl.22 and 23
10. KTB OKW, vol. IV, 1, p437; BA–MA RH 19 IV/247, KTB Sup Cmd–West, 3 Nov 1944; Jung, loc. cit., p111/112
11. KTB OKW, vol. IV, 1, p439; BA–MA RH 19 IV/247, KTB Sup Cmd–West, 10 Nov 1944; Jung, loc. cit., Anl.16
12. KTB OKW, vol. IV, 1, p439, 440; BA–MA RH 19 IV/247, KTB Sup Cmd–West, 18 Nov 1944; Jung, loc. cit., Anl.17
13. BA–MA RH 24-58/18, p22-48, KTB LVIII Pz.Corps, 7 Nov 1944
14. BA–MA RH 19 IV/247, KTB Sup Cmd–West, 16–18 Nov 1944; Jung, loc. cit., p114
15. KTB OKW, vol. IV, 1, p441–2; BA–MA RH 19 IV/242, KTB Sup Cmd–West, 20 Nov 1944; Jung, loc. cit., p114-116 and Anl.18
16. KTB OKW, vol. IV, 1, p441–2; BA–MA RH 19 IV/242, KTB Sup Cmd–West, 20 Nov 1944; Jung, loc,cit., p115 and Anl.19
17. KTB OKW, vol. IV, 1, p442 19443; BA–MA RH 19 IV/242, KTB Sup Cmd–West, 22 and 25 Nov 1944; Jung, loc. cit., p115/116 and Anl.20

18. BA–MA RH 19 IV/75, 81, Anl.871 and 82, Anl. 970, KTB Sup Cmd–West, 17 resp. 20, and 21 Nov 1944
19. Jung, loc. cit., p116; KTB OKW, vol. IV, 1, p443
20. BA–MA RH 19 IV/242, KTB Sup Cmd–West, 29 Nov 1944; Jung, loc. cit., p130; Operation Order printed as Anl.24 by Jung, is not as Jung assumes on p130, the draft of the order by Army Grp B, 29 Nov 1944, but the final order of operation by Army Grp B, 9 Dec 1944
21. BA–MA RH 19 IV/242, KTB Sup Cmd–West, 4 Dec 1944
22. BA–MA RH 19 IV/76 and 84, Anl.1543, KTB Supreme Command–West, 18 Dec 1944
23. KTB OKW, vol. IV, 1, p444; Jung, loc. cit., p117
24. KTB OKW, vol IV, 1, p446; BA–MA RH 19 IV/242, KTB Sup Cmd–West, 11–12 Dec 1944
25. Waldenburg, Siegfried von, pocket calendar
26. Holtermann, Dr. Arthur, letter Count von Schwerin, from Holtermann, 7 Dec 1944
27. Heiber, p713ff
28. Vogelsang, Fritz, diary, 22 and 24 Nov 1944
29. KTB 2d Bn./Arm.Art.Rgt. 146
30. Waldenburg, pocket calendar
31. KTB 2d Bn./Arm.Art.Rgt. 146
32. KTB 2d Bn./Pz.Rgt.16
33. KTB 2d Bn./Arm.Art.Rgt. 146
34. Vogelsang, diary
35. KTB 2d Bn./Pz.Rgt.16 and 2d Bn./Arm. Art.Rgt. 146
36. Waldenburg, pocket calendar
37. Vogelsang, diary
38. BA–MA RH 10/163, p29 and 30, doc. General Inspector of Panzer Troops
39. See ftnt. 38; BA–MA RH 19 IV/246, KTB Sup Cmd–West, 10 Dec 1944; KTB 2d Bn./Pz.Rgt.16
40. See ftnt. 38
41. BA–MA RH 19 IV/246, KTB Sup Cmd–West, 10 Dec 1944; Jung, loc. cit., Anl.29
42. Waldenburg, pocket calendar
43. Vogelsang, diary
44. KTB 2d Bn./Pz.Rgt.16
45. Waldenburg, pocket calendar
46. BA–MA RH 24-58/15 and 18, KTB LVIII Pz.Corps, beginning Dec 1944
47. Waldenburg, pocket calendar
48. BA–MA RH 19 IV/83, Anl.1324, KTB Sup Cmd–West, 6 Dec 1944
49. Waldenburg, pocket calendar
50. Waldenburg, pocket calendar; BA–MA RH 24-58/15, KTB LVIII Pz.Corps, 7 Dec 1944
51. Vogelsang, diary
52. Waldenburg, pocket calendar; Holtermann, letters, 7 and 28 Dec 1944 to Count von Schwerin from doc. Holtermann
53. KTB 2d Bn./Pz.Rgt.16, 30 Nov resp. 10 Dec 1944
54. BA–MA RH 19 IV/84, Anl.1403, KTB Sup Cmd–West, 11 Dec 1944; BA–MA RH 24-58/15, 16 and 32 KTB LVIII Pz.Corps; Waldenburg, pocket calendar; Various statements by individuals belonging to the division
55. Waldenburg, pocket calendar
56. Vogelsang, diary
57. Schwörer, Ernst, diary (date 4 Dec there certainly wrong, probably 8 Dec 1944)
58. Waldenburg, pocket calendar
59. BA–MA RH 19 IV/83, Anl.1380, KTB Sup Cmd–West, 9 Dec 1944
60. Waldenburg, pocket calendar
61. BA–MA RH 24-58/16, p70-71, KTB LVIII Pz.Corps, 10 Dec 1944; Order Arm.Art. Rgt. 146 to 3d Bn./146, 10 Dec 1944, 1850 hours from doc. Pz.Art. Rgt.146
62. BA–MA RH 19 IV/84, Anl.1419, KTB Sup Cmd–West, 12 Dec 1944
63. Vogelsang, diary
64. BA–MA RH 24-58/15 and 16, p78 and 79, KTB LVIII Pz.Corps, 13 Dec 1944
65. KTB 2d Bn./Arm.Art.Rgt. 146 and 2d Bn./ Pz.Rgt. 16
66. KTB 2d Bn./Pz.Rgt.16
67. BA–MA RH 24-58/15 and 16, p59-71, KTB LVIII Pz.Corps, 14 Dec 1944; Date of order 10 Dec 1944
68. Waldenburg, pocket calendar
69. Vogelsang, diary
70. BA–MA RH 24 -58/16, p84, KTB LVIII Pz.Corps, 15 Dec 1944
71. BA–MA RH 24-58/32, KTB LVIII Pz.Corps, 14 Dec 1944

72. BA–MA RH 19 IV/84, Anl.1450, KTB Sup Cmd–West, 14 Dec 1944
73. BA–MA RH 24-58/16, p88/89, KTB LVIII Pz.Corps, 15 Dec 1944
74. BA–MA RH 19/76 and 84, Anl.1453, KTB Sup Cmd–West, 15 Dec 1944
75. BA–MA RH 19 IV/84 and 244, KTB Sup Cmd–West, 15 Dec 1944; Jung, loc. cit., Anl.31
76. BA–MA RH 24-58/33, KTB LVIII Pz.Corps Qu, 15–16 Dec 1944
77. See ftnt. 76
78. KTB 2d Bn./Pz.Rgt.16
79. Kaspers, Walter, memories (unpublished)
80. KTB 2d Bn./Pz.Rgt.16
81. Waldenburg, pocket calendar
82. BA–MA RH 27-116/121, situation report for the armored motor vehicles of Pz.Rgt.16, 16 Dec 1944
83. Anl. to KTB 2d Bn./Arm.Art.Rgt. 146
84. BA–MA RH 24-58/18, p17-19, KTB LVIII Pz.Corps, 9 Dec 1944
85. Krüger, Walter and Dingler, Hans-Jürgen, MS B-321
86. Cole, Hugh M. *United States Army in WWII, The European Theater of Operation: The Ardennes, Battle of the Bulge* (Washington, DC, 1965), p136ff

CHAPTER 9, PART 2

1. BA–MA RH 24-58/16, 59-71, KTB 58th Pz.Corps 12 October 44
2. Langhäuser, Rudolf, MS B-27
3. BA–MA RH 24-58/18, 22-48, KTB 58th Pz.Corps 7 Dec 1944
4. BA–MA RH 27-116/127, 2a-doc. 116th Panzer Division, proposal Hauptmann Winter, Hans
5. BA–MA RH 24-58/15, KTB 58th Pz.Corps 16 Dec 1944
6. KTB 2d Bn./Pz.Rgt.16
7. BA–MA RH 24-58/16, KTB 58th Pz.Corps 16 Dec 1944
8. KTB 2d Bn./Pz.Rgt.16
9. Cole, 153; MacDonald, Charles B., *A Time for Trumpets, The Untold Story of the Battle of the Bulge* (New York: n.p., 1985), 130ff [hereafter, referred to as MacDonald IV]
10. BA–MA RH 19 IV/84, 163, KTB Sup Cmd–West, 16 Dec 44

11. BA–MA RH 24-58/16, KTB 58th Pz.Corps 16 Dec 1944
12. BA–MA RH 19 IV/84, Anl.1496, KTB Sup Cmd–West, 16 Dec 1944
13. BA–MA RH 24-58/15, KTB 58th Pz.Corps 16 Dec 1944
14. Langhäuser, loc. cit.
15. BA–MA RH 24-58/15, KTB 58th Pz.Corps 16 Dec 1944
16. Vogelsang, Fritz, diary
17. BA–MA RH 19 IV/84, 162, KTB Sup Cmd–West, 16 Dec 1944
18. Order 116th Panzer Division, Sect. 1a 16 Dec 1944 from doc. Arm.Art.Rgt. 146
19. KTB 2d Bn./Pz.Rgt.16
20. BA–MA RH 24-58/16, KTB 58th Pz.Corps 17 Dec 1944
21. Vogelsang, diary
22. Cole, loc. cit., 193ff
23. BA–MA RH 24-58/16, KTB 58th PzCorps 17 Dec 1944, and the following quotes.
24. Vogelsang, diary
25. BA–MA RH 24-58/15, KTB 58th Pz.Corps 17–18 Dec 1944, and the following quotes.
26. BA–MA RH 24-58/16, KTB 58th Pz.Corps 18 Dec 1944 and the following quotes
27. Kladde, 04 116th Pa.Div., Oberlt.Franz, Otto, in possession of author
28. KTB 2d Bn./Arm.Art.Rgt. 146
29. BA–MA RH 24-58/16, KTB 58th Pz.Corps 18 Dec 1944
30. BA–MA RH 27-116/127, 2a-doc. 116th Pz.Div., proposal Major Stephan, Eberhard
31. BA–MA RH 27-116/128, 2a-doc. 116th Pz.Div., proposals Oberlt. Andreis, Karl and Lt. Auert, Heinz
32. BA–MA RH 24-58/16, KTB 58th Pz.Corps, 18 Dec 1944 and following quote
33. BA–MA RH 19 IV/76 and 84, Anl.1558, KTB Sup Cmd–West, 18 Dec 1944
34. BA–MA RH 19 IV/76, 80, KTB Sup Cmd–West, 18 Dec 1944
35. BA–MA RH 24-58/16, KTB 58th Pz.Corps, 18 Dec 1944 and the following quote
36. BA–MA RH 24-58/16, KTB 58th Pz.Corps, 19 Dec 1944 and the following quotes

37. Vogelsang, diary
38. BA–MA RH 24-58/16, KTB 58th Pz.Corps, 19 Dec 1944
39. See ftnt. 38
40. BA–MA RH 24-58/15, KTB 58th Pz.Corps, 19 Dec 1944
41. BA–MA RH 24-58/16, KTB 58th Pz.Corps, 19 Dec 1944
42. KTB 2d Bn./Arm.Art.Rgt. 146
43. BA–MA RH 27-116/128, 2a-doc. 116th Pz.Div., proposal Oberlt. Steinmeier, Egon
44. Cole, loc. cit. 296ff; MacDonald IV, loc. cit. 488ff
45. Waldenburg, Siegfried von, MS A-873
46. Meurisse, André-Romain, in Houffalize 44 1945, published by Lessage, Jean-Marie, Houffalize, 1984, 15ff
47. Waldenburg, MS A-873; BA–MA RH 24-58/15 and 16, KTB 58th Pz.Corps, 19 Dec 1944
48. BA–MA RH 24-58/16, KTB 58th Pz.Corps, 19–20 Dec 1944
49. KTB 2dd/Arm.Art.Rgt. 146
50. KTB 2d Bn./Pz.Rgt.16
51. Kroll, Bernhard "Der Windhund" 1/59
52. BA–MA RH 24-58/16, KTB 58th Pz.Corps, 19 Dec 1944
53. See ftnt. 52
54. BA–MA RH 24-58/15, KTB 58th Pz.Corps, 19 Dec 1944
55. See ftnt. 52; BA–MA RH 19 IV/84, Anl.1585, KTB Supreme Command–West, 19 Dec 1944
56. BA–MA RH 24-58/16, KTB 58th Pz.Corps, 20 Dec 1944
57. See ftnt. 56
58. See ftnt. 56
59. Vogelsang, diary 20 Dec 1944 evening
60. Waldenburg, MS A-873
61. Guderian, Heinz Günther, handwritten notes to MS A-873, written in captivity, Allendorf, 1946, abridged vers. given to US Army historical div. by Waldenburg.
62. Krüger, Walter and Dingler, Hans-Jürgen, MS B-321
63. BA–MA RH 24-58/15 and 16, KTB 58th Pz.Corps 20 Dec 1944 and the following statements; Orders and reports Kladde, 04, 116th Pz.Div. see ftnt. 27
64. Siebert, Rudolf, *Die Schlacht in den Ardennen, Der Weg der Panzeraufklärungsabteilung 2, der 2. Panzer Division im Dezember 1944 als Vorausabteilung der Division nach Dinant,* (*The Battle in the Ardennes, The Path of Tank Reconnaissance Battalion 2, of the 2d Tank Division in December 1944, as Advance Battalion of the Division after Dinant*) manuscript
65. Cole, loc. cit., 308ff, 318ff, 352ff, 371ff, 427ff; MacDonald IV, loc. cit., 535ff; Wilmott, 631ff
66. Zander, Helmut and Kroll, Bernhard, *Briefe aus dem Jahr 1961*
67. Langhäuser, MS B-27 (date 21 Dec 1944, mistake)
68. BA–MA RH 24-58/16, KTB 58th Pz.Corps, 20 Dec 1944
69. KTB 2d Bn./Pz.Rgt.16
70. BA–MA RH 27—116/128, 2a-doc. 116th Panzer Division, proposal Major Tebbe, Gerhard
71. Cole, loc. cit., 353ff, mainly 358-359; MacDonald IV, loc. cit., 536; Hemmer, Albert, *L'offensive von Rundstedt dans la vallée de l'Ourthe, Les combats décisifs de Hotton* (*The offensive of von Rundstedt in the Ourthe valley, The Decisive Battles of Hotton*). (Stavelot, 1984), 51ff
72. BA–MA RH 24-58/16, KTB 58th Pz.Corps 21 Dec 1944
73. BA–MA RH 24-58/33, KTB 58th Pz.Corps, Sect. Qu 20 Dec 1944
74. BA–MA RH 24-58/16, KTB 58th Pz.Corps 20 Dec 1944
75. BA–MA RH 24-58/15 and 16, KTB 58th Pz.Corps 21–22 Dec 1944
76. BA–MA RH 24-58/16, KTB 58th Pz.Corps 21 Dec 1944
77. Ritgen, Helmut, information to the author
78. BA–MA RH 19 IV/84, Anl.1601, KTB Sup Cmd–West, 20 Dec 1944
79. Keitel, Wilhelm, and Jodl, Alfred, MS A-928
80. Freytag-Loringhoven, Berndt Freiherr von, letter to Generaloberst Guderian, 1950, in possession of author.
81. BA–MA RH 19 IV/85, Anl.1618, KTB Sup Cmd–West, 21 Dec 1944
82. BA–MA RH 19 IV/76 and 85, Anl.1644, KTB Sup Cmd–West, 22 Dec 1944
83. BA–MA RH 19 IV/76 and 85, Anl.1649, KTB Sup Cmd–West, 22 Dec 1944
84. Ba-MA Rh 24-58/15 and 16, KTB 58th Pz. Corps, 21 Dec 1944

85. KTB 2d Bn./Pz.Rgt.16
86. KTB 2d Bn./Pz.Rgt.16; Zander and Kroll, see ftnt. 66
87. KTB 2d Bn./Arm.Art.Rgt. 146
88. Vogelsang, diary
89. BA–MA RH 24-58/16, KTB 58th Pz.Corps, 21 Dec 1944
90. See ftnt. 89
91. BA–MA RH 19 IV/85, Anl.1627, KTB Sup Cmd–West, 21 Dec 1944
92. Vogelsang, diary
93. Cole, loc. cit., 378ff and 427-442; Hemmer, loc. cit., 111ff; MacDonald IV, loc. cit., 536
94. KTB 2d Bn./Pz.Rgt.16; BA–MA RH 27-116/127, 2a-doc. 116th Panzer Division, proposal Oberlt. Erdmann, Willi
95. BA–MA RH 24-58/16, KTB 58th Pz.Corps, 22 Dec 1944
96. BA–MA RH 19 IV/85, Anl.1661, KTB Sup Cmd–West, 23 Dec 1944
97. BA–MA RH 19 IV/85, Anl.1650, KTB Sup Cmd–West, 23 Dec 1944
98. BA–MA RH 24-58/16, KTB 58th Pz.Corps, 22 Dec 1944
99. BA–MA RH 19 IV/85, Anl.1643, KTB Sup Cmd–West, 22 Dec 1944
100. BA–MA RH 10 IV/85, Anl.1652-1655, KTB Sup Cmd–West, 22 Dec 1944
101. Junge, Oskar, report to the author; Kladde, 116th Pz.Div., 04 see ftnt. 27
102. BA–MA RH 27-116/128, 2a-doc. 116th Pz.Div., proposal Hptmn. Kroll, Bernhard
103. BA–MA RH 24-58/16, KTB 58th Pz.Corps, 23 Dec 1944
104. BA–MA RH 24-58/15, 16 and 17, KTB 58th Pz.Corps, 23 Dec 1944; KTB 2d Bn./Arm.Art.Rgt. 146
105. BA–MA RH 19 IV/85, Anl.1683 and 1689, KTB Sup Cmd–West, 23–24 Dec 1944; Siebert, see ftnt. 64
106. BA–MA RH 24-58/16, KTB 58th Pz.Corps, 23 Dec 1944
107. BA–MA RH 24-58/17, KTB 58th Pz.Corps, 23 Dec 1944
108. See ftnt. 107
109. Vogelsang, diary
110. BA–MA RH 24-58/16, KTB 58th Pz.Corps, 23 Dec 1944
111. Draper, Thedore. *The 84th Infantry Division in the Battle of Germany 1944–May 1945.* (New York, 1946), 95ff
112. BA–MA RH 24-58/15 KTB 58th Pz.Corps, 24 Dec 1944
113. Guderian, Heinz Günther, see ftnt. 61
114. BA–MA RH 24-58/15, KTB 58th Pz.Corps, 24 Dec 1944
115. BA–MA RH 27-116/128, 2a-doc. 116th Pz.Div., Gefechtsbericht *(battle report);* Pz.Rgt.16 Sect.1a, 28 Dec 1944, Anl. *zu Vorschlag Oberst Bayer, Johannes, für die Nennung im Ehrenblatt des Heeres (Addendum to proposal Oberst Bayer, Johannes, for nomination in Honor Roll of the army)*
116. BA–MA RH 19 IV/85, Anl.1704, KTB Sup Cmd–West, 24 Dec 1944
117. BA–MA RH 24-58/15 and 17, KTB 58th Pz. Corps, 24 Dec 1944
118. See ftnt. 115; KTB 2d Bn./Pz.Rgt.16
119. BA–MA RH 24-58/17, KTB 58th Pz.Corps, 25 Dec 1944
120. KTB 2d Bn./Pz.Rgt.16
121. See ftnt. 115; KTB 2d Bn./Pz.Rgt.16
122. BA–MA RH 24-58/17, KTB 58th Pz.Corps, 25 Dec 1944
123. BA–MA RH 19 IV/85, Anl.1720, 1724, 1725, 1742, KTB Sup Cmnd–West, 25–26 Dec.44
124. BA–MA RH 19 IV/85, Anl. 1742, KTB Sup Cmd–West, 26 Dec 1944; BA–MA RH 24-58/15 and 17, KTB 58th Pz.Corps, 25–26 Dec 1944
125. BA–MA RH 24-58/15 and 17, KTB 58th Pz.Corps, 25 Dec 1944
126. BA–MA RH 24-58/17, KTB 58th Pz. Corps, 26 Dec 1944
127. BA–MA RH 19 IV/76 and 85, KTB Sup Cmd–West, 25 Dec 1944
128. BA–MA RH 19 IV/85, Anl.1725, KTB Sup Cmd–West, 25 Dec 1944
129. KTB 2d Bn./Pz.Rgt.16
130. BA–MA RH 19 IV/76 and 85, Anl.1733, 1742 and 1744, KTB Sup Cmd–West, 26 Dec 1944; BA–MA RH 24-58/15 and 17, KTB 58th Pz.Corps, 26–27 Dec 1944
131. See ftnt. 121
132. See ftnt. 121
133. BA–MA RH 27-116/128, 2a-doc. 116th Pz.Div., proposal Lt. Weissflog, Hans-Joachim
134. BA–MA RH 27-116/128, 2a-doc. 116th Pz.Div., proposal Oberst Bayer, Johannes; BA–MA RH 27-116/128, 2a-doc. 116th

Pz.Div., proposals Oberstltnt. Zander, Helmut and Oberfeldwebel Pichler, Joseph

135. BA–MA RH 24-58/15, KTB 58th Pz.Corps, 26 Dec 1944

136. BA–MA RH 24-58/15 and 17, KTB 58th Pz.Corps, 26 Dec 1944

137. Cole, loc. cit., 547ff; MacDonald IV, loc. cit., 560ff; Draper, loc. cit., 95ff

138. MacDonald IV, loc. cit., 573

139. Vogelsang, diary

140. Report 116th Pz.Div., Sect. 1a, 29 Dec 44, BA–MA RH 24-58/17, KTB 58th Pz. Corps

141. Vogelsang, diary

142. See ftnt. 140

143. BA–MA RH 2 from 542, weekly report Sup Cmd–West, 30 Dec 1944

144. Holtermann, Dr. Arthur, letter to Generalleutnant Count von Schwerin 28 Dec 1944

145. BA–MA RH 24-58/17, KTB 58th Pz. Corps, 27 Dec 1944

146. BA–MA RH 19 IV/86, Anl.1766, KTB Sup Cmd–West, 27 Dec 1944

147. Waldenburg, MS A-874, (since from memory, not without errors); KTB 2d Bn./Pz.Rgt.16; KTB 2d Bn./Pz.Art.Rgt 146; Order 116th Pz.Div., Sect. 1a 26 December from doc.-Arm.Art.Rgt. 146; BA–MA RH 24-58/15 and 17, KTB 58th Pz.Corps, 27–30 Dec 1944

148. BA–MA RH 24-58/32, KTB 58th Pz.Corps, Sect. Qu, 23 Dec 1944

149. BA–MA RH 24-58/17, KTB 58th Pz.Corps, 27 Dec 1944

150. BA–MA RH 19 IV/85, Anl.1742, KTB Sup Cmd–West, 26 Dec 1944; KTB 2d Bn./Pz.Rgt.16

151. Vogelsang, diary

152. BA–MA RH 19 IV/85, Anl.1742, KTB Sup Cmd–West, 26 Dec 1944

153. BA–MA RH 19 IV/76, 115, KTB Sup Cmd–West, 26 Dec 1944

154. See ftnt. 153, 118

155. See ftnt. 153, 118 and 119

156. KTB OKW, vol. IV, 2, 1344

157. BA–MA RH 19 IV/86, Anl.1768, KTB Sup Cmd–West, 27 Dec 1944

158. BA–MA RH 19 IV/86, Anl.1783, KTB Sup Cmd–West, 28 Dec 1944

159. BA–MA RH 19 IV/86, Anl.1852, KTB Sup Cmd–West, 31 Dec 1944

160. BA–MA RH 19 IV/86, Anl.1784 and 1829, KTB Sup Cmd–West, 28 and 30 Dec 1944

161. BA–MA RH 19 IV/86, Anl.1802, KTB Sup Cmd–West, 29 Dec 1944

162. BA–MA RH 19 IV/86, Anl.1799, KTB Sup Cmd–West, 29 Dec 1944

163. Heiper, 338ff

164. Jung, loc. cit., 182, quote from Jodl-journal 29 Dec 1944

165. Guderian, *Memories,* 346ff (errors regarding dates and number of divisions from the West)

CHAPTER 9, PART 3

1. BA–MA RH 19 IV/86, Anl.1778 and 1782, KTB Sup Cmd–West, 28 Dec 1944; BA–MA RH 24-58/15, KTB 58th Pz.Corps, 28 Dec 1944

2. BA–MA RH 24-58/17, KTB 58th Pz.Corps, 29–31 Dec 1944

3. Waldenburg, pocket calendar

4. BA–MA RH 24-58/15 and 17, KTB 58th Pz. Corps, 29 and 30 Dec 1944

5. BA–MA RH 24-58/17, KTB 58th Pz. Corps, 29 Dec 1944

6. BA–MA RH 19 IV/86, Anl.1817, KTB Sup Cmd–West, 30 Dec 1944; BA–MA RH 24-58th/17, KTB 58th Pz. Corps, 30 Dec 1944

7. BA–MA RH 19 IV/144, KTB OBWest Sect.Ic 1 Jan 1945

8. BA–MA RH 24-58/17, KTB 58th Pz. Corps, 29-31 Dec 1944

9. BA–MA RH 24-58/17, KTB 58th Pc. Crps 30 Dec 1944

10. BA–MA RH 19 IV/86, Anl.1829, KTB Sup Cmd–West, 30 Dec 1944

11. BA–MA RH 19 IV/86, Anl.1784, 1791, 1804, from 29 Dec 1814 from 30 Dec. 1836 from 31 Dec 1944, KTB Sup Cmd–West, 29–31 Dec 1944; BA–MA RH 24-58/15, KTB 58th Pz.Corps, 29 Dec 1944

12. KTB OKW, vol.IV, 2, 977; Jung, 186; Haupt, Werner. *Rückzug im Westen 1944, von der Invasion zur Ardennen (Offensive Retreat in the West 1944, from the Invasion to the Ardennes Offensive).* (Stuttgart: n.p., 1978), 319ff Kurowski, Franz. Von den Ardennen bis zum *Ruhrkessel (From the Ardennes to the kettle of the Ruhr).* (Klagenfurt, 1979), 116

13. Elmshorner Nachrichten (*Elmshorn News*) from 2 Jan 1945
14. Waldenburg, pocket calendar
15. Wolff-Boenisch, Richard, diary from 30 Dec 1944
16. Schwörer, Ernst, diary, 31 Dec 1944
17. Vogelsang, Fritz, diary, 3 Jan 1945
18. Nagel, Helmut, reports to the author
19. MacDonald, Charles B. *United States Army in WWII, the European Theater of Operations, The Last Offensive* (Washington, DC, 1973), 22 and 43ff; MacDonald IV, 604ff [hereafter, referred to as MacDonald V]; Toland, John. *Ardennenschlacht 1940* (Deutsche Ausgabe: Neuauflage 1973), 344ff; Thompson, R. W., *Die Schlacht um das Rheinland* (Klagenfurt, n.d.), 146ff; Draper, excerpt in German translation without more details. *History of the 53d (Welsh) Division,* no further details known, 98ff
20. BA–MA RH 24-58/17, KTB 58th Pz. Corps, 2 Jan 1945
21. *History of the 53d (Welsh) Division*, 104 ff
22. *Die Geheimen Tagesberichte der Deutschen Wehrmacht im Zweiten Weltkrieg, 1939 to 1945* (*The Secret Daily reports of the German Wehrmacht in WW II*). vol. 12, 1 Jan–9 May 1945, Osnabrück 1984, 3 Jan 1945, 10
23. BA–MA RH 24-58/17, KTB 58th Pz.Corps, 3 Jan 1945
25. BA–MA RH 27-116/124, Final report by 116th Pz.Div. about Defensive Battles, 3–15 Jan 1945
26. Elterlein, Max Dieter von, diary and letters to parents; Löhe, Hans-Wilhelm, diary; Kirchner, Siegfried, recollections
27. KTB OKW, vol.IV 2, 1345
28. See ftnt. 27, 1346
29. Vogelsang, diary, 4 Jan 1945
30. See ftnt. 25
31. See ftnt. 26
32. See ftnt 21, 106ff
33. Waldenburg, pocket calendar
34. KTB 2d Bn./Arm.Art.Rgt. 146
35. Draper, loc. cit., see ftnt. 19
36. Vogelsang, diary
37. KTB 2d Bn./Arm.Art.Rgt. 146
38. See ftnt. 25
39. KTB 2d Bn./Arm.Art.Rgt. 146
40. See ftnt. 25
41. Waldenburg, Siegfried von, MS A-874
42. See ftnt. 21, 109f
43. BA–MA RH 27-116/128, IIa-doc. 116th Pz.Div., Proposal Hptm. Krüger, Erich
44. See ftnt. 21, 110
45. KTB OKW, vol.IV, 2, 1346 and 1353
46. Vogelsang, diary
47. See ftnt. 25
48. KTB 2d Bn./Arm.Art.Rgt. 146, 8 Jan 1945
49. Elterlein, see ftnt. 26
50. Varnholt, Otto, notes
51. See ftnt. 22, 9 Jan 1945, 28
52. See ftnt. 25
53. Heiber, p. 788; BA–MA RH 27-116/128, IIa-doc., 116th Pz.Div., Proposal Oberlt. Varnholt, Otto
54. See ftnt. 22, 10 Jan 1945, 30
55. See ftnt. 22, 10 Jan 1945, 30
56. Waldenburg, MS A-874
57. Elterlein, see ftnt. 26
58. Waldenburg, pocket calendar
59. Vogelsang, diary
60. See ftnt. 25
61. See ftnt. 22, 12 Jan 1945, 36
62. Waldenburg, MS A-874
63. See ftnt. 22, 12 Jan 1945, 36
64. See ftnt. 25, there Jan 13 incorrect, correct: 12 Jan 1945
65. Varnholt, notes
66. BA–MA RH 27-116/128, IIa-doc. 116h Pz.Div., proposal Hptmn. Banaski, Ernst
67. See ftnt. 25
68. KTB 2d Bn./Arm.Art.Rgt. 146, 12 Jan 1945
69. Vogelsang, diary
70. See ftnt. 22, 12–13 Jan 1945, 35 resp. 38
71. See ftnt. 22, 13 Jan 1945, 39 and 40
72. KTB 2d Bn./Arm.Art.Rgt. 146
73. BA–MA RH 27-116/128, IIa-doc. 116th Pz.Div., proposal Lt. Junge, Oskar
74. Draper, loc. cit., see ftnt. 19
75. See ftnt. 25
76. Waldenburg, MS A-874
77. Vogelsang, diary, 14 Jan 1945
78. See ftnt. 22, 14 Jan 1945, 42
79. See ftnt. 25
80. Ritgen, 263f.
81. See ftnt. 25
82. KTB 2d Bn./Arm.Art.Rgt. 146
83. Elterlein, see ftnt. 26
84. Varnholt, notes

85. BA–MA RH 27-116/128, IIa-doc, 116th Pz.Div., proposal Oberlt. Varnholt, Otto
86. See ftnt. 25
87. Waldenburg, pocket calendar
88. KTB OKW, vol.IV, 2, 1353
89. Lucht, Walter, MS B-769
90. Waldenburg, MS A-874
91. See ftnt. 25
92. KTB 2d Bn./Arm.Art.Rgt. 146
93. Elterlein, see ftnt. 26
94. Reprint "With the 2d Armored Division between Beffe and Houffalize," probably from Houston, Donald E., *Hell on Wheels: The 2d Armored Division* (San Rafael, CA, 1977)
95. See ftnt. 25
96. Vogelsang, diary
97. Wolff-Boenisch, diary, 17 Jan 1945
98. KTB 2d Bn./Arm.Art.Rgt. 146
99. Waldenburg, pocket calendar
100. Vogelsang, diary
101. Holtermann, Dr. Arthur, letter to Generalleutnant Count von Schwerin, 23 Jan 1945
102. Vogelsang, diary
103. See ftnt. 22, 17–28 Jan 1945, 51ff
104. Waldenburg, pocket calendar
105. See ftnt. 22, 19 Jan 1945, 58
106. KTB OKW, vol.IV, 2, 1352 and 1354,
107. Ibid, 1355
108. Waldenburg, pocket calendar
109. KTB 2d Bn./Arm.Art.Rgt. 146; KTB 116th Pz.Div, 25 January to 27 Feb 1945, BA–MA RH 27-116/132
110. Waldenburg, pocket calendar
111. Vogelsang,diary
112. Letter Lt. of Reserve Gerke to Oberlt. of Reserve Köhn, 27 Feb 45, copy in possession of author
113. KTB 116th Pz.Div., 25 Jan 1945, see ftnt. 109
114. Vogelsang, diary
115. KTB 116th Pz.Div., 27 Jan 1945, see ftnt. 109
116. KTB Arm.Art.Rgt. 146, 28 Jan–3 February 1945
117. KTB 116th Pz.Div., 28 Jan 1945, see ftnt. 109
118. KTB 116th Pz.Div., 29 Jan 1945, see ftnt. 109; Waldenburg, pocket calendar, 29 Jan 1945
119. KTB 116th Pz.Div., 29 Jan 1945, see ftnt. 109; Waldenburg, pocket calendar, 30 Jan 1945
120. KTB 116th Pz.Div., 31 Jan 1945, see ftnt 109
121. See ftnt. 22, reports from 30 Jan 1945ff
122. Guderian, *Memories,* 356
123. Ibid, 367

CHAPTER 10

1. MacDonald V, 4ff and 135ff
2. Ellis, L.F., *Victory in the West* (London, 1968), 250ff; Stacey, Charles Perry, *The Victory Campaign: The Operations in North-West Europe 1944-1945* (Ottawa 1960), 460ff; Thompson, R.W., *Die Schlacht um das Rheinland (The Battle for the Rhineland),* (Frauenfeld, n.d.), 190ff
3. BA–MA RH 19/IV/144, KTB Sup Cmd–West Ic, Daily report 5 Feb 1945; BA–MA RH 27-116/122, KTB 116. Pz.Div., 25 Jan-27 Feb 1945, entries from 4 Feb 1945, in future KTB 116th Pz.Div.; KTB OKW, vol.IV, 2, 1082 and 1083; Geyer, Rolf, MS B-147; Fiebig, Heinz, MS B-843; Schlemm, Alfred, *Mitteilungsblatt des Bundes Deutscher Fallschirmjäger e.V. und des Kameradschaftsbundes Fall-schirm-Panzerkorps H.G., mitte 1969, nach Bernhard, Herbert, 1945, Die Entscheidungsschlacht am Nieder Rhein* (Wesel, 1976), 59/60
4. Geyer and Fiebig, see ftnt. 3; Bernhard, loc. cit., 61; Bosch, Heinz, Der Zeite Weltkrieg zwischen Rhein und Maas, Geldern 1971, 190ff; *The Second World War between Rhine and Maas;* Busch, Erich, Die Fallschirmjäger-Chronik 1935-1945, Friedberg 1983, 88 and 154 *The Paratrooper Chronicle 1935–1945*
5. Geyer, MS B-147
6. KTB 116th Pz.Div., 1 Feb 1945
7. KTB 116th Pz.Div., 2 Feb 1945
8. KTB 116th Pz.Div., 2–4 Feb 1945
9. KTB 116th Pz.Div., 4 Feb 1945
10. Bernhard, loc. cit., 61; Franck, Burkhard, et.al., Text zur Battlefield Tour of Operation Veritable der Northag im Jahre 1982
11. KTB 116th Pz.Div., 4 Feb 1945
12. See ftnt. 11

13. KTB 116th Pz.Div., 1 Feb 1945; Order 116. Pz.Div., Sect. Ia 1 Feb 1945, docs. Arm.Art.Rgt. 146
14. KTB 116.Pz.Div, 5 Feb 1945
15. Vogelsang, Fritz, diary
16. KTB 2d Bn./Arm.Art.Rgt. 146, 5–10 Feb 1945
17. KTB 116th Pz.Div., 6 Feb 1945
18. KTB 116th Pz.Div., 7 Feb 1945
19. KTB 116th Pz.Div., 7–8 Feb 1945
20. KTB OKW vol.IV, 2, 1364
21. KTB 116. Pz.Div., 8 Feb 1945
22. BA–MA RH 2, vol.542, doc. OKH weekly reports Sup Cmd–West
23. KTB 116th Pz.Div., 10 Feb 1945
24. KTB 116th Pz.Div., 10–11 Feb 1945
25. Waldenburg, Siegfried von, MS B-215
26. See ftnt. 25
27. KTB 2d Bn./Arm.Art.Rgt. 146, 11 Feb 1945
28. Vogelsang, diary
29. See ftnt. 2 and text to Battlefield Tour as in ftnt. 10
30. Fiebig, MS B-843
31. Geyer, MS B-147
32. Bosch, loc. cit. 195/196; Busch, loc. cit. 141/142 and 154
33. Stacey, loc. cit. 476f; Ellis, loc. cit. 262
34. Bernstorff, Douglas Count von, MS B-601; Fiebig, MS B-843; Bosch, loc. cit. 196
35. Fiebig, MS B-843
36. Geyer, MS B-147
37. Bernstorff, MS B-601
38. KTB 116th Pz.Div. 12 Feb 1945
39. Waldenburg, MS B-215
40. KTB 116th Pz.Div. 11–12 Feb 1945; BA–MA RH 27-116/125, *Kampfbericht der 116th Pz.Div. 12 Mar 1945 über den Einsatz der Division am Nieder Rhein 11 February-9 Mar 1945, in Zukunft, Kampfbericht 116th Pz.Div.* (Combat Report of 116th Pz.Div. 12 Mar 1945, about the deployment of the division at the Lower Rhine 11 Feb.-9 Mar 1945, in the future, Combat Report 116th Pz.Div.)
41. Waldenburg, MS B-215
42. See ftnt. 40
43. See ftnt. 40
44. Bernstorff, MS B-601
45. KTB 116th Pz.Div. 13 Feb 1945
46. Befehl *(order)* Order of the 116th Pz.Div., Sect. Ia, 13 Feb 1945, 0100 hours for Defense on 13 Feb. English translation in Intelligence Summary 148 of 43d (Wessex) Division. Retranslated by the author; in paragraph 4c: the "1st Battalion" being relieved probably was 1st Battalion, Pz.Gren.Rgt.60
47. KTB 116th Pz.Div. 13 Feb 1945
48. Vogelsang, diary
49. KTB and combat report 116th Pz.Div. 14 Feb 1945
50. KTB 2d Bn./Arm.Art.Rgt. 146 14 Feb 1945
51. See ftnt. 49
52. BA–MA RH 19 IV/144, KTB Sup Cmd–West Ic 14 Feb 1945
53. KTB 2d Bn./Arm.Art.Rgt. 146 14 Feb 1945
54. Vogelsang, diary 14 Feb 1945
55. BA–MA RH 27-116/128, IIa-doc. 116 Pz.Div., Proposal Leutnant Käseberg, Herbert; Fellgiebel, Walther-Peer. *Die Träger des Ritterkreuzes des Eisernen Kreuzes, 1939–1945.* (Friedberg, 1986), 248
56. Combat report 116th Pz.Div., 14 Feb 1945
57. KTB 2d Bn./Arm.Art.Rgt. 146, 15 Feb 1945
58. KTB 116th Pz.Div. 15 Feb 1945
59. KTB and combat report 116th Pz.Div., 15 Feb 1945; KTB 2d Bn./Arm.Art.Rgt. 146, 15 Feb 1945
60. Document of 116th Pz.Div. for Wachtmeister Frey, Georg, 28 Mar 1945
61. BA–MA RH 27-116/128, 279, IIa-doc. 116th Pz.Div., proposal Hauptmann von Hütz, Leopold.
62. KTB 116th Pz.Div., 15 Feb 1945
63. BA–MA RH 27-116/128, IIa-doc. 116th Pz.Div., proposal Oberstleutnant Zander, Helmut; Fellgiebel, loc. cit., 455
64. BA–MA RH 27-116/128, IIa-doc.116th Pz.Div., proposal Hauptmann Schneider, Paul
65. Waldenburg, MS B-215
66. KTB and combat report 116th Pz.Div., 16 Feb 1945; KTB 2d Bn./Arm.Art.Rgt. 146, 16 Feb 1945
67. BA–MA RH 27-116/128, IIa-doc. 116th Pz.Div., proposal Oberlt. Gebauer, Josef.

68. KTB and combat report 116th Pz.Div., 16 Feb 1945; KTB 2d Bn./Arm.Art.Rgt. 146, 16 Feb 1945; Waldenburg, MS B-215; Vogelsang, diary 16 Feb 1945

69. KTB 116th Pz.Div., 17 Feb 1945; Waldenburg, MS B-215

70. KTB 116th Pz.Div., 17 Feb 1945; Bernstorff, MS B-601

71. *Die Geheimen Tagesberichte der Deutschen Wehrmachtführung im Zweiten Weltkrieg*, vol. 12, 182, report from 16 Feb 1945

72. Bernstorff, MS B-601; Busch, loc. cit., 142 (not quite without mistakes)

73. Stacey, loc. cit.; 478ff Ellis, loc. cit., 265ff; Thompson, loc. cit., 240ff; Withaker, W. Denis and Withaker, Shelagh, *Rheinland: The Battle to End the War* (Toronto, 1989), 80ff and 140ff

74. KTB 116th Pz.Div., 17 Feb 1945; Am Lindchen at road crossing southeast Gr.Ackershof

75. Vogelsang, diary

76. This and the following report about 18–19 Feb 1945, according to the KTB and combat report of the 116th Pz.Div.; KTB 2d Bn./Arm.Art.Rgt. 146, 18–19 Feb 1945

77. BA–MA RH 7, vol.385, 1-6, doc.OKH PA/P5 30 Apr 1945, proposal Major Jungwirth, Hans.

78. Fellgiebel, loc. cit., 247

79. Vogelsang, diary, 19 Feb 1945

80. Bernstorff, MS B-601

81. Bernstorff, MS B-601; Meindl, Eugen, MS B-051; Fiebig, MS B-843; KTB and combat report 116th Pz.Div., 17–18 Feb 1945

82. KTB OKW vol.IV, 2, 1364ff

83. Bernstorff, MS B-601; Ritgen, 271ff; Hudel, Helmut, MS B-768

84. KTB and combat report 116th Pz.Div., 19–20 Feb 1945; see ftnt. 83

85. KTB 116th Pz.Div., 20 Feb 1945

86. KTB and combat report 116th Pz.Div., 20–21 Feb 1945; Bernstorff, MS B-601

87. Withaker, loc. cit., 138/139; Thompson, loc. cit., 257f

88. Vogelsang, diary

89. Schwörer, Ernst, diary 18 Feb 1945

90. Stacey, loc. cit. 482ff; Ellis, loc. cit., 268ff; Withaker, loc. cit., 152ff

91. KTB 2d Bn./Pz.Ar.tRgt.146

92. KTB and combat report 116th Pz.Div., 22–23 Feb 1945

93. Vogelsang, diary

94. KTB and combat report 116th Pz.Div., 24–25 Feb 1945

95. Vogelsang, diary

96. MacDonald V, loc. cit., 145ff; Thompson, loc. cit., 259ff

97. KTB OKW vol.IV, 2, 1372ff

98. Ritgen, loc. cit., 276ff

99. KTB OKW, vol. IV, 2, 1373/1374

100. KTB and combat report 116th Pz.Div. 26 Feb 1945; report of Combat Group Tebbe for the period of 18 Feb–10 Mar 1945, copy with the author.

101. KTB 2d Bn./Arm.Art.Rgt. 146, 26 Feb 1945

102. Walter, Otto, Hauptmann and Cdr., 1st Bn., Parachute Infantry Regiment 7 in a letter to Bosch, Heinz, (see ftnt. 4)

103. KTB 116th Pz.Div., 26 Feb 1945

104. See ftnt. 103

105. See ftnt. 103 and control card General Staff Army, org. sect. of Army Pz.Jg.Sect. (38t,) 741

106. Vogelsang, diary, 26 Feb 1945

107. KTB 116th Pz.Div., 27 Feb 1945

108. Bernstorff, MS B-601

109. See ftnt. 107; Combat report Combat Group Tebbe (see ftnt. 100)

110. Combat report 116th Pz.Div., 27 Feb 1945

111. BA–MA RH 27 116/128, IIa-doc. 116th Pz.Div., proposal Hauptmann von Hütz, Leopold.

112. KTB 116th Pz.Div., 27 Feb 1945

113. Varnholt, Otto, notes

114. KTB 116th Pz.Div., 27 Feb 1945

115. Dörr, Manfred, Information from his file; Fellgiebel, loc. cit., 236

116. KTB 116th Pz.Div., 27 Feb 1945

117. Combat report 116th Pz.Div., 28 Feb 1945; Telephone log of duty officer with the Ia of the 116th Pz.Div., 28 Feb 1945, [hereafter, "log"]

118. KTB 2d Bn./Arm.Art.Rgt. 146, 28 Feb 1945

119. Bernstorff, MS B-601

120. Log, 28 Feb 1945

121. Log, 28 Feb 1945

122. BA–MA RH 7, doc.-OKH PA/P5, 28 Feb 1945; Proposal Generalmajor von Waldenburg
123. Combat report 116th Pz.Div. 1–2 Mar 1945
124. Log, 2 Mar 1945
125. Combat report Combat Group Tebbe, see ftnt. 100
126. Log, 2 Mar 1945
127. Waldenburg, pocket calendar
128. Combat report 116th Pz.Div., 3 Mar 1945
129. Log, 3 Mar 1945; Order 116th Pz.Div., Commander 6 Mar 1945, from doc. Arm. Art.Rgt. 146
130. Bernstorff, MS B-601
131. Stacey, loc. cit., 491ff; Ellis, loc. cit., 271ff; Withaker, loc. cit., 192ff; Thompson, loc. cit., 268ff
132. MacDonald V, loc. cit., 171ff; BA–MA RH 19 IV/144, KTB Sup Cmd–West Ic 2/-3 Mar 1945
133. Geyer, MS B-147; Schlemm, Alfred, MS B-084
134. Schlemm, MS B-084
135. KTB 2d Bn./Arm.Art.Rgt. 146, 4 Mar 1945
136. Schlemm, MS B-084
137. KTB OKW, vol.Iv, 2, 1612
138. Combat report 116th Pz.Div., 2/3 Mar 1945
139. Log, 3 Mar 1945, 1000 hours
140. Combat report, 3/4 Mar 1945
141. Waldenburg, Siegfried von, MS B-224
142. Combat report 116th Pz.Div., 5 Mar 1945
143. Log, 5 Mar 1945; KTB 2d Bn./Arm.Art. Rgt. 146, 5 Mar 1945
144. BA–MA RH 27-116/128, IIa-doc. 116th Pz.Div., proposal Oberleutnant Varnholt, Otto
145. BA–MA RH 27-116/128, IIa-doc. 116th Pz.Div., proposal Feldwebel Muster, Fritz; BA–MA RH 7, vol. 283, doc.-OKH PA/P5, 27 Apr 1945
146. Combat report 116th Pz.Div., 6 Mar 1945
147. KTB 2d Bn./Arm.Art.Rgt. 146, 6 Mar 1945
148. Log, 6 Mar 1945; Ritgen, loc. cit., 282; Hudel, MS B-768
149. Schlemm, MS B-084
150. Log, 6 Mar 1945
151. Waldenburg, MS B-224
152. Combat report 116th Pz.Div., 7 Mar 1945
153. KTB 2d Bn./Arm.Art.Rgt. 146
154. Log, 7 Mar 1945
155. Holtermann, pocket calendar, 7 Mar 1945
156. Combat report, 8 Mar 1945
157. KTB 2d Bn./Arm.Art.Rgt. 146, 8 Mar 1945
158. Log, 8 Mar 1945
159. Meindl, Eugen, MS B-051
160. Log, 8 Mar 1945
161. Meindel, Eugen, MS B-051, and 093
162. Schlemm, MS B-084
163. Meindl, MS B-093
164. Log, 9 Mar 1945
165. Log, 10 Mar 1945
166. Combat report, summary
167. MacDonald V, loc. cit., 176ff
168. MacDonald V, loc. cit., 183
169. Stacey, loc. cit., 522
170. KTB OKW, vol. IV, 2, 1165

CHAPTER 11

1. Log, 11 Mar 1945
2. Log, 12 Mar 1945
3. Waldenburg, Siegfried von, pocket calendar
4. Guderian, Heiz Günther, *Die Kämpfe der 116.-Panzer Division vom 24.3. bis 16.4. 1945 (The Battles of the 116th Pz.Div. from 24 March to 16 Apr 1945)* (The Ruhr Cauldron) MS B-713
5. Log, 11 and 15 Mar 1945
6. Zanzinger, Erich, diary
7. Vogeksang, Fritz, memories in addition to his diary
8. BA–MA RH 10/101, Blatt 59–61, order General Inspector of Panzer Troops, OKH/Gen St d H/Org Sect. Nr. I/1600 1945 g.Kdos. 25 Mar 1945
9. Log, 15 Mar 1945
10. Schwörer, Ernst, diary
11. Zanzinger, Erich, enclosure in diary
12. Order Pz.Rgt.16 Nr.15 1945 13 Mar 1945 doc. orders Pz.Rgt.16 in Tebbe docs.
13. Log, 15 Mar 1945
14. Order Pz.Rgt.16 Nr. 17 1945, 21 Mar 1945 see ftnt. 12
15. Order XLVII Pz. Corps, 26 Mar 1945 from doc. Tebbe, Gerhard

16. Information Tebbe, Gerhard; Stephan, Eberhard; Bröker, Ernst; Nommensen, Richard and diary Zanzinger
17. Waldenburg, pocket calendar
18. Vogelsang, loc. cit.
19. Waldenburg, pocket calendar
20. Wegmann, Günter, "*Das Kriegsende zwischen Niederrhein, Emsland und Teutoburger Wald im März/Apr 1945*," in *Osnabrücker Mitteilungen,* 83d vol., 1977, 152
21. Geyer, Rolf, MS B-414
22. Mattenklott, Otto, MS B-217; Karst, Friedrich, MS B-319; Wegmann, loc. cit. 152, 174, 203–/204
23. Wilmot, 734
24. Ellis, 282ff; MacDonald V, 296ff; Davis, Franklin, M. *Across the Rhine, World War II* (Time-Life: Alexandria, VA, 1980), 78ff
25. *Die Geheimen Tagesberichte der Deutschen Wehmacht im Zweiten Weltkrieg 1939–1945,* vol 12, 1 Jan–9 May 1945, Osnabrück 1984, 208ff; KTB OKW vol. IV, 2, 1165ff–also see ftnt. 24
26. Kesselring, Albert, MS T-123
27. Waldenburg, pocket calendar; Zanzinger, diary
28. Log, 23 Mar 1945
29. Guderian, MS B-713
30. Log, 24 Mar 1945, also the following quotes and declarations
31. Holtermann, pocket calendar
32. Waldenburg, pocket calendar
33. Log, 24 and 25 Mar 1945
34. Guderian, MS B-713
35. Zanzinger, diary; Schmeermann, Heinz, diary; Schwörer, Ernst, diary
36. Kaspers, Walter, diary
37. Log, 25 Mar 1945
38. Zanzinger, diary
39. Schmeermannn and Schwörer, diaries
40. Log, 25 Mar 1945
41. Log, 25 Mar 1945
42. Zanzinger, diary
43. Guderian, MS B-713
44. Log, 25 Mar 1945, also the following declaration
45. Ellis, loc. cit. 228ff; MacDonald V, loc. cit. 303ff; Davis, loc. cit. 83ff
46. Geyer, MS B-414; Wegmann, loc. cit. 175
47. Lüttwitz, Heinrich Baron von, MS B-198

48. MacDonald V, loc. cit. 306ff
49. MacDonald V, loc. cit. 315
50. MacDonald V, loc. cit. 316
51. MacDonald V, loc. cit. 317
52. Ibid
53. MacDonald V, loc. cit. 318 and 319
54. MacCormac, John, in the *New York Times,* 28 and 29 Mar 1945
55. Leach, Charles R., *In Tornados Wake: A History of the 8th Armored Division,* (Chicago, 1956), 1359ff; author unknown, *The Story of the 8th Armored Division,* (n.p., n.d.) 22 (probably precursor of "In Tornados Wake" right after end of war.)
56. MacDonald V, loc. cit. 357; Ellis, loc. cit. 293; MacCormac, loc. cit. 29 Mar 1945
57. MacDonald V, loc. cit. 351 and 347
58. Ellis, loc. cit. 296ff; MacDonald V, loc. cit. 339ff; Wilmot, loc. cit. 740ff
59. Zanzinger, diary
60. Log, 25 Mar 1945
61. Guderian, Heinz Günther, own memories; Kaspers, diary
62. Log, 25 Mar 1945
63. Guderian, MS B-713; Lüttwitz, MS B-198; Steinmüller, Walter, MS B-314; Lackner, Walter, MS B-508
64. Guderian, MS B-713
65. Log, 26 and 27 Mar 1945 0330 hours
66. Guderian, MS B-713; Log, 27 Mar 1945; Hammer, Ernst, MS B-195
67. Log, 27 Mar 1945
68. Zanzinger, diary
69. Guderian, MS B-713
70. Log, 28 Mar 1945
71. Schwörer, diary 28 Mar 1945
72. Guderian, Heinz Günther, memories
73. Tebbe, Gerhard, report to the author
74. Adam, Werner, post-war report, copied in *Der Grosse Kessel;* Mues, Willi, Erwitte/ Lippstadt 1984 267 and 591
75. Record of events, 9th US Army 27–30 Mar 1945
76. Log, 28 Mar 1945
77. Guderian, MS B-713; Log, Anl. Reconnaissance reports 28–30 Mar 1945
78. Geyer, MS B-414; Blumentritt, Günther, MS B-354
79. Zanzinger, diary
80. Log, 29 Mar 1945
81. Zanzinger, diary

82. Guderian, MS B-713; Log, 29 Mar 1945
83. Geyer, MS B-414
84. Lüttwitz, MS B-198
85. Wagener, Carl Gustav, MS B-593
86. Bayerlein, Fritz, MS B-396
87. Guderian, MS B-713; Log, 30 Mar 1945; Zanzinger, diary; Schwörer, diary
88. Log, 30 Mar 1945
89. Guderian, MS B-713
90. Elterlein, Max Dieter von, diary
91. Gillhaus, Karl Heinrich, post-war report
92. Log, annex to reconnaissance report 30 Mar 1945
93. Guderian, MS B-713; Log, 31 Mar 1945
94. Zanzinger, diary
95. Schwörer, diary
96. Bülow, Wolf-Dietrich von, MS B-199
97. Waldenburg, pocket calendar
98. Guderian, MS B-713
99. Ibid; Log 1 Apr 1945
100. Lüttwitz, MS B-198
101. Log, 1 Apr 1945
102. Guderian, MS B-713
103. Log, 1 Apr 1945
104. Elterlein, diary
105. Zanzinger, diary
106. Waldenburg, pocket calendar
107. Dunker, Rudolf, *Die Übergabe der Stadt Beckum, Bericht für die Stadtchronik der Stadt Beckum vom 1. Juni 1947;* Wegmann, Günter, *"Das Kriegsende zwischen Niederrhein, Emsland und Teutoburger Wald im März/Apr 1945, II. Teil,"* in *Osnabrücker Mitteilungen,* vol. 84 1978, 131ff; Inboden, August Wilhelm, letter to the author
108. Log, 2 Apr 1945
109. Guderian, MS B-713
110. Secret daily reports 30 Mar–2 Apr 1945; MacDonald V, loc. cit. 357ff and 379; Ellis, loc. cit. 319ff; Mues, loc. cit. 267ff. Mues based his reports of the battles on the history of the 8th Armored Division (see ftnt. 55) and on the 95th Inf.Div.; Fuermann, George M., Cranz, Edward F. *Ninety-Fifth Infantry Division History 1918 to 1946* (Atlanta, GA, n.d.)
111. HGr B, Situation evaluation 31 Mar 1945 1845 hours, copy with author
112. BA-MA RH 2 V 325, daily report West, 2–8 Apr 1945; Secret daily reports 31 Mar–4 Apr 1945; Estor, Fritz, MS B-581; Flörke, Hermann, MS B-329, 383, 607; Fretter, Pico, Maximilian, MS B-508, 569; Wagener, MS B-593; Mattenklott, MS B-217
113. Geyer, MS B-354; Blumentritt, MS B-354; Mottenklott, MS B-217
114. Zanzinger, diary
115. Schwörer, diary
116. Log, 3 Apr 1945
117. Tzschentke, Hans-Joachim in Mues, loc. cit. 237
118. Log, 3 Apr 1945
119. Dunker, loc. cit.
120. Zanzinger, diary
121. Guderian, MS B-713
122. Zanzinger, diary
123. Guderian, MS B-713
124. Varnholt, Otto, notes
125. Guderian, MS B-713
126. Log, 4 Apr 1945
127. Guderian, MS B-713
128. Zanzinger, diary 4 Apr 1945
129. Varnholt, notes
130. Guderian, MS B-713
131. Schwörer, diary 4 Apr 1945
132. Guderian, MS B-713
133. Log, 4 Apr 1945
134. Mues, loc. cit. 256
135. Ibid., 254
136. Secret daily reports, 4 Apr 1945
137. Guderian, MS B-713; Mues, loc. cit. 256ff
138. Varnholt, notes
139. Zanzinger, diary; Waldenburg, calendar
140. Guderian, MS B-713
141. Log, 6 Apr 1945, last entry!
142. Guderian, MS B-713; Mues, loc. cit. 267ff
143. Schmeermann, diary
144. Schwörer, diary
145. Zanzinger, diary
146. Elterlein, diary
147. Mues, loc. cit. 300 and 301
148. Guderian, MS B-713. In this report to the US Army, I dated the breakthrough south of Soest as the evening of 7 April. The different entries in diaries and the American documents show that it happened 6 April.
149. Hess, Karl, diary
150. Guderian, MS B-713
151. Mues, loc. cit. 243ff; MacDonald V, loc. cit. 363ff; Record of events of 9th Army 4–7 Apr 1945

152. Wirtz, Richard, MS B-714
153. Schwörer, diary
154. Zanzinger, diary
155. Mues, loc. cit. 301
156. Zanzinger, diary
157. Mues, loc. cit. 314
158. Varnholt, notes
159. Dunker, loc. cit.
160. Zanzinger, diary
161. Guderian, MS B-713; Lüttwitz, MS B-198
162. Guderian, MS B-713
163. Leach, loc. cit. 164, quoted from Mues 314
164. Dunker, loc. cit.; Mues, loc. cit. 315 and 317; Euler, Helmuth, *Die Entscheidungsschlacht an Rhein und Ruhr 1945,* (Stuttgart, 3d edition, 1981) 216ff
165. Schwörer, diary
166. Zanzinger, diary
167. Euler, loc. cit. 198–199; Meus, loc. cit. 318ff
168. Guderian, MS B-713; Lüttwitz, MS B-198; Hammer, MS B-195
169. Mues, loc. cit. 308ff
170. Zanzinger, diary
171. Waldenburg, pocket calendar
172. Schmeermann, diary
173. Schwörer, diary
174. Zanzinger, diary
175. Varnholt, notes
176. Zanzinger, diary
177. Guderian, MS B-713; Lüttwitz, MS B-198; Hammer, MS B-195; Bayerlein, MS B-396 and 836
178. Guderian, MS B-713
179. Lüttwitz, MS B-198
180. Guderian, MS B-713
181. Mues. loc. cit. 330ff
182. Schwörer, diary
183. Zanzinger, diary
184. Guderian, MS B-713
185. BA–MA RH 2 V 326; daily reports West 9 to 15 Apr 1945; Lüttwitz, MS B-198; Hammer, MS B-195; Wirtz, MS B-714; Zangen, Gustav von, MS B-849
186. Guderian, MS B-713
187. Zanzinger, diary
188. Mues. loc. cit. 334ff, 340ff, 584ff, based on report by Scherf, Walter; Ernst, Albert; Rose, Herbert; and the history of the 8th Armored Div.; Scherf, Walter, letters to the author 10 and 21 May 1988; Rose, Herbert, letters from the years 1980 and 1985

189. Lüttwitz, MS B-198
190. Secret daily reports 11 and 12 Apr 1945; BA–MA RH 2 V 326, daily reports West, 11 and 12 Apr 1945
191. Guderian MS B-713
192. Wirtz, MS B-714
193. Köchling, Friedrich, MS B-614
194. Ritgen, Helmuth, p307
195. Schwörer, diary
196. Zanzinger, dairy
197. Mues, loc. cit. 343ff and 468ff
198. Guderian, MS B-713
199. Ibid.
200. Dunker, loc. cit.
201. Waldenburg, Siegfried von, addition to MS B-713 30 October '47
202. Bayerlein, MS B-836
203. BA–MA RH 2 V 326, daily reports West 14 and 15 Apr 1945; Lüttwitz, MS B-198; Zangen, MS B-849
204. Guderian, MS B-713
205. Mues, loc. cit. 494 and 500
206. Ritgen, loc. cit. 308
207. Mues, loc. cit. 497
208. Guderian, MS B-713
209. Waldenburg, additions to MS B-713
210. Weyand, Josef, letter from 16 Nov 1987 with original note from 1945
211. Ibid.
212. Bayerlein, MS B-836
213. Elterlein, diary
214. Schwörer, diary
215. Elterlein and Schwörer, diaries
216. Mattischewski, Hans, diary
217. Mues, loc. cit. 520ff
218. Secret daily reports, 13 to 16 Apr 1945
219. Wagener, MS B-593
220. Wagener, Carl Gustav, "*Kampf und Ende der Heeresgruppe B,*" in *Wehrwissenschaftlicher Rundschau,* 10 1957
221. Guderian, MS B-713

CHAPTER 12
1. Guderian, MS B-713; Degenhard, Ernst, post-war report
2. MacDonald V, Map XIV; Record of events of the 9th US Army
3. Leisgang, Ambrosius, post-war report; Jordan, Justin, post-war report; Schmitz, Hebert, diary; Borgert, Wenzel, report to the author
4. Beckmann, Gustav, diary

5. Nommensen, Richard, letter to the author 1 July 1984
6. Löffler, Jürgen, H.G., report to the author
7. Degenhard, loc. cit.
8. Jordan, loc. cit.
9. Degenhard, loc. cit.
10. Brühl, Friedrich Count von, letter to the author
11. Beckmann, diary; Weissflog, Hans Joachim, post-war notes; Golly, Reinhard, post-war notes; Trösch, Franz, post-war notes; Borgert, reports to the author
12. MacDonald V, loc. cit., 379ff; Record of events of the Ninth Army; *The secret daily reports of the German Wehrmacht in WW II 1939–1945* vol.12, 1 Jan–9 Sep, Ossnabrück 1984, report from 6 Apr 1945
13. Estor, Fritz, MS B-581; Flörke, Hermann, MS B-329, 382, 383, 607; Fretter-Pico, Maximilian, MS B-568, 569; Mattenklott, Franz, MS B-717; Voigt, Horst, Dissertation of Situation Harz 17 August 1980
14. Kesselring, Albert. *Soldat bis zum letzten Tag.* (Bonn, 1953), 388ff
15. Estor, MS B-581
16. See ftnt. 13
17. Bradley, Dermot, Walther Wenck, Ossnabrück 1981, 335ff
18. MacDonald V, loc. cit., 386, 391, 401ff, map 6 on 403; Bornemann, Manfred, *Schicksals Tage in Harz.* (Clausthal-Zellerfeld, 1981), 27ff
19. Bornemann, loc. cit., 30
20. Estor, MS B-581; Mattenklott, MS B-217; G-2 periodic report #293 of 1st US ID, 11 Apr 1945. Copy in possession of author
21. Original order in possession of August, Count von Kageneck. Copy in possession of author
22. Bornemann, loc. cit., 37 and 38, 73 and 74
23. Beinlich, Joachim, unpublished dissertation, The End of the 9th Pz.Div.
24. Uhl, Dr. Hans, letter to the author 29 Sep 1988
25. Bornemann, loc. cit., 82
26. Beckmann, diary; Golly, post-war notes; Weissflog, post-war notes; Schmidt, Hans-Roland, reports to the author; Frickenstein, Karl-Heinz, diary
27. Beckmann, diary
28. Beckmann, diary
29. Bornemann, loc. cit., 88
30. See ftnt. 26.
31. Frickenstein, diary
32. Estor, MS B-581
33. Copy of original order in possession of author
34. Bradley, loc. cit., 340; Unrein, Martin, MS B-350; Mehner, Kurt, Draft for composition about Division "Clausewitz"; Bahr, Manfred, Battle of Ülzen and Panzer Division "Clausewitz" in combat troops-combat support troops, February 1982; Kurowski, Franz, Army Wenck, Neckargemünd 1967, 47ff; Gellermann, Günter Walter, Army Wenck, Inaugural dissertation, Cologne 1981, 25
35. Kempe, Hans, post-war report
36. See ftnts. 34 and 35
37. Leisgang, post-war report
38. N.a. *The Story of the 8th Armored Division,* (N.p., n.d.) 28
39. Bornemann, loc. cit., 49
40. Bradley, loc. cit., 348
41. Secret daily reports, 16 Apr 1945
42. Bradley, loc. cit., 350
43. Bradley, loc. cit., 358
44. Bradley, loc. cit., 366
45. KTB OKW, vol.IV, 2, 1581ff
46. Ellis, 327 and 331

INDEX

Abt, Ernst 85, 277
Adam, Theodor 492
Adam, Werner 199, 242–4, 246, 256, 415, 429, 437, 481
Agne, Karl 232, 484
Albert, Heinz 212
Alpers, Richard 488
Alsleben, Rolf 224
Ammermann, Theodor 483
Andreis, Karl 311, 487, 492
Appel, Hans 98, 216
Arnold, Helmut 476
Auert, Heinz 411, 494
Aufleger, Paul 490

Baecker, Horst 484
Baedeker, Dietrich 18, 79, 481
Banaski, Ernest 275, 355, 486
Bargstädt, Hans-Richard 108, 109, 112–13, 247
Bartels, Helmut 323, 488
Baselt, Dr.med. Gerhard 293, 480
Bauer, Anton 450
Baumgarten-Crusius, Werner 230, 331, 338, 488, 494
Bayer, Johannes 137, 203, 205–6, 211–12, 256–58, 264, 272, 274–88, 307–12, 314–18, 320–23, 326–28, 331, 332, 334–36, 368, 414–15, 485, 522
Bayerlein, Fritz 57, 432, 454–55, 460, 464–66
Beck, Ludwig 51
Beckmann, Gustav 191, 193, 220, 415
Bellmann, Wilhelm 491
Berger, Major 168, 170, 173, 180–81
Bergmann, Dr.med. Werner 527
Bernstorff, Douglas Graf von 412, 418, 435
Best, Eric 61, 482
Beug, Alfred 483, 488, 493
Beust, Henning Freiherr von 161
Bickert, Prof.Dr.med. Wilhelm 293, 309, 485
Bischoff, Karl-Peter 152, 309, 480, 485, 489
Bisping, Dietrich 480, 497
Bittrich, Wilhelm 100–01, 103, 183, 189, 201
Blaskowitz, Johannes 430
Blome, Josef 488
Blumentritt, Günther 27, 29, 31, 33, 52–53, 415
Bochnig, Helmut 181, 265, 278, 293, 483, 494
Bock von Wülfingen, Detlef 117
Bockhoff, Engelbert 122
Bohnert, Walter 486
Böke, August 197, 234, 258–295, 288, 280–281
Borgert, Wenzel 47, 281, 483, 487, 492
Bormann, Martin 161–62
Böttcher, Helmut 488, 493
Bradley, Omar N. 66, 74, 81, 87, 103, 129, 282, 369, 424, 441
Brandenberger, Erich 108, 114, 132, 152, 159–60, 176, 180 211, 237, 269

Brinkmann, Werner 292–93, 304, 371, 373–74, 376–77, 379, 481, 486
Brockhaus, Heinz 483
Brockmeier, Konrad 37
Bröker, Ernst 405, 415, 491
Brückner, Paul 239, 260, 269
Brühl, Friedrich Graf von 81, 84, 88, 293, 472, 475–76, 481, 490, 494, 530
Bruns, Walter 256
Bruns, Kampfgruppenführer 191, 193
Buhle, Walter 73 ·
Bunzel, Hans 486, 495
Burgdorf, Wilhelm 161–64
Büscher, Karl-Heinz 480
Buschmann, Hermann 484, 488, 493
Busse, Theodor 477
Butz, Willibald 480, 485, 489
Byrne, Bernard A. 410

Carlowitz, Hans-Christoph von 373, 489
Carstensen, Wilhelm 216, 482, 486
Charlemagne 148
Churchill, Winston S. 24, 478
Clemenceau, Georges 11
Collins, J. Lawton 129
Cramer, Hans 14

Davis, George H. 255, 257
Degenhard, Ernst 472, 476–77, 484, 488, 493
Degner, Joachim 482
Dieckmann, Heinrich 216
Diefenthal, Joseph 211, 225
Dierks, Eilhard 298, 492
Dietrich, Jospeh 39, 81, 83, 93, 162–63, 271, 287, 481
Dingler, Hans-ürgen 100, 293, 309
Dolezal, Leopold 243, 244, 245
Dollman, Friedrich 30–31
Doneit, Dietrich 482
Dorsch, Erwin 527
Drees, Karl-Heinz 495
Dreiling, Hermann 261
Drouven, Dr.med. Eugen 147, 504
Dunker, Rudolf 433, 435, 438–41, 444, 450–51, 463, 465

Eberbach, Heinrich 31–33, 74–76, 80–83, 85–86, 89, 98
Eckartstein, Gottfried Freiherr von 259–60
Einwächter, Hans 305
Eisen, Josef 240
Eisenhower, Dwight D. 24–25, 127, 282, 319, 369–70, 424, 441, 459, 474, 478
Elfeldt, Otto 65
Elisabeth, Zarin von Russland 133

Elterlein, Max-Dieter von 353, 358, 437, 448, 466
Engel, Herhard 2, 166, 181, 276, 278
Erdland, Alexander 480, 485, 489
Erdmann, Willi 214, 288, 292, 304, 481, 486
Ernst, Albert 457–58

Faeckenstedt, Ernst 149
Faith, Don C. 253, 255
Falck, Dr. Eberhard 480, 485, 489
Fallois, Gerd von Born- 475–76, 530
Fickessen, Jack W. 326
Fiebig, Heinz 115–17
Fischer, Otto 36, 59–60, 64, 76–77, 79, 482, 494
Fischer, Walter 415, 492
Flath, Karl-Hermann 481, 485
Flecke, Herbert 65, 79, 92, 482
Fleig, Raymond 245
Flörchinger, Karl 482
Franz, Otto 399, 485, 489
Frederick the Great, 133, 459
Frey, Georg 382
Freyer, Joachim 414
Fricke, Calus 450, 491, 527
Fried, Rudolf 145
Fritzschen, Joachim von 209
Froemel, Walter 415, 425, 491
Funck, Hans Freiherr von 56–59, 62, 64, 70, 87–89, 500
Fütterer, Friedrich 445

Gaiser, Eugen 262
Gärtner, Jakob 483
Gause, Alfred 56, 94, 100–01
Gebauer, Joseph 384
Gehlen, Reinhard 342
Geigenmüller, Helmut 293, 379, 472, 476–77, 487, 492
Gekle, Hermann 485, 490
Gerke, Heinrich 92, 227, 265, 306, 332, 487
Gerling, Rudolf 444, 452
Gerner, Julius 527
Gersdorff, Rudolf Freiherr von 68, 73, 86, 98, 114–15, 117, 124, 143, 144, 148, 155–56, 159, 175, 186, 211
Geyr von Schweppenburg, Leo Freiherr 8, 10–11, 31, 51
Gittermann, Horst 481, 485, 489
Goebbels, Joseph 400
Goerbig, Paul 474
Golly, Reinhard 473, 476, 493
Gorges, Gerd 482
Gottberg, Wilhelm von 429
Grohé, Josef 140, 148–49, 155, 503
Grollmann, Heinrich 7, 79, 98, 105, 139, 193–94, 234, 238–39, 264–66, 268–69, 274–75, 311–12, 315–16, 363, 366–68, 383–84, 419–20, 426–28, 432, 436, 454, 461, 484, 486, 491
Grünewald, Johannes 413

Grzonka, Hans-Joachim 332. 334
Guderian, Heinz 3–4, 31, 162–63, 283, 298, 340, 342, 368, 526
Guderian, Heinz Günther 12, 46, 59, 83, 163, 268, 297, 363–64, 480, 485, 489, 494, 500, 523
Günther, Arnold von 491

Hafemeister, Hans-Hermann 77–78
Hammer, Ernst 425
Hardenberg, Hasso Graf von 118
Harder, Ernst 348, 395, 401, 481, 486, 490
Harmel, Heinz 199
Hartlieb, Hubert 483, 487
Hartung, Karl 372, 480, 485, 489
Harzer, Walter 191
Hasenpatt-Prigge, Walter 488, 492
Hausser, Paul 31, 52, 56, 70, 87, 98, 501
Heestermann-Königsbeck, Wolfgang 488, 492
Heiberger, Kurt 194, 196, 200, 218, 482, 487
Heim, Hans 488, 492
Helldorff, Christoph von 481
Hellhammer, Otto 483, 487
Herring, Friedhelm 483
Heusinger, Adolf 3
Himmler, Heinrich 139, 148–49, 152–53
Hitler, Adolf 1–4, 9, 19, 21, 26, 29–33, 45, 49–54, 73, 81, 86, 101, 103, 111, 119, 124, 133, 137, 144, 152, 162, 166, 182–83, 250, 282–85, 287, 298, 301, 340–42, 344, 347, 351–52, 360–61, 365, 368, 388, 394–95, 403, 411, 417, 432, 474, 476, 478, 496, 511
Hodges, Courney, H. 98, 129, 219
Hoffman, Albert 162
Hölling, Karl-Heinz 188, 493
Holtermann, Dr. Arthur 11, 137–39, 155–56, 161–64, 166, 364, 480, 485, 489
Höltje, Wilhelm 431, 457, 461, 491
Holtkamp, Helmut 318, 482, 486, 490
Holzinger, Otto 451, 527
Honnie, Josef 154, 156
Hoppe, Günter 485
Horney, Wolfgang 484, 488, 493
Hossenfelder, Klaus 39, 98, 232, 484, 488, 493
Hübner, Eduard-Georg 398, 399, 494
Hübner, Friedrich 398, 400
Hütz, Leopold von 380, 382, 393, 397

Inboden, August-Wilhelm 230, 437, 444, 484, 488, 493
Irving, David 51
Issbrücker, Heinz-Jürgen 293, 484, 495

Jäger, Ernst 453
Jakobs, Oberfähnrich 200
Jansen, Quirin 146
Janske-Drost, Eberhard 1, 161, 199
Jeglinski, Erwin 493
Jochum, Karl 486

Jodl, Alfred 21, 29, 31–33, 74–75, 82, 94, 99, 119, 133, 180, 283–84, 286, 322
John, Erhard 293, 423, 487, 492
Junge, Oskar 527
Jungwirth, Han 384. 387, 400, 406, 408, 494

Kabitz, Eberhard 197
Kaden, Karl 482
Käseberg, Herbert 381, 494
Kaspers, Walter 487
Keitel, Wilhelm 119, 322, 477
Kempe, Hans 477
Keppler, Georg 107
Kesselring, Albert 164, 411, 417, 423
Ketteler, Josef Freiherr von 92, 415, 425, 490
Kimball, Edward A. 451
Kisker, Wilfrid 487, 492
Kleckel, Richard 232, 484
Kleer, Walter 154, 157
Klein, Feldwebel 201
Klinkenberg, Johann 145
Klosterkemper, Bernhard 425
Kluge, Günther von 31–33, 48, 52, 55–56, 58, 62, 64, 68, 73–75, 81–83, 85, 501
Knaust, Hans-Peter 191–92
Kobelinski, Herbert 413
Köchling, Friedrich 160, 509
Köhn, Kurt 326, 486
Kolb, Roland L. 356
Koppen, *Oberleutnant* (TSD) 527
Krass, Hans 492
Kratzsch, Hans 481
Krause, Leutnant 527
Krebs, Hans 112, 115, 117, 124, 137, 143–44, 148–49, 154–56, 159, 175, 179, 180, 182, 201, 210, 364
Krefeld, Rudolf 487, 491
Kreipe, Werner 283–84
Kremer, Max 147, 504
Kroll, Bernhard 261, 266, 306, 315, 328, 486
Krüger, Erich 351
Krüger, Walter 292, 296, 312–13, 316
Krümmling, Alfred 486, 491
Kuchenbuch, Frnz 332, 334, 359, 361, 367, 481, 485
Kuetgens, Dr. Felix 146–48, 504
Kuhlmann, Theo 482
Kühne, Klaus 415, 457, 481, 489–90
Kühne, Martin 168, 179
Kunstmann, Karl-Heinz 247
Kuntzen, Adolf-Friedrich 39, 76
Küpper, Walter 239, 485, 489
Kuschel, Gerd 88, 484
Kusenberg, Hans-Werner 195, 483, 488

Lademann, Gerhard 50
Lattmann, Martin 163
Lauer, Erich 251, 262

Lehmkämper, Wilhelm 482, 486, 491
Leiding, Alfred 77, 78
Lenz, Heinz 277
Leufen, Matthias 216
Lichtenfeld, Gottfried 486
Linde-Suden, Jörge-Achim von 228, 267
Lindner ?, *Oberstleutnant* ? 475
Linnarz, Victor 3
Löbbecke, Harald von 98, 113, 482
Löffler, Jürgen 206, 222, 225, 241, 260–61, 487
Lucht, Walter 360, 473
Ludeman, Richard H. 465
Lueder, Hans-Georg 62–65, 79, 481
Lüsse, Heinz 492
Lüttwitz, Heinrich Freiherr von 52, 343, 371, 373, 378–79, 389, 417, 425, 431, 441, 443, 446, 450–451, 454–55, 458, 464
Lutz, Gerhard 483, 488, 493
Lutz, Johann 253, 494

Maassen, Dr.med. Helmut 388
MacCormac, John 423, 424
MacDonald, Charles B. 238, 241, 249, 251, 258, 263, 269, 410
MacGraw, Oberleutnant 465
Manteufel, Hans-Georg 481, 485, 489
Manteuffel, Hasso von 231, 237, 273, 281, 287, 292, 296, 298, 312–13, 316, 321, 330–331, 363
Massman, Paul 483, 488, 492
Matern, Siegfried 488, 493
Mattenklott, Franz 149, 152
Mattischewski, Hans 467
Mehring, Dr.med. Werner 480
Meindl, Eugen 407–08, 412
Meiners, Detmar 483
Meyer, Dr. Alfred 155, 162
Meyer, Kuno von 155, 162
Michler, Kurt 483, 492
Mielke, Wilhelm 486
Möcklinghoff, Egbert 487
Model, Gerhard 482, 487
Model, Walter 85–86, 90, 92, 94–95, 99, 112, 115, 119, 122, 136–37, 153, 155–56, 159–64, 176, 182–83, 205, 207, 210–11, 213, 215, 219, 225, 231, 237, 258, 269, 281, 286–88, 294, 298, 339–41, 344, 363–64, 371, 432, 442, 448–49, 460, 467–69, 512
Möller, Wolfgang 482
Moltke, Helmuth Graf von 138
Montgomery, Bernard L. Viscount of Alamein 24, 98, 173, 282, 319–20, 369, 402, 416–17, 424
Müller, Gerhard 59, 186, 483, 488, 492, 522
Müller, Gerhard-Paul 75–77, 79, 91, 92, 121
Müller, Günther 216
Muntzig, Günter 527
Murray, William R. 410
Musculus, Friedrich-Heinrich 224, 226–27
Mussolini, Benito 19

Muster, Fritz 405, 494

Nagel, Helmut 137, 253, 261, 345, 482
Nelson, Gustin M. 308
Neubert, *Hauptmann d.Res.* 168
Neuhaus, Werner 482
Neusch, Erwin 492
Nitsch, Alois 61, 64, 76–78, 482
Noltensmeyer, Karl 241, 251, 450, 491, 527
Nommensen, Richard, 430–31, 433, 483, 487
Nürnberg, Hans 482

Oberfeuer, Kurt 482
Oehlmann, Paul-Hans 79
Orb, Helfried 218, 255
Osterroht, Helmuth von 130–31, 140, 150
Otten, Manfred 252

Packbier, Carl 147, 504
Palm, Baptist 248
Panneck, Günther 488
Patton, George S. 47, 63, 66, 74, 81, 90, 95, 98, 127, 319, 370, 417, 442
Pean, Dr. Ernst 6, 76–77, 79, 86, 89, 96, 125, 154, 261, 293, 483
Peetz, Reinhold 493
Pemsel, Max 27, 68
Penzler, Walter 481, 486
Pétain, Philippe 17
Petersen, Leutnant 529
Pfannkuche, Karl 79–80
Pich, Wolfgang 487, 492
Pichler, Josef 84, 243–44, 256–57, 323, 327, 335
Podlech, Joseph 428
Poppe, Max 474
Poschinger, Joachim Ritter von 358, 407
Poth, Erwin 23, 53, 483, 488, 492
Prem, Hans 48
Prophet, Gétain, Philippe 484, 488, 493

Quadt, Horst Freiherr von 276
Reinecke, Willi 359
Reinhard, Walter 71, 501
Remer, Otto-Ernst 296, 333, 519
Resch, Ludwig 483
Reunert, Emil 482, 486
Ribbentrop, Joachiim von 368
Ridgway, Matthew B. 442
Riedel, Dr.med. Carl 145
Rink, Herbert 211–212, 215–216, 218
Rink, Horst 490
Risse, Eberhard 88, 158–59, 288, 318, 481, 486, 494
Rommel, Erwin 9–10, 13–15, 19, 21–22, 26–27, 29–33, 37–38, 40–41, 43–45, 47, 51–53, 101
Roosevelt, Franklin D. 459
Rose, Herbert 457–58
Roseborough, Morgan 451
Rosenbaum, Dr.med. Paul 438–39

Röttger, Martin 481, 486, 490
Rudolph, Johann 444,489
Ruge, Friedrich 24
Rundstedt, Gerd von 19, 22, 28–31, 101, 112, 119, 137, 161–62, 180–82, 202, 211, 213, 219, 285–86, 298, 301, 395, 411
Ruppert, Hermann 338, 482, 486, 495

Säcker, Franz 483
Salmuth, Hans von 40, 44, 46
Sandkuhl, Wilhelm 63,225, 249–50
Schack, Friedrich-August 115, 135, 139, 148, 151–53, 157–60, 168
Schäfer, Hans 198
Schaller, Horst 243, 304, 447, 486
Schalon, Wilhelm 275, 286, 290, 491
Schelz, Josef 486, 490
Scherf, Walter 457
Schirmer, Kriegsfreiwilliger 206
Schlemm, Alfred 370–71, 383, 389, 399, 403, 408, 415
Schlewig-Holstein-Sonderburg-Glücksburg, Friedrich-Ferdinand Prinz zu 155, 186, 214, 268
Schliep, Jürgen 58, 483, 487
Schlotheim, Heinrich Freiherr von 481
Schmeer, Eduard 148
Schmeermann, Heinz 106–7, 195, 447, 454, 483, 492
Schmidt, Hans 102
Schmidt, Hans-Roland 475
Schmidthausen, Friedrich 452
Schmundt, Rudolf 3, 32
Schneider, Paul 383, 405, 486
Schneider, Wilhelm 309, 485
Scholz, Fritz 70, 80, 87–88, 91
Schörken, Otto 191, 195, 204, 230, 493
Schrom, Franz von 486
Schüler, Hulmut 80
Schulze, Heinrich 495
Schutow, Oberleutnant 424, 450, 491, 529
Schwerin, Gerhard Graf von 1–4, 6–7, 10, 17, 22–23, 50–54, 56–57, 63, 65, 71, 83, 93–104, 106–7, 109–10, 114, 116, 119–20, 132, 135, 137–39, 141–66, 177, 188, 364, 480, 495, 497, 500
Schwörer, Ernst 268, 294, 345, 390–91, 443, 447, 449, 452, 454–55, 460, 467
Seeger, Rudolf 487
Segebarth, Wilfried 483
Sesterhenn, Johann 246, 487, 492
Shakespeare, William 166
Simpson, William H. 417, 477
Speer, Albert 477
Speidel, Dr. Hans 11, 14–15, 22, 26–29, 31, 33, 36–37, 43, 48, 50–53, 71, 74, 81, 100–1, 112
Sperling, Max 172
Sponheimer, Otto 42, 499
Stachowitsch, Alexander 484
Stalin, Joseph W. 424
Stein von Kamienski, Albrecht 481

Steinmeier, Egon 77–78, 313, 483, 488, 492
Stephan, Eberhard 98, 118, 202, 246, 255, 276–77, 308, 310–11, 318, 334, 338, 372, 396, 399, 400–1, 414, 419, 425, 428, 487, 490, 494, 523
Stetzka, Karl-Heinz 79
Stoltenberg, Horst 486, 491, 529
Strackerjahn, Fritz 37, 69, 78, 482
Straube, Erich 106, 110, 415
Strickhausen, Heinz 204
Strickstrock, Josef 18, 481
Strube, Hans 155
Student, Kurt 233, 443
Stukenberg, Fritz 11, 184, 234–35, 480, 485, 489
Swenson, Karl-Heinz 482

Tanneberger, Willi 491, 495
Tebbe, Gerhard 2–3, 6,50, 290, 320, 335, 339, 392, 396–97, 402–3, 414–15, 418–19, 430, 466, 481, 489, 492
Templin, Horst 481, 486, 490
ten Hompel, August-Wilhelm 293, 435, 492
Thomale, Wolfgang 156, 258
Thomas, Friedrich 529
Thumbeck, Georg 495
Tielker, Karl-Ernst 483, 488, 492
Todt, Dr. Fritz 22
Trauden, Fritz 50
Trede, Edgar 529
Triantaphylides, Phidias 170, 196. 200–1, 482
Trierenberg, Wolf 110, 114
Tröster, Bruno 491, 529
Trotha, Wolf-Heinrich von 10–11
Tscheuschler, Günter 485, 489
Turowski, Erich 476–77
Twaddle, Harry L. 449, 462
Tzschentke, Hans-Joachim 198, 209, 444, 491

Uhl, Hans 475, 533
Unrein, Martin 477
Van Houten, John 449, 451
Varnholt, Otto 216, 240, 251, 359, 398, 405, 454, 488, 493
Vernhold, Josef 495
Vinke, Werner 293, 331, 338, 483, 487
Vogel, Wolfgang 491
Vogelsang, Fritz 6–13, 17–18, 36, 38–39, 41, 45– 46, 155–56, 158–59, 173, 178–79, 184–85, 189– 90, 195–96, 199, 203–4, 221, 224, 230, 232, 234–35, 248, 251, 263, 268, 270–72, 288–90, 292–95, 306–7, 309, 311–12, 316, 323, 325, 330, 336–39, 345, 347, 349, 352–53, 355, 357, 362–64, 366–67, 372, 374, 380–81, 386, 388, 390, 393, 396–97, 415, 435, 466, 480, 485, 489
Vöhl, Werner 492
Voigt, Gerhard 437, 461, 482, 491
Voigtsberger, Heinrich 8, 64, 89, 93, 137, 145, 149, 154, 156, 165–67, 176–77, 481, 495

Volckerts, Kurt 481

Wadehn, Walther 371
Wagener, Carl-Gustav 468–70
Waldenburg, Siegfried von 159, 165–66, 176–77, 179, 184–86, 188, 192, 197, 200, 203, 205, 222, 229, 231–34, 240, 244, 251, 264, 267–69, 287, 289, 292–94, 296, 304, 309–10, 313–14, 317–18, 320–21, 324, 343–44, 348, 353, 359–60, 362–63, 365–66, 368, 376, 379, 383, 386, 399–400, 404, 407, 412, 415, 427, 437, 444, 454, 463, 465–66, 485, 494, 507, 410, 417, 423
Wallace, Robert J. 446, 465
Warlimont, Walter 33, 52, 55, 62
Warnke, Werner 196
Watzdorf, Hans-Gottfried von 345, 356
Wegelein, Helmut 241
Wehking, Hermann 495
Weidemann, Gert-Axel 62, 197, 257, 276, 277, 278, 280, 481
Weinen, Albert 241
Weiss, Ernst-Werner 16, 200, 236, 482
Weissflog, Hans-Joachim 335, 475, 476, 490, 494
Wenck, Walter 442, 474, 477
Wendt, Kurt 39
Wessel, Karl 487, 492
Westphal, Siegfried 112, 144, 154, 182–83, 287
Weyand, Josef 465
Wich, Richard 490
Wiese, Rolf 125, 146, 153–54
Wilck, Gerhard 215, 225–26
Wilhelm, Hans 368, 484, 488, 493
Willerding, Gerhard 483, 488, 492
Willoh, Josef 493
Wilms, Otto 491
Winter, Hans 12, 240, 265, 269, 303, 306, 484, 487
Wirtz, Richard 449, 459–60
Wittich oder Wittish, Führer Volkssturm-Bn 532
Wohlgemuth, Wilhelm 483
Wolf, Lothar 6, 12, 82, 89–91, 92, 125, 132, 134–35, 155, 161, 293, 480
Wolff-Boenisch, Richard 42, 102, 216, 279, 345, 363
Wolter, Heinz 281
Wolters, Johannes 490

Zahn, Lothar 475, 532
Zander, Helmut 121, 137, 198, 200, 216, 266, 268, 292, 296, 315–16, 318, 320, 335, 383–84, 396, 482, 486, 494, 507, 523
Zangen, Gustav von 280
Zanzinger, Erich 415, 420, 424, 428, 431, 437, 443–44, 447–48, 450–54, 456–57, 460–61, 491, 528
Zehner, Kurt 57, 483
Zimmermann, Paul 139–40, 157

A Guide to Tactical Unit Symbols

Types of Units

Allied   Axis

Infantry

Mountain Infantry

Airborne

Volks-Grenadier

Armored Infantry/ Panzer Grenadier

Armor

Armored Recon/ Mech Cavalry

Engineers

Transport

Rocket Artillery

Artillery (Towed)

Artillery (Self-Propelled)

Anti-Aircraft Artillery

TD   PzJg   Tank Destroyer

German Equivalent

Signals

Maintenance

Medical

Combat Group (German) or Task Force (US)

Sizes of Units

•	Squad
••	Section
•••	Platoon
I	Company/Battery/Troop
II	Battalion/Squadron
III	Regiment
X	Brigade/Group/ Combat Command
XX	Division
XXX	Corps
XXXX	Army
XXXXX	Army Group

Examples

1st Battalion, 110th Infantry Regiment   1 [⊠] 110

Grenadier Regiment 951, 361st Volks-Grenadier Division   951 [v⊠] 361

Polish 1st Armored Division   1 (Pol.) [▭]

Combat Group Lueder, a regi-mental-sized *ad hoc* unit built around a panzer regiment headquarters of the 116th Panzer Division.   Lueder [▭] 116

Map 1

Overview of the Situation in the Supreme Command–West Area
of Operations as of 6 June 1944 and Rommel's Proposal of 3 May
for Deployment of I SS-Panzer and III Anti-Aircraft Corps

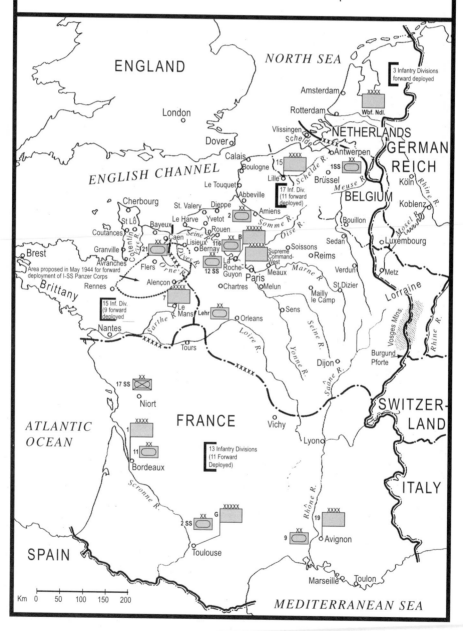

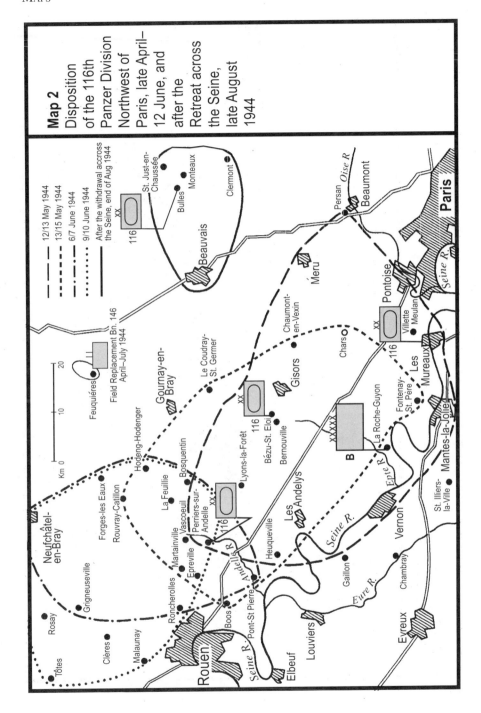

Map 2
Disposition
of the 116th
Panzer Division
Northwest of
Paris, late April–
12 June, and
after the
Retreat across
the Seine,
late August
1944

12/13 May 1944
13/15 May 1944
6/7 June 1944
9/10 June 1944
After the withdrawal accross the Seine, end of Aug 1944

Map 3
The Landing of 6 June 1944

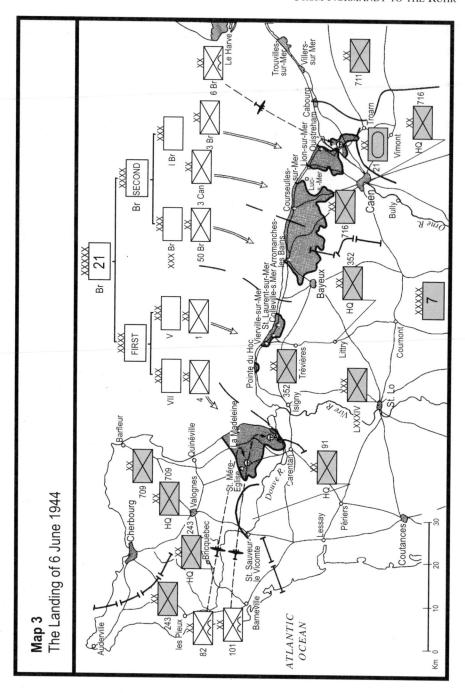

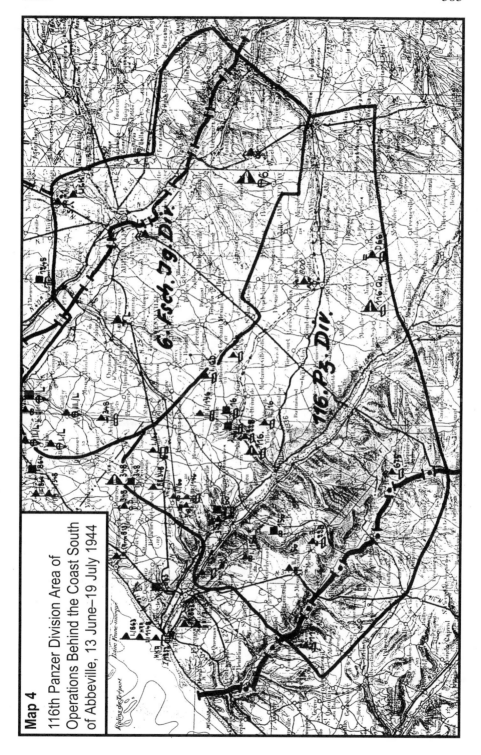

Map 4

116th Panzer Division Area of
Operations Behind the Coast South
of Abbeville, 13 June–19 July 1944

Map 5

116th Panzer Division Area of Operations Behind the Front
of I SS-Panzer Corps Near Caen, 22–28 July 1944

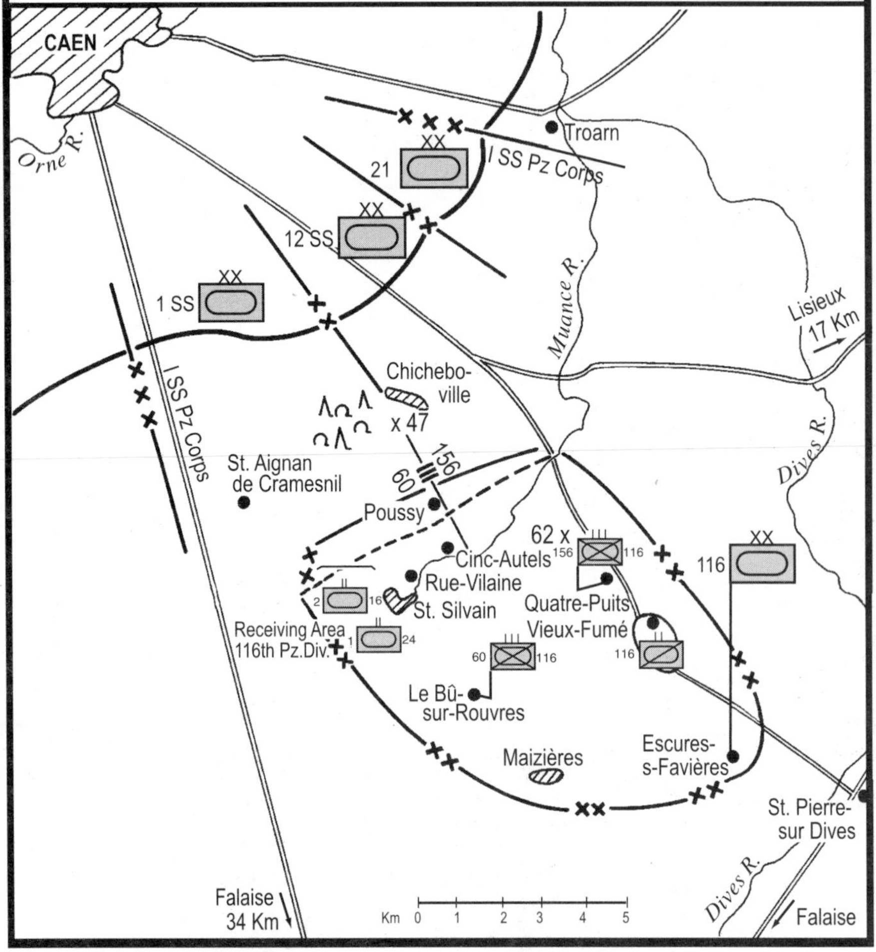

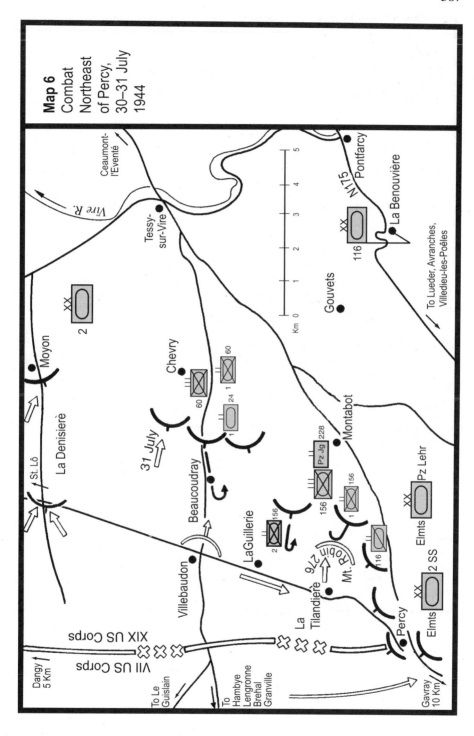

Map 6
Combat
Northeast
of Percy,
30–31 July
1944

Map 7
Combat in the Le Gast–St. Pois–Sée sector, 1–4 August 1944

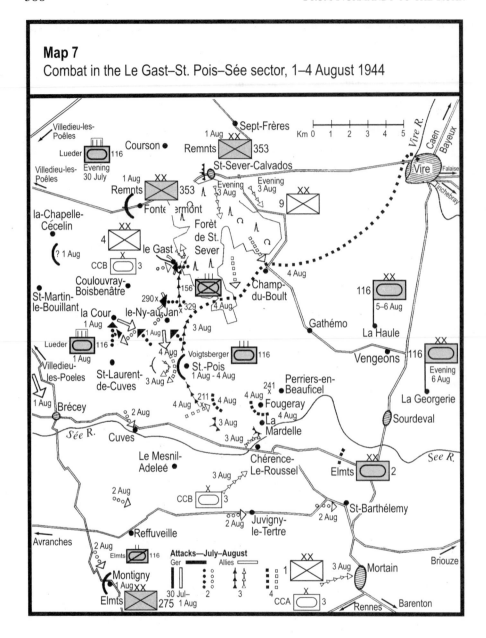

Map 8
Combat in the Champ-du-Boult–Perriers-en-Beauficel–
Chérancé-le-Roussel Sector and Counterattack
Toward Avranches, 5–11 August 1944

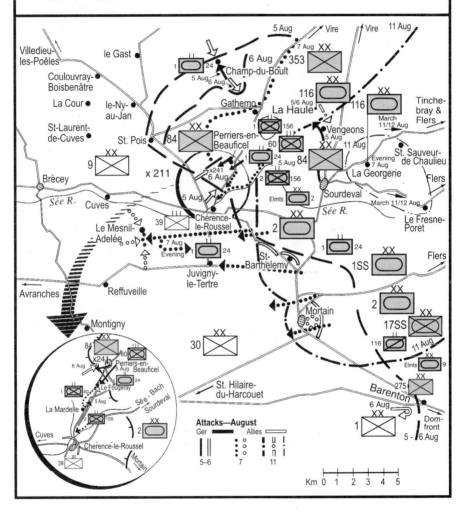

Map 9
Combat in the Sée–Argentan–Trun–Le Bourg–St. Léonard Sector, 12–20 August, and Breakout of the 116th Panzer Division from the Pocket Southeast of Falaise on the Night, 20–21 August 1944

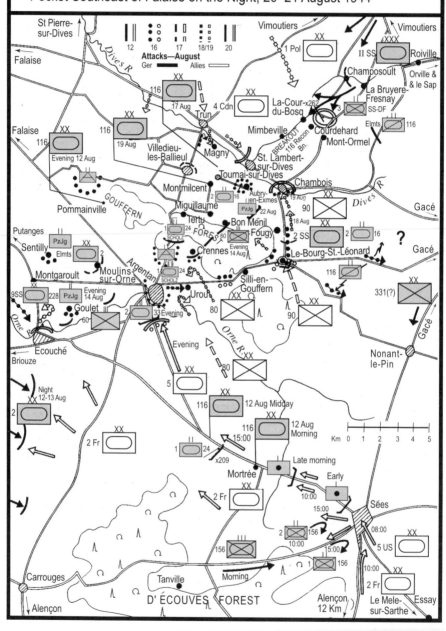

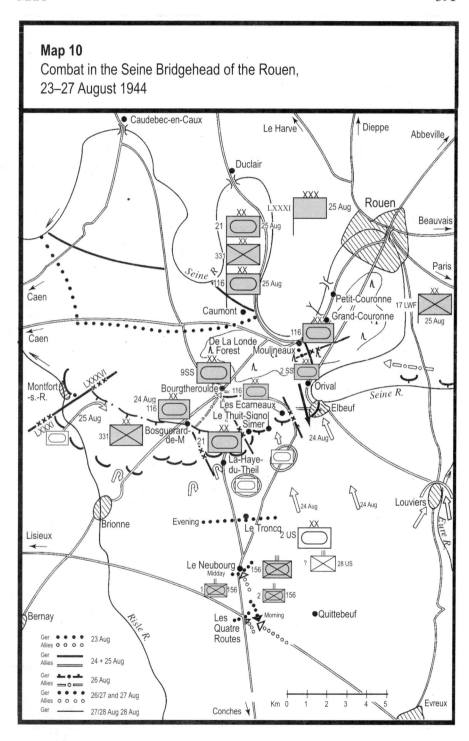

Map 10
Combat in the Seine Bridgehead of the Rouen,
23–27 August 1944

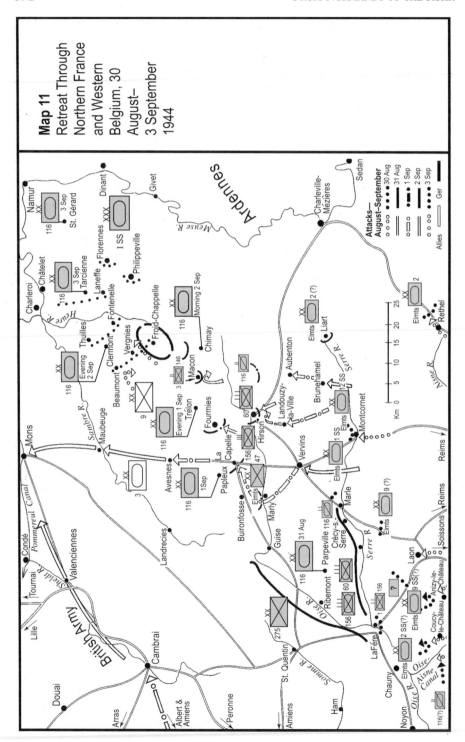

Map 11
Retreat Through
Northern France
and Western
Belgium, 30
August–
3 September
1944

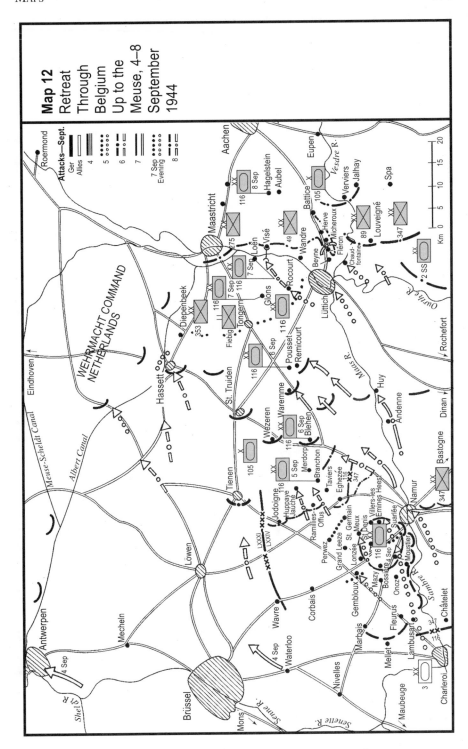

Map 12
Retreat
Through
Belgium
Up to the
Meuse, 4–8
September
1944

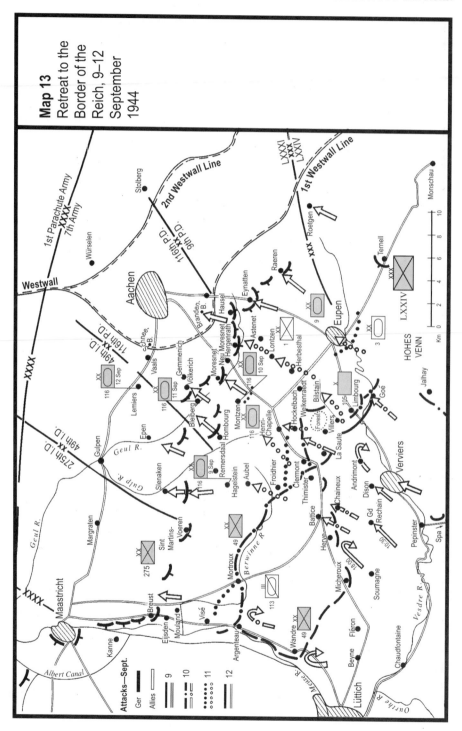

Map 13
Retreat to the Border of the Reich, 9–12 September 1944

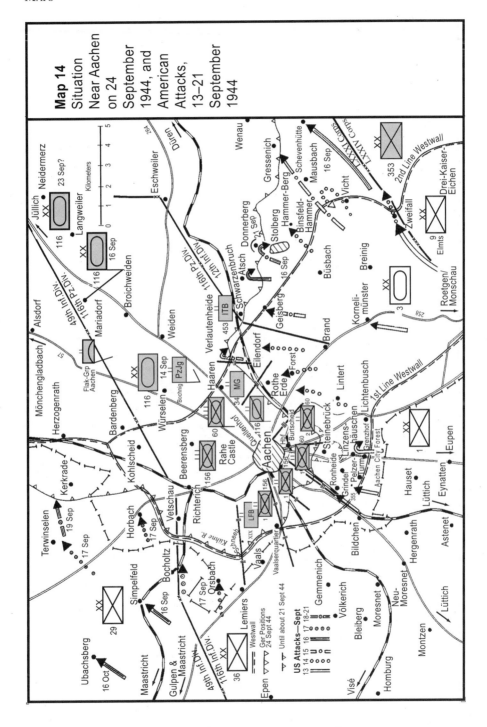

Map 14
Situation Near Aachen on 24 September 1944, and American Attacks, 13–21 September 1944

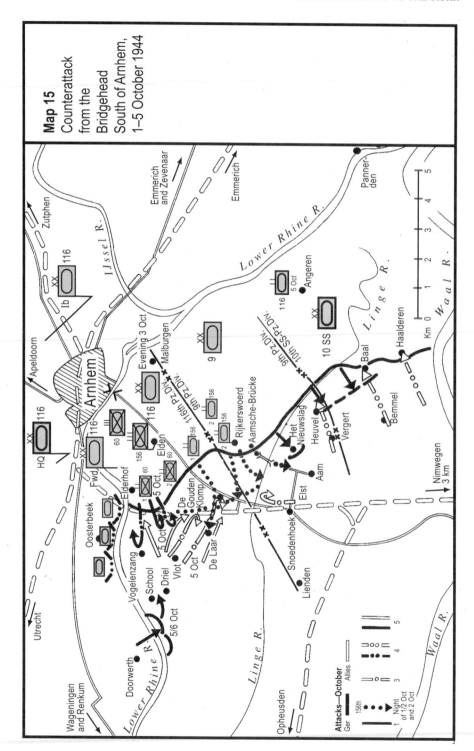

Map 15
Counterattack
from the
Bridgehead
South of Arnhem,
1–5 October 1944

Map 16
Aachen, Battle for Würselen, 11–22 October 1944

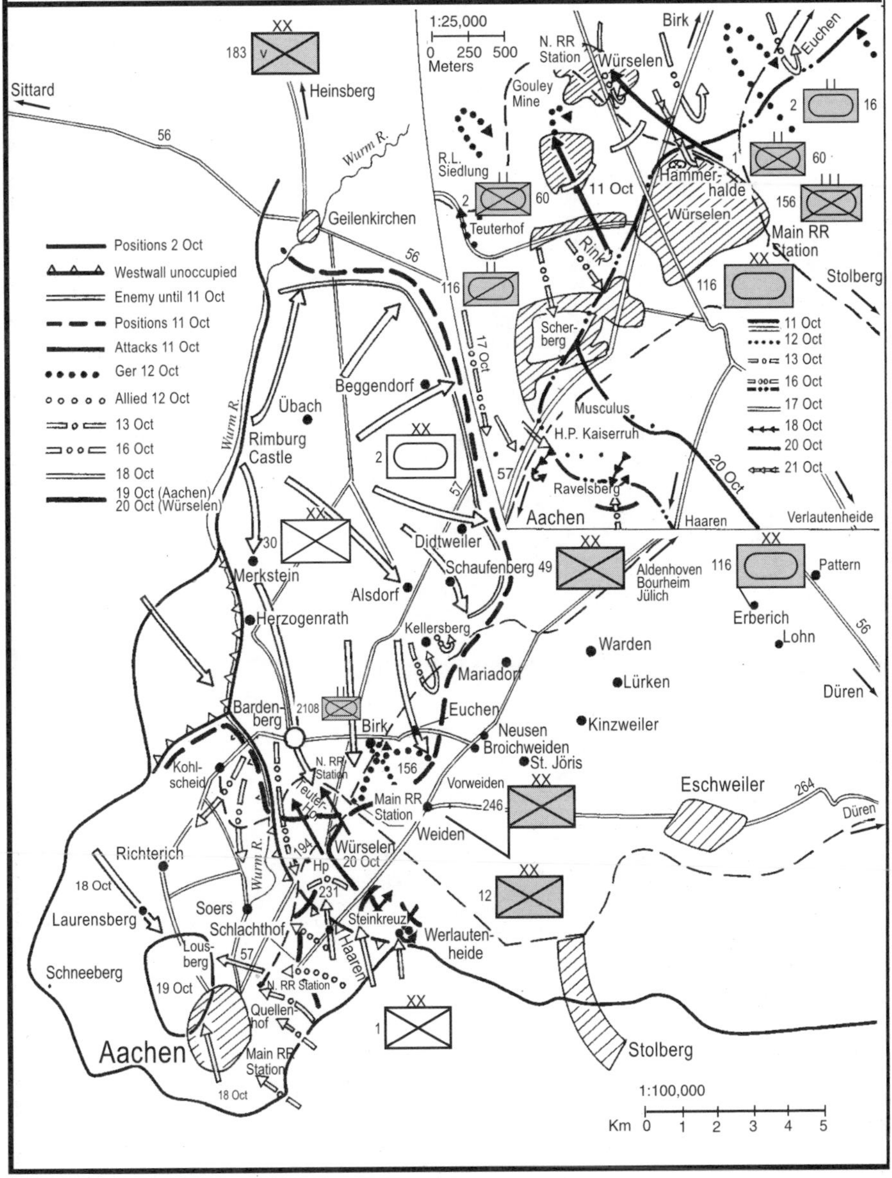

Map 17
Combat in the Hürtgen Forest, 2–15 November 1944

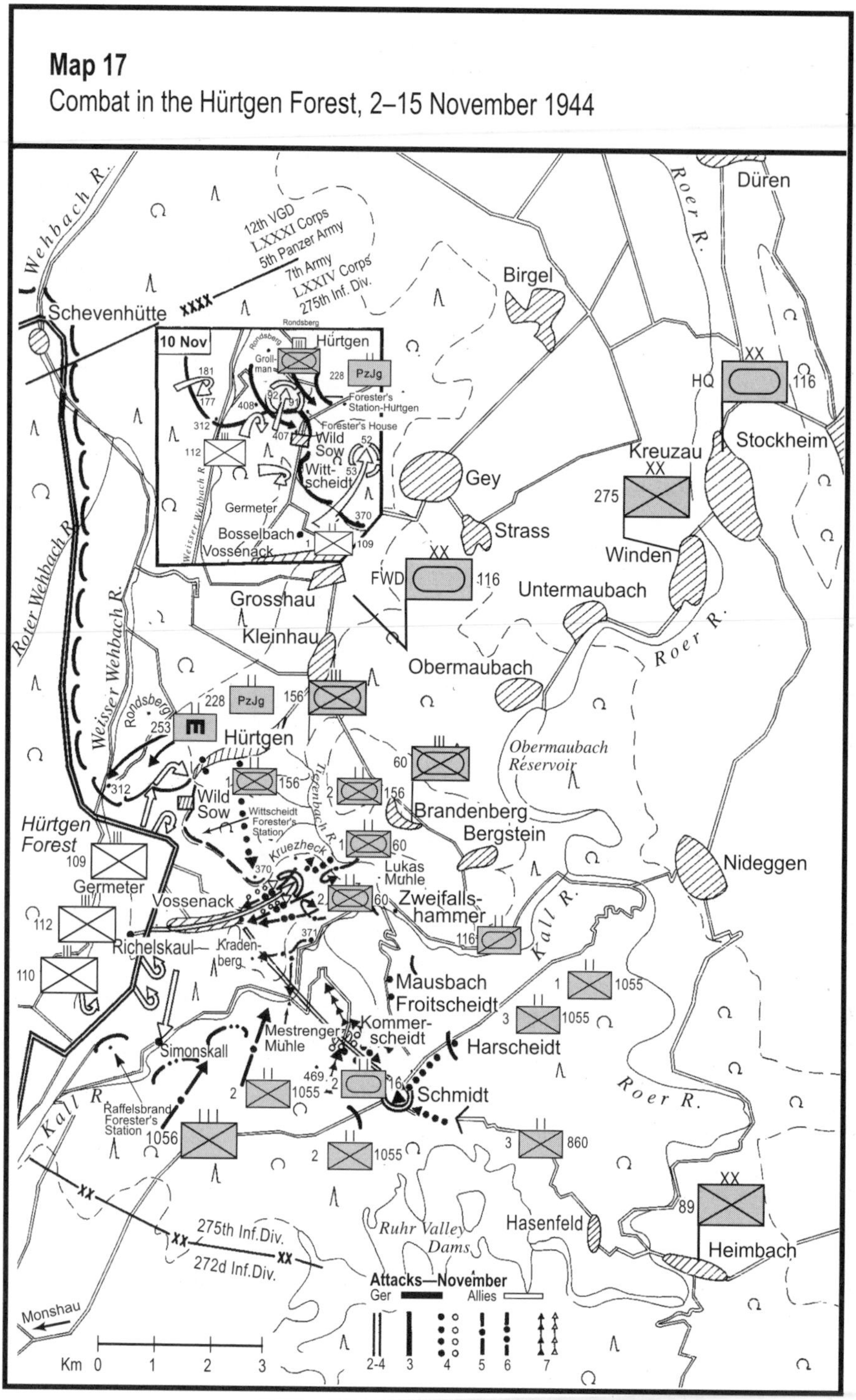

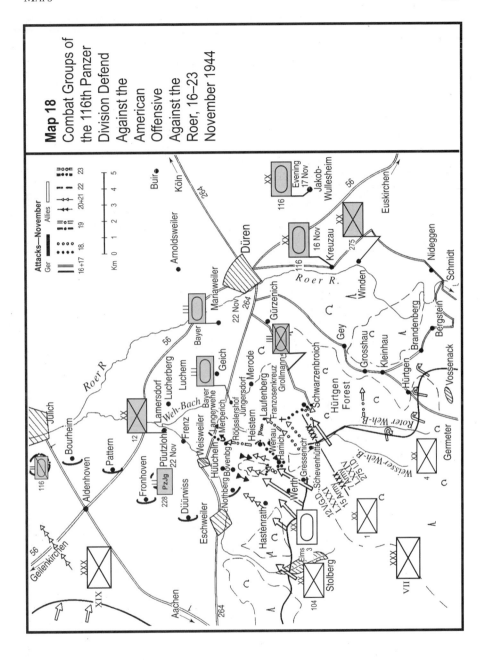

Map 18
Combat Groups of the 116th Panzer Division Defend Against the American Offensive Against the Roer, 16–23 November 1944

Map 19
Planning for the Ardennes Offensive

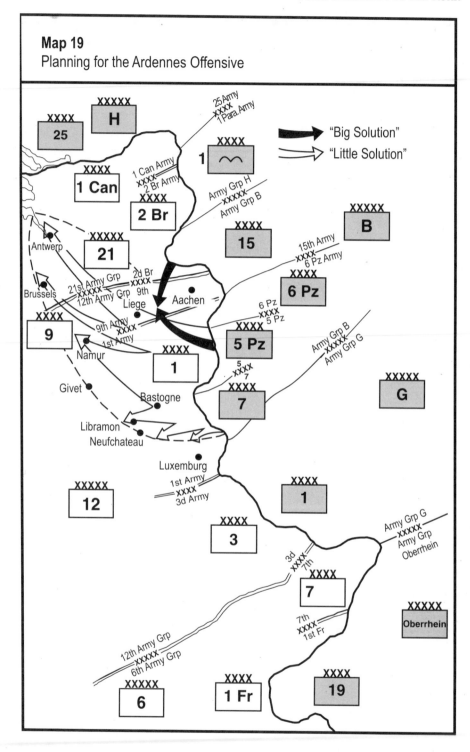

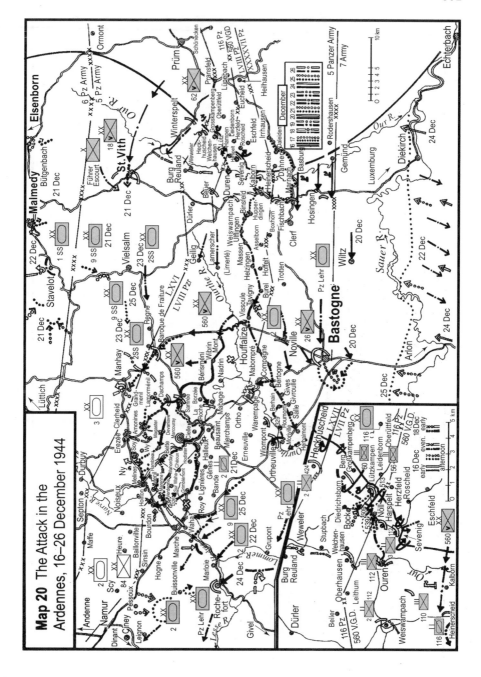

Map 20 The Attack in the Ardennes, 16–26 December 1944

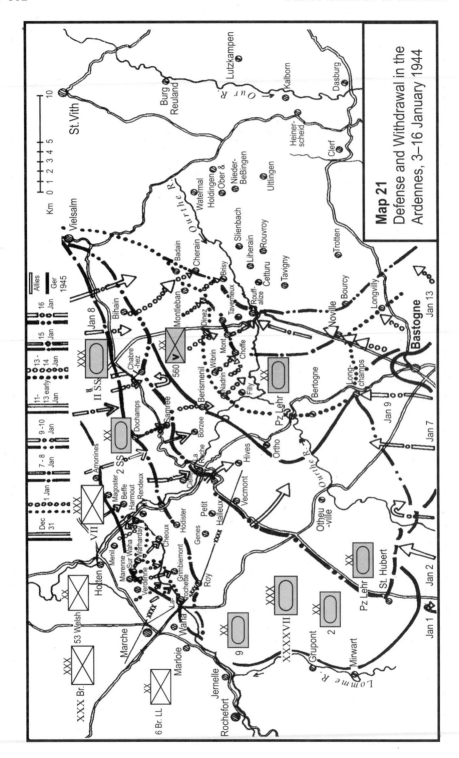

Map 21
Defense and Withdrawal in the
Ardennes, 3–16 January 1944

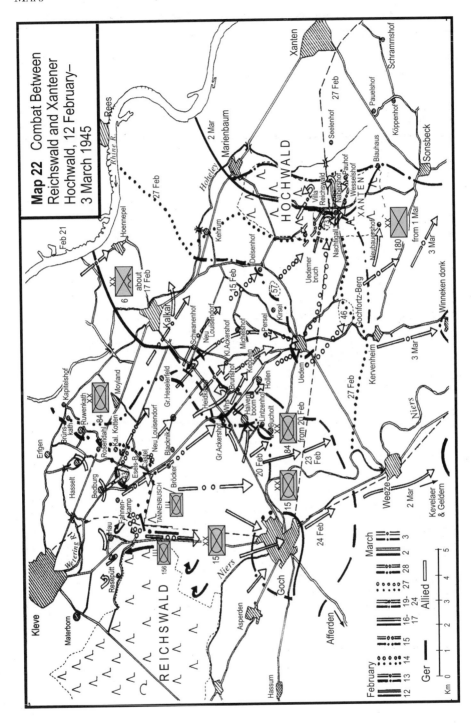

Map 22 Combat Between Reichswald and Xantener Hochwald, 12 February– 3 March 1945

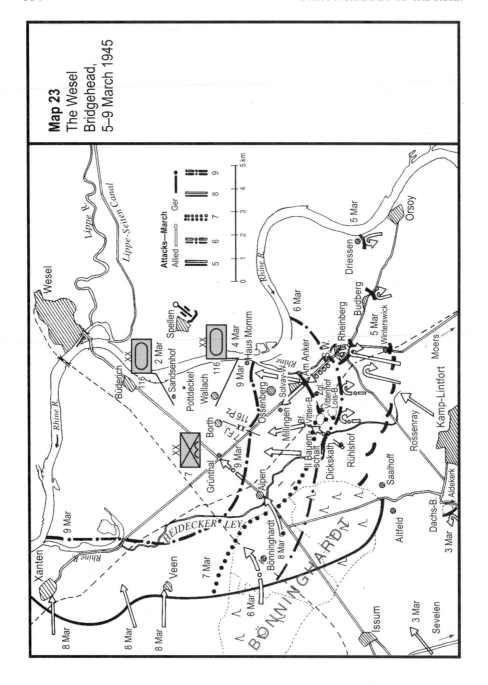

Map 23
The Wesel
Bridgehead,
5–9 March 1945

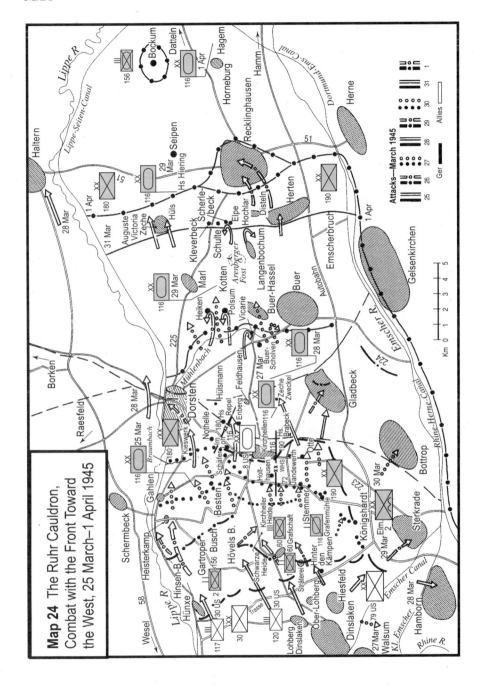

Map 24 The Ruhr Cauldron, Combat with the Front Toward the West, 25 March–1 April 1945

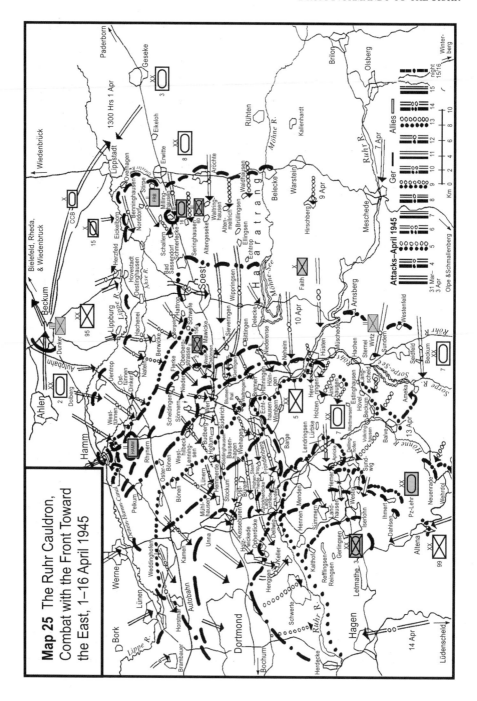

Map 25 The Ruhr Cauldron, Combat with the Front Toward the East, 1–16 April 1945

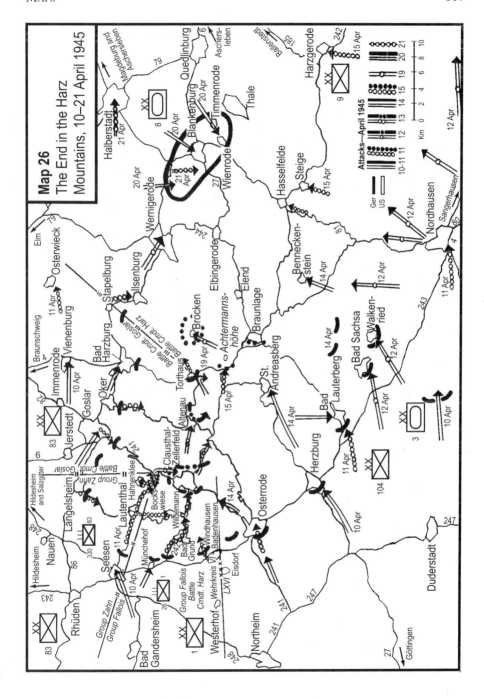

Map 26
The End in the Harz
Mountains, 10–21 April 1945

About the Author

Generalmajor Heinz Günther Guderian, Federal German Armed Forces (Retired), was born 23 August 1914 in Goslar, Germany, and is the son of *Generaloberst* and Mrs. Heinz Wilhem Guderian. After graduating from classical secondary school in Berlin-Zehlendorf, he joined Motorized Battalion 3 in Wünsdorf as a cadet on 1 April 1933. After being promoted to Leutnant on 1 April 1935, he served as platoon leader, battalion-and regimental adjutant, and company commander in Panzer Regiments 1 and 35. In the Polish Campaign of 1939, he earned the Iron Cross 2d and 1st classes, and was wounded twice during continued combat assignments in the 1940 campaign in the West.

After graduation from the War Academy in 1942, he served in general staff positions in armored units, and in May 1944, became the 1st General Staff Officer of the 116th Panzer Division. He served with the "Greyhound Division" in this capacity throughout the entire 1944–45 campaign in the West, such service only being temporarily interrupted by a third wound. Then-Oberstleutnant Guderian was awarded the Knights Cross on 5 October 1944 for leading the remainder of the Division out of the Falaise Pocket. In the *Bundeswehr,* the author served as commander of Panzer Battalion 3, later 174, and Panzer Brigade 14. As a general officer, he served in various capacities in the German Army staff, including Inspector of Armored Troops.

On 21 December 1972, General Guderian was awarded the Grand Merit Cross of the Order of Merit of the Federal Republic of Germany. Since retiring from active duty on 1 April 1974, he has been occupied with history in general, and producing the history of the 116th Panzer Division in particular.